The N
CO

About the Book

Angling is an ancie...........................or lost its
appeal. *Coarse fishing* is a subdivision of the sport and
it has a very large following. In this new and enlarged edition of a very popular book Peter Wheat
offers the right kind of down-to-earth advice which
will be found invaluable not only to the complete
newcomer, but also to the angler with a little
experience seeking to improve his ability to catch
more and larger fish. Without doubt, angling is an
absorbing, thrill-filled activity, but if the frustration
of constant failure which can so easily be the lot of
the beginner is to be avoided, it is essential to gain
at the very start a firm foundation of basic know-
how. This book provides that foundation.

About the Author

Peter Wheat is a lifelong angler who enjoys coarse,
game and sea fishing with equal enthusiasm. He lives
at Poole in Dorset and is a freelance writer and
angling consultant. Over the years his angling
articles have appeared in many magazines and
newspapers, and he has eleven published books to his
credit including *The Observer's Book of Fly Fishing* and
(with Ray Forsberg) *The Observer's Book of Sea
Fishing*.

The New Observer's Book of

COARSE FISHING

PETER WHEAT

DRAWINGS BY BAZ EAST

FREDERICK WARNE

First published by Frederick Warne
(Publishers) Ltd, London, England 1976

Copyright Frederick Warne (Publishers) Ltd
1976

Reprinted 1977, 1979, 1982
New revised edition 1984

Originally published as *The Observer's Book of Coarse
Fishing* in small hardback format.

Library of Congress Catalog
Card No. 74–21041

ISBN 0 7232 1681 9

Printed in Great Britain by
William Clowes Limited,
Beccles and London

Preface

This is essentially a book about the basics of coarse fishing, and its main purpose is to introduce the reader to the sport and assist him to a stage where he is able to catch fish fairly consistently.

I have endeavoured to cover the important points of the subject as comprehensively as is possible in a book of this size. To give scope for study of specialized aspects a list of books for further reading has been included at the back.

Acknowledgement is due to my good friend Baz East for drawings in the text. The black and white photographs are from my own collection.

I must also acknowledge the countless generations of anglers, past and present, who have both directly and indirectly given me my own meagre understanding of this fascinating sport. Of special mention: Francis Francis, Hugh Tempest Sheringham, Richard Walker, Bernard Venables and Fred J. Taylor.

And lastly, grateful thanks to the many friends with whom I have shared pleasantly memorable hours at the waterside. Particularly: Ron Barnett, Bob Church and the late David Carl Forbes. My enthusiasm has been quickened through fishing days spent in their company.

Peter Wheat

Contents

4: Final Matters

7

List of Black and White Photographs

Introduction

The seed of the sport of angling was sown far back in the Old Stone Age when fish hunting was one of man's principal food-gathering methods. Further back than approximately 8,000 BC, the human race really existed little better than the animals. They lived in small family groups, in caves and such like, and they survived under bitterly cold conditions by collecting berries, roots and edible plants, and by hunting animals and fish.

Earliest fishing techniques included spearing with bone harpoons and wooden lances fire-hardened or fitted with flint tips at their business ends, and net-ting and trapping. Also, though no evidence sur-vives to support it, it is quite feasible that paralyzing herbs were used to drug fish so that they floated to the surface for net collection—a method popular among certain native tribes to this day.

Exactly how important fish-catching was to Old Stone Age groups would largely have depended on the nearness or otherwise of lakes and streams. However, there is evidence to support the view that some family groups were quite prepared to venture many miles from their cave dwellings during the spring and summer in order to station themselves at vantage points along a river, and trap migrating salmon and trout on their journey upstream to the spawning redds. Traces of these prehistoric fishery sites have been found in France, and at New Ferry on the River Bann in Northern Ireland.

That fish were held in the highest esteem by our most ancient ancestors is obvious from the drawings and carvings which have survived on cave walls and antler bones. In France, for example, fish carvings dating to 12,000 BC exist which depict salmon, eel and pike, as well as other more carp-like species.

Perhaps the most remarkable of these piscatorial representations is a low-relief sculpture of a fish 3 ft (90 cm) long cut into the floor of the Grotte du Poisson in central France. Complete with proud dorsal, mouth, fins and gills, it is clearly a migratory species—probably salmon.

Also from France has come another interesting item—an antler stick depicting a shoal of four life-like fish swimming a river between the antlers and legs of two reindeer—a huntin' fishin' symbol if ever there was one.

Experts believe that early man carved and painted animal and fish pictures not solely for pleasure and beautification of his dwellings, but also as part of magical rituals which enabled him to catch them all the better. It makes me wonder if the paintings, photographs and stuffed carcasses which adorn the walls of anglers' dens have rather more primeval significance than mere decoration.

Old Stone Age fishermen went a hunting strictly for food; there was certainly nothing sporting about it. Pleasure fishing—rod, line and hook angling—was a much later development, and came about as a side effect of the Neolithic revolution, which began in south-western Asia—in areas such as Turkey's Anatolian plateau where wheat and barley grew wild, and where the ancestors of cattle, pigs, dogs, sheep and goats roamed abundantly.

Crop cultivation and animal breeding in this area led to a food-producing economy: farming. It was a far more settled way of life, with individual family groups joining together to work and to defend themselves against enemy attack. There was food to spare, more time for leisure activities, and greater security than ever before. It was the birth of civilization and, in my opinion, the birth of angling, too.

Obviously trapping fish for food remained fairly important to Neolithic man—especially in the embryo trial and error days of farming—and harpoons, nets, and traps closely similar to modern osier weels were commonly in use. So too were hooks, lines and crude stick-rods.

Hook materials included flint, thin wooden forks, bird-bone forks, animal bones, and even shells. At Shaheinab in the Sudan, Neolithic fishermen carved their hooks from Nile oyster shells.

Slowly but surely, over a span of several thousand years, the Neolithic stage spread across Europe, eventually reaching the shore of Britain some 5,000 to 6,000 years ago. The first farmers of this country settled in the fertile lands of Hampshire, Dorset and Wiltshire, and it is more than probable that pleasure fishing was enjoyed by them in rivers such as the Hampshire Avon, Dorset Stour, Test and Itchen.

With the growth of agriculture in Britain, hunting and fishing would consequently have become less important in advanced farming communities—fishing for the majority being but amusement to be enjoyed in the quiet hours between tilling fields and feeding domestic stock.

Today, Britain is just one of many countries able to claim angling as its largest participant sport. Adherents number in millions and a significant percentage of them angle fresh water for coarse fish species.

Indigenous sporting species which entered British waters following the close of the last Great Ice Age (about 10,000 years ago) include: roach, dace, rudd, grayling, perch, chub, tench, barbel, eel, bream and pike.

Sporting species introduced later by man include: common carp, crucian carp, catfish and zander.

'There is an indescribable fealty among fishermen greater than among any other group of men. There is devotion to the out-of-doors and relief from the grind of modern life that stamp them at once as men of spirit.'

HERBERT CLARK HOOVER

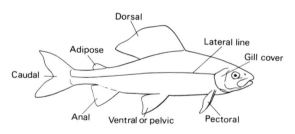

Fins and other external features of a fish

I: FIRST CONSIDERATIONS

Introducing the Quarry

From a wide variety of fishes inhabiting British waters a total of 16 coarse species can be selected as being of outstanding sporting value. Of these by far the best known and most popular is the roach, and therefore it will be appropriate to commence brief descriptions of the coarse angler's quarry with this fine fish.

The Roach

Family CYPRINIDAE *Rutilus rutilus*
Identification: A streamlined fish, deepening in the belly and hump-backing slightly as it increases size. The back is greeny brown with hints of metallic blue, flanks silver and underparts ivory white. Dorsal and caudal fins are reddish brown, pectoral fins orange red, and ventral fins coral red. The eyes are either watery red or wine red.

Distribution: Waters of every size and type. Common throughout England apart from Devon and Cornwall where it is rare, southern parts of Scotland and eastern Wales. Localized in Ireland but abounding in such waters as the Cork Blackwater, the Fairy Water near Omagh in Co. Tyrone, and the systems of Foyle and Erne.

Growth: Sizeable at 1 lb (450 g), a specimen at 2 lb (900 g). Although the species is capable of reaching weight in excess of 4 lb (1·8 kg), roach of 3 lb (1·4 kg) plus are rarely caught.

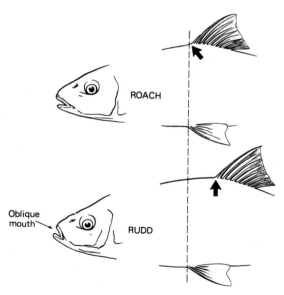

Points of identification between roach and rudd

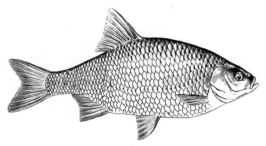

The Rudd

Family CYPRINIDAE   *Scardinius erythropthalmus*

Identification: Young rudd and roach are similar both in general shape and colour. They can be easily told apart by mouth shape and dorsal fin position.

The leading edge of the roach dorsal is rooted almost directly above that of the pelvic fins, whilst the rudd dorsal is set much further back towards the tail. The lower lip of the rudd protrudes beyond the upper lip, a feature absent in the roach.

In large rudd the body is deeper for length than that of roach, and the colouring is more distinctive: richly red fins and flanks of golden bronze.

Distribution: Stillwaters, canals and slow rivers. Prolific and large-growing in Ireland, less widely-distributed in England, absent from Scotland. The fens of Cambridgeshire, Norfolk, Lincolnshire and north Somerset, are traditionally fine rudd areas. Elsewhere in England waters where the species achieves notable weight are few and far between.

Growth: At 1½ lb (680 g) a good fish, at 2 lb (900 g) a specimen for English waters, and at 2½ lb (1·1 kg) a specimen for Irish waters. Few rudd weighing 4 lb (1·8 kg) or over have been caught, but nevertheless there is no doubt that 5 lb (2·2 kg) rudd exist —more so in Ireland.

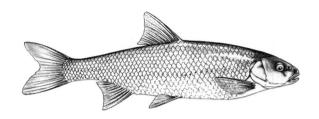

The Dace

Family CYPRINIDAE   *Leuciscus leuciscus*

Identification: The dace is a slimly built fish with a greeny brown back, silver flanks and a white belly. The fins are watery, but big dace in some rivers have red, orange or yellow in their pelvic and ventral fins.

Distribution: Rivers and streams. A few lakes also contain them. Widespread in England, absent from Scotland and the western parts of Wales. In Ireland abundant in the Cork Blackwater and the tributaries of this river.

Growth: This is the smallest of the sporting species. A 6 oz (170 g) dace is fair size, at 12 oz (340 g) a specimen. Dace of 1 lb (450 g) or over should be the subject of careful photographic record—if not a glass case.

The Crucian Carp

Family CYPRINIDAE   *Carassius carassius*

Identification: A short, deep, chunky-looking fish, with big scales, long high dorsal—convex on the top edge—and a caudal fin only slightly notched, almost spatular. The back is dark amber, the flanks golden bronze, and the underparts yellow splashed with reddish orange patches.

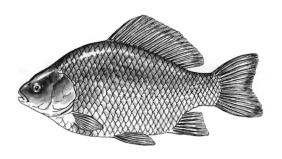

Distribution: Lakes, ponds, pits and slow rivers. Localized in England, southern and eastern parts mainly. Absent from Scotland, Ireland and Wales.
Growth: Excellent at 1½ lb (680 g). Crucian of 2 lb (900 g) plus are specimens. In a few choice waters live crucian weighing between 3 (1·3) and 6 lb (2·7 kg).

The Common Carp

Family CYPRINIDAE   *Cyprinus carpio*
Identification: Wild common carp are long, sleek fish, compared with domestic king carp strains imported from the continent which are short and immensely plump. All common carp possess four barbules—

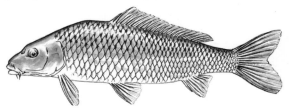

two on each side of the upper lip—and a long concave dorsal fin. The back is blue grey, the flanks brownly golden and the belly orange, yellow or white. Wild carp are always covered with big scales. King carp include, as well as fully-scaled fish, specimens which are partially scaled (mirror carp) and specimens with only two or three scales on each flank or no scales at all (leather carp).

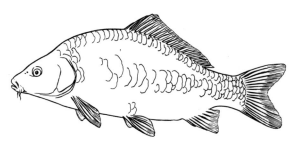

Partially scaled mirror carp

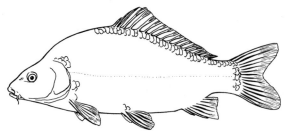

Partially scaled mirror carp

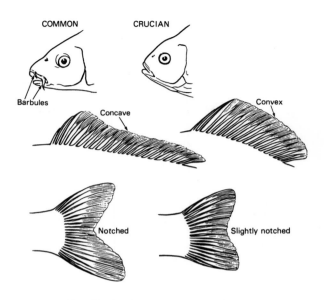

COMMON   CRUCIAN

Barbules

Concave   Convex

Notched   Slightly notched

Points of identification between common and crucian carp

The typical scale pattern of mirror carp is restricted to along the top of the back and the lateral line area. However, there are no hard and fast rules about this, and in some mirror carp the scaling is further restricted to only the top of the back apart from small groups near the gill covers and tail root. Such carp are nearly, but not quite, leather carp. There are also fully-scaled mirror carp.

Distribution: Lakes, ponds, pits, reservoirs, slow rivers and the backwaters of fast rivers. Stocked in many waters all over England, less common in Wales, Scotland and Ireland. Irish carp are resident in Reynella Lake, Co. Westmeath, and Cork Lough.

Growth: 'Wildies' are relatively small common carp. A 10 lb (4·5 kg) fish is an exceptional catch. King carp are not considered notable until they reach 15 lb (6·8 kg). Specimen weight is 20 lb (9 kg) for domestic strains. Carp as large as 51 lb 6 oz (23·3 kg) have been caught in England—from a water where fish at least 5 lb (2·2 kg) heavier have been observed at close quarters.

The Common Bream

Family CYPRINIDAE   *Abramis brama*

Identification: The bream is an instantly recognizable fish. Its body is deeply oval, humped, and compressed from side to side. The mouth is large and thick-lipped. Baby bream (anglers call them 'skimmers') are silvery fish. Fully mature bream are darker: black-backed with subdued silver-tinged bronze flanks and dull grey fins.

Distribution: Lakes, pits, reservoirs, canals and rivers. Widely distributed in Ireland, most parts of England and in many lochs of the Scottish lowlands.

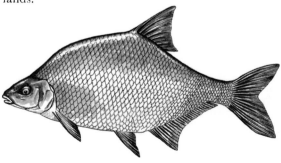

Growth: Big-growing, able to reach weights well above 10 lb (4·5 kg). Bream between 1 (450 g) and 6 lb (2·7 kg) are common catches, above 8 lb (3·6 kg) notable, and at 10 lb (4·5 kg) specimen size.

The Silver Bream

Family CYPRINIDAE   *Blicca bjoerkna*
Identification: A silver bream is difficult to distinguish from a young common bream. The shape of both species is basically the same and, as its name suggests, the silver bream is silver-flanked—little different from a 'skimmer'. Absolute identification must be left to experts, but an outward difference is found in ray counts of the dorsal and anal fins.

	Common Bream	**Silver Bream**
Dorsal		
Unbranched	3	3
Branched	9	8
Anal		
Unbranched	3	3
Branched	23–28	19–23

Distribution: Restricted to eastern parts of England. Very rare elsewhere.
Growth: Silver bream larger than 3 lb (1·3 kg) have been recorded, but the general run of fish weigh less than 1 lb (450 g). A 'silver' of 1½ lb (680 g) is considered a splendid catch.

The Chub

Family CYPRINIDAE   *Leuciscus cephalus*
Identification: A long sturdy-built fish. It has a big mouth set in a wide head and large scales. The back is olive green, the flanks dusky bronze and the belly white. All fins are dark with the exception of the coral red pelvic and anal fins.

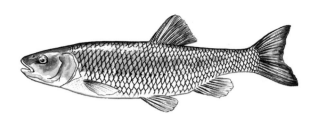

The following points avoid the confusion which frequently arises between small chub and big dace. The chub has a very big mouth compared with that of the dace, and a thicker, more blunt-headed appearance. The shaping of the fins is quite

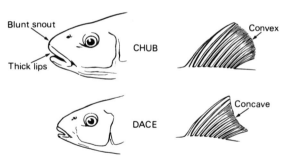

Points of identification between chub and dace

different too. The trailing edge of the chub dorsal is convex, that of the dace is concave. This difference also exists between the anal fins of the two species.

Distribution: Rivers and streams. Also found in a few lakes. Common throughout England apart from Devon and Cornwall. Less widespread (but very large-growing) in southern parts of Scotland. Rare in Wales and Ireland.

Growth: Average chub weigh between 1 (450 g) and 4 lb (1·8 kg). Five pounds (2·2 kg) is specimen weight for top-class chub rivers. It is probable that the species reaches 10 lb (4·5 kg) or more in British waters.

The Tench

Family CYPRINIDAE   *Tinca tinca*

Identification: One of the most beautiful of our freshwater fishes. A stout fish, short for its depth. It has thick, smoky blue fins (the caudal fin spatular), small crimson eyes, and a silk-smooth body of rich greeny bronze picked out with tiny close-packed scales. A rare ornamental variety, sometimes found in the wild, is the golden tench: bright orange or yellow all over, blotched with spots and patches of brown or black.

Distribution: Lakes, ponds, canals, reservoirs, pits, slow rivers and the slacker sections of fast rivers. Well distributed in England, less so in Wales, Scotland and Ireland—but heavy-growing in waters where it does occur, such as the River Shannon.

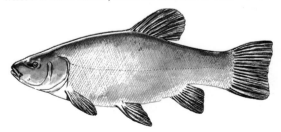

Male and female tench can be told apart by the shape of their pelvic fins. The pelvic fins on the male tench in the foreground are large and almost joined together. Those on the female are small and distinctly separate

Growth: Most tench caught by anglers range in size from 1 (450 g) to 5 lb (2·2 kg). A 5 lb (2·2 kg) tench is specimen weight. Tench above 6 lb (2·7 kg) are very difficult to catch. The species grows at least as heavy as 10 lb (4·5 kg) under perfect conditions.

The Grayling
Family THYMALLIDAE   *Thymallus thymallus*

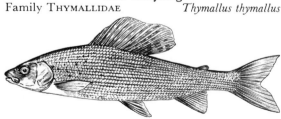

Identification: The grayling is a long streamlined fish, immediately identified by a large and colourful sail-like dorsal fin.   There is also, further down the back towards the tail, a small fleshy stub, the adipose fin, indicating that it is as much a game fish as a coarse fish.   The grayling is silver grey, marked over with darker lines running the length of its body. Its eyes are violet, a colour also mixed with subtle plays of blue and green in the shadings of the body.

Distribution: Well oxygenated rivers and streams. Widely scattered distribution in England, Wales and Scotland.   Also stocked in a few lakes.

Growth: A 1 lb (450 g) grayling is a satisfactory size from most rivers.   At 2 lb (900 g) it is big enough to be rated specimen weight.   And at 3 lb (1·3 kg) plus most definitely the catch of a lifetime.

The Perch

Family PERCIDAE   *Perca fluviatilis*

Identification: The aggressive nature of the perch is evident in its form and colour.   A hump-backed fish, rough-skinned, markedly bold in the shaping of its head and mouth.   The back is bronze green, flanks lighter, over-marked by strongly pronounced vertical stripes, and the belly bright white—sharply

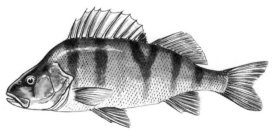

contrasting with coral red pelvic and anal fins. The base lobe of the caudal fin is also red. There are two dorsal fins, the leading one armed with pointed spines.

Distribution: Waters of every size and type. Common in England, Ireland, Wales and southern Scotland.

Growth: Perch are splendid fish at 2 lb (900 g) weight. A 3 lb (1·3 kg) perch is a specimen.

The Pike

Family ESOCIDAE   *Esox lucius*

Identification: A lean ferocious fish is the pike—a confirmed predator both in appearance and in habit. It has vast, flattened jaws packed full with tiny, razor-sharp teeth, and a projectile-like arrangement of fins designed to facilitate the quick bursts of speed necessary to trap lesser creatures. Its greenish body, flecked heavily with pale yellow spots, is camouflage which blends perfectly with weeds, reeds and undercut banks where it lies to ambush its prey.

Distribution: Every type of water. Abundant throughout Britain and Ireland apart from north Scotland.

Growth: How big the biggest pike is is anybody's guess. Forty-pound (18 kg) pike have been taken on rod and line in the past. But huge as these fish seem, it is still not outlandish to suggest that in the lochs and loughs of Scotland and Ireland lurk pike approaching twice this weight. Twenty pounds (9 kg) is accepted specimen size. Any pike bettering 10 lb (4·5 kg) is reward enough for a day's effort.

The Zander or Pike-perch

Family PERCIDAE   *Stizostedion luciperca*

Identification: The zander, or pike-perch as it is also called, is not a hybrid between pike and perch but a distinctly separate species. It is a lean fish, large-mouthed and toothy, with a sharp-spined double-dorsal fin and transparent pectoral and anal fins. The back is dusk green, the flanks olive streaked with darker vertical stripes and blotches, and the belly white. Eyes are noticeably large.

Distribution: Lakes, slow rivers and canals. Localized in England, chiefly the Great Ouse Relief Channel and neighbouring waters such as River Delph, Great Ouse, Old Bedford River and the Middle Level Drain. Also Woburn Abbey lakes, and Claydon Park lakes (private). Presently increasing and spreading rapidly.

Growth: Capable of reaching weights around the 20 lb (9 kg) mark. A zander is a good fish at 8 lb (3·6 kg) and a specimen at 10 lb (4·5 kg). Nearly all the fish of 10 lb (4·5 kg) or more so far caught have been taken from the Relief Channel.

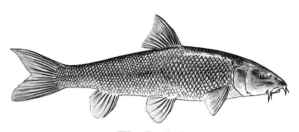

The Barbel

Family CYPRINIDAE   *Barbus barbus*

Identification: A species indigenous to fast rivers. The back of the fish rises quickly from the nose to the shoulders, then sweeps down in a smooth line to the tail. The underside is flat, slightly concave. It is this shape of body which enables the barbel to hold position on the bottom in swift currents—the flow forcing against the lift of the back serving to press the fish downwards in the water.

Flowing water pressures the barbel close to the bottom

As to colour, the dark back lightens golden brown or amber over the flanks, becoming cream white on the belly. There is often reddish orange in the tail and under fins. Four barbules, two on the nose and two at the join of the lips, hang down over a thick, underslung mouth.

Distribution: Fast rivers. A few lakes and reservoirs also contain barbel. In England the species is resident as far north as Yorkshire and as far south as Hampshire. It is not distributed further west than the Dorset Stour. Noted barbel rivers include: Dorset Stour, Hampshire Avon, Swale, Ure, Wharfe, Thames, Kennet, Lea, Bristol Avon and Severn. Stocking programmes have increased the distribution of the barbel considerably in recent years. The species is absent from Ireland, Scotland and Wales.

Growth: In top-class rivers a 10 lb (4·5 kg) barbel is a specimen. Elsewhere a 7 (3·1) or 8 lb (3·6 kg) fish is considered such. The barbel grows as large as 20 lb (9 kg) in the middle reaches of the Hampshire Avon.

The Eel

Family ANGUILLIDAE   *Anguilla anguilla*

Identification: A snake-like fish unlikely to be mistaken for anything else. Usually dark grey above and yellow beneath, becoming more silvery overall during the autumn migratory period. Apart from the small pectoral fins, the remainder of the fins have evolved to form a continuous fringe extending two-thirds along the back, round the tail-end, and almost for the same distance up the underside.

Distribution: Widespread throughout Britain in every type of water.

Growth: In less enlightened times many fanciful theories were produced to account for the presence of eels. They had never been seen to breed and none of their eggs had ever been found, so consequently the ideas put forward were wildly imaginative.

Aristotle suggested that they developed spontaneously from mud. Pliny stated that hairs from horses' tails were their origin. Yet another belief declared that dew falling in late spring, after being heated by the sun, brought forth eels!

Today, though we still have much to learn about the life-cycle of the eel, we do at least know the location of the breeding-ground and the route the eels take to reach this country. It is a fascinating sequence of events.

Both European and American eels breed in an area of the Sargasso Sea situated roughly halfway between the Leeward Islands and Bermuda. From this cradle the minute European larvae set course in the North Atlantic Drift bound for our shores. As they journey so they change in shape and colour eventually becoming elvers—4 in (10 cm) long wrigglers, black and worm-like.

The elvers swim up coastal rivers after a journey which has taken three years to complete during April and May, gradually spreading into waters of all types everywhere. The years pass, and the elvers mature to adulthood and continue growing until the urge to spawn sends them swarming back to the rivers and down to the sea in search of the Sargasso breeding-grounds. This migration commences in autumn, but whether or not they actually reach their ancestral home is a moot point. Some authorities believe they do; others tend to think they perish on the way and that it is only eels returning from America which manage to return and breed successfully—thereby making possible future eel stocks for British waters.

Most eels caught by anglers are small ones, called 'bootlaces'. Apart from eating purposes they are of little interest to anglers. As regards large eels, a three or four-pounder (1·3–1·8 kg) is a nice one; at 5 lb (2·2 kg) or over, specimen size. It is not known to what weight eels grow in Britain. Twenty pounds (9 kg) would not be an unrealistic estimate.

The Wels or Catfish

Family SILURIDAE   *Silurus glanis*

Identification: The wels, or catfish, could not by any stretch of the imagination be described as pleasant to look at. It has a big, flat, ugly head, and an extremely long, tapering, scaleless body. The mouth is massive, the lower jaw jutting out beyond the upper jaw, and there are six barbules: two long ones on the nose and four tiny whiskery ones beneath the chin. Of the fins, the dorsal fin is exceptionally small and the anal fin exceptionally long, fringe-like, extending half the length of the fish. A mixture of greys, greens and browns, mottled with irregular spotting, colours the upper parts. The lower parts are white.

Distribution: Strictly limited to a handful of still-waters in England. Claydon Park lakes (private)

31

and Woburn Abbey lakes are famous catfish preserves.

Growth: One of the largest species in the British Isles. In eastern Europe specimens have been recorded weighing 600 lb (272 kg). It is unlikely that catfish even one-sixth of that weight exist in England at the present time, but nevertheless, an 80 lb (36 kg) 'cat' is a possibility.

Legal Angle

Before setting out to catch coarse fish it is necessary first to obtain the legal right to do so. This right must usually be gained in two ways. (1) A rod licence, allowing the holder to participate in the sport of coarse angling. (2) A permit to fish a particular water from whoever controls the fishing rights.

Waters in England are administered by nine Regional Water Authorities, and in Wales by the Welsh National Water Development Authority. It is the R.W.A.s who issue, through tackle dealers, post offices, hotels and other agents, rod licences, valid for the length of one year, or a lesser period. An R.W.A. rod licence entitles the bearer to engage in coarse fishing, *using one rod*, anywhere within the issuing authority's area—providing permission of the person or body controlling the fishing rights is received first. If a second rod is required (a two-rod set-up is an advantage in some kinds of fishing) a second rod licence must be purchased.

A few waters are known as 'free waters'. That is to say, stillwaters and river stretches which can be legally fished by anybody in possession of a rod licence. Rather more private waters can some-

REGIONAL WATER
AUTHORITIES IN
ENGLAND & WALES

NORTHUMBRIAN

NORTH-
WEST

YORKSHIRE

SEVERN-TRENT

ANGLIAN

WALES
(W.N.W.D.A.)

THAMES

WESSEX

SOUTHERN

SOUTH-WEST

times be fished by applying to the owner and having that right granted at no cost. In such fortunate circumstances a rod licence is still of course required.

More usually, permission to fish must be paid for in the form of a day ticket, period ticket or season ticket, club membership subscription or syndicate share.

There are many ways of permit issue. By post, from a bailiff on the bank, from a tackle shop, from the home of the owner, or even from the local village store. Each water has a permit issue system which must be followed. Never start fishing without a permit assuming that 'somebody' will come along and collect the fee from you. Find out first if this is the system. If it isn't you may find yourself charged with an offence.

Now and then a water may be visited which does not require a rod licence. Here purchase of a permit automatically grants coverage, usually under a special rod licence—called a block or general licence—purchased by the owner or leaseholder from his R.W.A.

All this may sound a trifle complicated but in practice it is nothing of the sort. A visit to the local tackle shop and/or a letter to the secretary of the local angling club, will provide all the information required about licences and permits to fish waters available in your area. For waters further afield one can do no better than obtain a reliable reference guide such as *Where To Fish* (Harmsworth/Black). This invaluable publication, up-dated at intervals, is packed with information which is useful to anglers on holiday and those who frequently travel to distant fisheries in search of sport.

In England and Wales the coarse fishing season extends from the 16th June to the 14th March inclusive. Outside this period, with few exceptions, it is illegal to deliberately angle for coarse fish. Nevertheless, the legal period *can* vary for different areas and individual waters, and this being so I suggest you always check this point for yourself to make absolutely sure.

In Yorkshire, for example, the season starts and finishes earlier by over two weeks (1st June to the 27th February inclusive). Moreover, along rivers where both coarse and game fishing is practised (e.g. the Hampshire Avon) certain stretches remain closed until well into summer, and may also close earlier too, to cater for the needs of salmon and sea trout enthusiasts.

The important thing about all this, is never to fish anywhere without the correct rod licence and permit, or indeed out of season. To do so is to invite trouble and almost certainly, in these days of tighter restrictions, the possibility of a court summons. The modern view of poachers is not anything like as friendly as once it was!

Rod licences and fishing permits include rules and regulations printed on their backs. Always read these sections carefully because the information contained varies from area to area. What is perfectly correct for one water may be absolutely banned somewhere else.

In Scotland and the Republic of Ireland, there is no close season or rod licence for coarse fishing. Most places can be fished without any payment, after obtaining permission from the owner. There is also no close season in Northern Ireland, but local regulations concerning rod licences and permits must be checked.

As well as observing the regulations indicated on licences, permits, and in club rule books, bankside notices must also be obeyed—likewise the accepted code of behaviour in the countryside. Such points as shutting farm gates, not lighting open fires, not throwing away unstubbed cigarette ends, parking the car where it will not obstruct, and leaving trees, shrubs, field crops, flowers and every kind of animal, as undisturbed as possible, are essentials of conduct which should be second nature to every angler.

Removal of litter is very important. Not only does litter not look attractive, it also kills and injures wild birds, small animals and expensive domestic stock. Reports of such incidents are common.

Taking home personal rubbish, and picking up rubbish left by less thoughtful individuals, is a joint responsibility in which we all have a part to play. Lengths of line, hooks, bottles, tins, plastic bags and cups, are objects we cannot afford to ignore. They are proven killers and a direct reason why certain waters are closed off completely to anglers.

Absolutely everything should be done to ensure that the countryside and its inhabitants, including fellow anglers, remains peaceful, happy and content.

Dress and Approach

Young fish, and stunted fish in over-populated waters, are invariably easy to catch. They are always hungry and not at all cautious. Beyond a general understanding of simple methods, very little skill is required to coax them to take hook-baits.

Larger, older fish, are a different proposition. They do not feed all the time, and when they do they tend to remain exceedingly shy of any un-natural disturbance which even slightly alerts in them a sense of danger. Fish of good size are more difficult to catch than little ones, and to stand any chance at all with them it is essential for the angler to remain as quiet and out of sight as possible.

In this respect a choice of clothing requires consideration. Whatever is worn—and anglers are very individualistic indeed about dress—it should be of sombre colour. Country greens and browns for preference. True enough, good fish are caught from time to time by anglers wearing white shirts and light-coloured trousers, but such captures are few and far between compared with the high total of fish which bolt for safety after becoming alarmed by unusual movements along the bank.

Fish do not see as we see, but they do see enough to recognize the abnormal. Greens and browns are the natural colours of the countryside, and clad in these colours the angler is far more able to blend with the scenery than would be possible wearing 'whiter than white' gear. Personally, I would no sooner go fishing in a white shirt than I would attend a wedding in hob-nail boots and overalls!

Keeping movement to a minimum is just as important. Don't walk about more than you have to. And when you do, keep well away from the bank-edge and off the skyline. Make use of available cover. Keep movements slow. Above all tread lightly. Fish are acutely sensitive to vibrations through the water, and when these emanate from land they quickly get the message and fade away to the cover of weeds.

A point to remember is that a combination of foliage and terrain is just as useful a hide when you are in front of it, as it is when you are behind it. Dressed in camouflaged gear, with a bush, tree trunk or high bank to your rear, you can still remain 'out of sight' from fish literally swimming at your feet in clear, shallow water. For example, perched

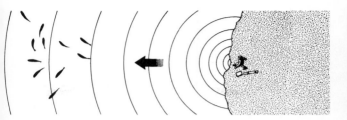

Heavy-footed movements scare fish

on the edge of a high bank an angler, and every movement he makes, is clearly outlined against the sky. But, by moving down in front of the bank he is able to make use of its face as an efficient means of back-camouflage, although much closer to the fish.

It is less likely that fish will be scared off when they are in deep or coloured water, or swimming far out from the bank, but the softly silent, unobtrusive approach, still remains sound tactics. The rule is never do anything which might even *possibly* put the quarry down, and that means the right clothes and the right approach on every fishing trip and in every situation. These are vital factors if you want to catch larger fish than run-of-the-mill tiddlers.

The bank face is useful back-camouflage

2: TACKLE, BAITS AND
METHODS

Bait Fishing Tackle

Rods

The majority of rods are manufactured from hollow tapering tubes of fibreglass, a highly versatile long-lasting material which has virtually taken over from older rod-building materials such as cane and tubular steel. Carbon-fibre and carbon composite rods are also available, but these are expensive compared with fibreglass equivalents and are not a recommended buy for complete beginners.

A 'glass' rod suitable for bait fishing has an overall length somewhere between 10 and 12 ft (3–3·6 m), a butt (handle) at least 2 ft (60 cm) long, and sliding fittings for attachment of the reel. The intermediate line guides, or rings, will be plain stainless steel ones finished with a hard chrome coating. Tip and butt rings will be lined with a friction-free material such as magnesium oxide.

The rod butt (handle) is surfaced with cork

Rods have two or three sections which fit tightly together. The simplest tubular fibreglass join is

known as 'wall-to-wall'—one section jammed inside
another. Metal ferrule and modern spigot ferrule
are more advanced types of join.

In putting a rod together check that the rings on
the different sections all line-up exactly. If the rod
has a metal ferrule the male part should be cleaned

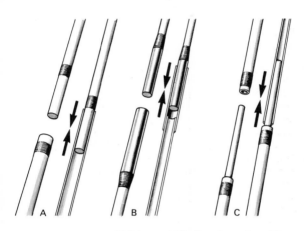

Ferrules: 'wall-to-wall' (A), metal (B), fibreglass spigot (C)

first and given a coat of spray-lubricant such as
WD-40 or AP-75 to ensure that the sections will
come easily apart again. A spigot ferrule requires
a coating of graphite (from a pencil) to prevent it
jamming. Do not force rod sections apart by
twisting them in different directions. A *straight*
pull is the correct drill.

To give you an idea of types of bait fishing rods,
here are descriptions of favourite rods from my own
collection.

Sight along the rod
to line up the rings

Float Rod: Length 12 ft (3·6 m), weight 12 oz (340 g), action fast and tippy. Three-piece with wall-to-wall ferrules. A rod suitable for float fishing with lines less than 5 lb (2·2 kg) test.

Avon Rod: Length 11 ft (3·3 m), weight 8½ oz (240 g), action right through the rod. Two-piece with spigot ferrule. An ideal rod for freelining and legering as well as float fishing, matched with lines between 2 (900 g) and 8 lb (3·6 kg) test. This is an excellent design for the 'one rod' angler.

Big Fish Rod: Length 10 ft (3 m), weight 12 oz (340 g), through action. Two-piece with spigot ferrule.

Big Fish Rod: Length 11 ft 6 in (3·5 m), weight 1 lb (450 g), through action. Two-piece with metal ferrules and a detachable butt.

Big Fish Rods, with lines between 8 (3·6) and 15 lb (6·8 kg) test are for pike, carp, eel and zander. Also for hard-fighting smaller-growing species such as tench, barbel and chub in snaggy conditions and in waters where they grow to very large size.

Heavy Deadbaiting Rod (Beachcaster): Length 12 ft (3·6 m), weight 1 lb 12 oz (790 g), steep-taper action. Two-piece with metal ferrule. In coarse fishing the only use for this sea rod is to enable large weighty deadbaits (e.g. herring, mackerel) to be cast long distance when pike fishing from the bank.

The illustrations show the rods I have described.

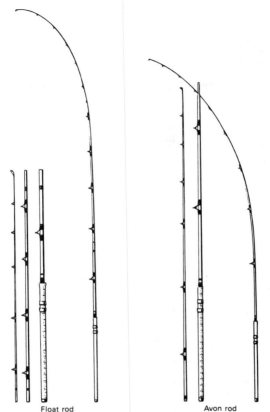

Float rod   Avon rod

From left to right, tip-actioned float rod, through
action Avon rod. Over page, through action big
fish rod, steep-taper heavy deadbaiting rod.

The action of a rod is the shape of its curve when

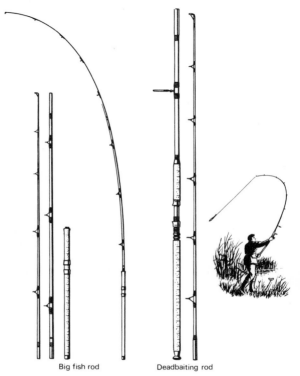

Big fish rod   Deadbaiting rod

under pressure. Different actions are produced by
varying the taper of the rod's length.

Rods are expensive and many newcomers to the
sport will not be able to afford more than one to start
with. Should this be the case, an Avon-type rod is
the most sensible choice. This design is suitable for
all small and middleweight species, pike in waters

where they do not grow much over 10 lb (4·5 kg), and carp in open, snag-free lakes.

For big pike, eels, carp in weedy waters and middleweight species in similar conditions, a big fish rod is essential kit. Without such a rod these fish are better left well alone.

Fibreglass rods require little maintenance beyond drying them out at room temperature when they get wet, giving them a fresh coat of rod varnish as required, and checking the rings regularly for signs of grooving. Grooved rings damage the line, weakening its test strength considerably, and must be replaced without delay.

Shop-bought rods have a high-gloss varnish finish. They are nice enough to look at but a positive menace in sunny weather. The varnish reflects the sun, giving off 'flashes' which send fish dashing for cover each time a cast is made. This problem can be dealt with by giving rods a coat of matt-finish varnish to dull the gloss varnish down. Rods so treated do not look particularly attractive but they do increase the chance of catching fish—which is what rods are for after all!

Reels
The fixed-spool reel is by far the most popular type on the market at the present time. Many different designs are available, left- and right-hand wind, at a range of prices to suit the pocket of every angler.

A main feature of this reel is the adjustable slipping-clutch which, providing it is set correctly, will yield line to a hooked fish the instant it pulls extra hard or goes off on a powerful run. It is a device which helps prevent line breakage.

To set the clutch slipping, the tension nut on the front of the spool is eased with the line under a

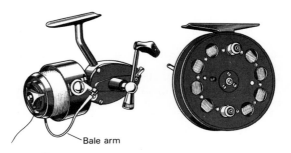

Bale arm

Fixed-spool reel (left) and centre-pin reel (right)

pressure approaching maximum test, until the spool just, and only just, begins to give line.

By placing the forefinger of the hand holding the rod against the rim of the spool a fine degree of control can be exercised over the slipping-clutch mechanism—lifting the finger when a fish pulls

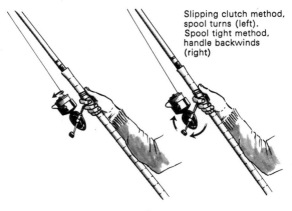

Slipping clutch method, spool turns (left). Spool tight method, handle backwinds (right)

hard and pressing it down firmly when pumping the rod up and down in order to wind line back on to the spool.

Alternatively, for anglers who do not like the slipping clutch routine (many don't) the spool can be screwed tight and the handle set to backwind (under finger-and-thumb control) against a running fish.

Line spools are interchangeable for fixed-spool reels and I suggest you buy several to allow a range of line strengths to be carried.

Fewer and fewer anglers use a centre-pin reel these days. The centre-pin design, although having some advantage over the fixed-spool with regard to tackle control when float fishing rivers is, in the final analysis, not nearly so versatile. It is also much more difficult to cast with efficiently.

By far the best plan for beginners is to learn the first principles of the sport with fixed-spool reels, and then later with two or three seasons' experience behind them, try a centre-pin as an alternative reel.

Side-cast reel, in casting position (left), and positioned for retrieving line (right)

The side-cast reel is a cross between the fixed-spool and the centre-pin. It is positioned as a centre-pin for retrieving line and playing fish, but for casting the drum twists round sideways so that the handles face up the rod and the line is able to slip freely over the edge in exactly the same way as from a fixed-spool. A large-diameter line-guide forms part of the fittings of this reel.

Side-casting unfortunately puts a multitude of turns in the line, and for this reason it is important to confine the use of side-cast reels to weightless tackle methods and terminal rigs which incorporate a large swivel at the top end for attachment to the main line. This swivel, plus winding the line firmly back on the drum through the fingers, virtually eliminates the turns completely.

Resting the butt against the forearm

48

For freeline deadbaiting in stillwaters I consider this type of reel second to none. The shallowness of the wide drum aids distance casting, and the centre-pin style of playing fish provides the sensitive control needed to handle big pike, eels and catfish.

All reels are mounted at the top of the butt so that the length of the butt rests comfortably against the underside of the forearm.

Lines

Nylon monofilament fishing line is available in a wide range of test strengths. If you have six spools for your reel this will enable you to carry the following breaking strains: 3 lb (1·3 kg), 5 lb (2·2 kg), 8 lb (3·6 kg), 12 lb (5·4 kg), and 15 lb (6·8 kg), with a spare spool available for any other test which might be required to suit a particular need. Each spool should be filled to the lip with at least 100 yd (91·4 m) of line.

To wind on a line, first fix the reel to the rod butt and attach the end of the line firmly to the spool. Then push a pencil through the hole in the container and get a friend to hold the pencil in such a way that the container revolves under pressure, as you transfer the line to the spool. Do this slowly keeping the turns tight. Care should be taken to spread the turns as evenly as possible as an aid to smooth casting, both for distance and accuracy.

Nylon monofilament has a nasty habit of losing strength quite suddenly, without warning, so test all lines regularly against a spring-balance. It may only be the last few yards (metres) of a line which has weakened, but check carefully because sometimes it is the whole line which needs replacing. It is sensible to commence each new season with fresh lines on all spools.

Fill the spool with
line to the lip

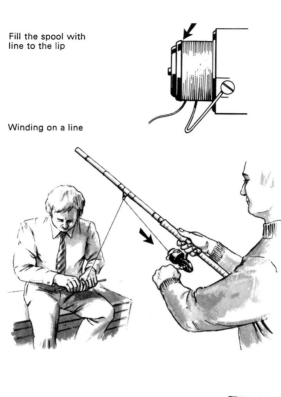

Winding on a line

Check line strength against a spring-balance

Hooks

These can be bought attached to lengths of nylon, but personally I prefer loose hooks of the 'eyed' type which are cheaper and more reliable. Hooks ranging from size 2 (the largest) down to size 16 will be required—a quantity of each size in separate grip-edged plastic bags.

Small hooks are usually sharp enough as bought, but larger hooks will certainly require additional

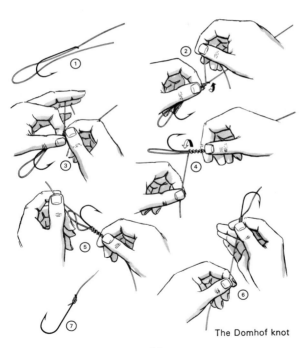

The Domhof knot

51

sharpening with a carborundum stone. Throw out any hooks which are spotted with rust, soft in the wire, or otherwise suspect. It is far better to be safe than sorry! Eyed hooks are attached direct to the reel line for maximum reliability. The Domhof knot is suitable for hooks with turned down eyes and the tucked half-blood knot for hooks with straight eyes.

The illustration (page 51) shows how the Domhof knot is tied. The end of the line is threaded through the eye and a loop formed along the length of the hook's shank (1). Several turns are then taken round the top of the shank with the right hand whilst the left hand retains the loop in place (2). Now the finger and thumb of the right hand are used to hold the turns firmly so that the left hand can be freed (3). Between three and five more turns are then made down the shank—making sure they do not overlap each other (4). The end of the line is tucked through the loop (5). The end of the line is pulled to remove the loop and tighten the turns (6). Neat and strong, the completed Domhof knot (7).

For pike and zander fishing a selection of three-point hooks will be needed for making up the wire traces for live and dead baiting methods. These treble hooks are numbered according to size exactly the same way as single hooks are.

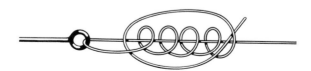

The tucked half-blood knot for straight eyed hooks

Turned down eyed hook (left). Treble hook (right)

Trace Wire

When baiting with live or dead fish, or when lure fishing, for sharp-toothed predators such as pike and zander, some form of wire trace will be required between the main line and the hooks. Trace wire is either single-strand or multi-strand—the latter type also available nylon-coated. Single-strand wire is reliable for deadbaiting but, in my experience, is not so suitable for livebaiting or lure fishing because of its tendency to kink. A livebait as it swims about can cause kinking and so can a large, lightweight spoon which may double-back on itself. For lures and livebaits I prefer multi-strand wire which is soft and supple: plain for lures and nylon-coated for livebaits. I also use nylon-coated wire for most of my deadbait rigs.

On pages 92–98 will be found details of simple wire rigs and how to make them.

Simple floats from porcupine quill and balsawood

Floats

The purpose of a float is to indicate bites, to present the bait as naturally as possible at the depth the fish are feeding and, as required, to carry additional casting weight.

Float patterns are many and I appreciate that the vast array available in a tackle shop (including wagglers, duckers, sticks, zoomers, windbeaters and darts, etc.) can bewilder the tyro. Enough to say at this point that it is not necessary to own hundreds of floats to catch fish. A handful of different patterns will suffice to begin with, and these will be mentioned in the parts of this book dealing with basic methods and practical fishing. (See pages 102 and 130.)

Floats are made from such materials as bird quills, porcupine quills, cane, balsawood, cork, wire, reed, elderpith and nylon, or often a combination of two or three of these materials. (See page 53.)

To attach a float to the line a small ring is whipped to the lower end and a rubber band (float cap) is added near the tip. For some methods this ring is most useful, but for straightforward attachment there is nothing to beat two strong rubber bands—one near the tip and one near the base.

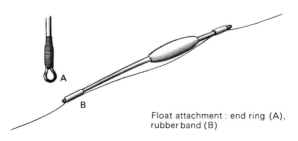

Float attachment : end ring (A), rubber band (B)

This allows quick interchange of floats to be made without the need to take down the terminal tackle.

Float caps are bought in packets of assorted sizes. Be a bit choosy about the brand. Float caps must be long enough and strong enough to grip the float against the line firmly and prevent it sliding down during casting and retrieving. Depth setting must be kept exactly right to catch fish with a float rig, and weak float caps can spoil the presentation very easily.

Lead

To 'cock' a float, make it stand in the water with just the right amount of tip showing above the surface; lead split-shot is added to the line beneath the float. The line is placed in the split and the split closed with either finger pressure or thin-nosed pliers—but not too tight because this can damage the line and even cut it through.

Split-shot is available in different sizes. The largest is called swanshot. Other sizes include AAA, BB, and microshot. There are also types of shot which are numbered according to their size. An easy way to obtain a supply of shot is to buy a multi-compartment dispenser containing six different shot sizes.

For float fishing use only soft-lead shot. If you cannot close the split with average finger pressure, it is not soft enough. Most shot is round, but another type, a very splendid type for float work, is called 'mouse droppings'—elongated shot made from super-soft lead.

Apart from its use for float fishing, lead-shot is also used when legering to make a simple form of leger weight known as the link-leger. There are a number of variations on the same principle, but I make my link-legers as follows. A 2 in (5 cm)

55

length of monofilament, test strength slightly less than the main line, is attached to a tiny two-way swivel, and to this 'tail' is added swanshot made from hard lead. By varying the amount of shot it is possible to balance the weight of the link-leger exactly right for the swim being fished, adding or subtracting shot as required.

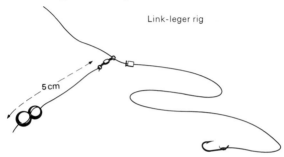

Link-leger rig

5 cm

I use the link-leger for both stillwater and river fishing. I consider it an outstanding general-purpose weight. To attach it to the line, the line is threaded through the top eye of the swivel, a plug-stop is added, and finally the hook is tied on.

Split-shot, and, from left to right, three leger weights: Arlesey bomb, drilled bullet, swivelled coffin lead

Other leads to have in the tackle box include Arlesey bombs and swivelled coffin leads. Carry a few of each in $\frac{1}{4}$ oz (7 g), $\frac{1}{2}$ oz (14 g), and $\frac{3}{4}$ oz (21 g), sizes. For piking, $\frac{1}{2}$ oz (14 g), 1 oz (28 g), and 2 oz (56 g) drilled bullets are handy leads.

New leads are shiny. They dull quickly in the water, but if you want to avoid every chance of scaring fish, leave them in a jar of vinegar overnight. That will do the trick.

As bought, a coffin lead is not swivelled. Insert a two-way swivel for half its length inside one end of the lead and bang it firm with a hammer.

Plastic plug-stops
To hold the leger weight up the line at a set distance from the hook some form of stop is needed. One or two split-shots is a commonly used method, but a better device is the plastic plug-stop. This consists of a stiff plastic band fitted with a specially shaped plug. The line is threaded through the band and the plug jammed in to hold it tight.

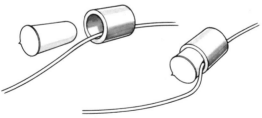

Plastic plug-stop

Swimfeeders
These are fished in place of the leger lead—with the additional advantage that they feed the swim with groundbait and hookbait samples.

57

The basic swimfeeder is a transparent plastic tube perforated with holes and weighted by means of a lead strip. There is a loop of nylon at one end and to this loop a link-swivel is added. The main line is threaded through the eye of the swivel.

In operation one end of the tube is plugged with groundbait, a 'middle' of hook bait samples is added, and then a cap of groundbait to seal it. Cast out, the groundbait breaks-up and the contents are spilled out on the bottom right where the hook-bait is lying.

The open-end swimfeeder is best for stillwaters. The type more suitable for rivers is known as a block-end swimfeeder, designed to let the feed out in a slow trickle rather than all at once.

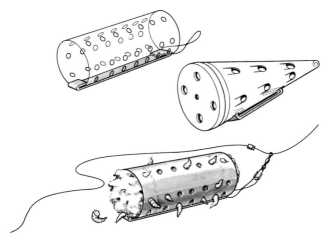

Top : open-end swimfeeder. Centre : Polycone block-end swimfeeder. Bottom : open-end swimfeeder primed with bait

An advanced block-end design is known as the Polycone. This type is attached by threading the line through a central hole and retaining it above the hook, running leger style, by means of a plug-stop or split-shot. The Polycone discharges its contents at a slower rate than the open-end, and it has a shape which is less likely to roll along the bottom or to lift in swift water—features very important in a swimfeeder used for river fishing.

Another excellent block-end feeder is the Feederlink. Designed by Peter Drennan, this is one of the very best for legering in rivers.

Rod Rests

Some fishing methods require the rod to be rested steady, either because the technique is delicately sensitive or because there will possibly be long waits between bites—bites from species which hang on

Rod rests

long enough to allow the angler time to pick up the rod and strike. Rod rests are used for this purpose.

A rod rest for front support has a groove beneath the fork so that the line can run freely out. The back rest is a plain half-moon shape. Telescopic rests (front and back) allow for fine adjustment. They should have stout shafts and strong tips.

Front and back rests are angled so as to bring the rod butt close alongside the angler. This arrangement enables the rod to be picked up and a bite struck all in one movement.

Landing Nets

Apart from the smallest tiddlers, a landing net will be required to lift fish from the water. A triangular-framed landing net with 32 in (81 cm) arms is a reasonable size for most species apart from the very

David Carl Forbes carefully unhooks a tench. The wet mesh of the landing net helps prevent damage to the protective slime coat of the fish

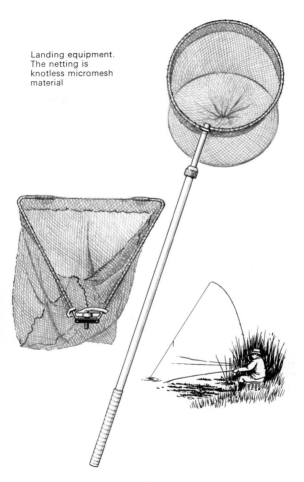

Landing equipment. The netting is knotless micromesh material

largest carp and pike, etc. For big fellows a landing net with 42 in (106 cm) arms is a more adequate size. Round-framed nets are also available and these are useful for netting fish from thick weed as they penetrate the growth more easily than triangular-framed nets.

The handle should be strongly built, featuring a reliable screw-fitting for joining to the frame. An extending handle is priceless when attempting to net a fish from across a wide margin of weed or soft marsh.

How to net fish correctly is explained in the chapter dealing with handling fish. (See pages 166–168.)

Polarized Glasses

A pair of these glasses is a marvellous angling aid. They absorb reflected glare so that only useful light reaches the eye. When the sun is strong on the water the surface loses its brilliant sheen and it becomes easier to see the float clearly and bite indications.

Polarized glasses also enable the angler to see right through the surface, deep into the water—as far as the bottom, providing the depth is not too great or the water too murky. In this way big fish can be pinpointed and fished for specifically. For maximum effect, wear a wide-brimmed hat or eye shield.

Plummets

The typical plummet is a cone-shaped lead weight with a ring at the pointed end and a thickness of cork let into the base. It is used to discover the depth of a swim when float fishing. The hook is threaded through the ring and secured in the cork. By casting out several times and adjusting the float either up or down until just the right length of tip pokes above the surface, the tackle can be set to

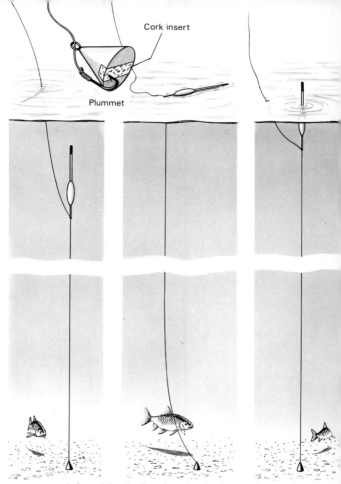

Left to right, the float is under depth, over depth and at correct depth

swim depth. A plummet is mainly useful for stillwaters of great depth rather than shallow lakes and
rivers.

Seats
Collapsible seats suitable for angling purposes come
in many shapes and sizes. The main requirements
of any seat is that it should be both strongly built

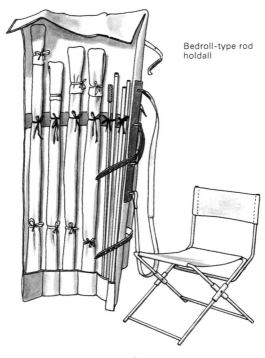

Bedroll-type rod
holdall

and comfortable. Low seats, which allow advantage to be taken of minimum cover, are better for daytime fishing than high ones. At night, all types of seat, bedchairs included, can be used.

Choose a design which features a backrest for additional comfort. If it also has armrests, make sure it is wide enough to sit in without becoming so firmly stuck that when you stand up to play a fish the seat remains with you! This can happen if you are wearing thick clothing.

Rod Holdalls

Rods, rod rests, landing net and umbrella, can be carried in a holdall fitted with a shoulder strap. Three main patterns are available: one with zip-up top, one with a full length zip which opens up wallet-style, and one which opens right out like a bedroll. The choice is yours, but having tried them all I now prefer the latter, which gives easier access to everything. It features individual sections for rods, rod-rests, landing net and umbrella, all securely held and protected.

Arrangement of tackle

Tackle Carriers

Tackle boxes, baskets and haversacks are used to carry tackle, bait and refreshments. The choice is again one of personal opinion. Boxes and baskets have the advantage that they can also be used to sit on, but large haversacks hold far more gear.

Other Tackle

Scissors, knife, torch, thermometer, old towelling and a first-aid kit are essentials. An anti-sting spray such as Wasp-eze should be included in the first-aid kit.

A large umbrella, complete with metal pegs and guy ropes to stake it firmly down, and a waterproofed canvas sheet, are further accessories which make the coldest rain-filled day pleasantly bearable —even if the fish do decide not to bite!

Tackle should be arranged so that essential items are close to hand. The illustration (page 65) shows a proper layout of gear. An umbrella (A) is both a shelter from the rain and a windbreak. It should always be staked down, to prevent it blowing away, with guy ropes and metal pegs (B). Floats, hooks and shot (C), hook baits (D), hand-towel (E) and groundbait (F) are all items which should be located within arm's reach. The mouth of the keepnet (G) is best positioned so that the fish can be slipped inside without the need to stand up. If a rod rest (H) is used it should be angled so that strikes can be made firmly over the shoulder. Never commence fishing without first fitting up a landing net (I) and placing it on the bank where it will be ready for instant action when needed.

Choosing Tackle

By far the most sensible plan is to visit a recommended tackle shop, in the company of a knowledgeable angling friend if possible, and let the dealer advise you in your selections according to what you can afford.

Tackle dealers are keen anglers themselves, and what is more they rely for their livelihood on clients who return regularly. They cannot afford to give bad advice or mislead, and their after-sales service and deep knowledge of local angling cannot be equalled by any form of mail-order tackle buying or by traders selling tackle purely as a sideline.

Casting

Short casts are made underhand. The terminal tackle hangs down rather less than the length of the rod, with the bale-arm open and the forefinger against the spool rim to prevent the line spilling free. As the rod top is moved down and outwards, a sharp flick is given to the tackle and at the same time the forefinger is lifted to release the line.

Longer casts are made across the body. The bale-arm is switched to the open position, and the

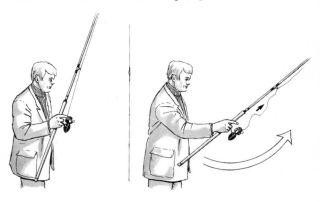

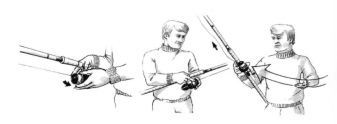

line retained by a forefinger. In a single movement
the rod is brought across the body and, as the terminal rig straightens out astern of the angler, the
rod is brought back again to point in the direction

of the cast. As that angle is reached the forefinger
is lifted to free the line and send the terminal tackle
on its way.

Alternatively the cast can be made away from the body.

Distance casting a deadbait with a beachcaster and side-cast reel combination is actioned as follows. First, the deadbait is set to hang down approximately half the length of the rod, and the reel drum turned to the casting position with the forefinger of the hand nearest to the reel pressing against the rim of the drum as a line stop.

Now the angler positions himself and his tackle (1). A pendulum action is imparted to the bait, first away from the body (2), and then back towards the body (3), *directly in line with the length of the rod*. On the second outward swing (4) the angler stretches well over ready to propel the bait forward by pulling down on the butt end with the left hand and pushing upwards from under the reel with the right hand (5). The angle of the body and the rod are shown (6) as the tackle is released.

Note the changing position of the head as the cast develops. This cast is made slowly, without jerk, and with maximum power applied from position 5 right through until the bait is released.

Hookbaits and Groundbaits

Bread

The most versatile of all baits. *Bread flake* is a piece torn from the inside of a fresh loaf pinched round the hook-shank to hang down soft and flaky over the hook. A pinch of flake combined with maggots forms a highly successful 'sandwich bait'.

Bread crust is a chunk torn or cut from the outside of a loaf so that a portion of the white remains attached. To use this bait the hook is inserted from the crust side, turned, and brought back through so that the bend of the hook rests against the inside part. Crust can be fished freeline at the surface, or anchored with a leger weight at any depth from bottom to surface.

Bread cube is a shape about the size of a sugar lump, with or without the outer skin attached. Notable as bait for big roach.

Bread paste is made by removing the crust from a three-day old loaf, wrapping the white inside a clean cloth and giving the contents a thorough soaking. As much water as possible is then squeezed out and the bread, still in the cloth, is worked with the fingers until it is a soft smooth paste.

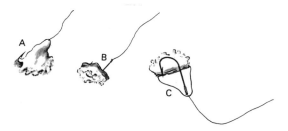

Bread flake (A), bread crust (B), balanced crust (C)

Balanced crust combines a buoyant crust with enough paste added to the hook-shank to sink it ultra-slowly.

Caddis larvae
These are the grubs of the caddis fly which live along the bottom of rivers and lakes in little tubes which they construct from twig fragments, leaf remains and grit. A caddis grub must be extricated carefully and nicked on the hook through the tip of the tail.

Cheese
Cheddar cheese, in cube or paste form, is a fine general-purpose bait. Chub, roach, barbel, carp and tench, have special liking for it. All other kinds of cheese can be used—the softer, strong-smelling ones, mixed with bread paste.

Crayfish
Supplies of these small freshwater lobsters are obtained after dark, from certain rivers, by the drop-net method. A suitable drop-net can be made from the wheel rim of a child's cycle by adding a narrow-mesh bottom, three or four steadying wires and a length of cord for lowering and retrieving the apparatus. A fish such as a herring is attached firmly in the middle of the net as lure, and the trap is then dropped to the bottom against the edge of the bank.

It is advantageous to have a number of nets out along a suitable stretch. Each net is left for at least 30 minutes and then retrieved quickly. With any luck several crayfish will have crawled over the netting to eat the bait-lure; they must be picked up between finger and thumb across the back before they have a chance of scuttling off into the vegetation.

A second way of catching crayfish is to wade a

Crayfish drop-net baited with a dead fish (arrowed)

small stream turning over the larger stones under which they rest during daylight hours. As the crayfish are exposed, pin them down with a forked stick to be lifted out with the fingers.

A crayfish bait is fished freeline on a size 4 hook passed through the tail-end segment from the under-side. Lead is only added if the weight of the bait is not enough to hold position against the strength of the current. Crayfish can be kept alive in a large bucket of water, if the water is changed frequently.

Creepy-crawlies
This category includes such animals as beetles, woodlice, caterpillars, dockgrubs and snails.

Giant grass-hoppers (when they can be found) are fine bait for chub

These, and similar small creatures, are well worth trying as bait.

Elderberries
Ripe for picking from late summer onwards. The berries can be used straight off the tree, nicked lightly on fine-wire hooks to avoid bursting, for roach, dace, chub and barbel. To preserve elderberries for out-of-season use put them in either syrup or a solution of one part formalin to ten parts water.

Elvers
These young eels, just a few inches long, can be collected from coastal rivers during spring. Preserve them in a formalin solution or keep them alive in an old bathtub. They can also be obtained throughout the summer months by searching weed clumps and underneath the bank with a collecting net. Elvers are fished on float and leger rigs. The live ones should be killed first by dipping them in boiling water. A freshly dead elver hooked through

73

the head and long-trotted down the length of a weirpool in June is first-class bait for chub—and barbel too, when the mood takes them.

Fish baits
Minnows, loach, ruffe, bullhead, bleak, gudgeon, roach, rudd, dace, carp, bream, chub, perch, herring, mackerel and sprat, are all baits for catching predators: pike, perch, zander, eels, chub and catfish.   Using live fish as bait is banned in Ireland.

Flies
Alive and dead, flies of various kinds can be used to catch surface-feeding fish.   Freshly hatched bluebottles are outstandingly suitable and easy to obtain. All that is required is an airtight tin full of casters (chrysalid stage) left in a warm spot to hatch.   If kept in the container the majority of the flies remain in a doped state, unwilling to fly.   This makes possible their removal one at a time for the hook without risk of the whole lot swarming free.

Freshwater mussels
Found in both stillwaters and rivers they can be harvested with either a long-handled rake or a forked stick and glass-bottomed observation tube. Never remove more than you absolutely require, and return any left at the end of the day.   Keep them alive in a keepnet.   The shell is opened with a knife and the soft flesh threaded as firmly as possible on the hook.   When removing the flesh keep an eye open for pearls.   Freshwater mussel pearls of quality are worth a great deal of money.   Mussel bait is deadly for tench and bream on the right day.

Hempseed
To prepare hempseed it should be soaked for a few hours, then boiled in water with soda added until

the husks split exposing the white kernels.   Fine-wire hooks are used when single-seed float fishing for roach and dace, the bend of the hook being pressed into the white split to hold the seed in place. Hempseed is also legered for barbel and chub—two or three grains on a big hook.

More controversy surrounds the use of hemp as bait than all the other baits put together.   A lot of nonsense has been preached about the seed drugging fish and making fisheries 'one-bait-only' waters, and consequently it is banned in some places.   Check this point locally before using it.

When fishing with round split-shot and hempseed on the hook false bites are often registered caused by fish sucking the shots in mistake for seed.   This irritation can be avoided by shotting the tackle only with mousedropping split-shot or coiled lead wire. Lead wire is attached by threading the line through the coil and holding it in place with a single dust-shot or plug-stop.

Wheat, pearl barley, corn on the cob, macaroni, tares and long-grain rice, are baits prepared in much the same way as hempseed.

Lead wire coil for hempseed fishing

Tinned sweetcorn

This bait requires no preparation, simply impale one or more grains on a fine-wire hook.   Sweetcorn attracts large fish of many species, and at the same time avoids the little ones.

Maggots

Without doubt the most popular bait.   Maggots, or gentles, are the larvae stage of the bluebottle fly. All species apart from confirmed predators can be caught on them, including large specimens.

Maggots are fished single, double, or as a bunch of a dozen or more, legered and float fished.   The smaller maggots of the house fly (squats) and the greenbottle fly (pinkies) have purpose as free-feed when hookbaiting with bluebottle maggots.

Casters is the angler's name for chrysalids, the stage which maggots pass through prior to hatching as mature flies. They are yellow at first, becoming bright orange and then dark red prior to transformation.   Casters are fished neat or in conjunction with maggots; two maggots and a single caster is a typical sandwich bait.

Some casters float and some sink.   It is important when feeding a swim with them as groundbait that only sinkers are used.   Floaters and sinkers can be divided by tipping them into a bucket of water and skimming off those which remain at the surface.

Floating casters are, however, bait for surface fishing methods.   Scattered on the water they attract such fish as rudd and dace.

Meat baits

Sausages are excellent bait for barbel, carp and chub.   I prefer the small skinless varieties, uncooked, lightly fried or lightly boiled, whole or cut into chunks.   Sausage meat is equally good mixed with bread or sausage rusk to form a paste.

76

Cubes of tinned meats and liver are other proven meat baits. And so too are exotic 'stink baits' concocted from cat and dog foods mixed with rusk, bread, and anything else which is meaty smelling.

Potatoes
Mainly bait for carp, but also at times used for tench, bream and chub. Tinned potatoes are best for short-range freeline fishing, and larger un-skinned potatoes for distance casting and for reducing the interest of other potato-loving species when angling solely to catch carp.

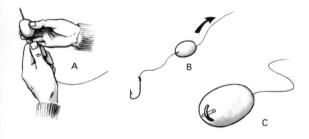

Baiting with potato bait

Potatoes are prepared by boiling them until they are soft, as soft as would be required for table. To bait a potato the line is threaded through with a baiting needle (A). The hook tied on and pulled back against the bait (B). At short range the bait is tossed out by hand, but for rod casting a shock absorber is needed between the hook-bend and the bait. A piece of crust or half a matchstick is suitable for this purpose (C). Carp are caught on both skinned and unskinned potatoes. A thick disc-shape, because it sinks slowly, is ideal when fishing

Potato disc, for a muddy or weedy bottom

over thick mud or bottom weed. It is less likely to become hidden.

For species other than carp, cube portions of potato work well. In order to hand-cast a potato,

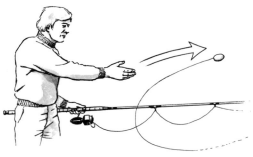

Hand-casting a potato

the bale-arm of the reel is disengaged so that line can run freely, and the rod is pointed in the same direction as the bait is to be thrown.

78

Silkweed

Silkweed, or rait, is a soft algae found growing on weirpool stonework and similar places. It is collected and kept fresh in a bucket of water to be used by draping a little over the hook and float fishing it at about mid-depth. Silkweed appeals to roach and chub, less often, dace and barbel too. Most of the success I have had with silkweed has been experienced on hot days during low-water conditions.

Slugs

A deadly bait for big chub, legered or freelined. The brown slugs with orange frills catch fish, but the smaller black slugs which creep river banks on damp mornings are even better. Slugs are sticky creatures and should be handled as little as possible. The cleanest way is with a pair of tongs made from two lengths of wood to which strips of rough sandpaper have been glued.

Wasp grubs

Superb late-summer bait float fished for roach, dace, chub and barbel. During August–September is the period to search for nests. Once one has been located, wasp powder obtained from a chemist should be put down at its entrances to kill the wasps. Twilight is the time for this, when the wasps are back in the nest and least active. On the following day the nest can be dug out and baked to toughen the grubs held within. Baking is simply accomplished by putting the nest in a container placed inside an outer vessel holding boiling water and simmering it there for a short spell.

Worms

Lobworms can be collected in quantity in return for a little after-dark hunting. All that is required is a torch with a subdued beam, a bag or tin to hang round the neck, and access to a close-cropped lawn or verge. Shortly after full darkness lobworms come to the surface and lie half out of their holes. By stepping lightly, shining the torch a little way ahead, the shiny bodies of the worms can be spotted in the grass. To make a capture, first make sure which end of the worm is which, and then grab it at the point where it enters the ground, trapped between finger and thumb. Do not pull too hard or the worm will break. Maintain a steady pressure and as the worm is felt to relax its grip draw it slowly clear. Many worms can be gathered this way in less than an hour, but never take more of them than absolutely needed.

Lobworms are fished whole, in sections, and as bunches of three or four, legered, freelined and float fished. To be really effective bait a lobworm must look right on the hook. It is not much use jabbing 12 in (30 cm) of worm back and forth through its body until it resembles a sticky brown lump rather than the fish-appealing creature it was

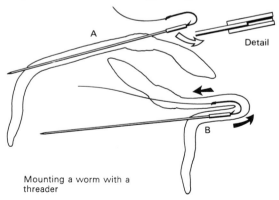

Mounting a worm with a threader

before. A threader gadget designed by big-fish hunter John Stadon is a boon for attaching lob-worms properly. It can be made in a few minutes from a 4 in (10 cm) baiting needle and a ¼ in (6 mm) length of metal tube of slightly larger diameter than that of the needle. The needle's eye is snipped off and in its place the tube is pushed on and pinched firm so that half of it remains hollow.

To thread a worm the point of the needle is inserted into the thick band of skin called the saddle and carefully pushed down the inside of the body for several inches before being brought out again through the side. The hook-point is then pushed into the tube's hollow and the worm eased gently up the needle, round the bend of the hook and along the line until the needle is free. This treatment fixes the worm, leaving just the hook-point exposed to the bend and the line coming out of the saddle. The worm is firmly attached for casting but at the same time alive and full of attractive movement.

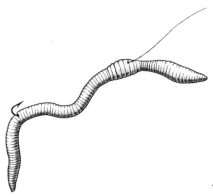

Worm bait

Air-filling a lobworm with a hypodermic needle

To make a lobworm float, inject several segments with air through a hypodermic needle. If only the head end is air-filled and the hook inserted at the other end, it will half-float—the tail waggling the hook enticingly sub-surface.

Smaller worms, brandlings, redworms and gilt-tails, found in dung heaps, under old sacking, lawn mowings, leaves and stones should also be tried as bait.

Worms require no special preparation. New

Baits: maggot (A), caster (B), elderberry (C), hempseed (D), pinched bread flake and maggots (E), caddis larva (F), silkweed (G)

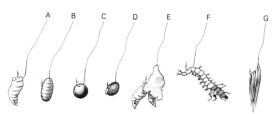

from the ground, retained in damp moss, grass or loam, they remain lively for several days at least.

Groundbait

To gather fish to the area of water being fished (the swim) and to encourage those already there to feed, groundbait is introduced. This is done at the start of a session and then at intervals. For some species (e.g. carp, tench and bream) groundbaiting pro-

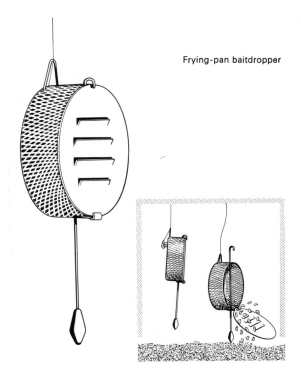

Frying-pan baitdropper

grammes are undertaken lasting several days or longer before the spot is actually fished. Pre-baiting is not always a success, but it does produce satisfactory results often enough to make it a worthwhile proposition prior to the start of the season for anglers living close enough to the water who can get permission to do so.

Groundbaiting at its simplest is the introduction of hookbait samples such as handfuls of maggots, paste balls and chunks of floating crust. To get hook samples down fast in deep lakes and river swims where the current is swift, a baitdropper is used. This device, attached to the end of the line, has a compartment for filling with hookbait which opens on impact with the bottom. A popular design is the frying-pan baitdropper (page 83). It is attached by passing the hook through an eye situated at the top of the pan and sticking the point of the hook in a cork block at the back. The bait-dropper is swung out underarm and as it falls a catch lifts on contact with the bottom to open the flap. A baitdropper should never be used with a fragile rod as it will impose too severe a strain on the tip section. Other types of hook-sample distributors include specially designed catapults and throwing sticks for long-range baiting.

A throwing stick is a device used to throw light-weight hook samples far out from the bank. A length of bamboo, metal or fibreglass tubing is all that is required to make this item of tackle. A wooden plug is glued 4 in (10 cm) inside one end, and it is in the compartment so formed that bait samples are placed, maggots, stewed wheat, etc. A throwing stick is wielded at arm's length with a firm movement of the forearm and a final flick of the wrist. With practice it is possible to bait-up at fairly long distance very accurately indeed with this

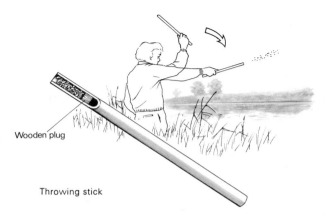

Wooden plug

Throwing stick

useful piece of equipment.

One way of naturally groundbaiting a river swim is described as 'raking the bed'. For this method an ordinary garden rake is employed; the plan is to wade out well above the swim and rake the sediment and gravel enough to send down a flow of particles and food creatures dislodged from the bottom. This is a reliable means of getting a dace shoal feeding when the river is running low and crystal clear.

Cloudbait is a fine white groundbait which, as its name suggests, clouds the water, attracting fish but not over-feeding them. Its use is largely restricted to stillwaters and canals.

Stodge groundbaits are used when fishing for bottom-feeding shoal fish (e.g. tench, bream, carp and chub) in order to spread the bottom of the swim with enough food to hold their interest for as long as possible. The deeper the swim, the faster its current, the stiffer the groundbait must be mixed.

Plenty of quality branded groundbaits are available from tackle shops made from ingredients balanced to suit every kind of water and situation. Follow the mixing instructions on the bag, adding hook samples, and you will find most of these groundbaits satisfactory.

Here are a couple you can make yourself:

Cloudbait
Fine sausage rusk or breadcrumbs, well soaked.

Stodgebait
Coarse sausage rusk, mixed with either a branded groundbait or chicken meal.

Hookbaits are carried in various plastic bait boxes. It is important that maggot containers have well-perforated lids to prevent the maggots sweating and turning sour. Large plastic buckets are used for mixing groundbaits and carrying livebaits, etc.

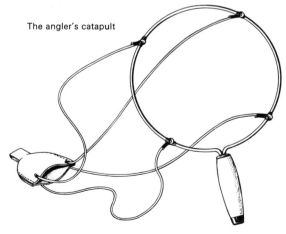

The angler's catapult

Margin fishing

Freelining Methods

Freelining is a term covering methods in which the line is weightless apart from a baited hook, or a wire trace rig in the case of pike, zander and eel fishing.

Margin fishing is a simple form of freelining which catches carp at night. Carp patrol the margins of lakes during the hours of darkness and by listening for the slurpy noises they make, sucking food from the surface, their movements are tracked and a floating bait lowered ahead of them.

Margin feeders can be stalked along the bank. An easier tactic is to remain in one place and wait for them to come to you. Put the rod in rests with the tip poking out over the water and a crust or air-filled lobworm bait on the surface directly beneath. The line should be slack but held clear of the water.

If fingerling rudd or roach make a menace of themselves nibbling crust bait off the hook, pull the bait up an inch (2·5 cm) clear of the water and lower it down only when a carp moves close by.

Rod and line strength is measured according to the size of carp in the lake and a consideration of snags and weedgrowth in the area being fished. A matchbox-size crust or large lobworm on a size 2 hook makes an ideal duo at the business end.

Roach, rudd, bream and tench are other fish which feed in the margins at night. Providing big carp do not inhabit the water, tackle strength can be scaled down to catch these smaller species.

Try bottom-fished baits as an alternative to floating baits.

Freeline casting requires heavy baits such as wetted crust, potato and paste-ball. Again the rod is placed in rests, but now with a loop of line pulled down between reel and first ring held by a bite-indicator. For carp the bale-arm of the reel is left open to give line freely—a wise precaution because carp frequently run with the bait at great speed.

Silver foil bent tube-shape over the line is a good indicator. It is important that the tube is at least 3 in (7·6 cm) long to overcome line twist and the possibility of a line-breaking jam at the butt ring

With the bale-arm open a running fish takes line freely

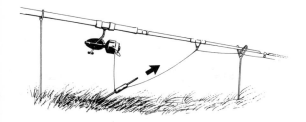

Knitting needle method of holding a tube indicator

as a fish runs out line. In windy weather, light-weight indicators need greater securing to stop them swinging about giving false bite indications. A method of doing this with a foil tube is to stick a knitting needle in the ground beneath the rod pointing directly towards the butt ring. The tube, mounted on the line, is pushed over the needle. When a bite occurs the tube is lifted clear.

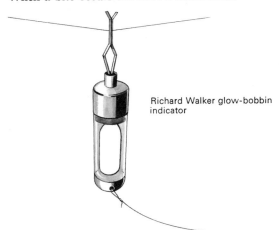

Richard Walker glow-bobbin indicator

The Sundridge Electronic
Bite Alarm designed by
Chris Brown. (*right*)
Powered by a small
battery, the Sundridge
indicator is fitted with a
buzzer and light. (*above*)
The head screws on to a
standard bank stick
positioned above the
butt ring of the rod. The
line runs behind the
antenna, which is set to
the required sensitivity
by means of a screw
adjuster

Electric indicators fitted with lights and buzzers
are used for carp at night. Glow-type indicators
for other species. A glow indicator, such as the
Richard Walker glow-bobbin, should be secured to
the back-rest by a length of thread so that when
flicked off on the strike it will not be lost in the
foliage or water. (See page 89.)

Fish lily-beds during hot summer afternoons. Carp seek these spots for food and shelter, and they can be enticed to take a freelined floating bait tossed to lie in a clear space of water between the pads.

Lily-beds are jungles of stems and roots. Extra-strong tackle is essential: heavy-duty rod, size 2 hook, line at least 15 lb (6·8 kg) test—even when the carp run no larger than 3 (1·3) or 4 lb (1·8 kg).

Strike immediately the bait is sucked under, hold tight, and quite literally drag the fish back through the growth. A tug-of-war of this nature is a real test of nerves should the carp hooked happen to be a very big one!

The above methods are also suitable for canals, sluggish rivers and backwaters of fast rivers.

Trotted crust is a productive freeline technique for river chub during the summer months. Gain the interest of chub by sending down the current a few loose chunks of crust. Watch their progress carefully and when they start getting pulled under follow with a further crust chunk on a size 2 hook and 5 lb (2·2 kg) test line. When a chub takes the bait, pause a second or two, then strike the hook home with a firm sweep of the rod. To help keep the line on the surface, spray it with a water repellent (e.g. WD-40 or AP-75) or lightly grease with vaseline.

Freeline pike deadbaits, herring, mackerel and freshwater bait-fish of similar size, in still and slow-flowing waters. Set the rod in rests with the bale-arm off (drum in casting position if a side-cast reel is used) exactly the same as for carp. A main difference is that a pike run is left longer than a carp run before striking to give the pike the time it needs to turn the bait headfirst into its mouth.

A lily-bed jungle where carp lie during hot afternoons

Deadbait rigs are many, and there is not space to even begin to mention them all. Suffice to describe just one. It is made from a 24 in (60 cm) length of 14 lb (6 kg) multi-strand or nylon-covered trace wire as follows:

First, a two-way swivel is secured to one end of the wire for attachment of the rig to the main line.

With multi-strand wire this is done by taking the end twice through an eye of the swivel and binding it in tight close turns around its main part for at least half an inch (12 mm). Nylon-covered wire is taken only once through the eye, then twisted in open turns along the main part and fused as a hard join by moving a match up and down the twists to melt the nylon covering. This join should be about 1½ in (38 mm) long.

Next, a size 6 long-shank hook is threaded on the wire, followed by two medium size treble hooks. To complete the rig a third treble hook is secured

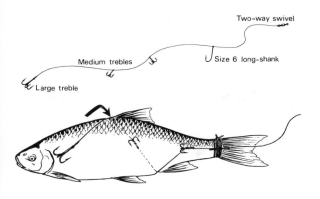

Two-way swivel

Medium trebles

Size 6 long-shank

Large treble

Deadbait rig

to the free end of the wire in the same manner as the swivel was.

To mount a bait, the end treble is hooked in its side near the gill-cover and the wire taken over its back. Here the first of the running trebles receives two twists of the wire before being inserted in the flank halfway along the length of the fish. The wire is then taken under the bait and the same

Hooking positions

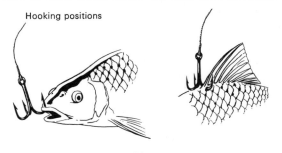

process repeated with the second running treble, inserted in the opposite flank nearer to the tail. Finally the wire is twisted several times round the shank of the single hook which is fixed deeply through the tail root to be held in place with a few turns of thread.

Always puncture the swim-bladder of a freshly killed bait or it may fail to sink. For fish of small-herring size make up rigs which have only one running treble.

Freeline pike livebaits from a boat to search

Dapping

deep corners of lakes. Lower the bait over the side, giving line gradually as it swims downwards. A single-treble trace hooked through the top lip or the front root of the dorsal fin allows the bait maximum freedom of movement. (See page 93.).

Dapping live insects in the surface film over the heads of surface-feeding chub, roach, rudd and dace is never an easy method, but nevertheless it produces plenty of good fish from overgrown canals and small streams. The angler must remain undetected by the fish and yet get close enough to them to dibble insects from above.

Dap insects freeline-style in windless conditions. Add a small drilled bullet stopped by a split-shot 12 in (30 cm) from the hook when extra control is needed. Hook-size for dapping matches the type of insect to be dibbled. Line tests: 3 lb (1·3 kg) for dace, roach and rudd; 5 lb (2·2 kg) for chub.

Stillwater Legering Methods

Leger stillwaters with a link-leger or Arlesey bomb to cast lightweight baits over a distance and to sink buoyant ones. The length of line between hook and stop-shot is called the trail. It is adjusted to suit the bite-pattern of different fish and to present buoyant baits at predetermined depths above bottom.

For example, crust is a very buoyant bait. With a trail length of 2 in (5 cm) it will lift just off-bottom. On the other hand, a trail length of 36 in (91 cm) in 36 in (91 cm) of water will float it on the surface.

Depth versatility of legered buoyant baits is something to keep in mind when fishing a lake.

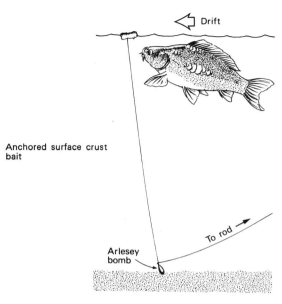

Drift

Anchored surface crust
bait

To rod

Arlesey
bomb

Typical advantages are (1) Over a bed of thick
weed a buoyant bait can be suspended above the
growth so that it is completely exposed to fish
passing by. (2) Surface anchored, a buoyant bait
is presented with the line totally submerged—
excellent in windy conditions and a reasonable
answer to the problem of carp crafty enough to
circle a bait before approaching it to make sure it
is not attached to anything 'dangerous'!

Eighteen inches (45 cm) is an average trail for
non-buoyant baits. Be prepared to make changes
when fish give bites which are consistently missed
no matter how quickly they are struck at. A trail

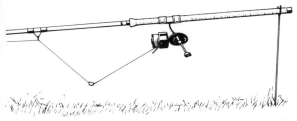

Bread paste dough-bobbin indicator

variation of a few inches can make all the difference, turning slight pulls and plucks into bold takes.

Rod rests and bite-indicators are used for still-water legering. Reel bale-arm closed for roach, rudd, crucian carp, tench and perch. Reel bale-arm open for common carp, pike, zander, eels and catfish.

Keep the weight of the leger lead as low as possible to cast the distance and to counteract any wind-created surface drift.

The open-end swimfeeder is often employed in place of a leger for lake fishing. It is an arrangement well proven for tench, roach, rudd and bream.

Fix the trail length at 12 in (30 cm), put the rod in rests, and add a dough-bob indicator to the loop between reel and first ring. Leave for a few minutes to allow the groundbait plugs to soften, then bring the swimfeeder back 12 in (30 cm) to expel the contents from the tube in a patch on the bottom with the hookbait right in the middle of the 'hot-spot'.

Swingtips, quivertips and springtips are sensitive bite indicators which screw into the tip of the rod. They are useful for both stillwater and river legering.

Left: multi-treble rig for pike and zander. Right: single hook eel rig.

Leger small fish, sprats, young rudd and roach, etc., for pike and zander on fine-wire traces incorporating two or three tiny trebles inserted along the flank.   For eels use a single-hook wire trace, the wire threaded through the bait [a 4 in (10 cm) dead roach] with a baiting needle so that the bend of the hook rests in the corner of the mouth.   Micro-fish baits (minnow size) are lip-hooked: to nylon for perch, to fine-wire traces for other predators.

River Legering Methods

Leger rivers to present baits along the bottom. Cast a leger of the right weight downstream and

The baited hook, cast to A, rolls with the current to B

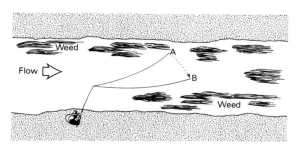

across so that it rolls the bait to a spot where it is judged the fish are most likely to be . . . under the bank further below . . . alongside a clump of reeds . . . in a slack at the tail-end of an island, and so on.

By altering the length and angle of each cast, and by lifting and lowering the rod with pauses between movements, a rolling leger can be made to search every inch of the river bed.

Leger leads used for the rolling technique include Arlesey bombs of $\frac{1}{4}$ oz (7 g), $\frac{1}{2}$ oz (14 g), and $\frac{3}{4}$ oz (21 g) sizes and swanshot link-legers. The latter have the advantage of being finely adjustable to meet the needs of many different swims and the varying strengths of current flowing through them.

Upstream legering is a more difficult method than downstream legering but ideal for those clear channels at the tails of large weedbeds which prove awkward to fish downstream. It is equally ideal for catching 'lippers'—chub and roach which lift the bait and tug it hard but fail to take it properly. When legering downstream 'lippers' pull the rod hard over cast after cast, and yet striking merely results in the bait being plucked away from the culprit. Upstream legering means the strike is made downstream, giving greater chance of the hook dragging back into the fish's lip.

An upstream leger lead (link-leger) must just, and only just, hold bottom against a reasonably taut line. When a fish picks up the bait, turning downstream with it, the weight of the leger should be sensitive enough to dislodge immediately, offering no resistance at all. As the line falls suddenly slack, wind the line tight again as quickly as possible and strike. If you are really on the ball

Rod and line falling slack (arrowed) is indication of a bite when upstream legering

you can also be up on your feet and backing away at the same time.

Rod position when legering downstream is at an angle down and across river, with the fingertips of the free hand holding the line above the reel to feel bites. Bites are invariably felt before they are seen when legering with the current so this point should never be neglected. The forefinger of the hand holding the rod rests against the spool of the reel as additional control when striking bites.

Feeling for a bite

The rod is placed in a long front rest for upstream legering, facing towards where the bait lies with the tip pointing high in the air.

Static legering is required when there is need to cast a bait to a spot in the river and have it remain in position against pressure from strong currents. A case in point is when fish are gathered beneath a stretch of bushes overhanging the far bank, and the current across width is so fierce that a rolling leger bait is carried past them too fast to be investigated. Under such circumstances a swivelled coffin leger lead is used, as heavy as conditions demand. This presentation is not nearly so sensitive as the rolling leger or upstream leger, but used in the right places it still catches plenty of fish.

Legering fish on the outer margin of slacks bordered by fast water is another purpose for the swivelled coffin lead. Deadbaits mounted on the rigs already described. Livebaits lip-hooked on single–treble rigs.

Block-end swimfeeders are an alternative to leger leads. For some species, especially barbel, swimfeedering is extremely productive.

The block-salt weight is used to cast tiny weight-less baits long distance—yet still fish them on a free-line. A cube of salt is cut from a block, grooved, and clove-hitched to the line about 18 in (45 cm) from the bait. After casting, the salt cube dissolves within seconds of touching water leaving the bait drifting weight-free. The addition of a split-shot sinks the bait slowly, a calm weather presentation for deep waters where fish cruise at many levels.

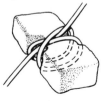

Block-salt casting weight

Stillwater Float Fishing Methods

Quill floats and balsa floats are ideal for fishing swims less than 8 ft (2·4 m) deep during calm windless periods. They are attached with rubber bands top and bottom, and shotted so that just the barest tip remains above surface.

Space the shot on the line as follows: a big shot at quarter-depth, another of similar size at mid-depth, and two or three smaller ones spread out below. By moving the distance of the bottom shot from the hook, the rig can be adjusted to indicate bites clearly; a difference of an inch (2·5 cm) or less is sometimes enough to transform shy dips and trembles on the tip into firm pulls which plunge the float right under.

Depth setting (float to hook distance) puts the bait either on the bottom or off-bottom to suit the habits of the species fished for.

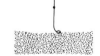

Shotting lay-out

Float size is selected for casting distance. A near-bank swim can be fished easily with a small lightly-leaded float but a swim further out will require a float big enough to carry the amount of shot necessary to cast a bait that far. To counter surface drift, the line should be treated to make it sink by pulling it through a synthetic mud ball of fuller's earth mixed with detergent and a little glycerine.

The lift-method is an important technique for near-bank fishing. The tackle consists of a short length of peacock quill attached by a rubber band at the bottom end and a single large shot pinched on

Lift-method

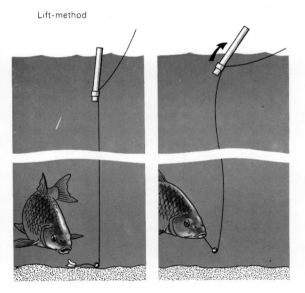

2 in (5 cm) above the hook. Depth is set greater than the water, and after over-casting the swim the tackle is drawn slowly back until the float cocks upright. The rod must be placed in rests for this ultra-sensitive style of fishing.

As a fish sucks the bait upwards it also lifts the shot. The float rises and starts to keel over. Strike as the float 'grows' through the surface and before it has time to lie flat.

This method was perfected for tench fishing by Fred J. Taylor, but it works just as well for other species. It can be scaled up or down according to how shyly the fish are biting.

Antenna floats of small size with long stems and balsa bodies are used for fishing swims exposed to soft breezes. If conditions are not too bad the line is simply threaded through the bottom ring and held in position with plug-stops either side of the ring. For stronger breezes a dust-shot is pinched on above the float to sink the line away from the influence of surface drag.

Windy weather floats are larger antenna-types. A well-known pattern, called an onion, is a crowquill fished upside down with the addition of a short cork body placed low on the stem.

Shotting these floats correctly is a task which should be taken care of at home to save valuable fishing time. This can be done in a bath or rain barrel by attaching a short piece of nylon to the ring and pinching on the amount of lead desired below the float plus an extra dust-shot. Twists of lead wire are added to the stem directly above the ring to cock the float leaving 1½ in (3·8 cm) of tip above the surface. Pre-test shotting is best left attached to serve as a reminder of the exact shot necessary to balance the float perfectly.

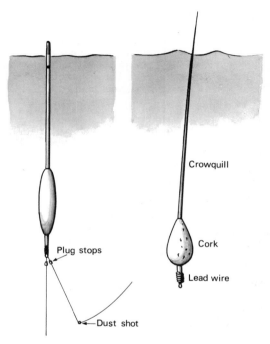

Plug stops

Dust shot

Crowquill

Cork

Lead wire

Antenna float rig   Crowquill onion float

To make the rig, a plug-stop is fixed on the line.
The line is then threaded through the ring of the
float and a hook is attached.   All shot go on the line
beneath the float, apart from the dust-shot which is
added 12 in (30 cm) above the plug-stop as a line
sinker.

A typical windy weather float in my box balances
a swanshot and an AAA size shot.   The swanshot

is set at mid-depth and the AAA shot either just off-bottom with a 12 in (30 cm) tail or right on the bottom with a shorter tail of 6 in (15 cm).

The float has freedom of movement between top-shot and plug-stop—the plug-stop being positioned to mark depth setting. During casting the float rests against the shot, sliding up-line as the tackle settles in the water until it meets the plug-stop.

Deep water floats are antenna-types with a large shot-carrying capacity fished slider-style in water where the depth approaches the length of the rod or is deeper. To fish a deep-water slider it is essential to understand how to tie Billy Lane's special stop-knot. It is made from a 6 in (15 cm) piece of nylon in this manner.

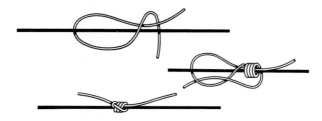

Billy Lane stop-knot

Points to note about the knot are: (1) It must be pulled really tight. (2) The ends should be trimmed off not less than 1 in (25 mm) long. (3) Tied correctly, it moves when the line is tight but holds position firmly when the line is slack.

To rig slider tackle the line is threaded through the ring of the float and the hook is tied on. Shotting consists of a top-shot 5 ft (152 cm) from the hook, a bottom shot 1 ft (30 cm) from the hook, and

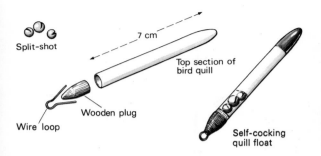

Split-shot

7 cm

Top section of
bird quill

Wooden plug

Wire loop

Self-cocking
quill float

in-between, at 4 ft (1·2 m) from the hook, the remainder of the shot grouped together. A stop-knot is whipped to the line at the estimated depth, and by trial casting with a plummet the exact depth is discovered—setting the stop to either hang the bait an inch (2·5 cm) clear or to have the bottom shot brushing the lake bed.

Self-cockers and semi-cockers are floats which carry weight in their bodies. They are usually attached bottom-end only, for presenting slow-sink baits to upper-level feeders like rudd and dace.

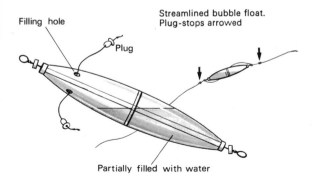

Filling hole

Streamlined bubble float.
Plug-stops arrowed

Plug

Partially filled with water

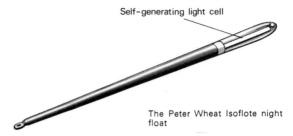

Self-generating light cell

The Peter Wheat Isoflote night float

Bubble floats are either round or torpedo shaped, transparent, designed to be part-filled with water to give weight. They are used in a number of ways but chiefly as a controlling aid when fishing surface baits. They are held in place on the line by plug-stops placed one at each end. (See page 107.)

The Isoflote is a float with a self-generating light cell (Betalight) in its tip for night fishing. In shape,

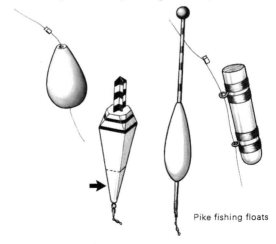

Pike fishing floats

size, weight and shot capacity it is closely similar to a balsa float of about one swanshot size. It can be seen at a range of 10 yd (9 m). An Isoflote is expensive to lose, so the hook-length *below* the float should be 1–2 lb (450–900 g) lighter than the mainline. It will break, without loss of the float, if the hook snags the bottom or up a tree.

Pike floats for stillwater and river fishing include the following.

Left to right, a drilled cork bung, a self-cocking float made from a Dutch gar-float (the arrow points to the heavily leaded section of its body), a longstemmed antenna type, and a slider constructed from a metal cigar tube.

River Float Fishing Methods

With slight modifications, float methods suggested for stillwaters can be used in sluggish canals and the slacker areas and backwaters of rivers. But, for float fishing the runs and glides, a quite different approach is required.

Typical Avon floats

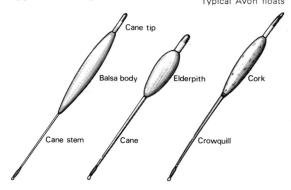

Cane tip

Balsa body   Elderpith   Cork

Cane stem   Cane   Crowquill

Swimming the stream or trotting involves casting out the tackle with the bait set deep enough to trip bottom, letting it move downstream for a distance, and then retrieving it back to be cast again. When the distance covered in this way is 30 yd (27 m) or more it is described as long-trotting.

For a slow or medium current in water less than 6 ft (1·8 m) deep, large quill and balsa floats fixed top and bottom with strong rubber bands are satisfactory. Deeper, stronger-flowing swims, however, require more substantial floats to take the shot-load needed to get the bait down. These floats, called Avons, have a cane or quill stem and a body of cork, balsa or elderpith. (See page 109.)

In very deep swims (e.g. tidal sections of rivers) it

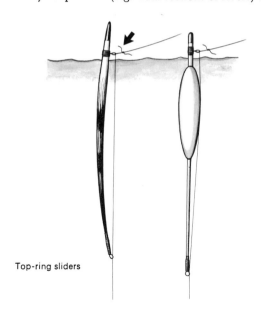

Top-ring sliders

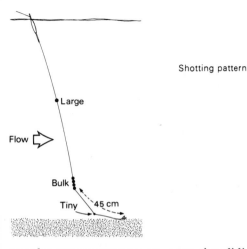

Shotting pattern

Flow

Large

Bulk

Tiny

45 cm

may become necessary to use a top-ring sliding float to fish bait along the bottom. The nylon stop-knot is depth-set so that when it is drawn against the ring by the weight of the shot the baited hook will be just tripping bottom.

Always choose the lightest float possible for the conditions, shotted so that about $\frac{1}{2}$ in (12 mm) of tip is above the surface.

The shotting pattern for river fishing is very much a matter of personal opinion. Plenty of anglers like to space the shot out along the line with shot-size gauged smaller and smaller towards the hook. Other anglers, myself included, are satisfied to group the bulk of shot together about 18 in (45 cm) from the hook, and have single shot situated one big one between bulk-shot and float and one tiny one between bulk-shot and hook. The position of the latter shot is adjusted to present the bait as naturally as possible.

The cast is made across river and a little up-stream. The bale-arm is then 'turned in' to take up slack and bring the float back into the correct path for moving downstream. All this takes but a brief moment to perform, and then the bale-arm is opened to let line be taken as the float moves with the current. Just how quickly line leaves the reel is controlled either by the forefinger of the hand holding the rod being pressed against the edge of the drum (slow rivers) or by the line passing through the fingers of the free hand (fast rivers). The whole idea is to check the passage of the float enough to keep the tail ahead and the bait bumping bottom.

Sometimes fish lie high in the water and must be angled for with the bait set shallow, but most often it is along the bed of the river where they will be feeding—the larger species definitely so.

Mending the line means correcting the down-stream bow which forms in the line by flicking it upstream. There is a knack in doing this without disturbing the float and jigging the bait unnaturally which comes with experience. Careful manipula-

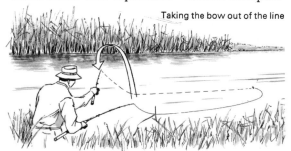

Taking the bow out of the line

tion of the rod is needed to lift line from the water and mend the bow, but it is important that this is carried out to keep the line between rod and float straight and thereby allow the float an unchecked passage through the swim, presenting the bait naturally. A bellying line, commonly caused by the float travelling slower than the speed at which the line is leaving the reel, also tends to cushion the power of the strike, particularly when striking at long-range.

Line strength for trotting depends on the type of river fished and the size of fish it holds. A point to remember is that if a big float is to be used, and the trot made over 30 yd (27 m) of water, it is vital that a strong line test is selected, even for roach and dace. Striking as hard as is needed to set a hook at 30 yd (27 m) puts the line under severe strain, and anything weaker than 4 lb (1·8 kg) test is likely to snap.

Bites when trotting frequently stab the float under fast and decisive, but it should never be thought that the float *must* become totally submerged to indicate that the bait has been taken properly. Other significant signs to watch for include: the float lift-

A strikeable indication when trotting

ing, the float sinking but not going right under, and the float bobbing off-course from the line of trot. Striking at every movement of the float which looks unusual soon develops an ability to distinguish between the true bites of fish and false knocks caused by the hook dragging bottom or hitting weed.

Striking a bite and getting a hooked fish immediately under control is very easy with the forefinger method; the float dips and instantly pressure is applied to the drum with the forefinger as the strike is made.   At exactly the same moment the bale-arm is shut to 'collect' the line from the finger.

When paying out line with the free hand, a bite is connected by holding the line firmly with the fingers, striking, and then passing the line from the free hand to be clamped against the butt by the forefinger of the hand holding the rod.   The bale-arm is then turned-in with the free hand to make the final pick-up.

In both cases the drill is extremely fast, and though it may sound awkward and perhaps not completely effective, it is, in fact, perfectly reliable procedure.

Stret-peg a slacker strip of water along the river

Stret-pegging

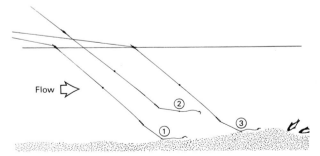

Flow ⟹

margin by casting downstream close to the bank and drawing the tackle back far enough to straighten the trail right out with the bait resting on the bottom some way below the float.

At intervals of a few minutes lift the rod top high enough to dislodge the tackle, and let out a further foot (30 cm) of line as it is lowered so that the bait reaches a fresh area further down the bank. With inch (2·5 cm) long lobworm sections on the hook this searching method is sound for roach and perch under floodwater conditions. It should be noted that variations in the level of the bottom do not spoil the stret-pegging style of swim searching.

The streamlined bob-float is a handy general-purpose float to have in the tackle box. Its thick shape is perfect for trotting baits in swirly water, rocky shallows, weirpool tails, etc., where many currents conflict. It is especially good for hunting perch, chub and barbel with minnows or bleak as hookbait.

Streamlined bob-float

Fish baits trotted mid-depth in rivers—also canals and drains if they flow—work well for pike and zander. Let the tackle ahead a short distance and then walk behind it for as far downstream as is advisable. Retrieve the tackle and start again from the top end.

Undercut banks, reedbeds and the mouths of bays and inlets, should be given extra attention. Pike love these spots and they 'hole-up' in them fully expecting to make meals of small fish passing by.

Float-tip colours include fluorescent red, orange and yellow. Antenna stems can be seen more clearly if they are striped alternately with bands of black and white topped by orange or red blob-tips.

Completely black floats are, surprising as it may seem, first-class indicators during the half-light period before full darkness. A black float at gloaming can be seen more easily against the silver grey-ness of the water at this time of day than a float of any other colour.

Floats for shallow water fishing should be matt varnished below the tip. A high gloss finish glinting the sun can scare fish which are moving only a few feet away.

Lure Fishing

Strictly speaking, all hook baits are lures. The term 'lure fishing', however, includes only methods in which baits—artificial and natural—are spun, wobbled, or otherwise worked through the water in a fish-like manner, to entice the interest of predators.

Types of lure include spinners and plugs (artificials), and dead fish (naturals). Many hundreds of different artificial patterns have been devised, to search at every depth from surface to bottom and in some cases adjustable for a range of depths. A few patterns are fitted with anti-snag wires over the treble hook to prevent it catching up in weed. The wires collapse as a fish grabs the lure.

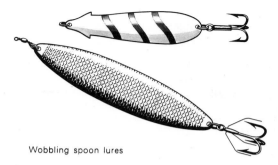

Wobbling spoon lures

Specialist lure-fishers take huge collections of lures to the waterside, neatly arranged in special, multi-compartment tackle boxes. For general angling nothing like so vast an array is required to catch fish and to experience the pleasure of this fascinating branch of the sport.

Rods for lure fishing from the bank should be long, at least as long as 10 ft (3 m), to assist in giving the baits life-like action, as well as to control large fish over the top of snag-filled margins.

An Avon-action rod meets the needs of zander and smaller species, whilst a carp or light pike rod has the additional backbone required to handle the larger fish and heavier lures of pike fishing.

A single-handed baitcaster rod of 5 ft (1·5 m), 6 ft (1·8 m) or 7 ft (2 m) length, is a pleasant-to-use weapon when boat fishing. It has the kind of

The Devon minnow—a spinning pattern

lively action which makes a 5 lb (2·2 kg) pike feel like a fish of at least twice that weight.

Reels of fixed-spool design are fine for casting lures; the shallow-drum Mitchell range is outstanding. For a crank-handled baitcaster rod a good type of reel is a spincast. This reel, which resembles a closed-face fixed-spool, fits on top of the rod. To cast with it, the thumb of the hand holding the rod pushes down a spring lever on the back of the reel which is released as the lure is propelled out on the forward movement.

Crank-handled baitcaster rod mounted with a spincast reel

Lines between 3 (1·3) and 15 lb (6·8 kg) test are employed in lure fishing. A choice of strength depends on all the usual considerations: size of fish, amount of snags in the water, and the weight of bait/terminal tackle.

Between 3 (1·3) and 5 lb (2·2 kg) test is average for rudd, perch and chub; 8 lb (3·6 kg) for zander and small pike; and 10 (4·5) to 15 lb (6·8 kg) for big-pike hunts.

Traces are necessary to prevent line twist, caused by a lure which spins, badly fouling-up the line and creating a bird's nest. Length of trace is between 1 (30) and 3 ft (90 cm). For zander and pike it should be wire.

At one end is a two-way swivel for attachment to the main line, and at the other end a link-swivel for quick-change baiting. As a broad guide, the strength of the trace should be equal to that of the main line.

Anti-kink devices further help to prevent line twist by forcing the swivels to turn, which otherwise would not always happen. When light spinning with small baits a plastic anti-kink vane is sufficient. For bigger lures, distance casting, and to get a bait deep down in a strong current, an anti-kink lead is the usual form. The Wye lead, fitted with a link-swivel, and the foldover lead, are common forms.

It will be found helpful at times to use a vane combined with a small amount of lead. Lead is added by 'half-blooding' a nylon tail to the bottom eye of the vane and pinching on swanshot.

All plugs are not fish-like imitations. Some imitate such creatures as frogs and tiny swimming rodents. (See page 120.)

Top: Wye Lead. Centre: shotted plastic anti-kink vane. Bottom: foldover anti-kink lead

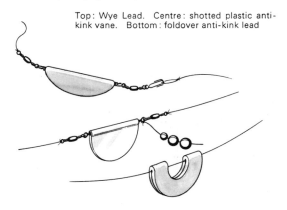

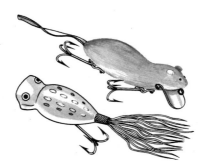

Top: Rodent-imitating lure. Bottom: frog-like
surface-popper lure

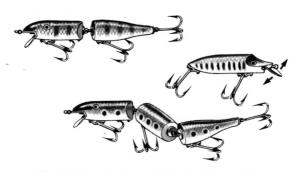

Fish-imitating plug lures. The single-joint model has a lip
adjustable to different running depths (arrowed)

Small fish are spun by mounting them on flights.
A typical flight, as illustrated, has a paired spinning
vane, two treble hooks on short wire lengths and,
centrally, a weighted spear. The spear is pushed

Spinning flight

down the throat of the bait to bring the vane in contact with the bait's mouth, and the hooks are inserted one on each side. To hold everything secure, turns of fine wire are taken along the length of the bait.

Drop minnow tackle is not difficult to set up. Thread the line through the bait from the tail to the mouth with a baiting needle, add a long-shanked number 6 hook to the end, two or three split-shot nipped on the shank, and pull the hook

Drop minnow fishing

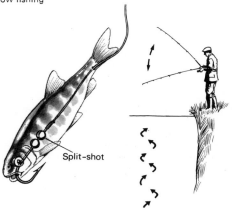

Split-shot

back into the bait until the bend of the hook rests against the corner of its mouth.

Fish a drop minnow for chub and perch in back-waters and sidestreams. Action the retrieve by raising and lowering the rod top to zig-zag the bait along an upright plane. Bring the bait towards the surface slowly, wind the rod down again, and then let the bait fall quickly to the bottom.

Snap-trolling is a sink-and-draw method similar to drop minnow but used with bigger, pike-size baits. The rig for snap-trolling is constructed from an 18 in (45 cm) length of multi-strand wire by adding a barrel lead to one end, threading on two number 8 treble hooks and a single hook, and adding a swivel at the opposite end.

These hooks are held in place by twisting the trace wire three times round each shank so that the points face away from the leaded end, and by binding them over with fine wire. Hooks are positioned to suit the length of the bait: the first treble inserted near the head, the second halfway down the flank, and the single in the tail-root.

Mount the bait by pushing the lead inside the bait's mouth, fixing the hooks, and twisting a few

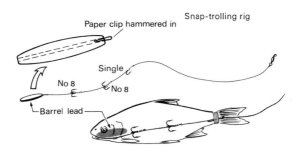

Paper clip hammered in

Snap-trolling rig

Single

No 8

No 8

Barrel lead

turns of fuse wire at the root of the tail for maximum security. If the mouth of the bait is big (e.g. a chub bait) the lips are sewn roughly together to hold the lead in place.

Holes amid thick weed in stillwater or river, pikey-looking margins and small streams, are places to try with snap-trolling gear. The bait is swung out and allowed to fall to the bottom. Providing the amount of lead for size of bait is judged correctly, it will fall diagonally and move fish-like through the water.

Keep in mind that this is not a long casting method, but an under-the-bank method. Although the bait is mounted backwards it is fished forwards.

Wobbled deadbaiting is a long casting method. The rig is a number 2 treble hook attached to an 18 in (45 cm) length of multi-strand wire. To the eye of the number 2 are trailed two number 8 treble hooks fixed on short lengths of wire—one length a trifle longer than the other.

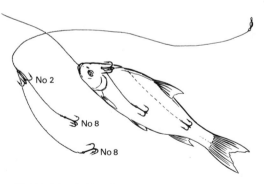

Wobbled deadbaiting rig

123

Retrieving a wobbled deadbait

The main wire is threaded with a baiting needle from behind the skull of the fish, through and out of its mouth and pulled to bring the number 2 treble hard against the bait's back. Trailing trebles are inserted one in each flank, and a swivel is added in the normal way for securing to the line.

Impart life to the bait by swimming it as erratically as possible with horizontal zig-zag movements of the rod top and sudden changes in speed of retrieve. But never retrieve over-quickly unless pike are feeding really well.

Takes when snap-trolling or wobbled deadbaiting may be felt or seen. Immediately you are aware that a fish has 'latched on', let out a little line, dwell a short pause and strike.

Float-spinning combines a fly-spoon or similar size lure with float tackle. The float is trotted down the stream or cast out across the lake, and then brought back with pauses at intervals to allow the lure to 'hang' in the current (river) or flutter down (stillwater).

Chub and perch respond well to this technique, and so too do lake rudd. Experiment with depth settings. The illustration shows the retrieve action

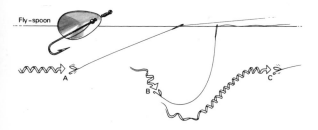

of a fly-spoon being worked beneath a float in a river (A). In a stillwater, a pause in the retrieve (B) sends the fly-spoon fluttering downwards. With the commencement of the retrieve (C) the fly-spoon lifts sharply. This falling, lifting, flashy activity of the lure is extremely attractive to fish-eating species.

The colour of artificial lures is commonly silver or gold, often over-marked with eye-catching spots and stripes. Plugs include patterns outlandishly gaudy and patterns which cleverly imitate the fish which predators feed upon. These, and silvery naturals such as sprats, chub, dace and roach attract predators because, as they are worked, they radiate the flashes and sounds of fish in distress.

Each lure pattern is different in shape, weight and action. And each must be fished in its own way to be effective. Trials with varying retrieve speeds and under differing weather conditions are always worthwhile experiments. Some lures attract fish better on dull days, while others are just as productive on bright days. It is all a matter of trial and error to find out which should be used when.

Above all, when fishing a lure, try to imagine its passage through the water. Make it move as a fish does as far as possible—either wounded, or as a bold invader of a predator's lair. Pike attack lures not only for food, but also because they get annoyed when strange creatures keep buzzing past their noses!

A pike of 10 lb (4·5 kg) taken on a silver wobbler lure

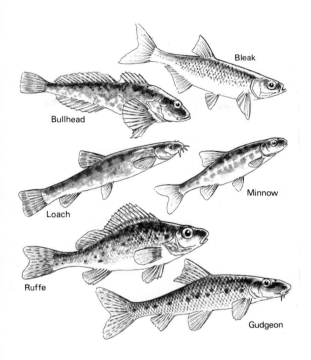

Bait species

Bait Fish

Bait fish are fish which do not grow large enough in themselves to be a sporting proposition, but which can be used on the hook to catch other, more interesting species.

Bleak: Common fish in some rivers where they form vast, greedy-feeding shoals. Easily caught in quantity with fine float tackle and maggot bait set between mid-water and surface. Bleak average no more than an ounce or two (28–56 g).

Gudgeon: Another fish weighing only a few ounces. Gudgeon are bottom feeders. They occur in lakes, but more frequently in swift-flowing rivers. To be caught by float fishing baits of worm and maggot close to the bottom. Groundbaiting and raking the river bed will quickly encourage a shoal of gudgeon to feed.

Ruffe: This species, rarely exceeding 4 oz (113 g) weight, prefers still or slow-flowing water. In rivers where they occur (e.g. Thames) they are really a lot harder to avoid than to catch in any slack or slow run which has become their home. Worms are bait enough; lightly legered or float fished.

Telescopic minnow trap

Minnow: The smallest of the bait fish, widely distributed in rivers. Most easily taken in quantity with a minnow trap—a telescopic container with an entrance designed so that fish can enter without trouble but find extreme difficulty in getting out again.

Minnows (and fry of other species) are attracted to the trap by baiting a chunk of bread inside it. The trap is lowered down the edge of the bank or on a gravel shallow where minnows are congregated. It should be angled on the river bed with the entrance hole facing into the current.

When several minnows have become imprisoned, the trap is lifted and the captives transferred to a water-filled bucket or thick plastic bag.

Loach and Bullhead: Two species found in brooks. Collect by wading with a net upstream searching weedbeds and beneath stones. Fished dead, legered or freelined, these tiddlers make grand bait for big chub.

3: PRACTICAL FISHING

On Catching Fish

Coarse fishing is an enjoyable pursuit at any time of the season and in every type of water. But the sport is at its best when it offers a reasonable chance of contact with fish of good average size.

As I write, a roach of 2 lb (900 g) stares down at me from its glass case on the wall. I do not normally kill fish to make trophies of them, but that roach I did keep because it was my very first 2 lb (900 g) roach and as such a significant milestone in my angling life. I caught it by long-trotting double-maggot down a glide of Hampshire Avon towards the close of a November day when most of the other fish which had come to the net had been chub.

Extra big specimens are often hooked 'out of the blue' like that, when least expected. And this being fact it would be quite untrue to say that an element of luck does not play a part in successful angling.

The aim of the game is to reduce this need of luck. One should constantly strive to improve knowledge and ability, mastering as far as one is able, fishing in the right way, at the right time, in the right places and with the right baits, so that the odds weigh in favour of success through personal effort rather than good fortune alone.

Stunted fish and young fish are easy to catch because their numbers are great and they must eat frequently, continually, to avoid starvation. The

instincts of these small fish are relatively unde-
veloped. They cannot afford to be over-particular
about what they will, and will not eat. Their
attitude towards baited hooks is suicidal to say the
least, and they can be an outright menace when the
intention is to catch larger fish.

I shall say no more of tiddlers, but confine my
remarks to fish of reasonable size which are an
entirely different proposition. Although they also
eat—to a greater or lesser extent—all the time, their
main feeding periods are much more clearly defined.
Such key factors as water temperature, oxygen
content, light intensity and food availability, affect
the feeding habits of different species in different
ways—influencing the depth at which main feeding
takes place and the part of each 24-hour period
when it occurs.

Each species is unique in its feeding pattern. It
is true that some species are so closely akin in
evolutionary development that only minute points
of feeding indicate them apart, but other species are
widely separated: classed as evening–dawn feeders,
night feeders, day feeders, 'round the clock' feeders,
etc.

Quite obviously many good fish are caught in
circumstances which do not make them conform to
accepted feeding patterns. It should be remembered, however, that these captures *are* exceptional
and in no way relate to the *typical* habits of fish—
the habits which anglers need to understand to be
successful.

Coarse fishing seems to get categorized into
summer fishing and winter fishing—a division rather
of weather change than of calendar date.

Just so long as conditions remain mild, summer
methods and tactics continue to apply no matter
how late in the year. It is not until water tem-

perature plunges, as air temperature decreases and cold winds and rains begin to prevail, that the transition takes place which requires different methods and swims to suit the changed moods of fish living from then on in low-temperature conditions.

All sporting species can be caught during summer months, but in winter not all of them feed regularly enough to be worthy of serious effort to catch them. These dormant species are only ever likely to be caught during the cold months when breaks in the weather bring the water temperature up high enough to stir them back to activity for brief periods.

Extremes of water temperature, high or low, can reduce the feeding of all species to almost nil. For example, during hot, summer afternoons, the temperature of a lake may go up so high and the oxygen content drop so low, that only small rudd remain prepared to feed. In winter, the temperature of a lake may become so far reduced that the whole fish population becomes dormant, unmoving, totally disinterested in feeding. These high–low extremes do not affect river fish quite so noticeably.

Knowing about the effects of weather on fish is information basic to catching them above tiddler size. A point to keep in mind is that once you are able to catch fish of good average size regularly, you can expect to catch extra big specimens occasionally. Moreover, chances of this happening are further increased by specializing for a single species in a water where it is known to reach great size.

Choice of venue is very important. Red-letter specimens simply cannot be caught if they are not in the water, any more than a silk purse can be made out of a sow's ear!

The following brief notes are intended only as an introductory guide to catching the individual species. I assume that fish of good average size (and larger) are in the water, and that it is fish of this quality which the reader desires to catch.

Small Species

Stillwater Roach

Tackle: Avon rod. 3 lb (1·3 kg) line. Size 8 and 10 hooks.

Hookbait: Breadcrust cubes, small worms, sweetcorn, pinched flake combined with maggots—size 10 hook. Whole lobworms—size 8 hook.

Groundbait: A billiard-ball size lump approximately every 15 minutes. Mix groundbait 'tight' and lace with maggots. When legering, mould the groundbait round the lead.

Methods: Float fish on the bottom during daytime. Leger after dark.

Remarks: Roach dislike light. Seek them in deep water and weedbed holes during daytime, and try shallower water at night. Use rod rests and a dough-bob indicator for legering, bale-arm closed.

Strike as soon as the float goes right under (as it lifts for the lift-method) and (legering) when the bobbin is moving smoothly to the rod. Expect to miss bites; stillwater roach often 'lip' the bait without taking it properly.

River Roach

Tackle—for trotting: Float rod. 3–4 lb (1·3–1·8 kg) line.—for long-trotting: Avon rod. 4 lb (1·8 kg) line. Size 8, 10, 12 and 14 hooks.

Hookbait: Breadcrust cubes, pinched flake—size 10 hook. Maggots—size 12 and 14 hooks. Silkweed

—size 10 and 12 hooks.　Whole lobworms—size 8 hook.

Groundbait: Little but often.　It is most important not to over-bait a roach swim.　Throw maggots in as loose feed or put them down with a bait-dropper as additional attraction to balls of groundbait.

Methods: Float fishing and legering.

Remarks: Search the clear channels between the weeds with either trotting tackle or a sensitive leger rig on summer days.　Also try silkweed float fished at mid-depth in weirpools run.　Come evening, trot open water of slower flow near weed.　Should roach still be feeding at full darkness, switch to light legering.　A cube of breadcrust static on the bed of a swim where roach night-feed is a tactic which often pays off in the shape of a larger specimen or two.

From autumn onwards, roach gather as vast shoals—to be discovered by long-trotting deeper, smoother runs, where weed has died down.　Winter roach fishing remains good all day if the sky is overcast, but dusk to darkness is still *the* period for catching bigger fish.　After-dark legering is even more deadly at this time of year than it is in summer. Roach are most happy in a water temperature of not less than 42°F (5°C).　Below this minimum they do not feed so actively.

Dace

Tackle—for trotting and dapping: Float rod 2–3 lb (·9–1·3 kg) line.—for long-trotting: Avon rod. 3–4 lb (1·3–1·8 kg) line.　Size 12, 14 and 16 hooks.

Hookbait: Maggots and various insects.

Groundbait: Feed the swim with loose maggots and white groundbait.　Also rake the river bed above the swim to dislodge small creatures and colour the water.

Methods: Float fishing and dapping.

Remarks: Dace love light. Trot fast water for them on sunny, summer days, and also dap insects along narrow, overgrown streams. Through the winter period dace share deeper water with roach. The sharp difference between the feeding habits of the two species can be noted when fishing swims they share together.

Between morning and afternoon the catch will commonly consist of dace plus a few roach of small size. But by evening, as light intensity weakens, the dace cease feeding to be replaced—after a short lull —by roach feeding as eagerly as were the dace before.

Following a mild winter, dace return to shallow water before the end of February to spawn.

Rudd

Tackle: Avon rod. 4 lb (1·8 kg) line. Size 8, 10 and 12 hooks.
Hookbait: Maggots, worms, breadcrust cubes and pinched flake—hook-size matches bait-size.
Groundbait: Decoy crusts thrown or anchored alongside reedbeds and lily-patches. Maggots and

Crust attractor for rudd

chrysalids catapulted out. For rudd lying deep, small balls of groundbait. When anchoring crusts the best method is to secure them to the stems of rush or reed with strands of water weed. Never use old fishing line or any kind of rot-proof thread as these materials are a deathtrap to birds and animals. *Methods:* Slow-sink, self-cocking float rigs. Margin methods for summer nights. Shotted float and leger rigs in winter.

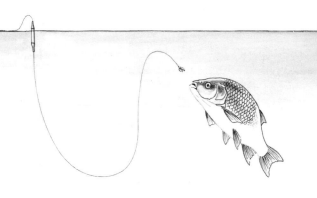

Rudd rig

Remarks: When the weather is warm rudd feed on or near the surface. Once a shoal has been pinpointed, cast out a slow-sink bait as close to the fish as possible. The float, a self-cocker, should be attached to the line with long, valve-rubber sleeves top and bottom, adjusted so that they protrude beyond the float ends to prevent the hook tangling the float as the tackle flies through the air.

Maggots as bait are an advantage because they cannot be nibbled off the hook easily—something which happens frequently with bread as bait. Worm is a selective bait particularly ideal when large and small rudd are mixed together.

A boat is always helpful. Apart from the increased coverage of the water which being afloat gives, it also enables baits to be cast from angles and distances which makes possible a high degree of accuracy coupled with minimum disturbance of the shoal.

From the bank, a heavily weighted float, 5 lb (2·2 kg) line and a carp rod, may be tackle strength needed to reach the fish.

In winter, rudd move to deep water, remaining near the bottom. Here they seem to prefer baits fished an inch (2·5 cm) off-bottom. Buoyant baits can be legered this distance on a short trail, but non-buoyant baits will need to be cast out on float tackle to achieve the same presentation.

Allow bites to develop properly before attempting to set the hook. The rod is held or put in rests according to how the fish are feeding.

Crucian Carp

Tackle: Avon rod. 3–4 lb (1·3–1·8 kg) line. Size 10, 12 and 14 hooks.

Hookbait: Maggots, flake, maggots and flake combined, sweetcorn, worms and hempseed.

Groundbait: Liberally feed the swim with balls of groundbait laced with hook samples whilst fishing. It is advantageous to pre-bait prior to dusk and dawn.

Methods: Float fishing with the bait on or near the bottom, day and night. Leger only at long range or when the wind is extremely strong.

Remarks: Crucian offer superb sport during summer. They live as shoals in thick weed and beneath lily-pads and these are the obvious places to try for them. Crucian disclose their presence by jumping clear of water and belly-flopping loudly back again, also by sending up patches of tiny bubbles as mud is nosed deeply for food.

Dusk to midnight and first light to mid-morning

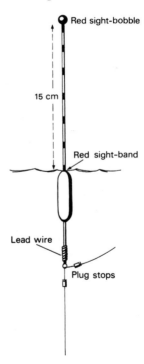

Red sight-bobble

15 cm

Red sight-band

Lead wire

Plug stops

The author's crucian float design

are major feeding periods. They sometimes will feed right through the day if conditions remain warm and dull.

Timing the strike is the most difficult part of catching crucian. The float tours across surface in half-a-dozen different directions, sinking and rising again and again before properly sliding away. It can take as long as five or ten minutes for a bite to develop to strikeable stage—the bait in the mouth instead of held gently between the lips.

Never strike simply because the float is moving. Wait for it to submerge completely or, at the very least, go under as far as the tip.

All my crucian floats are home-made antennas fixed bottom end only, balanced with twists of lead wire at base to cock upright with 6 in (15 cm) of stem above surface. The bait and a single small shot rests on the bottom.

Each float is painted with a red band sight-blob, alternate bands of black and white, and a red band at surface point. The long stem is an excellent interpreter of running bites, and the lower red band an aid in spotting another type of bite which crucian give by sucking the bait in on the spot but failing to run with it. When this happens the float hardly moves; only the red band dips beneath the surface. Should the float sink like this, remaining so for a little time, I tighten the line and strike as soon as the weight of a crucian is felt at the other end.

A lift rig indicates these delicate-looking bites better but unfortunately is not suitable for dealing with more typical crucian takes.

Crucian become torpid in winter. Should they feed, the bites are generally fast, up-and-down jabs and these fish must be struck without a moment's delay. The rod is put in rests for crucian fishing.

At night an Isoflote float is substituted for the antenna.

Grayling

Tackle: Float rod. 3 lb (1·3 kg) line. Size 12, 14 and 16 hooks.

Hookbait: Worms and maggots.

Groundbait: Loose feed with maggots when maggots are hookbait. Otherwise no groundbaiting is necessary.

Method: Trotting.

Remarks: Grayling are caught winter and summer with trotted baits. They remain active in the coldest weather, and it is then, in the depths of winter, that trotting is most enjoyable. For long-trotting, line test should be increased to 5 lb (2·2 kg).

Grayling are as fond of lying in turbulent waters as in smoother pools, and as the system of fishing is to work the water over, searching many swims of varied depth and character, the float should be thick-bodied—a streamlined version of the grayling-bob float, for example.

Grayling fight with a strange corkscrewing action, made possible by the largeness of the dorsal fin. They use the spread of this fin to such good effect that even quite small fish feel very heavy indeed.

The fight from a 2 lb (900 g) plus grayling remains memorable for a lifetime.

Gilt-tails, cockspur worms, are considered top bait by expert grayling fishers. These worms can be found beneath damp heaps of lawnmowings which have started to rot down.

Perch

Tackle: Avon rod. 5 lb (2·2 kg) line. Size 4, 6 and 8 hooks. Bar-spoon spinners fitted with large treble hooks and small plugs.

Hookbait: Lobworms and small fish.

Groundbait: Perch can be attracted to a swim by cloudbaiting it heavily.

Methods: Freelining, legering, paternostering, float fishing and lure fishing.

Remarks: Perch are opportunist feeders. Summer finds them hidden in thick weed, feasting, as the urge takes them, on fry and small fish. A big perch spotted attacking tiddlers may possibly be caught with a worm, fish bait or spinner, so it is sound planning when fishing lakes noted for perch, but trying to catch other species, to have a spare outfit set up ready for perch should a pack of them put in an appearance. They move mainly at dawn. Undercut banks along clear-flowing rivers sometimes have perch in residence which can be 'teased' to grab a worm freelined or twitched on a split-shot weighted line at first light.

Perch in deep lakes live at the bottom of the deepest parts in winter. Successful methods include running leger and running paternoster rigs

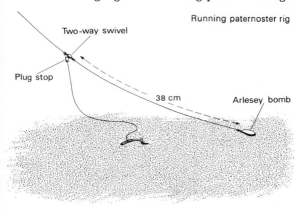

Running paternoster rig

Two-way swivel

Plug stop

38 cm

Arlesey bomb

baited with lobworms. The rod is put in rests with the bale-arm left open and a bite indicator such as a tube of silver foil.

Bites need plenty of time to develop. Let line run out without resistance. Do not strike too hard or put too much force against the fish in case the hook-hold is a poor one. It often is with a big perch. Deep-water perch are not fighters and a carefully measured retrieve is all that is required to subdue them.

River perch in winter shoal in slacks, backwaters, mouths of sidestreams and mini-pools formed by reedbeds part-submerged beneath floodwater. Use freelined, legered and paternostered baits in these places. Elsewhere perch take over strips of slow water along the reeds. Any stretch of river which has deepish water under the bank and a reedy margin, *may* hold perch. The striped pattern of camouflage which makes perch such showy individuals out of the water blends perfectly against a backcloth of reed stalks, so it is not surprising that in such places they position themselves ready to pounce out and attack small fish which venture close—feeding habits which the worm fisher can take full advantage of.

The approach to the reeds should be softly quiet in order to avoid one's movements being transmitted to the fish. It is also essential to work the float down the edge close enough to the stalks to brush against them.

Different depth settings from mid-water to inches off-bottom should be tried, and changes of bait also. Sometimes a lob-tail will do the trick, while at other times it will be a small whole worm which they want or perhaps a full-grown lob if the mood takes them. Search a section of reeds fully, then move a short way downstream and try again. If perch are at home and feeding they will not need further stimulation than the hook-worm dancing past them.

Strike when the float is carried right under and play the fish firmly away from the reeds—either well upstream or well downstream—for netting. The less the actual perch holt is disturbed the more chance there will be of catching lots of perch.

Middleweight Species

Chub
Tackle: Avon rod.   3–6 lb (1·3–2·7 kg) line.   Size 2, 4, 6, 8, 10, 12, 14 and 16 hooks.—Big chub in snaggy streams: Carp rod.   7–10 lb (3·1–4·5 kg) line.   Size 2 and 4 hooks.
Hookbait: Bread, maggots, sweetcorn, cheese, worms, crayfish, elvers, meat baits, slugs, small fish and insects of all kinds.
Groundbait: Crust chunks, surface fishing.   Loose-fed hook samples, and groundbait balls laced with hook samples, float and leger **methods.**
Methods: Freelining, float **fishing,** legering and dapping.
Remarks: Chub are quarry for **all** seasons.   Providing the current strength allows, heavy baits such as slug, crayfish, elvers, bunches of lobworms, and dead fish, can be freelined or light legered in every part of the river system at any time of the year in expectation of chub.

Floating baits—freelined crust, bubble float controlled, air-filled lobworms, dapped insects—catch chub on summer days and warm winter days when these fish will be watching the surface for food coming downstream.

Float fishing and legering with cheesepaste, sausage, bread, worms and maggots as hookbaits,

143

Strike sequence for 'lipping' chub

takes chub lying in weirpools and streamy runs (summer) and deeper-water slacks (winter). Mild winter spells are opportunity for baiting swims heavily and long-trotting maggots and pinched flake for shoal chub of 1 to 4 lb (450 g–1·8 kg) class.

When the water temperature drops low, chub habitually continue feeding long after other species have ceased. Under these conditions size of bait should be kept small.

Float bites are usually full-blooded enough to slam the float down. Leger bites vary between rod-bending pulls and tiny tweaks not always easy to identify quickly enough to connect with. One type of bite which always presents a problem is the slow take which brings the rod top over a foot (30 cm) or more yet leaves the angler striking at thin air—no matter how quickly he manages to respond.

Bites of this nature are frustrating. They give the appearance of being 'sitters', but in fact are exactly the opposite. The only compensation, at least in my experience, is that chub which produce them are not shy. Quite often they will continue 'lipping' baits cast after cast for a couple of hours at least.

A strike sequence which works is to sit with the rod pointing upriver and across held in one hand, with the other hand controlling a loop of line taken from between reel and butt ring held at arm's length. As a bite is felt this loop is gradually eased out as the fish moves away. Once it has all been taken up and the rod commences to bend, the rod is brought round until it points downstream. As the bend increases the strike is executed.

Plenty of bites are still missed in this way, but at least enough are connected to prove that giving line is far better than quick-striking when chub are in a playful frame of mind.

Always hold the rod when chub fishing, feeling for bites with the fingers when freelining or legering.

Tench

Tackle: Avon rod. 4–7 lb (1·8–3·1 kg) line. Size 6, 8, 10 and 12 hooks.—For big tench in weedy lakes: Carp rod. 8–10 lb (3·6–4·5 kg) line. Size 6 and 8 hooks.

Hookbait: Breadcrust cube, pinched flake, maggots, flake and maggots combined, sweetcorn, worms, freshwater mussels and meat baits.

Groundbait: Pre-baiting days, even weeks, before the start of the season, is traditional preparation for catching this species. It is a ploy which does not always increase sport, but at least it is an excuse to be at the waterside!

Tench are lovers of weedy areas, and swims are cut from the thickest-grown parts with sharp hook-blades and weed rakes. A good swim-shape is triangular with a narrow channel leading back to the bank. A suitable weed rake can be made quite easily by lashing two garden rake heads back to back with soft wire. Two scythe blades screwed

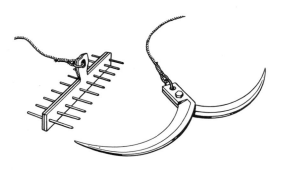

Tools for preparing swims

together make an excellent cutting implement. These tools are attached to lengths of thick cord. They are thrown out, allowed to sink, and then retrieved slowly. By varying the angle and length of each throw the area to be cleared is enlarged to the shape and size required. Great care should be taken when using these tools as careless throwing can lead to a nasty accident. For the same reason double-check that the cord is attached securely.

Tench swims are profusely baited with stodge and hook samples before and during fishing. Raking the bottom at the start of a session, despite the noise and disturbance it creates, actually attracts tench. However, raking should not be carried out if the bed is layered with stinking mud as this has quite an opposite effect to that intended, for obvious reasons.

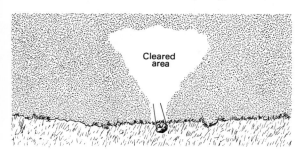

Cleared area

A tench swim located in thick weed

Methods: Float fishing, freelining and legering—particularly legering with a swimfeeder. Swimfeeder legering, with maggots on the hook and in the tube, is regarded as an outstandingly lethal method for tench.

Remarks: Without doubt, tench fishing is most rewarding at the beginning of the season. Indeed, it makes the perfect, dawn-on-the-sixteenth, start and many are the anglers who would not consider any other fish to open with.

By midsummer, tench are difficult to tempt in numbers. They prefer minute forms of natural food to the baits of fishermen. A move to deeper-water swims can sometimes extend the best of tenching longer; tench in the deeps are those which

Bob Church weed dragging a tench swim

failed to move out to the weedy spawning shallows, and among them are hefty specimens of great weight and fighting ability.

Autumn, as natural food decreases, and early March if the weather is mild, are further periods worthy of concentrated tench fishing.

Stillwater tench hibernate, but those in rivers remain active because changing conditions force them to move, using up energy and needing food to replace this lost energy.

A B C D

A tench bite. The strike is delayed until the float is completely submerged

Tench feed avidly between dawn and mid-morning and between dusk and midnight. Exceptionally, tench continue feeding throughout a day or night. Bites when laying-on with float or running leger tackle are 'sitters' as a rule. The float wiggles, then slides smoothly away; or, legering, the bobbin jumps fast to the butt. Shy-biting tench are common from July onwards, the lift-method being one answer to this development.

The rod is put in rests for tench fishing. Use a dough-bob indicator for day legering and a glow-bob indicator at night.

Zander

Tackle: Avon or carp rod. 8–10 lb (3·6–4·5 kg) line. Wire traces fitted with treble hooks of small size. Spinners and plugs.

Hookbait: Small fish.

Groundbait: Cloudbait—to attract small fish to the swim. Balls of stodge mixed with fish oils and mashed herrings—to attract zander.

Methods: Freelining, float fishing, paternostering and lure fishing.

Remarks: Zander remain active summer and winter. They are peculiar in that they prefer dirty-coloured water to feed in. I believe their marvellous eyesight is a reason for this, coupled with other well-developed senses. Zander simply find their food easier to catch in coloured water—the very time when other species are most vulnerable to attack. It is probably for the same reason that zander feed at night.

All pike methods scaled down catch zander. They are poor fighters compared size for size with pike though, and for this reason it is important not to use over-powerful tackle.

Barbel

Tackle: Avon rod. 4–7 lb (1·8–3·1 kg) line. Size 4, 6, 8, 10 and 12 hooks.—For sections of rivers known to hold barbel well in excess of 12 lb (5·4 kg) (e.g. middle Hampshire Avon): Carp rod. 8–12 lb (3·9–5·4 kg) line. Size 4, 6 and 8 hooks.

Hookbait: Bread, cheese, maggots, meat baits, hempseed, sweetcorn, worms, crayfish, elvers and small fish.

Groundbait: Large balls of stodge well-laced with hook samples. Maggots and hempseed thrown in loose and put down with a bait-dropper.

Methods: Float fishing and legering—particularly swimfeeder legering.

Remarks: In summer, barbel feeding mainly takes place between late afternoon and early morning. Length of the feeding spells varies greatly according to weather conditions. Later in the year barbel indulge more frequently in bouts of daytime feeding. It is known that barbel in some rivers continue to feed at night in winter (e.g. notably the barbel in the Thames) but more normally the activity of this species after the end of autumn is reduced to spasmodic bursts of middle-of-the-day feeding.

Trotting and legering are methods equally as good for barbel. A choice between the two is made according to which of them is more suited to the needs of an individual swim.

Barbel give decisive float bites. Leger bites vary between gentle trembles (which cannot be seen on the rod but register only through the finger tips) and 'smash takes' capable of dragging an unattended rod into the water. Whether the rod is held or put in rests when legering depends entirely on how firmly the fish are biting.

Eels

Tackle: Heavy carp rod. 10–12 lb (4·5–5·4 kg) line. Size 4 single hook attached to trace wire.

Hookbait: Dead fish—a fish of 4 in (10 cm) is about right size.

Groundbait: Fish chunks and balls of stodge mixed with mashed fish and fish oils.

Methods: Freelining and legering.

Remarks: To bait a dead fish the trace wire is threaded with a baiting needle through the body from mouth to vent before the top swivel is twisted on. The fish is then pulled down so that the bend of the hook is against the corner of its mouth. A split-shot is pinched on close to the vent to retain the bait in this position. Casting weight, if needed, is added in the form of a small, streamlined lead, threaded on the wire before threading the wire through the bait. The weight is pushed deep inside the fish.

Fishing for big eels (nobody fishes seriously for small eels unless they like eating them!) is a pursuit of summer and autumn months. During the day, put out a bait in the deepest water which can be found. At night, when big eels are moving, swims of lesser depth on the edge of deep water should be tried.

The rod is put in rests with the bale-arm open and an indicator attached. Silver foil is a satisfactory indicator for daytime; at night use a bite alarm.

An eel runs with a bait before swallowing it, so allow plenty of time for this to happen. When you strike, hang on tight. A big eel is a fantastically strong animal to tangle with.

Migrating eels weigh between 1½ lb (680 g) and 3 lb (1·3 kg). But eels far larger swim British waters and it is these which big-fish specialists hope to catch. Quite probably giant eels are abnormal; they are fish which have not matured properly and do not experience the spawning urge. It is also possible that eels which have slipped into waters they cannot escape from grow big before they die.

Bream

Tackle: Avon rod. 4–6 lb (1·8–2·7 kg) line.—For snaggy conditions and waters where bream grow as large as double-figures: Carp rod. 7–9 lb (3·1–4 kg) line. Hook sizes 6, 8, 10 and 12.

Hookbait: Bread, cheese, maggots, worms, sausage paste and freshwater mussels.

Groundbait: Large balls of stodge laced with hook samples introduced frequently. Heavy pre-baiting in known hot-spots is advantageous.

Remarks: There are several ways of locating a bream shoal. For a start, the fish roll at the surface prior to feeding, and below where they are last seen is the place to put a hookbait. Faint discoloration of the water also signals bream, rooting pig-like in the mud. Angle upstream of discolorations in moving water.

A location method which bream expert Peter Stone and his friends use is known as the 'cross-over'. It involves several anglers spacing themselves about 10 yd (9 m) apart along the bank. All fish hard for ten minutes and then, if no bream have been caught, the angler furthest upstream moves down

10 yd (9 m) below the end angler and tries again. This system of searching continues at ten-minute intervals until bream are found or the day ends. If bream are located, the anglers muster together as a group to take equal advantage. As bream shoals are often vast there is plenty of fish for everybody.

Spots where bream feed include weirpools, underwater ledges, bulrush beds, areas of submerged lily and deeper holes in shallow lakes. Because bream shoals wander about a great deal, it is possible, in smaller stillwaters, to learn the pattern of their patrol well enough to be able to groundbait an area along the path and halt their progress—at least for as long as groundbait supplies last.

Bream eat enormous quantities of food, and quite honestly it is impossible to over-bait a bream swim. A full sack-load, if it can be carted to the waterside, would certainly not be overdoing things. Once groundbait runs out, the bream move on and you will catch no more. The importance of heavy groundbaiting is as cut and dried as that.

Bream live in many different swims and bite in many different ways. Consequently there is always need to adjust basic float fishing and legering to deal with these changing circumstances. Such techniques as trotting, laying-on, lift-method, stretpegging, static legering and legering with a lead light enough to sink the bait slowly, are all methods which will be found useful at various times and places.

Should method and bite-pattern allow, the rod can be put in rests with the bale-arm closed. Add a dough-bob or glow-bob as indicator when legering from rests.

Bream feed day and night. In winter, river bream remain active. Those in stillwaters tend to hibernate.

Big Species

Common Carp

Tackle: Carp rod. 8–15 lb (3·6–6·8 kg) line. Size 2, 4, 6 and 8 hooks.

Hookbait: Bread, cheese, freshwater mussels, maggots, sweetcorn, meat baits, potatoes, worms and 'exotics'.

Groundbait: Hook samples thrown or catapulted, and balls of stodge laced with hook samples.

Methods: Freelining and legering.

Remarks: Carp in hard-fished waters have a habit of remaining far out from the bank during the hours of daylight and must be fished for at long range. They are easier to catch after dark because they then move in closer to the bank.

When legering, the rod is put in rests with a silver foil tube indicator; the bale-arm is open. At night the silver foil is replaced with an electric bite alarm. Carp run with the bait, but there is absolutely no reason to let them run very far. As soon as the line is moving, turn in the bale-arm, wait for the line to tighten, and drag, rather than strike,

A carp angler's pitch

the hook home, as the weight of the fish is felt.

In winter it is a good idea to scale the size of bait right down, and to strike at twitch bites. Twitch bites are quick jerks of the indicator caused by carp sucking in and blowing out the bait quickly. Carp often play with baits in this manner when the water is cold.

To hit twitches the bale-arm is closed and a dough-bob or glow-bob indicator is hung about 6 in (15 cm) beneath the rod. Strike fast the moment the indicator moves. An important point is to set the reel to backwind—just in case a carp does charge off with the bait fast. Should this happen with the reel in anti-reverse, either the rod will finish up in the water, or the line will snap.

Twitch bites, of course, also result from little fish nibbling at the bait and bigger fish brushing past the line. The only way to discover the difference is to strike at them.

Carp are often twitch-biters in over-fished public fisheries, no matter what the water temperature is. They also shy away from ordinary baits, and this in turn has lead to the invention of what are collectively called 'exotic baits'—baits concocted from ingredients completely different from those commonly used on the hook. Successful carpmen keep their bait recipes secret for one *very good* reason; once they become general knowledge, used by everybody, they cease to be 'different' and no longer catch carp so effectively.

Exotics are invented by experimenting with edible ingredients which it is thought might appeal to carp, and trying out the resulting 'mixes' to see how the fish respond to them. Plenty of free samples should be introduced to the water as part of these trials. Tinned cat and dog foods are often used in 'something new' carp baits.

Pike

Tackle: Pike rod. 8–15 lb (3·6–6·8 kg) line. Wire traces fitted with treble hooks.—For long-casting herring and mackerel baits: Beachcaster. 15–18 lb (6·8–8·1 kg) line. Side-cast reel.

Hookbait: Fish.

Groundbait: Fish chunks and balls of groundbait mashed with herrings and scented with fish oils.

Methods: Freelining, legering, float fishing and paternostering. Lure fishing with spinners, spoons, plugs and moving deadbaits.

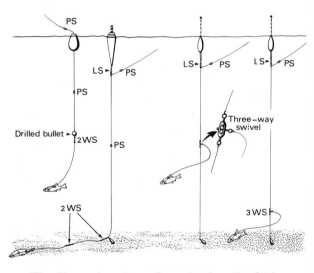

The illustration shows float rigs for pike fishing. The one on the left is ideal for trotting live and dead baits in rivers. Next to it is a deadbait rig for stillwater work which features a self-cocking float.   On the right are two paternoster rigs.   By comparing them it will be seen that by varying the length of line between the leger lead and the three-way swivel it is possible to fish the livebait at any depth between near-surface and bottom.

The paternoster rig is suitable for both stillwater and river fishing in any swim where it is desirable to restrict the bait's movement to a small area such as a clear hole in an otherwise snaggy section of water.   PS = plug-stop,   LS = link-swivel,   2WS = two-way swivel,   3WS = three-way swivel.

Jardine snap-tackle

The Jardine snap-tackle livebait rig is attached by sticking the small hook on the end treble just astern of the gill cover of the bait and the small hook of the top treble through the leading root of the dorsal fin. The top treble is adjustable along the wire to accommodate baits of different shapes and sizes. Between the main line and the snap-tackle a wire trace is added, attached by a link-swivel to the wire-loop.

Remarks: Pike are extremely fit and lively during summer, and from a purely sporting point of view it is my opinion that lure methods are preferable to bait fish methods at this time of year.   Summer pike are everywhere in the water, and hunting systematically with lures is a deeply satisfying way of finding them out.

The author with a brace of big pike weighing 20 lb 4 oz
(9·1 kg) and 17 lb 8 oz (7·8 kg), taken in February

From autumn to the season's end, although pike
still respond to lures, bait fish methods come into
their own for catching pike of larger size. Every
method has its day, but I am firmly convinced that
freelining herring and mackerel baits in stillwaters
of shallow depth is the number one approach if you
want to connect a pike of 20 lb (9 kg) plus.

By the time the season is beginning to draw to a
close, pike will already be gathering in groups as
preparation for entering the spawning areas.
Some groups consist almost entirely of females [the
majority of pike weighing upwards of 10 lb (4·5 kg)

are females] and if such a group as this can be
marked down it is possible to catch a number of
specimens between 10 (4·5 kg) and 30 lb (13·6 kg)
plus in the space of just a few weeks.

Isolated slacks along stretches of fast-flowing
rivers are places to try for big-pike groups. In
stillwaters the groups are not so easily located because they roam about quite a bit. The effort is
still worthwhile nevertheless.

I remember a friend of mine visiting a gravel-pit
regularly for several winters without even one big
pike falling to his rod. Then he stumbled on an inform hot-spot where his first three runs to deadbaits
yielded two pike of over 20 lb (9 kg) each, inside
the space of half-a-day's fishing!

Catfish

Tackle: Beachcaster. 15–30 lb (6·8–13·6 kg) line.
Wire traces fitted with single hooks.
Hookbaits: Worms and small fish.
Groundbait: Balls of groundbait mashed with herrings
and fish oils.
Methods: Legering and freelining.
Remarks: Because catfish are so rare in this country
very little is known about them. It is known,
however, that they reach enormous size in the lakes
at Woburn Abbey, and that they pack tremendous
strength.

Angling for catfish is undertaken with the rod in
rests and the bale-arm open. One of the major
problems is getting a firm hook-hold. Catfish often
fail to take the bait properly and missed runs are a
consequence. The strike should be delayed as long
as possible.

Catfish are warm water feeders, only ever likely
to be caught when the temperature rises above
60°F (15°C).

Lighter strength tackle, a carp rod and 10 lb (4·5 kg) line, is adequate for dealing with small catfish in open water, but such gear could never be expected to subdue monster 'cats'—fish weighing as much as 60 (27·2) to 80 lb (36·2 kg).

Handling Fish

Playing
Small fish are easily and quickly brought under control by applying gentle rod pressure and turning the handle of the reel. The only point which must be watched for is that a fish does not come to the surface and flap about—disturbance capable of scaring off the remainder of the shoal. This activity can be avoided by keeping the rod top low towards the water and winding back slowly.

Big fish, and the bigger and tougher they are the more this applies, must be 'played' long enough to tire them before any attempt is made to lift them out. Exactly how an individual fish is played depends largely on the type of swim where it is hooked. If a fish is hooked amid thick weed or close to snags, quite obviously it cannot be allowed much line at any time during the fight. Clearly this is the reason why strong rods, lines and hooks are required when fishing such parts as lily 'jungles'.

In open water, lighter tackle can be used and the fish allowed to exhaust itself by running against rod pressure; the slipping-clutch of the fixed-spool reel is set tight enough to give line only in the event that the fish tugs extra hard or puts on a sudden burst of speed.

The fighting habits of fish vary from one species to the next but, broadly speaking, they consist of strong runs interspaced with lulls, when the fish moves more slowly or allows itself to be brought in close to the bank.

As examples, I will outline the typical fight patterns of two of the strongest species in fresh water—barbel and carp.

First barbel: We will imagine that a 6 lb (2·7 kg) class barbel has been hooked 10 yd (9 m) downstream in fastish water. Immediately it will feel heavy as it thumps against the arched rod, and inevitably your heart starts to quicken its beat. This is the very time to remain calm to resist the impulse to pull hard on the rod and try to drag the fish in. At this stage, too great a pressure will send the barbel off on a mad run downstream, forcing you to run also to keep up with it—if it hasn't broken free of course!

Steady pressure is what is wanted. Enough to keep the fish moving and sapping energy, but no

Downstream pressure is applied as the barbel fights upstream of the angler

more than that. With luck the fish will fin up-stream, going above the spot on the bank where you are standing. This manoeuvre is favourable because downstream pressure can then be applied to coax the fish to fight both the rod and the current. This action serves to exhaust it, so that when eventually it does fall back it will be tired—perhaps even ready for the net. Should the barbel remain downstream, walk down the bank, keeping contact by taking in line as you go, and get well below the fish that way.

The fight from a barbel of this size may last minutes or for as long as a quarter of an hour. There will be quiet periods when the fish pushes against the current neither giving nor taking line, other times when it will be brought almost as far as the net, and crucial moments which leave you weak at the knees when panic moves send line screaming from the reel.

Played out and on its side, the barbel is ready for the net

Keep patient, keep cool, and above all try to be always downstream of the fish. Eventually, after what will almost certainly seem an eternity, the barbel will tumble on to its flank and be ready for netting.

Two developments to beware of: (1) A barbel which allows itself to be brought straight to the bank after being hooked. *Watch out for a long run.* The fish could be either big or foul-hooked in a fin; not realizing at first that anything is wrong. If you do get a run of this kind, do not try to stop it too abruptly or you will part the line for sure. (2) A barbel which is exhausted, but gives one last dash to the centre of the river just as you are about to net it out. An exhausted barbel on a long line can be a difficult customer because it no longer has the ability to resist the current properly. Gradually it drags off downstream, and if you do not react fast, run after it and pressure it back to the bank, you could be in real trouble.

Patience is a virtue when playing barbel. A double-figure specimen can take as long as an hour to beat even on correct strength tackle. In my opinion, if you can handle barbel you can handle any fish in the river. They do not come any stronger than this species.

Now carp. This time the fish is a ten-pounder (4·5 kg), hooked in a lake swim where a patch of lilies grows to the right and a fallen tree rests in the water to the left. The strike has been made, and after a second or two to think about it the fish has powered off hard and fast straight out from the bank towards open water. No snags or thick weed to worry about so the fish can be let run against medium pressure. Eventually it slows up, and by pumping the rod—lifting and lowering it and winding in line on the downward strokes—you find it can

(*above*) A swirl, and the carp makes off on a second run

(*below*) Steady pumping brings the carp closer and closer

be brought grudgingly back towards the bank. Occasionally the slipping-clutch grates a yard or two of line as the fish shakes its head, but otherwise it is a time to breathe deeply and calm down (an angler would not be an angler if he didn't shake a bit when he hooks a good fish!).

Just as you are beginning to wonder if the carp has had enough, it suddenly wakes up and off it goes again on a second run; this time it moves more to the left and not so far. You start to pump the rod, but the resistance is more stubborn. The fish, in fact, has started to 'kite'—turning broadside on to where you are standing and using the depth of its body to cruise towards the fallen tree. Now there *is* cause for concern. If the fish reaches the tree it will cut the line the moment it makes contact with the rough bark.

Straightaway the rod is swung parallel to the bank pointing away from the tree and sidestrain is applied to as much as the tackle will stand. At first it has no result, the fish keeps on course towards the tree. But then, as the greater pressure begins to drag it off balance it veers round and starts coming back to the bank yet again.

Steady pumping brings it closer and closer. A few short runs are counteracted without trouble. Then it sees the approaching net, senses acute danger and crashes off with all its remaining strength towards the lilies. Sidestrain is applied in the opposite direction, and though the fish does enter the stems a little way the taut line rips through the foliage and it is soon free again—this time flopped on its side as a truly beaten fish.

Summing up: Let a big stillwater fish run if it has a mind to, and the area it is in is snagless. Apply sidestrain when the situation looks dangerous. Retrieve line by pumping. Never attempt to wind line back against a running fish to stop it—rather finger the edge of the drum to slow it up. And above all, stay calm.

Netting
Very small fish can be taken from the water by swinging them out on the line. When doing this it is essential to have enough line between rod-tip and fish to allow the fish to come back into the hand.

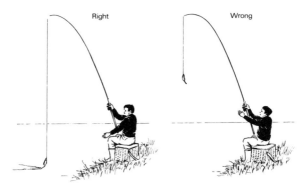

Swinging a small fish out on the line

Fish heavier than about half-a-pound (226 g) should be netted. To net a fish, the landing net is submerged deeply and the fish drawn over the rim. The net is then lifted to engulf the fish inside the mesh. By remaining seated the angler is less likely to frighten other fish which might be feeding in the swim.

Never attempt to put the net under the fish. Always bring the fish over the net. To get a big

Netting a fish

fish from water to bank, first make sure it is fully enclosed, then lay the rod down, and grip frame and mesh with both hands for lifting out.   It is helpful when handling an exceptionally big fish to have a friend take care of the netting for you—but be absolutely sure he understands the procedure, and does not attempt to lift the net until he is told to do so.   This is vitally important to avoid completely any confusion which might arise.   The rule is that the man with the rod controls the man with the net.

Unhooking
Handle fish with wet hands or with a damp cloth when unhooking them.   If the hook is so far back

Artery forceps being used to unhook a small roach

that it cannot be retrieved with the fingers the best tool to use is a pair of artery forceps.

To unhook pike and zander special tools are required: a selection of mouth gags of various sizes (points taped over to avoid undue injury); a pair of pliers and a pair of end-snips fitted with long handles; and a model-maker's knife blade also mounted on a long handle.

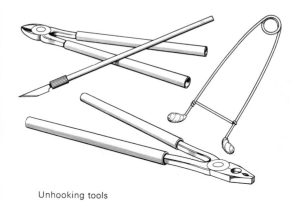

Unhooking tools

First pull the pike clear of the netting and, if it is large, wrap it in a wet sack or old bath towel. Hold the body of the pike still, and insert as small a gag as possible to open its mouth wide. The hooks, even when quite far back, can be removed with the pliers. If you sit on the ground by the pike, you can control its movements with your own body and work really close in without fear of getting bitten. Care must be taken not to damage the fish by applying too much pressure.

Unhooking a pike

The knife blade sometimes helps when it is necessary to remove a hook nicked in loose skin, but if the hooks are so far back that they cannot be seen at all it is advisable to cut through the wire with the snips as far down the throat as possible.

An important aspect of piking, which quite honestly I cannot emphasize enough, is *never* to purposely delay the strike so long that a pike has time to swallow the hooks down to the stomach.

Handlifting a pike

Far better to strike early and risk missing a secure hook-hold, than gut-hook and sentence a fine, sporting fish to an early death.

Incidentally, it is not absolutely necessary to use a net to land small pike and zander. A fish of either species as large as 10 lb (4·5 kg) can be removed from the water by gripping it with one hand firmly across the back, astern of the gill-covers, and hoisting it out. (See page 171.)

Photographing

Photographing the catch is the ideal way to preserve a permanent record of notable specimens and memorable bags. *For the sake of the fish it must be carried out carefully*. Don't keep fish out of water longer than absolutely necessary. Don't let them flap about on dry ground. Don't squeeze them tight or hug them against rough clothing. Don't hold them at peculiar angles which could damage their vital organs (e.g. upside down).

The most sensible plan is to have the camera ready for instant use all the time. This means that as soon as a big fish is unhooked it can be photographed and slipped back into water in a very short space of time.

Before sliding out a bag of fish for photographing, soak the area (short soft grass for preference) and keep a bucket of water on hand to wash the fish over with. It takes time to put (say) a couple of dozen dace back in the water and some of the fish left until last can dry out if the day is hot. *Never throw fish back*.

Weighing

Catches of fish are best weighed still in the keepnet. After the fish have been let free the keepnet is then weighed again and its weight is deducted to get the accurate weight of the fish.

A big crucian carp weighed accurately in a plastic bag on dial-clock scales

Big fish can be weighed individually in a thick plastic bag or soft-mesh knotless bag, subtracting the weight of the container afterwards, of course.

Spring-balance scales and dial-clock scales are used to weigh fish. The latter type is more accurate and also adjustable so that the weight of the container can be compensated before weighing the catch.

Retaining and Returning

For various reasons it is necessary to retain fish for a period following capture before returning them in good condition.

Hard-fighters such as barbel and tench benefit greatly from being rested in a keepnet to recover strength and balance, particularly when they are going to be returned to a river of strong current. I

Ron Barnett gently returns a fine 12 lb (5·4 kg) carp caught by the author

have seen, for example, barbel floating belly-up and slowly dying, not because they were injured, but because they had been released too soon to be able to combat the swift-flowing current.

Notable specimens caught at night must also be retained in order to photograph them properly on the morning after. True, it is possible to picture fish in the dark, but it is never an easy exercise. It takes a lot of fiddling about and adjusting this and that. And if you want to use a flash gun without scaring other fish in the swim and annoying fellow anglers, it calls for a long walk away from the water carrying both camera gear and the trophy fish.

Returning a fish

Clearly it is essential for matchmen to keep what they land, and it is equally clear that in certain circumstances when pleasure fishing it can spoil the swim to return caught fish among those which are still to be caught.

Keepnets should be of large size, staked out along the bottom so that fish have plenty of room to move and change position. Wide-mesh knotted keep-nets are a menace because the roughness of the knots removes scales and protective slime and the width of the mesh causes fin-split. Such injuries can lead to the death of the victims—perhaps even the spread of disease to other fish and a resulting widespread fatality.

In recent years a new type of keepnet has been introduced to the market made from knotless micro-mesh material. Extensive testing has proved how superior these nets are for preserving fish in perfect order. This is the only type I would personally recommend.

If a big fish is to be returned straight to the water it should be handled with extreme care; hold it between the hands on an even keel until it is able to wiggle clear. Stroking the flanks lightly helps aid recovery. When returning a big fish to a river it is vital to hold it with its head pointing upstream directly into the current. If a fish is held with its head pointing downstream for any length of time it will die. (See page 175.)

Carp and other big fish may be retained in *open-weave* hessian sacks or industrial nylon keepsacks— one fish per sack. An ideal keepsack, 5 × 4 ft (1·5 × 1·2 m), is punched all over (corners included) with $\frac{1}{4}$ in holes to ensure good water flow, and pegged out in water at least 3 ft (·9 m) deep on a hard bottom. In hot weather, retention time should not exceed one hour.

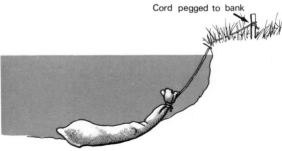

Cord pegged to bank

The sack method of retaining carp individually

4: FINAL MATTERS

Sporting Divisions

Coarse fish are hunted for the pleasure and interest which comes from trying to catch them, and for the feelings of excitement and satisfaction which follow whenever the attempt is successful. Few of the coarse species have any real value at table; even the edible ones are very little eaten apart from eels. Coarse fishing is really just a 'catch and return' activity, and few are those who purposely seek coarse fish to eat.

It goes without saying that coarse fishing is fun for everybody who participates but, in the jargon of the angler, the term 'fun fishing' takes on special meaning; it describes the activities of non-specialists—the vast ranks of those who simply go fishing for the balm of catching a few fish and 'getting away from it all'.

Personally, I think this is what fishing is really all about and the way to enjoy it. It does not necessarily follow, of course, that the knowledge and ability of 'fun fishers' has to remain limited. Through practical angling, observation, and a study of thoughts and ideas expressed by fellow anglers in books and articles, it is possible to become proficient to the point where, providing they are in the water, specimen fish can be caught in return for little increased effort.

Many friends of mine have long lists of notable catches to their credit, yet strongly deny they are anything but 'fun fishers'. They know the basics of the sport well enough to take advantage of every opportunity which comes their way, but that is as far as their 'specimen hunting' inclinations go.

'Specimen hunting' is a significant division of coarse fishing—highly specialized these days. Some specimen hunters are happy to seek big fish of all species, according to season and what big-fish water they can obtain access to. Other specimen hunters specialize in just one or two species; they learn everything they can about the habits of their chosen quarry and strive always to improve tackle, methods and baits to catch them with.

The pinnacle of achievement for many specimen hunters is the breaking of a British record. Yet, ironically, few indeed are records topped by fish caught by anglers who, at time of capture, confidently thought themselves in with a chance of beating the best for a certain species.

To increase knowledge of big fish and big fish waters, specimen hunters band together in groups—both locally and nationally. Many specimen hunters also belong to the National Association of Specialist Anglers, formed in 1982 when the old style National Association of Specimen Groups was disbanded.

The N.A.S.A. is open to all serious anglers including matchmen. Further details from the secretary, Des Taylor, 20 Grampian Road, Stourbridge, West Midlands, DY8 4UE.

Famous national single-species groups—with memberships including both specimen hunters and non-specimen hunters of proven ability—include The Tenchfishers', the Chub Study Group, The Barbel Catchers' Club, The National Anguilla Club (eels), the British Eel Anglers Club, The Carp Society, and the British Carp Study Group. The latter group is by far the most advanced in the country, printing its own magazine, *The Carp*, and operating a special advisory service to answer the carp fishing problems of non-members. This service is open to all, and requests for information should be made to the secretary, Peter Mohan, Heywood House, Pill, Bristol, BS20 0AE.

Mr Mohan is also secretary of the Carp Anglers Association, an organization open to all who are interested in carp fishing—even those who have still to catch their first carp. There are two divisions of membership—senior and junior—with the junior section limited to under 16's.

Another excellent single-species group is the Pike Anglers' Club, with a membership divided into senior members (highly experienced pike anglers) and associate members (less experienced anglers including beginners and youngsters). It, too, publishes its own magazine.

Specimen hunting is a first-class approach for really keen anglers. But be warned, do not let the hunt for bigger and bigger fish get out of hand. It is so easy to become dissatisfied with results if they fall short of expectations, and the result is that the enjoyment of 'going fishing' ceases to have meaning.

There is a true story of one specimen hunter who dearly wanted to catch a 20 lb (9 kg) carp. He tried very hard for several years, with tackle and methods unquestionably excellent, and because of his ability he landed a high total of carp weighing between 10 lb (4·5 kg) and 19 lb 12 oz (8·9 kg). The 20 lb (9 kg) target eluded him though, and eventually a matter of 4 oz (113 g) caused him to suffer a nervous breakdown.

The moral, if you fancy taking up specimen hunting after learning the ropes for a few seasons, is to set your sights high by all means, but never to forget that small fish are worth catching too. Enjoy the fun of small fish and the big fish will follow—without any loss of mental health!

'Match fishing' is a third division of coarse angling. Matches are fished as individual events and team events, in leagues and as annual championships. Most matches are 'pegged down' with each participant restricted to a single spot on the bank by drawing a ticket with a number on it corresponding to the number on a peg stuck in the ground at that spot. Less frequently matches are fished as 'rovers', allowing those taking part to select their own swims by going off, one from each team at few minute intervals. In winter, 'fur and feather' matches take place, sometimes solely for pike. Boxing Day is a popular date for these contests.

Years ago match winners received a copper or brass kettle, or other metal ornament as prize, and it was easy to judge how good a particular matchman was from the amount of 'shine' in his front parlour.

Modern match fishing is quite different. Major fixtures are sponsored with big-money prize lists, and top matchmen put a lot of behind-the-scenes effort into winning important events. Match 'stars' often speak of a season's success in terms of money won rather than in terms of good fish and notable catches. It is not everybody's idea of what angling should be about, but nevertheless, for those who find pleasure in competing against fellow anglers as well as against fish, match fishing is *the* sporting division with greatest appeal.

Fly Fishing

There has not been space in this book to deal with fly fishing. Special rods and lines are required, and the casting style is quite separate from all other forms of casting. Coarse fish caught with fly tackle and imitations of insects and fish constructed from fur, feather and silk, include rudd, dace, chub, grayling, bleak, pike, barbel, carp and perch. Further information is contained in my book *The Observer's Book of Fly Fishing* (Warne).

Lines and Baited Hooks Kill

Nylon monofilament fishing line has a habit of losing its strength, and as some anglers know to their cost a big fish hooked on last year's line is often lost in the first moment that pressure is applied. On the other hand, nylon line does not rot, and though it may deteriorate, becoming as weak as cotton, it still remains strong enough to kill birds and animals which become entwined in it.

Sad pictures of birds are published which prove just how fatal fishing line is to wildlife; pictures depict robins and finches hanging by their legs from monofilament tangled in tree branches, and blackbirds and thrushes strangled in their undergrowth homes.

But not only the smaller birds. A goosander drake, reported in a past issue of *Birds*, the magazine of the Royal Society for the Protection of Birds, apparently died in the agony of total starvation with its beak clamped tight by a chunk of monofilament no longer than 5 ft (1·5 m).

Angling is getting a bad name because of the menace of unwanted line left unthinkingly along the bank, and it is a stigma which can only be removed by practical action: *take home every piece of waste line and burn it.*

In awkward casting spots, trees are decorated with hooks, spinners, floats and nylon lengths, and these also should be removed if at all possible.

Another kind of monofilament menace is created by anglers who will insist on fishing fine lines in snaggy water for big-growing species. Apart from the fact that beating a heavy carp or barbel from a lily-bed or thick streamer weed on light gear is very much a trust-to-luck affair, it also means that when breaks occur (they often do) long trails of line are left threaded through the growth—definite traps for coots, moorhens, swans and ducks, as they paddle about up-tailing to feed on the weed.

Baited hooks out of the water are killers, too. Anglers leaving swims for any length of time should wind their tackle in and clean the hook of bait. After all, a bunch of maggots is an open invitation to a friendly robin, a crust to a swan, half a sausage to a dog or cat. Such incidents really do happen, believe me!

★   ★   ★

The Anglers' Co-operative Association

This organization was founded in 1948 by angler and barrister John Eastwood, KC. It is a voluntary body and its aim is to fight water pollution through the common law, the legal and administrative costs being shared by anglers and others interested in the conservation of rivers and lakes and the fish they contain. Apart from membership subscriptions it has no other means of support.

Since its formation the ACA has fought over 1,000 serious cases of pollution, losing only one and that merely because of a technicality.

Not all anglers are members but **all anglers** should be. The ACA is the most successful safeguard we have in the constant battle against those who thoughtlessly and carelessly defile precious water. A membership of over 10,000, including 1,000 angling clubs and associations, believes this to be true.

For further information write to the ACA, Midland Bank Chambers, Westgate, Grantham, Lincs. NG31 6LE, or in the case of Scotland to 10 Corrennie Drive, Edinburgh. Currently the ACA handles over fifty cases of pollution at any one time. That kind of action takes money—your money. A year's subscription to the ACA costs less than the price of ticket and bait for a decent day's fishing, so there is no excuse for not giving this organization the support it deserves.

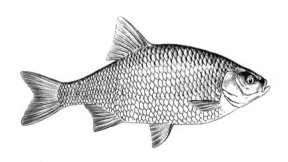

Size of Fish in British Waters

Species	Quality	Specimen	Possible Maximum Size
Roach	1 lb (·45 kg)	2 lb (·9 kg)	4½–5 lb (2–2·2 kg)
Rudd (England)	1 lb (·45 kg)	2 lb (·9 kg)	5 lb (2·2 kg)
Rudd (Ireland)	1½ lb (·68 kg)	2½ lb (1·1 kg)	5 lb (2·2 kg)
Dace	6–8 oz (170–226 g)	12 oz (340 g)	1½–1¾ lb (·68–·79 kg)
Crucian Carp	1 lb (·45 kg)	2 lb (·9 kg)	6–6½ lb (2·7–2·9 kg)
Common Carp (Wild)	4 lb (1·8 kg)	10 lb (4·5 kg)	20 lb (9 kg)
Common Carp (King)	8 lb (3·6 kg)	20 lb (9 kg)	60–70 lb (27·2–31·7 kg)
Common Bream	4 lb (1·8 kg)	10 lb (4·5 kg)	16 lb (7·2 kg)
Silver Bream	8 oz (226 g)	1½ lb (·68 kg)	4 lb (1·8 kg)
Chub	3 lb (1·3 kg)	5 lb (2·2 kg)	10–12 lb (4·5–5·4 kg)
Tench	3 lb (1·3 kg)	5 lb (2·2 kg)	12–15 lb (5·4–6·8 kg)
Grayling	1 lb (·45 kg)	2 lb (·9 kg)	5 lb (2·2 kg)
Perch	1 lb (·45 kg)	3 lb (1·3 kg)	6–8 lb (2·7–3·6 kg)
Pike (River)	5 lb (2·2 kg)	15 lb (6·8 kg)	40–45 lb (18·1–20·4 kg)
Pike (Stillwater)	8 lb (3·6 kg)	20 lb (9 kg)	70 lb (31·7 kg)
Zander	5 lb (2·2 kg)	10 lb (4·5 kg)	20–25 lb (9–11·3 kg)
Barbel	5 lb (2·2 kg)	10 lb (4·5 kg)	20 lb (9 kg)
Eel	2 lb (·9 kg)	5 lb (2·2 kg)	20 lb+ (9 kg)
Catfish	Not widely enough distributed to offer comparisons		80 lb (36·2 kg)

Books for Further Reading

Catch More Roach and Rudd by James Randell. Wolfe Publishing

Successful Roach Fishing by David Carl Forbes. David & Charles

Catch More Dace by Peter Wheat.   Wolfe Publishing

The Carp Strikes Back by Rod Hutchinson. Wonderdog Publications

Rod Hutchinson's Carp Book by Rod Hutchinson. Hudson-Chadwick Publishing

Carp Fever by Kevin Maddocks. Beekay Publishers

Carp For Everyone by Peter Mohan. David & Charles

Quest For Carp by Jack Hilton.   Pelham Books

Carp by James A. Gibbinson.   Macdonald & Janes

Catch More Bream by Dennis Kelly.   Wolfe Publishing

The Complete Chub Angler by Ken Seaman.   David & Charles

Fishing for Big Chub by Peter Stone. Beekay Publishers.

Tench by Fred J. Taylor.   Macdonald & Janes

Fishing For Big Tench by Barrie Rickards and Ray Webb.   Rod & Gun Publishing

Catch More Tench by Bob Church.   Wolfe Publishing

Grayling by Reg Righyni.   Macdonald & Janes

Catch More Perch by Barrie Rickards.   Wolfe Publishing

Fishing For Big Pike by Ray Webb and Barrie Rickards.   Black

Pike by Fred Buller.   Macdonald & Janes

Catch More Pike by David Allen.   Wolfe Publishing

Pike by Jim Gibbinson.   Osprey Publishing

The Fighting Barbel by Peter Wheat.   Benn

Catch More Barbel by Ken Cope.   Wolfe Publishing

Fishing As We Find It.   Peter Wheat (editor). Warne

Catch A Big Fish. David Carl Forbes (editor). Newnes

In Search of Big Fish by Frank Guttfield. EMAP

Match Fishing by Dave Burr and Jack Winstanley. Hamlyn

Match Angling. John Carding (editor) Pan Angler's Library

Match Fishing To Win by Billy Lane and Colin Graham. Macdonald & Janes

Pelham Manual of River Coarse Fishing by Peter Wheat. Pelham Books

Still-Water Angling by Richard Walker. David & Charles

Small Stream Fishing by David Carl Forbes. Newnes

Irish Coarse Fishing by James Williams. Black

Billy Lane's Encyclopaedia of Float Fishing by Billy Lane and Colin Graham. Pelham Books

Rigs and Tackles by Fred Buller. Macdonald & Janes

The New Encyclopaedia of Coarse Fishing Baits by Colin Graham. Macdonald & Janes

Angling and The Law by Michael Gregory. Charles Knight

Where To Fish 1982–83. D. A. Orton (editor). Harmsworth/Black

British Freshwater Fishes by M. E. Varley. Angling News (Books)

Modern Specimen Hunting by Jim Gibbinson. Beekay Publishers

The Observer's Book of Fly Fishing by Peter Wheat. Warne

The Observer's Book of Sea Fishing by Peter Wheat and Ray Forsberg. Warne

Angling Newspapers (published weekly): *Angling Times, Angler's Mail*

Index

187

Mist

Persuasion

These three gorgeous men are very persuasive!

Three passionate novels!

In April 2008 Mills & Boon bring back
two of their classic collections, each
featuring three favourite romances
by our bestselling authors…

MISTRESS BY PERSUASION
His Pretend Mistress by Jessica Steele
Stand-in Mistress by Lee Wilkinson
The Millionaire's Virgin Mistress
by Robyn Donald

HER SECRET CHILD
The Secret Love-Child by Miranda Lee
Her Secret Pregnancy
by Sharon Kendrick
Riccardo's Secret Child
by Cathy Williams

Mistress by Persuasion

HIS PRETEND MISTRESS
by
Jessica Steele

STAND-IN MISTRESS
by
Lee Wilkinson

THE MILLIONAIRE'S
VIRGIN MISTRESS
by
Robyn Donald

◎™ MILLS & BOON®
Pure reading pleasure

*All the characters in this book have no existence outside the
imagination of the author, and have no relation whatsoever to anyone
bearing the same name or names. They are not even distantly inspired
by any individual known or unknown to the author, and all the
incidents are pure invention.*

*Harlequin Mills & Boon Limited,
Eton House, 18-24 Paradise Road, Richmond, Surrey TW9 1SR*

MISTRESS BY PERSUASION
© by Harlequin Enterprises II B.V./S.à.r.l 2007

His Pretend Mistress, Stand-In Mistress and *The Millionaire's
Virgin Mistress* were first published in Great Britain by Harlequin
Mills & Boon Limited in separate, single volumes.

His Pretend Mistress © Jessica Steele 2002
Stand-In Mistress © Lee Wilkinson 2002
The Millionaire's Virgin Mistress © Robyn Donald 2003

ISBN: 978 0 263 86123 5

05-0408

*Printed and bound in Spain
by Litografia Rosés S.A., Barcelona*

HIS PRETEND
MISTRESS

by

Jessica Steele

100 Reasons to Celebrate

We invite you to join us in celebrating
Mills & Boon's centenary. Gerald Mills and
Charles Boon founded Mills & Boon Limited
in 1908 and opened offices in London's Covent
Garden. Since then, Mills & Boon has become
a hallmark for romantic fiction, recognised
around the world.

We're proud of our 100 years of publishing
excellence, which wouldn't have been achieved
without the loyalty and enthusiasm of our
authors and readers.

Thank you!

Each month throughout the year there will
be something new and exciting to mark the
centenary, so watch for your favourite authors,
captivating new stories, special limited
edition collections…and more!

Jessica Steele lives in the county of Worcestershire with her super husband, Peter, and their gorgeous Staffordshire bull terrier, Florence. Any spare time is spent enjoying her three main hobbies: reading espionage novels, gardening (she has a great love of flowers) and playing golf. Any time left over is celebrated with her fourth hobby, shopping. Jessica has a sister and two brothers and they all, with their spouses, often go on golfing holidays together.

Having travelled to various places on the globe researching background for her stories, there are many countries that she would like to revisit. Her most recent trip abroad was to Portugal where she stayed in a lovely hotel, close to her all-time favourite golf course. Jessica had no idea of being a writer until one day Peter suggested she write a book. So she did. She has now written over eighty novels.

CHAPTER ONE

SHE was panicking so wildly she could barely manage to turn the knob of the stout front door.

Her employer—soon to be her ex-employer—coming into the hall after her gave her extra strength. 'Don't be so...' he slurred, but Mallon was not waiting to hear the rest of it. With shaking hands she yanked the door open and, heedless of the torrential rain deluging down, she went haring down the drive.

She did not stop running until her umpteenth glance behind confirmed that she was not being followed.

Some five minutes later Mallon had slowed to a fast walking pace when the sound of a motor engine alerted her to the fact that Roland Phillips might have decided to pursue her by car. When no car went past, panic started to rise in her again.

There was no one else about, nothing but acres and acres of unbuilt-on countryside so far as she knew. As the car drew level she cast a jerky look to her left, but was only a modicum relieved to see that it was not Roland Phillips.

Had she been hoping that the driver would be a female of the species, however, she was to be disappointed. The window of the car slid down, and she found herself staring through the downpour into a pair of hostile grey eyes.

'Get in!' he clipped.

Like blazes she'd get in! She'd had it with good-looking men. 'No, thank you,' she snappily refused the unwanted offer.

The grey eyes studied her for about two seconds. 'Suit

yourself!' the mid-thirties man said curtly, and the window slid up and the car purred on its way again.

Though not at any great speed, Mallon noticed as, shock from Roland Phillips's assault on her starting to recede a little, she also noticed that, with a veritable monsoon raging, only an idiot would drive fast in these conditions.

She trudged on with no idea of where she was making for, her only aim to put as much distance as possible between her and Roland Phillips at Almora Lodge. So far as she could recall there was not another house around for miles.

Her sandals had started to squelch, which didn't surprise her—the rain wasn't stopping; the sky was just emptying about her head.

That she was soaked to her skin was the least of her worries. She hardly cared about being drenched. Though she did begin to hope that another car might come by. If its driver was female Mallon hoped she would stop and give her a lift.

More of her shock receded and, feeling cold, wet, and decidedly miserable, Mallon half wished she had accepted a lift with the grey-eyed stranger.

A moment later and she was scoffing at any such nonsense. She'd had it with men; lechers, the lot of them! She had known some prime examples in her *ex*-stepfather, her *ex*-stepbrother, her *ex*-boyfriend, without the most recent example of that ilk, her *ex*-employer.

The rain pelted down, and, since she couldn't possibly become any more sodden, Mallon stopped walking and tried to assess her situation. She supposed she must have put a distance of about a mile or so between her and Almora Lodge. She had sprinted out of there dressed just as she was, in a cotton dress—too het up then to consider that this was probably the wettest summer on record—and without a thought in her head about nipping upstairs to collect her handbag. Her only thought then had been to put some space between her and the drunken Roland—call me Roly—Phillips.

Mallon resumed walking, her pace more of a dejected amble now as she accepted that, new to the area, she had no idea where she was going. Her only hope was that someone, foolhardy enough to motor out in such foul weather, would stop and offer her a lift.

Surely no one with so much as a single spark of decency would leave a dog out in such conditions, much less drive on by without offering her a lift?

Perhaps that was why the grey-eyed man had stopped? He hadn't sounded too thrilled at the notion of inviting her drenched person to mess up his leather upholstery. If, that was, his sharp-sounding 'Get in!' had been what you could call an invitation.

Well, he knew what he could… Her thoughts broke off as her ears picked up the purring sound of a car engine. She halted—the rain had slackened off a little—and she turned and watched as the car came into view.

She eyed the vehicle warily as it drew level, and then stopped. The window slid down—and at the same time the heavens opened again. Solemn, deeply blue eyes stared into cool grey eyes. He must have driven in a circle, she realised.

The man did not smile, nor did he invite her into his car, exactly. What he did say, was, 'Had enough?'

Mallon supposed that, with her blonde hair plastered darkly to her head, her dress clinging past saturation to her body and legs, she must look not dissimilar to the proverbial drowned rat.

She gave a shaky sigh. It looked as though she had two choices. Tell him to clear off, when heaven alone knew when another car would come along, or get into that car with him. He looked all right—but that didn't mean a thing.

'Are you offering?' she questioned jerkily.

His answer was to turn from her and to lean and open the passenger door. Then, as cool as you please, he pressed a button and the driver's window began to close.

Feeling more like creeping into some dark corner and having a jolly good howl, Mallon hesitated for only a moment or two longer. She still felt wary, but she also felt defeated.

She crossed in front of the vehicle and got in beside the stranger. When he stretched out his hand nearest her she jumped nervously. The man gave her a sharp glance, her wariness of him not missed, she gathered. Then he completed his intention of turning on the heater and directing the warmth on to her.

Instinctively she wanted to say she was sorry—but for what? She roused herself—all men were pigs; he would be no exception, and she would be a fool to think otherwise.

They had driven about half a mile when he asked, 'Where are you going?'

The car had a good heater and she supposed she could have thanked him for his thoughtfulness. But she didn't want to get into conversation with him. 'Nowhere,' she answered tiredly.

He gave a small snort of exasperation. 'Let me put it another way. Where would you like me to drop you?'

He was exasperated? Tough! 'Anywhere,' she replied. She hadn't a clue where she was going, where she was, even—none of the area was familiar territory.

He turned his head, grey eyes raking her. 'Where have you come from?' he questioned tersely.

She was feeling warmer than she had been, and while she was still wary, she felt a shade more relaxed. To her ears this man was sounding a touch fed up because he had bothered to act as any decent human being would to a fellow person and had bothered to pick her up at all. But she had a feeling that if she didn't soon answer he would open the door and tip her out. It was warm in the car. Somehow she felt too beaten to want to squelch out in the rain again.

'Almora Lodge,' she said. 'I've come from Almora Lodge.'

She wondered if he knew where Almora Lodge was, but realised he probably did when he asked, 'Do you want me to take you back there?'

'No, I don't!' she answered sharply, tartly. She drew a very shaky breath, and was a degree more in control when she added. 'No, thank you. I don't want to go back there—ever.'

Again she felt grey eyes on her, but was suddenly too tired and too emotionally exhausted to care. He said nothing, however, but motored on for a couple of miles, and then started to slow the car down.

Alarm rocketed through her. Apart from a large derelict-looking building to the right, which stood in what looked like the middle of a field, there seemed to be no other dwelling for miles.

He slowed the car right down and steered it to what appeared to be the only respectable part of the derelict property—mainly the stone pillars either side of a gateless entrance that declared 'Harcourt House'.

'Where are you taking me?' she cried fearfully, her imagination working overtime. She could lie buried for years in the rubble hereabouts, or in one of those about-to-fall-down-looking outbuildings, and no one would be any the wiser!

In sharp contrast to her panicking tones, however, his tone was calm and even—if a shade irritated. 'Like Sinbad, I appear to be lumbered,' he answered, which—recalling the tale of the old man of the sea who refused to get off Sinbad's back—she didn't think was very complimentary. 'You don't know where you want to go, and I'm not in the mood to play guessing games. I'm stopping off here to pick up some of my gear and…'

'You live here!' she exclaimed in disbelief.

'I live in London. I'm having this place rebuilt,' he said heavily, going on, 'I hadn't intended to come down this weekend, but with this rain forecast I came down last night to check if a bad part of the roof had been made sound.' That, it appeared, was all the explanation he had any intention of making. Because he was soon going on, 'I've a couple of things to do inside that may take some while— you can either stay in the car incubating pneumonia until I can drop you off at the first shelter for homeless persons I come to, or you can come inside and dry off what's left of your frock while you wait for me in a heated kitchen.' So saying, he drove round to the rear of the house and braked.

Mallon stared at him for several stunned seconds, the homeless persons bit passing her by as her glance went from him and down over her dress.

With horrified eyes she saw that her dress was torn in several places. The worst tear was where the material had been ripped away in her struggle, and her bra, now transparent from her soaking, was clearly revealing the fullness of her left breast—the pink tip just as clearly on view.

'Oh!' she cried chokily, her cheeks flushing red, tears of humiliation not far away.

'Don't you dare cry on me!' he threatened bracingly, about the best tone he could have used in the circumstances, she realised. 'Come on, let's get you inside,' he said authoritatively and, taking charge, was out of the car and coming round to open the passenger door.

She did not immediately get out of the car. She'd had one tremendous fright—she was not going to trust again in a hurry. Thankfully the rain had, for the moment, abated. The stranger was tall and he bent down to look at her as stubbornly, a hand hiding her left breast, she stayed where she was, refusing to budge.

'You won't...?' she questioned, and discovered she had no need to complete the sentence.

Steady grey eyes stared back at her and every bit as though she had asked, did he fancy her enough to try and take advantage? his glance skimmed over the wreck she knew she must look, and 'Not in a million years,' he said succinctly. Which, while not being in the least flattering, was the most reassuring answer he could have given her.

He left her to trail after him when she was ready, opening up the rear door and entering what she could now see was a property that was in the process of undergoing major rebuilding.

Mallon stepped from the car and, careful where she walked, picked her way over builders' paraphernalia. The rear hall was dark and littered with various lengths of new timber. It was a dull afternoon. Up ahead of her an electric light had been switched on. From this she knew that, electricians having been at work, Harcourt House was no longer as derelict as it had once been and, if the front of the house was anything to go by, it appeared still to be.

Holding her dress to her, she followed the light and found the grey-eyed man in the act of switching on an electric kettle in what, to her amazement, was a superbly fitted-out kitchen.

'Your wife obviously has her priorities sorted out,' Mallon commented, hovering uncertainly in the doorway.

'My sister,' he replied, opening one of the many drawers and placing a couple of kitchen hand towels on a table near Mallon. 'I'm not married,' he added. 'According to Faye…' he paused as if expecting the name might be familiar to her—it wasn't—'…the heart of the home is the kitchen. With small input from me, I left her to arrange what she tells me is essential.'

As he spoke, so Mallon began to feel fractionally more at ease with the man, though whether this was his intention she had no idea. She found she had wandered a few more steps into the room, but her eyes were watchful on him while he made a pot of tea.

'There's an electric radiator over there,' he thought to mention. 'Why not go and stand by it? Though, on second thoughts, since you can't stand there nursing your wet frock to you the whole time, why don't I go and find you a shirt to change into while you drink your tea?'

Mallon didn't answer him but, discovering a certain decisiveness in him, she moved out of the way when he came near her on his way out. She was still in the same spot when he returned, carrying a shirt and some trousers, and even a pair of socks.

'There's a drying machine through there—that will eventually be a utility room,' he informed her, and added, 'There's a lock on the kitchen door. Why not change while I go and check on a few matters?'

Mallon was in no hurry to change. She felt this man was being as kind as he knew how to be, but she wasn't ready any longer to take anyone at face value. Eventually she went over to the kitchen door and locked it, presuming that, since the place was uninhabited apart from work hours Monday to Friday when the builders must traipse in and out of the place, it had been a good idea to be able to lock in the valuable kitchen equipment.

Quickly, then, Mallon made use of the towels. She was past caring what she looked like when, not long afterwards, her dress tumbling around in the dryer, she was warm and dry in the garments the man had brought her. She was five feet nine inches tall, but he was about six inches taller. She rolled up the shirt sleeves and to prevent the trousers dragging on the floor she rolled the legs of those up too—but she was stumped for a while as to how to keep them up. That matter was soon resolved when, her brain starting to function again, she vaguely recalled that some of the timber in the hall had been kept together by a band of coarse twine.

By the time she heard the stranger coming back, she had the largest of the hand towels wound around her now only damp hair, and was feeling a great deal better than she had.

She found a couple of cups and saucers, discovering in the process of opening various cupboards until she came to the right one that his sister, Faye, had not only organised the kitchen but had stocked it with plenty of tinned and packet foods as well.

Mallon had unlocked the kitchen door, and as the man came in she informed him, half apologetically for taking the liberty, 'I thought I'd pour some tea before it became stewed.'

'How are you feeling now?' he asked by way of an answer, taking up the two cups and saucers and carrying them over to the large table. He pulled out a chair for her, but went round to a chair at the other side of the table and waited for her to take a seat.

'Warmer, dryer,' she replied, trusting him enough to take the chair he had pulled out for her.

'Care to tell me your name?' he asked when they were both seated. She didn't particularly—and owned up to herself that she had been so thoroughly shaken by the afternoon's happenings she didn't feel at her sunniest. 'I'm Harris Quillian,' he said, as if by introducing himself it might prompt her to tell him with whom he was sharing a pot of tea.

'Mallon Braithwaite,' she felt obliged to answer, but had nothing she wanted to add as the silence in the room stretched.

He drained his cup and set it down. 'Anything else you'd like to tell me?' he enquired mildly.

Not a thing! Mallon stared at him, her deep blue eyes as bright as ever and some of her colour restored to her lovely complexion. She drew a shaky breath as she began to realise that she owed this man more than a terse No. He need not have stopped and picked her up. He need not have given her some dry clothes to change into. She acknowledged that it was only because of the kindness of Harris Quillian that she now felt warm and dry and, she had to admit, on her way to having a little of her faith in human nature restored.

'Wh-what do you want to know?' she asked.

He shrugged, as though he wasn't all that much interested anyway, but summed up, 'You're a young woman obviously in some distress. Apparently uncaring where you go, apart from a distinct aversion to return to your last port of call. It would appear, too, that you have nowhere that you can go.' He broke off to suggest, 'Perhaps you'd like to start by telling me what happened at Almora Lodge to frighten you so badly.'

She had no intention of telling him anything of the sort. 'Are you a detective?' she questioned shortly.

He shook his head. 'I work in the city. I'm in finance.'

From the look of him she guessed he was high up in the world of finance. Must be. To have this place rebuilt would cost a fortune. She still wasn't going to answer his question, though.

He rephrased it. 'What reason did you have for visiting Almora Lodge in the first place?' Stubbornly she refused to answer. Then discovered that he was equally stubborn. He seemed set on getting some kind of an answer from her anyhow, as he persisted, 'Almora Lodge is almost as out of the way as this place. You wouldn't have been able to get there without some form of transport.'

'You *should* have been a detective!' She was starting to feel peeved enough not to find Mr Harris-financier-Quillian remotely kind at all!

'What panicked you so, Mallon, that you shot out of there without time to pick up your car keys?'

'I didn't have time to pick up my car keys because I don't have a car!' she flared.

He smiled—he could afford to—he had got her talking. 'So how did you get there?'

She was beginning to hate this man. 'Roland Phillips picked me up from the station—three and a half weeks ago!' she snapped.

'Three…' Harris Quillian broke off, his expression darkening. 'You lived there?' he challenged. 'You lived with Phillips at Almora Lodge? You're his mistress!' he rapped.

'No, I am not!' Mallon almost shouted. 'Nor was I *ever*!' Enraged by the hostile suggestion, she was on her feet glaring at the odious Harris Quillian. 'It was precisely because I wouldn't go to bed with him that I had a fight with him today!' A dry sob shook her and at the instant Harris

Quillian was on his feet. He looked about to come a step closer, perhaps to offer some sort of comfort. But Mallon didn't want any sort of comfort from any man, and she took a hasty step back. He halted.

The next time he spoke his tone had changed to be calm, to be soothing. 'You fought with him?' he asked.

'Well, in truth, I don't think he actually hit me.' Her tone had quieted too. 'Though I shouldn't be surprised if I'm not nursing a few bruises in a day or two from the rough way he grabbed me,' she admitted. 'It was more me fighting him off, fighting to get free of him. He'd been drinking but he'd lost none of his physical strength.'

'You managed to get free before…?'

'Y-yes.' Her voice was reduced to a whisper—she felt quite ill from just remembering. Then realised she must have lost some of her colour when her interrogator said, 'It might be an idea if you sat down again, Mallon. I promise I won't harm you.'

Whether he would or whether he wouldn't, to sit down again suddenly seemed a good idea. Some of her strength returned then, sufficient anyway for her to declare firmly, 'I don't want to talk about it.'

Harris Quillian resumed his seat at the other side of the table, then evenly stated, 'You've had a shock. Quite an appalling shock. It will be better if you talk it out.'

What did he know? 'It's none of your business!' she retorted.

'I'm making it my business!' he answered toughly. Just because he'd picked her up in a monsoon and given her shelter! He could go and take a running jump! 'Either you tell me, Mallon,' he went on firmly, 'or…' Mallon looked across at him, she didn't care very much for that 'or'. 'Or I shall have to give serious consideration…' he continued when he could see he had her full attention '…to driving you to the police station where you will report Roland Phillips's assault…'

'I'll do nothing of the sort!' Mallon erupted, cutting him off. While it would serve Roland Phillips right if the police charged him with assault, there were other considerations to be thought of. A charge of assault, and its attendant publicity, was something Mallon knew, even if she was brave enough to do it for herself, would cause her mother grave disquiet. But her mother, after many years of deep unhappiness, was only now starting to be happy again. Mallon wasn't having a blight put on that happiness.

Obstinately she glared at Harris Quillian. Equally set, he looked back. 'The choice,' he remarked, 'is yours.'

Mallon continued to glare at him. He was unmoved. What was it with him? she fumed. So he'd given her a lift, given her dry clothes to put on—she took her eyes from him. Her dress—albeit torn—would be dry by now. Her glance went to the kitchen windows, despair entering her heart—the rain was pelting down again with a vengeance!

'I worked for him,' she said woodenly.

'Roland Phillips?'

'He advertised for a live-in housekeeper, clerical background an advantage,' she answered. 'I needed somewhere to live—a live-in job seemed a good idea. So I wrote to apply.'

'And he wrote back?'

'He phoned. He works as a European co-ordinator for a food chain. He said he was seldom home, but…'

'You agreed to go and live with him, without first checking him out?' Harris Quillian questioned harshly.

'Hindsight's a brilliant tool!' she exploded sniffily, and started to feel better again—it was almost as if this determined man was recharging her flattened batteries. 'He said he needed someone to start pretty much straight away. Which suited me very well. He said he was married and...'

'You met his wife?' Quillian clipped.

'She was abroad. She works for a children's charity and had just left to visit some of their overseas branches. I didn't know that until I'd arrived at Almora Lodge, but it didn't bother me particularly. Roland Phillips works away a lot too. In fact I'd barely seen anything of him until this weekend.'

'Is this the first full weekend he's been home?'

Mallon nodded. 'He arrived late on Friday. He...'

'He?' Quillian prompted when her voice tailed off.

'He—well, he was all right on Friday, and yesterday too,' she added. 'Though I did start to feel a bit uncomfortable—not so much by what he said, but the innuendo behind it.'

'Not uncomfortable enough for you to leave, then, apparently!' Quillian inserted, and Mallon started to actively dislike him.

'Where would I go?' she retorted. 'My mother remarried recently—it wouldn't be fair to move in with them. Besides which I hadn't worked for Roland Phillips a full month yet. Without a salary cheque I can't afford to go anywhere.'

'You're broke?' Quillian demanded shortly, and Mallon decided that she *definitely* didn't like him. It was embarrassing enough to have to admit to what had happened to her, without the added embarrassment of admitting that, since she couldn't afford alternative accommodation, she had nowhere to rest her head that night. 'He forgot to leave any housekeeping. I used what money I had getting in supplies from the village shop a mile away.'

'You never thought to ask him for some housekeeping expenses?'

'What is this?' she objected, not liking his interrogation one little bit. But when he merely looked coldly back at her, she found she was confessing, 'It seemed a bit petty. I thought I'd leave it until he paid me my salary cheque and mention it then. Anyhow,' she went on abruptly, 'Roland Phillips had too much to drink at lunchtime and—and...' she mentally steadied herself '...and seemed to think I was only playing hard to get when I told him to keep his loathsome hands to himself. It was all I could do to fight him off. It didn't occur to me when I managed to get free to hang around to chat about money he owed me! I was through the door as fast as I could go.' Mallon reckoned she had 'talked out' all she was going to talk out. 'There!' she challenged hostilely. 'Satisfied?'

Whether he was she never got to know, for suddenly there was such a tremendous crash from above that they both had something else momentarily to think about.

A split second later and Harris Quillian was out in the hall and going up the stairs two and a time. Mallon followed. There was water everywhere. He had one of the bedroom doors open and Mallon, not stopping to think, went to help. Clearly the roof was still in bad shape somewhere, and with all that rain—that crash they had heard was a bedroom ceiling coming down.

'Where do you keep your buckets?' she asked.

An hour later, the mopping up completed, the debris in the bedroom confined to one half of the floor space, Mallon returned to the kitchen. In the absence of abundant floor cloths, she had used the towel from around her head to help mop up the floor.

Fortunately her hair was now dry, and she was in the act of combing her fingers through her blonde tresses when Harris Quillian came to join her. Whether it was the act of actually doing something physical, she didn't know, but she was unexpectedly feeling very much more recovered. Sufficiently, anyhow, to realise she had better assess her options more logically than she had.

'Thank you for your help,' Harris Quillian remarked pleasantly, his grey eyes taking in the true colour of her hair. 'You worked like a Trojan.'

Mallon couldn't say he had been a slouch either, tackling all the heavy lifting, fetching and carrying. 'It was a combined effort,' she answered. For all she knew she looked a sketch—tangled hair, any small amount of make-up she had been wearing long since washed away, not to mention she was wearing Quillian's overlarge shirt and trousers, and, thanks to paddling about in water upstairs, was now sockless. 'I'd better start thinking of what I'm going to do,' she commented as lightly as she could.

'So long as you don't think about going back to Almora Lodge!' Quillian rapped, at once all hostility.

Oh, did he have the knack of instantly making her angry! 'Do I look that stupid?' she flared. But, knowing she was going to have to ask his assistance, had to sink her pride and come down from her high horse. 'I was—er—wondering—um—what the chances were of you giving me a lift to Warwickshire?' she said reluctantly.

'To your mother's home?' he guessed.

'There isn't anywhere else,' she stated despondently.

'But you don't want to go there?'

'She's had a tough time. She's happy now, for the first time in years. I don't want to give her the smallest cause for anxiety. Especially in this honeymoon period,' Mallon owned. 'But I can't at the moment see what else I can do.'

There was a brief pause, then, 'I can,' he replied.

Mallon looked at him in surprise—wary surprise. 'You can?'

'Smooth your hackles for a minute,' he instructed levelly, 'and hear my proposition.'

'Proposition!' she repeated, her eyes darting to the door, ready to run at the first intimation of anything untoward.

'Relax, Mallon. What I have to suggest is perfectly above board.' She was still there, albeit she was watching his every move, and he went quickly on. 'You need a job, preferably a live-in job, and I, I've just discovered, appear to need—a caretaker.'

'A caretaker!' She stared at him wide-eyed. 'You're offering me a caretaker's job?'

'It's entirely up to you whether you want to take it or not, but, as you know, I'm having the place rebuilt. I could do with someone here to liaise with plumbers, carpenters, electricians—you know the sort of thing. Generally keep an eye on everything.' He broke off to insert, 'Someone to mop up when the roof leaks. I've just witnessed the way you're ready to pitch in when there's an emergency. Later on, I'll need someone here to oversee painters and decorators, carpet fitters, furniture arrivals.'

He had no need to go on; she had the picture. But she had just had one very big fright with one employer and, while it would suit her very well to caretake for a short time—it would give her the chance to have a roof of sorts over her head while she looked for another job—she had been gullible before.

'Where's the catch?' she questioned, trying not to think in terms of this being a wonderful answer to her problems. If she accepted this caretaking job it would mean that she wouldn't have to go and intrude on her mother and John Frost at this start of their married life together. She...

'Apart from the fact that this kitchen is about the most comfortable room in the house, there is no catch,' Harris Quillian replied. 'You and I have a mutual need...'

'Where would I sleep?' Mallon interrupted him suspiciously.

Grey eyes studied her for a second or two. 'You don't trust men, do you?' he said quietly.

'Let's say I've had my fill of men who seem to think that I just can't wait to get into bed with them!'

'You've had bad experiences apart from Phillips?'

Mallon ignored the question. Her experience with Roland Phillips was the worst, but she had no intention of telling Quillian of her ex-stepfather, ex-stepbrother nor her fickle-hearted ex-boyfriend.

'Where would I sleep?' she repeated stubbornly, vaguely aware that she must be seriously considering the job offer.

'At the moment there are only two bedrooms habitable—and they're not yet decorated. One should be sufficient for you,' Quillian stated. 'Though at present only one of the bedrooms has much furniture. Obviously it's my bedroom for when I stay weekends.' Again she darted a quick look to the door. 'But I'll be returning to London this evening, so it would be all yours until I can get another bed sent down—probably tomorrow or Tuesday.' She relaxed slightly, and he asked, 'You wouldn't mind being here on your own?'

'I'd welcome it!' she answered bluntly, truthfully, hardly able to believe this sudden turn of events.

'Good,' he said, and she warmed to him a little that he appeared not in the slightest offended that she had just as good as said that she wouldn't mind if he left her on her own right now—that she'd rather have his space too, than his company. 'Should you accept, I'll get my PA to arrange some furniture first thing in the morning. By the end of the week you would be comfortably set up in your own bedroom.'

'You'll be—here again next weekend?' she questioned stiltedly, and found herself on the receiving end of his steady grey-eyed look.

'Are you always this cagey?'

'Apparently not—or I wouldn't be in the situation I'm in now!'

He took that on board, then documented, 'So you're worried about me staying overnight in the same house with you?' Mallon made no answer, and after a moment he informed her, 'The reason I bought this place was so that, eventually, I'd have somewhere away from London to un-wind at the weekends. Harcourt House is obviously far from finished, but if you'd agree to stay on, ready to con-tact me or my PA with any problems—more ceilings com-ing down, builders needing chasing, that sort of thing—then, should I come down on a Friday evening, or on a Saturday, I'd undertake to drive you to a hotel and come and collect you shortly before I go back to London again. How does that sound?'

'How long would it be for?' she enquired, realising she should be snatching at his offer, but traces of shock from the terrible fright she'd had were still lingering. 'When I get my head back together I shall want to look around for something more permanent,' she explained.

'I can't see the builders being finished in under three months. Though I wouldn't hold you to that length of time if you find the right job sooner.'

Mallon took a deep breath. 'I'd like to accept,' she said, before she could change her mind. And, the die cast, she suddenly again became aware of the way she was dressed. 'My clothes!' she exclaimed. 'I can't go around wearing your shirt and trousers for the next three months!'

'Then I suggest I drive you to Almora Lodge to collect your belongings,' Harris Quillian said coolly.

'You'd come with me to…?' she began fearfully.

His jaw jutted. 'I wouldn't contemplate letting you go on your own,' he grated positively, and took his eyes from her to glance at his watch. When he looked at her again, Mallon could not help noticing that there was a steel-hard glint in his eyes all at once. Then, to her absolute amazement, he icily announced, 'Apart from anything else, I think it's more than high time I went and had a word with my brother-in-law.'

Mallon stared at him speechlessly, her brain refusing to take in what it was he was saying. 'Brother-in-law?'

Harris Quillian moved to the kitchen door, all too obviously keen to be on their way. 'Roland Phillips,' he stated quite clearly, 'happens to be married to my sister Faye.'

Mallon looked at him open-mouthed. She could not remember just then all that she had said to Harris Quillian. But what she did know was that she had told him, exceedingly plainly, that his sister's husband had assaulted her with violating, adulterous intent!

Anger started to surge up in her—anger against Quillian. How dared he allow her to tell him all she had? He must have known that she would never have said a word to him about Roland Phillips had she know he was Roland Phillips's brother-in-law!

More, she realised, Harris Quillian had deliberately kept that information to himself to get her talking. Must have! He'd purposely… He… How *dared* he?

CHAPTER TWO

MALLON felt angry enough to bite nails in half. 'You should have said!' she erupted furiously. 'You let me tell you everything I did, while all the time...'

'It wasn't the truth?' he cut in sharply, entirely unmoved by her anger. 'You're saying now that you were lying?'

'I wasn't lying. You know full well I wasn't lying!' she retorted—did he think she went out walking in a cloudburst wearing only a cotton dress just for the fun of it?

'Then what the blazes are you getting so stewed up about?' Quillian demanded.

'Because, because...' She faltered. Then she rallied. 'I wouldn't have told you anything of what I had if I'd known you were related to him!'

'Only by marriage!' he gritted, the idea of being related by blood to that worm plainly offensive to him.

'You won't say anything to your sister?'

'Give me one good reason why I shouldn't.'

Mallon stared at him angrily. 'If you can't see that to tell her might do irreparable harm to her marriage...'

'Harm has already been done. My sister and that apology for a man separated three months ago.'

Mallon's anger went as swiftly as it had arrived. 'Oh,' she murmured. 'H-he never said. He let me think she, his wife, had only recently left on an overseas trip to do with her work.'

'Did you see any evidence of Faye being around?'

'We're back to hindsight again,' Mallon muttered wearily. '*Now*, now that I *know*, I can see that there hadn't been a female hand about the Lodge for some while.'

'It was in need of a clean and tidy-up when you ar-rived?'

Understatement. 'Let's say it was fairly obvious he hadn't advertised for a housekeeper a minute too soon. Are he and your sister legally separated?'

Harris Quillian shook his head. 'It's a trial separation as far as Faye is concerned. She's hoping that, once they're through what she terms a cooling-off period, they'll get back together again.'

'Oh, grief!' It amazed Mallon that anyone with a grain of intelligence should fall for, let alone want to marry and stay married to, a man like Roland Phillips. 'It won't help if you tell her about me,' Mallon said.

'You're suggesting that I don't tell her? You think it would be better for her to go back to him without being aware of what he's capable of?' Harris questioned grimly.

'She may well know, but love him enough to forgive...'

'What he tried to do to you is unforgivable!' Harris chopped her off harshly.

Mallon let go a shaky breath. 'I—w-wouldn't argue that,' she had to agree.

The subject seemed closed. 'Ready?' he said. 'We'll go and get your clothes.'

Mallon suddenly had an aversion to putting on the dress that Roland Phillips had tried to tear from her. She knew then that she would never wear it again. She wouldn't have minded borrowing a comb, but Harris wasn't offering, and she wouldn't ask. 'I look a sight,' she mumbled.

'Do you care?'

It annoyed her that he too thought she looked a sight! He needn't have agreed with her. 'Not a scrap!' she an-

swered shortly, and, delaying only to put on her sodden
sandals, she joined him at the door.

The nearer they got to Almora Lodge, though, and
nerves started to get the better of her. So that by the time
Harris had pulled up outside the house, she had started to
shake.

'You'll come in with me?' she questioned jerkily when
all those terrible happenings began to replay in her head,
refusing to leave. Suddenly she felt too afraid to get out
of the car.

'I'll be with you most every step of the way,' he replied,
his expression grim.

The front door was unlocked. Harris didn't bother to
knock but, tall and angry beside her, he went straight in.
There was no sign of Roland Phillips.

'I'll be one minute,' Harris said. 'If you see Phillips
before I do, yell.'

Mallon waited nervously at the bottom of the stairs
while Harris headed in the direction of the drawing room.
She waited anxiously when he went from her sight. Then
she thought she heard a small short sound that might have
been a bit of a groan, then a thud—but she had no intention
of venturing anywhere to find out what it was all about.

And, true to his word, barely a minute later Harris appeared. He *was* with her every step of the way too as they
went up the stairs. He stayed close by while she packed
her cases and retrieved her handbag.

She had been all knotted up inside, certain that at some
stage Roland Phillips would appear, if only to find out who
was invading his property. But she was back in the car
sitting beside Harris Quillian—and had seen nothing of her
ex-employer. She started to feel better.

'Thank you,' she said simply as they left Almora Lodge
behind.

'My pleasure,' he replied, and at some odd inflection in his tone, almost as if it *had* been a pleasure, Mallon found her eyes straying to his hands on the steering wheel. The knuckles on his right hand were very slightly reddened, she observed.

'You saw Roland Phillips, didn't you?' she exclaimed as the explanation for that groan and thud suddenly jumped into her head. 'It wasn't very nice of him to mark your hand with his chin like that!' The words broke from her before she could stop them.

'Worth every crunch,' Harris confirmed.

Mallon turned sideways in her seat to look at him. Firm jaw, firm mouth, steady eyes; she was starting to quite like him. 'You didn't need much of an excuse to hit him,' she commented, guessing that because, at heart, his sister wanted to get back with her husband, Harris had previously held back on the urge to set about Roland for the grief he had caused Faye. However, Roland's behaviour today had given him the excuse he had been looking for.

'True,' Harris answered. 'Unfortunately he was still half sozzled with drink, so I only had to hit him once.' She had to smile; it felt good to smile. By the sound of it, Roland Phillips had gone down like a sack of coals.

Harris carried her cases up the stairs when they arrived at Harcourt House. The two habitable bedrooms were side by side. He placed her cases in the room as yet without a bed, and showed her the other room.

'Faye has seen to it that there's plenty of bed linen, towels, that sort of thing, so I'll leave that side of it to you.' And, when Mallon stood hesitantly in the doorway, he went on casually, 'I'll arrange for locks to be put on both these bedroom doors tomorrow.' Then, taking up what was obviously his overnight bag, he announced, 'Now I should think about leaving.'

Mallon began to suspect he had a heavy date that night. She wished him joy. She went downstairs with him, looking forward to the moment when he would be gone and she could change out of his clothes and into her own.

'You've been very kind,' she began as he accompanied her into the kitchen. 'I don't quite honestly know what I would have done if you hadn't done a circle round and picked me up.'

'You're helping me too, remember,' he said, and, taking out his wallet, he handed her a wad of notes. 'In view of your past experience, I think it might be as well if you accepted your salary in advance rather than in arrears.'

'I don't want...' she began to protest.

'Don't give me a hard time, Mallon. I've an idea you're going to earn every penny—if only by keeping an army of builders supplied with tea and coffee.' He smiled then, about the second time Mallon had seen him smile. This time it had the strangest effect of killing off all thought of protest. 'While we're on the subject of sustenance, fix yourself dinner from anything you fancy in the cupboards. It's there for your use, so eat heartily.' His glance slid over her slender figure, her curves obvious even in her baggy outfit. Mallon stilled, striving to hold down a feeling of panic. Then her large, deeply blue and troubled eyes met his steady grey ones, and he was no longer smiling. 'You have a beautiful face, Mallon, and a superb figure.' He brought out into the open that which she was panicking about. 'And you've had one hell of a fright today. But, trust me, not every man you meet will be champing at the bit for your body.'

She swallowed hard. This man, while sometimes being curt with her, sharp with her, had also been exceedingly kind. 'As in—n-not in a million years?'

He laughed then, and suddenly she relaxed and even

smiled at him. She knew he had recalled without effort that he had answered 'Not in a million years' when she had earlier delayed leaving his car in fear that he too might have wicked intent. 'Something like that,' he answered.

'Then go,' she bade him, but, remembering he was now virtually her employer, 'Sir,' she added.

And he, looking pleased that her spirit seemed to have returned, was unoffended. Handing her his business card, 'Contact me if you need to,' he instructed. 'You'll be all right on your own?' he questioned seriously. 'No fears?'

'I'll be fine,' she answered. 'Actually, I'm suddenly starting to feel better than I have in a long while.'

Harris Quillian stared down at her, studying her. Then, nodding approvingly, he took up his overnight bag and his car keys. 'I may be down on Friday,' he said, and was gone.

Her sleep was troubled by dark dreams that night. Mallon awoke a number of times, feeling threatened and insecure, and was awake again at four o'clock, although this time dawn was starting to break. And, with the light, she began to feel a little more secure.

She lay wide awake looking round the high-ceilinged uncurtained room. As well as not having curtains, the room was as yet uncarpeted, but there was a large rug on the floor and, against one wall, a large oak wardrobe.

Mallon could tell that, once the building work was completed, furniture and furnishings installed, Harcourt House would revert to what had once been its former glory. She liked big old houses—she had been brought up in one.

Her eyes clouded over. She didn't want to dwell on times past, but could not help but think back to her happy childhood, her loving and loved parents and the plans they had made for her future—all of which had turned to dust nine years ago.

*S*he had been thirteen when she and her mother were wondering whether to start dinner without waiting for Mallon's father. He'd been a consultant surgeon and worked all hours, so meals had often been delayed. 'We'll start,' her mother had just decreed, when there had been a ring at the doorbell. Their caller had been one of his colleagues, come to tell them that Cyrus Braithwaite had been in a car accident.

The hospital had done everything they could to try and save him, but they must have known at the start from the extent of his injuries that they were going to lose him.

Mallon had been totally shattered by her adored father's death; her mother had been absolutely devastated and completely unable to cope. With the help of medication, her mother had got through day by day, but Mallon could not help but know that Evelyn Braithwaite would have been happier to have died with her husband—that perhaps it was only for her daughter's sake that she'd struggled on.

Some days had been so bad for her mother that Mallon would not consider going to school and leaving her on her own. The first year after her father's death had passed with Mallon taking more and more time off school. Her studies had suffered and, having been at the top of her year, her grades had fallen; but she'd had higher priorities.

Her father had been dead two years when her mother had met Ambrose Jenkins. He was the antithesis of Mallon's father: loud where her father had been quiet, boastful where her father had been modest, work-shy where her father had been industrious. But, at first, he'd seemed able to cheer her mother, and for that Mallon forgave Ambrose Jenkins a lot. She'd found she could not like him, but had tried her hardest to be fair, recognising that because she had thought so much of her father she could not expect any other man to measure up.

So when, within weeks of meeting him, her mother told
her that she and Ambrose were going to be married,
Mallon had kissed and hugged her mother and pretended
to be pleased. Ambrose had had a twenty-seven-year-old
son, Lee. Mallon had found him obnoxiously repellent.
But, for her mother's sake, she'd smiled through the wedding and accepted that Ambrose would be moving into
their home.

What Mallon had not expected was that Lee Jenkins
would move in too. By then she was a blossoming fifteen-
year-old, but, instead of being proud of her beautiful
blonde hair and curvy burgeoning figure, Mallon had been
more prone to hide her shape under baggy sweaters and to
scrape her hair back in a rubber band. For never a day had
seemed to go by without her stepbrother making a pass at
her.

To say anything about it to her mother, after the most
unhappy time she had endured, was something Mallon had
found she just could not do. Though she had to admit that
she'd come close that day Lee Jenkins came into her room
just as she had finished dressing.

'Get out!' she screamed at him—a minute earlier and
he would have caught her minus her blouse!

'Don't be like that,' he said in what he thought was his
sexy voice, but which she found revolting, and, instead of
leaving her room, he came further into it and, grabbing a
hold of her, tried to kiss her.

She bit him—his language was colourful, but she cared
not. Once he let her go and she was free of him, she wasn't
hanging about.

She was badly shaken, and wanted to confide in her
mother. But, somehow, protective of her still, Mallon
could not tell her. Instead she took to propping a chair

under the knob of her bedroom door at all times whenever she was in there on her own.

Then, horror of horrors, her mother had been married for only a year when her stepfather cast his lascivious glance on Mallon. At first she couldn't believe what her eyes and instincts were telling her. That was until the day he cornered her in the drawing room and, his eyes on her breasts, remarked, 'Little Mallon, you're not so little any more, I see.' Coming closer, his slack mouth all but slobbering, he demanded, 'Got a kiss for your stepdaddy?'

She was revolted, and told him truthfully, 'I'm going to be sick!'

She *was* sick, and later sat on her bed and cried, because she knew now, more than ever, that she could not tell her mother. Her parent would be destroyed.

Mallon sorely wanted to leave home. It wasn't home any more anyway. But money, which she had never had to particularly think of before, had been tight for some while. She knew that her father had left them well provided for, but only a few days ago her mother had suggested she might like to take a Saturday job, and Mallon had asked if they were having some temporary financial problem. Her mother had replied, 'I'm afraid it isn't temporary, Mallon, it's permanent,' and had looked so dreadfully unhappy Mallon had been unable to bear it.

She knew without having to ask where all the money had gone. Ambrose Jenkins had been spending freely, too freely, the money her father had invested. Incredibly, there was little of it remaining.

Lee Jenkins was as work-shy as his father, and had to be a constant drain on what resources her mother had remaining. Determined not to be a drain on those resources herself, Mallon left school and got herself a job.

As jobs went it wasn't much: a clerical assistant in a

large and busy office. But, for her age, it didn't pay too badly. Though it wasn't sufficient to pay rent as well as keep her should she attempt the enormous step she wished to take and leave home.

The following two years dragged miserably by, and when she saw how badly her mother's marriage was faring, Mallon was glad she had not left home. Her mother started to realise what a dreadful mistake she had made in marrying Ambrose Jenkins, but did not seem to have the strength to do anything about his by then quite blatant philandering ways. Mallon knew her mother was suffering. But, feeling powerless to do anything about it, Mallon wanted to be there to support her when she finally did cry Enough!

While Mallon was doing everything she could to cold-shoulder both father and son without her mother being aware—which would only make her even more wretched—it was not her stepfather's habit of staying out nights and weekends, and coming home only to be fed and laundered, that brought things to a head. But money.

Both the Jenkins men were out that Wednesday when Mallon came home from work and found her mother in tears. 'Oh, darling!' Mallon cried, going over to her. 'What's the matter?'

Plenty, she learned in the next five minutes. Ambrose and her mother were splitting up, but that, it seemed, was not the reason for her mother's despair. But, as she explained, because she had foolishly listened to Ambrose Jenkins eighteen months ago when as near penury as made no difference, he had told her of a business venture that would almost immediately earn them double. It would, however, mean a quite substantial investment.

Evelyn Jenkins was not used to working with money, she had never needed to. But, aware that something needed to be done to get them solvent once more, she had been persuaded to borrow, using their lovely home as collateral.

It had all ended in tears. The upshot being that now, eighteen months later, the business venture had folded. With no more money forthcoming, Ambrose was leaving, and even the house no longer belonged to her mother. 'We've got to leave here,' her mother wept. 'This lovely house your father bought for us!'

Oddly then, though maybe because having reached rock bottom the only way was up, and perhaps aided by thinking of her gentleman former husband, Evelyn Jenkins seemed to gather some strength. Mallon could only guess at the inner torment her parent must have been through before she had confided in her. But the next morning, before Mallon could say she intended to take the day off work and start to look for somewhere to rent, her mother was telling her how she intended to contact a firm of lawyers that day to see if there was anything to be done.

Mallon hurried home that night to hear that John Frost, the head of the firm her father had always used, and who knew the family, had initially dealt personally with her mother. After a detailed check of all the paperwork he had passed the opinion that she had been criminally advised, had put a doubt on the fact that the money had been invested anywhere but in Ambrose Jenkins pocket, and had concluded that Evelyn Jenkins had a case for suing him.

Since, however, that man appeared to not have any money, there seemed no point whatsoever in taking that route. 'I think I would rather divorce him,' she decided. Mallon could only applaud her decision.

There followed months and months of upset. Ambrose wanted to behave like a single man, but didn't want to be divorced, apparently, and so was as obstructive as he knew how to be; which was considerably.

Although divorce was not John Frost's speciality, and he had handed the case over to someone whose subject it was, John Frost was always there to smile and encourage when her mother went to his offices to pursue the matter of the protracted proceedings.

Mallon and her mother moved into a tiny flat, the rent of which took quite a chunk out of Mallon's salary. She was not complaining—it was a joy not to have to live under the same roof as the Jenkins duo. A joy not to have to continually be on her guard against the loose-moralled, lascivious pair.

Her mother's divorce was finalised on Mallon's twentieth birthday. John Frost, by now something of a friend, took them to dinner to celebrate.

Finances were extremely tight and her mother did try to support herself, but she had never had to work outside of the home, and it was all too apparent that she neither enjoyed nor was cut out to stand in a shop serving all day, or to sit in an office trying to get to grips with a computer. Mallon couldn't bear it—her father would have been utterly distraught that life should have treated his beloved Evelyn this way.

'You don't have to go out to work, you know,' Mallon insisted. 'We can manage.'

Her mother looked uncertain. 'I have to contribute something. It isn't fair...'

'You do contribute. You're a wonderful homemaker.'

'But...' Evelyn Jenkins tried to argue, but Mallon could see that her heart wasn't in it. And eventually, with Mallon using every persuasion she could think of, her mother gave in—and for about eighteen months more they limped along on Mallon's salary.

Then suddenly everything started to improve. Mallon and her mother went out to dine with widower John Frost a few times, and invited him to their small flat in return. It didn't take much for Mallon to see that John was keen on her mother, and Mallon liked how protective he was with her.

The next time he asked the two of them to dine with him Mallon found a convenient 'work' excuse at the last minute, and left it to John Frost to persuade her mother that he would be equally delighted to take her out without her daughter.

On the work front matters were looking up too. Mallon had made steady progress and was rewarded with promotion to another department. With the move came a very welcome raise in salary which meant that she and her mother could begin to renew the odd item here and there that had worn out. While not riches—they still had nothing in the bank—her pay rise made life just that little bit easier.

With her move to a new department Mallon met two people she would be working with. Natasha Wallace, a pleasant if plain girl of about her own almost twenty-two years, and Keith Morgan who was three years older.

Mallon became friends with both of them. And, with John Frost and her mother seeing just a little more of each other—John taking care not to rush Evelyn—Mallon started to go out and about with Natasha; sometimes Keith would go with them.

Mallon had been well and truly put off men by the behaviour of Ambrose and Lee Jenkins, and while it did not particularly bother her she just could not see herself entering into any kind of a relationship with any man.

Which was why it came as something of a surprise to her that, four months into her friendship with Natasha and Keith, she began to realise that she had some quite warm feelings for Keith. Feelings which, to her further surprise and pleasure, she discovered were returned.

They did not always go out as a threesome. When
Natasha started to put in some extra practice for a violin
exam she was about to take, Keith and Mallon went out
more and more as a twosome.

Even now as she lay wide awake in Harris Quillian's
bed Mallon felt sick in her stomach as she recalled how,
only three months ago, their feelings for each other starting
to take over, she had been on the brink of committing
herself to a very intimate relationship with Keith Morgan.

It had started on a Saturday when Natasha had been
busy with her music and Mallon and Keith had been to
the cinema. Keith had been kissing Mallon goodnight
when he'd suddenly begged her to go away with him. 'I
want to go to bed with you—you must want the same,' he
urged. Oh, help—it was such a big step! 'You know you
want me as much as I want you.'

She said no, but week after week for the next two
months he again and again urged her to go away with him.
Then one Saturday he told her he loved her. It was what
she needed to hear.

She agreed, albeit, it was with a rather shaky 'Y-yes,'
that she answered.

Keith didn't waste any time and told her on Monday
that he had arranged their romantic tryst for the coming
weekend, and would pick her up from her home on
Saturday morning.

Why couldn't she tell her mother? Her mother had met
both Keith and Natasha and would have understood.
Mallon later wondered—could it be that at heart she had
known that something was not quite right? But just then
she managed to convince herself that, after the dreadful
years her mother had endured, and with everything going
so right for her just now—she seemed to be spending more

and more time with John Frost—she did not want to give her parent the smallest cause to worry about her.

Mallon made her way home from work on Friday and made up her mind to tell her mother that night. For heaven's sake, Keith would be calling for her in the morning!

Her mother wasn't in but had left a note saying that John had phoned and had particularly wanted to discuss something with her, so could she meet him later that afternoon? She didn't think she would be late back.

Mallon hoped not. She was on edge, and knew that feeling wouldn't go away until she had told her mother her plans. When each hour ticked away and her mother didn't appear, Mallon guessed that John had taken her mother to dinner.

Which proved correct when, just after ten, John Frost brought her mother home. 'Um—we've got something to tell you,' Evelyn Jenkins said, but didn't have to—Mallon could see the joy they shared with each other.

'We're going to be married,' John could hardly wait to tell her. 'Is that all right with you, Mallon?'

She hadn't seen her mother looking so happy in years. 'You know it is!' Mallon beamed, and forgot all about Keith Morgan when she went over and the threesome embraced.

John had brought some champagne in with him and they talked for an age as the newly engaged couple shared with Mallon that they had steadily got to know each other over the years, and saw not one single reason to wait. They would marry next month and Mallon would give up the flat.

'Give up the flat?'

'Your mother will be moving into my home, Mallon,'

John answered. 'It's my wish that you move into my home too.'

'Thank you,' she answered, not wanting to blight this happy time for them. But she somehow knew, much as she liked John and much as she would miss her mother dreadfully, that her place was not in her mother's new home. This, after all she'd been through, was a special time for her mother.

'That's settled, then.' John smiled, and went on to outline how he'd telephoned his married daughter in Scotland and she was flying down tomorrow for a family celebration dinner.

'Oh!' Mallon exclaimed. Oh, grief, she had forgotten all about Keith Morgan!

'Don't say you can't make it, darling. Did you have some other arrangement?'

'Keith—er…'

'I'm sure he'll understand. This is a family occasion, after all.' Evelyn Jenkins beamed.

'Of course. I'll give him a ring,' Mallon said with a smile and realised, perhaps because of her mother's lovely news, that she didn't feel unduly upset that her weekend with Keith was off.

He did not understand when she rang him. Instead, he was furious. 'I've booked the hotel!' he protested angrily. 'Your mother's been married before—what's so special now?' If he couldn't see, Mallon wasn't about to try and explain.

'I'm sorry,' she apologised. 'I'll see you on Monday.'

The celebratory dinner went wonderfully well. John's daughter, Isobel, was as thrilled as Mallon that the two had finally decided to marry.

By Monday, feeling uncomfortable that she had let Keith down, Mallon went to seek him out to apologise again and to try and make him see how important it had been to her mother that she had been there.

'Keith,' she began, going over to his desk.

'Mallon, I...' he said at the same time, for no reason she could think of, looking almost sheepish.

''Morning, Keith!' They both turned to see Natasha standing there, looking more animated than Mallon had ever seen her. Natasha grinned at them both but addressed Keith when she said, 'I thought you'd like to know I didn't get into trouble when I got in last night.'

Mallon stared at her, and then smiled. What was more natural? She had let Keith down and Natasha was an old chum. 'You were out with Keith last night?' she commented, still feeling a touch uncomfortable, but glad that Keith hadn't had a totally dull weekend. Though... Suddenly some instinct in Mallon started to quiver. She knew *she* was feeling uncomfortable, but what the Dickens was Keith looking so uncomfortable about? 'You've been out with Keith on a Sunday before,' Mallon commented slowly. 'What was so different about last night?'

Keith found his shoes worthy of inspection, while Natasha answered, 'Only the fact that I didn't go home at all on Saturday night.'

Something inside Mallon froze. 'Now that is different.' Somehow she managed to make her tone light. 'You went away with Keith?' she asked, a very personal question she knew, but she needed some answers here.

Natasha's eyes sparkled. 'It was wonderful, wasn't it, Keith?' He didn't answer.

There was only one other question which, in normal times, Mallon would not have dreamed of asking. 'Did you sleep together?' she asked, her light tone gone.

Natasha looked a shade put out but, possibly because of

their past friendship, answered honestly, if a shade coolly, 'We did. That was rather the whole point of going.'

Mallon looked at Keith. He did not deny it. 'We'd better get on with some work.' She left them and went to her desk. She was deaf to Keith Morgan's entreaties when he explained he had been so very angry with her for letting him down, but that it was her, Mallon, that he loved.

Mallon knew then that she was at a crossroads in her life. She no longer wanted to work in the same department with Keith and Natasha. She felt deeply, instinctively, that she should not live with her mother and John Frost when they married, but knew if she insisted on staying on in the flat alone that her mother would be upset. And she had endured more than enough upset already.

Over the next few days Mallon figured it out. She still wasn't any happier working with Natasha and Keith—but no one was going to know it. What she needed, Mallon decided, was a clean break, a new job, a…

Suddenly she had it. The only excuse her mother was likely to accept for her not moving in with her and John would be if she said she had applied for a job in another area.

Mallon looked at the state of her finances. She wanted to treat her mother to a really lovely outfit to be married in. More genius arrived. How about if she found a live-in job? Brilliant! She could then spend her final month's salary on something really gorgeous for her mother. And living in, board and lodgings obviously taken care of, she could limp along quite well on any money left over until pay day.

Mallon got out of Harris Quillian's bed, musing how she had thought everything through. Then, opting for the job advertised for housekeeper, clerical background an advantage, in preference to one for a hotel receptionist because of her lack of training in that area, she had acted. Had *she* made a mistake! She had still been feeling very much let down by Keith Morgan's behaviour when, on top of it, she had met that reptile Roland Phillips. Grief, was she ever off men—permanently!

Mallon went to one of the bedroom windows and stared out. The rain had stopped, thank goodness. If it stayed dry perhaps the roofers could come and take a look at... Harris Quillian had been kind, she suddenly found herself thinking. When she came to think about it, more than kind. Her mother would have been overwrought had Harris given her a lift to her mother's new home.

She had a lot to thank him for, Mallon knew. Not least his generosity in giving her all that money. Salary, he'd called it. But he had trusted her not to do a flit at the first opportunity. Though, from his point of view, he could afford to trust her not to run off with the family silver. She turned to look back into the uncarpeted room, and found she was smiling—there was hardly anything worth pinching.

Mallon decided to investigate the water heating system. She had been weary enough last night and had endured sufficient water on her body from her drenching to think it wouldn't matter if she went to bed without first showering. But it wouldn't surprise her to find that brand-new shower in the bathroom was not yet functional.

It was functional, she discovered, and she had a lovely time standing under the warm-to-hot spray. Harris Quillian thought she had a beautiful face and a superb figure, she found herself idly musing—and abruptly stepped out from the shower. For goodness' sake—as if she cared!

Not that there had been anything 'personal' in his remarks. She put his comments from her—she was sure he'd had a heavy date last night. No doubt with some luscious

sophisticate. He certainly wasn't the least bit personally
interested in the likes of one Mallon Braithwaite. He
couldn't have made it plainer that he wanted the place to
himself at weekends. Which, she sighed, unsmiling,
couldn't suit her better.

She had unlocked the front and rear doors and was in-
vestigating the refrigerator, glad to see that Faye Phillips
had stocked her brother up with cartons and cartons of the
sort of milk that kept for months, when Mallon heard the
first of the builders arrive.

Shortly afterwards there was a knock at the kitchen
door. 'Miss Braithwaite? It's my firm that's doing the rebuilding. I'm Bob Miller,' he introduced himself. 'Mr
Quillian's been on to us. We had a bit of rain yesterday,
didn't we?' he understated.

She took to Bob Miller, a muscly sort of man of about
fifty. He didn't seem to question who she was or why she
was there, but just accepted it. 'You could say that,' she
agreed.

'All right if I come in and take a look at the ceiling that
came down yesterday?'

'Of course. Er…' She remembered Harris's remark yesterday about keeping an army of builders supplied with tea
and coffee. 'Shall I make some tea?'

Bob gave her a wide grin. 'Now that's the way to start
the week,' he accepted.

It was a busy week too. Had she at any time wondered
what she would do all day, then she had no difficulty in
filling those hours. Throughout the week she met Cyril,
the carpenter, who as well as doing his other work fitted
locks on two bedroom doors and put security catches on
all bedroom windows. She also met Charlie, Dean, Baz
and Ron, who were excellent with plumbing stonework,
and electrics. And Ken, who was something of an intel-

lectual, and who liked working out in the open air. There was Del too, who had a lovely tenor voice, and who sang throughout most of the day. And lastly Kevin, the 'gofer'.

It was Kevin who gave her a lift in 'the van' when he had to visit the building suppliers in town. 'Take as long as you like,' he offered cheerfully as he dropped her off at the supermarket. 'I'll be ages.'

Mallon purchased fresh fruit and vegetables and other provisions, and also bought a newspaper, plus stationery and postage stamps. She studied the situations vacant column when she got back, but there was little there of interest to her. Still, Harris had suggested that the builders would be there for three months, so there was no particular hurry. And anyway, this time, she didn't want to rush into the first likely job she saw.

Apart from the bed Harris had promised, several other items of furniture arrived that week. Mallon directed the sofa and one of the padded chairs to the drawing room, which was, as yet, like the bedrooms uncurtained and uncarpeted. The wardrobe, desk and another padded chair were carried up to her room, and, since she more or less lived in the kitchen, she had another easy chair put in there.

She found that as well as thinking frequently of her mother and John Frost, and trying not to think of the likes of Keith Morgan and Roland Phillips, she thought a good deal of Harris Quillian too.

Contrary to his comment about her incubating pneumonia, she had not so much as sneezed. In fact, given that she was still having the most ghastly dreams, and had once or twice had to leave her bed to go and sit in the safe haven of the kitchen until she was more at peace, she had never felt better.

Would Harris really have driven her to a police station to report his brother-in-law for assault? she wondered. But, since his sister was apparently hoping to go back to her husband once their trial separation was over, Mallon thought it doubtful.

Harris had said he might come down on Friday, so on Friday morning Mallon packed a bag ready to move out for the weekend, then went in search of Kevin. He was frequently trundling off in the van to a village shop two miles up the road 'for the lads'.

'Would you give me a lift the next time you're going to Sherwins?' she asked him.

'Pleased to,' he answered in his cheery way. And twenty minutes later came to the kitchen door looking for her.

She made various purchases at Sherwins, who seemed to keep a supply of absolutely everything, and by that evening there was a vase of flowers standing in the hearth, and, with a few rugs scattered about, the drawing room was looking quite homey.

But Harris Quillian did not appear, and Mallon went to bed that night aware of the oddest pang of disappointment. She immediately scoffed at any such notion—but slept badly.

She was glad to leave her bed on Saturday morning. Bob Miller had said his men would be working that morning. Mallon showered and dressed in jeans and a tee shirt and went downstairs to get busy.

One of the men had brought her a bag of plums. By midday she had two plum pies made, and was just thinking of making a batch of cakes—they'd be gone in seconds, she knew, but they were a good-hearted bunch of men— when, glancing to the kitchen window, she saw a car glide by with Harris at the wheel.

She hadn't expected to see him until at the earliest next Friday now. Suddenly she was smiling—only then did she realise that she was pleased to see him.

CHAPTER THREE

MALLON heard Harris coming along the hall, and unexpectedly felt ridiculously shy all at once. He was as she remembered him when, tall, broad-shouldered and steady-eyed, he came into the kitchen.

She felt oddly tongue-tied, and he did not speak straight away, but stood in the doorway just looking at her, as if it was the first time he had seen her. Only then did it dawn on her, as his glance went over her gleaming blonde head and down over her tee shirt and denim-covered long legs, that this was the first time he had seen her with her hair looking anything other than soaking wet or dry and in a tangle.

'I polish up quite well,' she said in a rush, feeling self-conscious suddenly. It was the first time too that he had seen her with her nose powdered and wearing dry clothes that were her own.

She tensed as soon as the words were out, realising she might have invited a personal remark. He smiled, disarmingly, and she had an idea he knew she wished she had kept silent.

Any feeling of tension swiftly disappeared, though, when the closest he got to a personal remark was to say, 'I was going to take my bag upstairs, but I couldn't resist the smell of home baking.'

She felt self-conscious again. For goodness' sake, pull yourself together. 'Del brought me a bag of plums,' she found herself answering, and could have groaned at how stupid she felt she sounded. 'He's a plasterer.' She found

47

she couldn't shut up. 'There are a few buckets and bowls
on the landing in case we have another cloudburst,' she
gabbled on. 'One part of the roof has been repaired, but
there are a few fresh leaks, and the roofer-tiling man can't
get here before Monday.' Stop it! Stop it! 'Would you like
a coffee?' she changed tack to ask abruptly—and instantly
felt her sudden change of tone to almost snappy might
have offended him.

But no. 'I'd love one,' he replied. 'I'll just take my bag
up, and you can fill me in on anything I need to know.'

She was glad to see him go; it gave her a chance to get
herself back together again. Good grief, what was the matter with her? She had never felt shy or tongue-tied in a
man's company before! Tongue-tied? It sounded like it,
the way she had rattled away! Was it nerves? Surely her
experience with Roland Phillips hadn't shattered her confidence to that extent! She most earnestly hoped not,
though acknowledged she had previously received a few
wounds from her experiences with men like her ex-
stepfather and his son, not to mention the faithless Keith
Morgan. She probably still nursed a few non-physical
scars, without taking on any more from Harris's brother-
in-law.

Mallon had the coffee made when Harris came back into
the kitchen, and thought she had herself all of one piece
again—until he observed casually, 'I see the bed has arrived.'

'You've been in my room?' she questioned, at once hostile.

His casual demeanour vanished. 'I'm not allowed to
check my instructions with regard to windows and doors
have been carried out?' he questioned, a shade toughly.

Mallon looked from him and into her coffee. What was

wrong with her? It was his house; he could do what he jolly well pleased. Silence between them stretched.

Then, his tough tone gone, 'You're upset,' he commented mildly.

She looked up. 'You make me sound like some touchy diva. I'm sorry,' she apologised, and tried to explain. 'I just—like my privacy.' She had no intention of explaining further that it had begun years ago, when she'd had to prop a chair under the knob of her bedroom door to keep would-be intruders out.

'You're a strange mixture,' Harris offered pleasantly.

She didn't thank him for it. 'I'm supposed to ask how?'

Her belligerence didn't touch him. 'You welcome me with the smell of home cooking—then give me the cross-and-garlic treatment in case I get the wrong idea.'

Nothing escaped him, she saw, but didn't care for his summing up. 'The cooking wasn't for you in particular, even if you are welcome to it,' she retorted, and had suddenly had enough. 'I've a bag packed. I'll go.'

'Where?' he asked in surprise, his expression hardening. 'You're not leaving just because...'

'I'm not *leaving* leaving. I'm going to a hotel overnight,' she explained. 'You said... You've forgotten!' she accused.

'No, I haven't,' he denied. 'I just thought, on account of our—scratchy—start, that you were not intending to come back.' Again his tone altered. 'You're welcome to stay if you want...' he began.

'I don't want!' she cut in bluntly.

'Pardon me for mentioning it,' he retorted pithily. 'Forgive me for feeling guilty that I appear to be turning you out,' he added curtly.

Mallon didn't want to apologise, didn't want to be always in the wrong—and that was how this man made her feel. Without looking at him, without bothering to finish her coffee, she marched stiff-backed out from the kitchen and up to her room.

It took but a few seconds to collect the bag she had packed and in no time she was on her way back down the stairs again. By the time she had reached the hall, however, Harris Quillian had come out from the kitchen and was standing there, car keys in hand. When she neared him he stretched out a hand for her overnight bag.

'I was going to ask Kevin if he could drive me into town,' she said, hanging on to her bag. 'He very often goes for building supplies and things they're short of.'

'I'll take you,' Harris answered evenly, and before she could marshal up any sort of an argument he had taken her overnight bag, and she was seated beside him in his car and they were driving out between the stone gateposts of Harcourt House.

Why, though, did she want to argue? Mallon found she was silently questioning. Harris had been nothing but kind and decent to her. Suddenly she felt quite dreadful, and, 'I'm sorry,' she blurted out, and when he momentarily took his eyes off the road to glance at her, she went on, 'I don't know why I'm so...' she searched for a word, and used his; it seemed to serve for how she felt '...so scratchy.'

'I do,' he surprised her by answering, his eyes once more on the road up ahead, his tone mild.

Mallon stared at his profile. 'You do?'

'Could it be you're still suffering with some trauma from what happened to you last Sunday?'

Mallon thought about it. That soaking as she'd sped and then trudged through the torrential rain had been traumatic enough without all that had gone before. All this week she had experienced horrendous flashbacks of Roland Phillips's lust-filled face as he'd tried to tear her clothes from her. It came to her then that it was unlikely that anyone would recover instantly from something like that.

'You could be right,' she conceded thoughtfully, but, not wanting to stress the point, felt she should admit, 'I have been having flashbacks and the most awful dreams.'

'You've not been sleeping well?'

'It's not as if I have to get up to go to work in the morning,' she answered lightly.

'According to Bob Miller, when I spoke with him Thursday, you're always up and about and have the kettle boiling when he arrives at seven forty-five,' Harris drawled.

He'd got her there. 'I didn't know you'd got your spies about!'

'Have you gone all scratchy again?' Harris asked, but it wasn't annoyance she heard in his voice, but teasing. She found she liked his teasing.

'I shan't say sorry again,' she told him with a smile. But was serious when she went on, 'For all you've been so kind, you...'

'Hey, you'll be giving me a halo next!'

'I doubt you're that saintly. But it was...good of you to stop last Sunday the way you did.'

'Water under the bridge. The main thing now is to see if there's anything to be done about those flashbacks and dreams. Would you see someone professional? I can arrange...'

'Heavens, that's not necessary! I wouldn't have told you if I'd thought you'd take it so seriously!'

'It is serious, Mallon. You're on edge with me a lot of the time. I don't want you to end up afraid of men because of what my brother-in-law tried to do to...'

'For goodness' sake!' she exclaimed irritably. 'I'm not afraid of men! I'm chatting to one or other of the builders all day!' she went on indignantly. And, when Harris Quillian didn't interrupt, she found she was storming on, 'I might be a bit cautious sometimes, a touch watchful, but that's not all down to Roland Phillips, as ghastly as...' She broke off, hating Quillian again that he had made her angry enough to be heedless of what she was saying.

And hated him some more when it became clear he wasn't going to pretend he hadn't heard what she had just said. 'You've had a similar experience?' he questioned harshly. Turning sharply to look at her. 'That makes Phillips's actions doubly heinous!' he gritted.

'I don't want to talk about it. And it was nothing nearly as bad, anyway,' she answered snappily. 'Watch where you're going,' she ordered bossily. 'In fact...' she went on when she could see that they had arrived in the main street in town '...you can drop me off here and I'll...'

He ignored her—and she wanted to thump him. Never had she met such a man. She wanted to find her own hotel. A bed and breakfast place in her view would be just ideal. But, no, he had to take her to the smartest hotel in town!

When he halted the car in the car park of the Clifton Hotel, Mallon was determined she was not going to go in. She looked stonily at him—he looked stonily back. 'Don't give me a hard time, Mallon,' he said—a shade wearily, she thought, and all at once she felt dreadful. Without question he must work hard and put in long hours to be the success everything about him spoke of him being, and had probably left London for Upper Macey and Harcourt House with the hope of being able to unwind for some hours before he went back into the cut and thrust of his financial world again.

'I'm...' She opened her mouth to say she was sorry, then was unsure why she wanted to apologise, so said instead, 'It looks a bit plush. How do you think the jeans and tee shirt will go down?'

Suddenly warm grey eyes were smiling into wide deeply blue eyes. 'You're a snob, Mallon Braithwaite,' he teased.

'I'm not,' she denied, adding, deliberately ungrammatically, 'I've just been brought up proper.'

He started to grin, her heart gave the most unexpected thump, and she looked quickly away. She found the door catch, and by the time Harris had taken up her overnight bag and was coming round to her, she was out of the car.

He had obviously used the Clifton Hotel as his base in the initial stages of negotiating the purchase of Harcourt House and subsequent on-site meetings with architects and planners, Mallon gathered. Because he was greeted by name and it seemed as though nothing would be any trouble for him.

In no time she found she was booked into the busy hotel and Harris was standing looking down at her. 'I'll come and collect you tomorrow,' he said, and she felt guilty at putting him to so much bother.

'I'll get a taxi back,' she insisted.

'Are you casting aspersions on my driving?'

She smiled; it turned into a laugh. 'I wouldn't dare,' she replied, and felt secure, and continued to feel so even when his glance strayed to her upward-curving mouth.

After he had gone Mallon felt strange, not bereft exactly, and couldn't put her finger on quite how she felt; but she missed him.

Up in her hotel room she scorned such nonsense. She was just feeling a bit cut adrift that was all. She didn't know anyone here and, well, her life had changed fairly dramatically recently. Apart from changing her job and parting with a boyfriend she had, until not so many weeks ago, always lived with her mother.

Thinking of her parent, Mallon picked up the telephone. Her mother had rung her at Almora Lodge ten days ago, so she had better call in case her parent thought to phone Almora Lodge again.

She had rung not a moment too soon, Mallon discovered, when her mother heard her voice. 'I was going to ring you!' the new Mrs Frost exclaimed, sounding well, extremely happy, and pleased to hear her.

'Everything all right with you?' Mallon asked.

'Couldn't be better. John's such a love. I'd quite forgotten how true gentlemen behave,' Evelyn Frost confided, and Mallon, her emotions welling up, felt choked. Those dreadful years her mother had endured when living with Ambrose Jenkins must have been truly awful. 'How are things with you?' her mother asked. 'Have you seen much of your employer this week?' She meant Roland Phillips, Mallon knew, having told her during their last telephone conversation that he was seldom home.

'I haven't seen him since last Sunday,' Mallon answered, finding it totally beyond her to blight her mother's new-found happiness—she would be fearfully upset if she knew even the barest details of her running away from Roland Phillips. She would be equally upset, and would probably insist she came home straight away to live with her and John, should Mallon tell her the whole of it and how she came to have a new employer.

Mallon had a long chat with her parent and finally replaced the phone, growing even more convinced that her mother had done the right thing in marrying John Frost— Ambrose Jenkins didn't bear comparison.

Aware that the charge for staying overnight in the Clifton Hotel was going to make quite a hole in her finances, Mallon opted to go out and buy a sandwich for her lunch. She had a look around the shops while she was

out, and popped into a supermarket for some flour and a
few other odds and ends.

She was back in her room well before it was time for
dinner and had thought she might go out for a snack somewhere. Then found she was wondering what Harris was
having to eat. She hoped he was helping himself to the
plum pie—and realised she was thinking of him with some
affection.

Good grief! She barely knew the man! True, he had
been more than kind. But, anyway, he was probably far
from starving. He had a car; if he didn't fancy cooking for
himself, he could always drive into town for dinner.

Maybe he would come to the Clifton Hotel for a meal.
That settled it; she *would* go out. Perhaps, though, he had
a lady-friend locally; he was footloose and fancy-free after
all.

All at once Mallon was feeling restless. Blow him. The
hotel's dining room would be big enough for both of them.
She had earlier unpacked her overnight bag. She went over
to the wardrobe and took out the smart trousers and top
she had hung there.

The hotel dining room, when she went down, was fairly
crowded, she observed. Apart from couples and foursomes
there was one very large party, plainly celebrating something. But Harris Quillian was not there.

Mallon got on with the meal she had ordered, and by
the time she was eating her pudding she had realised that
the big party were a family party celebrating a golden wedding anniversary. She wasn't particularly looking in that
direction, but could hardly miss the huge bouquets of flowers that were carried over to that table, or miss that the
sprightly, if mature, couple—who didn't look anywhere
near old enough to have been married for fifty years—

standing together to cut the anniversary cake and to be photographed.

She opted to take her coffee in the hotel lounge and felt less restless on leaving the dining room than when she had entered, though found as she sipped her coffee that she was again thinking of Harris Quillian. The fact that, at around thirty-five years or so, he was unmarried spoke of some pretty fleet footwork, she decided, and again found she was wondering if there was some female locally who had tipped his decision to purchase the Upper Macey property. On reflection, she thought not. If he was quite content with his bachelor status, thank you, he was hardly likely to put it in jeopardy by having anything remotely suggesting a 'steady' woman-friend locally.

'Is this seat taken?'

She looked up to see a pleasant man of about twenty-five had come on a hunt for spare chairs. 'Please take it,' she said with a smile, and discovered that he was in no hurry to dash away, until someone needing the chair reminded him of his duty.

Ten minutes later Mallon was thinking of returning to her room when the man came back. By that time there was another chair free close by. She thought he was going to take it over to his party, but he instead brought it to where she was sitting.

'Have you any objection if I sit here for a few minutes?' he asked. 'Just say, and I'll go.'

He seemed harmless enough, and it wasn't as if she was in the room on her own. His party were but yards away on the other side of the room. 'Won't your companions be expecting you back?'

'It's my grandparents' golden wedding,' he replied, and explained, 'All the family are taking a trip down memory lane.' He smiled. 'I'm not old enough for such goings on.'

Over the next twenty minutes Mallon got to quite like Tony Wilson. He was pleasant without being pushy, lived and worked about eight miles away, and had opted to stay overnight in the hotel with his family. Mallon saw no reason not to be as open as him when he asked if she was on holiday in the area, and told him that she was only there overnight.

'What sort of work do you do?' he wanted to know.

'I'm doing a temporary house-sitting job at the moment,' she felt able to tell him, explaining, 'There are deliveries and builders, things like that.'

'The owners are away most of the time?' Tony queried.

'The owner came home this morning,' Mallon answered.

'And gave you the weekend off,' Tony accepted.

Mallon thought it was time she went and made her acquaintance with the paperback thriller she had purchased in the supermarket. 'Some of your family are looking over this way. I think your presence is required.'

Tony glanced back to where someone so like him he had to be his father had his eyes on him. Tony waved, and, turning back to her, invited, 'Come with me. Come and join the party.'

'Wouldn't dream of it,' she answered, the idea of gate-crashing a special golden wedding celebration unthinkable.

'They'd love you to.'

She shook her head, almost said she had a good book waiting, then realised that might sound rude. 'No, but thank you,' she said, and smiled because he was nice.

Her book didn't live up to its blurb, or perhaps it was that she was suddenly feeling restless again. Having tried without success to get into it, Mallon put her book down and went and had a long soak in the bath, letting her mind wander until it all at once struck her that for most of the time she had been thinking of Harris Quillian.

58 HIS PRETEND MISTRESS

True, he had been kind to her, more than kind to her. Generous too, insisting on paying her wages in advance the way he had. But, remembering that he had been more than sharp with her on occasions, she decided that he did not deserve so much attention in her head.

More bad dreams invaded her sleep that night and Mallon awoke glad to leave her bed. She showered and dressed, exchanging yesterday's white tee shirt for a fresh one, observing from the grey skies that it looked as though they were going to pay today for yesterday's sunshine.

The threatening rain arrived, in torrents, while she was in the dining room having her breakfast. Did roofers work in the rain? she wondered, and hoped so, otherwise, if this kept up, she would be spending much of her time tomorrow emptying buckets and bowls.

She smiled at the thought, and realised, quite crazily, she fully admitted, that for all the plushness of this hotel she was ready to go back to Harcourt House. In fact, for all its far from finished state, she was actually looking forward to returning. Whoa, there, she instructed herself, now don't start getting attached to the place. In three months' time—sooner if the right job came up—she would be leaving.

She was in a thoughtful mood as she left the dining room. She had no idea why Harcourt House should have any effect on her at all. With the exception of a few of the rooms most of the place was in a mess. If the electricians weren't cutting off the power for some reason or other, then the plumbers were cutting off the water while they worked on whatever new problem had presented itself. And that was without the constant banging and crashing of work in general as the builders went about their business. And yet, when she cared more for peace and quiet than all the hammering and hollering that went on, Mallon owned she sometimes came near to feeling quite tranquil in Harris Quillian's home.

She went to her room and packed her few belongings but, unsure what time Harris would come for her, she left her bag in her room while she went down to Reception to pay for the hotel's services.

'The account is settled,' the receptionist informed her when she asked for her bill.

'Settled? There must be some mistake. I...'

'Mr Quillian left instructions for the account to be sent to him.' The receptionist smiled. 'I wouldn't dare hand it over to you.'

Mallon was just about to inform her that she would jolly well have to when Tony Wilson came up to her, and the receptionist turned to deal with someone else.

'I was hoping I'd see you this morning,' he said frankly, and as someone else came up to the reception desk they moved a few steps out of the way. 'You went off in such a rush last night, I didn't get chance to ask if perhaps you might like to come out with me one evening? We could have dinner somewhere if...'

'I'm sorry, Tony.' She stopped him right there. As nice as he was, it would be a very long time before she so much as considered going out with anyone again. But, because he was so nice, and had such an open way with him, she tried to be honest too as she told him, 'I've only recently broken up with someone—I'm not ready to date again yet.'

'Oh, I'm sorry,' Tony replied, but wasn't ready to give up. 'Perhaps if you gave me your phone number we could talk on the phone? Get to know each other a little. You could get to know me...'

'No,' she interrupted him, and he could see that she meant it.

But he still wasn't giving up. 'Will you be here in this

hotel next weekend?' he wanted to know—and Mallon just had to laugh.

And at that point she all at once became aware that they had company. She half turned. Severe grey eyes were boring into her. 'Harris!' she exclaimed in surprise. She hadn't seen him come in, hadn't heard him approach, and in actual fact hadn't expected him to be at the hotel so early.

He did not, she rather thought, look exactly delirious to be there. Tony hadn't moved, and Harris, having switched his gaze to him, was not saying a word but was just standing there looking at him. She realised she had no choice.

'Tony, this is—my employer, Harris Quillian. Harris, Tony Wilson,' she completed, and stood by while the two civilly acknowledged each other.

Then Harris was bluntly asking, 'If you're ready?' and Mallon again felt the urge to thump him.

'I'll just pop up and get my bag,' she said politely, and had Tony Wilson for an escort to the hotel lifts.

'You're sure about that phone number?' he pressed as they stood waiting for the lift to arrive.

'Positive,' she answered, and glanced over to see that Harris Quillian was staring unsmiling at the two of them. In direct contrast, and doubting she would ever see Tony Wilson again, she gave Tony her best smile.

She wasn't smiling as she went up in the lift, though. Okay, so Quillian was obviously in a hurry to get back to London, but it wasn't her fault that he'd had to come out of his way to collect her. She would have been more than happy to have returned by taxi. In fact she had said she would. So it was his fault, not hers.

Having established that fact, Mallon collected her overnight bag, gathered up the plastic carriers of her purchases of yesterday, and rode down in the lift. It annoyed her that he wasn't standing around waiting impatiently for her but was in conversation with the receptionist—who was all but drooling at his charm.

'Ready when you are,' Mallon interrupted brightly.

He turned, glanced at her shopping bearing the super-market logo. Although he took her overnight bag from her, as he said goodbye to the receptionist so he seemed to say goodbye to most of his charm. Mallon decided she cared not, and walked ahead of him out of the hotel.

She anticipated a silent drive back to Harcourt House. For a while all that could be heard above the purr of the car's engine was the fast speed of the windscreen wipers as they dealt with the downpour. But then, in his unfriend-liest tone yet, Quillian demanded to know, 'Who was that?'

'Who?' She knew full well whom he might mean but, while he might be in a rush to get back to London, she was not feeling very friendly either and was in no hurry to co-operate.

'Wilson!' he replied curtly.

'A fellow guest.'

'You met him yesterday?'

What *was* this? She decided she would not answer, but, on thinking about it, had to suppose there must be some point to this third degree. 'That's right,' she replied at last.

'You had dinner with him?'

'No.'

'But you've arranged to see him again.'

'No, I haven't!' she denied sharply.

'Where does he live?'

'Quite close.'

'You've told him where you live?'

'Am I likely to?' Mallon retorted heatedly. She'd had just about enough of this. Though, hang on a minute, per-haps the whole point of all this was that Quillian didn't want his address given out to all and sundry—or to any chance acquaintance. She could only suppose that as she liked her privacy, so did he like his.

Mallon had thought, her answer satisfactory, that Harris Quillian had finished with the subject. But she was proved wrong when, still in a demanding frame of mind apparently, he snarled, 'You've given him your phone number?'

It gave her great pleasure to be able to answer loftily, 'It may have escaped your notice, but we don't happen to have a telephone.'

Had she thought her lofty tone might annoy him, however, she discovered she was mistaken. In fact his voice had lost its harsh edge and was almost pleasant when he enquired, 'You don't have a mobile?'

'No,' she replied, and wished the journey to end so that he could clear off back to London.

A couple of minutes ticked by, then—and she was sure it wasn't to make amends for being so bossy with his questioning—Harris Quillian was observing, 'You've been shopping, I see.'

'I needed some flour and stuff,' she replied politely, if woodenly.

'I never thought of that. I shall have to let you have some housekeeping money.'

Honestly! This man! 'Are you deliberately trying to provoke me?' Mallon demanded crossly.

Harris turned to glance at her. 'What did I do?' he asked, and seemed genuinely not to know.

'It's enough that, besides all that money you gave me last week, you'll pay my hotel bill!' she flared.

'Ah!' he murmured. Then said softly, 'Proud Mallon, are you going to forgive me for treading on your sensitivities?'

Her anger went in a moment—she couldn't understand it. She had an urge to smile, and turned her head to look out of the side window just in case he was giving her another brief glance and caught her smiling.

But it was no good. Something was bubbling up inside of her, and she turned back to look at him. 'Why do I want to laugh?' she asked.

Harris glanced her way again, and after a moment's thought, suggested, 'Because basically, at root, you've a sunny temperament. Life recently, and I suspect not so recently, hasn't given you a happy time—your sunny side is only now starting to reassert itself.'

That slightly winded her. 'I didn't ask for in-depth psychoanalysis!' she offered stiffly, no longer feeling like laughing.

But he laughed. She felt miffed that he should. 'Was that what I did?' She didn't deign to answer. He was not a bit bothered, but went on, 'May I compliment you on what *you* did?'

That stirred her interest. 'What did I do?' she asked, puzzled.

'You've started to make Harcourt House look a little more like home.'

She stared at him, and, yes, felt a little flattered that he must have noticed she had changed the linen and put out clean towels. 'You've been in the drawing room?'

'The flowers were an added touch,' he confirmed, and suddenly all animosity between them seemed to have disappeared.

Mallon could not understand the warm glow she experienced to see Harcourt House again. Even in the rain the house seemed to welcome her. 'Have you time for coffee before you go?' she asked Harris as he carried her bags of groceries into the kitchen.

Placing the carriers down on the kitchen table, he looked over to her. 'I'm going somewhere?' he asked.

'You're...' She broke off—hadn't he, last Sunday, said something about collecting her from her hotel shortly before he went back to London again? Whatever, the unexpected surge of pleasure she felt that he was apparently meaning to stay around for a few hours more gave a hiding to her earlier wish that he would clear off back to London. 'I'll take my bag up,' she said, and headed for the door. Grief—she was *pleased* he was staying around!

Any wondering about what was going on that she should feel so pleased was abruptly abandoned when, on reaching the landing, she saw that the bowls she had yesterday strategically placed to catch any rain leaks were now full enough to be close to overflowing.

Dropping her bag where she stood, Mallon opened the door of the nearest, as yet unfinished room with an adjoining bathroom, and carefully picked up the nearest bowl. Because it was so full she had to carry it carefully, but once she had tipped the contents away into the bath she did a speedy turnabout to replace the bowl before the incessant dripping rain could do much damage.

She carried out the same procedure with the next bowl, going slowly while it was full. This time, though, when she swung about in her hurry to replace the bowl, she cannoned straight into Harris, who had obviously come up the stairs, assessed the situation, and was immediately lending a hand.

Unfortunately, while her bowl was empty, his was full. With Mallon going full pelt into him, Harris had small chance of depositing the entire contents of his bowl into the bath. With a great deal of speed and dexterity, a good half found its intended target while the remainder went over Mallon and the floor.

The water was cold and Mallon reeled back. But even as she gasped from the sudden shock of it, she would have laughed. Her mouth did begin to curve upwards. But then her eyes went to Harris, and she no longer felt like laughing. Because he wasn't looking at her face, but to where the water had tipped down the front of her.

Stunned, she followed his gaze and nearly gasped anew; her tee shirt, that had a few minutes ago been more than adequate cover, now clung to her like a second skin and was now revealing the full curves of her breasts and where the shock of cold water had made their tips stand out in hardened peaks. Harris Quillian was just standing there and staring at her breasts as if fascinated!

The bowl dropped from her hands, its clatter as it hit the floor bringing his eyes abruptly upwards to her shaken expression. 'Mallon, I…' he began, but she wasn't waiting around to hear anything.

She pushed past him, taking to her heels, barely knowing where she was heading until she found herself in the sanctuary of her room.

But it wasn't a sanctuary, because Harris had followed her. 'Get out!' she yelled at him, alarm bells going off in her head, pictures haunting her—she'd screamed the same thing at Lee Jenkins all those years ago!

Harris's answer was to come swiftly up to her and take a firm grip on her upper arms. 'Calm down,' he instructed, and she tried to get free. 'I'm not going to hurt you. You're safe with me. Safe,' he repeated. 'Get that into your jumpy head. You're safe.'

Mallon stared at him. His grey eyes were holding hers firmly as he concentrated on making her believe him, that she was safe, that he would not hurt her. She ceased struggling, but was still watching him warily.

'Listen to me,' he continued, when he could see he had her full attention. 'Things like that happen. Fact. Anyone would have looked at you to see what damage had been done. Fact. You're distrustful, and I can see why. But try to trust that I just happen to be a male with...'

She'd had enough of being lectured. 'With eyes that can't help lingering,' she butted in antagonistically, and discovered that her words had more strength than any pushing and shoving she had done to get free of his grip.

A harsh glint came to his eyes, and abruptly he let go his hold on her. 'You're impossible to get through to like this!' he rapped, and, turning sharply about, he went striding from her room.

The next sound she heard was the purr of his car being driven down the drive. She went mutinously to the window and was in time to see Harris steering the vehicle through the stone pillars.

No doubt he had changed his mind about not rushing to return to London. Well, she was glad, glad, glad. With any luck he would forget to ever come back.

CHAPTER FOUR

MIRACULOUSLY the rain had ceased at some time during the night and Mallon awoke to a gloriously sunny morning. She wished she had awakened feeling as sunny. Harris had suggested that basically she had a sunny nature; nightmarish dreams during the night had clouded her morning.

She left her bed in a sombre frame of mind, her bad dreams not the only cloud on her day. Yesterday, because of her attitude, Harris had curtailed his visit. He had come down to unwind a little and she had put the kibosh on that.

Feeling very ashamed of herself, Mallon went over the events of yesterday that had led to Harris departing early. 'You're safe with me. Get that into your jumpy head,' he had said. But she had been in no mind to be lectured and he hadn't hung around—perhaps thinking that the best way to calm her fears was for him to absent himself.

Mallon spent that Monday in making tea for the builders and in feeling thoroughly mortified at the way she had behaved with Harris yesterday. She knew she was not going to feel any better until she had apologised.

Strangely, bearing in mind she had an uncomfortable weight on her conscience, that night she had her first dream-free sleep in a long while. She awoke on Tuesday to another sunny morning and went to one of her windows to look out at the peace and serenity of it all—before the builders came—and could not help but realise that Harcourt House had been built in a most wonderful spot.

With the improvement in the weather, so Mallon's 'sunnier' side began to reassert itself. So much so that when she saw that one of the builders had left a newspaper lying around, she borrowed it. The only live-in job that remotely appealed—and in all honesty it wasn't all that appealing—was a hotel receptionist's job. She now thought she would be able to do that sort of work but, did she want to?

The knowledge that in less than three months she would have to find somewhere to live and work, if she didn't want to go and park herself on her mother and John, prodded her into putting pen to paper. But it was Thursday before Mallon, impatient with herself for her delaying tactics, firmly decided to go and post her application.

She was uncertain how near or far was the closest post-box, and went to see if Kevin and the van were anywhere about. He was usually gone, or going, somewhere. The van was not to be seen. 'Kev won't be back for a couple of hours,' Dean informed her helpfully. 'If it's urgent, though, you can borrow my bike,' he offered.

Mallon knew that Dean was a cycling enthusiast. 'Are you sure?' she asked.

'It's not my best bike,' he answered with a shy smile.

And five minutes later, able to prove the old adage 'You never forget how to ride a bike' Mallon was having a lovely time pedalling up the road. She did not see a post-box until she was almost at Sherwins' shop. But, having popped her letter inside the postbox, she was enjoying herself so much that on her way back she investigated the various lanes *en route*. By the time Harcourt House came into view, Mallon had a feeling she would be very reluctant to leave the area.

Having departed with more determination not to wobble off the bike than with style, Mallon pedalled back up the drive with both style and speed—but only to have to concentrate on not falling off in her surprise when, at one and the same time, she spotted Harris and his large car.

She sailed straight past him and went to return Dean's bike. 'Thank you, Dean,' she said with a smile.

'You can borrow it any time,' he replied, which she thought was lovely of him, and she thanked him again, but owned to feeling all kind of churned up inside; and knew it had nothing to do with the fact that this was the first time she had ridden a bike in years.

She was approaching the rear entrance when Harris came round the corner and joined her. 'Whose chariot?' he enquired by way of greeting.

'Dean's,' she answered. And, realising that that probably didn't mean very much to him. 'Charlie's mate,' she added, 'the plumber.' They entered the house and, when she just knew Harris wasn't asking for an explanation found she was burbling on, 'I borrowed it to go and post off a job application.'

Harris halted. She halted with him. 'You're not happy here?' he asked.

Mallon stared at him, then glanced pointedly around at the clutter of builders' essentials lying around in the hall. Added to that was the general banging and clattering going on, and she didn't have to say a word—they both laughed.

To share laughter with him did funny things to her insides. 'I'm just about to make some coffee,' she invented. 'Would you like one?'

'I thought I'd have to make my own,' he accepted, and smiled at her, and she went hastily in front of him to the kitchen.

'You're not working today?' she asked when they were seated at the kitchen table, their coffee in front of them, a sudden feeling of being on edge starting to get to her. 'Sorry, that was stupid, you obviously are.' Would he wear a business suit purely to come and have a look at a building site, for goodness' sake?

'You're nervous of me?' he asked, too shrewd by half in her view. But, when only a short while ago his quick perception might have bothered her, strangely, just then, it didn't.

'Not nervous,' she answered, and, as if to prove it, sent him a smile. 'What I am feeling is awkward and guilty because I know I owe you one big apology, and I don't know the best way to go about it.'

Grey eyes fixed on her lovely deep blue ones. 'Such honesty,' he said quietly, adding, 'I appreciate it, Mallon. But don't feel awkward—I take it, since there's not much here worth breaking, that the apology you owe me is personal?'

'You know it is. You came here last weekend to unwind, but my—jumpy—behaviour last Sunday drove you back to London earlier than you intended.'

'You've been feeling guilty about that?' he questioned seriously.

She nodded. 'And ashamed,' she confessed.

'Oh, Mallon, Mallon,' he said softly. 'You've been through such a foul time. It's only natural that you're going to be jumpy on occasion.' He left his chair and, coming over to where she was sitting, he looked down at her and, smiling, tapped her gently on her nose, and stated, 'And I shouldn't have let it get to me that you can't trust me enough to believe me when I tell you that you're safe with me.'

'Oh, Harris, I...' she began helplessly, realising only then that he was far more sensitive than she had seen. But he had moved a few steps away and was transferring his coffee cup and saucer from the table to the draining board.

'Don't worry about it,' he instructed, and, going on to another subject entirely, 'I thought I'd take some time out this morning to come and have a look around and check a few things out with Bob Miller. I could take you for a quick lunch in town afterwards if you're interested?'

She did like him so. A quick lunch didn't sound so good for his digestion, but it pleased her that he had asked. 'Or I could fix you something here?' she offered.

'Thank you, I accept,' he said without hesitation, and she smiled and he went to inspect the rebuilding progress so far.

By the sound of it he wanted to start back for London as soon as he'd eaten. Which she translated as meaning that he wouldn't mind having his meal more or less straight away. Pasta seemed the order of the day.

Harris was back a half-hour later. 'Ready to eat?' Mallon asked.

'I'm impressed,' he commented, and was appreciative too when they sat down to eat. 'You'd no idea you'd be feeding me this lunchtime, but this is excellent.'

'Oh, just something I threw together,' she laughed, thankful she'd found a tin of salmon in a cupboard which, with the pasta, some milk and Roquefort cheese, made a tasty impromptu meal.

She owned she was feeling happy. Though, nearing the end of the meal, when Harris explained that he'd come down today because he would not be there at the weekend, she experienced the oddest sensation which, had she not known better, she would have said was one of disappointment.

Which was quite, quite, utterly ridiculous, she determined. Especially since as soon as he came in she would have been off to a hotel, and would see nothing of him at the weekend anyhow. And why, for heaven's sake, would she want to see him? Crazy wasn't the word for it.

Putting such thoughts aside, Mallon strove to remember what they had been talking about. His property, this property, and his visit today to inspect it, that was it. 'What made you choose this particular area?' she asked. 'Was it because your sister…?' Her voice tailed off. But Harris, it seemed, was right on her wavelength.

'Faye wasn't living in Lower Macey then,' he took up, bringing out into the open what Mallon was reluctant to. 'She spotted Almora Lodge on her first visit here. When she discovered the owners were renting it out while they're abroad for a year, she persuaded Phillips to take it.' Harris paused, and then quietly asked, 'You've seen nothing of him, I hope?'

'No, thank goodness,' she answered abruptly, bleakly, and guessed her expression must have given away that she regretted having instigated this conversation and did not want to be reminded of his brother-in-law.

But, even so, Haris wasn't prepared to leave the subject, and asked, 'How about those bad dreams?', clearly associating her night-time horrors with Roland Phillips's assault on her.

Mallon made a determined effort to buck up. 'They've gone,' she answered cheerfully.

'Completely?'

'Haven't had one since…' She had been about to say Sunday night, but, feeling sensitive to Harris suddenly, did not want to remind him of their spat last Sunday, so changed it to, 'For three nights.'

She could tell he had immediately done the calculation and that his arithmetic was spot on, but all he said was, 'Keep up the good work.' And then he asked, 'Do you want a hand with the washing up?', although he was plainly about to leave.

And Mallon wanted to laugh and actually did feel light-hearted. 'I think I'll be able to manage,' she replied sunnily—and he left.

She missed him when he had gone, and wondered if she had gone soft in the head. Why, she barely knew the man! What the Dickens was she thinking of?

What she was thinking of, she discovered on Saturday morning, was Harris. He seemed always to be popping into her head. Well, why wouldn't he? she argued. If it hadn't been for him that day she had run from Roland Phillips, heaven alone knew what she would have done.

The builders were working that morning, and it was a lovely day. There was much noise going on, more than usual, or so it seemed, and Mallon thought it a good idea to take a walk. She took her purse with her. If she saw a telephone kiosk she would ring her mother.

Out on the country road, she walked along, her mind absently engaged in wondering what Harris was doing this weekend. Did the fact that he wasn't coming down to Harcourt House mean that he was heavily engaged with some woman? Mallon—ridiculously, she owned—felt a touch irked at the very idea—then became aware of a car approaching from behind.

There was no pavement. She stepped from the road and onto the grass verge. But instead of the car passing, as she'd expected, it started to slow down. She was about to turn to see if some stranger to the area wanted to ask directions, when she heard a voice that turned her blood to ice!

'Can I give you a lift?'

It was Roland Phillips's voice! She was sure of it! She wanted to run, and did not answer. Then the car was pulling in front—and he had recognised her.

'Well, well! As I live and breathe, Mallon Braithwaite!' She kept on walking. He drove alongside of her. 'Now what, I wonder, are you doing in these parts?' She tried to ignore him, but found that his evil brain was clearly up to checking that the only property along that route was the one owned by his brother-in-law. 'Don't tell me you're staying at Harcourt House!'

She wouldn't dream of telling him anything, but dread entered her heart; she didn't want this man knowing where she lived, or that this weekend she would be there on her own.

'You're living with Harris Quillian?' he chortled. 'Now isn't that a turn-up for the books.'

'I'm his caretaker!' Mallon stopped to reply, anger taking the place of fear.

'That's a new name for it!' Mallon realised that Roland Phillips was a man who *would* think like that, and wished that Harris had hit him harder. 'Is he down this weekend?' Roland Phillips asked, to strike fear into her heart again.

'I'll give him your regards when I get back, shall I?' she managed to stay composed long enough to enquire, looking pointedly at Roland Phillips's chin in the hope that the memory of Harris thumping him hadn't disappeared in a bleary haze.

She gathered that it hadn't when he gave her a spiteful look, and put his foot to the accelerator and drove on. She had been enjoying her walk, but all her pleasure had abruptly departed. She turned about and returned to the house.

The builders departed just after midday and, left on her own, Mallon wished she had asked them to take her into town. Any one of them would have done so, she was fairly sure. It wouldn't have taken her long to find some place to stay.

Against that, though, and for all it was sunny now, the weather had been extremely changeable of late, and it did not follow that it was going to stay sunny. As she had told Roland Phillips, she was there at Harcourt House in the capacity of caretaker. Which meant she needed to be on site, at least in case fresh leaks appeared.

Mallon went up to bed that night feeling full of anxiety and praying that her ex-employer had remembered, and believed her, when she had intimated that Harris was around that weekend.

She made doubly sure that her bedroom door was locked and did something she hadn't had to do since she and her mother had parted company with the Jenkins pair—Mallon placed a solid chair under the door handle. Before she climbed into bed, while perfectly aware that she couldn't see Roland Phillips, drunk or sober, shinning up a drain-pipe, she checked that her bedroom windows were locked.

That night her dark dreams returned, and left her so shaken that she couldn't even leave her room to go down to her usual haven of the kitchen.

She was never more glad to see Monday arrive and, with it, the return of the builders. She went with Kevin into town and did some shopping, and tried a couple of times to phone her mother, but she was out, probably shopping herself, Mallon realised.

As the week went on, so Mallon slowly began to get back to the way she had been before she had taken that walk last Saturday. As yet, however, she hadn't been able to say goodbye to the returned dreams and flashbacks.

There was a letter for her on Friday. The receptionist's job she had applied for had been filled. Mallon admitted that she was not overly upset—her dormant sunny tem-perament seemed to be waking up again. Even the fact that the weather had turned dull, and that Charlie had turned the water off when she had some laundry in the washing machine didn't bother her unduly.

'Got a bit of a problem,' Charlie explained, and explained in detail while she tried to keep up with his plumbing talk.

Anticipating that Harris would arrive at some time on Saturday morning, Mallon cadged a lift with Kevin when he popped in to say he was going to Sherwins and did she want anything. She returned with fresh vegetables and chicken pieces, with the idea of making a large casserole. She would have some for her dinner that evening—then, if Harris didn't want to go out or start foraging for his meal tomorrow, he could have the rest of it. If he didn't, it would keep in the fridge for her meal when she returned on Sunday.

The last of the builders had gone by five-thirty. At six o'clock the casserole was in the oven and was coming along nicely, when she heard the sound of a car pulling up. One of the builders returning for something he had forgotten? Or—she felt a glow of anticipation suddenly—had Harris come down today instead of tomorrow?

Unsure if her feeling of warmth was in evidence in her eyes and face, Mallon turned her back on the windows. Harris usually passed the windows in his car, but that wasn't to say that some builders' plant wasn't blocking the way. If it was Harris and he was walking by, he might glance in.

She had herself under control when she heard someone coming along the hall. If it was one of the builders he could have taken what he'd come back for and gone. If it was something he had left inside, she was sure that whichever one of them it was would have called out.

The kitchen door opened, but as she turned and glanced to the door, so the colour drained from her face. 'This place is taking shape!' Roland Phillips remarked, coming further into the kitchen.

Mallon felt sick in the pit of her stomach. 'What do you want?' she asked bluntly.

'Don't be like that, Mallon. I've come to do you a favour.'

'I don't need your favours!'

'Yes, you do. Your mother rang.'

'My m...'

'Shame on you, Mallon.' He tut-tutted. 'Couldn't you bring yourself to tell her you'd left me in the lurch?'

'I thought it best not to tell her why I left!' Mallon retorted. Oh, heaven help her, she was here all alone, not a builder in sight—and Roland Phillips had got that lecherous look in his eyes! 'She would have insisted I went to the police.' Mallon thought it would do no harm to warn him.

'Don't be like that, my dear,' he replied, his eyes going over her figure. 'You know I've always fancied you.'

'You don't know me!' she answered shortly, backing away as he came closer.

'Whose fault is that?' he complained, and as he took another step nearer, and she smelt his alcoholic breath, Mallon had nowhere else to go. 'Why can't we...?' he began, but the rest of it was lost in the roar of sound from the doorway.

'What the hell are you doing here?' Harris Quillian demanded, his face like thunder.

Roland Phillips jerked round. 'I—I...' he started to bluster. Then got his second wind and edged away from Mallon, his prey, to challenge, albeit not very aggressively, 'If you'd got a phone here I wouldn't have had to bother to come at all. I came to tell Mallon that her mother had phoned.'

Harris wasn't interested. 'I don't want you anywhere near here,' he told him curtly, holding the kitchen door

wide. 'Get out, and stay out!' And, his tone icy and determined, he snarled threateningly, 'Set so much as one
foot on this property again…and I shall come looking for
you.'

He didn't say what he would do when he found him.
He didn't have to. Roland Phillips quite plainly knew that
his brother-in-law didn't go around making empty threats,
and didn't hang around to say goodbye. He went at speed.

By then Mallon, although she owned to feeling a shade
weepy in her relief that Harris had arrived tonight instead
of tomorrow, though still shaken was starting to recover.
'I wasn't expecting you until tomorrow!' she exclaimed.

But was shaken anew that it seemed Harris had put his
own interpretation on having seen her and his brother-in-
law so up close together. 'Obviously!' he rapped.

'Obviously?' she repeated, thunderstruck. 'You can't for
a minute think…!'

'How did Phillips know you were here?' Harris Quillian
demanded.

And Mallon *did* want to weep. How could he? How
could he? But her spirit, badly shaken on two counts, was
aided by sudden fury. Somehow, she managed to control
her fury, and it was with dignity when, not deigning to
answer him and passing the oven as she went, 'Turn that
off at seven!' she ordered. 'I'm going to pack!'

The pig, the absolute total pig! She sailed from the
room, head held high, and stormed up the stairs. She was
so incensed she only just remembered to sidestep the
dodgy floorboard on the landing that Cyril had pointed out
that morning, and arrived in her room growing more and
more outraged. So outraged, in fact, that she slammed the
door with such force the windows rattled.

She was unrepentant; she didn't care. The place was a
disaster area anyway, with its disintegrating floorboards,

haphazard plumbing, perished plaster in most bedrooms that left only two habitable. Mallon was too het up as she got out her cases to want to think of its beautiful setting and how gloriously fabulous it was going to look when all the work had been completed.

How dared Harris-rotten-Quillian think that she had *obviously* contacted Roland Phillips to come over as soon as the last workman had gone because Harris-rotten-Quillian would *obviously* not be arriving until the morning?

Hurt and angry, and feeling more like bursting into tears than ever, Mallon had just taken a couple of dresses out from the wardrobe when her bedroom door opened and the object of her hate came in. She knew the chair was in the way—it was a heavy chair and by skirting round she was spared from nightly having to drag it across the room. Harris nearly fell over it.

Good! 'I leave the chair there—usually lodged under the doorknob—to keep out unwanted intruders!' she told him acidly, going over to one of the open suitcases on the bed and starting to fold the first of the dresses into it.

Harris watched her for a moment or two, then said, 'I'm not very good at saying sorry.'

Huh! 'Even when you know you're in the wrong?'

'Do you really prop that chair under your doorknob at night?'

She shrugged, intended to tell him nothing—but the words were coming anyway. 'I went for a walk last Saturday. Your brother-in-law was driving by. He stopped, and realised where I was living. That chair has been under the doorknob ever since.'

'Oh, Mallon,' Harris mourned helplessly. 'I'm a swine.'

'*Obviously!*' she agreed, and wondered if she was losing it when, having tossed his word back at him, she wanted to laugh.

'I *am* sorry,' he stated softly.

'There—that didn't hurt, did it?'

'If I lend you my mobile phone to ring your mother, will you forgive me?'

Mallon hesitated. 'I—might,' she mumbled.

'Your mother doesn't know you no longer work for Phillips?'

'I rang her—from the Clifton Hotel. I couldn't tell her. She'd worry.' Mallon's anger was draining away. She started to fold the second of the dresses.

'You don't have to leave!' Harris said suddenly, and Mallon knew, her anger gone, that she did not want to leave. 'In fact, you don't have to go anywhere this week-end.'

'You're staying here?' She was weakening; she knew she was.

'Until Sunday,' he confirmed. 'Try to trust me, Mallon,' he urged. She rather thought that she did trust him already. She looked across to him, looked straight into a pair of steady grey eyes. Then, as they stared at each other, a smile, a winning smile of such charm broke from him that she felt momentarily powerless. 'Please stay,' he urged, and, teasingly, 'I know you're just going to hate me like blazes if, come your return on Sunday, there's none of that delicious-smelling casserole left.'

She wanted to smile in return, but wouldn't. Though owned that, rather than referring to her going and never coming back, he was making it easier for her to return on Sunday—should she still decide to go now.

'Are you saying you won't take me t-to a hotel?' she asked, thereby agreeing, she realised, that she was not intending to leave permanently.

'You know that's not what I'm saying. What I am saying is, given the impossibility of the conditions here, you manage to make the place more and more comfortable each time I visit. It seems poor recompense that you should leave just because I've arrived.'

He was saying, she saw, that from his point of view she was welcome to stay. But that, should she go, it would be only her choice. To stay, she knew, would be to tell him that trust him she did.

'You no longer think I purposely invited your brother-in-law here?'

'I never did,' Harris replied promptly.

'Oh?'

'So I got mad. I wanted an excuse to hit him. When he scuttled away without a fight—I just needed someone to release my fury on.'

'And I happened to be the nearest.'

'That doesn't make me a very nice person,' he volunteered.

She wanted to deny that. Thinking of his amazing goodness to her, she wanted to tell him so, but felt shy suddenly. 'That halo I gave you did slip a bit,' she agreed. Then smiled as she told him, 'But nobody's perfect.'

Harris returned her smile, and to be friends with him once more did her heart good. 'You want to exchange those cases for a weekend bag?' he suggested.

Mallon shook her head. 'If it's all the same with you…' she took a deep breath '…I'll stay and share that casserole with you.'

Harris nodded, satisfied, then showed her the particular peculiarities of his mobile, and left her. She dialled her mother's number with no idea how to explain why she did not want her to again try and get her on Roland Phillips's number.

'Hello, Mum, it's me,' she opened.

'Oh, Mallon. What a relief! Mr Phillips said you weren't

working for him any longer when I rang. Where on earth are you? I've been worried...'

'Oh, Mum, there's no need. I'm not far away from Lower Macey. Only a few miles up the road from that other job.'

'What happened?'

Mallon, while hating to mislead her parent, replied by saying that she hadn't taken to Roland Phillips all that well, and now had a better job working for his brother-in-law, supervising the builders—she was glad brilliant supervisor Bob Miller couldn't hear her—and also overseeing the delivery of furniture, fixtures and fittings to the property. 'It's only a temporary job,' she explained, 'but I really love it.'

'Well, as long as you're happy. You know that there's always a home here for you.'

'Of course. How's John?'

As the phone call was ending, Mallon's mother pressed her to give her new employer's name and, since there was no phone there, the address where Mallon could be contacted. Her mother wanted Mallon to have a word with John, as well.

'Did I hear your mother say you were working for Harris Quillian?' John asked, and, when she confirmed that she was, it transpired that John knew of him, for he went on to say, 'Well, we've no need to worry about you there. Harris Quillian is head of Warren and Taber Finance. A straighter man you'd never find.'

After her telephone call, John reiterating that there was a home there for her any time she liked, Mallon washed her face, applied her usual light make-up and brushed her blonde hair. She felt she would like to have changed into a fresh dress, but Harris didn't seem to miss much and she didn't want him to think she had changed on account of him being there. Besides, who dressed up to eat in the kitchen?

Harris wasn't around when Mallon went back down the stairs again. But she knew he wouldn't be very far away. There were still a couple of hours of daylight left. He would be around somewhere, having a look at how the work had progressed since he was last down.

Mallon had the casserole, some potatoes and broccoli all ready to serve when she heard him approaching the kitchen. 'Everything okay?' she enquired when he came in.

'Some parts of the rebuilding are going on faster than others,' he answered, confirming that he'd been having a look around.

'While I think of it, there's a very dicey floorboard on the landing,' Mallon reported, taking the casserole pot over to the table.

'I noticed it.'

It was true, she mused, he did never miss a thing. She supposed he hadn't got to be head of a finance company by missing very much.

'Where did you learn to cook?' he asked midway through the meal. 'I haven't spotted a recipe book anywhere around.'

'I'm not sure you need much of a recipe book for a casserole,' Mallon answered lightly. 'I've always cooked,' she said without thinking.

'Your mother didn't care to?'

Was he probing to know her background? Mallon eyed him carefully. Or was he just being polite? 'My father's death devastated her,' she replied, seeing no harm in answering in. 'My mother lost interest in everything when he died.'

Harris eyed her in that steady way he had. 'Even you, her daughter?' he enquired quietly.

Mallon could feel herself bridling but, because most of the time she quite liked the man, she decided he was just keeping some sort of conversation going between them 'It was because of me she decided to live on without him,' she replied—a shade coolly, it had to be admitted.

'How old were you when your father died?'

'Thirteen,' Mallon replied, and, remembering back, 'He was a lovely man, quiet, gentle—a wonderful surgeon, so everyone said.'

'He was a consultant?'

'The best in all fields. It's no wonder my mother... ceased to function for a while.' But Mallon did not want to dwell on those unhappy days, and went on brightly, 'My mother married again recently, I think I mentioned it, and, after some truly dreadful unhappy years, is happy again now. And that's what matters.'

'You're saying that there is now no place for you?' Harris queried shrewdly.

'That's exactly what I'm *not* saying,' Mallon denied. 'Only this evening, when I phoned them—your phone's over there by the way—' she broke off to point to the end of the worktop '—they both said that there was a home there for me with them.' And, before he could say anything to that, 'But naturally I prefer living here,' she added dryly.

'Rotting floorboards and all,' Harris took up, his mouth curving in a hint of a smile, not offended in any way. 'You were living with your mother prior to her remarriage?' he asked.

'We had a small flat.' Mallon again saw no reason not to answer. 'My mother would have been upset had I said I wanted to keep the flat on rather than move in with her and John. But it was true that I was looking for a job change.'

'So you made believe you'd be happier doing a live-in housekeeping job?'

'It wasn't all housekeeping. True, Almora Lodge took some clearing up, but I'm not used to being idle and R-Roland Phillips's study was a mess too. He suggested I should sort things out for him, get his backlog of filing filed, that sort of thing. He...' Abruptly, she stopped. She didn't want to think about Roland Phillips, much less talk about him. 'Del brought me some more plums from his trees yesterday. I made a fresh pie, or there's cheese for afters?'

Harris eyed her silently for some seconds, then quietly stated, 'Do you know, Mallon, I rather think I got the better part of the bargain when I asked you to stay on here.'

His remark pleased her, pleased her so much she didn't know what to say. She wanted something sharp and witty but there was nothing there, only a tremendous feeling of shyness. She swallowed hard, and then managed, 'And you think that sort of remark gets you out of the washing up?'

'There's a dishwasher here somewhere,' he murmured, good humour there in his fine grey eyes.

Mallon declared that they hadn't used sufficient dishes to warrant the dishwasher, and later Harris did the drying while she washed and rinsed—and again that feeling of shyness crept over her. It seemed so intimate somehow, standing so close next to him. She moved her position, taking half a step away. Good heavens, what in creation was going on with her? Intimate! For goodness' sake, what was she thinking? Harris was merely helping with the washing up—he'd be astounded if he knew what had just gone through her head.

She turned from him, checking that everything was neat and tidy. 'I think I'll go to bed!' she announced shortly, suddenly feeling more aware of Harris than she had of any man, and that, most peculiarly, included Keith Morgan.

She looked up at Harris, and found he had his eyes on her, that steady look of his fixed on her again. 'You usually go to bed this early?' he asked. It was still daylight outside.

'N-not usually. But you're here to caretake tonight, so I feel free to go up and finish my book.'

'You could bring your book down to the drawing room,' he suggested mildly.

'I'll—um—see,' she mumbled, but left the kitchen knowing that she wouldn't be coming down from her room with her book—she had an uncomfortable feeling that he knew it too.

It wasn't as if she didn't trust him, she reasoned, when up in her room she tried to make sense of her emotions. It had to be emotional, this feeling of being at one with him one minute, and shy and a touch diffident with him the next.

She did trust him; she knew that she did. So much so that, knowing that there were just the two of them alone in the house, that night she restored the heavy chair by the door to its former home. She realised a couple of hours later, when she lay down to go to sleep, that her trust in Harris must have been instinctive and complete, because she had not locked her door and, remembering that it was unlocked, she couldn't think of one good reason to get out of bed to go and lock it.

Having gone to sleep in a fairly tranquil frame of mind, her dreams that night, in contrast, seemed doubly violent. Mallon was gasping and panicking in her sleep. She seemed to know that she was dreaming, that it wasn't real, but as panic held her firmly down she could not find a way through to the surface. Dark forces were squashing her; she was drowning. Her breathing stopped, there was no more air; she could take none in. Then, just when she knew she must suffocate, she broke through—and surfaced.

With a gasp of terror, Mallon came awake, fighting for breath. She inhaled on a noisy gulp of air and struggled to sit up, and gradually her laboured breathing started to ease. She was all right; she was all right. It was a dream, only a dream—but she didn't want to go back to sleep again, didn't want it to start all over again.

In fear she got out of bed and went to the window, intending to open it wide. She needed air, cool cold air. Then her brain started to function again. Harris was next door. The sound of a window opening might disturb his sleep.

Mallon turned away, knowing she should go back to bed, but she couldn't; her fears of it all starting up again were too real. She grabbed up her cotton robe, glad then that she had taken the chair away from the door and had no need to start moving furniture about.

It was still dark when she quietly opened her door, but she didn't want to put the light on in case Harris heard any small sound or perhaps opened his eyes and saw a line of light. Just in time she remembered the ropy floorboard, and, avoiding it, found her way to the banister and held on to it as a guide all the way down the stairs.

Having safely negotiated her way to the bottom, Mallon knew of the perils in the way of builders' materials lying about, but felt she could safely put a light on now.

She was by then wide awake and did not want to return to her room, to fall asleep again and to again awake in panic. She went quietly along the hall to the outside door. Harris had locked up tonight.

Mallon unlocked the door and went and stood outside

in the cold night air, breathing deeply until after about five minutes she began to feel calmer. Calm enough to return indoors anyway.

Taking care to be quiet, she stepped back inside and re-locked the outside door. She knew that she still didn't want to return to her bed, and, as she had on several occasions before in the middle of the night, she headed for the kitchen. Strangely, though, she saw that the kitchen door was ajar and that the light was on.

She realised that Harris must have forgotten to turn off the light before he'd gone to bed—though she couldn't remember noticing the light was on. Mallon put that down to the fact that she had been in something of a state earlier.

But, on pushing the door open, she was staggered to see Harris standing at the kitchen sink calmly filling the kettle with water. 'I disturbed you!' she exclaimed at once.

'Can't a man make a cup of tea in his own kitchen without you kicking up a fuss?' he enquired pleasantly.

She felt dreadful. The poor man had come down to Harcourt House for a rest, to unwind, and here he was up in the middle of the night, and it was all her fault. 'I'm sorry,' she apologised, feeling utterly miserable, and turned about to go back up to her suddenly much detested bed. But his voice delayed her.

'Bad dream?' he asked, and she turned back.

'I—thought I'd said goodbye to them, but they returned,' she admitted.

'When?' he enquired, spooning tea into the teapot. 'When did they come back?'

'Last Saturday night.' She did not seem to have the energy just then to prevaricate.

'The Saturday you were out walking and met Phillips again,' Harris remarked, not having to pause to calculate, she realised. But he made no further comment on that subject, but invited, 'Come and sit down and share a pot of tea with me. Unless you'd prefer something stronger.'

'Tea would be fine,' Mallon answered. But barely had she agreed to stay and drink tea with him than she suddenly became aware that, where she was nightdress and cotton-robe-clad, Harris wore only a robe. From his nicely shaped legs showing beneath and the vee of dark hair at his chest, it would seem that he had little else underneath. Abruptly she went and took a seat at the kitchen table.

'Sugar?'

'What?'

'Do you take sugar?' Harris enquired.

'Er—no,' she replied, and made stern efforts to get herself more of one piece. 'I didn't think I'd made any noise. I didn't want to disturb you.'

'You didn't. I was awake, wondering if I started moving around I might wake you—when I heard a few isolated sounds that indicated you might be in trouble.'

'Oh, Harris, I'm a mess, aren't I?'

He looked at her, and then brought two cups of tea over. 'No, you're not,' he answered, pulling out a chair and sitting down opposite her. 'What you are is traumatised by what happened to you, or would have happened to you had you not been able to escape from Phillips.'

Mallon stared at him. Harris seemed so understanding somehow. She felt then that she could talk to him about absolutely anything. 'But—I should be over that by now, surely?'

'Not at all,' he disagreed, sending her a gentle smile. 'You're highly sensitive, Mallon. You went to live and work at Almora Lodge in good faith—your faith that Phillips was a decent man was cruelly shattered.' Harris broke off, and then, his grey eyes holding her deeply blue ones, refusing to let her look away, said deliberately, 'It hasn't been of any help that something similar happened to you before.'

'No, it didn't!' she denied sharply, her calmer mood swiftly vanishing.

Annoyingly, Harris stayed quiet, his eyes still holding hers, still refusing to allow her to look away. 'Forgive me,' he said, but didn't look particularly sorry. 'You said, that day we met, that you'd had your fill of men who seemed to think you couldn't wait to get into bed with them.'

'Do you forget nothing either?' Mallon erupted.

'Either?' he queried.

'I've already seen that you don't appear to miss much!' she retorted. He had rattled her; she didn't see why she shouldn't try to rattle him.

But, no, he stayed calm, stayed cool, and not one whit out of countenance. 'I haven't missed that, while there's a warmth in you that wants to get out, you are very often— troubled—in case that warmth is taken advantage of.'

He was psychoanalysing again; she didn't like it. 'What sort of night-time reading do you have by the side of your bed?' she asked sarcastically.

He smiled, it was a lovely smile, and something inside her seemed to melt. And when, gently, he asked, 'What happened, Mallon, to make you so defensive?' while she wanted to hotly deny she was in any way defensive, she found that she could not.

'N...' She tried anyway, but the word 'nothing' refused to leave her lips. 'I...' she tried again. Then found she was relating, rather shakily, it had to be admitted, 'Two years after my father's death my mother married again. It was a disaster from almost the first.'

'What went wrong?' Harris prompted, his tone quiet.

'He, Ambrose Jenkins, was more interested in my father's money than in making my mother happy,' Mallon replied, and looked away from Harris as she relived that dreadful time. 'By the time the marriage was over, there was no money left. Even the lovely house my father had bought was gone.'

'You and your mother moved into your small flat without this man?'

Mallon nodded. 'And without his odious son!' she declared.

'But his son lived with you in your previous home?'

'That's where I learned the value of propping a chair under my bedroom doorknob if I wanted any privacy.'

'He tried to seduce you?' Harris questioned gently.

'It didn't get beyond him trying to make a grab for me when no one else was around.'

'How old were you?'

'When it began? Fifteen. Though it didn't start with his father until I was sixteen.'

'His father! G...' Harris bit off whatever expletive had been on his tongue.

'He was more verbal than grabbing.'

'What was your mother doing all this time?' Harris wanted to know.

'Doing?' Mallon flicked a glance at him. 'Nothing. She didn't know. Besides, I made jolly certain I was never alone in the same room with either of them.'

'Good for you. But—you didn't tell your mother what you were having to put up with?'

'How could I? She had barely been functioning after my father's death. She later on realised her new husband was a lecher, but to know then that she had married such a man, brought him into our home, and that he and his equally lecherous son were both casting their lascivious gaze in my direction, would have finished her.'

'And so you bore it all alone?'

'It's over now,' Mallon said, and actually found a smile. 'But it's left its scars.'

'I'll cope,' she said lightly.

'I'm sure you will,' he agreed.

And she liked him so well then, as she looked into his warm grey eyes, she actually felt quite a lump in her throat. Abruptly she got to her feet. 'Do you mind if I don't drink my tea after all?' she asked, conversely then feeling somehow that she needed the sanctuary of her own room.

Harris got to his feet too, his tea untouched also. 'What's wrong?' he wanted to know.

'Nothing,' she answered. Then, staring up into his good-looking face, she confessed, 'I've shared, told you things just now, that I've never told another living soul.' She smiled. 'I think I feel a little light-headed.'

'Your confidences are safe with me,' he quietly assured her.

'I know,' she replied, and did.

'Come on, let's get you back to bed. You've got to be up early in the morning.'

She laughed, the sauce of it! He was here—he was good at making tea. Let him make Bob Miller his first brew. Switching off the downstairs lights, and then switching on the stairs and landing lights, Harris went up the staircase with her.

'Watch that floorboard,' he warned when they turned on to the landing.

She recalled how he had noticed it previously but glanced at him to remind him that *she* had been the one to tell him about that floorboard! But, not looking where she was going, her foot unerringly found that rickety floorboard. It gave way and she started to fall knowing, as she grabbed at air, that nothing was going to save her.

Something did, though. Or rather, Harris reached for her

to try and hold her, but in his efforts he wasn't looking where he was walking either, and he caught his foot in the same floorboard—and they both went down.

Mallon was about to laugh, to apologise, to say something light—perhaps something about his hazard-strewn house. But then she became startlingly aware of his body moving over the top of her, his weight pressing down on her through the thin covering of her nightdress and cotton robe—and she wasn't stopping to think that his weight might be just temporary while he recovered and attempted to find his feet.

'Get off me!' she shrieked, her hands pushing at his chest.

'Shh-shh,' he quieted her, and as she looked up at him and saw nothing of the lust in his face that she had seen in the faces of Ambrose and Lee Jenkins, or Roland Phillips, so her world started to right itself. 'Never in a million years, remember?' Harris murmured.

And she felt ashamed of herself. 'Sorry,' she mumbled. But suddenly the feel of his body over hers was creating the oddest of sensations in her. 'I—do trust you,' she managed. 'It's j-just that…'

'Old habits die hard.'

'Something like that,' Mallon replied, and as Harris made to get up, so she stared up at him. He hesitated, his eyes on her eyes, his glance going down to her mouth, and back up again to her eyes.

Then, unhurriedly, his head was coming down, and tenderly he placed his mouth over hers. Mallon felt the warmth of his kiss, and was not conscious of breathing. All she knew was that this gentle kiss from his wonderful mouth was totally thrilling. She wanted to kiss him back, but was afraid to move lest she break some spell. So she just lay there, closer to him than she had ever been to any man, and too soon Harris was breaking his kiss.

He looked down at her. 'There's nothing to worry about, Mallon,' he assured her, his tones soothing. 'I—um—think you needed to be kissed, and—' he smiled '—while it wasn't such a great chore—did anyone ever tell you what an invitingly sensational mouth you have?—that kiss was a prelude to nothing.'

Her heart was thundering like crazy. 'I—er…' Her voice was husky, but she wasn't surprised. 'If you'll let me up?' she requested, and searched desperately for some suitably light remark. And, as he got to his feet and helped her up, 'Let me know when you think *you* need to be kissed,' she said, 'and I'll see what I can do about it.' It wasn't brilliant or witty, but it was the best she could do in the circumstances.

She went to her room without another word, and, closing the door, leant against it, her head in a whirl. She had been kissed with more passion, but never so wonderfully. Harris had said that his kiss had been a prelude to nothing. But—she hadn't wanted that kiss to lead to nothing! She had wanted him to kiss her again, and again! Heavens above, what on earth was happening to her?

CHAPTER FIVE

By MORNING Mallon had her head back together again. While she was still slightly amazed at the emotional feelings Harris had aroused in her when he had kissed her so tenderly, so wonderfully, last night, she was able to convince herself that, clad as they had been, in the situation they'd been in when they had fallen in a heap together, something of the sort was not unlikely to happen.

She would watch out in future, of course. Not that the same thing would happen again. She was never ever going to leave her room in the middle of the night. Nothing, not even the vilest screaming nightmare, would make her.

She owned she was feeling just a touch out of sorts that morning. A fact not helped by the event that her shower had gone temperamental on her—she'd have a word with the plumber if he were about. Harris had said she had 'needed' to be kissed. So, okay, he had also said that it wasn't such a great chore, but his remark wasn't very complimentary, was it? Now she came to think of it, it was a downright cheek! She would prefer to be kissed because he just couldn't help it, rather than from some 'there-there, that'll make you feel better'-type diagnosis.

She there and then decided to avoid him as much as possible. It was too late now to wish she had gone to a hotel last night. And it would draw too much attention to her feeling out of sorts if she suggested she should stay at a hotel tonight.

Having washed and dressed, Mallon went downstairs to find that Harris must already be up and about—the cups and saucers they had left on the kitchen table last night had been washed and put away at any rate.

She glanced through the kitchen window and saw him in conversation with Bob Miller. Bob was earlier than usual—had it been pre-arranged he should be early, or had Harris phoned him that morning?

Mallon was not left wondering for long. She had just made a pot of tea when Harris came into the kitchen, his glance going over her long-legged trim shape in her jeans and tee shirt.

'How's my favourite caretaker?' he asked easily, coming over and looking down into her face as if to assess for himself how she was.

'Never better,' she answered lightly—no way was he going to know that he bothered her in the slightest. 'Baz brought me some new laid eggs from his hens yesterday. Boiled or scrambled?' She met his glance, but just had to look at his truly wonderful mouth, and felt her heart give a little leap when she saw his lips start to curve upwards. She looked swiftly away.

'I haven't had a newly-laid boiled egg in years,' he replied.

Mallon poured some tea and handed Bob Miller his through the kitchen window, and, feeling unsettled and jumpy inside, she got busy setting the eggs to boil.

'Have you heard from the job you wrote after?' Harris enquired conversationally when they were seated at the table.

'Are you asking me to leave?' she asked jerkily, and knew she was more jumpy—about him—than she had realised. Especially when he looked at her in some surprise.

'What brought that on?' he asked, and, when she went a touch pink with embarrassment, 'Haven't I just said that you're my favourite caretaker?'

'So...' She shrugged. 'I heard—they didn't want me.'

'Their loss is my gain,' he replied, and she just didn't need his charm. 'Talking of leaving, though,' he went on, 'it might be an idea if you made yourself scarce today.'

Solemnly she looked at him. 'But you're not asking me to leave?'

'Definitely not,' he replied, and informed her, 'There is more than one rotting floorboard on the landing. I've arranged for all the old wood to be taken up and a new floor put down today. It's only a guess, but I'd say the noise is going to be fairly horrendous.'

Mallon was used to the builders' racket, but she saw his point. 'Thanks for the tip-off.'

'I could drive you into town—you could shop to your heart's content,' he offered.

But there was a restlessness in her which Mallon couldn't understand, and all she knew was that to sit beside him in the close confines of his car was not part of her avoid-him-as-much-as-possible plan.

'It's a lovely day. I think I'll go for a walk—a long walk,' she answered, and immediately recalled how last Saturday she had been taking a walk when she had seen Roland Phillips again.

Grey eyes assessed deeply blue eyes. 'Would you like company?' Harris asked carefully, and, because she was feeling all at once extremely sensitively tuned in to his wavelength, it seemed to Mallon that Harris was remembering Roland Phillips too.

She answered slowly, but truthfully, 'I think there are some things I should do on my own.'

Harris smiled encouragingly. 'That's my—er—care-taker,' he said. But she felt a warm glow and inordinately pleased.

She set off as soon as the breakfast things had been

cleared away, and walked steadily along green leafy lanes. She wasn't making for anywhere in particular, but she had some money with her should she come across a shop.

As she had remarked to Harris, it was a lovely day, and, having endured enough rain, it was a pleasure to be out in the sun. He had offered to walk with her and she had declined, but he was in her head so much on that walk it was just as though he was there walking along beside her.

Mallon had no idea how far she had walked until all at once she recognised that she was in the area of Sherwins' shop. It seemed as good a stopping place as any.

Though as she rounded the bend to the shop, so she recognised someone coming out from Sherwins and going over to his parked car. Roland Phillips. What she could have done, because he hadn't yet seen her, was to have doubled back and disappeared down the side lane she had just come from, and stayed there until he had gone by.

She did hesitate, it was true, but suddenly she was remembering Harris saying 'That's my caretaker' and she knew that to run away was no way to slay her personal dragons.

She went on; he saw her and he stopped. 'Well, if it isn't my brother-in-law's little playmate,' he remarked nastily, his eyes doing a thorough inspection of her nevertheless. Mallon went to walk past him without a word—he didn't seem to like it. Though, ever with his eye to the main chance, 'I'm going your way. I'll give you a lift if you like?'

'No, thank you.'

'Come on—don't be stuck up,' he said, and tried to delay her by placing a hand on her arm.

Mallon found his touch revolting but, instead of being afraid, she suddenly discovered she was growing angry. 'Take your hand off me!' she ordered cuttingly.

'Don't be like that!' he answered with what he thought was a winning smile—and Mallon was all at once as angry with herself as she was with him. To think she had let this excuse for a man, this oily weasel, cause her such ghastly nights!

'I do not like you,' she started to grow furious enough to tell him. 'In fact I find you totally repulsive.' And, her indignation never higher, 'Normally I wouldn't lower myself to speak to the likes of you,' she told him scornfully. 'But I'll make an exception this once to tell you that if you ever come near me again, I shall not hesitate to report your attack on me to the police.'

He didn't like it. She didn't care, and, since she had nothing else she wanted to say to him, she pulled her arm from his slackening hold and went to take a browse round Sherwins.

From Sherwins she started to make her way back to Harcourt House. Had she thought about it she would have assumed she would have felt like bursting into tears after her encounter with Roland Phillips—but she felt more elated than anything else.

It was so good not to feel afraid any longer, and while it was true that physically that disgusting man could get the better of her, he was an intelligent man. Intelligent enough anyhow to know that any sniff that he had assaulted a woman and his executive job with a very well-thought-of company would be decidedly rocky, to say the least. She wondered why she hadn't reasoned that out before, and could only suppose that fear of the man had numbed her brain.

The nearer she got to Harcourt House, however, and thoughts of Roland Phillips began to fade. Thoughts of Harris began to dominate her head, instead. She wondered what he was doing while the carpenters were busy putting

down a new timber landing. And unexpectedly felt quite
churned up that, having come down to Harcourt House to
relax, he might have been driven out by the noise and
returned to London.

Her eyes scanned the drive for his car as she passed
between the stone pillars of his Upper Macey residence.
Most of the builders had finished for the day, but Bob
Miller's vehicle was there out front, so too was Cyril's car
and two others, but neither of them belonged to Harris.

She told herself she wasn't worried. Good heavens, why
should she worry? Harris had every right to come and go
as he pleased. But when, with the front door open, she
could have gone indoors that way, she opted to go round
to the rear of the house. His car wasn't there either.

Mallon went into the kitchen, her earlier feeling of ela-
tion completely gone. If anything she was feeling a shade
flat. Though, of course, she knew that was only because,
extra carpenters brought in, the noise was occasionally
deafening.

At half past four the floor was down and the building
workers went on their way. Since they wouldn't be back
until Monday, Mallon got out the broom and, after sweeping the landing, she swept the stairs and the downstairs
hall. Some of the dust and debris went out of the rear door,
but the dust and debris that was nearer to the front door
she swept out that way.

She was in the act of sweeping off the front steps when
an electrical wholesaler's van drove in through the gates.
She stood watching, hoping that the driver hadn't seen her
from the road and called in to ask for directions to somewhere—apart from Sherwins and Almora Lodge, she was
a stranger in these parts herself.

'Miss Braithwaite?' the driver got out to enquire, and
before she could answer, 'Got your TV for you,' he said.

She opened her mouth, but started to smile—Harris's car was coming up the drive. She turned her attention back to the TV man. 'Er—you'd better bring it into the kitchen. I don't think we've got the necessary point in the drawing room.'

'You have,' he assured her. 'One of our chaps came out earlier today.'

'The drawing room it is, then.' She showed him where to take the television set, and was in the kitchen when Harris, having stopped to have a word with the man, followed her into the kitchen.

He came nearer. 'How was your walk?' he asked evenly, his eyes searching her face as if for anything untoward.

She smiled. She felt good, and didn't want to talk about Roland Phillips. 'Fine,' she answered, and, because Harris seemed to be expecting more of a comment than that, 'I thought you'd gone back to London.'

'Oh, dear, does that mean you're glad or sorry?'

As if she'd tell him! 'That's some television set.' He turned away, but as he strolled out of the kitchen, she was sure he had a smile on his face. She guessed he had gone upstairs to inspect the new landing floor.

She thought she might go up too, and change out of the clothes she had worn all day, but suddenly she felt shy, and while she knew she was being totally ridiculous, she just couldn't get past that barrier of shyness. It was there on the landing that they had last night fallen together and he had kissed her and...

Mallon blanked off such thoughts. For goodness' sake, it had been a kiss, and, while it hadn't been the sort of kiss one gave a maiden aunt, it hadn't been very sexual either.

She concentrated her mind on dinner. She had purchased some minced beef in Sherwins—she hoped Harris liked spa-

ghetti bolognese. When she heard him come down the
stairs and go in the direction of the drawing room, Mallon
slipped out of the kitchen and up to her room to change.
She would dearly have loved to take a shower, but had
forgotten to have a word with the plumber.

Washed and changed into a cotton dress, Mallon went
downstairs again and found the television installer had
gone and that Harris was coming into the kitchen with a
couple of boxes of what looked like groceries.

'What have you got there?'

'Probably all the wrong things, but since you wouldn't
come with me, what's a mere male to do when he inves-
tigates and, I admit, gets carried away, in a supermarket?'

She had to laugh, and was still smiling when she saw
that his glance had gone to her mouth. How dear he was.
Dear! Suddenly astonished by the way her thoughts were
going, Mallon's smile abruptly departed. She felt awkward
all at once.

'Do you like spaghetti bolognese?' she asked shortly,
and knew he was staring at her as though trying to figure
out what had so suddenly gone wrong. But, when she was
certain he would demand to know why she had, on an
instant, changed from smiling to stilted, he let it go.

'Spaghetti bolognese is one of my passions,' he replied
mildly. And she knew then that it wasn't and that he was
lying.

But she didn't feel like laughing, and after some minutes
he went from the kitchen, and a minute or so later she
heard the muted sound of the television set.

When about an hour and a half later Harris joined her
in the kitchen for dinner, Mallon knew that she was feeling
more tense than awkward. She had never felt this way
before and couldn't understand it. She thought she might

have been able to understand it better had she not liked Harris. But she did like him, very much.

When Harris kept up a smooth flow of conversation throughout the meal, she gradually managed to say good-bye to her inner feeling of tension. She was truly interested when he told her of his plans for the house and how, once the house had been restored, he had plans for the outbuildings. Indeed she had started to feel quite relaxed, so relaxed that she was unsure when the conversation had changed and they began generally discussing books they had both read.

But Harris was standing next to her, drying the dishes as she washed them, when that uncomfortable feeling of tension came over her again.

'That's the lot, I think,' she said, taking a look around to see if they had missed anything. And, all chores done, she thought it best to make herself scarce before he noticed she was uptight about something. She felt she knew him well enough by then to know that he would ask why she was uptight. And how could she tell him when she didn't know why herself?

'I think you've earned an evening sitting in front of the television,' Harris teased, turning to her.

She looked at him, and her heart did a crazy little flip, and she knew then that she felt so fidgety, so on edge, that it was completely beyond her to sit silently with him in the drawing room.

'I—um—think I'll go up,' she answered, feeling dreadful that her voice had come out sounding as stilted as she was feeling. 'I've come to a good part in my book,' she lied.

Harris looked back at her, but his tone was mild when, after surveying her for a second or two, 'We needn't have the television on, if you'd prefer to bring your book down,' he suggested.

Oh, grief, this was terrible. What on earth was the matter with her? 'I think I'll have an early night,' she replied, and, thinking to end the conversation, she went to skirt round him, but only to find he had moved and had stepped in front of her.

'Something the matter, Mallon?' he asked quietly, and she felt worse than ever.

'Nothing,' she replied, sincerely hoping he would allow her to leave it there. 'Honestly,' she added, staring up at him, her deeply blue eyes troubled.

'You know you don't have to worry?' he said, and, looking at her sharply, 'Would you like me to leave?'

Her breath caught. No, she did *not* want him to leave. 'No, I wouldn't!' she answered equally sharply.

'You do know I'm not like Phillips?'

'Of course I know!' she exclaimed. 'And I'm not in the slightest worried! I just want... Goodnight,' she said abruptly.

Harris stared at her for perhaps a second longer, then stepped out of her way. Mallon went quickly. Oh, why, oh, why couldn't she be natural with him? What in creation was it about him that made her so restless one minute, so uptight the next?

She reached the privacy of her room, and knew restlessness again when she experienced an incredible urge to go downstairs again to assure Harris that she trusted him completely, and felt not one moment's disquiet with just the two of them alone under the same roof.

That compulsion, that urge, was so strong that only by telling herself that he would think her some kind of nut who had exaggerated out of all proportion his need to know she was not in the slightest worried, stopped her from giving in.

She picked up her book and took it over to the window seat. Always before she had admired the view from that window and some of its tranquillity would wash over her.

But, with that feeling of restlessness upon her, Mallon could find no tranquillity. Neither could she become involved in her book. She put it down, yet needed something to do.

She went into the bathroom and cleaned her teeth and washed her face, and wished her shower was working. She tried it anyway—there was no joy, it still wasn't working. Harris had a shower in his bathroom? No! She rejected the idea before it was born. And then remembered that there was a bathroom across the landing.

A minute later and to have a shower suddenly became a must. She went and opened her door and listened. Without any carpets or furnishings to deaden the sound, the faint noise of the television wafted up from the drawing room. Mallon quietly closed her door and without more ado slipped out of her clothes and into her cotton robe. She grabbed up her soap and a towel and in no time went from her room and across the landing, only to find that the bathroom door needed more than a push to open it.

She gave it a thump with her hip—it opened. Closing the door after her, she was soon testing to see if she was getting her hopes up over nothing. Success—the shower was in beautiful working order! In moments she had tied her hair to the top of her head, and was stepping in.

Bliss! Having been deprived of a shower all day, Mallon stood with water cascading over her shoulders for an age before she got busy with the soap. But all good things must come to an end and she finally rinsed the suds away and turned off the shower.

Her thoughts were anywhere as she slid back the shower door prior to stepping out. But as she did step out onto the bathroom floor, so she raised her eyes from watching where she was treading—a must in this never-knew-when-it-was-going-to-jump-up-and-bite-you, hazard-filled house, she had discovered—and she gasped in absolute horror. Because standing there, looking totally thunderstruck, was Harris. She had not a stitch on!

He was shirt and trouser-clad and with a towel thrown over his shoulder. He had obviously just come in and had that moment turned after closing the door after him. For a split second he gazed in stunned fascination at her naked body. Mallon froze. Then, as scarlet colour rioted and seemed to be her only covering, she let out a squeal of anguish and leapt to race past him on her way to the door.

Harris, at once reading her intent, swiftly stepped to the right—out of her way. Unfortunately, Mallon charged to the left, and they collided. He put out a hand to save her, but his touch scalded her, and, her sights set on that door, she pushed him out of the way. She made a lunge for the door—and found it stuck fast!

But, while she was panicking wildly, Harris was getting everything together and had spotted her robe where she had left it. He snatched it up and suddenly he was there at the door with her. 'You're all right, Mallon,' he attempted to soothe her, arranging her robe over her naked shoulders. 'You're safe,' he went on calmly. 'Nothing's going to harm you.' He raised her robe a little and, finding the armholes, 'Put your arms in,' he instructed, but even as—some of her panic starting to fade—she tried to do as he said, it just wasn't happening.

'You try getting wet arms into thin cotton!' she erupted. But, albeit that it wasn't easy, because she insisted on having some of the material to cover up her front when he lent a hand, he made a better job of it than she did. In no time she was covered. He even managed to find the tie belt.

'There,' he said, and Mallon discovered that she must have turned around, because she was suddenly facing him and was looking up into his warm grey eyes. 'All tied up like a Christmas parcel,' he gently teased.

Unbelievably, she found she was smiling, and guessed that that was perhaps his intention. 'I meant to have a word with the plumber. My shower wasn't working this morning,' she explained.

'Neither was mine,' Harris replied, adding, 'When I heard what I thought was your shower in operation, I thought what a good idea, and came to see if this one was in business.' He smiled then, and asked, 'All right now?'

'Y-yes,' Mallon stammered. She was over her shock, but with him so close she was suddenly very much aware of him. 'I'll go,' she said, and turned, ready to give the doorknob another hard tug.

But Harris reached for the doorknob at the same time and, even as he remarked, 'Another job for the carpenters,' and went to move her to one side, he unthinkingly put an arm about her thinly clad shoulders.

The feel of his hand over her hand, the feel of his arm across her shoulders, seemed to cause her to freeze again. She wasn't moving anyway. But supposed that somehow she must have moved—half turned at any rate—towards him. And Harris must have half turned to her too, because all at once they were facing each other again, staring at each other. Staring into one another's eyes.

His hand came away from hers, and she took her hand from the doorknob. 'Mallon.' He murmured her name. Then slowly his head started to come down. Mallon could not have turned from him then had her life depended upon it. And when his mouth met hers, his kiss was what she wanted.

His kiss was gentle, and was over almost as soon as it had begun. But as he broke that gentle kiss he drew her closer to him and, as if he could not resist, he buried his face in her neck. 'You smell wonderful,' he breathed, and while her heart started to beat a crazy rhythm, he pressed his lips to her throat. She felt his grip on her waist tighten momentarily, then Harris was pulling back, straightening up, and taking a pace back. His warm grey eyes studied her deep blue ones and softly he asked, 'Are you going to forgive me for being a mere male?'

Her feelings of panic were a thing of the past, but to be close to Harris like this was sending all sorts of conflicting messages to her. 'I—think I should go,' she decided, her decision very shaky because, staggeringly, she didn't think she wanted to go at all!

'You're not scared of me?' he questioned, his hands falling to his sides.

Mallon felt anything but scared. More, she wanted his hands back on her waist—they'd seemed, just then, to be-long there. 'Not at all,' she told him with a smile, and added, perhaps a little less honestly, 'I don't—I mean—I know it was only a small kiss, but I don't want to go any further.' Small kiss! It was blowing her *mind*!

Harris returned her smile and took perhaps another half-step away as he commented, 'Little Mallon Braithwaite—' she'd always thought herself quite tall '—I don't think you've been very far with any man, have you?'

She could have taken exception to his question, but didn't. Suddenly she was feeling happy. And, incredibly, given that she was standing there in her thin robe and nothing else, she felt happy and comfortable with him again—and, once more, able to tell him anything.

'I came close once,' she confessed. And saw he looked interested.

'I do hope, Miss Braithwaite, that, having given me that surprise, you're not going to leave it there.' She laughed. 'When was this?' he wanted to know.

'Oh, a couple of months or so ago.'

'What happened?' Harris persisted.

And Mallon, strangely, now, finding nothing wrong with being dressed the way she was while having this conversation, discovered too that it didn't hurt one tiny bit as she told him, 'He said he loved me. We'd arranged to go away together one weekend. Only at the last minute I couldn't go—so he took my friend instead.'

'Oh, Mallon, you poor love,' Harris murmured.

'Well, she was his friend as well. The three of us worked together.'

'That was your reason for leaving your job?' he questioned, as perceptive as ever. But, no longer smiling, he didn't wait for her to answer but asked abruptly, 'Did you love him?' And, when she did not answer quickly enough, 'Are you still in love with him?' he demanded.

Mallon stared equally solemn-faced at Harris, a gasp of surprise taking her as, like a thunderbolt, it shatteringly at that moment dawned on her why her emotions had been so all over the place just recently. 'No,' she said, and knew it for a certainty. 'I was never in love with him.'

'But, you being you, you must have been extremely fond of him to have contemplated going away with him?'

'It seems ages ago now.' Mallon dismissed the subject lightly, and saw that Harris had taken on board that it was all in her past, dead and buried. 'I'd better go and leave you to your shower,' she said, though she did not want to do anything of the kind.

'Am I allowed to kiss you better before you go?' His good humour appeared to have returned.

Mallon smiled up at him. It didn't hurt—there was nothing to kiss better. Her non-fling with Keith Morgan didn't hurt a bit now, and she was happy. But, because she couldn't help it, and it had been a sort of an invitation anyway, she went forward and stretched up and kissed Harris on his cheek.

Only as she went to pull away Harris, probably thinking to steady her, placed a hand on her ribcage—and she found his touch through the thin material of her robe electric. Their faces were close as they stared at each other, and by mutual consent, naturally, it seemed, they moved together and his mouth was over hers. This time his kiss was nothing like the other two times he had kissed her. It started out gentle and tender, just a meeting of lips, but all at once Mallon was giving in to her need to touch him and, as her arms went around him, so Harris eased her into his arms. As their bodies touched, so his kiss deepened.

Nor did it stay at one kiss. He held her to him, her thin covering no covering at all as he kissed her throat once more, and then again claimed her lips.

'Sweet Mallon,' he murmured, and drew back to look into her eyes. Then, as if he could not resist, 'My dear,' he said softly; and when she was aching for him to kiss her again, her ache was eased when, again, warmly, his kiss intensifying, he lingeringly embraced her again.

Her arms went up and around him when his hands caressed over her back. She loved the feel of his caressing hands, especially when his hands pressed her closer to him.

Tenderly he kissed her throat, tracing kisses up to her ear, one hand caressing to the front of her, moving slowly upwards until gently, gradually, her right breast was captive in his hold.

She leaned her head against his shoulder, his touch as he moulded her breast doing mindless things to her, enchanting her. He kissed her again, his hand lingering, his fingers teasing the hardened nub of her breast.

Then, as if the cotton of her robe was too much of an intrusion, he took his hand from her breast. While holding her close with one arm, while kissing her and seeming to draw the very soul from her as she responded fully, he caressed her spine. Then, while moving, caressing, caressing tenderly up to her throat and down, that hand gently slipped inside her robe.

Mallon felt his sensitive touch capture the naked silken skin of her right breast, and as those sensitive fingers teased at the hardened peak a whole gamut of emotions started to explode within her. She started to sink from the emotion of what he was doing to her, of what he was drawing from her, and a gasp of drowning broke from her.

But her gasp of sound, faint though it had been, reached Harris and he stilled. Although his hand lingered on the wonderful swollen curve of her breast for a second longer, then he reluctantly dragged it across the hardened tip, and finally removed it from her. Then he pulled back to look into her face.

'You're in no danger,' he quietly assured her.

'I...' was about all she could manage as his hands settled on her waist. He straightened up to look searchingly into her disturbed blue eyes, and she was left fighting desperately hard to get herself together. 'I don't want you to kiss me again,' she lied.

'I should think not too,' he answered. 'Disgraceful behaviour.' But he was serious when, allowing some daylight between their two bodies, he said, 'I mean what I said, Mallon—you're safe.'

'I know,' she answered, and turned from him, but was

in such a turmoil she had less chance than before of opening the stuck door.

Harris came to the rescue and tugged the door open for her to pass through. 'You're all right, Mallon?' he asked before he let her go.

How could he be so calm when she was such a riot of jangling nerve-ends? 'I'm fine,' she assured him. 'Don't worry.' With that she walked by him and to her bedroom.

Safe? He had aroused such a clamour of out-of-control feelings and emotions in her. But, all too clearly, with that quiet assurance of, 'You're in no danger,' he had been supremely in control of his own feelings and emotions the whole of the time. He had kissed her and she had been emotionally all over the place. But their exchange of kisses had not disturbed him in the slightest! Look how easily he had let her go!

Safe? What was safe about being in love with a man who just did not want to know?

CHAPTER SIX

HARRIS was in her head the moment Mallon awakened on Sunday. She *was* in love with him. It was a fact. It would not go away. The only mystery was—how had it taken so long for her to realise what had been going on inside her? It had started from the first week that she had known him!

Explained, now, were those moments of shyness, of feeling tongue-tied, awkward, but oh, so joyful to see him. This was why she had felt so restless on occasions. This was why... She found herself reliving again his kisses, his touch.

How on earth had she ever imagined that what she felt for Keith Morgan had been love? The fact that he had soon found solace elsewhere when she hadn't been able to go away with him had hurt at the time, but Mallon could only ponder, had it been more hurt pride than anything else? Perhaps she'd experienced a little pain too that he had revealed himself as being fickle and coming from a similar stable to Ambrose and Lee Jenkins.

Whatever, now that she knew the strength of her feelings for Harris—her love for him—Mallon knew that what she had felt for Keith had been nothing remotely like love.

Mallon left her bed to wash and dress, wondering if she had perhaps been looking for an excuse not to go away with Keith that time. She certainly hadn't protested too much when she hadn't been able to go—in fact, she couldn't remember protesting at all.

But Keith Morgan was far from her head when, having

to pause first and take a deep breath, Mallon opened her bedroom door.

Sounds below told her that Harris was up and about, and for some seconds she felt such a confusion of emotions, wanting to see him, eager to see him again, yet all of a sudden so overwhelmingly shy to see him, that she just could not move.

But, knowing that she could not stand there dithering all day, she took another deep breath and started off along the landing with no idea of what she would say to Harris. She had last night lyingly told him that she did not want him to kiss her again, but oh, how she had wanted him to kiss her—and to go on kissing her! He had aroused needs and desires in her, and she had wanted to make love with him; had he refused to accept her lie, then she didn't know what would have happened. She hadn't been at all scared; that was one thing she knew for certain.

So how was she supposed to greet him? Was she supposed to just breeze in with a bright Good morning? She could still feel the enrapturing imprint of his caressing hand on her breast, for goodness' sake!

Mallon's dilemma of how she was to greet him, after what to her had been a great degree of intimacy last night, evaporated into nothing when she went into the kitchen. A little too shy to look directly at him for a moment, her eyes went instead to his weekend bag standing on the kitchen table, his car keys next to it!

Dread smote her like a blow. All too plainly, Harris was on the point of departure. 'You don't have to leave because of me!' came blurting from her before she could stop it, her eyes shooting to his.

She wanted to retract the words as soon as they were out, but it was too late. She wanted to run, to hide, but Harris was smiling. 'Because of you?' he queried lightly.

But she knew that he knew quite well what she was referring to, though whether he was teasing her she was too churned up to know. But the fact that they'd had, for the want of better words, an amorous encounter, was out in the open—and Mallon did the only thing left to her. She grinned as she suggested, 'If you promise to never again enter rooms without first knocking, I'll promise to never again prance around n…with nothing on.'

He grinned in return. But then his grin went into hiding, and he was all seriousness when he questioned, 'You slept all right? No—ill effects?'

She hadn't slept so well, but not because she had been worried or afraid. But what she was afraid of now was that if she told him just how unworried and unafraid she had been, she might give away something of how she felt about him.

'Oh, Mallon, my dear,' Harris murmured when she delayed too long in her search for some neutral kind of answer. 'You should have slept soundly. You were never in that sort of jeopardy!'

Had he been trying to calm any fears he thought she might have had, then Mallon did not thank him for it. He was as good as telling her that had she not called a halt to their lovemaking, then he would have done so. Either that or he was saying that she did not have as much sex appeal as she might think she had!

From another, desperate, pride-backed somewhere, she found another grin. 'That's all right, then,' she answered brightly, not caring at all to be as good as told that she came way down in the desirability stakes. And, just to let him know that she didn't care a hoot whether he went or stayed, 'Anything caustic you want me to tell the plumber tomorrow?'

She dared a glance at Harris and thought she saw a hint

of admiration in his eyes at her manner. But she wasn't into trusting her imagination just then—though she all but crumbled when he answered, 'Just tell him that through his negligence the two of us could have got into a great deal of trouble.'

Mallon had to laugh—she rather thought Harris had meant her to. But the next second she didn't feel at all like laughing because he was picking up his bag and car keys. 'Drive safely,' some proud being she was just starting to get to know bade him.

His answer was to come close and drop a light kiss on her cheek in passing. 'Bye,' he said, and went.

How long after he had gone she stood there with her hand pressed against the cheek he had kissed, Mallon didn't know. What she did know was that she, who had never particularly craved other company, was lonely. Not lonely for anyone else—just lonely for Harris.

Somehow she limped through the rest of that day, Harris rarely out of her thoughts. Wasn't love supposed to be joyful? She supposed it would be—if that love were returned. Fate gave a scornful laugh. Fat chance!

On Monday, the plumber sorted the showers out, and her day was brightened on Tuesday when a telephone engineer came to install a telephone. It was a nice surprise. Harris had said nothing about having ordered the service.

That evening Mallon made use of it by ringing her mother and at the same time giving her the telephone number and having a lovely chat. Her mother was extremely happy, and it did Mallon's heart good to hear her sound more bubbly than she could remember her being since Mallon's father had died.

The next few days dragged by, but when Friday arrived Mallon started to feel all agitated inside with anticipation.

Harris had driven down last Friday. Perhaps he would drive down today.

She went to bed that night nursing disappointment. She had seen no sign of him, neither had he telephoned. Saturday dawned bright and sunny. Mallon felt pretty much the same. Harris might come today!

But he did not come that day either, nor the next day. The phone stayed silent all weekend, and Mallon endured endless pangs of wanting to see him, and of having him constantly in her head.

The sunny weather turned into a heat wave, and on Monday Mallon started to look forward to the weekend, hoping that, should Harris come down—and surely he must—the weather would hold. She doubted he was able to spend very much time during the week out of doors.

When the builders departed on Monday, she got out the broom and gave the drawing room a sweep and a dust. With the builders hard at their labours, she could have spent her day sweeping and dusting. She was in the drawing room early on Tuesday morning, checking the room over, when for the first time ever the telephone rang—and she all but jumped a mile.

With her heart starting to race, even though she told herself it would be her mother, Mallon went to answer it. 'Hello?' she answered, her voice calm enough. But her heart started to thunder when she recognised her caller's voice.

'Everything going as planned?' Harris enquired coolly.

'No problems,' Mallon replied. She knew she had a smile in her voice—she couldn't help it.

'Good,' he answered, and Mallon, sensing that his call was about to end, desperately wanted to ask if he would be down at the weekend. But couldn't.

'What's your weather doing?' Had she really asked that?

Was she so desperate to keep him on the line she was
asking about *weather*! 'I expect you're enduring the same
heat wave we are.' Shut up! Shut up! 'The joiners have
made a lovely job of that piece of banister that needed
turning,' she adopted a bright tone to tell him cheerfully.
'Er—did you want to have a word with Bob? I think he's
around somewhere. I can go and find...'

'No need. If you tell me there aren't any problems, I'm
sure it's so,' he answered, and rang off.

Mallon put down the phone and was in such an emotional stew that just then she had to be on her own. The
builders were good and gave her as much privacy as they
could, given that they were in and out of the house the
whole time. She went up to her room and shut herself
away.

Why hadn't she asked him if he was coming down at
the weekend? Or even when he might next be down? It
would have been a perfectly normal question to have
asked, surely?

When she felt she had herself back together again,
Mallon took herself off for a walk, knowing that her love
for Harris had made her vulnerable. Vulnerable and proud
that he should not see so much as a glimmer of her feelings
for him. So that what had once been normal was now
questioned, just in case she might be giving herself away.

She returned to Harcourt House. She had hoped that her
walk might make her feel better, but it had not. What did
make her feel better, however, was to glance out of the
kitchen window at lunchtime, just in time to see Harris's
car glide by.

Emotional colour immediately flooded her face, so she
was glad it would take him a minute or two to get to the
kitchen. Hello stranger? No. Today's not Friday or Saturday, is it? No.

Her rehearsed greetings vanished into thin air when, tall, good-looking and with the jacket of his business suit in one hand, Harris walked into the kitchen. 'What are you doing here?' she asked, her heart drumming; she loved him so much! 'Not, of course, that, since you own the place, you can't come and go as you please,' she said lightly, with a small laugh.

Harris did not laugh. In fact there wasn't so much as a smile about him when he stated, 'Talking of problems—I have one I need to discuss with you.'

Alarm instantly filled her. He was going to ask her to leave; she knew that he was! But she didn't want to leave, not now! Not now that she knew she was in love with him. Was that it? Had he seen her love? Was that why he had come personally to tell her to go? Pride suddenly became her ally. He might *think* she was in love with him—she was going to see to it that he had very serious doubts about that.

'I was going to make myself a coffee and a sandwich. Are you in a rush?' she asked pleasantly. It had only been a temporary job anyway. She would tell him that. Should she tell him first that she was leaving before he told her to go? She rather thought that she might.

'A sandwich would be fine,' he answered evenly, and Mallon got out bread, butter, cheese and ham—and reconsidered. She loved him so much; she mustn't be hasty. Perhaps he hadn't come to give her her marching orders. Perhaps... But why...?

She made a plate of sandwiches for them both, but all at once she had no appetite. He draped his jacket over the back of a chair and she made a pot of coffee.

'So what's the problem?' she asked when they were seated at the kitchen table. 'Nothing too serious, I hope.'

Harris placed a sandwich on his plate, and looked across to her. And then said, 'It's Faye.'

Relief drenched her—it didn't sound as if Harris was telling her goodbye. 'Your sister?' she asked, striving to keep her voice level.

He nodded. 'Faye rang me, shortly after I'd phoned you,' he replied. 'It afterwards occurred to me that, if she was passing this way, she might call in to see you.'

Mallon hadn't a clue what he meant by that. Passing this way, Faye would obviously be *en route* to Almora Lodge. But what was Harris saying—that he didn't want his sister to know that Mallon was here at Harcourt House? Was he, after all, asking her to go? 'You couldn't have rung me back and discussed this over the phone?' Mallon asked, her awful feeling of insecurity causing her to go on the attack.

Harris looked at her, his expression solemn. 'It isn't as simple as that,' he replied.

What wasn't? Mallon stared back at him, then all at once something clicked, and, 'Why would your sister call here—to see me?' she asked. And, annoyed suddenly, she exclaimed indignantly, 'You don't want me to tell her what a lecherous swine her husband is. That's it, isn't it? Well, of course I wouldn't!' She was outraged. 'Thanks very much for your high opinion of me!' she snapped.

Only to have her indignation and her feelings of outrage instantly pricked, when Harris replied, 'It's because I hold you in high regard that I've chosen to take time off to come and see you rather than phone.'

Oh, Harris! He held her in high regard! 'Er...' She tried to think clearly. 'So—er—what's the—um—problem?' she asked with what thinking power she had left.

'The problem is that my sister, as clever as she undoubt-edly is, is still in love with that low-life she married. I've tried to set her straight—it only made for bad blood between us. So, for the moment, that leaves me having to stand back unable to do anything but just be there to support her as and when I feel called upon to do so.'

Mallon guessed it went very much against the grain for him to stand back, and she could only admire him that, when he must care a lot for his sister, he would do that.

'You—feel the need to support her now about something?' Mallon sifted through what he had said so far, and might be implying.

'The crux of the problem is that Faye, while still hoping to salvage her marriage, got to hear that Phillips has a mistress,' Harris began. 'She had just been in contact with him and was close to being hysterical when she rang me this morning, wanting to know how I could let her down so badly by having her husband's mistress...' He broke off, but was looking directly into Mallon's serious blue eyes when he ended, '...living here in my house.'

'*Me!*' Mallon exclaimed, her mouth falling open in shock. 'He t-told her that *I* was his m-mistress?'

'Incredible, isn't it?'

Mallon was very near speechless. 'The reptile!' she gasped, and then recalled the last time she had seen Roland Phillips. 'I did this!' she blurted out.

'You did this?' Harris challenged—and she rushed on.

'He's paying me back. I saw him...'

'When?' Harris cut aggressively through what she was saying. 'When did you see him? Has he been here again?' he demanded.

'No!' Mallon answered. 'It was—er—the other Saturday.'

'The day after I told him not to come here again?'

Mallon nodded. 'I'd gone for a walk. I think to prove to myself that I wasn't scared.'

'I remember,' Harris inserted, his tone quieter. He continued to be gentle as he asked, 'How did you feel when you saw him?'

She smiled then. 'Not scared,' she answered. 'What I was, was angry. I got stroppy anyway and told him I found him totally repulsive and something to the effect that, were it not for the fact of telling him that if he ever came near me again I would report him to the police, I wouldn't lower myself to speak to the likes of him.'

'You did that?' Harris asked, and she basked for a moment in what she thought was admiration in his eyes. But his expression was changing as he questioned, 'How have you been sleeping?'

With Harris so much in her head, the fact that she loved him so much but that he would never love her, badly, was her answer. 'I haven't had one single, solitary bad dream since, if that's what you're asking,' she replied. 'But we're digressing. Naturally, should your sister call, I would most definitely let her know that I'm not her husband's mistress. I'll...'

'You won't have to,' Harris interrupted. But, oddly then, he paused for a moment before he added, 'I've already convinced her of that.'

Normally Mallon would have accepted that, and would perhaps have said something to the effect that that was all right, then. But something—maybe something in his pause—perhaps something in her heightened sensitivity to him—had her questioning.

'And—she believed you? Just like that?' They were talking here of a woman who was very much in love with her husband. Would Faye, no matter how much of a rat that man might be, believe, with no evidence, that the woman her husband had said was his mistress was not—purely on her brother's say so? Particularly as the said

mistress was living only a few miles up the road from him?
'How?' Mallon asked. 'How did you convince her?'

'Ah,' Harris murmured, and Mallon instinctively knew
she was not going to like his answer, whatever it was. Her
instinct was proved right, even if he did preface it with,
'As I mentioned, Faye was close to being hysterical. The
only way I could think to calm her down was to tell her
that you were not *his* girlfriend—but mine.'

Mallon stared at him staggered. 'Mistress!' she exploded. 'You said *mistress*! You told your sister I was your
m...' She couldn't believe it. 'What else did you tell her
that she was likely to believe?' she questioned with sharp
sarcasm, her eyes flashing sparks.

Harris met her angry gaze full on, but did not duck from
answering. 'I tried to keep as near to the truth as possible,'
he owned.

'Oh, it sounds like it!' she flared hostilely.

'I was wrong. I know I was wrong. But she was hurting—I've sort of got used to picking her up and making
her feel better when she's fallen down. It's second nature
to me, I suppose.'

Mallon felt herself beginning to soften. She made herself
toughen up. He was outrageous! What he had told his sister
was outrageous. 'So?' Mallon questioned belligerently.

'So I told her you had worked for Phillips for a few
weeks, mainly when he was out of the country. That you
had walked out on him when he'd come home and made
a pass at you.'

Well, that was true. 'Go on,' Mallon invited stonily.

'I said I was driving by and, as you didn't have transport, offered you a lift to the station, but that before we
got there I offered you a job here and—um—things went
on from there.'

'Just as if I was any sort of—fl-floozie, who'd hop into bed with any...'

'Of course not!' Harris cut her off sharply.

'Not much!' Mallon cried, and, starting to get too stewed up to sit still any longer, she shot to her feet—and so did he. As toe to toe they faced each other, she erupted again, 'Then—after your phone call—you realised that your sister might belt down here to have it out with her husband, and that she might also take it into her head to call in here and say hello to me. And you couldn't have that, so you hot-footed it down here...'

'I wanted to tell you personally. I...'

'You have!' Mallon snapped, and, too het up suddenly to stay talking to him, she announced angrily, 'I'm going for a walk!' She was over by the door when she threw over her shoulder, 'I hope, if you've any decency, that you'll be gone by the time I get back!'

She set off at a brisk pace, but within five minutes the heat of the day caused her to slow down. She was still angry with Harris, though. Why couldn't he have told his sister the truth? So, okay, Faye had been hysterical, but who did Harris Quillian think he was, telling his sister that she was his mistress? Even if his sister was hurting quite desperately and in urgent need to know that by no chance was he housing her husband's mistress.

The thought of Faye Phillips's dreadful hurt weakened Mallon a little. Poor Faye. She had been hoping to be reconciled with her husband—but, by the look of it, he didn't want to know. Mallon pushed such weakening thoughts away from her. She wanted to stay angry. Even if Harris Quillian had grown up looking out for his sister, that still didn't give him the right to go round telling her what he had—even if it had calmed her and made her feel a little better.

Mallon had walked for about a mile when she realised she was feeling calmer herself. She even began to wonder what she had got so stewed up about? True, she didn't want to be thought of as any man's mistress, but, it was only a name after all. *She* knew she wasn't. *He* knew she wasn't, and, oh, hang it—she'd said she hoped he'd be gone by the time she got back.

Mallon turned about, trying not to see the funny side of it. It was his house, when all was said and done. He could come and go as he pleased—and she had more or less ordered him out!

She made her way back to Harcourt House knowing that, while inwardly she might still be a little angry with him, that she might not even like him very much just then, she still loved the swine. If he had gone, heaven alone knew when she might see him again.

There was a car on the drive Mallon did not recognise when she reached Harcourt House. She took little notice of it. With so many expert tradesmen about there seemed always to be some different car or other parked about. Anyhow, there was only one car she was interested in seeing.

It was still there. She breathed a sigh of relief—and could afford to be angry again. Harris must have heard her coming along the hall, for he suddenly appeared from the drawing room.

Her intention to turn into the kitchen without a word was thwarted, however, when Harris smilingly called, 'I'm glad you're back. We have a visitor.'

Mallon halted, the smart-looking car on the drive and her earlier spat with Harris and its contents merging with that '*We* have a visitor', and starting to mean something.

'How nice!' she answered pleasantly, unsure how sharp Faye Phillips's ears were—if Harris Quillian was waiting for a smile, though, he'd have a long wait. She went towards him, but was glad he had the sense not to put an arm across her shoulders as he escorted her to the drawing room.

A tall dark-haired woman, about ten years younger than Harris, was standing watching the door when they went in. 'You must be Mallon,' she said. For all she smiled her greeting, Mallon thought Faye looked sad and vulnerable and, if she wasn't mistaken, just a little red around the eyes, as if she had recently been crying.

Harris introduced them and Mallon smiled brightly, and said, 'Hello,' adding, 'I'm sorry I wasn't here when you arrived. I popped out for a walk.'

'While I did a building inspection,' Harris slipped in.

'I should have let you know I was stopping by,' Faye said apologetically to Mallon, hesitated, and then added, 'You've probably guessed I've been to see Roly.'

'I thought perhaps you might.' Mallon could see no point in pretending otherwise. But, not wanting Harris's sister to dwell on something that had clearly been, and still was, very painful to her, 'Have you eaten? I can get you…'

'I couldn't eat a thing.' Faye Phillips smiled.

'But you don't have to dash back, I hope?' From what Mallon could see, the woman was in need of large doses of TLC.

'Oh, that's kind of you. The setting here is so tranquil.'

'You must stay as long as you like,' Harris invited.

'Are you sure?' Faye turned to Mallon and confided, 'I feel a bit of a wreck, actually. While I do have a meeting in London early tomorrow morning, I wouldn't mind at all relaxing down here overnight. Would that be all right with you, Mallon?' she asked. 'Harris mentioned about a month ago that, albeit undecorated and minimally furnished, he now has two bedrooms just about habitable.'

Mallon's thoughts were quickly into how she would give her Harris's room, when he answered his sister's question for her. 'Of course you must stay. You'll be able to get to know each other. You'd like that, wouldn't you, Mallon?' he asked.

'I'd be delighted to have your company,' Mallon assured Faye, knowing she had no option and hoping that, since Faye knew of her employment with Roland Phillips and her 'involvement' with Harris, she'd barely have to be on her guard, if at all.

Which would all have been fine but for two things: Harris checking his watch and commenting generally, 'I shall shortly have to think about getting back to London,' and his sister objecting strongly to the idea.

'Oh, you can't!' she cried.

'I can't?' he queried, with a brother's teasing expression on his face.

'You've come down to be with Mallon. I shall feel dreadful if you go back because I'm here,' she wailed. 'I can have the spare room, can't I, Mallon? And...' Her voice tailed off. The unhappy woman looked so near to tears again that Mallon couldn't bear it, because it seemed to her that Faye had probably got an overnight bag with her and had hoped, expected, to be staying overnight at Almora Lodge.

'Certainly you can,' she declared cheerfully, and looked at Harris, fully expecting him to gently insist that he had business in London that just would not wait.

But, to her utter astonishment, 'We can't have Faye feeling like that, can we, Mallon? It looks as though matters financial in London will have to wait.'

Mallon was still staring at him uncomprehendingly when Faye said that, since they hadn't known she was coming, the room wouldn't be ready, and began to insist

on making up the bed herself. Only then did it dawn on
Mallon that, while other bedrooms in the house were in
the process of being replastered, they were nowhere near
ready for anyone to sleep in them.

Even while she was quickly mentally switching Faye
over to have the one habitable guest room—her room—
Mallon was startlingly realising that there was only *one*
other bed in the house!

Her eyes shot to Harris, but from the way he stared
urbanely back she knew that he had also done the two-
beds-divided by-three-people calculation. 'I wouldn't
dream of letting you.' She found she was answering Faye's
insistence to make up her own bed. But, very much aware
that Faye thought she and her brother slept together,
Mallon still expected Harris to intervene. When he did no
such thing, Mallon started to get angry. Though bearing in
mind that the best way to convince Faye that she was not
her husband's mistress was to let her believe she shared a
bed with Harris, Mallon managed to hide her anger by
adding, 'Though since I'm hot and sticky from my walk,
and need a shower, I wouldn't mind if one of you nipped
out to the supermarket for me.'

'I'll go,' Faye offered at once. But before Mallon could
begin to wind up to what she would say to one Mr Harris
Quillian, once the two of them were alone, he was offering
to go to into town to the supermarket with his sister.

'Perhaps you'd like to give me a list,' he suggested.

She'd like to give him a punch on the head! Mallon
concocted a list and handed it to him. He glanced at the
first item and his lips twitched and Mallon again felt the
need for physical violence. He thought the first item—'I
hate you, Quillian'—was funny!

'We'll go now,' he told his sister, and as Faye took a
step towards the door so Harris came over to Mallon and

bending down, on the pretext of kissing her cheek, he breathed in her ear, 'Promise you'll still be here when I get back?'

Her insides felt all wobbly at the firm hold of his hands on her arms, at the touch of his wonderful mouth against her cheek. Though, from some stronger somewhere, she managed to grit beneath her breath, 'Don't tempt me!' As he stepped back, she smiled at Faye. 'Bye.'

Mallon stood motionless for a minute or two after they had gone. It was, she admitted, tempting to leave. That monster Quillian didn't deserve any better. Against that, though, and aside from the fact that she had nowhere else to go if she didn't want to go and park herself on her mother and John, she still loved the monster.

Leaving the drawing room, Mallon went up the stairs to survey the two habitable bedrooms. She had no intention of sharing a bedroom with him, though—she just couldn't. She remembered her responses to him that Saturday when he had come for a shower just after she'd had hers. No! It was impossible. She wouldn't! She couldn't. If he kissed her again…! Stop it! Why would he kiss her again? Get your head together, do.

Mallon started work on the two rooms. But, even as she worked, she knew it wouldn't come to sharing a room with him. There was no mistaking his sister's look of vulnerability, but she had seemed reasonably calm—well, certainly not hysterical, as Harris said she had been when she had phoned him. Perhaps, while they were out, Harris would tell Faye the truth of their arrangement here. Perhaps he would tell her that she was his caretaker and nothing more than that.

But Faye was hurting, was hurting very badly. What better way to convince her that she did have his total support, that he was not housing her husband's mistress? What better way to convince her...?

Mallon took her toiletries out from the one bathroom and transferred them, along with some of her belongings, into the next-door bedroom and bathroom. Any items remaining in the wardrobe and drawers could, she felt, quite understandably be put down to her spreading out while waiting for the bedrooms to be fully furnished.

Making up both beds with fresh linen, Mallon became more and more sure that Harris would have come up with a pretty good explanation while he and Faye were out. Though the weakening thought did start to creep in that, if the worst did come to the worst and she did have to share a room with him, then, since the weather was so hot, and nobody would want many clothes on the bed, he could have the duvet for a mattress on the floor.

But she quickly cancelled that soft-hearted thought; it wouldn't come to that. While it was true that Faye was distressed and must inwardly be hurting dreadfully—and it was also true that Harris was doing the very best he could to take care of her—Mallon started to grow more and more confident that, by the time they returned, he would have told Faye all that there was to tell her.

Perhaps they'd have a laugh about it before he went back to London, Mallon mused when at last she was able to take a shower, though since she was using Harris's bathroom she first locked the door. She even smiled to herself, knowing that she had been worrying needlessly. In fact, so certain did she become that she had nothing at all to worry about, she determined that, once she'd finished her shower, she would set about moving everything back into her own room.

Once she had dried off and changed into fresh underwear and a fresh dress, though, she remembered that Kevin usually called in at the kitchen around now. Ostensibly to fill his kettle, but in reality looking for a cup of tea.

She was half minded to let him make his own tea, but he was such a willing lad and was always pleased to give her a lift in the van to anywhere she wanted to go. So, instead of moving her belongings back to her own room, she went downstairs to make Kevin a cup of tea.

The tea was just made when Harris's car went past the kitchen window. 'Here comes the boss,' Kevin announced. 'I'll take my tea outside, then I'll go and see how my horses have done.' Kevin liked his daily small flutter on the races. 'Want anything bringing back?' he asked.

'Not today,' she answered with a smile, and was pouring his tea when Harris and his sister appeared with plastic carriers of shopping.

As Kevin took his tea with him, Mallon looked to Harris and Faye. They were not smiling as if about to tell her that all had been revealed, and Mallon waited.

'Harris said you liked flowers.' Faye found a smile, and handed her a lovely bouquet of yellow roses.

'Thank you. Aren't they beautiful!' Mallon exclaimed, taking them from her. She waited. Still nothing. 'I've made some tea,' she announced.

'Shall I get my overnight bag in first?' Faye asked, confirming for Mallon that the poor woman had half anticipated that she would be staying overnight at Almora Lodge.

'You didn't tell her?' Mallon challenged as soon as Faye Phillips was out of earshot.

'Tell her?'

Mallon had a momentary, and joyful, vision of Quillian with a cauliflower ear. She controlled herself. 'Why can't you tell Faye the truth about…?'

'About Phillips? You'd like me to tell her that her husband, the man she is so besotted with, assaulted you, tore your clothing, and the devil alone knows what he would have attempted had you not been able to get away?' he challenged harshly. 'You can see how she is now. What do you think it would do to her to know that?'

Mallon's anger faded into nothing. 'You don't think she has an idea what he's capable of?' she questioned in a half-hearted attempt not to be defeated.

'I strongly suspect that she has,' he answered. 'But she's heard as much about him just lately as she can take. I honestly don't think she's up to taking much more. I've done what I can—she has to sift through everything now in her own quiet time.'

'And will she?'

'She will. She has a fine brain. I don't think she's far off realising that she's been totally blinkered where Phillips is concerned.' Harris looked seriously at Mallon when he added, 'Faye and I came close to being enemies when she wouldn't listen to my telling her some truths about him. I've since had to swallow down my natural instincts and go along with her because...'

'Because you need her to know you'll be there to support her when the scales finally fall from her eyes,' Mallon cut in without thinking.

'Oh, Mallon, you understand so well,' he murmured, and, when she had quite forgotten why she had been angry with him, or, in fact, that she had ever been angry with him at all, he added softly, 'In fact, my dear, as well as being beautiful on the outside, you have an inner beauty that hits me time and time again.'

Mallon stared at him, her heart racing. Did he really think that about her? She felt weak at the knees. But then quickly realised that, whether he did or whether he didn't, it was still miles away from him being in love with her.

If she didn't want him to know what effect his words had on her, then she had better get her act together—and be sharp about it!

'So where did you suppose you might be sleeping tonight?' she asked pithily.

Harris looked at her, annoying her afresh that, instead of being put out, there actually seemed to be a hint of humour in his grey eyes. 'Ah, Mallon, you wouldn't have me sleep in my car, would you?' he asked.

She smiled the sweetest smile. 'Of course not,' she answered nicely, and, her sweet tone fading, she retorted, 'For preference I'd have you sleep in a ditch!' He had just burst out laughing when his sister returned. Mallon transferred her attention to Faye. 'Your room's all ready, I'll come up with you, if you like, while Harris puts the shopping away.'

Against all the odds, dinner that evening—chicken and vegetables with custard tart, and cheese and biscuits to follow—was a surprisingly pleasant meal. Mallon could only put the fact that the meal seemed so without strain of any sort down to the fact that all three of them were making an effort.

She knew that *she* was making an effort. In her empathy with Faye she had bottled down her tremendous inner disquiet about having to share a room with Harris. She had searched and searched for alternatives, and in truth had come up with many: drawing room sofa, duvet on floor of one of the uninhabitable bedrooms, even putting the duvet in the bath—though, bearing in mind how tall Harris was, Mallon couldn't see herself putting him through that.

Faye too was making every effort, chatting cheerfully, responding brightly to the flow of conversation Harris instigated time and again. If occasionally her eyes clouded over in moments of forgetfulness of her surroundings, and that heartbreaking vulnerability showed through, then Faye seemed to recollect where she was and returned to being bright and cheerful again.

And Harris, Mallon had to concede, was a super person to have at the dinner table. Bearing in mind that he knew both her frailties and his sister's, he was charming and witty, so that by the end of the meal Mallon, if not forgetting her worries, had to some extent put them to the back of her mind.

Those worries came rushing to the fore, however, once the meal was over and the used dishes were in the dishwasher and everything was once more spick and span. The three of them had moved to the drawing room with a suggestion that they watch some television. But Faye appeared to have too much going on in her head to be able to sit watching the small screen.

'If no one minds, I think I'll go to bed,' she said, getting to her feet. 'I've an early start in the morning,' she excused.

'Would you like a warm drink to take up with you?' Mallon offered.

'No, but thank you all the same,' Faye declined. However, she found a smile as she in return offered, 'Since I shall be away so early, I'll bring you a cup of tea up before I go.' And while Mallon was making a mental note to be up before the birds in the morning, Faye wished her and Harris goodnight and, closing the drawing room door after her, she went up to her room.

Mallon knew all about being unable to settle to watch television. Five minutes later she gave up all pretence of trying to concentrate on the programme. She turned to look at Harris, and found he wasn't watching the television at all, but was watching her.

Without more ado he got up and switched the television

set off. Then he came and stood looking down at her. 'You'll be all right with me, Mallon.' He'd brought out into the open the worries which had been stewing away inside of her.

'Do I have to?' she blurted out. 'I mean, is it strictly necessary for—for you to share my room?'

'Can you think of an alternative?' he asked in return, ignoring that in actual fact she would be sharing *his* room, the one he used whenever he came down to Harcourt House.

'You obviously can't,' she replied, realising that he must have searched as hard as she had for a solution that wouldn't upset his sister—she was upset enough already.

'You've been so good about all this,' Harris stated warmly. 'It seems poor recompense that you should have to share that bed with me. P...'

'Hold it right there, Quillian!' Mallon erupted, and was on her feet. 'Who said anything about sharing the bed?' It gave her the greatest pleasure to be able to tell him, 'You can have the duvet—it might help to soften those hard floorboards.'

Her small feeling of triumph never breathed life. The least she'd expected was a scowl; what she got was a laugh. 'Heartless wench!' he called her nicely. But, as he came close up to her and looked deep into her lovely eyes, he was unsmiling as he assured her seriously, 'You're safe with me, Mallon. I'm not like Phillips, or your ex-boyfriend, or any other licentious male of your acquaintance.'

Mallon rather thought she knew that. 'You're still sleeping on the floor!' she snapped, and thought that to follow Faye's example and go upstairs was a very good idea. 'Goodnight!' she bade him shortly, and went at speed. If he answered, she didn't hear him.

In his room, which for that night she now regarded as hers, Mallon quickly showered and got into her nightdress. After listening for sounds that might indicate Faye was wandering around, and on hearing none, Mallon tossed the duvet off the bed and onto the floor. Looking at the jumbled heap, conscience made her go over and spread it out. She tested it with her hands. The floor felt rock-hard! Even with the rug she then went and placed under it it was barely any better. She toughened her soft heart—he still wasn't going to share her bed.

After placing a pillow on the floor, Mallon climbed into bed, a solitary sheet on that hot night her only covering. She lay down, but was still awake at one in the morning. Harris definitely wasn't going to share her bed—he hadn't come up the stairs yet.

An hour later, when she had started to form the view that he must have decided to sleep on the sofa in the drawing room—perhaps with the intention of telling Faye that they'd had cross words or something—Mallon's ears, alert for every sound, heard Harris almost silently enter the bedroom.

The only light in the room was from the moonlit sky and the illuminated dial on the bedside clock, but, even so, Mallon closed her eyes and concentrated on making her breathing sound regular. She was overwhelmingly aware of him quietly moving around and was glad as his eyes became accustomed to the darkness that he found his 'floor bed' without bumping into anything.

'Goodnight,' he said, to let her know he knew she was awake. She didn't answer—but went to sleep with a smile on her face.

Mallon awoke feeling cold. She glanced at the clock and saw that it was ten past three. She looked over to where Harris was. She was cold—and he'd got the duvet. She heard him. He was restless; she guessed the floor was getting harder by the second.

Ten minutes later he was still restless, and she knew couldn't be asleep. She had gone from feeling cold to feeling thoroughly chilled. She wondered if he was cold too.

Oh, this was ridiculous! 'Give me your pillow,' she commanded.

She'd said it quietly, just in case he was asleep. But a moment later his pillow landed. Mallon got out of bed and placed his pillow at the foot of the bed. Then she went and got into bed under the sheet.

She swallowed, her courage failing her. Then she shivered and her brain decided this was all completely crackers—she trusted him, for goodness' sake. 'Your pillow's at the bottom of the bed if you want to share the duvet,' she said in a low tone, not wanting to wake Faye, should the poor woman be asleep.

Mallon heard Harris move, then the duvet came over her. His shape loomed out of the semi-darkness but, just when she was about to have second thoughts about the wisdom of what she had done, Harris, his voice threatening, warned her, 'You lay one finger on me, Mallon Braithwaite, and I'll yell the house down!'

What could she do? She stifled a laugh, then didn't feel at all like laughing as his bare leg made contact with her bare leg. 'On *top* of the sheet!' she ordered on a hiss of sound.

'Sorry, your honour,' he answered, and dutifully complied.

She loved him, and started to feel less cold. When she started to actually feel warm, Mallon went to sleep. She awoke with a start to find that dawn had broken and that two things seemed to have simultaneously brought her awake. One, the sound of teacups tinkling in saucers, the other, the feel of Harris moving to get under the sheet with her—not at the bottom of the bed, where he should have been, but at the top!

'*Get...*' was as far as she managed to shriek before Harris clamped a hand over her mouth, silencing her. She wriggled violently to get away, her bare—*bare?*—thigh brushing against his bare thigh.

'Faye's at the door with the tea tray!' Harris hurriedly whispered.

Mallon fumed impotently as he took his hand away. But, unused to being found in bed with anybody, Mallon couldn't take it, and as Faye tapped softly on the door and came in, so Mallon ducked her head beneath the covers.

The side of her face brushed against Harris's hair-roughened chest and, while she realised he was naked from the waist up, she hoped with all she had that he was wearing *something*!

'I'd make a useless waitress!' She heard Faye laugh as she apologised for spilling tea into the saucers. But whatever Harris said in reply Mallon didn't catch—her attention was suddenly riveted elsewhere as she realised that with one hand splayed against Harris's chest, as though to push him away, her fingers were touching his right nipple.

'You'll be all right?' she heard Harris ask his sister, but Mallon didn't hear what Faye said this time. Somehow, as if fascinated, Mallon found that her forefinger was exploring his nipple.

She traced the circle of it, the tip of it, and had the most wild notion all at once to put her lips to it. She wouldn't, though. Not with Faye in the same room. But, come to think of it, wouldn't it be safer to do that while Faye was there?

Moments later and suddenly some devilment seemed to come alive in Mallon. After all, this situation was none of her making. She moved her head, her lips parting as she came into contact with Harris's nipple. She kissed it. Kissed it again. Touched it again. And then took the tip inside her lips. All at once she found pleasure in playing with his nipple, the tip of her tongue finding it totally fascinating. She kissed it, and teased at it with her tongue and lips.

Indeed, so taken up was she with what she was doing that a gasp of shock left her when, abruptly, the covers were pulled back from her head and, 'Just what do you think you're doing?' Harris enquired quietly. As, abruptly, any remaining feeling of devilment Mallon had experienced promptly departed.

'Wh-where's Faye?' she asked shakily.

'On her way back to London by now, I shouldn't wonder.'

'Oh. Um—sorry.' Mallon apologised for making free with his nipple. Then thought, Hang on here—it was her space that had been intruded upon. 'I just thought I'd pay you—um—back a little.' She excused what she only then started to realise was out-and-out wantonness.

Harris was lying on his side and stared down at her. 'And how would you feel if I did done the same to you?' he questioned and while her colour flared and her heartbeats started to race, 'Sorry,' he apologised. 'I couldn't resist that. One of us had better get up.'

They both went to leap out of bed at the same time—and collided. Her nightdress must have ridden up during her sleep and she felt the length of his bare thighs against her.

'Oh,' she cried—but it wasn't a wail of panic.

Though she supposed that there must have been a hint of panic in there somewhere, because Harris was gently calming her, 'Hush, you're all right,' while at the same time backing his body from her.

Mallon looked up at him and somehow had the weirdest feeling that she didn't want to be all right. 'I'm not worried,' she told him honestly.

'You're sweet,' he said, and smiled, and moved a little further back. Though, prior to leaving the bed, he went to place a light kiss on the end of her nose. Only, intending to back away too, she moved as well—and somehow their lips met.

It was a brief meeting of their two mouths, and they both pulled back, staring into each other's eyes. The next Mallon knew was that she had moved forward and so had Harris—and unexpectedly she found herself in his arms.

It was where she longed to be, and she could not help but put her arms around him, and as he held her close, so she moved closer still. She felt him burying his head in her neck, in her hair, and then she felt his mouth on hers again, gently seeking this time; seeking, finding, gently giving, gently taking as her lips parted.

She loved him so, and that love seemed to consume her as, with gentle tender hands, she caressed his broad shoulders. Again Harris kissed her, trailing kisses down her throat. 'You're exquisite,' he murmured, and she thrilled at his words, at this closeness.

She wanted to be closer to him still and dared to move that little bit nearer, feeling his warmth, feeling his hard chest against her breasts.

When Harris drew back to look into her face she could do nothing but smile, her lips parting, inviting his kisses.

Oh, my darling, she thought, enraptured when, accepting that invitation, his head came down again and he kissed her. She felt his hands at her back, caressing, moving round to the front, caressing still, this time searching.

His left hand found her right breast, and she sighed from the pure pleasure of his touch. 'Oh!' she sighed, enchanted, and kissed him and held him close. As their kiss broke, so his sensitive fingers moved up to the tiny pearl buttons of her nightdress, unhurriedly unfastening.

Returning again to her mouth, his kisses became more passionate. She felt his hands caress the nakedness of her breasts and, as her heart leapt, she smiled shyly up at him in full agreement to his touch. She pressed closer to him, uncaring then of anything but her love for him and the magic of desire he was drawing from her. She wanted him, it was that simple, and she had not the smallest objection to make when he slid her nightdress from her shoulders and down past her waist.

He held her closely to him then, the broad expanse of his naked chest against her swollen breasts, kissing her deeply for long ageless seconds. 'Sweet Mallon,' he murmured, caressing her—and Mallon never wanted him to stop.

More, when he kissed her breasts, first one, then the other, his gentle fingers circling the hardened tips in much the same way her finger had circled his nipple, he evoked in her an untamed need for him.

Then Harris was lying over her and Mallon thrilled at this new closeness, her hands going to his waist, to the material of his shorts. More enchantment was hers when his hands moved her nightdress yet further down and away from her. She felt the thrill of his tender touch as he caressed her naked buttocks and, her heart in overdrive, she wanted to know more of his skin too, wanted to place her hands inside the back of his shorts and press him to her.

She wanted him. More and more she wanted him. 'Harris.' She spoke his name huskily, wanting him so badly, yet at the same time feeling suddenly shy.

'Mallon?' he responded to the unspoken question in her voice.

'I—um...' She didn't want to talk; she wanted to kiss him. So she kissed him and, because this was such new territory for her, she pulled back to look at him, and smiled as she told him, 'I—um—think I'm in need of a little guidance here,' and immediately wished she hadn't.

Because as Harris lay over her—looked down at her, feasted his eyes on her face with her thick blonde hair all tousled around her head—he all at once stilled, glanced away from her; and then groaned an agonised kind of groan.

'What did I say—do?' she asked, completely bewildered.

But Harris had moved from her and was lying on his stomach, his face in the pillow. 'I said you'd be safe,' he groaned. She didn't want to be safe.

'That's...'

'Mallon, don't talk. Just do me a favour.' Anything. Anything at all. 'Get out of bed—now,' he requested through what seemed to be clenched teeth.

'G-get out...'

'Now!' he repeated urgently. But she didn't want to. She wanted him. She loved him. She wanted his hold, his touch. She wanted to be held in love for just a while.

That was when reality, cold reality, which she didn't want, started to force its terrible way in. Hang on here— Harris didn't love her. He had never pretended that he did. The love was all on her side!

'Please, Mallon,' he urged, his tone strained. 'Go now!'

Mallon drew a shaky breath. She still did not want to go. But Harris wanted her to go. He didn't love her. The love was all on her side. Mallon stirred and, dragging herself away from him, got out of bed.

'Consider it done,' she managed croakily—and fled.

She reached her room, her head in a whirl. She knew that she could trust him. But what rocked her, and shook her to her foundations, was that nobody had told her that she shouldn't trust herself!

CHAPTER SEVEN

THAT phrase was still rocking her minutes later when Mallon stood beneath the shower and tried to get her head together. *She could trust him—but she couldn't trust herself.* Oh, Harris, Harris, what had he done to her? Her body still ached for him and, had he not told her to go...

Mallon was still trying to get herself into more of one piece when, dried and dressed, she had to face the most unpalatable truth—it was time to leave. Oh, how she did not want to go. But oh, how she recognised that go she must.

She knew she had been in a bit of a state when she had first come to Harcourt House—it seemed Roland Phillips made a practice of going around wrecking women's lives—but she was all right now. And she had Harris to thank for that. Just as he was doing all that he could for his sister, he had invented a job for the bedraggled wretch he had seen walking along in the pouring rain, and in doing so had begun a healing process for her.

So, fine, she had made Harcourt House a little more liveable-in than it had been, but her continued presence here was not, strictly speaking, necessary. Should there be a delivery of more furniture or carpets, or anything at all, then there were always at least four men on site who could direct delivery people.

It was with a deep sadness in her heart that, having already delayed as long as she could, Mallon left her room. She had so many mixed feelings about seeing Harris again. Yet, if she was to leave and never to see him again after that, she so desperately needed to see him now—just the one more time.

A kind of panic hit her then that, for all she hadn't heard his car, Harris might have already left! Hurrying up her steps, she went down the stairs and into the kitchen. His car was outside—and so was he. Oh, heavens, it was still early, but he appeared to be on the point of leaving.

Mallon swallowed hard. She badly wanted to go out to him—she could tell him she was leaving—but suddenly she felt too paralysed to move. Then she saw Harris take a glance to the kitchen window. He saw her, and started to move. He was coming back in.

Oh, grief! While wanting so desperately to hide, Mallon also quite desperately needed some contact with him. His expression when he entered the kitchen was almost stern. But as Harris looked across at her, he smiled suddenly. 'You okay, Mallon?' he asked.

Devastated, if you want to know. 'Absolutely,' she answered brightly.

Her insides were already in a giant upheaval, but that was before Harris went on to bring out into the open what her suddenly pinkened skin was all about! 'You know that our—um-bed-share—was never meant to end that...' He broke off, and it seemed to her that, when Harris was usually so confident about everything, this time he was having to search to find the right words. 'Have I harmed you?' he asked abruptly, his smile gone.

Oh, Harris! Her heart went out to him for his sensitivity. 'Not a bit!' she assured him. 'Other than...'

'Other than?' he quickly took up, his searching grey eyes scrutinising her face.

'Other than you've restored my faith in men.' She felt she owed him that honesty.

'*I* have?' he exclaimed in surprise.

She hadn't wanted to mention the amorous time they had shared. Indeed, had she been asked, she would have said she'd have sprinted like crazy away from doing so. But she had learned of Harris's sensitivity, and it seemed to her then that he was blaming himself for what had happened when she knew full well that, by taking liberties with his person—albeit that she'd started them only to pay him back—*she* had been the instigator.

So she took a brave breath and told him openly, 'You taught me this morning that not all men are like my former stepfather or his son, or Keith Morgan or Roland Phillips. And...'

'Oh, Mallon—does that mean you really do trust me?'

'Of course,' she answered without hesitation, and smiled. But, while being so open with him, she could not be so open as to tell him of the shattering truth she had discovered—that it was herself she did not trust. 'It was my fault,' she freely admitted. 'Though I fully intended to be up bright and early.'

'As did I,' Harris chipped in. 'Blame it on the previous sleepless hours that, were it not for the rattling teacups, I'd probably still be asleep now. As it is, I can't tell you how sorry I am that I—overstepped the mark.'

She wanted to say something light, a Think nothing of it would have done, but the words got stuck in her throat. So she drew breath to tell him what she had to tell him. 'Harris, I...' Was as far as she got, because, almost as if he knew what she had been preparing to say, he interrupted her.

'This won't make any difference?' he asked.

'Difference?'

'You wouldn't dream of leaving me?'

Oh, Harris! She was weak. She knew she was weak. Even as she knew that he wasn't asking about her leaving him, but about leaving his employ, Mallon was listening to her heart and not her head.

And, 'What sort of a girl do you take me for?' she answered lightly.

'You'll stay?'

'Of course.'

He looked relieved. 'Good,' he said, and looked about to come over and kiss her cheek. But he checked himself, and instead said, 'I'd better get off.' Giving her a warm smile, he turned about.

Mallon collapsed onto a kitchen chair once he had gone. She was weak, pathetic, and should have told him that she wasn't staying. But she loved him—and that seemed to have stripped away her backbone.

Anyhow, this job had never been permanent, she argued to her name-calling self. So surely she wasn't being all *that* spineless when any week now she would have to face doing what today she had put off doing.

She set the kettle to boil ready for when Bob Miller arrived, but her thoughts were far from making a pot of tea and more to do with the fact that the last time Harris had left he had kissed her cheek. This time, maybe to try and reassure her that she had nothing to fear, he hadn't come anywhere near.

Mallon spent the next two days knowing what she already knew anyway, that she did not fear anything about Harris. He was in her head the whole of the time. He was there in her thoughts when she got up in the morning, there when she went to bed at night.

She rang her mother, and had quite a long chat—and Harris was still there. She thought of him while she chatted to the workmen, when she went to Sherwins in the van with Kevin. In fact there was little room in her head for anyone but Harris.

It just wasn't good enough, she told herself countless times. She shouldn't be spending her days just dwelling on thoughts of him. She should be thinking of looking for a career. Thinking in terms of what she would do when she left Harcourt House as, inevitably, she would have to.

The trouble was that she couldn't think of a career. She had no idea what she wanted to do apart from stay somewhere near Harris for the rest of her life. Pathetic? Pathetic wasn't in it! she scolded.

Mallon wondered if he would come down that weekend and rehearsed how she would be cool, but friendly, the next time she saw him. He must not kiss her again—she would be lost. Not that he'd shown any desperate need to kiss her when he had left on Wednesday.

She got out of bed on Saturday, determined that she wasn't going to strain her ears that day listening for the purr of his car as she had yesterday.

By ten o'clock, when she realised her ears were at full pitch without her even being aware of it, Mallon took herself off for a walk. But by eleven she was hurrying back— Harris might have arrived while she was out!

He had not arrived, indeed he never did, and she went to bed that night after giving herself another severe talking to.

Mallon woke up on Sunday, showered, dressed and went downstairs to start her day, pushing one Harris Quillian Esquire firmly out of her thoughts. She had better things to do, she decided, than to mope around thinking solely about a male of the species who couldn't even be bothered to pick up the phone to tell her he wouldn't be coming down this weekend.

When the unfairness of that thought hit her—good heavens, she was nothing more than the hired help; why on earth would Harris ring to apprise her of his weekend plans?—Mallon locked up the house and took herself off for yet another walk in disgust.

She determined, positively, that today there would be no rushing back. She had done that yesterday and had been so disappointed for her trouble. Today she ignored the road, deciding to walk over fields instead.

It was two hours later when, not in the slightest hurry, Mallon made her way back to Harcourt House. It had been good to be outside. She had picked an armful of wild flowers and grasses and thought how they would brighten up the hearth in the drawing room.

She ambled up the drive and unlocked the front door, feeling certain that she hadn't once thought of Harris—in all of ten minutes. Intending to go down the long hall and into the kitchen, where she would find a vase to arrange the flowers, Mallon was barely through the front door when she heard voices coming from beyond the open drawing room door—one male, one female.

She halted. Her immediate reaction was to break out in smiles—Harris was home. Her next reaction was for her smile to dip. If Harris had brought his sister with him and intended to stay overnight, there was *no way*—he could use whatever excuse he liked, but absolutely, positively, set-in-stone definitely, no way—Mallon Braithwaite was going to share a room with him!

Feeling shy suddenly though striving for an air of pleasant detachment, Mallon, with the intention of popping her head round the drawing room door to say Hello, had started to go along the hall when Harris stepped out from the drawing room.

She blushed and caught his glance on her scarlet face. 'Mallon,' he said softly.

'I didn't expect you today,' she blurted out.

'Is it inconvenient?' he enquired, a teasing kind of look in his eyes.

'Not at all!' she answered briskly. Though more gently, 'Is Faye with you?'

He shook his head, and at his next words Mallon's world collapsed. 'I've brought Vivian. Come and meet her.'

Vivian! How Mallon kept her shock from showing, she never knew. It went without saying that he had women-friends. It just hadn't occurred to her that he would bring any of them down here! She smiled and went with him to the drawing room. She did not want to meet Vivian. No way did she want to meet the woman.

As Mallon knew she would be, Harris's lady-friend was an elegant, immaculately turned-out woman. She was a brunette of around thirty—and a sophisticated orchid type. So much for standing there with an armful of wild flowers!

Harris performed the introductions smoothly and with charm, adding pleasantly, 'Mallon has made this place much more like home with her feminine touch.' Mallon, glancing around the sparsely furnished room with its floor-boards bare apart from a scattering of rugs, wanted to hit him.

'I'd better put these flowers in water,' she said with a smile—Vivian Holmes hadn't a hair out of place; Mallon had been climbing stiles and scrabbling around picking flowers and grasses. She wanted out of there with all speed! 'Would you like coffee?' From somewhere, the manners borne of her upbringing came to trip her up.

'Love some,' Harris replied. 'I'll just show Vivian around the rest of the house.' Mallon couldn't get to the kitchen fast enough.

Mechanically she got out a large vase and filled it with water, while cruel jealousy threw spiteful darts at her. How could he have brought that woman here? He was showing her over the house, for goodness' sake! How could he?

Mallon's sense of fairness tried to get through. Harris had every right to bring whomever he pleased. It was his property. It was nothing to do with her.

Maybe not, but he could whistle for his lunch if he thought she was going to make it! She was caretaker, not cook. If he was so enamoured of Vivian Holmes that he had brought her down so he could show off his house, then let Vivian cook his lunch—and his dinner too, come to that.

Mallon let go a juddering kind of sigh. Vivian Holmes would probably turn out to be an excellent cook. She looked the type who did *everything* well. Mallon blanked her thoughts off, or thought she had, and then the most horrendous notion hit her. If they were staying here to lunch and dinner—what was to stop them staying the night?

Oh, she wasn't having that! It was for certain Harris wouldn't be expecting her to move out of her room to make way for his 'guest'. Mallon knew, without having to think about it, that Harcourt House, with its two habitable bedrooms and two beds, was just not big enough for the three of them. If Vivian Holmes was staying, Mallon Braithwaite was going.

She had the coffee percolating when she heard them walking about on the bare boards overhead. What were they doing up there? They'd been gone for an age!

Eventually Harris and his companion came down the stairs, and he brought her into the kitchen. Mallon poured three cups of coffee and, while they sat at the table drinking it, Harris invited Vivian's comments on the kitchen. 'Most of the ideas in here are Faye's,' he told her, and somehow Mallon managed to keep her expression even.

Vivian had obviously met Faye. Did that signify that Vivian had been Harris's lady-love for some while? Mallon rather thought it did. More than that, Vivian was probably the one with whom Harris spent his weekends when he didn't come down to Harcourt House. True, Faye was under the impression that one Mallon Braithwaite was his mistress, so she might only have met Vivian briefly and have had no idea how serious things were between them. But...

'...and what do you think, Mallon?' Mallon looked across at Vivian and realised that the woman was asking her opinion of the kitchen.

'I think Faye has done an excellent job,' she replied, and discovered, as Vivian pointed out one or two fixtures which could be altered, that, even though the woman was acting as if she was ready to move in and take over at any given moment, her ideas were sound.

More, as Vivian included her in her discussion with Harris, Mallon found that in other circumstances she could quite like her. But that still didn't mean that she was hanging around if Vivian was staying the night.

Though, partly because she was starting to like the woman, and partly from manners, but mainly because she needed to know how long they intended to be there, Mallon queried, 'Will you be here for lunch?' and found herself staring into a pair of gently contemplating warm grey eyes.

But even as her heart did a tiny flip he looked quickly away, his glance resting on Vivian, and for an insane instant Mallon had the impression that he had forgotten Vivian Holmes was there. But, just to prove how insane that thought was, he smiled at Vivian and replied for the both of them. 'I think not. In fact I think we'll get off now. You've seen enough, Vivian?' he enquired, and that,

Mallon thought, said it all. Abundantly plain for all to see was that at some later date, when all the work was completed, Vivian was going to move in with him and make Harcourt House her home.

Somehow or other Mallon got through the next five minutes. She was glad they were going. She couldn't be more pleased they were going. So pleased they were going that she smiled as she said goodbye to Vivian, and positively beamed when she said goodbye to Harris-get-out-of-bed-now-Quillian. He hadn't been thinking of Mallon Braithwaite when he had urged her to 'Please, Mallon. Go now' but an honourable man, he'd been thinking of Vivian Holmes, his lady-love!

'I'll see you when I see you,' Mallon called cheerfully, as she watched him follow Vivian out of the kitchen. Honourable! Stuff his honourableness!

She was hurting, but even so she couldn't resist a last look at Harris as he and Vivian went by the kitchen window to his car. Then Mallon promptly turned her back on the window. If he happened to glance through, which of course he wouldn't, then he would see that already he and his companion had gone from her mind and that she had her attention on the kitchen cupboards, in which she was looking for something.

Mallon might not have been looking through the window but her ears were tuned in, listening for the purr of the car's engine, listening to hear it start up and as it departed fade away. Only then would she feel able to let down her guard.

But, listen though she did, and impatient though she was for that sound—for them to be gone—she did not hear any sound of a car's engine. What she did hear was the sound of footsteps—and she froze. They were coming back in!

Fearing that she didn't have another smile left in her,

Mallon turned to face the kitchen door. Correction. *They* were not coming back in. Vivian must still be in the car because, tall and straight, and oh, so dear, Harris came in alone.

He came in, came close, and only a couple of feet away he stopped. Silently, and for several seconds, they just stood and stared at each other. Harris fixed his gaze on her and Mallon, sure it wasn't just her imagination, felt a kind of tension in the air between them. She struggled to break it, to find her voice, but her throat was suddenly so dry that her voice came out sounding all husky and sort of choky.

'You—forgot something?'

Grey eyes looked down into deeply blue eyes. 'You—seemed a bit—out of sorts,' he said quietly—and Mallon knew that if this clear thinking man wasn't to guess precisely why she was 'out of sorts', then she had better buck her ideas up.

She did manage to find another smile. 'Who, me?' she queried. Though, because she feared he might be too astute to be fobbed off, she went on, 'How would you feel if you came in looking as though you'd been playing in the dirt and had to shake hands with someone who was the last word in elegance?'

His answering smile was slow in coming but eventually made it. 'It bothered you? Vivian...'

But Mallon didn't want to hear what he had to say about Vivian, and laughed lightly as she told him, 'It's a woman thing.' And again found he was studying her.

'That's all? You're not worrying over anything?' he pressed.

'Not a thing.'

'You're sleeping well?' he queried and, after a thoughtful moment, 'You're not losing any sleep—having bad dreams because I lost my head a little last…'

'Of course not!' she cut in. She did not need him to go into that time they had shared his bed together, thank you very much. 'Good grief, I'm not such a hothouse flower…' She broke off, hothouse flower bringing to mind orchids, bringing to mind Vivian. 'Shouldn't you be going wherever it is you're going?' And please don't tell me where that is because I don't want to know.

Nor did she need it when he suddenly came a step closer and took her hand in his. It wasn't fair because she was melting under his touch—and yet was so weakly in need of his touch that she just didn't have the strength to do as she knew she should and pull her hand out of his hold.

'You're sure you're all right about—everything?'

Oh, absolutely. You in here holding my hand, your elegant girlfriend sitting out there waiting for you—what could be more right? 'Positive,' Mallon answered and, pride belatedly arriving, she pulled her hand out of his grip and took a step away.

'You would tell me?'

Mallon found a light laugh. 'I can see, Harris, that you'd like to set yourself up as my trauma physician. But I just didn't have a problem coming to terms with the fact that, in a given set of circumstances, certain biological urges— er—need to be restrained.'

Any hint of a smile left his expression and Mallon could see that he didn't care very much for what she had just said. But, even so, he stayed long enough to ask, 'May I take it that you've forgiven me my lack of restraint in that department?'

Mallon smiled, a genuine smile this time. If there was a tinge of relief in her smile that she had been thinking *not* about his lack of restraint in the 'biological urges' de-

partment but about her own, only she would know about
it.

'It's no big issue, Harris, honestly,' she said, and impulsively, quite forgetful that he had his woman-friend sitting in his car waiting for him, Mallon went forward,
stretched up, and kissed him.

It was a mistake. She knew it as soon as their mouths
touched. A shock of electricity bolted through her. But, as
she immediately went to pull back, firm hands came to
grip her arms, and she was once more staring straight into
a pair of warm grey eyes.

'Th-there!' Mallon whispered on a gasp of breath.
'Completely forgiven.'

Harris continued to grip her arms, then, a second or two
later, he said gruffly, 'I'd better go,' and went.

In the following twenty-four hours Mallon went over
Harris's visit again and again. Her memories were bittersweet. How dared he bring another woman into what was
her home? she fumed, in what she knew was an irrational
moment. But why shouldn't she be irrational if she wanted
to? Why should she be rational? She loved the swine.

But he didn't know that she loved him—nor would he,
for heaven's sake! She had seen his sensitivity—she'd just
die if he ended up feeling sorry for her. Oh, she wouldn't
have that.

Her pride dipped as she recalled the way he had left
Vivian in the car and had come back. Mallon sighed hopelessly as she thought of how his fine sensitivity had picked
up—for all her efforts to the contrary—that she might be
out of sorts about something. He needn't have come back.

Did that mean that he cared? Just a little? Oh, come on,
Mallon, for goodness' sake! Did it look as though he
cared? Have you forgotten Vivian Holmes? Vivian of the
'I'll show Vivian the rest of the house'. Vivian of the

JESSICA STEELE   157

subtle suggestions for alterations to the kitchen. Vivian of the 'You've seen enough, Vivian?'.

Well, if she hadn't, Mallon had. More than enough. Especially when she thought of Vivian moving in and taking up residence at Harcourt House. Mallon went hot and cold all over when it struck her that, for all she knew, Vivian might be planning to arrive, complete with suitcases, this coming weekend!

Mallon awoke on Tuesday morning and knew, without having to think about it any more, that this was the end. She glanced at the wall that separated her room from Harris's room and knew she just wouldn't be able to bear it if Harris and Vivian came down on Saturday and stayed overnight—in his room.

Mallon left her bed knowing indelibly that, before Vivian moved in with her suitcases, she, Mallon Braithwaite, would be moving out with hers.

Before Bob Miller had arrived, Mallon had her bedlinen and towels in the washing machine and had been on the phone to the railway station checking train times. There was a train departing at twelve-fourteen which would deposit her at the railway station in her mother's home town.

It was early to ring her mother, but not too early to pack. Mallon tried to be positive as she got her belongings together and fought to keep unwanted thoughts at bay. But the knowledge that she was severing all ties with Harris and would never see him again was crucifying, so that when at eight-thirty she dialled her mother's telephone number Mallon had never felt so unhappy.

'Hello darling,' her mother answered her greeting, and sounded so warm and wonderful that Mallon almost burst into tears.

'Can I come home?' she asked chokily.

'Are you crying?' Evelyn Frost asked in alarm.

Crying, weeping, bleeding on the inside—yes, all of that. 'Can I come?'

'Of course you can; you know that,' her mother answered and, when she had never been the practical one, she put aside any concern she felt and surprised Mallon by asking, 'How are you getting here? Do you want John and I to come for you?'

'No, no, that's all right,' Mallon replied, and, feeling more in control now, 'I'm catching the twelve-fourteen train—and I'm not crying.'

She went in search of Kevin after her call. 'No problem,' he answered when she had said that she needed to be in town for midday and that if he were going that way any time would suit.

With the assurance that Kevin would give her 'a call', Mallon took her suitcases into the kitchen. She made sure everywhere was as tidy as it could be, given the circumstances, and with her laundry tumble-dried, ironed and put away by ten-thirty, she went to look for Bob Miller.

She found him just as he was about to drive off to another job he was working on some miles away. She explained, cheerfully and with a smile, that she was leaving Harcourt House and had thought, even though she knew he had some keys, that she would leave her set of keys with him.

His expression said he was curious, but when Mallon wasn't any more forthcoming he pretended to be aghast as he quipped, 'You mean you're going—leaving me to make my own morning tea?'

'You'll survive,' she replied, and, after arranging to give the keys to Kevin for him to pass on to him, she returned to the house.

She was undecided what to do about letting Harris know he had lost his caretaker. She wanted to phone him; she had his number. But he might not be in, or in a meeting and unavailable. He had been so good to her, taking her in the way he had and giving her shelter. The least she could do in return was to try to speak personally to him. Though what reason for leaving she was going to give she had no idea. It positively wouldn't be the truth, that was for certain.

In the end Mallon took out her writing paper, knowing that the only reason she wanted to ring him was because she was looking for an excuse. She was aching for the sound of his voice. And that really *was* pathetic! She must be strong, and strong started here.

There was not much time to spare when, with difficulty, she at last managed to write her note. She thanked Harris for his kindness, but stated that she felt now was the time to move on. She sealed the envelope knowing she wouldn't be seeing him again so he would not be able to question her decision. To think that he would do was, she realised, just so much pie in the sky—then Kevin came into the kitchen.

'Do you want these putting in the van?' he asked, seeing her cases down by the door.

'I'll carry one,' she answered—and just then the telephone rang.

'I can carry these, no trouble,' Kevin assured her. 'I'll see you when you've finished on the phone, no sweat.'

He had disappeared before Mallon could decide whether or not she wanted to answer the phone. But who did she think it would be, for goodness' sake? She had been churned up inside about leaving before the phone had started to ring; she was doubly so when she went to answer it.

Her mother had insisted that she and John would pick her up from the station when she arrived. But her mother

hadn't consulted John about it. Perhaps they'd discovered
John had to be elsewhere at that time. Perhaps her mother
was ringing to say for her to take a taxi from the station
after all.

She was certain that it would be her mother—so why
was she feeling so shaky? 'Hello?' she enquired down the
mouthpiece.

'How's life in sunny Upper Macey?' Harris asked, and
Mallon had to sit down.

He sounded so warm, sounded in such good humour.
'Fine,' she answered. 'Actually…' She couldn't get the
words out.

'Actually?' he queried and, as astute as ever, his tone
changing, 'What's happened?' he wanted to know.

'N-nothing. The roof's still on.'

'What's happening—with you?' he insisted, and she
knew she was imagining it, but he made it sound as if the
house could fall down for all he cared—so long as she was
safe.

Oh, wishful thinking! She knew then that she was going
to have to tell him. 'I'm leaving,' she announced bluntly.

'Leav…' He broke off, and, obviously looking for reasons himself, 'Has Phillips been around again?' he demanded. 'I know he's working from home this week. If…'

'He hasn't been near,' she replied quickly, guessing that
knowledge had reached him from Faye.

'Then what…?'

'I—just think it's time to go, that's all,' she butted in,
and, loving him, wanted him to beg her to stay.

'You're not afraid? Nothing's upset you? I haven't upset
you? If…'

'It's not you,' she said quickly. Oh, how could she lie
to him—how could she not? 'And… And I'm not upset.'

'You are!' he contradicted forcefully.

'I just think…I want to go.'

There was a short silence. Then, 'We'll talk about this at the weekend,' Harris decreed. 'I intended to come down on Friday…' Alone?

'I'm leaving—now,' Mallon cut him off—and very near had her ears blasted for her trouble.

'*You can't!*' he roared.

So she was a good caretaker! Tears pricked her eyes as she quietly replaced the receiver. The phone rang again. This time Mallon did what she should have done the first time. She ignored it. She went to the kitchen and tore up the note she had written. It was no longer needed.

Having locked up as far as was practicable, bearing in mind that the builders would want to come in and out, Mallon went out to the van with the phone still ringing in her ears. Kevin kept up a lively chatter all the way to the railway station, and once there insisted on carrying her cases on to the platform.

'Are you coming back?' he asked as Mallon handed him her set of keys.

'I may do,' she answered, and thanked him and said goodbye, knowing that she had just uttered the biggest lie of all. She wouldn't be going back. She had left Harcourt House for good. It was a permanent leaving. And—it hurt.

Proving that the second telephone call must have been from Harris, her mother and John were at the station to meet her and Mallon had no need to take a taxi.

Her mother looked worried, but Mallon could not bear that anything should blight her mother's new-found happiness so hugged her, and kissed John, and told them cheerfully, 'It's good to be back—but I'm not stopping too long.'

'You know you're welcome for as long as you like,' John replied. 'It's your home now.' Mallon smiled at him for saying so, but knew she would make her own home somewhere else.

Once they were inside the house John carried one of her cases up to the room her mother had prepared for her and Mallon took the other case. 'I'll leave you to settle in,' John said with a contented smile, but while he went back down the stairs her mother stayed behind.

'What happened, Mallon?' she asked. Perhaps because she was so happy herself, she had observed that, for all her daughter's cheerful front, underneath Mallon wasn't at all.

Mallon straightened from the suitcase she had just unfastened and looked over to the dear soul who, since her marriage to John, seemed to have grown in confidence and no longer needed her daughter to protect her. 'I...' Mallon began, ready to evade the question. But, looking at her mother, found it impossible to lie to her. 'I fell in love with him,' she said simply.

'Harris Quillian?' Mallon nodded. 'And he?' her mother asked.

'He has a lady-friend. I thought it best to leave,' Mallon replied.

'Oh, darling,' her mother cried, and came and gave her a hug.

Mallon dully carried on with the business of living. Later that day she was helping prepare the evening meal when her mother slipped up and mentioned that they had been going to eat a little earlier because...

'Because?' Mallon queried, smiling at her parent's look of guilt but eventually dragging from her that her mother and John had tickets for the theatre that evening, but had decided against using them.

'We don't think it will be much of a play after all,' Evelyn Frost ended.

'That's why you booked your seats, was it?' Mallon teased, and, fully aware that the only reason they had decided not to go was because she had come home, she said firmly, 'I wouldn't hear of you not going.'

'But—you're upset!'

'No, I'm not. I was,' Mallon agreed—her mother had known that much. 'But I'm all right now.'

It wasn't easy to persuade her mother that she would be more upset if they stayed home than if they went to the theatre, but at last her mother gave in and they had an early meal.

The house was quiet after her mother and new stepfather had gone and Mallon knew she should be glad of the peace and quiet. But, although the builders would have left Harcourt House for the day now, she had grown used to having them crashing and banging about the place, and wanted to be back there. Though a second later and she owned that, in all honesty, it wasn't the builders' racket she wanted to get back to—just the house.

Harcourt House where, at any given moment, Harris might telephone. Where, at any given moment, Harris might drive up, might arrive, walk in. She half wished she had not left, but knew that alternative: to have stayed and heard, endured, watched his relationship with Vivian Holmes would have been untenable.

She had been right to leave. Mallon stiffened her backbone to endorse that firmly, but that didn't make it hurt any less. She had cut Harris out of her life, left him— without any forwarding address. He might guess she had gone to her mother's new home, but he had not the remotest idea where her mother lived, and neither did he know her mother's new name. Mallon bit her lip hard as fate cackled—Harris was likely to come looking?

She was glad she had insisted that her mother leave her

to see to the dinner dishes. Aside from not wanting to give her parent extra work, it gave Mallon something to do. She felt she needed to keep busy; it might help her to stop thinking of Harris Quillian.

It did not. By eight-thirty the kitchen was immaculate. Mallon went to the drawing room and over to one of the comfortable chairs, but no sooner had she sat down than she stood up again. She couldn't settle.

She went upstairs for her book and came down and read one paragraph—and found her thoughts had drifted off to how Harris hadn't wanted her to go. Her insides went all soft on her when she thought of how he'd said, 'We'll talk about it at the weekend. I intended to come down on Friday'. Malevolent intelligence reminded her that he might well be intending to visit Harcourt House—but not alone.

Which was precisely the reason why she had left—because she knew she wouldn't be able to bear seeing him with Vivian Holmes. It wasn't mere jealousy, Mallon knew that, torturous though jealousy was. It was more—self-preservation. If he was going to be happy with Vivian, good luck to him. She just didn't want to be around to witness it.

Feeling despair starting to descend on her like some dark cloud, Mallon once more pushed Harris out of her head. Positive. Be positive, she willed herself, and determined that she would set about making herself a new life. First thing tomorrow she would check with the agencies, buy a paper and see what situations were vacant. She…

The doorbell sounded. Her mother hadn't said she was expecting anybody to call. Mallon left the drawing room and went along the hall. With her fingers on the door lock, her thoughts on telling whoever it was that she'd be pleased to take a message for either her mother or John,

Mallon pulled back the heavy front door—and got the shock of her life!

She went scarlet, then, as her colour began to fade, she went pale. The caller was there for neither her mother nor her stepfather. But tall, business-suited, and with grey eyes that weren't looking in the least friendly, there stood the man she had only recently mused had no earthly idea where she had gone!

'H-how—did you find me?' Mallon gasped. Her colour might be returning, but her brain seemed incapable of thinking further than that.

Harris Quillian stared uncompromisingly down at her, 'With difficulty,' he gritted. 'And not a little abandoned pride.' And, his glance searching her face, though what he was looking for she hadn't a clue, 'I need to talk to you, alone,' he stated in clipped tones. 'We'll talk in my car,' he informed her tautly.

CHAPTER EIGHT

MALLON was still staring at him, totally stunned, when Harris took a step back, as if expecting her to step forward to go with him to his car. 'You w-want to talk to me?' she questioned faintly—about as much as she was able to manage as her brain started to function again and one thought after another chased through her head: how had he found her? He hadn't known her mother's new address—or even her old one for that matter. Why had he bothered? And—what was there to talk about?

'I do,' Harris answered grimly, repeating succinctly, 'Alone.'

Alone? Without her mother and her husband there? Did that mean that Harris wanted to give her a ticking off for leaving without notice? Surely not? Though it sounded very much that way. From the tough look of him he wanted to give her a 'telling off', but intended sparing her the humiliation of taking it with others present.

'I...' She opened her mouth to tell him what he could do with his 'telling off', but—and she admitted she was weak where he was concerned—she didn't want him to go away again—not just yet. Soon enough he would walk away from her life for ever. 'You'd—um—better come in,' she invited.

'I said, alone,' Harris reminded her shortly.

'My mother and John are out. Unless you intend to murder me, we can talk alone inside.'

The answer she received was a kind of grunt. But when she half turned, Harris took a step forward. She held the

166

door while he crossed the threshold and, closing the door, she led the way into the drawing room, her heart still hammering away at seeing him so totally unexpectedly.

Once in the drawing room she turned to face him, intending to challenge why had he bothered to come to see her. But as her glance went to his face, grim still and without a doubt hostile, he was, even so, very dear to her.

'Have you eaten?' she found she was asking instead. From his business suit she guessed he had come straight from his office.

'Who wants food?' He spurned her offer none too politely. So it was to be pistols at dawn? She could have asked him to take a seat, but it didn't look as if he would be there that long. 'Why did you go?' Harris demanded abruptly.

He wanted an explanation—she didn't have one; her brain was seizing up again. 'I was never going to stay!' she responded. Then, gaining her second wind, 'You knew that,' she challenged. 'You knew that the job was never going to be permanent.'

Harris looked back at her, annoyed with her, she knew. Then, suddenly, as he looked into her deeply blue eyes, his harsh look seemed to soften and he ventured, 'I thought we could talk—you and I?'

Oh, Harris, don't! She needed to be tough, and he was making that difficult. 'We—could,' seemed to be forced from her. And remembering, 'I've discussed things with you, told things to you that I've never told another living soul. But...' Feebly, she broke off. Broke off, feeling that she had said too much, that already she had said *much* too much.

'So what happened to that?' he wanted to know. 'What happened to that trust you had in me that you had to run away without even talking to me about it first?' His glance was fixed steadily on her when he accused toughly, 'You wouldn't have let me know anything about your plans had I not chanced to telephone!'

Mallon didn't like his digging, his chipping, nor that 'run away' statement. 'Will you have a seat?' she said in a rush. 'Perhaps I can get you a drink if you don't want anything to eat.'

She did not like it, either, that he saw too much when he instructed harshly, 'Don't be nervous with me, Mallon. I don't like it. Especially since you know I would never harm you.'

If only that were true! She was harmed. She did hurt; he was the cause. She went over to one of the well-padded chairs. Although it seemed he had refused her offer of a drink, when she sat down Harris, closer than she would have liked, came and took possession of a chair next to her.

There were only a few yards separating them when, still searching to exonerate herself without giving herself away, Mallon thought she could safely explain, 'I did write you a note.'

'I didn't find it.'

'You've...?' He'd been down to Harcourt House? 'I—er—after your phone call... When I told you I was leaving—well, there didn't seem any point in leaving a note. I tore it up,' she said. But found that the question she had previously denied would not stay down. 'You've been to Harcourt House?'

'Of course I've been there!' he grated—and proceeded to totally astonish her when he added shortly, 'I was half-way down there when Bob Miller contacted me on my car phone to say that you'd already left. It seemed to...'

'Just a minute!' she interrupted on a gasp of sound. And

when she could see she had his full attention, she went on. 'Bob Miller wasn't there when I left!'

'I know he wasn't.'

Mallon wasn't sure her jaw did not fall open as something else all at once struck her. 'You didn't—didn't—um—leave your office to go down to Upper Macey just because…?' She broke off. Of course he hadn't! Love must have softened her brain. 'I'm sorry, that was a stupid question.' Grief, he dealt in million-pound deals—as if he'd desert his business just because she'd told him she was leaving!

But, 'I did,' she clearly heard Harris reply. And, if that wasn't enough to have the blood pounding in her ears, he caused emotional colour to flood her face when he added, 'I delayed only long enough to contact Bob Miller on his mobile, then I took off.'

'Y-you t…?' Words failed her. She supposed she had been a competent caretaker, even a good caretaker, but *that* good? So good that Harris would leave his business to charge down to Upper Macey to see her, to ask her to reconsider? No—common sense reared its sharp hand to give her a slap—don't be ridiculous. She was a caretaker, not some high-flying executive at Warren and Taber Finance. 'You—said you rang Bob Miller.' She managed to latch on to something fairly sensible.

'I rang his mobile. He wasn't at Harcourt House but at one of his other jobs some ten or so miles away.' Mallon had known that. 'He said you had discussed handing over the keys into his safe-keeping.' Harris paused and then, with that steady grey-eyed look she knew so well, said, 'I didn't care at all for the finality of that.' Her lovely blue eyes widened slightly. 'I told him to get back to Harcourt House immediately and to stop you from leaving.'

Fresh shock made her gasp. 'Stop me from leaving?' she echoed faintly.

'By the time he got there, you'd gone.'

Mallon's insides were having a wild time within her, her emotions haywire as she strove to be calm and to tell herself that Harris was a kind and sensitive employer and that he would act so towards any member of his staff. But, against that, her brain was insisting, Oh, come on, Mallon, do you really believe that? But if she didn't believe that…then didn't it follow that for Harris, a businessman of some note, to drop everything to chase down to see her, to try to stop her from leaving, it must mean—mustn't it—that he cared a little for her?

Her mouth did fall open in shock. Even as she was discounting that Harris could possibly care, the notion caused her some shock. 'You—er…' was as far as she could get before her brainpower returned to scoff. As if! 'You—er—decided to carry on down to Harcourt House anyway?' was the best she could come up with—that much had already been established when Harris had referred to not finding any note from her when he'd got there.

'It was my only option,' he answered, his eyes steady on hers. 'When I realised I didn't know where in blazes you were heading, that I had no address, apart from somewhere in Warwickshire—and then only if you were making for your mother's new home—I was left hoping you might have left some clue to your whereabouts in your room or somewhere else in the house.'

'You checked my room?' she questioned faintly, trying desperately not to see anything in Harris's actions that just wasn't there.

'I checked everywhere,' he replied.

'Nothing?'

'Not a clue!' he answered heavily.

Oh, heavens, it sounded as if he had been quite keen to find her! 'B-but, you did find me.' She smiled, still trying to show a cool front. 'You're here now.' And because, even though her insides were all of a tremble, her curiosity would not stay down, 'How *did* you find me?' she just had to ask.

Harris seemed to relax just a trifle for the first time since he had arrived, and with a hint of a smile answered, 'As I mentioned, with difficulty, and not a little abandoned pride. Though I have to say that a little abandoned pride was well worth the cost if it meant I could find out what I wanted to know.'

Crazily, her heart just refused to listen to the logic of her sober brain, which cautioned, This can't mean what you think it means—that Harris cares a little for you. 'My address?' she queried, her voice barely above a whisper.

'Your address,' Harris confirmed. 'I was in the drawing room, those wild flowers you picked on Sunday still fresh in the hearth, as I tried not to despair that I might never find you.'

Had he not referred to his visit on Sunday in the same breath as his despair that he might never find her, Mallon thought her heart would have leapt straight out of her body. But he had mentioned the two together and, by reminding her of Sunday, when he had brought his woman-friend, Vivian Holmes with him, it negated for Mallon any crass thoughts and feelings she might otherwise have had.

'I—er—must have left some clue after all,' she commented stiffly, and saw Harris frown at the change in her.

But, determinedly, he kept to his purpose, although by then Mallon was confused as to know what purpose that was—she certainly wasn't going back to be his caretaker again. Then he revealed, 'I was quite desperately trying to think of anything you had ever said that would hold a clue.

I knew your old home was in Warwickshire, and that was about it. So I went back to the very beginning, how we'd met when you ran away from my brother-in-law. But still couldn't find any clue. That was until I remembered how you'd said you had written to Phillips applying for the job. The moment that I realised Phillips had once had your old address, I was on my way to see him.'

'Oh, Harris!' Mallon murmured involuntarily, realising then that this was what he'd meant by abandoning a little pride. It would have gone very much against the grain for him to ask Roland Phillips for anything. 'You—must have wanted my address pretty badly.'

Harris looked at her for long, long seconds, his expression unsmiling. 'I did,' he said simply.

Her throat went dry. 'He—er—gave it to you without any—er—fuss?'

Harris did smile then. 'I wouldn't say without any fuss. Though to begin with he said that if you'd written he didn't know where the letter was. When I told him you'd done some filing in his study...'

'You remembered I'd told you I cleared up his study?'

'Didn't I say I went over everything you'd ever said, looking for clues as to where you might be?' He did not wait for an answer, but continued, 'After a short discussion that went along the lines of Phillips still having a job when his employers heard from my company if he didn't let me loose amongst his files, he allowed me into his study.'

'You found my letter in a file marked General Correspondence?'

Harris nodded. 'Then I had to sit outside your old address for a couple of hours, waiting for the new tenants to come home in the hope they had your mother's forwarding address. But, after that, the rest was relatively easy.'

Mallon stared at him, a roaring starting in her ears.

Surely she could no longer deny what everything was telling her—that Harris did care—a little?

'You—went to all that trouble?' she questioned huskily.

Harris looked levelly at her. Then, quietly, he told her, 'It was important to me.' Mallon's eyes were fixed on nowhere but him when slowly, carefully, he added, 'You are important to me, Mallon.'

Such a rush of emotion hit her then that she couldn't sit still, and she jerked to her feet. Keeping her back to him, so he should not read the flood of emotion in her face, she took some steps away.

She was vaguely aware of hearing him move. Then knew he was close behind her when, over her shoulder, he soothed, 'Now don't be alarmed. I know I came on too strong when we shared a bed a week ago, and if that's what frightened you away we'll take things more...'

Mallon turned to face him. He looked worried, strained, and it was too much. If she was the one to be left with her pride in ashes, so be it. Even though she still found it difficult to believe that he'd dashed down to Harcourt House, sunk his pride to go and ask his detested brother-in-law for a favour and had then come to look for her—how could she let Harris think himself the villain of the piece?

'Oh, Harris,' she said softly. 'What a poor memory you have of that morning.'

He stared at her, but that look of strain did not lessen. 'I didn't terrify the life out of you?' he asked.

She shook her head, and even managed to find a smile. 'So, okay, I'll admit I'm not the smartest in the—er—bed department, and that I've probably got a lot to learn there. But, as I remember it, you were the one who ordered me out, not the other way around.'

Some of the strain seemed to go from him, but he was

still questioning when he asked, 'And nothing that happened that morning has worried you, made you feel awkward, ill at ease with me…?'

'The only thing that has been bothering me is that, while I knew that I could doubly trust you, I discovered that I…' She hesitated. However, he seemed to be suffering too, and she loved him too much for that. 'I discovered that I couldn't—er…' She took a breath, and plunged. 'I couldn't trust myself.'

Harris stared at her for perhaps one age-long second, Then he said softly, 'My dear, are you saying that, had I not turned you out, you'd have willingly…?'

'I couldn't have stopped myself,' she admitted honestly.

'Oh, love,' he murmured, and stretched out his arms for her. Her heart fluttered wildly as she went to him. She felt his arms about her and it was sheer bliss to be held by him. 'Is that why you ran away?' he leaned back to ask, looking deeply into her eyes. 'Because you didn't trust yourself alone under the same roof with me?'

He did care! He must care, mustn't he? Everything about him, every look, everything she knew about him, said that he wouldn't be here now, holding her this way, if he didn't care. But, while Mallon knew that she trusted him completely, a modicum of self-preservation lingered, and she found that she could not be as open with him as he perhaps would have liked.

'Not—quite,' she admitted after some moments of staying silent.

'You ran away for some other reason?' Harris queried, as sharp as she knew him to be. Mallon felt then that she would prefer not to say anything else at all. To do so would be to tell him that she loved him and, while she was growing more and more to believe that he did care a little for her, that was a long, long way from the totally deep and all-consuming love she had for him. 'You're not going to tell me, are you?' he asked gently. 'Not even when we've always been able to talk, you and I.'

She laughed lightly and had no idea when her arms had gone around his waist—it felt so good, so natural just to be standing there holding each other like this. 'There are some things a girl doesn't even tell her best friend.' She smiled.

He smiled too, and then bent to gently kiss the corner of her mouth. 'Not even,' he said on straightening, his grey eyes warm on her, 'when you know that—I've fallen for you—in quite a big way?'

Involuntarily her eyes shot wide. Her throat went dry as she looked back at him. Oh, Harris, Harris, Harris, I love you so. She checked. Steady. This was all so incredible. Steady. What did 'fallen for her in a big way' mean, exactly?

'You—um—wouldn't care to expand on that a little, I suppose?' she asked, having to search and find every scrap of control.

But he looked equally wary, before manfully biting the bullet. 'If I know my Mallon, you wouldn't issue an invitation like that unless you have some kind of—feeling for me.' Oh, my word, he was getting close.

She hesitated. 'S-so?' she stammered, realising, even as she said that small word, that it was tantamount to admitting that she did have some kind of feeling for him.

He knew it too, she realised, when his grip on her tightened before he allowed himself a small smile. Then he said, 'It began one rain-soaked day when I stopped to offer you a lift. You refused at first...'

'But you did a circuit and came round again,' she supplied in a whisper.

'I told myself I was being stupid—somebody else would

have come by and you'd have accepted a lift with them. But was that rain on your face—or tears? I was in no particular hurry.'

'You took me in,' she said softly. 'Not only gave me a lift, but gave me a job too.'

'Why wouldn't I?' he asked, and, his expression going grim, he continued, 'Phillips, regrettably, is linked to my family—and you'd been assaulted by him!'

'You were so kind.' Mallon smiled, and, because she didn't want him looking so grim, she leaned forward and stretched up and gently kissed him.

'Oh, Mallon, Mallon,' Harris murmured when she pulled back. But his grim expression had gone and there was a trace of a smile on his face when he went on, 'I don't know about being kind. All I thought I was doing at the start was doing my small bit to get you back on a more even keel after your distressing experience. What I hadn't anticipated I'd be doing would be spending so much time in the week that followed with you so much in my head.'

Mallon stared at him in delight. 'You thought of me sometimes?'

'Often,' he replied. 'That first Saturday when I came down to Harcourt House it somehow didn't seem to sit well with me that I was there and you were in a hotel.' He smiled as he confessed, 'I know I couldn't settle until I'd come to get you the next day. For my sins only to be annoyed that, while I'd been thinking how you must have been put off men, you'd been spending time with some man named Wilson!'

'Wilson?' Mallon queried. 'Oh, Tony Wilson!' she remembered.

'How could you?'

'How could I what?'

'Here am I, growing all irritated over the man—and you can barely remember who he is!'

'You're—irritated over…?'

'I believe it's called jealousy,' Harris replied, a light of such tenderness in his eyes that her heart seemed to turn right over.

'You were jealous?' she asked incredulously. 'But we barely knew each other.'

'My dear,' Harris replied softly, 'there just isn't any logic to the way I feel about you. I was glad one minute that there wasn't a phone in the house so Wilson couldn't call you. But I couldn't get a phone installed quickly enough to stop Phillips coming around with telephone messages. I was, by turns, jealous, then angry. But I knew that I liked to find you at Harcourt House so much that I didn't care at all for the notion of you packing with the intention of spending a second weekend at the Clifton Hotel.'

'You asked me to stay,' she recalled.

'And,' he took up, 'when I couldn't resist giving in to my need to kiss your irresistible mouth, I had to pretend that the need was yours.'

'You rat!'

'Love me?'

Mallon backed away from that one. 'You were saying?'

Harris took time out to gently touch his mouth to hers. Then, his grip on her firming, he drew back to say ruefully, 'I shouldn't have done that. Just as I shouldn't have kissed you that Saturday when we both had the idea of taking a shower.'

'I remember.' She smiled. Would she ever forget it? It was the night she had realised she was in love with him.

'That was the night I told you that you were in no danger—but didn't think to mention that—I was.'

'You were in danger?'

'Of falling in love with you, my darling,' Harris murmured tenderly.

'Oh,' Mallon whispered on a gasp of breath.

'I wasn't admitting it—not then,' he owned.

'Of course not.' Had he really said he had been in danger of falling in love with her?

'But I had never felt like that before—as if I was losing some of my control. I realised I needed to leave in order to sort myself out.'

'And did you? Sort yourself out?'

'Not then. All I knew then was that the moment I was apart from you I wanted to be back with you. I was constantly pulled to go down to Upper Macey—and was constantly fighting it. Only when I recognised what my true feelings for you were did I see that, while visions of your beautiful body threatened my self-control, it wasn't just your body I was enamoured with but you and your inner loveliness.'

'You're—enamoured of me?' Mallon asked shyly.

Harris looked down into her face, seemed to love looking at her, and then said tenderly, 'Dear Mallon Braithwaite. My darling Mallon Braithwaite. What do you think it is that I've been telling you for the last ten minutes if it's not that I love and adore you to total and complete distraction?'

'Oh, Harris,' she sighed.

'Do you mind?'

'Not at all,' she answered breathlessly.

'And—do you think you could love me a little in return?' he asked carefully, going urgently on when she seemed too shy to answer, 'I know you've been harmed in the past, but I'll never harm you. You know...' But Mallon, while feeling more than a little euphoric, was sud-

denly bombarded by a recollection of how she had felt
bruised and harmed by his visit a couple of days ago. All
warmth for him left her face. 'What's wrong?' Harris demanded at once. 'Tell me…'

'What's your relationship with Vivian Holmes?' Mallon
butted in, her rosy feeling of belief in his love starting to
painfully crumble.

'I don't have a relationship with her!' Harris denied,
without having to think about it.

'That's why you brought her down to Harcourt House
last Sunday, was it, because you don't have a relationship
with her? That's why you showed her all over the house,
asked her if she'd seen enough, listened to her…?'

'Vivian Holmes is one very well thought of interior designer,' Harris butted in this time.

Mallon's mouth formed an 'O'. 'But…' she began,
though as she started to relive the time last Sunday Vivian
being an interior designer did seem to fit. 'You didn't say,'
Mallon argued as she got herself together a little. 'I would
have thought you'd have mentioned…'

'You're right, of course,' he agreed, and the corners of
his mouth started to curve in a hint of a self-deprecating
smile. 'And normally I probably would have said she was
an interior designer come to have a look around. But you'd
got me in a stew, Mallon,' he confessed.

'I—had?'

'Believe it, my love. I'd so wanted to see you, yet knew
I should stay away. But I had to come to see you because
I couldn't stay away. For the first time in my life I felt
vulnerable. There have been times when I just wanted to
quietly hold you, and others when I've quite desperately
wanted to make love with you. It was after our lovemaking
a week ago that I started to feel I could no longer trust
myself to be alone with you and began to grow fearful that

you might leave if the same thing happened again. Yet what guarantee did I have that, in that obstacle course of a house, some other floorboard might not trip us up or some other minor accident would occur, and, alone with you there, I might find you in my arms?'

Mallon stared at him thunderstruck. 'You—brought Vivian Holmes down because...'

'Because I couldn't stay away any longer. Though it was Faye I rang first to ask to come with me because I felt I shouldn't risk being alone with you.' He smiled then. 'I was in a state about you—but you'd been through enough, my darling.'

Mallon had a feeling that if Harris went on like this for much longer her backbone was going to melt. 'But—Faye didn't want to come?'

'She'd got some business she was in the middle of, and since I'd merely asked if she fancied just coming along for the ride, not making anything big of it, of course...'

'Of course.' Mallon found she was smiling again. 'So you rang Vivian...' She broke off when Harris shook his head.

'I was growing more and more desperate to see you, and in the process of wondering if I dared risk going down to Upper Macey anyway, Faye rang to say her friend Vivian had just phoned for a chat during which—Faye in the past apparently having gone into raptures about Harcourt House—Vivian said she was just dying to see it.'

'That's when you rang Vivian?'

Harris placed a tender kiss to the side of Mallon's face. 'That's when I rang her. I told her I had my own ideas about the place but that I'd welcome hearing any suggestions she had to offer. So...' his look became rueful '...I came and I saw you, and I felt some gigantic thump in my chest when you came in looking absolutely adorable with your arms full of wild flowers, and I wished Vivian Holmes a hundred miles away.' He smiled then as he added, 'I wanted you all to myself, Mallon Braithwaite.'

'You came back,' Mallon said softly. 'You left Vivian in the car and came back.'

'I needed some time alone with you. And you kissed me, and I wanted to hold you, and to go on holding you. I, my dear, was feeling more vulnerable than ever.'

'You—w-were?' Mallon asked shakily.

'Oh, yes,' he owned, and confessed, 'Which left me having to return to London when I didn't want to go at all. Which consequently had me making plans to go down to Upper Macey at the weekend and deciding—if you weren't happy with me sleeping under the same roof—to pick you up from the Clifton early in the morning on Saturday and Sunday. Only...'

'Only?' Mallon prompted, her head spinning, her heart racing with all he was saying.

He kissed her again, and held her that little bit closer. 'Only I couldn't wait until Friday evening to hear the sound of your voice.'

'Ah,' she whispered. 'So—you rang me at Harcourt House this morning.'

'And knew—the instant you said you were leaving—that I couldn't let you. That I love you with everything that's in me. That I can't let you go.' Harris paused to place a gentle, almost reverent kiss on her brow before going on, 'When I realised that I didn't have a clue where to find you I broke out into a cold sweat. I had to find you. Life without you, my dear love, would be unbearable.'

'Oh, Harris!' Mallon sighed.

'Does that mean that you're—glad I found you?' he wanted to know.

Mallon laughed lightly; she just had to. 'You know I am,' she answered.

'As in—you love me a little?'

Oh, she loved him, loved him, loved him. 'As in—I love you a lot.'

'Oh, my darling,' Harris breathed, and, as if he had been holding himself in check for far too long, he drew her close up against his heart and held her so for long ageless moments. 'You're sure?' he asked urgently, pulling back to look into her face.

'I've been sure ever since that night we shared the same shower room,' she answered honestly.

'You knew *then*?' He seemed astounded.

'There were indications along the way,' she replied. 'But that was when I knew.'

'Sweet love,' he breathed, and kissed her, held and kissed her, and kissed her again, until at last he drew away and, with his arms around her, guided her over to the sofa where they sat close. Then he kissed her again, and said those magical words she thrilled to hear. 'Mallon, Mallon, I love you so,' he told her, and when she bathed in the glow of his love but was too choked to say anything, he prompted, 'And you…?'

Mallon beamed—and found her voice. 'And I love you, so much,' she answered, and kissed him, and was kissed in return.

'Thank heaven!' he murmured, and, after holding her close for many minutes, confided, 'I didn't know whether I should call here tonight or early in the morning. But my soul was in torment, and it just seemed beyond me to leave seeing you until tomorrow—even if,' he added with a lopsided kind of grin, 'I was unsure of my reception.' She smiled lovingly at him, and he went on, 'I stood there, when you opened the door, desperately trying to gauge from your expression if I was about to make the biggest fool of myself of all time.'

'Oh, Harris!' She had never thought to hear him sound so uncertain over anything. 'Thank you for braving it,' she said from her heart, and admitted, 'I've been in a bit of—er—torment myself, over you.'

'Oh,' he breathed softly. 'I'm so very sorry.' As though to wipe away any pain she had endured, he tenderly kissed her. But, looking into her eyes, his expression grew solemn. 'Why did you try to leave me?' he asked. 'You are going to tell me?' he pressed.

Mallon went a little pink as she confessed, as she knew she must, 'I thought that if you came down to Harcourt House at the weekend you might bring Vivian Holmes with you. I'm sorry, Harris, but the thought of you and her s-sleeping in the room next to me was more than I could take.'

Harris was hugging her close up to his heart before she had finished. 'Oh, sweetheart,' he murmured. But, drawing back to look into her sunny blue eyes, 'You were—jealous?'

'You sound surprised.'

He grinned cheerfully. 'Such a notion had never occurred to me.'

She kissed him because she loved him. She could hardly believe what was happening, and because she wanted to see his face she drew back this time. Then she heard the sound of a car on the drive.

'It sounds as if my mother and John have come home early. Um…'

'Um?' Harris queried.

'I—er… Well, my mother wanted to know what had happened to bring me home. I told her I was in love with you…' Harris's beam of a sudden smile caused her to break off. But she felt she had to tell him the rest before her mother came in. 'I also told her that you had a lady-friend.'

'You meant Vivian Holmes?' Mallon nodded, and he smiled and said, 'Then, my darling, it looks as if I shall have to untell her. Perhaps I'd better do that before I ask her.'

'Ask her?' Mallon queried when he didn't add anything.

'Well, I suppose it's your mother I ask. Though it could be your stepfather. Do you know?'

'What?' Mallon asked, by then feeling totally confused.

'It's customary, I think, to ask a parent for the hand of their daughter. I've never done this before, but I'd like to get it right.'

'Hand?' Mallon queried faintly.

'We are getting married, aren't we?' he asked, his expression all at once never more serious. Mallon swallowed hard, her heart thundering. She hadn't thought... 'You will marry me?' Harris pressed. 'I won't rush you if...'

'I'd love to marry you,' she answered chokily.

He exhaled a held in breath. 'Good. Thank you, my love,' he murmured, and, bringing her left hand to his mouth, he kissed it. 'Perhaps by the time we come home from our long honeymoon Harcourt House will be ready for its mistress.'

Mallon gasped. 'Me?' she said in wonder.

'Only you,' Harris replied, and tenderly kissed her.

'Oh, Harris,' Mallon cried. Mistress of Harcourt House, wife to its master! Oh, how wonderful!

STAND-IN MISTRESS

by

Lee Wilkinson

Lee Wilkinson lives with her husband in a three-hundred-year-old stone cottage in a Derbyshire village, which most winters gets cut off by snow. They both enjoy travelling and recently, joining forces with their daughter and son-in-law, spent a year going round the world 'on a shoestring' while their son looked after Kelly, their much loved German shepherd dog. Her hobbies are reading and gardening and holding impromptu barbecues for her long-suffering family and friends.

Don't miss Lee Wilkinson's exciting novel, *Mistress Against Her Will,* out in July 2008 from Mills & Boon® Modern™.

CHAPTER ONE

'AND the installation work could be carried out without delay?'

'Yes, certainly.' Cool and efficient-looking in a charcoal-grey suit, her slim, nylon-clad legs neatly crossed, Joanne was quietly confident.

There was a brief pause while the burly managing director of Liam Peters thought it over.

'Well, if your company can give me the kind of service you've just outlined, Miss Winslow, I believe we can do business,' he said pleasantly.

'I'm sure we can,' she promised.

Elbows resting on the arms of his chair, hands steepled, he stared at her across the desk.

Smooth sable hair framed an oval face with good features—dark blue eyes, widely spaced, a generous mouth, a straight nose, and a determined chin.

Not exactly beautiful, he decided, but an interesting face, full of character.

'In that case I'll expect your team of technicians to be here first thing Monday morning to talk to me.'

'They will be,' she assured him, and smiled.

That smile made him revise his previous opinion.

Rising to his feet, he accompanied her to the door of the outer office and they shook hands cordially.

Barely restraining the impulse to jump for joy and shout 'Yippee!' she made her way sedately out of the newly completed office block and into Fulham Road.

She was immediately engulfed by the golden brightness of an early-September afternoon and the ceaseless roar and bustle of London's traffic.

After months of worry, as the economy declined and the company her brother had built up began to founder, things seemed to be looking up.

For over five years Steve had struggled to make Optima Business Services successful, but the recession had meant less work and put a severe strain on the company's slender financial resources.

The first really tricky patch had been weathered by mortgaging their house. But the second squall, coming fast on the heels of the first, had threatened to sink them.

Then, just that morning, Steve had been promised a substantial injection of cash by MBL Finance, an international investment company who specialised in helping small businesses.

Now, heaven be praised, she had as good as secured what promised to be a lucrative contract to set up a large new communications network.

About to head in the direction of the nearest tube station, Joanne glanced at her watch. She was surprised to find it was twenty minutes to five. At this time on a Friday there was no point in going back to their Kensington offices.

She was less than ten minutes' walk away from where they lived, so she might as well go home and start preparing a meal for when the rest of the family got in. Turning, she headed for Carlisle Street, and the house she shared with her brother, Steve, her sister, Milly, and Milly's husband, Duncan.

Milly would no doubt be home by now, packing. The young couple were moving to Scotland, where Duncan, a newly qualified doctor, had recently been offered a position at a practice in his home town of Edinburgh.

A furnished flat above the surgery went with the post, and the journey by overnight sleeper meant they would be in Edinburgh by seven-thirty tomorrow morning, which would allow them plenty of time to get settled in over the weekend.

What had made the offer even more acceptable was that one of the receptionists had recently left, and Milly had been given the chance to take over her job.

Even so, she had seemed edgy and unsettled, less than enthusiastic about moving so far north, and her obvious reluctance had caused some trouble between herself and Duncan.

When she protested, with some passion, that she liked the secretarial job she had now and didn't want to leave, Duncan had pointed out quietly that before she married him he'd made it quite plain that he planned to return to Scotland.

Unable to deny this, she had resorted to tears, and, when they did no good, ragged outbursts of temper. But to Joanne's immense relief, Duncan, as steady and level-headed as Milly was wild and wilful, had largely ignored her tantrums.

When Joanne reached Carlisle Street, which was quiet and tree-shaded, lined by old and elegant town houses with porticoed entrances, she walked down it with her usual feeling of nostalgia.

Number twenty-three had belonged to her parents. A happy family home, its front room had been used as an office, with a gold-lettered sign in the window that read: 'John and Jane Winslow. Solicitors.'

Then five years ago the pair had died together in a train crash in Mexico, while on a second honeymoon.

Milly, the youngest of the family, had been only thirteen at the time. Instead of returning to university for the autumn term, Joanne had joined her brother's business venture so she could be on hand to look after both of them.

Steve had protested that at twenty-two he was old enough to look after himself, but had been only too pleased to have the running of the house taken off his hands.

Joanne climbed the steps, put her key in the lock, and let herself in. She had expected to hear pop music blaring, but the house was still and silent. It seemed Milly wasn't home after all.

When she'd changed from her business suit into trousers and a top, she made her way down to the pleasant, airy kitchen.

Having plugged in the kettle for a cup of tea, and opened up the stove, she began to prepare the evening meal. Lisa, Steve's secretary, and now his fiancée, was coming home with him tonight, so they could make it a family celebration.

With that thought in mind, Joanne found a couple of bottles of sparkling wine and put them in the fridge.

She was in the middle of adding a breadcrumb and pine-kernel topping to the cheese and broccoli bake when Milly appeared in the doorway.

Petite and pretty, with red-gold hair, bright blue eyes and a figure like a pocket Venus, she was usually sparkling and vivacious, dressed up to show off her charms.

Now, wearing scruffy jeans and a shrunken T-shirt, she looked edgy and in low spirits as she slumped down at the table.

'I didn't realise you were home,' Joanne remarked. 'No music.'

'Didn't feel like playing any.'

'Still worrying about the move?' Joanne asked with some sympathy.

When Milly said nothing, she added reassuringly, 'I'm sure there's no need to. Once you've settled in and made some new friends you'll be fine.'

Her face sullen, Milly muttered, 'What about my job? You know how much I enjoy it…'

Rather than go to college, Milly had chosen to take a secretarial course. Quick and intelligent, despite her some-what flighty ways, she had done well. On completing the course, she had found a job with Lancing International, filling in for one of the secretaries who was on maternity leave.

She had proved so efficient that when the new mother failed to return she had been offered the post on a permanent basis.

'Well, I'm sure you'll find your new job interesting,' Joanne said soothingly.

Milly snorted. 'Depressing, more like. Who wants to be stuck in a doctor's surgery day and night?'

Letting that go, Joanne poured them both a cup of tea and sat down opposite, before enquiring, 'Finished packing?'

'I haven't even started.'

'If you need any help let me know.'

'I'm not sure whether I'm going.' The words were spoken defiantly.

As lightly as possible, Joanne said, 'I don't see you have much choice. All the arrangements are made. And, after all, Duncan is your husband.'

'You don't need to remind me. I wish I'd listened to you when you said I was too young to get married.'

Joanne's heart sank. It was true that, thinking Milly too immature, she had at first opposed the marriage. But Duncan had seemed both sensible and stable, and the pair had been so very much in love, that she had finally given her blessing.

'Duncan and I have quarrelled so much lately that I'm beginning to wonder if the whole thing was a mistake,' Milly added miserably.

Hiding her dismay, Joanne said calmly, 'You know perfectly well that you're only feeling this way because of the move.'

Taking a gulp of her tea, Milly shook her head. 'There's more to it than that.'

'Stuff and nonsense,' Joanne said briskly.

'You don't understand. I think I'm in love.'

'As you've only been married for a few months I should hope so.'

'I don't mean with Duncan. I still care about him, of course, but I think I've fallen for someone else.'

'If it's Trevor, he will be flattered.' Joanne tried to make a joke of it.

Diverted, Milly pulled a face. 'What you see in that pompous git I can't imagine... You may not be Miss World but you could do better than him.'

'Thanks,' Joanne said drily.

'Duncan doesn't rate him either,' Milly added, as though that settled it. 'He has about as much charisma as a worm without any charisma.'

'I certainly wouldn't call Trevor a worm,' Joanne objected mildly.

'Neither would I, on second thoughts. He's too picky and bossy. He'd want to tell you what to do all the time.'

'I'll bear that in mind. I should hate to marry the wrong man.'

'Like me, you mean?'

'Don't be an idiot!' Joanne exclaimed with a sharpness born of fear. 'You haven't married the wrong man. Duncan is exactly what you need.'

'But I keep trying to tell you... I've fallen for someone else.'

Taking a deep breath, Joanne said, 'Well, if it isn't Trevor, you'd better tell me who it is.'

'My boss. Brad Lancing... Now, he *is* charismatic.'

'Brad Lancing!'

'He's absolutely gorgeous! Handsome, clever, and totally charming... He has the most fascinating eyes you've ever seen... And that mouth...' Milly practically drooled.

So that explained Milly's moods, her reluctance to leave her job. Joanne groaned inwardly.

Seeing the look on her sister's face, Milly said, 'You think I'm just being a fool, don't you?'

'According to Steve, Lancing is a married man with children, so the answer's yes.'

'Steve's wrong. I know for a fact that he *isn't* married and he *hasn't* any children. He's a thirty-year-old bachelor.'

Unsure which version to believe, Joanne countered, 'And you're an eighteen-year-old married woman.'

'Age doesn't matter, and I don't feel married when I'm with him. I feel…well…*wonderful*.'

'Oh, Milly,' Joanne said helplessly, 'don't you know that a lot of women fall for their boss, while most bosses scarcely notice their secretary?'

'Brad notices me,' Milly assured her triumphantly. 'The two nights I told you I was working late, I was having dinner with him.'

Suddenly scared half out of her wits, Joanne croaked, 'You didn't go any further?'

'No, I didn't. But from some of the things he said, and the way he looked at me, I know he wanted to.'

Joanne gritted her teeth. When Milly had first started to work for the company, Steve had mentioned that Lancing had a bad reputation as far as women were concerned.

But she hadn't worried, never dreaming that a sophisticated man like him would be even remotely interested in a girl who was just eighteen, and newly married, to boot.

He must be a complete and utter swine, and totally without scruples.

'Surely you realise a man like that is only out for what he can get?' she said desperately. 'And when—'

'Don't tell me, I know… When he's got it he won't respect me. Well, I'm fed up with being *respected*. I want some excitement in my life, and if this trip to Norway does come off…' She stopped speaking abruptly.

'What trip to Norway?'

'If it turns out to be necessary, Brad will be going to Norway for six weeks or so on business. He's asked me to go with him.'

Tight-lipped, Joanne demanded, 'As what?'

'His secretary, of course,' Milly answered demurely.

'But you're no longer working for him. You've given in your notice.'

Milly shook her head. 'I haven't said anything about leaving. I haven't made up my mind about going to Scotland...' Seeing the look on her sister's face, she faltered to a halt.

Joanne's cup rattled into the saucer. 'You can't seriously mean that you're willing to risk destroying your marriage because of a silly infatuation?'

'Oh, but I—'

'Hasn't it occurred to you that Brad Lancing probably only wants a brief fling? Another notch on his bedpost? Even if I'm mistaken about him being married, he has a reputation as a Casanova... And what about your wedding vows?'

'I was too young to tie myself for life.'

'At the time you assured me you were ready for the responsibilities of marriage.'

'Well, I thought I was.'

'So did I. And so did Duncan. But if you're stupid and immature enough to jump into bed with the first man you regard as *gorgeous*, we were obviously wrong.'

Flushing, Milly hit back. 'Oh, you've always been so prim and proper. If you're not careful you'll end up an old maid, or married to someone as narrow-minded as Trevor.'

'Suppose you leave me out of it.' Joanne tried to speak calmly. 'It's *your* future we're discussing...and Duncan's. He absolutely adores you. Have you thought what this will do to him?'

'I never wanted to hurt him,' Milly said unhappily. 'But I don't seem able to help myself. I keep thinking about this wonderful trip to Norway and what I'll lose if I don't go.'

'Try thinking about what you'll lose if you *do* go. A future with a good man who loves you, who'll stand by you; a home of your own, and a chance to make a life together in a beautiful part of the world...

'Suppose you give up all those things and this *wonderful trip* doesn't materialise?'

Seeing the uncertainty on her sister's young face, Joanne pressed home her advantage. 'You can't expect Duncan to wait around tamely to see whether his wife is going to Scotland with him, or to Scandinavia with another man.'

Milly bit her lip. 'I'll know by tonight if the trip's on. Brad's been away on business for over a week, but he said he'd be back this evening and if the Norway trip needed to go ahead he'd call me.'

'Here?'

'Yes. You see, there's not much time. If it is all systems go, we'll be travelling tomorrow morning.'

'What if he doesn't call?'

Milly twisted her wedding ring round and round her finger. 'I don't know. I may go to Scotland... I'm not sure—'

The sound of a key turning in the lock cut through her words, and a moment later a voice called cheerily, 'Milly, darling, I'm back.'

Scrambling to her feet, Milly said urgently, 'Jo, you won't say anything to Duncan until I've made up my mind?'

'Not a word. But if you don't want him to start asking awkward questions, I suggest that while I finish getting dinner ready you go up and make a start on some packing.'

As the girl hurried away, her bright-blue eyes clouded with worry, Joanne rose heavily to her feet and collected the cups and saucers.

Damn Brad Lancing! she thought violently as she rinsed and dried them. How *could* he encourage someone who was obviously just an easily-led young girl, and *married* into the bargain?

Milly might have imagined herself in love with him, but if he hadn't taken her out to dinner and dangled the bait of this Norwegian trip in front of her she wouldn't be seriously contemplating leaving Duncan.

Standing wringing the tea towel between her hands as though it was Brad Lancing's neck, Joanne was still mentally castigating him when the wall-phone, just by her head, rang.

She picked it up on the first ring and gave the number distractedly.

'Miss Winslow?' a clear, well-modulated voice asked.

'Yes.'

'Brad Lancing. The Norwegian trip is on. I'll be pleased if you'll have dinner with me tonight, so we can discuss the travel arrangements...?'

A red mist forming in front of her eyes and the blood pounding in her ears, Joanne was about to tell him who she was, and exactly what she thought of him, when a sudden sense of caution brought her up short.

Would that be wise?

Rather than giving up, a man like him, with no sense of shame, might only keep on trying to contact the girl he had obviously marked down as his next conquest, and somehow she must prevent that at all costs...

While her thoughts raced frantically, part of her mind registered the fact that the attractive voice was going on, 'I'll be at Somersby's at seven-thirty, if you can make it?'

About to say coldly that she couldn't, Joanne hesitated. Then, reasoning that if she agreed, as he doubtless expected, he would have no cause to argue or phone again, she adopted Milly's slightly breathy way of speaking, and said, 'Yes, I'll be there.'

'The address is Grant Street, Mayfair. Take a taxi.'

A second later she heard the receiver at the other end being replaced. It seemed he was a man of few words. Which was a blessing. If he'd tried to engage her in conversation it would have been difficult to keep up the pretence.

Even worse, Milly might have put in an appearance, and so long as she believed he hadn't rung she could well decide to go to Scotland.

Once there, and settled into her new life, surely this temporary infatuation would die a natural death?

Feeling somewhat more cheerful, Joanne went back to preparing the meal.

Everything was in the stove, and she had just started to set the table when a most unwelcome thought presented itself. Brad Lancing had said *Somersby's at seven-thirty*... If no one turned up, would he ring again to find out why?

Her blood ran cold. That could prove disastrous.

At seven-thirty they would still be sitting down to their meal, and, expecting him to ring, Milly would hardly hold back and let her sister fob him off.

Well, there was only one thing for it, Joanne decided; she would have to keep the appointment. At least it would give her a chance to tell him to his face just what she thought of men like him...

She heard the sound of the front door closing, and footsteps crossing the hall. A moment later Steve and his fiancée appeared in the doorway.

An inch or so under six feet, and slimly built, Steve was dark-haired and blue-eyed. With a thin, intelligent face and good features, he just missed out on being handsome.

But he was so genuinely *nice* that Joanne had often wondered why he hadn't been snapped up. Except he worked so hard that, until a few months ago, there had been no time for a woman in his life.

Then Lisa, small and blonde and as sweet as she was pretty, had come to work for him.

It had been love at first sight, and now with a baby on the way—unplanned, they had admitted sheepishly, but very much wanted—they were busy making arrangements for a late-October wedding.

Sniffing appreciatively, Steve said, 'Something smells

good.' Then with undisguised eagerness, 'How did things go with Liam Peters?'

'Monday morning, first thing, you can send in the troops.'

He gave a whoop of joy and, seizing hold of her, whirled her round until she was breathless.

'Looks as if you've had some good news,' Duncan remarked as he and Milly joined them.

'You're not wrong… And we're going to have a real celebration! There should be a couple of bottles of bubbly somewhere.'

'It's already in the fridge,' Joanne said.

'Clever girl!' Taking a bottle, Steve eased out the cork, poured the wine and, having handed a glass to each of the others, raised his own in salute.

'Here's to us, and particularly Jo, who's managed to swing the deal with Liam Peters, as well as finding time to take care of us all and cook some marvellous meals.'

There was a little burst of cheering, and they all drank. The bubbles made Milly sneeze, and then laugh.

Drawing a deep breath, Joanne took the plunge. 'I *hope* it's a marvellous meal tonight. I'm sorry to say I won't be here to share it.'

Seeing the surprise on all their faces, she added hurriedly, 'Trevor forgot it was tonight Milly and Duncan were leaving for Scotland, and he booked expensive seats at a special concert he knew I particularly wanted to go to.'

Perhaps the explanation was a little fulsome, but it was the truth, as far as it went.

What she failed to add was that, on discovering what he'd done, she had paid for her ticket—Trevor wasn't one to waste money—and suggested that he take his mother instead.

Milly, clearly disappointed, moved closer to her fair-haired husband, who put his arm around her.

Please God, things would work out, Joanne thought,

watching them together. Milly was too young to mess up her life.

'Well, if you won't be here on our last night,' Duncan said cheerfully, 'we shall expect you to be our first visitor when we get settled in.'

'Done!'

'Lisa's staying over,' Steve said; as he opened the second bottle of wine, 'so I won't need to turn out to drive her home…'

Afraid of being late in case Brad Lancing was the impatient sort who might call to see where she'd got to, Joanne left the others talking, and, having rung for a taxi, slipped upstairs to shower and change.

Needing to keep up the pretence of her concert-going, she put on her best silk suit, made up with care, fastened pearl studs onto her neat lobes, and swept her dark hair into an elegant chignon.

When she came down again, Duncan whistled, and Milly nodded approvingly. 'Not bad. Though I have to say it's wasted on Trevor.'

Then a little tremulously, 'Well, I guess we'll be gone before you get back…'

So she had decided to go. Joanne said a silent prayer of thanks.

With her emotions running high, and feeling the prick of tears behind her eyes, she hugged her sister and brother-in-law and said as brightly as possible, 'Have a good journey… And as soon as you're ready for visitors, let me know.'

'Will do,' Duncan assured her.

The doorbell announced the arrival of the taxi, and after more quick hugs all round, Joanne said, 'Well, enjoy your meal,' and fled before she could disgrace herself by crying.

Somersby's proved to be a select and stylish restaurant above an art gallery. The taxi dropped Joanne at the awninged entrance, and, her heart beating fast, she climbed a flight of red-carpeted stairs.

At the top, a uniformed attendant was waiting to open the heavy glass doors for her.

As she crossed the luxurious foyer she went over in her mind all the things she intended to say to Brad Lancing. When she had, hopefully, made him squirm, she would walk out.

No, that wasn't the way to do it. It would be almost three hours before Milly and Duncan started for the station, and in that time, left to his own devices, Lancing might phone and throw a spanner in the works.

She just couldn't chance it. Somehow she needed to keep him occupied until Milly was safely on the train.

But how?

That still undecided, Joanne found herself facing another dilemma. She had no idea what he looked like. She pictured him as floridly handsome, with bold eyes and a sensual mouth. Possibly even a moustache.

Apart from Duncan, who was good-looking in a boyish, wholesome way, she and Milly had never shared the same taste in men, Milly tending to go for the more blatantly sexual.

Oh, well, if she just walked in, hopefully there wouldn't be too many men sitting alone waiting for their dates. But it was only seven-twenty-five; suppose he hadn't yet arrived?

As she hesitated in the doorway, the *maître d'* appeared at her elbow. 'Good evening, madam.'

'Good evening. I'm joining a Mr Lancing.'

Inclining his head, he murmured, 'If you'll come this way?'

Rehearsing in her mind what she was going to say, Joanne followed as he led the way to a small, secluded table in an alcove, where a man with thick dark hair was sitting.

He glanced up at their approach, and then rose politely to his feet.

Over six feet tall and broad-shouldered, his face lean and tanned and, apart from a certain toughness, almost ascetic, he was so unlike the florid, thickset man she had visualised that for a moment she wondered confusedly if the waiter had made a mistake.

But, stopping by the table, he murmured discreetly, 'Your guest, Mr Lancing.'

Somehow Brad Lancing's appearance threw her, and instead of the words she had been rehearsing, wits completely scattered, she found herself stammering, 'M-Mr Lancing… I'm Miss Winslow…but, as you see, the wrong one.'

He raised dark, well-marked brows. 'Not the one I was expecting, admittedly, but equally charming.'

Hating him on sight, she explained a shade breathlessly, 'I'm Milly's sister.'

'You're nothing at all like her,' he observed dispassionately.

'No.'

'Won't you sit down?'

'Thank you.'

He remained on his feet until the *maître d'* had pulled out her chair and settled her, before resuming his own seat.

At least the brute had manners, she conceded.

'I'm afraid I'm the bringer of bad tidings,' she said as soon as they were alone.

His eyes were every bit as fascinating as Milly had said. A clear dark green, and put in with a sooty finger, they made her breath quicken as they rested on her face. 'Nothing too dreadful, I hope?'

'Milly can't come,' she informed him in a rush.

'I see.' Then like a rattlesnake striking, 'You're the Miss Winslow I spoke to on the phone.'

Shaken by his perspicacity, she found herself admitting, 'W-well, yes.'

'In that case you're not the wrong one at all.' He smiled a little, drawing her attention to his mouth.

Firm and controlled, yet passionate, it had a combination of warm sensuality and cool austereness that might have made almost any woman drool, and Joanne realised all too clearly why Milly fancied herself in love with him.

She was dragging her gaze away with an effort, when he said softly, 'Tell me, Miss Winslow, why did you pretend to be your sister?'

'I—I didn't...'

Ignoring her instinctive denial, he insisted, 'Of course you did. You even imitated her voice.'

Weakly, Joanne said, 'It was just a joke... She wasn't there, and I...'

'You were simply answering for her?'

'Yes.'

'Do you always answer for your sister?'

'No, of course not... But I knew she'd want to come...'

'So why isn't she here?'

'Well, just before she was due to start, she had an emergency call from an elderly aunt,' Joanne improvised wildly. 'Poor Aunt Alice had just had a bad fall and was refusing to go into hospital. Milly is very fond of her...'

Just for an instant Joanne thought she saw a gleam of unholy amusement in those clear green eyes, but his face showed no trace of a smile as he said, 'I know how these family relationships can be.'

'She wasn't sure how long it would take to get Auntie settled,' Joanne ploughed on, 'and she thought she might possibly have to stay the night.'

'So you came in her place?'

'Well, yes... I thought I'd better come and explain in person.'

'Much nicer and more *friendly* than simply phoning,' he agreed drily.

It was quite obvious what he was thinking, and suddenly she knew exactly how to play it.

Desperate situations called for desperate measures. If she could flatter his ego, pander to his vanity, make him believe she fancied him, he might ask her to have dinner with him.

If he did she should be able to string him along until Milly was safely out of his clutches. *Then* she would have the pleasure of telling him exactly what she thought of him.

Trying for a spot of girlish confusion, she admitted, 'I must confess, I've been hoping to meet you.'

'Really?' he murmured, a glint in his eye.

'I've heard such a lot about you from Milly.'

A look she couldn't decipher crossed his face, before he asked ironically, 'Can any secretary be relied on to say good things about her boss?'

'Surely that depends on the boss?' Joanne's answer was a little sharp, and, reminding herself of the role she had decided to play, she gave him a coy glance from beneath long, silky lashes, and added, 'If he happens to be a man like you...'

As though genuinely curious, he asked, 'So what exactly did...Milly...say about me?'

'She said you were clever, charismatic, and totally charming.'

Just for an instant he looked disconcerted. Then he observed lightly, 'I might find that description difficult to live up to. However,' he went on with a touch of self-mockery, 'rather than let the ''world of bosses'' down, I'll try...'

At that moment one of the waiters came up and handed them both a leather-covered menu.

'Oh...' Joanne made to rise. 'I really ought to go and let you have your meal in peace.'

He asked, as she'd been hoping he would, 'Won't you stay and dine with me?'

'Well, I…'

'Unless your fiancé would object?'

He had sharp eyes, she thought as she answered, 'No, I'm sure he wouldn't.'

'Then please, do stay.'

'Thank you, I'd like to.' She made no attempt to hide the eagerness.

'Would you care for a drink while you look at the menu? Champagne, perhaps?'

The glass of wine she had drunk earlier, combined with all the emotional turmoil, had made her feel strangely light-headed, but she managed a smile, and agreed, 'That would be lovely.'

He signalled the wine waiter and gave the order.

Within moments, the man was back with a bottle of the finest champagne in an ice bucket. Having gently twirled the bottle for a moment or two, he removed the wiring, eased out the cork, and poured the smoking wine into two flutes, before departing soft-footed.

Joanne was watching the bubbles rise, when her companion raised his glass and, his eyes smiling into hers, said softly, 'Here's to an exciting evening.'

She smiled back, and took a cautious sip. With a bit of luck he would get more excitement than he'd bargained for!

CHAPTER TWO

PLAYING for time, Joanne sipped her champagne and scanned the menu for as long as she dared, before choosing a melon starter and a main course of avocado and prawns.

The order given, Brad Lancing fixed her with his handsome eyes, and asked, 'By the way, as your sister's spokeswoman, can you tell me if she still intends to go on this Norwegian trip?'

Caught wrong-footed, Joanne hesitated, then said lamely, 'Well, I think she'd like to.'

Picking up on that uncertainty, he explained, 'You see, there's not much time. I have two seats booked on a plane that leaves Heathrow at lunch time, and if your sister is likely to be still tied up with...your auntie I shall need to find myself another secretary.'

And one who was willing to be his bed-companion, no doubt, Joanne thought sourly.

Hoping to give him as much trouble as possible, she assured him, 'I'm quite sure Milly won't want to let you down.'

Recklessly, she added, 'And if by any chance she can't come, I might even volunteer for the post myself!'

A devilish gleam in his eye, he refilled her glass and said, 'I might hold you to that. But you'd need to come prepared. The nights can get pretty chilly.'

'Oh, I'm sure I could cope.'

'Have you much experience?'

Loathing both him and the *double entendre*, she gave him a come-hither look and cooed, 'Oh, yes, lots.'

'Where are you working now?'

Reluctant to provide too much personal information, she said briefly, 'Optima Business Services.'

'Owned by Steven Winslow.'

It was a statement not a question, but she answered, 'That's right.'

Brad Lancing seemed to know a great deal. But perhaps Milly had told him?

'So you act as your brother's secretary?' he pursued evenly.

'I've been Steve's personal assistant for over five years.'

Reacting to her tone, he said, 'I see.' Then, a challenge in his voice, 'And are you a good PA?'

'If I wasn't I wouldn't have kept the job. Neither of us believes in nepotism.'

As soon as the words were out it struck her that she had been replying as *herself*, rather than the kind of woman she was pretending to be.

Giving him a flirtatious glance, she said in her best girly voice, 'But *I'm* not very interesting… I'd much rather talk about *you*, Mr Lancing.'

His firm mouth twitched. 'Won't you call me Brad?'

'I'd love to, if you call me Joanne.'

'It will be my pleasure.'

Taking a sip of her champagne, she smiled at him over the rim of the glass. Then, recalling something Milly had once said, she leaned towards him and murmured in a husky voice, 'I've always found handsome, powerful men like you a real turn-on.'

The 'like you' was her own contribution.

An expression that might have been amusement flitted across his face, making her wonder if she was overdoing it, but it was gone in an instant, and she decided it must have been self-satisfaction.

Someone as vain and egotistical as he undoubtedly was would lap up any amount of flattery.

He must have been looking forward to a romantic evening with a girl who thought he was wonderful, and being a womaniser, he would no doubt have seduction on his mind.

Well, let him believe she was a pushover. The shock would be all the greater when he discovered that instead of the sex kitten he was hoping for, she was a cat with claws.

For the next hour or so, while they ate what turned out to be a very good meal, Joanne flirted with him shamelessly. Hanging on his every word, she touched his sleeve from time to time and occasionally let her foot nudge his under the table.

Avoiding questions about herself as much as possible, she made an effort to keep the conversation centred on him.

It proved to be harder than she had anticipated.

Most men, even the nicest ones, were usually happy to keep their egos inflated by talking about themselves, but Brad Lancing, while prepared to discuss the business scene, seemed unwilling to divulge anything remotely personal.

Perhaps he was married after all?

If he was, she pitied his poor wife.

'I suppose you must travel an awful lot?' Joanne enquired as the waiter brought the liqueur coffees Brad had ordered.

'Not as much as I used to. These days I only travel if I believe my presence is really essential.'

'Your wife must be pleased about that,' she remarked idly, taking a sip of her coffee.

Those green eyes pinned her, making her go oddly fluttery. 'I'm not married,' he told her coolly, 'nor have I ever been remotely tempted to put my head in the silken noose.'

'Oh…'

With a gleam of mockery, he added, 'Who was it said, "Love all and marry none"?'

'Whoever it was, I understand you follow their advice to the letter?' The sharp words were out before she could prevent them.

'I have until now,' he admitted easily. Then with a side-long glance, 'You sound as if you disapprove?'

She answered the question with another. 'Who was it said, "Gather ye rosebuds while ye may"?'

'Now, that one I *can* answer. Herrick.'

His voice, as well as being attractive, was educated, but, not having put him down as a man who would take much interest in poetry, she was surprised by his knowledge.

'Do you agree with the sentiment?' he pursued.

'I suppose so,' she admitted, 'though I haven't had much time for gathering rosebuds.'

'Why not?'

She replied briefly, 'When our parents died in a train crash I left college to take over the running of the house.'

'How old were you then?'

'Nineteen.'

'And you went to work for your brother at the same time?'

'Yes.'

'How many were there in the family?'

'Just three. Steve, who's the eldest, myself, and Milly, who was only a schoolgirl.'

'So you've been a mother to your younger sister?'

'You could say that.'

Seeing he was about to probe further, she forced a bright smile, and changed the subject. 'I understand that you'll be in Norway for six weeks or so?'

'That's right.'

'It seems a long time for a business trip. Are you planning a new project?'

'No. Just sorting out a family business that's been in existence for generations.'

'A family business?' she echoed in surprise. 'Surely Lancing isn't a Norwegian name?'

'No, it was my mother who came from Norway. Her father was Norwegian and her mother English. An only child, she lived with her parents in Bergen until she met and married my father.

'After that she only returned to Norway for holidays, though the family remained close until she was killed in an accident just over a year ago.

'When my grandfather died shortly afterwards he left me the Dragon Shipping Line and hotel business he'd spent his entire life running.

'Since then there have been quite a few problems, and a while ago I sent one of my best men over there to deal with them.

'Paul was fairly sure he was well on his way to sorting them out without needing me, but during the last couple of months things have started to go wrong again.

'Then this morning something more serious happened that made up his mind that he needed my help, and he contacted me to say he thinks I should go after all.

'If the problems *had* been resolved I would probably have left my trip until the spring. But as it is, I can't let things drift until then.'

Starting to feel more than a little woozy, she asked, 'Why spring?'

'Because, though September is a wonderful time to hike in the hills, Norway is particularly beautiful in the spring when the ice is breaking up and the rivers are in spate…

'You see, as well as dealing with the business side, it's my intention to take some time off and have a break.

'Due to pressure of work I haven't had a proper holiday for a couple of years, and I haven't been to Norway for more than a few days at a time on business.

'I'm very fond of my mother's homeland, so the thought of taking a real holiday there is an enticing prospect…'

Enticing enough to almost make Milly leave her husband, Joanne thought bitterly.

He raised a winged brow. 'Judging by your expression, you don't think so?'

'Not at all,' she disagreed hastily. 'I've always thought Norway must be wonderful. Which part are you going to?'

'Bergen. Have you ever been there?'

'No.'

'Have you done much travelling?'

'Not since my parents died. Though I did have a long-weekend break earlier this year.'

'Where did you choose to go?'

'I was hoping to go to Rome, but Trevor favoured Amsterdam.' Now, what on earth had made her tell him that?

Picking up her left hand, he examined the diamond solitaire she wore. 'Trevor being your fiancé?'

After a brief hesitation, she said, 'Yes.'

He stroked over her knuckles with his thumb, sending a shiver through her. 'But obviously he's not the jealous type?'

'No.' Restive beneath his touch, she withdrew her hand, and glanced a shade muzzily at her watch. Milly and Duncan should be away from the house in the next five minutes or so...

'You seem eager to leave,' Brad commented lightly.

She was. Her mission accomplished, she couldn't wait to end the charade and escape. 'Well, if you need to make a fairly early start tomorrow...'

'Yes, you're quite right,' he agreed, signalling the waiter. 'It's time we were making a move.'

High time. Drawing a deep breath, she turned to tell him exactly what she thought of him, but just at that instant the waiter arrived.

While Brad paid the bill, and added a generous tip, she glanced around. There were still quite a few people within earshot, and, disliking the idea of making a scene in the quiet restaurant, she decided to wait until they were outside.

When she had picked up her bag he drew back her chair, and she rose to her feet a shade unsteadily. A hand cupping her elbow, he escorted her out of the restaurant and across the foyer.

Distinctly light-headed, she had to make herself concentrate as they descended the red-carpeted stairs. A couple of steps from the bottom, she stumbled, and he was forced to steady her.

At the entrance, a sleek grey limousine was drawn up, a liveried chauffeur holding open the door. Before Joanne could gather her wits Brad had handed her in and was sitting beside her.

'I'd intended to get a taxi,' she said in belated and breathless protest as they drew away.

'Oh?'

Without turning his head, the chauffeur asked, 'Straight home, sir?'

'Yes, please, Gregory.' Brad touched a button and the glass partition between the driver and his passengers closed. A moment later blinds slid into place, covering both the partition and the windows.

Taking immediate advantage of the softly lit intimacy, he caressed her silk-clad knee.

Flinching away in a sudden panic, and wishing desperately that she hadn't been foolish enough to get into the car in the first place, Joanne announced as firmly as possible, 'I live in Fulham, and I—'

'Yes, I know.' He drew her close, and an instant later his mouth was covering hers.

Shocked by the suddenness of the move and by the tumult of feeling his kiss evoked, for a moment or two she made no attempt to free herself.

When, remembering just *who* was kissing her, she pulled herself together and began to struggle, his arms merely tightened and he deepened the kiss.

Terrified now, she began to struggle in earnest, but he was so much stronger than she had realised, and he held her easily.

Tearing her mouth free, she gasped, 'Leave me alone. I don't want you to touch me...'

Looking completely unruffled, he remarked, 'From the way you've been behaving, I rather thought you were inviting it.'

'Well, you were wrong. I want to go home,' she added shakily.

'That's where we are going.'

'*My* home,' she insisted.

'Somehow I'd got the impression that, in spite of being engaged, you'd intended to come home with me.'

Her heart throwing itself against her ribs, she said hoarsely, 'Well, you were wrong! I'd like you to tell your chauffeur to stop and let me get out right this minute.'

Raising his dark brows in mock-surprise, he queried, 'So what made you change your mind?'

'I haven't *changed my mind*. I—'

'I'm pleased to hear it.'

Ignoring the interruption, she rushed on, 'I haven't *changed my mind* because I never had the slightest intention of going home with you.'

His voice holding more than a hint of soft menace, he said, 'I wouldn't like to think you'd been leading me on just for the hell of it.'

She swallowed hard. 'I haven't been leading you on just for the hell of it—'

'Well, as you have undoubtedly been leading me on, perhaps you'd like to tell me why?'

'Because I needed to keep you occupied, to prevent you contacting Milly,' she admitted in a rush.

He smiled grimly. 'So your sister was at home all the time? Oddly enough I never did believe in poor Auntie Alice...

'But I'm afraid I don't understand why you were prepared to go to such lengths to stop me contacting my own secretary?'

'If you *had* spoken to her she would have dropped everything and come.'

'I see,' he said slowly. 'And you thought she might be…keeping my bed warm tonight?'

'I know she would.'

'You don't know anything of the kind.'

'She's infatuated with you.'

'And you blame me for that?'

'Of course I blame you. She told me how you'd taken her out to dinner, and the way you'd looked at her.

'If I hadn't discovered what was going on, and happened to intercept your phone call, she would have risked everything to be here.'

He frowned. 'Risked everything?'

Into her stride now, Joanne rushed on, 'Steve told me you had a rotten reputation as far as women were concerned, but I never dreamt that even a swine like you would go after a girl who's only eighteen and married into the bargain—'

'Married?' He sounded startled.

'Don't pretend you didn't know.'

Her face full of contempt, she lashed out at him verbally. 'You're a miserable, womanising bastard, and totally without principles!

'You dangled the bait of a Norwegian trip in front of her until she was almost prepared to break up her marriage and go to Norway with you, rather than move to Scotland with her husband—'

'Would you care to slow down a little…? I'm getting confused. I thought she lived with you?'

'She does, and so does her husband… Or rather they *did*. They'll soon be on their way to Edinburgh to live, and hopefully Milly will be well out of reach of lecherous men like you…' Running out of breath, Joanne stopped abruptly.

'Now I'm beginning to understand,' Brad said evenly.

'Presumably they're taking the night sleeper, and you wanted to keep me occupied until your sister was safely on board and couldn't change her mind...'

'That's right.' Joanne made no secret of her triumph. 'Now, if you'll ask your chauffeur to stop and let me get out...'

When he made no move she threatened shakily, 'If you don't I'll start screaming.'

Calmly, he said, 'Even if I allowed you to scream, I doubt very much if anyone would hear...'

Recalling both his strength and his total lack of scruples, she shuddered.

'And I can't help but feel you owe me...'

When she said nothing he pointed out, 'You seem quite certain that your sister would have been sharing my bed tonight.'

'Well, I'm not Milly,' she cried desperately.

'But earlier you agreed that you'd come in her place. You even boasted that you were experienced.'

Watching all the colour drain from her face, he observed mockingly, 'Now you're acting more like a frightened schoolgirl than a woman with lots of experience.'

He ran his hand up her thigh and, his voice smooth as satin, queried, 'You did say "lots"?'

She pushed his hand away, and seeing the gleam in his eye, realised he was enjoying baiting her, getting a little of his own back.

Suddenly afraid of how far he'd go, she begged, 'Please don't.'

'That's better,' he applauded.

'Will you let me get out?' Despite all her efforts her voice shook betrayingly as she added, *'Please.'*

His dark, well-shaped head tilted a little to one side, he pretended to consider. Then he said ironically, 'As you're asking so prettily, and I don't want to add kidnapping to my list of crimes, I'll be happy to take you home. Where do you live, exactly?'

She gave him her address.

He pressed a button, and, speaking into a small grille, ordered, 'Gregory, I'd like you to go straight to Fulham and drop Miss Winslow at twenty three Carlisle Street.'

'Thank you,' she said through gritted teeth.

Settling himself back into his seat, Brad turned to her and asked seriously, 'Suppose I told you that you're totally mistaken about my relationship with your sister? That as far as I'm concerned she's simply a nice girl and an efficient secretary?'

So now he was trying to excuse himself, make himself out to be whiter than white.

As she remembered the way he had slid his hand up her thigh Joanne's blood boiled.

'Knowing what kind of man you are, I wouldn't believe a word of it,' she said contemptuously, and moved as far away from him as the seat would allow.

For a while they sat in a silence that, keyed-up as she was, soon became nerve-racking. Bracing herself, she stole a sideways look at his clear-cut profile.

It was cold and set, and she realised that he was quietly, but furiously, angry.

But then he was not only a man whose lies had been summarily rejected, but also a hunter deprived of his prey.

Serve him right, she thought with immense satisfaction. Let him go to bed frustrated for once.

He turned his head and glanced at her. As he caught sight of her gleeful expression, his own face hardened even more.

At that precise moment the limousine slowed down, drew into the kerb, and stopped.

The instant the chauffeur opened the door, Joanne scrambled out without a backward glance, only to find Brad close on her heels as she crossed the broad pavement.

Accompanying her up the steps, he waited impassively

in the lamp-lit porch while she found her key, then, taking it from her nerveless fingers, he opened the door.

'Thank you.' Her voice was cold, and, dropping the key back into her bag, she turned away.

'Before you go,' Brad said silkily, 'in view of the expectations you raised, I think at the very least I'm entitled to a goodnight kiss.'

Stepping over the threshold, he pinned her back against the door panels.

'Get your hands off me, you—'

Ignoring her protest, he covered her mouth with his and kissed her deeply.

His kiss was insolent, punitive, and by the time he finally lifted his head she was dazed and breathless.

Looking down into eyes that brimmed with tears of rage, he said, 'As you're convinced I'm a lecherous, unfeeling brute, I thought you'd be disappointed if I didn't act like one.'

As he moved back she lifted her hand and slapped his face as hard as she could. Then, catching her breath in a kind of sob, she fled into the house, banging the door behind her.

Trembling in every limb, she sank down limply onto the hall chair, and, taking a tissue from her bag, scrubbed repeatedly at her lips, as if trying to remove every last trace of his kiss.

Damn Brad Lancing to hell! she thought furiously as she listened to the car door slam and the limousine drive away. He had to be the most obnoxious man she had ever met, and if she never saw him again it would be too soon. He was immoral and arrogant and quite unscrupulous...

Seething futilely, she sat mentally flaying him, until the worst of her agitation had subsided and she had returned to a state of relative calm.

Everywhere was quiet and, apart from the hallway, the house seemed to be in darkness. Presuming that Steve and

Lisa had gone to bed, she bolted the door and made her way upstairs.

As she reached the landing Steve's bedroom door opened. 'I know this sounds dead nosy,' he admitted with an unrepentant grin, 'but we happened to see you getting out of a posh limousine…'

Oh, hell! Joanne thought helplessly. In the circumstances, the last thing she wanted was to have to explain where she had been, and why.

It wouldn't be fair to tell anyone else about Milly's involvement, especially now everything was, hopefully, going to be all right.

'I can't imagine it belonged to Trevor?' Steve pursued.

'No,' she said after a moment.

As Lisa appeared at his elbow he added, 'The man who got out with you…while not in the least like Trevor, looked strangely familiar…'

'Did he?' she stonewalled.

'Though I've only seen him once—Milly pointed him out one day when I picked her up from work—he's not a man one would easily forget…'

When she said nothing, his voice teasing, Steve urged, 'Come on, Sis, give. Can't you see we're both dying of curiosity to know what you were doing out with Brad Lancing?'

Caught off balance, and unable to think of any satisfactory explanation, she admitted boldly, 'I was having dinner with him.'

Steve whistled softly. 'So you were *lying* about Trevor and the concert tickets?'

'Not exactly. He did get some tickets, but I told him I couldn't go.'

Frowning, Steve said, 'I know the engagement isn't *official* but this isn't like you, Sis…'

Joanne groaned inwardly. Now, on top of everything else, Steve thought she was cheating on Trevor.

She wished, not for the first time, that, even at the risk of hurting his feelings, she had refused point-blank to wear Trevor's ring until she had come to a firm decision.

When she said nothing, sounding baffled, Steve commented, 'I didn't even realise you knew Lancing.'

'I only met him recently.'

'Why did you…? No, don't tell me, I can guess why you kept it a secret. You didn't want to upset Milly when she'd developed this schoolgirl crush on the guy…'

So Steve had been aware of Milly's infatuation, but, judging by his casual tone, he hadn't appreciated what terrible consequences there might have been.

But, showing he *had*, he went on, 'The trouble is, men like him aren't to be trusted. If he'd turned on the heat things could have been difficult, to say the least.'

Then awkwardly, 'I know it's none of my business, Sis, but if you intend to go on seeing Lancing you will take care, won't you?'

'I'm almost twenty-five,' she pointed out a shade tartly. 'Old enough to know what I'm doing…'

That was a laugh.

'And if it sets your mind at rest, I'm unlikely to be seeing him again. Tomorrow he's going to Norway for six weeks on business.'

Briskly, she added, 'Now I'm off to bed. Goodnight, you two.'

Escaping into her own room, she closed the door firmly behind her, and went through to the bathroom to strip off her clothes.

What a night! she thought wearily. The only thing she could hope was that she had managed to discomfit Brad Lancing as much as he had annoyed her.

Rather than falling for him, as Steve seemed to fear, she had found him hateful and despicable. The few hours spent in his company were some of the worst she had ever had to endure.

Remembering the unpleasant little scene in the car, the way he had run his hand up her thigh and, his voice smooth as satin, queried, 'You did say "lots"?' she shuddered. He had deliberately gone out of his way to frighten and humiliate her.

Joanne brushed out her long dark hair and pulled on a voluminous cotton nightie, before cleaning her teeth more vigorously than usual.

Then, climbing into bed, she switched off the light, closed her eyes, and endeavoured to put Brad Lancing right out of her mind.

After more than an hour she was still wide awake and, in spite of all her efforts, still thinking about him, repeatedly going over in her mind everything he had said and done.

Especially that last devastating kiss.

She could still recall the way his mouth had ruthlessly mastered hers; smell the subtle scent of his aftershave; taste the hint of liqueur and the freshness of his breath; feel the way every nerve in her body had tightened in response.

Just thinking about it was enough to stir her senses and, she was horrified to realise, make a core of liquid heat start to form in the pit of her stomach.

No! She tried hard to deny it. How could a man like that, a man she both loathed and despised, arouse a desire that a decent, upright man like Trevor had never been able to awaken?

It was *unthinkable*.

Disturbed and wholly dismayed, she tossed and turned restlessly, finally drifting into an uneasy doze around dawn.

Joanne was trawled from the depths by a persistent sound that it took her a moment or two to identify as the doorbell.

It was almost certainly the postman, who was tending to come early these days, and she didn't want Steve to be disturbed. Working as hard as he did, he liked to sleep late at the weekend.

Stumbling groggily out of bed, she pulled on her dressing gown and, tying the belt around her slender waist, padded barefoot down the stairs.

All the time the bell kept ringing with a maddening persistence that grated on her nerves. So much *noise*, and he probably only wanted to deliver one of those aggravating packets that gave themselves importance by saying, 'Please do not bend...' and then contained just junk mail.

Having drawn back the bolts, she threw open the door, and burst out crossly, 'Will you please stop ringing the bell? My brother's still in bed and...'

The words died on her lips.

Brad Lancing was standing there wearing a well-cut suit and a matching shirt and tie. Freshly shaved, his thick, dark hair parted on the left and neatly brushed, his green eyes clear and sparkling with health, he looked dangerously attractive and virile.

Before she could slam the door in his face he took his finger off the bell-push, and strolled in as if he owned the place.

As, the wind taken completely out of her sails, Joanne stepped back, he closed the door behind him and stood gazing down at her, his six-foot frame easily dwarfing her.

Straight-faced, he studied her shiny nose, the dark, silky hair tumbling round her shoulders, her demure Victorian nightdress and gown, her slim bare feet, and commented, 'Just up, I see.'

Infuriated by his obvious amusement, she demanded, 'What are you doing here?'

'Can't you guess?'

'It's too early in the morning for guessing games,' she informed him curtly, 'so perhaps you wouldn't mind just telling me what you want?'

His eyes glinted at her tone. 'You.'

'What?' she said stupidly.

'I'll be setting off for Norway around lunch time today, and I need a secretary. As it's the weekend and too late to make other arrangements, I've decided to accept your offer.'

'Offer? What offer?'

'Surely you remember offering, "If by any chance Milly can't come, I might volunteer for the post myself"?'

'I wasn't serious.' She took a step backwards and, a panicky edge to her voice, repeated, 'Of course I wasn't serious.'

His dark, winged brows drew together in a frown. 'That's a pity, because when I said I might hold you to it, I *was*.

'Now, clearly your sister isn't in any position to come, so the job's yours.'

Knowing he'd noted that touch of panic, and determined to stay cool, Joanne said, 'Thanks, but I already have a job.'

'I'm sure that, for the next six weeks or so, your brother could find himself another PA.'

With polite finality, she said, 'Even if he could, I wouldn't be taking up your offer.'

The door to the kitchen was ajar, and, glancing in at the comfortable-looking high-backed chairs drawn up in front of the stove, Brad suggested, 'Rather than stand here, suppose we go through and have some coffee while we talk about it?'

'I've no intention of making you coffee, and I don't want to talk about it.'

Stepping past him, she held open the front door. 'Now, if you'll please leave.'

When he made no move to go, losing her cool, she cried, 'Go on, get out! If you don't leave this instant I'll call Steve and get him to throw you out.'

'Are you sure that's wise?'

Though his tone was mild, it was undoubtedly a threat,

and she hesitated. There was something about his firm mouth, the set of his jaw that, despite his quiet manner, his veneer of charm, made him formidable.

She shivered.

Steve was far from being a seven-stone weakling, but she sensed instinctively that he would be no match for this man.

As she stood irresolute, Brad Lancing took control once more. Closing the door, he put a hand beneath her elbow and urged her towards the kitchen.

Digging in her toes, she said mutinously, 'As far as I'm concerned, there's nothing to talk about. You are the last person in the world I would choose to work for.'

He shook his head almost regretfully. 'Ah, but you see, you don't have a choice. At least not if you care what happens to Steve's company.'

'What do you mean, "care what happens to Steve's company"? Of course I care.' She was aware that the note of panic was back in her voice.

'Then we do have something to talk about.'

He strode into the kitchen, leaving her to follow in his wake, demanding anxiously, 'What *could* happen to Steve's company?'

Ignoring the question, he asked, 'Would you like to make some coffee?'

'I've already told you, I wouldn't.'

He indicated one of the armchairs. 'Then perhaps you'd like to sit down?'

'I don't want to sit down. I want to know what you're talking about.'

Plugging in the electric kettle, he began to calmly assemble the cafetière and mugs. 'When we're both sitting down with a cup of coffee, I'll be happy to explain.'

CHAPTER THREE

SEEING he meant to have his way, she bit her lip and sat down, watching him with angry eyes.

His movements were deft, assured as he spooned coffee into the cafetière and filled it with water. She wondered abstractedly how such a masculine man could look so at home in a kitchen.

It was the last thing she had expected.

A lot of wealthy men with a staff of servants to wait on them had probably never even seen the inside of a kitchen.

As though aware of her hostile scrutiny, he turned and cocked an eyebrow at her. 'Milk and sugar?'

'Just milk, please.' She forced herself to answer civilly.

He handed her a mug of coffee and, putting his own on the stove where he could reach it, sat down in one of the high-backed chairs and regarded her quizzically.

Because he was well-groomed and smartly dressed, with her hair tumbling round her shoulders she felt dishevelled, and at a distinct disadvantage in what Milly referred to as her 'little orphan Annie' garb.

In a reflex action, she tucked her bare feet beneath her voluminous skirts, and saw him smile.

Gritting her teeth, she said as calmly as possible, 'Now you've got what you wanted and we're both sitting down with a cup of coffee, perhaps you'll tell me what could possibly happen to Steve?'

Brad answered with a question of his own. 'I understand your brother's having a hard struggle to keep his company afloat?'

'What makes you think that?'

'It's true isn't it?'

'It *was* true. But now things are looking up.'

'Really?' he drawled.

'Yes, really! Not only has Steve found an investment company willing to put money into Optima, but we've also just secured a contract to install a large new communications network.'

'For Liam Peters?'

Wondering how he knew, unless Milly had told him about the negotiations, she said, 'Yes.'

'What would your brother do if both those opportunities were to fall through?'

A chill running down her spine, she demanded, 'Why should they fall through?'

As though she hadn't spoken, Brad went on smoothly, 'With the house mortgaged up to the hilt, and scarcely enough money in hand to pay the staff their next month's wages—'

'Who told you that?' she broke in angrily.

'After I'd dropped you off last night I spent a little while checking up—'

'Well, wherever you got the information—'

'I got it from the horse's mouth, so to speak.'

'I don't know what you mean.'

'You've just told me your brother was promised a loan by an investment company?'

'Yes.' Shaken as she was by a sudden nameless fear, her voice was barely above a whisper.

'Before agreeing to lend a business money, the first thing an investment company does is obtain a very clear picture of their client's current financial situation, as well as the business's future prospects. MBL is no exception—'

'How do you know it was MBL…?' Almost before the words were out, she froze.

Watching the dawning look of horror in her deep blue eyes, he waited quietly.

With a courage he was forced to admire, she sat up straighter and lifted her chin. 'What does the M stand for?'

'Michael. Though the family have always used my middle name.'

'You don't happen to own Liam Peters too?'

'It's a subsidiary of Lancing International.'

'But surely you don't control their policies, or interfere in their internal decisions?'

'Not normally. But if I wanted to, all it would take is a word in the right ear.'

While the full enormity of what he was saying sank in she sat staring straight ahead, feeling curiously numb and empty.

She could hear herself asserting 'You are the last person in the world I would choose to work for'.

And his response: 'Ah, but, you see, you don't have a choice. At least not if you care what happens to Steve's company'.

After a moment she said carefully, 'There must be more ethical ways to acquire a secretary?'

'I'm sure there are. But, as I don't want just *any* secretary, it's a case of needs must...

'You see, as this will be part-holiday, I want not only an efficient PA, but also a companion. I don't find there's much pleasure eating alone, sightseeing alone, spending the evenings alone...'

So this was what Milly had been asked for.

'I'd like someone intelligent to talk to, someone to share things with—'

'If you mean your bed, I won't sleep with you,' she broke in sharply. 'I won't be your mistress.'

He laid it on the line. 'If you really want to save your brother, you'll do anything I want you to do. Be anything I want you to be.'

'I've got a fiancé.'

'That didn't seem to worry you last night.'

Head bent, she clenched her hands together until the knuckles showed white. Then, looking up, her eyes so dark they appeared almost black, she moistened dry lips, and asked, 'Why me?'

He laughed, as though that was a silly question.

And perhaps, in the circumstances, it was.

'Shall we call it poetic justice? You deprived me of a perfectly good secretary—'

'But Milly wasn't free to—'

Taking no notice of the interruption, he went on relentlessly, 'And with no personal knowledge of what kind of man I really am, you attacked and reviled me.

'I'm afraid I don't take kindly to being called a lecher and a liar, and my motto has always been, ''Don't get mad, get even.'''

And this was his way of doing it. To use and humiliate her.

Feeling as though her blood had turned to ice in her veins, she shivered, seeing now, with hindsight, that it had been playing with dynamite to incense a man as ruthless as Brad Lancing.

Of course, he *might* be bluffing. For an instant she clung to the thought. But if she refused, and he *wasn't*, it would not only be the end of the company Steve had worked so hard to make successful, but the end of the road for them all.

There weren't that many jobs about. With no money coming in they would find it impossible to keep up the high mortgage payments...

Added to that, it might well put the young couple's wedding plans in jeopardy, and with a baby on the way the whole situation could become a nightmare...

And it would be all her fault.

If only she had had more sense...

But it was too late for regrets, and, having got into this

mess, how could she let Steve and Lisa and the loyal, hard-working staff at Optima suffer because of *her* stupidity?

The answer was, she couldn't.

If she hadn't meddled in the first place she would never have met Brad Lancing and none of this would have happened... But something even worse *might* have done.

At this very moment, Milly, rather than being safely in Scotland, might be wrecking not only her own life but also Duncan's, by going to Norway with a womanising swine who would drop her the minute he had had his fun.

It didn't bear thinking about. At least *this* way there would only be herself who would suffer...

She had looked up to give Brad Lancing her answer, when the door opened and Steve walked into the kitchen wearing a short navy-blue towelling robe.

Barefoot, his dark hair rumpled, he rubbed the back of his neck and yawned widely. 'I could do with a coffee if there's any made?'

'There should be some in the pot.' She was surprised by how steady her voice sounded.

'Thanks. Lisa's still asleep so I'll...' The words tailed off as he caught sight of Brad. 'Sorry, I didn't realise you had a visitor.'

'An early one, I'm afraid.' Brad rose to his feet and held out his hand. 'I'm Brad Lancing... You must be Steve.'

The two men shook hands. Neither smiled, and Steve's face had a cool, guarded look.

Joanne took a deep breath. 'Mr Lancing called to—'

'Brad, please... There's no need for formality outside the office.'

'Brad,' she tried not to stumble over the name, 'called because he's in need of a secretary...'

As she paused momentarily, searching for the right words, Steve said, 'Well, as Milly's in Scotland, I fail to see how—'

Hearing the faint suggestion of antagonism in her

brother's tone, Joanne broke in hastily, 'You don't understand... Somehow there's been a mix-up—'

'What kind of a mix-up?'

'Milly failed to hand in her notice, and apparently no one realised she was leaving so soon. Brad is going to Norway today, and, as there's no other secretary available, I've agreed to go in Milly's place,' she finished in a rush.

Looking taken aback, Steve demanded, 'What about your own job?'

'Lisa could take over for the few weeks I'll be away. She said only yesterday that she didn't have enough to do.'

Seeing by Steve's face that he was about to argue, Joanne said decidedly, 'I'm sure she'd jump at the chance to get some added experience. And, as Milly has let Brad down, I feel I owe it to him.'

'I don't see that it's *your* responsibility to make up for Milly's misunderstanding.'

'Perhaps not.' Then knowing she had to convince him it was what she *wanted* to do, she added, 'But I'd very much like the chance to see something of Norway.'

'I can't imagine your *fiancé* will care for the idea of you being away so long.' It was obvious that Steve had emphasised the relationship for Brad's benefit.

With more confidence than she felt, she said, 'He'll understand when I explain about Milly.'

'You're going to ring him?'

'Yes.'

She would have to make time to break the news. Trevor was already seriously displeased with her over the concert tickets, and this *desertion*, as he would no doubt see it, certainly wouldn't help matters...

Feeling too stressed at the moment to cope with what she felt sure would be an angry and hostile reaction, she chickened out. 'But not now. He's taking his mother to Bournemouth for the weekend. When I'm sure he's back I'll decide on the best way to break it to him.'

'Well, of course, it's up to you,' Steve said with obvious disapproval. 'How soon will you have to start for the airport?'

'As soon as possible.' It was Brad who answered. 'There's a lunch-time flight from Heathrow to Bergen via Oslo.'

'You'll be based in Bergen?'

'Yes. I'll give you the address and phone number.' Then to Joanne, 'You won't have had breakfast yet, but we'll get something to eat at the airport.'

She nodded, and rose to her feet.

'How long will it take you to pack and get ready?'

'Half an hour or so. I can't say exactly,' she answered shortly.

Catching his eye, and suddenly daunted by the gleam of anger she saw there, she added, 'But I'll be as quick as I can.' Then was annoyed with herself.

'Two things... Don't forget your passport...'

Seeing what might be a way out, she was about to say she hadn't got one, when she recalled telling him about the trip to Amsterdam. Sighing inwardly, she wished she had kept her mouth shut. But it was too late now.

'And do pack a raincoat.'

Rattled, because it sounded like an order, she asked sweetly, 'What about gumboots?'

'Good idea,' he answered, straight-faced. 'It can be very wet in Bergen.'

Bested, she made a rapid retreat.

Steve followed her into the hall and, his blue eyes worried, said urgently, 'I just hope you know what you're doing.'

'At my age I should do,' she answered levelly.

'Look, Jo, I'm well aware that you're no silly schoolgirl, but you will watch your step, won't you? Brad Lancing has—'

'If you're going to say a wife—' she began.

'I'm not. It appears my informant was mixing him up with his cousin, *Blake* Lancing, who works for the firm, and who *has* got a wife and family...

'But what I intended to say when you interrupted me was, Brad Lancing has loads of sex appeal and, where women are concerned, apparently, not too many scruples.'

'So?'

Looking uncomfortable, Steve came to the point. 'Though I wouldn't have thought you were his type, he may have designs on you...'

Joanne was smiling a little at the old-fashioned phrase, when he added, 'And in some respects you're more naïve and vulnerable than Milly, and less able to take care of yourself.'

'Thanks a lot,' she said wryly.

'Listen to me, Sis,' Steve persisted. 'Lancing's a wealthy, sophisticated man, way out of your league. He's a heart-breaker, with a reputation for loving 'em and leaving 'em—'

'Don't worry, I know all about his reputation,' she interrupted firmly.

'And you still intend to go?'

'Yes.'

Steve sighed. 'I just don't want you to get badly hurt.'

'I won't.'

He looked unconvinced.

'Don't worry about me.' She gave him a hug. 'I'll leave you to explain things to Lisa. But I'll make the time to have a quick word with Milly before I go.'

Looking surprised, he said, 'In view of her crush on Lancing, I didn't think you'd want to tell her.'

'I've no intention of telling her, but if I don't get in touch to make sure they've arrived safely she might ring after I've gone.'

'Yes, I see what you mean.'

'If I can keep her in ignorance for the time being, all

well and good. Knowing Milly, she'll want to set about redecorating the new flat, so for the foreseeable future she's likely to be wrapped up in her own affairs.'

'Well, if she does ask where you are we'll stall her and let you know, then you can give her a ring…

'Hang on, we're forgetting something. What about your birthday?'

'Oh, no,' Joanne groaned. 'She's sure to get in touch for that… Well, if at all possible, I'd like you to hide the fact that I've gone to Norway with Brad. I should hate to unsettle her.'

'Tell you what, I'll swear blind you've gone to Paris with Trevor.'

He turned to go back to the kitchen as his sister hurried up the stairs.

When Joanne had showered and dressed in a smart suit and a white tailored blouse, and taken her hair into a neat coil, she set about unearthing her case from the depths of the built-in wardrobe.

Steadfastly refusing to think about what lay ahead, she packed as quickly as possible, putting in only what she considered to be essentials.

As she closed the lid and fastened it she noticed Trevor's ring, and wondered, Would it be best to leave it at home?

But if she took it off Brad might get the wrong idea. No, she would keep it on and hope that it might act as some kind of safeguard.

Though, since she knew the kind of man he was, that could well be a vain hope.

Gathering up her belongings, she carried her case downstairs and stood it in the hall while she rang Milly, who answered with a grudging, 'Hello?'

'Hi! So you're home?'

'Oh, it's you! I thought it was another patient. We've

had two calls already and the surgery doesn't open until nine.'

Deciding to ignore that, Joanne asked, 'Did you have a good journey?'

'Very good. Slept the whole way, and the train got in on time. There's a supermarket just round the corner from here, so we did a quick shop and were in the flat before eight-thirty.'

'What's it like?'

'Quite spacious and not badly furnished, but most of the walls are a boring beige, which means one of our first jobs will be to redecorate.

'Most of the boxes we sent ahead have already arrived and are waiting to be unpacked, so we've an awful lot of work to do before we can get properly settled. I hate unpacking! I'm at the stage where I can't find a thing...'

As Joanne listened to a string of complaints both the men appeared in the hall. Steve, usually one of the most even-tempered of people, was looking more than a little flushed and aggressive, while Brad appeared to be as cool as a proverbial cucumber. She wondered what they had been saying to each other.

'At the moment,' Milly was going on, 'the kettle seems to be missing, which is a dratted nuisance...'

'Well, I'd better let you get on and look for it.' Joanne made her voice as cheerful as possible. 'I'll be in touch before too long to—'

'Jo,' Milly broke in, 'has Brad been in touch?'

'No, he hasn't,' Joanne lied hardly, and, meeting those green eyes, saw by the mockery in them that he knew quite well what question she'd been answering.

Biting her lip, she added quickly, 'Here's Steve to have a word. Take care, now. Love to Duncan.'

As she handed the receiver to her brother he gave her a one-armed hug, and whispered, 'If you need rescuing, just let me know.'

Brad picked up her case and, like a programmed robot, she led the way to the door. On the threshold, she turned to blow Steve a kiss.

The morning was clear and sunny, and as they descended the steps a playful breeze snatched a handful of bright leaves from a silver birch and swirled them around their heads like confetti.

They could be a couple leaving on their honeymoon, she thought with bitter irony.

While the chauffeur stowed her case, Brad helped her into the limousine and, taking a seat by her side, regarded her quizzically.

Running a finger beneath the lapel of her smart charcoal-grey business suit, he asked, 'Do you always dress to make a statement?'

She answered primly, without looking at him, 'I try to wear what's suitable for the occasion.'

'Then I shall certainly look forward to tonight.'

Suppressing a shudder, she moved as far away from him as possible, and the journey to the airport continued without another word being spoken.

While the silence stretched Joanne went back over the last hour or so, trying to come to terms with the appalling situation she found herself in; trying to find some way of escape.

Without success.

In spite of racking her brains, she could find no solution. It seemed she would be forced to go through with it. But how exactly was she going to play the hand her own stupidity had landed her with?

She considered briefly whether she could refuse to have any social contact. If she just did her job, carried out orders, spoke to him as little as possible and then only about business...

But common sense told her that wouldn't help matters.

In fact, being difficult, while it might give her a certain satisfaction, could only make a bad situation worse.

After all, if she shared his meals and his evenings, listened when he wanted to talk, appeared to conform, it didn't mean she had surrendered.

If she remained coolly polite, and acted in a civilised manner, as though he was simply her employer, it might make things more bearable.

And if he *had* intended to force her to share his bed, he might change his mind and find someone else.

As Steve had pointed out, Brad Lancing was a man with loads of sex appeal. There must be plenty of women who would be only too delighted to be his sleeping partner. So was there anything to be gained by trying to coerce an unwilling one?

He had no real interest in *her*. She was far from beautiful, not at all the kind of woman to attract a man like him. The only thing he wanted was revenge.

Don't get mad, get even.

Remembering his words, the confidence she had been trying to build began to crumble away.

But somehow, whatever happened, she would have to cope. And the only way she could do that was to refuse to think ahead. She must ignore what *might* happen, and find some means of getting through the here and now relatively unscathed...

Having thought it through, and made her decision, Joanne felt a little more settled by the time they reached the busy airport.

While the chauffeur dealt with the luggage she accompanied Brad to the desk to check in for their flight with something approaching equanimity.

Formalities completed, he said, 'We've got about an hour before our flight will be called, so I suggest we go and have something to eat.'

'How long will the journey take?' she asked as he led

her through the bustling throng of people to the nearest restaurant.

'The flight to Oslo takes about an hour and three quarters, and that's followed by a short hop across country to Bergen.

'Norwegian time is an hour ahead of ours, so, taking everything into account, we should arrive just nicely for dinner.'

As soon as they were seated and had each scanned the menu a waiter appeared at their table with a pad and pencil.

Turning to Joanne, Brad suggested, 'Though it's closer to lunch time than breakfast, what about bacon and eggs and all the trimmings?'

Finding she was suddenly ravenously hungry, she agreed, 'That sounds fine,' and caught his look of surprise.

As the waiter whisked away, without thinking she asked, 'Were you expecting me to go on hunger strike?'

His eyes, a clear dark green with very black pupils, looked amused. 'No, but I noticed you ate very little last night.'

'I wasn't hungry then.' She had been so intent on playing her part, and there had been so much adrenaline pumping into her bloodstream, that she hadn't wanted to eat.

'It occurred to me that you might be one of those tiresome women who prefer to live on raw carrots and lettuce leaves.'

'Before too long you might wish I was.'

He raised an enquiring brow. 'Why's that?'

'If I feel stressed I tend to eat more, and, as you'll presumably be paying for my food...'

He laughed, and she noted again that his mouth and teeth were excellent. 'I think the budget will stand it.' Slyly, he added, 'And it's a well-known fact that certain...shall we say...*activities* burn up quite a large number of calories.'

Watching her cheeks turn the colour of poppies, he went on with smooth satisfaction, 'So we'll have to make sure you get plenty of exercise. What would your brother think if I took you home all roly poly?'

Knowing that if she let herself be thrown by his teasing she would only be playing into his hands, she fought back. 'That's unlikely. Even without…exercise, I have the kind of metabolism that burns off fat…'

She saw a gleam of admiration in his eyes as she added, 'Steve is the same. Whereas Milly—'

'Can't look at a biscuit without putting on weight? Yes, she mentioned it… And before you get all indignant, it was a casual remark made at the office during a coffee break.'

At that moment their breakfast arrived.

'All the trimmings' included fresh orange juice, toast and marmalade, and a large pot of coffee.

As they tucked in Brad observed, 'I noticed that you and your brother are very alike physically… And I strongly suspect in character as well.'

He added the rider with a dryness that made her ask sharply, 'Why do you say that?'

A glint in his eye, he asked, 'Why do you think?'

Remembering how she'd smacked his face, a look of horror dawning, she whispered, 'He didn't…?'

'No, he didn't. But I got the impression he would have liked to take me on. Judging by what he said, he seems to share your very poor opinion of me…'

Her heart sank. Steve, with no idea what harm this man could do to him—and to his business.

Brad's smile was grim. 'And, though he managed to stay quiet and relatively civil, he warned me off in no uncertain terms.

'Having pointed out, yet again, that you were engaged to be married, he added that if I laid so much as a finger on you I'd have him to reckon with.

'He seems to think that you're sweet and inexperienced and might be in danger of losing your girlish innocence—'

'You didn't tell him the truth?' she broke in anxiously.

'What? That you've had *lots* of experience? No, I thought it might shock him.'

She bit her lip. 'You know what I mean. That you'd coerced me into coming… I don't want him to worry.'

'His only worry is that you might be vulnerable, and in danger of not only losing your fiancé, but also falling in love with me. If he'd known you hated the sight of me and…' Breaking off, he queried, 'I take it you *do* hate the sight of me?'

'What do you think?'

Laughing at her vehemence, he went on, 'And had only agreed to accompany me under duress he would have consigned me to hell-blazing rather than let you come. I must say, I admired his guts.'

'He cares about me,' she said simply.

Their journey proved to be pleasant and uneventful, and, tired from her virtually sleepless night, Joanne slept for most of the first part and dozed for the second, Brad only wakening her as they began their descent.

They came in to land at Flesland Airport through low cloud and rain.

'Though it's usually mild on the coast, it's wet for over two hundred days in the year,' Brad told her. 'Luckily the weather seldom seems to spoil the lovely views.'

As soon as the formalities were over they collected their luggage and made their way to the exit. Outside the air was warm and shrouded with mist and gentle rain.

There was a taxi rank close by, and as an empty vehicle drew up Brad handed their cases to the driver and, having given the man directions in fluent Norwegian, helped her in.

Joanne was vaguely surprised that no car was waiting for him. She would have expected the firm to have sent one.

As though reading her mind, he said, 'I wanted to keep

our arrival a secret until I've had time to talk to Paul Randall and assess the situation.'

'It all sounds very cloak-and-daggerish,' she remarked.

'You could say that,' he agreed lightly.

When he made no attempt to elaborate, after a moment or two she changed the subject. 'I don't like to appear terribly ignorant, but where exactly *is* the airport?'

'About twelve miles south of Bergen. When there's not a lot of traffic it takes somewhere in the region of thirty minutes to drive into the centre of town.

'It's a great pity there was so much low cloud today, otherwise you would have had a good view from the air.

'Bergen is known as "the city of the seven hills" because, as well as being beautifully situated on the coast, it's enfolded at the crook of seven mountains and fishboned by seven fjords...'

Driving on the right, their windscreen wipers steady as a metronome, they left the airport along with a fair number of other vehicles, including the *Flybussen*, which Brad translated as the airport bus.

Rain virtually obscured the view from the taxi windows, isolating them, cutting them off from the rest of the traffic and the outside world.

She was suddenly very aware of him, of how close he was sitting, and the fact that his thigh was almost brushing hers. Finding the intimacy overpowering, but unwilling to admit it, she tried surreptitiously to inch away.

The corner of his long mouth twitched, convincing her that he had noticed and been amused by her manoeuvre.

Flustered, needing something to say, she asked, 'Where are we staying?'

'There are plenty of good, modern hotels, but I thought we'd stay at Lofoten.'

'Lofoten?' she echoed uncertainly.

'The house my mother was born in. It's not far from the centre of town, and within walking distance of the harbour and the offices. That being the case, I decided it would make as suitable a base as any.

'Lofoten's a large place, and it needed to be, as my great-great-great grandparents had numerous offspring, quite a few of whom ended up in Chicago.

'After my grandfather's death, as I didn't want to part with the house, and there was no point in letting it stand empty, it was turned into a small hotel...'

Slanting her a glance, he queried mockingly, 'Relieved?'

'Yes,' she said boldly. And she was. For an uncomfortable minute she had visualised being quite alone with him. At least in a hotel there would be other people close by.

CHAPTER FOUR

ONCE past the electronic-toll inner ring road that surrounded downtown Bergen they drove through the modern part of the town and were soon in the centre.

Peering through the rain-misted taxi window, Joanne saw that most of it appeared to be old and historic.

As they crossed the end of the long, narrow harbour Brad said, 'This is Torget, Bergen's market-place. It's also known as Fisketorget.

'At the turn of the last century fishermen in wellington boots and women in long aprons used to gut the fish catch here.'

Beyond a sprawl of crooked streets lined with a hotchpotch of picturesque architecture that seemed to house a plethora of antiques shops they came to a slightly more open area.

'Here we are,' Brad said as the taxi drew up in front of an old and rambling two-storey wooden building. Standing on the edge of what appeared to be spacious walled grounds, it was painted red-ochre, and had long, smallpaned windows, arched at the top.

'This has been the family home for several hundred years,' he told her, a note of quiet pride in his voice. 'The fabric itself hasn't altered much, though the house has seen quite a few changes in its time.'

Set back from the road with a smoothly pebbled frontage brightened by tubs of late-summer flowers, it was sturdily built of clapboard, with ornate shingles and overhanging eaves. A board above the entrance porch said simply, 'Lofoten.'

Standing on the narrow pavement in the gentle rain,

while Brad paid the driver and dealt with their luggage, Joanne stared up at the roof-ridge, fascinated by the family of carved, intertwined dragon-like creatures that cavorted there.

Noticing her absorption, he asked, 'Like the Lofoten dragons?'

Turning to him, she breathed, 'They're wonderful. They have so much character.' Pointing, she added, 'Look at the expression on that little one's face, he looks quite pained.'

'Can you see why?'

Returning her attention to the roof, she laughed. 'Yes! That big one's standing on his tail.'

Gazing into her glowing face, where moisture beaded her eyebrows and long lashes and a drop of water trickled down her cheek, Brad thought in surprise, *Why, she's beautiful,* and had to subdue a sudden impulse to kiss her.

Showing no sign of tearing herself away, despite the softly falling rain, she exclaimed, 'Oh, just look at the baby!'

'I agree, he's delightful,' Brad said drily. 'But, on a strictly practical note, your hair's wet now, and if we stand here much longer we'll both be soaked to the skin...

'Though, on the plus side, we could always share a hot tub, then have the pleasure of rubbing each other down...'

Galvanised by his rider, she reached the porch ahead of him.

Making no attempt to hide his grin, he suggested, 'If you'd be kind enough to release the door catch?'

Wondering crossly how he could so easily destroy her composure, rattle the cool, level-headed woman she had prided herself on being, she obeyed.

He shouldered open the heavy door and led the way into a large foyer, deserted except for a woman at the reception desk.

The floor, ceiling, and walls were all of old smoky-gold

wood. In the centre a handsomely carved staircase led up to a balustraded landing.

Used as she was to carpets and floor coverings, Joanne's first impression was of rustic simplicity and a certain austereness. Yet at the same time there was an air of homeliness, of welcome, which was largely engendered by a green-and-blue tiled stove shaped like a giant beehive that threw out a glowing warmth.

In front of the stove was a jewel-bright woven mat that matched the curtains at the windows, a leather settee and several chairs the colour of maple syrup, and a sturdy little coffee-table. To one side was an alcove stacked high with logs that smelled of pine.

Looking up from a computer screen, the fair-haired woman at the reception desk smiled a greeting, and said in excellent English, 'Mr Lancing...how very nice to see you! What a pity it is raining.'

He put the cases down and, returning her smile, asked, 'How are you, Helga?'

'I am very well. I hope it is the same with you?'

'Indeed it is.' An arm around Joanne's waist, he drew her forward. 'This is Miss Winslow.'

He hadn't said *my secretary*.

Glancing at Joanne's engagement ring speculatively, Helga said, 'It is nice to meet you, Miss Winslow.' Again there was that friendly smile.

Joanne managed to smile back.

'I'm sorry it was such short notice,' Brad said.

'Your suite is always kept ready for you,' Helga assured him, 'so it is not a problem. I will call Edvard to deal with your cases.'

'Don't bother, I'll take them.'

He turned to Joanne and, an unmistakable challenge in those green eyes, asked, 'Ready, darling?'

Since deciding at the start of the journey how to play her

hand she had gone through the motions like an actress forced to audition for a role she neither liked nor wanted.

Now the journey was over, they had arrived, and suddenly this was no longer just a role she could back out of, it was all too real. But for everyone's sake she *had* to go through with it...

Somehow she forced her unwilling legs to follow him as he led the way over to the small lift. The cases taking up quite a lot of floor space, they stood very close together as, creaking and wheezing asthmatically, the lift climbed to the next floor.

When they reached the landing Brad turned left down a passageway and, dropping one of the cases briefly, opened the door at the end and ushered her into a living-room.

It was comfortably furnished and homely, with a huge leather couch, two armchairs, a television and stereo, a grandmother clock, and a series of well-stocked bookcases.

Situated between the windows was a fireplace and in it, complementing the central heating, a tiled stove, a smaller version of the one in the lobby. To each side was a stack of logs, and in front of it a thick white goatskin rug.

A door to the left opened into a room with a desk and an array of expensive computer equipment. Another door led into the bathroom.

Putting down his own case, Brad told her casually, 'As you might guess, this was originally a second bedroom, but I decided it would be a lot more useful as an office.'

Joanne's heart sank like a stone. Until that minute she had been clinging to the faint hope that she might have a room of her own.

Perhaps it was the fact that there was only one bedroom that had made him avoid introducing her as his secretary. Calling her simply Miss Winslow had allowed Helga to draw her own conclusions.

He opened a door to the right and, his eyes on her face,

as though to gauge her reaction, added, 'However, this is plenty big enough for both of us.'

Putting her case on a low chest, he continued conversationally, 'I originally chose rooms at the rear of the house because it's quieter, and the view, when you can see it, is better.'

The *en suite* bedroom, with windows looking out over a terrace and what appeared to be a fairly extensive garden, was airy and pleasant. It had light, modern furniture, two walk-in wardrobes and a king-sized bed topped by a sumptuous-looking duvet.

Her thoughts suddenly focused on the coming night, Joanne found herself staring at the bed, mesmerised, unable to look away.

She could visualise Brad joining her there. Naked. Instinctively she knew that he wouldn't wear pyjamas. He would have a good body, firm and muscular. His hands—until then she hadn't realised she had noticed his hands—were strong and well-shaped with long fingers and neatly trimmed nails. Skilful hands, no doubt...

Erotic images began to form in her mind, sending heat surging through her entire body. A heat that, she was horrified to realise, wasn't caused totally by dread and aversion, but held an unwelcome measure of excitement.

Noting that her eyes were fixed on the bed, with no change of tone he asked, 'Which side do you prefer?'

She stiffened and forced herself to look away. 'I prefer to sleep alone.'

'Always?'

'Always.'

'What about Trevor?'

'Trevor isn't the kind of man who...' She broke off. Knowing that she'd already broken the news to Trevor—she'd said no! Joanne shivered as a drop of cold water ran from the dark hair at her nape and trickled down her neck.

Seeing that shiver, he said, 'You can tell me about Trevor later. At the moment you need to dry your hair.'

She had intended to wash it this morning... But 'this morning' now seemed to belong in another life.

'I'd like to take a shower.' She spoke the thought aloud.

A devilish glint in his eye, he asked, 'Feel like sharing one?'

'No, I don't. I agreed to be your secretary, not your mistress!'

'Pity. Still, it's early days yet. When you get to know me better—'

'I still won't want you!'

Seeing his grin, she wished she'd ignored him instead of rising to the bait.

Glancing though the window, he observed, 'The rain seems to be easing off and the clouds are lifting, which means a fine evening. If you like, I'll book a table and we'll have dinner out and do a spot of sightseeing.'

'That would be nice,' she agreed politely.

He ran lean fingers over his chin. 'I'll need to shave, and I've a few things to set up. I also want a quick word with Paul Randall.

'People tend to eat fairly early here, so shall we say about an hour?'

She nodded.

His hand on the latch, he turned. 'By the way, there's no need to dress up. Something pretty and informal will do fine...'

Though it was politely phrased, she recognised it as an order.

'And it might be as well if you bring a jacket in case it turns cool later on.'

When the door had closed behind him she took off her suit and tailored blouse, and opened her case to find her wash bag.

It was just as well he didn't want her to dress up, she

thought wryly, surveying the clothes she had packed. She hadn't a thing that was really dressy with her.

Apart from another business suit, a raincoat, a fleece, some woollies, and a designer jacket she'd pushed in on impulse, she had nothing but jeans, skirts and tops.

She might just as well stick with what she had been wearing.

Going through to the surprisingly luxurious bathroom, she pushed home the small bolt—just to be on the safe side—and, trying to keep her mind fixed on the immediate future, stepped into the shower cubicle.

But as she showered and shampooed her hair, try as she might, her recalcitrant thoughts kept straying to the coming night with a combination of dread and fascination.

What on earth was the matter with her? she wondered irritably. This was so out of character, so *unlike* her.

Even when she was younger, unlike a lot of her friends, she had felt no impulse to dabble, to experience for herself what she had been led to believe was a potentially explosive force. Several of the older boys had tried to interest her but, rather than be attracted by their sweaty hands and hot mouths, she had been repelled.

And as she got older she had been unable to respond in the way her boyfriends wanted, and she had come to the conclusion that some vital spark was missing from her make-up.

Tired of being tried and found wanting, she had avoided serious petting. Then after the death of her parents she had had no time for a social life.

Deciding regretfully that she probably wasn't destined to have a husband and children, she had settled on a career.

Then, at the beginning of the year, a business acquaintance had introduced her to Trevor Wilky, and a steady, low-key relationship had developed that had given her cause to think again about her future.

But what this nightmare she was caught up in would do to that relationship she dared not begin to think...

Sighing, she turned off the water and, stepping from the scented shower-stall, reached for a towel to wrap turban-wise around her head while she dried herself and pulled on a bathrobe.

Amongst the bathroom's plush fittings were a cream hair-dryer and a styling-brush.

Wondering if they had been installed for the women Brad brought here, she dried her hair, pulled her own brush through it, and took it up into its usual neat, shining coil. Then, going through to the bedroom, she put on fresh un-dies, and the suit and blouse she had taken off earlier.

With a clear, creamy skin and well-marked brows and lashes, she needed very little in the way of make-up. A dab of compressed powder to stop her nose shining, a hint of blue eye-shadow, a touch of lip-gloss, and she was ready.

Picking up her shoulder bag, she ventured into the living-room. At first she could see no sign of Brad, then through the half-open door of his office she glimpsed him at his desk, his dark head bent over some papers.

The heels of her neat court shoes were rubber-tipped and made no sound, but as though sensing her presence he glanced up.

Leaving what he was doing, he rose to his feet and joined her in the living-room. Freshly shaven, his hair still a little damp from the shower, he had changed from his suit into smart-casual clothes, and looked relaxed and handsome.

His gaze swept over her from head to toe and back again in silence, taking in her suit and blouse and her businesslike hairdo.

His chiselled lips tightened and, meeting his eyes she read the displeasure in their cool green depths.

'You said there was no need to dress up,' she reminded him defensively.

'That's true,' he agreed, his tone even. 'But I also specified something pretty and informal. The suit you're wearing is neither.'

'Well, I'm afraid it will have to do,' she said coldly.

She saw the displeasure turn to anger.

'While ideal for business, it could hardly be described as appropriate for an evening out. Everyone will think you're my secretary.'

Scared of his anger, and despising herself for being scared, she said, 'I am.'

'Only when we're at the office. At all other times you will please dress as though you were fulfilling the other half of your brief.'

Angry in her turn, she said shortly, 'I'm afraid I don't have anything tarty enough for a mistress.'

'Then we'll need to do some shopping. In the meantime, I'd like you to take off the things you're wearing and change into something more suitable for dining out.'

Standing her ground, she said, 'I've no intention of taking them off...'

Her words ended in a gasp as, disposing of her handbag and jacket, with great deliberation he began to undo the buttons of her blouse.

His fingers brushed against her breasts, and, trying to push his hands away, she gasped, 'What are you doing?'

'Taking them off for you.'

In desperation she insisted, 'But I haven't *got* anything more suitable...'

He finished undoing the buttons, and in spite of her resistance began to tug the blouse free from the waistband of her skirt.

'In that case, we'll stay in after all. I'll have a meal sent up, and we'll think of something else to do to pass the evening.'

Scared stiff of what that 'something else' might be, she assured him shakily, 'It's the truth... You can come and look for yourself if you don't believe me.'

Dragging the edges of her blouse together, she led the way into the bedroom, and threw open the lid of her case.

He had a quick rifle through it and, selecting a silky skirt patterned in brown and rust, a cream top with a cowl neck-line, a pair of strappy sandals and her fun-fur designer jacket, said coolly, 'These are fine. Now, do you need any help to get into them?'

'No, I don't—and I'm only changing to shut you up!'

'Then I'll leave you to it.'

With shaking hands she took off what she was wearing and dressed in what he had chosen, while admitting she had been silly to oppose him.

Such opposition got her nowhere, and only made things worse. If she could only tell him to go to hell and walk out. But for Steve's sake, she couldn't. Brad was the mas-ter. He held the whip and was quite prepared to crack it.

As soon as she was ready she picked up her jacket and reluctantly returned to the living-room.

He was standing with his back to her, looking out over the dusky garden, apparently deep in thought.

Pausing, she noticed afresh how broad his shoulders were in comparison to his hips, how symmetrical and supple the line of his spine.

She knew by now that he was light on his feet, easy and graceful, yet carrying with him an air of authority, a self-confidence that amounted almost to arrogance.

Joanne sighed. Her mother would have undoubtedly classed him as a man's man and a woman's darling.

There was no denying he was a superb male animal, and the fact that she couldn't fault him physically only made her hate him more.

He turned at her approach, and nodded his approval. 'A great improvement.'

'I'm so glad you think so,' she said with saccharine-sweetness.

The glint that appeared in his eye made her wish she could learn not to provoke him.

'There's just one more thing…' He moved towards her, and suddenly he was much too close for comfort.

Before she could begin to guess his intention he spun her round and began to deftly remove the pins from her hair.

As the thick, silky mass came cascading around her shoulders he remarked with satisfaction, 'That's better.'

Tossing the pins aside, he turned her to face him and, holding her upper arms, stood looking down steadily into her stormy eyes.

Only when her gaze fell beneath his did he add, 'I much prefer your hair loose. It makes you look a great deal more feminine.

'And I do like my women to look feminine.'

Such a masculine man would, she thought, while bitterly resenting the way he had phrased it.

'Now, if you're ready to go?'

Biting her lip, she allowed herself to be helped into the fun-fur jacket and escorted down the stairs and across a lobby now lit by hanging lamps.

It was no longer deserted. A party of new arrivals clustered round the desk, and an elderly couple sat in front of the glowing stove drinking coffee.

When they got outside it was to find the evening was clear and dry and comparatively mild. Only the still-damp pavements showed it had been raining.

Tucking her hand through his arm, Brad said, 'I thought a stroll as far as the Rosenkrantz Tower, to stretch our legs, then dinner on Bryggen.'

'Bryggen?'

'The quay. An historic place. The buildings there are on the World Heritage list. They also form a major tourist attraction, and house boutiques, museums and restaurants.'

As the dusk thickened lights began to spring up everywhere. Traffic was busy and bustling, and laughing groups of people thronged the pavements, looking all set to paint the town.

'Is there much nightlife?' Joanne asked as they walked.

'Quite a lot. Most of it's in the centre, and at weekends the harbour area in particular tends to get crowded.'

'Nightclubs, that sort of thing?'

'There's everything from piano bars to discos, as well as the kind of cosy meeting place where you can go for a drink and find earnest students and the local intelligentsia.

'The piano bar at the Kirkenes is well worth a visit. I'll take you there tomorrow night...'

While she looked around her with unfeigned interest they walked until they got to the short and sturdy Rosenkrantz Tower.

Thinking it looked a bit like a folly, she asked, 'What was its purpose?'

'It was built in the middle of the fifteen-hundreds by Erik Rosenkrantz as a fortified official residence.'

Standing a few feet away, a camera slung around his neck, a balding tourist who had followed them there appeared to be listening with interest.

When Joanne had had time to admire the picturesque tower they turned and retraced their steps until they reached Ovregaten.

'Ovregaten forms the back boundary of Bryggen,' Brad told her. 'All these narrow passages are where the citizens of Bergen used to live in the fourteenth century.'

Glancing around while she listened, she noticed that the tourist, who had apparently followed them back, was once more listening.

'After several disastrous fires,' Brad went on, 'the surviving buildings on Bryggen are mostly reconstructions, the oldest dating from around seventeen hundred...'

He pointed out a row of wooden structures, whose gables

faced the harbour. Topped with triangular pastry-cutter roofs, they were painted red, blue, yellow and green.

The harbourside was illuminated, and the modest buildings, along with the stocky tower and the yachts lining the pier, were reflected in the still water.

'Isn't it wonderful?' she breathed.

'It's renowned for being one of the most beautiful cityscapes in Northern Europe.'

Hearing the quiet pride in his voice, she knew he loved his mother's homeland.

When they reached the restaurant Brad had chosen it proved to be an old timber building with crooked floors and a lively Wild-West-saloon-bar-type ambience.

They were greeted at the door, and Joanne was relieved of her jacket, before they were led to a secluded booth beneath a wooden balcony, and handed large menus.

'What a fascinating place,' she said as she settled herself on the bench.

'I thought you might like it.'

Catching sight of the balding tourist who had followed them to and from the Rosenkrantz Tower being turned away, she commented, 'It seems we were lucky to get a table.'

'I see our friend didn't.'

She was surprised by the satisfaction in his voice.

'At such short notice we wouldn't have if they hadn't known me,' he added.

'With two of the best chefs in town, and a traditional menu that features marinaded moose and roast reindeer, it's always booked well ahead by locals and tourists alike.'

When she remarked on the fact that a lot of the well-, but casually, dressed clientele were speaking English he explained, 'English is taught in the schools here, so a lot of Norwegians speak it fluently.'

After studying the menu she refused the more exotic dishes, and settled for grilled salmon and a fruit dessert.

While they sipped a cocktail and waited for their food to arrive, keeping to impersonal topics, they conversed with an ease that surprised her.

He was an intelligent and stimulating companion who, instead of talking down to her, as Trevor quite often did, treated her as his intellectual equal.

There was an interesting edge of irony and a certain dry humour to his observations that she found refreshing, and, without being in the least arbitrary, he had clear and well-formed views on most things.

Views that she could find no fault with. In fact, to her even greater surprise, she agreed with many of them.

Nor could she fault his behaviour.

There was nothing to be seen of the man who had set himself out to seduce Milly, the libertine who had run his hand up her thigh.

Correct and courteous, he was a charming host who showed not the slightest sign of overstepping the mark, and as the meal progressed she found herself in real danger of enjoying his company.

But a leopard didn't change its spots.

She was reminding herself what kind of man he really was, and how much she loathed and despised him, when he glanced up and caught her eye.

'I don't need to ask what you're thinking,' he remarked sardonically. 'You have a very expressive face.'

Cursing his perspicacity, she felt the betraying colour rise in her cheeks.

At that moment, to her very great relief, their coffee was brought and served.

But it seemed as if, suddenly, the whole mood of the evening had changed, and Joanne found herself wishing that the uncomfortable little incident had never taken place.

Gnawing at her bottom lip, she was wondering how to break the lengthening silence and get back on some kind of reasonable footing, when Brad said, 'You were going to tell me about your fiancé.'

With no particular wish to talk about Trevor, she tried to wriggle out of it. 'There's not much to tell... And I've no idea where to start.'

'You could start by telling me what he looks like.'

Brad's earlier easy manner had vanished as though it had never been, and there was a coolness to his voice that made it clear he was responding to her tacit animosity.

But, having caused this new and hostile mood, she would somehow have to cope with it.

Which meant fight, or surrender.

Unwilling to either take him on or surrender totally, she chose a middle course. Even then, as she might have expected, it proved to be a running battle, with her doing the running.

His eyes on her face, Brad pressed, 'Is he tall or short, fat or thin, dark or fair?'

'He's tall and fair and quite nice-looking.'

'Quite nice-looking... As striking as that!'

'Do you *have* to be so sarcastic?'

With a mirthless grin, he said, 'I'm afraid a lukewarm description like that brings out the worst in me. But do go on, and I'll try to restrain myself.'

Like hell you will! she thought. Stifling the urge to say it aloud, she asked, 'What exactly do you want to know?'

'To start with, how old is he?'

'Thirty-six.'

'So he's past the impetuous years of youth.'

Trevor was so admirably sober and steady that Joanne couldn't believe he had ever been impetuous.

When she said nothing, Brad queried, 'And you're what? Twenty-five? Eleven years is quite a big difference.'

Sounding defensive, she said, 'I'll be twenty-five in a few days' time. But in any case I've never considered that age matters.'

Changing tack, Brad asked, 'I take it Trevor's an only child?'

Flustered by the question, she asked, 'What makes you think that?'

'I got the impression that he's something of a mother's boy.'

'There are worse things to be,' she said icily. 'At least Trevor's decent and upright, which is more than you can say for *some* men.'

He let that go, and asked satirically, 'Apart from the fact that he's decent and upright, what makes him your Mr Right?'

'We share the same interests.'

'Which are?'

'Reading...music and the arts...the theatre in particular.'

'No sports or outdoor activities?'

'Trevor isn't the sporty type.'

'Doesn't he even watch sport on the television?'

'No.'

'What about you?'

'I don't watch it either.'

He acknowledged the retort with a glinting smile, before rephrasing the question. 'Do *you* indulge in any outdoor activities?'

'I enjoy hiking and swimming.'

'Do you like skiing?'

'I've never had the chance to try.'

'If you had the chance, would you take it?'

'Yes.'

'And leave Trevor at home?'

When she remained silent, he said, 'Tell me about his faults. One can't weigh up a person without knowing their faults.'

All in all, Trevor had few really bad faults. Apart from wanting to lord it a bit, and having a tendency to tell her how to run her life, he had proved to be the ideal man-friend.

The main criterion was, though pleasantly attentive, he neither pressured her to sleep with him, nor demanded the kind of response she knew herself to be incapable of.

Having what she guessed was a lower than average sex drive, he had appeared perfectly satisfied with companion-ship, and a few less-than-passionate kisses.

'He hasn't got…' about to say 'many serious faults', she changed it to '…any serious faults.'

'A veritable paragon.'

'I'm lucky to have him,' she said firmly.

'How long *have* you had him?'

'We met about seven months ago.'

Reaching across the table, Brad picked up her hand and moved the solitaire from side to side with his thumb. 'And you've been engaged, how long?'

She wondered briefly whether to tell him the truth, and decided against it. If he had a speck of decency left, the belief that she had a fiancé might serve as some kind of protection.

Removing her hand, she answered evasively, 'Not very long.'

'How long is ''not very long''?'

'A couple of weeks.'

'Does his mother approve?'

'Yes, she does,' Joanne said shortly.

'Perhaps she thinks it's time he was safely married to a *nice* girl. It's just as well she doesn't know that you've led her darling boy astray.'

'I haven't done anything of the kind,' Joanne protested indignantly.

'Surely you and Trevor have slept together?'

Without considering what Brad would make of it, she answered truthfully, 'No, we haven't.'

'Not even when you went to Amsterdam?'

'No.' Half expecting Trevor to suggest a double room, she had been bracing herself to agree, when, in the end, he had booked two singles.

Watching her face, Brad asked drily, 'Why not? Don't tell me he didn't want to… Or did Mother come along to keep an eye on her boy?'

'No, she didn't!'

'So why didn't you sleep together?'

'Not everyone has the "let's jump into bed" mentality. Trevor is happy to wait until we're married.'

'Is he, now? And what about you? While you're waiting, are you getting your fun elsewhere?'

'No! I certainly am not!'

He shook his head pityingly. 'You must be terribly frustrated. No wonder you offered to take—er—Milly's place.'

Well, she'd walked right into that one, she thought grimly, and denied through gritted teeth, 'I didn't mean it.'

'So you said. But I really think, things being as they are, you might quite enjoy it… In fact, I'll make absolutely sure you do.'

A slow, suffocating heat filling her, she shuddered.

His head tilted a little to one side, he queried, 'Is that a shiver of anticipation?'

'No, it isn't,' she said thickly. 'It's a shudder of loathing.'

But she was shaken afresh to realise that wasn't altogether true.

Turning her head, she looked anywhere but at him.

He smiled ironically. 'With a face that mirrors your feelings and your every thought, I'm afraid you don't make a very good liar… And when you refuse to look at me, like now, I know it's because you daren't.'

CHAPTER FIVE

WHILE she was still struggling to regain her equilibrium he asked, 'As a matter of interest, when are you getting married?'

Somehow she managed to answer, 'We haven't yet set a date.'

'Ah, well, that kind of decision needs careful thought. There's no point in rushing into it.'

'I'm so glad you approve.'

He got his own back by touching a fingertip to her hot cheek, then pulling it away and blowing on it.

Watching her soft mouth tighten, he suggested, 'Why don't you tell me about the actual proposal? How long had you been expecting it? I gather women know these things.'

Having presumed that Trevor was a born bachelor, his proposal had come right out of the blue. Though in retrospect she realised that she should have at least *suspected* his reason for ordering champagne—as far as he was concerned, an unusual and reckless extravagance.

'I hadn't been expecting it.'

'A *surprise* proposal! And, I suppose, being the model of excellence he is, he found a bench in some rose garden and went down on one knee?'

'No, he didn't.'

His voice mocking, Brad said, 'If I ever decide to propose to someone I really ought to know how it's done. So tell me, what did he do…?'

Trevor had taken her to one of the best restaurants in London and, clearing his throat, begun rather pompously, 'We get on very well together, wouldn't you say?'

'Yes,' she had agreed, a little puzzled by his manner. 'What makes you ask?'

'I want us to get engaged.' Before she realised his intention, he had taken her hand and slipped a diamond solitaire onto her third finger.

Taken completely by surprise, she blurted out, 'What about your mother?'

'Mother approves.'

'Oh…' she said a bit blankly.

'I've got a good job. I could take care of you and give you everything you and our children might need.'

'Well, I…'

'From the way you get on with Cousin Jean's twins, I know you're fond of children.'

That wasn't strictly true. She wasn't fond of children *en masse*, but as individuals she found them interesting and, in most cases, lovable.

'You'd like a family, wouldn't you?'

'Yes, but I—'

'You see, Mother's decided it's high time I got married and gave her some grandchildren.'

Someone else she could rule.

Pushing away that uncharitable thought, Joanne said carefully, 'If you don't mind, I'd like to think about it.'

Hurt that she hadn't jumped at the chance—as his mother had assured him she would—Trevor said huffily, 'I really don't see what there is to think about.'

Not wishing to wound him in any way, she explained seriously, 'Before I commit myself I have to be sure I could be the sort of wife you need.'

His blue eyes complacent, he told her, 'Mother seems to think you're exactly what I need. She's satisfied that you're a girl with good morals. The kind that doesn't play around.'

Recognising that as the highest accolade, Joanne said, 'I'm flattered, really I am. All the same I want to be certain I'm doing the right thing before I say yes.'

With a touch of irony, she added, 'I should hate to let you, or your mother, down.'

Somewhat mollified, he agreed, 'I suppose it makes sense to be absolutely sure.' Then magnanimously, 'Very well, take whatever time you need…'

When she attempted to slip off the ring he stopped her. 'I went to a great deal of trouble to choose that particular ring…'

It was the safe, conventional choice she would have expected a man like Trevor to make.

'Mother was convinced you'd like it, and so was I…' He sounded as disappointed as a child whose gift was in danger of being spurned.

'I *do* like it,' she assured him. 'But it wouldn't be right to wear it until I've made up my mind…

'Suppose I decide not to marry you?'

Unable to seriously believe such a thing could happen, he said comfortably, 'I'm sure you won't…'

And he was probably quite right, she conceded. Common sense said she should agree. Where would she find another decent man who had Trevor's attributes? A man who suited her half as well as he did?

If she couldn't bring herself to marry him she might as well accept the fact that she would never have a husband and children…

'Now the ring's on your finger, promise me you'll wear it while you're making up your mind,' Trevor went on. 'We would be *so* disappointed if I had to take it back.'

'Very well, I promise,' she answered reluctantly.

He smiled, showing teeth that were white and even. His mother had once told her how long he'd had to wear braces to produce such a perfect result. 'Knowing you as I do, I have no doubt at all that you'll make me a perfect wife…'

But as far as Joanne was concerned, even at the end of the evening, defying common sense, a little niggle of doubt still lingered…

*   *   *

Getting no immediate response to his question, Brad pursued, 'Or perhaps *you* proposed to him?'

Knowing he was just needling her, she said stiffly, 'Trevor took me out to dinner and ordered champagne, then he produced a ring and asked me to marry him.'

'With a declaration of undying love, presumably?'

Suddenly chilled by the thought that love had never been mentioned, she lied, 'Of course.'

'And you love him?'

'Why else would I have agreed to marry him?'

He shrugged. 'That depends on whether you think love is important?'

'What do you think?' The question was a challenge.

He answered seriously, 'As a matter of fact I think it's *very* important. So long as the other necessary ingredients are present, love is the glue that sticks a marriage together.'

Amazed that a man like him should think that way, she asked, 'What do you regard as "the necessary ingredients"?'

'Shared interests, sexual compatibility, respect, a liking for each other's company.'

Unable to argue with that, she found herself saying, 'I think so too.'

'So, swept off your feet, you accepted?'

'Yes,' she retorted defiantly.

Brad passed lean fingers over his smoothly shaven chin and, his voice thoughtful, remarked, 'That's a somewhat different version to the one your sister gave me.'

Startled, Joanne demanded, 'What version did Milly give you?'

'She said that Trevor had proposed, but you hadn't given him an answer, and she was hoping that when you had had time to think it over you'd turn him down.

'If I remember rightly, she described him as a pompous git.'

Caught on the raw, Joanne retorted, 'Even that's better than being a lying hypocrite, and that's what you are.'

His firm mouth tightened, and a steely glint appeared in those clear dark-green eyes.

Refusing to be intimidated, she rushed on, 'Don't you remember saying that I was mistaken about your relationship with Milly? That as far as you were concerned she was simply a nice girl and an efficient secretary?'

'As a matter of fact I do.'

'Well, that hardly sounds like the kind of conversation any ordinary secretary would have with her boss.'

'I agree that it wouldn't be if it had happened in the office—'

'So presumably it was when you took her out to dinner?'

'I didn't "take her out to dinner".'

'She told me you'd taken her out to dinner *twice*.'

'They were business dinners,' Brad said, his voice even. 'Both times there was someone else present, which I think you'll agree hardly counts as a romantic tête-à-tête.'

'I really don't see why you needed a secretary—' Joanne began.

'The meetings had been instigated by a man I didn't altogether trust,' Brad broke in firmly. 'I decided to have a secretary along to take notes so that the next day he couldn't wriggle out of what had been said and promised.'

'Are you trying to tell me the kind of conversation you had with Milly went on in front of someone else?'

'On the second occasion my client was delayed, and while Miss Winslow and I waited we had a drink and talked. Apart from a bit of family gossip, that's all there was to it.'

He made it sound so reasonable, so *credible*.

But, recalling how, when she had asked Milly, 'You didn't go any further?' Milly had answered, 'No, I didn't. But from some of the things he said, and the way he looked at me, I know he wanted to,' Joanne felt a fresh surge of anger.

Watching her face, Brad commented, 'You obviously don't believe me.'

'No, I don't,' Joanne informed him hardly. 'Milly told me differently.'

'Well, as it appears to be your sister's word against mine, and I'm sure you trust her implicitly—'

'Yes, I do...'

But even as she spoke, a little demon of doubt reminded Joanne that Milly was, at times, prone to exaggeration. To occasionally seeing things as she *wanted* them to be, rather than as they really were. If she fancied herself in love with her boss, might she not have read more into the situation than was warranted?

For a moment Joanne wavered. Could she have been mistaken about Brad Lancing?

Then came the memory of the way he had run his hand up her thigh, and her face hardened in condemnation. No, she wasn't mistaken. She knew from her own experience just what kind of man he was...

'Then perhaps we should change the subject.' Brad sounded resigned, almost bored.

'Perhaps we should,' she agreed icily.

'Tell me,' he resumed after a moment, 'how do you think Trevor will react to the idea of his fiancée running off without a word as soon as his back is turned...?'

'You did say he'd taken his mother to Bournemouth?'

Ignoring the last provocative question, she said, 'It won't be without a word. I have every intention of phoning him after the weekend.'

'Suppose he takes it into his head to ring you at home tomorrow?'

'If he does, I'm sure Steve will explain.'

Only, knowing Trevor, he wouldn't ring.

On the rare occasions they had had a minor difference

of opinion, unable to believe he could be in the wrong, he had always left it to her to make the first move.

This time, unfortunately, the difference of opinion had developed into a major incident. When she had refused to go to the concert with him he had accused her of caring more for Milly than she did for him.

Finding he couldn't move her, he had been at first petulant, then downright angry. 'Why do you keep on mothering her, giving up everything for her? I know it's her last night at home, but you don't have to be there. She doesn't need you any longer. She's a married woman now, not a child...'

In spite of all her efforts to smooth things over, it had ended in what his mother was pleased to call 'a little fall-out'.

'In any case, I'll talk to him on Monday,' she added flatly.

'So what will you tell him? The whole truth?'

Horrified, she cried, 'No, of course not.'

'I thought you said he wasn't the jealous type?'

'He isn't... But for everyone's sake I want him to believe it's strictly business.'

'Even if he believes that, won't he be concerned that you're spending six weeks in Norway with a man who—according to you and your brother—has a bad reputation as far as women are concerned?'

'Yes, he might be.'

'Only *might*?'

'He trusts me.'

'Then all I can say is, he's a fool.'

'How dare you suggest...' Suddenly remembering the previous night, the way she had acted, she broke off abruptly, colour flooding into her face.

'Exactly,' Brad said softly.

'But I'm not really like that...' she blurted out. 'I was just trying to...'

'Tease?' he suggested when she hesitated.

'Protect Milly.'

'Are you quite sure Milly needs protecting?'

'When there are unscrupulous men like you around, yes, she does.'

'Funny, but she didn't strike me that way at all. In fact, I got the distinct impression that she's quite capable of taking care of herself. Maybe more so than you are.'

It stuck Joanne that Steve, who knew them both a great deal better, had said much the same thing.

'Most of the ''experienced'' women I've known,' Brad went on thoughtfully, 'have been sophisticated and hard as nails. Well able to take care of themselves. Or else the kind of girl one could only describe as weak, or promiscuous… In my opinion you're none of those things. Which I find distinctly intriguing…

'I'd also be fascinated to know why a girl who admits to having had lots of experience should choose to marry a man with no red blood in his veins.'

Watching her face, he smiled a little. 'Unless, of course, you lied about being experienced, and are really afraid of sex…'

Before she could find her voice, he added, 'Later, when we go to bed, no doubt I'll be able to solve the mystery.'

As she listened to his words that strange, tumultuous excitement she'd experienced earlier, and which had been lurking at some subconscious level in her mind, surfaced. Her breathing quickened and her heart began to throw itself against her ribs, while every nerve in her body sprang into life.

Brad stopped speaking and glanced up as a small party passed on their way to the door.

While they had been talking the restaurant had steadily emptied until now they were one of only two couples remaining.

'Are you about ready to go?' he queried politely.

'Yes, quite ready.' Though the words were positive enough, her voice shook a little.

'Then I think it's time we were moving.'

He signalled the waiter, and paid the bill, before rising to pull back her chair.

A few minutes ago she had been only too eager to escape Brad's interrogation, but now, reminded afresh of what lay ahead, she got to her feet all of a tremble, her stomach churning.

At the door he draped her fur jacket around her shoulders and, with a proprietary gesture, took her hand and tucked it through his arm.

The evening had remained fine and mild. Above their heads a clear indigo sky was spangled with stars, and a full moon floated like a pale silver balloon.

Once they were moving, the adrenalin pumping into her bloodstream made her walk at a faster pace than normal.

Though he was appreciably taller than she was, he adjusted his stride to suit hers, and they moved easily together, only the occasional brush of thigh against thigh making her falter and the breath catch in her throat.

After a little while he remarked slyly, 'You seem to be in a hurry to get back.'

As she made a determined effort to slow her pace he went on, 'It's a good thing our friend isn't still trying to follow us.'

It took her a moment to catch on. 'You mean the tourist who—?'

'I very much doubt if he was a tourist. I think he'd been paid to watch us. Which means the opposition knows we're here.'

'Oh.'

'Don't look so concerned. It was bound to happen sooner or later.'

His arm tightened, giving her hand a little squeeze. 'And

with much more exciting things to look forward to, who can worry about business problems?

'Unfortunately I only managed a few words with Paul earlier, so before I can forget work and concentrate solely on pleasure, I shall need to contact him again...

'However, I'll try not to keep you waiting too long,' he promised softly, 'and once I've joined you, we'll have the whole night before us to experiment, to find out what gives you the most pleasure...'

The last thing she wanted to do was *enjoy* what was about to happen to her, she thought frantically. But in spite of her normal frigidity, she might be in danger of doing just that.

No, she couldn't let herself enjoy it! The only way she could keep any vestige of pride or self-respect was to remain unmoved, to *suffer* it.

'I don't want to *experiment*...' she began hoarsely. Then, covered in confusion, tried again. 'In the circumstances I'm not concerned about...'

'Your own pleasure?' he suggested as the sentence tailed off. 'Oh, but I am. I've never cared for the ''wham bam, thank you, ma'am'' approach. My own satisfaction is geared to how much my partner is enjoying what's happening...

'No, I suggest we take it nice and slow and easy, that way we'll both gain.' A shade sardonically, he added, 'And once you're into your stride you can show me just how much experience you have got...'

Her throat and mouth dry, chills running up and down her spine, Joanne wondered frantically if it would be best to stay silent or to fight back?

Common sense answered that he was deliberately baiting her, and rising to the bait would just be playing into his hands.

But it might help if she could steer the conversation away

from the coming night. At least it would give her some temporary relief from his tormenting.

Taking a desperate grip on what little remained of her composure, she began as evenly as possible, 'With regard to your business problems, at present I know so little...'

Sighing, he gave her a mocking sidelong glance. 'It's a shameful waste of a lovely night to talk business.'

Focusing straight ahead, she stated firmly, 'If I'm to act as your secretary it would be as well if you put me in the picture.'

Suddenly serious, he agreed, 'You may be right...

'Well, in a nutshell, the problems the Dragon Line have been experiencing were at first thought to be the ordinary, everyday problems that trouble any business. But gradually it became clear there was more to it than that...'

'A form of industrial sabotage?'

'Yes, though on a fairly small scale. That's when I sent Paul over to try and sort things out.

'He laid a trap and caught the person responsible, a cargo-handler named Mussen. The man was aggrieved because his brother, who he firmly believed to be innocent, had been discharged from the DL hotel staff for petty pilfering.

'On my instructions, after a good talking-to, Mussen was allowed to keep his job, which, with an ailing wife and four young children, he badly needed.

'His brother was also reinstated at a somewhat lower level with a promise that, after a six-month probationary period, he should have his old post, as chief desk clerk, back.

'That should have put an end to the problems, and for a while it seemed to have done. Then more worrying things began to happen...'

Only half listening, unable to wean her thoughts away from what the coming night might bring, Joanne asked abstractedly, 'What kind of things?'

'Mostly mechanical failures. For instance, the *Midnight Dragon* car ferry was unable to sail because the main doors couldn't be made watertight.

'Then a steam valve stuck, causing an explosion in one of the boiler rooms—though without any serious casualties, thank the lord...

'Because this time the sabotage could have had very serious consequences, we considered calling in the police. But both Mussen and his brother had alibis, and after digging around for a while Paul couldn't find any real evidence to prove that the boiler-room incident had been anything but accidental.

'After some thought we decided to hang on, and keep everything under wraps. The DSL has an excellent safety record, and if that sort of thing got out it would only destroy confidence and do a great deal of harm to the line's reputation.'

'But that wasn't the end of the problems?'

'No. Things were quiet for a while, and we both hoped that the situation was back to normal. But we were wrong. Over the last couple of weeks it's all started up again.

'A ship's security officer who disturbed an intruder was attacked and left suffering from mild concussion... And in the early hours of yesterday morning a fire broke out in a storeroom of one of our hotels.

'Thanks to an alert and well-trained night security guard, it was dealt with quickly. The damage was kept to a minimum, and, even more importantly, none of the guests were disturbed.

'Only the guard and the manager know about it and they'll keep it to themselves...'

By now they had reached the area of crooked streets and picturesque architecture that Joanne recognised as being not far from the hotel. In a few minutes they would be back. The thought made her palms grow clammy and turned her knees to water.

Making an effort to keep her mind on what he was telling her, she asked, 'You don't think the fire could have been accidental?'

'The guard, who is an ex-fireman, was quite satisfied that it had been started deliberately…'

At that moment they reached the hotel and, pausing on the pavement, Joanne tilted back her head to gaze up at the family of dragons silhouetted against the night sky.

'Would you like to meet the rest?' Brad asked.

'The rest?'

'The rest of the Lofoten dragons.'

He ushered her round the side of the building and through a high wooden gate into a leafy, lantern-lit garden.

An enchanted garden, Joanne found herself thinking as she gazed around her.

The moonlight bleached the scene, turning trees and plants alike to a weird, unearthly silver. Only within the pools of light cast by the lanterns did the autumn colours come to glowing life.

A flight of shallow steps led down from the paved terrace to several different levels. On one side, and seeming to spring from nowhere, a shallow stream chuckled along a fern-hung gully, while paths wound between rocky out-crops, and climbed to secret places.

Brad took her hand, his touch sending a quiver through her, and led her down a moonlit path until they came to a humpbacked bridge that spanned the stream.

On the far side was a wooden summer house, the lantern-lit porch furnished with a couple of reclining chairs.

Having settled her into one, he dropped down beside her and, waving a hand at the rising ground opposite, said, 'There! What do you think?'

They blended in so well that even in the bright moonlight it took her a little while to spot them, and when she finally did surprise made her laugh aloud.

The rocky hillside was swarming with dragons of all

shapes and sizes. A whole family of them, from monsters to babies. Some obviously playing; others sleeping; one peering at them from the undergrowth; another scratching itself.

All different characters. All friendly.

'Aren't they marvellous!' she exclaimed.

'I used to love them as a boy, then when I got to be a teenager and put away childish things, I decided they were a bit twee...'

'And now?'

'Now I think they suit the place.'

'How do they come to be here?'

'The ones on the roof date from when the house was built, but the rest were commissioned when the garden was landscaped some seventy years ago.

'My grandfather, who was the youngest child in the family, and the only boy, loved dragons. They were put here to please him; which they did for the rest of his days.'

It was a nice story, and told in a wonderfully romantic spot. There had been an absence of romance in her life, Joanne thought, and unconsciously sighed for what she had missed.

As though answering that sigh, Brad commented, 'It's a beautiful night.'

'Yes,' she agreed.

With a teasing glance, he added, 'Ideal for lovers, wouldn't you agree?'

Reaching across, he took her hand and, raising it to his lips, dropped a kiss into the palm.

The romantic little gesture made her tremble and set her yearning. Scared stiff by her own treacherous reactions, she snatched her hand away and said jerkily, 'No, I wouldn't.'

Catching hold of her jacket, which she was still wearing loose around her shoulders, she jumped to her feet.

He rose too, seeming to tower over her. 'So what would

you consider ideal? A change of scene? A new moon to wish on? A different companion?'

'The latter.'

'Well, at least you're being honest. Which is a change from last night. Then you said, and I quote: "I've always found handsome, powerful men like you a real turn-on."'

Cupping her chin, he tilted her face and studied it in the lantern-light, before saying with evident satisfaction, 'Yes, I should just think so!'

His words made her fiery blush deepen even more.

He laughed softly and, his voice considering, asked, 'So, if you don't want to enjoy a little kiss what shall we talk about?'

'I really don't know,' she muttered.

'Last night you knew. If I remember rightly, you said, "I'd much rather talk about *you*, Mr Lancing".'

He gave such a good impression of the 'girly' voice she had used that if she hadn't been so wound-up she would have laughed.

Damn him! she thought vexedly. Oh, damn him!

When she remained silent he sighed theatrically. 'Well, if we can't find anything to talk about I'll just *have* to kiss you.'

Releasing her chin, he drew the edges of her jacket together over her breasts, trapping her arms inside, while he stood gazing down at her thoughtfully.

Her dark eyes looked wide and frightened, and the soft fur gave her face a lovely, luminous quality that he found quite enchanting.

As she stared up at him he asked with smooth mockery, 'All braced for the ordeal?'

A surge of nervous excitement dried her mouth and made butterflies dance in her stomach as, holding her breath, she waited with a kind of helpless hunger, horrified to realise that she *wanted* him to kiss her.

Experienced as he was, he must have known, but even so he took his time about it.

When he finally bent his dark head, and touched his lips to the corner of her mouth, she froze into complete immobility.

After a moment his lips began to travel lightly over hers, bestowing a series of soft plucking kisses that tantalised and tormented without satisfying her hunger for him. When they moved away to graze over her jaw and the soft skin beneath her chin, trembling, eyes closed, lips a little parted, she waited in an agony of suspense.

Then, so unexpectedly that she staggered, she found she was free.

'There, now, the ordeal's over,' he told her cheerfully. 'That wasn't so bad, was it?'

Instead of relief, she felt a blinding anger.

He'd done it purposely of course. Setting her up. Making her wait. Deliberately teasing her.

'Dear me,' he murmured, 'you look quite disappointed. Did you want me to kiss you properly? Or would *you* like to kiss *me*?'

'I'd sooner cut my throat.'

Swinging on her heel, she set off back across the bridge and up the path towards the house.

He caught her up and, walking by her side, kept pace effortlessly. Though she refused to look at him, she felt convinced that he was smiling.

When they reached the terrace he said, 'We can go in this way,' and, opening one of a pair of doors that weren't unlike French windows, ushered her into what appeared to be a breakfast-room.

'Would you like a nightcap of any kind before we go upstairs?'

'No, thank you.'

The minute the words were out, she wished she had said yes. It would have given her a little more breathing-space.

'Then we can go this way.'

He escorted her through to an inner hall, up a back stair-case, and along a short stretch of corridor to their suite. Having let them into the living-room, he switched on the light and dropped the latch behind them, making her feel trapped.

As she hovered uncertainly he slipped her jacket from her shoulders and, moving aside her curtain of dark, silky hair, touched his lips to the warmth of her nape.

Shuddering, she turned at bay.

Looking anything but concerned, he suggested, 'If you'd like to go ahead and get ready for bed, I'll join you as soon as I've had a word with Paul.'

Her stomach tied itself in knots.

She'd die if he touched her.

She'd die if he didn't.

'Please don't hurry on my account,' she said fervently.

He laughed. Despite the fact that she was easy to scare, she didn't lack either courage or spirit.

'In fact, if you *never* come it will be too soon—'

The words ended in a little gasp as he took her face between his palms and, running his fingers into her hair, quoted, '"Methinks the lady doth protest too much."' Then sardonically, 'Can it be that you really fancy me?'

Frightened to death in case he had guessed the conflict-ing emotions that filled her, she muttered, 'I *loathe* you.'

A glint in his eye, he said, 'Now you've hurt my feel-ings... And just when I thought we were getting on well.'

Bending his head until his lips were only inches from hers, he suggested, 'I think I should have a kiss to make up for it.'

'I don't want you to kiss me,' she said thickly.

'Would it help if you pretended I was Trevor?'

'No, it wouldn't.'

'Thank the lord for that,' he said piously, and before she could catch her breath his mouth was covering hers.

If she had expected the same kind of punitive kiss she'd been subjected to the previous night, she couldn't have been more wrong.

Gentle, rather than forceful, his mouth coaxed and beguiled, his tongue-tip tracing the outline of her lips before slipping between them to tease the sensitive inner skin.

When, unable to hold out against him, her lips parted, he deepened the kiss.

Like a lighted match being dropped into a pool of petrol, fire exploded inside her, and for perhaps the first time in her life she knew what it was like to be consumed by passion. A white-hot passion that seared her very soul and melted every bone in her body.

As he felt her grow limp his arms went around her and his kisses became ardent and demanding, asking for, and getting, a response that only served to add to the conflagration.

When he finally lifted his head, unable to stand, she clung to him, dazed and devastated, only gradually becoming aware that somewhere close at hand a phone was ringing.

Though he was breathing as if he had just run a race, his recovery was light years ahead of her own. Steering her to the nearest chair, he pushed her into it, and went into his office.

She was vaguely aware that he was speaking, without making any sense of the words.

After a moment or two he returned to say, 'That was Paul. I need to talk to him, so if you'd like to go to bed…?'

She looked up at him, a hectic flush on her cheeks, her eyes wide and unfocused, and got unsteadily to her feet.

'I'd better give you a hand.' Stooping, he picked her up and carried her through to the bedroom, setting her down carefully.

Having switched on the bedside lamp, he drew the

greeny-blue folk-weave curtains and asked, 'Do you need any help to get undressed?'

Made speechless by the effortless way he'd carried her, she shook her head.

'Then I'll join you as soon as I've finished talking to Paul.'

The door closed quietly behind him.

CHAPTER SIX

SHAKEN to the core, Joanne found it was several minutes before she could pull herself together enough to go through to the bathroom and prepare for bed.

As she creamed off her make-up she looked at the woman in the mirror. Though the dark hair and eyes, the shape of the face and the features were the same, it was a stranger who stared back at her.

In place of the usual pale composure there was a pink flush lying along the high cheekbones, and the blue eyes were so dark they looked almost black.

The mouth too was different. Instead of the starved, pinched look she had started to glimpse at times, it had the soft ripeness of a mouth that had just been thoroughly kissed.

She had got used to thinking of herself as a woman who lacked something, who was next-door to frigid. A woman to whom sexual love and passion would always be a stranger. Someone *incomplete*.

Now her whole conception of herself had been changed, and for good.

If the man who had worked this miracle had been anyone other than who he was she would have gone down on her knees and given thanks.

Perhaps she still should, she thought, there was a lot to be thankful for. For the first time in her life she felt emotionally whole. Complete.

Though Brad Lancing was lecherous and rotten to the core, there was something inside her that responded to his maleness, that sang into life when he touched her.

If only she could feel that kind of passion for a decent

man; a man she could love and marry, who would make a good father; a man she could spend the rest of her life with.

Catching sight of the ring on her finger, she thought of Trevor, and knew without a doubt that he wasn't that man.

The kind of blazing response she had given Brad would frighten poor Trevor half to death. He wasn't emotionally equipped to handle it.

Nor inspire it, for that matter.

He was the sort of man who felt more at home with a nice, steady, low-key existence. Narrow and grey.

Seeing things clearly now, she guessed that the main reason, maybe the *only* reason, he had asked her to marry him was that he believed she was safe and undemanding. That she wouldn't rock the boat by asking for more than he could give.

The same reasons that had made her consider accepting him.

She sighed, it just showed how emotionally unawakened, how blind, she must have been to even *think* of accepting a man who was willing to marry only because his mother wanted grandchildren.

Sighing, she admitted what she had always known. Trevor was still tied to his mother's apron strings, and even if he married he would allow his mother to keep on running his life...

No, now she knew what it was like to feel whole, she couldn't marry Trevor, and she could only be thankful that, rather than accepting his proposal, she had asked for time to think. It would make it somewhat easier to give him back his ring.

If only she hadn't agreed to wear it in the first place...

The fact that she *had* would no doubt add to his anger and disappointment, but it was much too late for regrets, and common sense told her that he himself wouldn't be seriously hurt, only his pride.

Though what if, by turning Trevor down, she lost out

completely? As Milly was fond of pointing out, she was no Miss World. What if no other man ever wanted her, except perhaps for a brief fling?

Even now, with her new-found confidence in herself, she knew she wasn't the type to go in for affairs.

But if she was going to live at all she wanted some colour and excitement and love in her life, so she would take the chance.

When she had brushed out her hair she started, naked, for the bedroom. Her hand was on the doorknob, when she froze.

She had been so taken up with Brad's effect on her that she hadn't given any thought to the man himself. Suppose he was already lying there in bed, waiting for her?

Her throat closing up with a mixture of nervousness, anticipation and embarrassment, she stood rooted to the spot, listening to her own breathing and heartbeat.

Now she knew what a devastating effect his kisses had on her, she doubted her ability to stay unmoved. And after her helpless response he must feel very confident that, sexually at least, she would make the kind of companion he wanted.

But after teasing her about her 'experience' it might come as a shock when he discovered, as he was bound to, how utterly *inexperienced* she was.

After a minute or so, knowing it was necessary to get a grip, she read herself the Riot Act. There was no way she could stay lurking in the bathroom indefinitely. If Brad decided to come looking for her it would make her feel both stupid and cowardly.

The least she could do was go out there and face him with her head held high. Pulling on a towelling robe, she tied the belt and, filled with a kind of panicky excitement, threw open the door.

The bed was empty, and so was the room.

She hardly knew whether to be relieved or sorry. In some

ways the *waiting* was the worst. It would surely be less traumatic to get it over with.

Having hung the robe back behind the bathroom door, she took Trevor's ring from her finger and dropped it into one of the case's zipped inner pockets, before finding a nightdress and pulling it on.

A mid-calf-length shift made of ivory satin, it had shoe-string shoulder straps and was split down to the waist, the two halves of material held together by a series of matching bows.

Complete with a second, coffee-coloured nightie, and a matching negligee, it had been a so-far unworn Christmas gift from Milly and Duncan.

'I thought it was time you had something young and glamorous,' Milly had said bluntly, 'instead of those dreadful little orphan Annie things you wear.'

But Joanne had been happy with her Victorian cotton nighties, until Brad had appeared so obviously amused.

When she had been packing, remembering that amusement, a kind of perverse pride had made her take the satin rather than the cotton.

Now she was glad she had.

Putting the negligee on the bottom of the bed, she climbed in and, pulling up the duvet, hesitated. Should she sit up with the light on?

But if she did she would appear to be waiting for him.

Perhaps it was better to switch it off and look settled?

Deciding on the latter, she turned off the lamp and snuggled down, closing her eyes. Surely he would hurry through his business? Though she was anything but experienced, she hadn't the slightest doubt that he had been as aroused as she was.

Her whole body newly awakened and eager, totally unable to relax, the waiting seemed endless.

She found herself thinking ahead. How it would be when

he came to her... When he kissed her and touched her...
When he made love to her...

In the darkness her cheeks grew hot.

Only it wouldn't *be* love, she reminded herself. It would
be lust... That sobering thought should have depressed her,
but somehow it failed to. Knowing only too well what kind
of man he was, she still wanted him with a hunger that
amazed her.

Though the common-sense part of her knew that she
would bitterly regret it later, pride seemed a cold companion compared to the urgency of her need.

In the past, when Milly had got involved with unsuitable
boys, Joanne had wondered vexedly why the girl hadn't
exercised more self-control.

Now she knew.

Impatiently, she switched on the light and looked at her
watch. More than an hour had gone by. What on earth
could be keeping him?

Pushing back the duvet, she got out of bed and opened
the door into the living-room. The curtains were drawn
across the windows and the room was in semi-darkness,
apart from the red-gold glow thrown out by the stove.

He must be working at his desk.

But the door to his office appeared to be slightly ajar,
and she could see no lights burning there either.

Curiosity made her pad across to push the door wider
and peer inside. Brad wasn't at his desk and the room was
empty. He must have gone out.

Disappointment bitter on her tongue, she turned.

He had made the couch up as a bed and was lying on
his back, the covers pulled up to his hips, his hands clasped
behind his head. Beneath the dark brows his eyes gleamed
in the firelight.

Above the waist he was wearing nothing, and the same
below, she guessed. He looked like an advert for some
sexy, masculine body-splash.

Totally disconcerted, she just stood and stared at him.

'Well, well, well…' he murmured. 'I thought you would be asleep by now.'

Somehow she found herself saying, 'I couldn't sleep.'

'Frustration is hell,' he agreed, his voice wry. 'But, as you've come to me, I guess we can do something about it.' He held out his hand.

Shamefaced and desperately self-conscious, she stood rooted to the spot, making no attempt to take the proffered hand.

'Come here,' he ordered softly.

Still she made no move.

'If I have to come and get you…'

He left the threat unfinished, but it was enough to get her unsteady legs working, and as though mesmerised she took a few steps towards the couch.

'Closer,' he said inexorably.

When she was standing beside him he reached out and lightly stroked the smooth ivory satin covering her upper thigh, making every nerve in her body leap in response.

'Though I thought the Victorian look had a certain charm, I must say I prefer this. It's a wonderful combination of virginal and sexy.'

Her mouth desert-dry, she waited.

He picked up her left hand. 'I see you've taken off Trevor's ring.'

Thinking ruefully that he didn't miss a thing, she said, 'I decided it was a mistake to wear it.'

'Why was it a mistake?'

'Well, I…I realised I didn't care for him enough.'

'You told me you loved him.'

'Perhaps love was too strong a word. I'm…fond of him.'

'But he loves you?'

'I don't think so.'

'When I asked if you'd received a declaration of undying love, you said yes.'

'It wasn't true,' she admitted. 'Love was never mentioned. He regards me as *suitable*.'

'So the engagement's off?'

'It was never really on,' she admitted.

'Then your sister's version was the right one?' he remarked with satisfaction.

Joanne nodded mutely.

'Good.' Surprising her, he added, 'I wasn't altogether comfortable with the idea of making off with another man's fiancée...

'Tell me, why did you wear the ring?'

'Trevor had put it on my finger, and to please him I agreed to keep it on while I made up my mind. Now I have.'

'And this is your final decision?'

'Yes. In the circumstances I've decided I can't marry him.'

'In the circumstances...' Brad repeated softly. 'If it wasn't for the *circumstances*, would you have married him?'

She answered truthfully, 'I might have done.'

Watching his brows knit together in a frown, she added, 'But I realise now that it would have been a sad mistake.'

'I must say, I'm pleased. A marriage like that would never have worked.'

Curiously, she asked, 'What makes you think so?'

'For one thing, you're much too warm and passionate for a cold fish like Trevor...'

It gave her the strangest feeling to hear herself referred to as *passionate*...

'And for another, marriage should involve a twosome, rather than a threesome.

'I'm only amazed that you ever considered accepting him in the first place.'

So was she now.

Weakly, she said, 'We had a lot in common...or at least I thought we had...'

Surprising her, Brad remarked, 'I imagine we two have a great deal more. To start with, let's see how sexually compatible we are...'

Tense and waiting, she started to tremble.

He gave the hand he was still holding a sudden jerk, so that with a startled squeak she fell half on top of him.

Throwing an arm around her, he held her to his bare chest and, growling, buried his face against her throat.

That kind of playful rough and tumble was the last thing she had expected and, her dignity momentarily outraged, she put her hands flat-palmed against his chest and tried to lever herself away.

Laughing, he rolled, pinning her beneath him so that she was squashed and breathless. Then, finding the tender spot where neck and shoulder meet, he gave her a love bite.

His mouth, and the warmth of his naked body through the thin satin sending shudders of desire running through her, she made a half-strangled protest.

'Don't you like to play?' he asked seriously.

'It's just that you took me by surprise...'

'I intended to. It releases the tension.' He kissed the tip of her nose. 'Didn't Trevor ever play love games?'

'No.'

'What about your other lovers?'

Uncertain how to answer, she stayed silent.

Lifting a dark brow, he hazarded, 'Or maybe there haven't been any other lovers?'

When she still said nothing he added, 'Never mind, in a little while I'll find out to my own satisfaction...and yours too, I hope. But first I want to look at you...'

His weight lifted, and a moment later, finding his feet, he had scooped her off the couch and laid her down on the thick goatskin rug that lay in front of the stove.

His face intent, absorbed, he untied the bows holding the

bodice of her nightdress together and, slipping the straps
from her shoulders, eased it past her waist and over her
hips.

As he stared down at her body lit by the firelight's glow
he caught his breath. Long-legged and slender, her skin
flawless, her breasts small and firm and beautifully shaped
above a narrow waist and flaring hips, she was the loveliest
thing he'd ever seen.

'You look as perfect as a golden statue,' he said softly.

'I'm anything but perfect,' she objected breathlessly. 'I
have a mole.'

'So you have.' He sounded fascinated. 'Which makes
you even more perfect. I've never really fancied making
love to a statue.'

Bending his head, he kissed the small dark mole that lay
like a beauty spot on her flat stomach, before nuzzling his
face against the softness of her breasts.

The slight roughness of his skin added an extra dimen-
sion to the pleasure, and she gasped.

Lifting his head a little, he said, 'Bristles can be ruinous
to a delicate skin. If I'd realised I would have shaved again.
I still can if you—'

'No! No, you don't need to…' She couldn't bear it if he
left her now. As he hesitated, as if not totally convinced,
she added fervently, 'I *like* it, really I do,' and heard his
quiet chuckle.

Then, closing his eyes, as though to add to the tactile
pleasure, he let his lips rove over her breast, searching
blindly for a nipple.

When, finding one, he took it into his mouth and suckled
sweetly, she began to make soft little mewing sounds in
her throat, and when his hand slid downwards to explore
and add to her pleasure she found herself imploring,
'Please… Oh, please…'

But, refusing to hurry, he led her through a maze of
sensual delight, taking time to touch and taste every inch

of her, leaving her whole body alive and quivering with sensation.

When she thought she could stand no more of such exquisite torment and begged him hoarsely to stop he laughed softly, and said, 'My little innocent, I've only just started.'

By the time she felt the weight of his body, into sensual overload, she was convinced she could experience nothing further. But once again he proved her wrong by entering her and lifting her to heights of ecstasy she'd never even dreamt of.

Afterwards, lying with her head pillowed on his shoulder, his body half supporting hers, the glow from the stove warming her bare flesh, she knew herself to be completely and utterly happy.

His cheek resting on her hair, he asked gently, 'Why did you tell me you'd had lots of experience?'

'I'm not sure,' she admitted. 'It just seemed to be part of the game we were playing.'

'A game you had no stomach for, judging by the look on your face. Tell me, Joanne, how many lovers have you had?'

'None apart from you,' she admitted.

'That's what I thought, but I could hardly believe it. Did something happen to put you off sex?'

'No. It was just that nothing *good* happened. I didn't seem able to respond... I began to think I *couldn't*...but still part of me wanted a home of my own and children...'

'So that's why you considered marrying a man like Trevor?'

'Yes.'

He shook his head. 'Such a colourless existence might well have destroyed a woman like you... Or at least done you as much harm as I have.'

'You haven't done me any harm,' she denied, yawning.

'Through forcing you to come to Norway with me, I've altered the course of your life.'

Heavy lids drooping, drifting on a warm sea of contentment, she said thickly, 'I can only be grateful for that.'

She was deeply asleep when he finally eased himself
free, and, having collected her nightdress, stooped to gather
up her slight weight, murmuring, 'Better take you back to
bed. It'll soon start to get cool.'

When he had carried her though to the bedroom he
tucked her in, dropped her nightie over a chair, and bent to
kiss her softly before switching off the lamp.

Bright sunshine was slanting in through a chink in the curtains when Joanne drifted slowly and languorously to the
surface, aware that she was in bed, but with no recollection
of how she had got there.

Her last memory was of lying in Brad's arms in front of
the glowing stove. The euphoria she had felt then was still
with her.

Encased in a golden bubble of happiness, she sighed and
stretched luxuriously. Her body felt tender in places, but as
sleek and satisfied as a cat sated on cream. Her mind, still
in a blissful dreamlike trance, was as yet undisturbed by
the realities of the situation.

For a moment or two she lay savouring this wonderful
and extraordinary feeling of joy, then, needing to see the
man who had given her such a priceless gift, she turned her
head.

The pillow beside her was smooth and undisturbed. For
whatever reason, Brad had returned to the couch rather than
share the bed.

Frowning, she wondered why. Surely it couldn't be on
ethical grounds?

Or could it?

In some ways he was turning out to be not at all the kind
of man she had first thought him.

Though he had ruthlessly coerced her into coming to
Norway with him, he had admitted that he wasn't altogether

comfortable with the idea of 'making off' with another man's fiancée…

Still, she had explained that there was not, and never had been, a real engagement, so what was the problem?

At least she and Brad were grown adults and free, and if it was the circumstances that were troubling him, as he had pointed out, *she* had gone to *him*, so he couldn't be accused of forcing her in any way…

She had gone to him… The remembrance of that should have made her cringe, should have made her feel ashamed and humiliated.

But somehow it didn't.

For once in her life she had acted completely out of character, brushing aside both common sense and propriety.

She should be eaten up with remorse, but even the sight of her nightdress hanging over a chair couldn't make her feel sorry. Couldn't make her regret what had happened.

And surely Brad wouldn't?

Though he must have known how totally naïve she was in sexual matters, he had clearly enjoyed making love to her. So why had he returned to sleep alone on the couch? Why hadn't he got into bed beside her?

If he *had* she could have snuggled up against him, let her bare leg brush his… This time *she* could have touched *him*, let her fingers find the small leathery nipples, and the ripple of muscles beneath the smooth skin, run her hand down his flat belly to play with the dark, silky curls of pubic hair…

Shocked by her own unbridled sensuality, she jumped out of bed and hurried naked into the bathroom to clean her teeth and shower.

As she stood beneath the jet of hot water, soaping her breasts and recalling how Brad's hands had caressed and fondled them, all at once she thought of Milly, and felt absurdly guilty.

But why should she feel guilty?

It wasn't as if she had set out to steal the man her sister fancied. Her only concern had been to save Milly's marriage, and hopefully she had done just that.

Now the young pair had started a new life in Scotland, with a bit of luck Milly would soon have forgotten the foolish crush she had had on her boss.

Though it was ironic in the extreme that, having saved Milly from such a dangerous and potentially destructive relationship, she had been unable to save herself.

And now she wouldn't even if she could.

When Joanne had dressed in an oatmeal linen skirt and top, she brushed out her black hair and, after the briefest hesitation, left it loose around her shoulders.

As her lover liked it…

The thought sprang into her mind, sending a fizz of excitement through her. She had never imagined herself having a lover. And certainly not a wonderful sensual man like Brad.

Heading for the living-room, her heart beating faster, she wondered what he would do, how he would treat her. Would he hold out his hand and smile? Or would he take her in his arms and kiss her?

In the event he did neither.

When she opened the door and walked into a room full of fresh air and sunlight, he tossed aside the paper he was reading, and rose to his feet, gravely courteous.

Dressed in stone-coloured trousers and a black polo-necked sweater, he looked so virile and attractive that he took her breath away.

Though she hadn't been able to wait to see him, the moment their eyes met she found herself blushing painfully.

'Good morning. I hope you slept well?'

While pleasant and friendly, neither his tone nor his attitude were remotely lover-like.

'Y-yes, thank you.' Disconcerted, she found herself stammering slightly.

'I was about to give you a call. Breakfast should be here any minute.'

Right on cue, there was a tap at the door.

'Come in,' he invited.

The door opened to admit a young, fair-haired girl wheeling a breakfast trolley.

'Thank you, Lys. You can leave it there. I'll see to it.'

She gave him a quick, eager smile and left without a word, closing the door quietly behind her.

Pushing back the couch, from which the bedding had been removed, Brad pulled the trolley in front of the open window and placed a chair at either end.

Then, turning to Joanne, who was hovering uncertainly, he asked, 'Where would you like to sit?'

'I don't mind in the slightest,' she answered, and took the chair he pulled out for her.

He sat down opposite and raised an enquiring brow. 'Tea or coffee?'

'Coffee, please.'

In spite of—or maybe *because* of—the previous night's intimacy, they were acting like two strangers, she thought in dismay as he lifted the coffee-pot and filled both their cups.

'Now, what would you like to eat?'

The trolley was set with crusty bread, jam, cold meat, various cheeses, and fish.

She was about to plump for bread and jam when, a gleam in his eye, he suggested, 'If you feel brave enough, why don't you sample the herring?'

Her heart lifting in response to that hint of devilment, she agreed, 'I'd love to.'

He helped her to a generous portion, and passed her the plate.

Accepting it with a word of thanks, she added quizzically, 'I strongly suspect you were hoping to call me a coward?'

He smiled at her, and her heart turned right over. 'A coward is the last thing I'd call you…though I admit to being surprised. None of the females I've known would touch it. Though it's extremely tasty.'

Watching him help himself to some, she said, 'As a matter of fact you're preaching to the converted. I adore kippers.'

He threw back his head and laughed. 'I'm beginning to realise you're a woman of many parts.'

Very conscious of him, of his powerful masculinity, she tried hard to concentrate on her meal, but each time her eyes inadvertently strayed in his direction she found he was watching her.

Growing uncomfortable beneath that steady scrutiny, and needing something to say, she asked, 'Did you get in touch with Paul Randall?'

'Yes.' Brad frowned.

'Something wrong?'

'There was another spot of trouble during the evening. Nothing major, but enough to slightly injure a crew member, and prevent one of the ships from sailing.

'The problem is, the longer this sabotage goes on, the more chance there is of someone getting seriously hurt.'

'And you really don't think that whoever's behind it will stop?'

Brad shook his head. 'Mr X, if I may so call him, has been stepping up the attacks. I strongly suspect with the intention of bringing me over here.'

'Why should he want to do that?'

'It's always easier to deal with the opposition on home ground. But I may yet surprise him by winning.'

'I don't see how you can hope to win when you don't know where the next attack's going to be.'

'Certainly an open, all-out war would be a lot easier to fight.'

Wryly, he added, 'That's no doubt why this person prefers an undercover campaign. As you remarked when we were leaving the airport, it's all very cloak-and-daggerish…'

Seeing her faint shiver, he said reassuringly, 'There's no need to worry. I can't imagine you'd be in the slightest danger.'

'Which means *you* might?'

'Though it may sound melodramatic, there is a possibility. Paul has already had a bit of bother which might, or might not, have been an accident.'

'What kind of bother?'

'The brakes on his car failed. Luckily he was back home and just coasting into the garage, so the only damage was a cracked headlight.

'I've suggested he keeps quiet about it, and gets the car properly examined to see if the brakes have been tampered with.'

Getting to his feet, he stretched, lithe as a big cat. 'But that's enough of problems… As it's Sunday, I thought rather than work I'd play hookey.'

Wondering if that meant he was going to leave her to her own devices, she said, 'Oh.'

'What's the matter? Did you want to work?'

She shook her head.

'Then as it's such a lovely day, I'll take you up Mount Floyen. At the top there's a look-out point that gives you a bird's-eye view of the town.'

His manner was that of a pleasant, slightly detached host, but still she felt her spirits soaring. He wasn't intending to walk away and leave her. They would be together.

And, strangely enough, being with him was the only thing that really mattered.

'There's no rain forecast,' he went on, 'so you shouldn't need more than a jacket with you, just in case it turns cool.'

'I'll get one,' she said eagerly.

Each wearing a light jacket, they walked for perhaps half

a mile through the sunny and pleasant streets of Bergen, until they came to what appeared to be the glass entrance to a station.

'Floyen is over a thousand feet above sea-level,' Brad told her, 'so most people take the *Floybanen*.'

The cable car was busy with rucksack-laden tourists, but they got a seat without too much difficulty.

Disturbed by the pressure of his muscular thigh against her own, Joanne stared determinedly through the window as they climbed steadily.

There were several intermediate stops on the way to the top but, totally distracted, her mind on other, more personal, things, she took in very little.

At the top Brad helped her off, and, taking her hand, led her out onto an airy platform apparently suspended in space.

She gasped at the view. Spread far below them, glowing with autumn colours, Bergen looked like a perfect scale model, its necklace of green and gold islands set like gems in a sea of lapis lazuli.

'Isn't it magnificent?' she breathed.

He smiled. 'I've always thought so.'

Having stood for quite a time admiring the view, they strolled the length of the platform and turned towards a small village.

As they reached a wooden bench Brad instructed, 'Wait here a minute.'

Obediently Joanne sat down and watched his broad shoulders disappear into a shop.

When he returned he was carrying two long, curly cones. Handing her one, he said with a grin, 'I couldn't let you miss out on one of my favourite boyhood treats.'

Sitting side by side in the sun, they started on the delectable concoction of ice cream mingled with candied oranges, apricots, cherries and nuts.

Nibbling around the top of her crisp cone, as she had

often done as a child, she thought about the man by her side.

Brad had called her a woman of many parts. Now she was beginning to realise that the same could be said for him. The worldly, sophisticated man she knew had vanished, to be replaced by someone carefree and boyish.

Someone she could love.

CHAPTER SEVEN

No! REMEMBERING his playboy reputation, remembering Milly, how could she possibly think that?

She could *never* love Brad.

Sexual attraction was one thing. Physical. Fleeting. A surface magnetism that would eventually wither and die for lack of roots. No emotions needed to be involved. Except the obvious.

Real love was something totally different. Deep and lasting, a seed that, having once taken root, grew and flourished and transformed completely. An emotion that, if one was lucky, would change and endure, and last a lifetime.

Though how would she know that? She who had never been in love... Yet she *did* know, and what she felt for Brad was merely sexual attraction, she told herself firmly.

All the same, he was completely irresistible.

Glancing surreptitiously at him, she saw that his eyes were narrowed against the sun, the thick, sooty lashes almost brushing his hard cheeks; his dark hair was slightly ruffled, and there was a fragment of apricot on his lower lip.

While she watched him, fascinated, he gathered it up neatly with the tip of his tongue, and then, as if sensing her regard, turned his head to glance at her. Though she felt the colour rise in her cheeks, she was unable to look away, caught and held by those eyes. Fascinating eyes, the colour of deep mossy pools, with a ring of even darker green surrounding the iris, and tiny flecks of gold swimming in their clear depths.

As she gazed at him, mesmerised, he broke the spell by saying lightly, 'Aren't we a messy pair?' and, leaning for-

ward, licked away a smear of ice cream from the corner of
her mouth.

That erotic little action made her heart start to race and
her stomach fold in on itself.

Looking hurriedly away, she returned her attention to her
ice-cream cone and, finishing it to the last crumb, sucked
her sticky fingers like an urchin.

Brad reached for his jacket and, having fished in the
pocket, produced a small bottle of water and a packet of
tissues. When he'd dampened a wad, he handed her half.

'Thank you. Were you ever a boy scout?'

Grinning, he wiped his own hands and said, 'No. It's
experience that's taught me to be prepared.'

Cleaning her fingers, she said contentedly, 'That was absolutely delightful.'

'And so are you.'

She caught her breath audibly, oddly moved by the
sweetness of the unexpected compliment, and her hands
weren't quite steady when she handed him the tissues to
dispose of.

Dropping them into a nearby litter bin, he suggested
gravely, 'I thought we might go for a walk now, if that
suits you?'

'That suits me fine,' she agreed, and rose without looking
at him, afraid he would see the turmoil of emotions that
filled her.

'I doubt very much if that weirdo has bothered to follow
us up here,' Brad went on, 'but if he has it'll give him
some exercise.'

He sounded so laid-back about it that, unwilling to tar-
nish the brightness of the day, Joanne refused to worry.

Tucking her hand through his arm, he added, 'If we take
a circular route we'll be back in this area just in time for
a late lunch.'

'Sounds ideal.'

It was a perfect autumn day, still and balmy, the thin

golden air exhilarating as champagne as they took a sun-dappled path through the scented pine woods.

Enjoying the movement and the feel of the springy carpet of brown pine needles beneath their feet, they walked mostly in companionable silence, with only the odd remark being passed.

It was approaching two o'clock when, having almost completed the loop, they reached a fairy-tale hotel perched on a tremendous overhang.

'I thought we'd have lunch at the Trondheim,' Brad said. 'There's a wonderful view from the terrace.'

It was so idyllic that, too happy to speak, she nodded wordlessly.

After freshening up they were shown to a table for two beneath a gaily-striped umbrella. There they were served with a delicately chilled white wine and an excellent salad.

The leisurely meal over, they were just drinking their coffee, when a well-dressed blonde woman of statuesque proportions advanced on their table, crying, 'Brad, darling! Where on earth have you been? I've been trying to get hold of you to invite you to my party, but your office told me you were away… Why didn't you let me know you were coming?'

'Erika…' Tossing his napkin onto the table, he rose to his feet.

She was somewhere in her early twenties, Joanne guessed, and almost as tall as he was. High heels brought her eyes on a level with his. A moment later she had thrown her arms around his neck and was kissing him full on the lips.

For a moment he stood perfectly still, then, unwinding her arms, he stepped back and surveyed her. Silvery hair hung straight and glossy, framing an oval face with perfect features and eyes of a pale, glacial blue.

'Erika, you're looking as beautiful as ever,' he remarked with cool politeness.

Then, turning to his companion, 'Joanne, may I introduce Ms Reiersen? Erika, this is my secretary, Miss Winslow.'

'How do you do?' Joanne murmured.

The blonde's glance slid over her dismissively, and without deigning to reply she said to Brad, 'How long have you been here?'

'We flew in yesterday.'

'I'm seriously angry that you came to Bergen without letting me know. Daddy will be too.'

'It was a spur-of-the-moment decision.'

'Well, I'll forgive you if you come to my party.'

'When is it?'

'Tonight…so, you see, you're just in time… It's to celebrate my divorce. As of now, I'm a free woman.' She displayed her ringless fingers.

'Well, I—'

'I know Daddy will expect you to be there.'

At Brad's slight frown, she added hurriedly, 'Even though it's a party I'm sure he'll want to talk business, but I won't let him monopolise you, I promise…

'Oh, and Paul Randall will be coming, so you really can't let the side down.'

Joanne found the blonde's desperation, and the reason for the party, both sad and pathetic.

A young chap appeared by her side, fair-haired, bearded and brawny, and with a hostile glance at Brad asked, 'Are you about ready, Erika?'

Ignoring him completely, she put a beautifully manicured hand on Brad's arm and urged, 'Promise me you'll be there…'

'I take it the invitation includes Miss Winslow?'

'Why on earth should you want to bring your secretary?' she asked rudely. Then, 'You *will* come?'

His tone regretful, Brad said, 'I'm afraid I've already promised Miss Winslow that I'll take her to the Kirkesen tonight.'

'Well, I'm sure she won't mind—'

'I really don't mind—'

The two women spoke simultaneously.

He shook his head. 'As Miss Winslow is new to Norway, I don't want to leave her sitting in a hotel room on her own.'

'For heaven's sake,' Erika burst out petulantly, 'she's not a child. She can go out on her own if she wants to...'

Apparently seeing by his face that she was wasting her breath, she said ungraciously, 'Oh, very well, bring her if you must. I'll expect you about seven.'

She presented her mouth for his kiss.

He gave her a chaste salute on the cheek.

Obviously disappointed, she turned away.

Her young partner, scowling his displeasure, moved to follow her.

Brad sat down again, remarking, 'Not a very sociable young man at the best of times, and jealousy does nothing to improve his manners...

'And, speaking of manners, I apologise for Erika's rudeness. I hope you don't dislike her for it.'

Sounding tolerant, he added, 'You see, she isn't altogether to blame. She's always been Daddy's little girl and allowed to get away with anything.'

'Of course I don't dislike her. In fact I felt rather sorry for her. It can't be much fun having one's marriage break up.'

'Especially after two other relationships ended in disaster. But that kind of upbringing doesn't encourage the willingness to compromise. Nor does it create a good basis for wedded bliss. And unfortunately she chose to marry her own cousin, which meant they shared a lot of the same faults.'

'How long did the marriage last?'

'They separated after just a few months.'

Just a few months… And now she was celebrating being single again…

As though reading her mind, Brad added, 'To me, divorce smacks of failure. I don't see it as a good reason for having a party. Still, we won't need to stay too long.'

Heartily disliking the whole situation, Joanne said, 'I really think you should go alone.'

'I don't want to go alone. I happen to want you with me.'

'It's very kind of you to be concerned about me, but I really don't mind if you leave me.'

'I've no intention of leaving you.'

She gave up trying to be diplomatic, and said flatly, 'And I've no intention of going to the party when Ms Reiersen so obviously doesn't want me there.'

'Erika may sound a little ungracious, but I'm sure she'll be more than happy to see both of us,' he assured her smoothly.

'Like hell!' Joanne muttered under her breath.

'In any case, *I* want you to go.'

She bit her lip, determined that this time he wouldn't get his way. Wild horses wouldn't drag her to that party.

Watching her mutinous face, he asked, 'Now, would you like some more coffee?'

'No, thank you,' she said distantly.

'Then I think we should be making a move. It's possible to walk down to town via Fjellveien, but I think we've done enough walking today. Especially as we'll no doubt be dancing tonight,' he added deliberately.

When she made no comment, apparently accepting her silence as submission, he tucked her hand through his arm, and they made their way back to the cable car, only to find they had just missed it.

As, forced to wait half an hour for the next one, they sat in silence Joanne found herself wondering about his relationship with Erika. Judging by the way the blonde had kissed him, it must have been a close one.

Had been? Or *still was*? Brad had said something about the young chap being jealous.

But surely any close relationship must have ended, or presumably Brad would have told the blonde he was coming to Bergen…?

It was almost a quarter past six by the time they reached Lofoten. 'I expect you could do with a cup of tea?' Brad suggested.

Having half expected to be hurried straight up to his suite, Joanne relaxed, and asked, 'When did you learn to mind-read?'

A gleam in his eye, he answered succinctly, 'As far as *you're* concerned I find it easy.'

Annoyed with herself for giving him an opening, she wished she had simply said 'Yes, please.'

The lobby was empty, and when Helga looked up to smile and greet them Brad ordered a pot of tea.

Then, having settled Joanne in front of the stove, he said, 'There's something I need to do before we go up, but I'll try not to be long.'

A moment later he had disappeared back through the main entrance, and she caught just a glimpse of him walking quickly past the small-paned windows.

She had finished her second cup of tea and was starting to wonder where on earth he'd got to, when he returned.

'Would you like some tea?' she asked.

He shook his head. 'No time. It's almost seven o'clock now, and you've got some getting-ready to do!'

'If you think for one minute I'm going to that party—' she began fiercely.

'Shhh…' He put a finger to her lips and, glancing in Helga's direction, added quizzically, 'We mustn't fall out in front of the staff… Now, the lift's not here, so the stairs will be quicker.'

The wooden treads creaked comfortably under their weight as, stoking the fires of anger and defiance, she accompanied him up to their suite.

As soon as the door had closed behind them he said, 'Now, we both need to shower and change, and I must order a taxi, so if you want to have a row, make it snappy, because we haven't a lot of time.'

As though to add weight to his words, the grandmother clock chimed the hour.

'I don't want to have a row,' she said as calmly as possible.

'Good. In that case, we can both start getting ready.'

She defied him. 'I've no need to get ready. I really don't want to go to the party.'

He shook his head reprovingly. 'Perhaps you've forgotten, it's what *I* want that counts, and I want you to go with me.'

'I want to stay here.'

'But you don't have a choice,' he said flatly. 'Now, please go and get ready.'

'I won't.'

Though his expression didn't change, she could feel the force of his anger and was suddenly scared stiff of it.

But what could he do to her? He wouldn't hurt her.

Or would he? Even as the thought crossed her mind she knew with certainty that, no matter how badly provoked, he would never physically harm a woman.

It was only the mean and cowardly, the *inadequate* men who took their anger out on someone weaker than themselves.

He came over to her and lifted her chin so that she was forced to look at him. 'Do as I say, Joanne,' he insisted quietly.

Blue eyes clashed with green.

For a moment she tried to stare him out, but his will-power proved stronger than hers. Her eyes were the first to drop and, her nerve suddenly cracking, she turned and fled.

When she had showered she brushed out her hair and swirled it on top of her head in an elegant chignon, before making up with care.

He wouldn't be able to accuse her of not trying to look her best, she thought with satisfaction. Though there was one thing that he seemed to have forgotten, and she had deliberately left it until the last minute to mention. She had absolutely nothing to wear to a party. Especially a posh one. And she had little doubt that it *would* be posh.

Rather than have her look totally out of place, he would be forced to let her stay behind.

There was a tap at the door, and his voice queried, 'How are you doing?'

'About ready.'

Pulling on her negligee, she went through to the living-room, where Brad, looking breathtakingly handsome in evening dress, was fastening his bow-tie.

As he glanced up she said sweetly, 'There's just one thing...I haven't got *anything* to wear.'

A knock cut through her words.

Brad opened the door, nodded his thanks and, passing over a fifty-krona tip in exchange for a package, closed it again.

Handing Joanne the large, flat box, he said calmly, 'How about this?'

With the infuriating knowledge that she had been out-manoeuvred, she put the box on the couch, tore off the silver and gold paper and removed the lid.

For a moment she stared down at the contents silently, then, with an odd tightness in her chest, lifted out the dress.

It was exquisite.

Ankle-length, and made of pure silk chiffon, it was the same deep blue as her eyes, and striking in its simplicity.

One shoulder was completely bare, while climbing over

the other, and running down the bodice to the thigh-length slit in the skirt, was a trail of small silver ivy leaves. There was a silver-lined matching wrap.

The designer label said simply: Tessin.

Never in her wildest dreams could she have afforded a dress like that.

'If you dig a little deeper,' Brad said, 'you should find some accessories.'

Beneath the dress there were silk stockings and gossamer undies, and to one side, carefully wrapped in tissue paper, a pair of silver sandals and a small evening purse.

How on earth had he managed to conjure up things like that on a Sunday? she wondered dazedly.

He answered her unspoken question. 'I have a friend who lives above her own boutique. Luckily it's just along the street...

'As there wasn't much time, having told Ingrid your size, I was forced to leave the shoes and undies to her. The only thing I personally chose was the dress. I hope you like it.'

Starting to realise the full implications, Joanne said stiltedly, 'It's beautiful, but I can't possibly accept such an expensive gift.'

'It isn't a gift. Nor is it for services rendered.' As the colour rose in her cheeks he went on, 'By the time this trip is over you'll have more than earned it...

'And I *do* mean for your secretarial skills,' he added sardonically.

Watching her soft lips tighten, he came over and took her hand, stroking the soft palm with his thumb. 'Please, Joanne, will you get dressed and come with me?'

Disconcerted because he'd *asked* rather than *ordered*, she took a steadying breath, and said, 'I don't understand why you want me.'

'For one thing Paul will be there, and I'd like you to meet him. For another, we have to consider poor Knut.'

'Poor Knut?' she echoed blankly.

'The young man Erika had in tow. He's been in love with her for a long time now, but I'm afraid she just uses him.'

'I don't see what difference *my* being there will make.'

'If I go alone, what do you think will happen?'

Put like that, Joanne had no doubt. It had been obvious at lunch time that, with Brad present, Knut came a very poor second.

Knowing full well that Erika would be anything but pleased, she squared her shoulders and agreed. 'Very well, I'll come.'

He used the hand he was still holding to draw her closer and, bending his head, kissed her lightly on the mouth. 'That's my girl.'

Her whole being made radiant by that fleeting kiss, she took the box and its contents through to the bedroom and put on her new finery as swiftly as possible.

Everything fitted to perfection. Which suggested a degree of experience on Brad's part that she preferred not to contemplate.

Settling the dress into place, she struggled to fasten the tiny, invisible hand-sewn hooks and eyes that ran down the back. She had managed to fasten two thirds of them, before admitting she would need Brad's help with the rest.

Stepping in front of the long mirror, she caught her breath, picturing her family's surprise at the transformation. Who would have thought she could look like this?

The beautiful material clung lovingly to the slender curves of hips and bust, but, though the bodice was daringly low, and she was bra-less, the dress was so well-cut that she felt completely at ease wearing it.

Well, *almost* completely.

Seeing how, when she moved, the skirt parted just enough to give a tantalising glimpse of a silk-clad leg, she thanked her lucky stars that her legs were in such good shape.

When, having gathered up her wrap and purse, she returned to the living-room, for what seemed an age Brad regarded her in silence.

Wondering if he was disappointed, she said hesitantly, 'I'm afraid I haven't any jewellery.'

With a slightly husky note in his voice, he assured her, 'You don't need any jewellery. It would be gilding the lily. You look absolutely stunning just as you are.'

Happiness and the warmth of his approval heady as vintage champagne, she said, 'I'm afraid I couldn't fasten all the hooks and eyes.'

'Then allow me.'

She turned her back.

They could have been a long-married husband and wife, she thought as with deft fingers he proceeded to complete the task.

But, as though to disprove that image, he lightly gripped her shoulders and, having touched his lips to the warmth of her nape, traced the exposed length of her spine with his tongue-tip.

Little shivers of excitement were still running through her as he turned her round and, saying, 'Mustn't spoil the lip gloss,' kissed the tip of her nose. Then, putting the wrap around her shoulders, he escorted her down to the waiting taxi.

Their destination was out of town, and during the drive, apparently deep in thought, Brad said nothing.

Joanne occupied her time by wondering what he was thinking, and worrying, just a little, about the coming evening.

The Reiersens' house was a huge old place situated at the top of a wooded incline. Blazing with lights, it was more like a castle than a house, Joanne decided as they left the road and wound their way up an imposing drive.

When their taxi stopped at a paved area crowded with cars Brad helped her out and, after a brief conversation with the driver, escorted her up a wide sweep of stone steps to a large, studded door.

He tugged on the bell-pull and the door was opened by a middle-aged manservant, who bowed his head politely and took Joanne's wrap.

As they made their way into the wood-panelled hall a waiter approached with a loaded tray, and Brad helped them both to a glass of champagne.

On their right, an archway led through to a large, chandelier-hung ballroom, where a crowd of people were gathered in laughing groups, sipping their drinks and talking.

It was a warm night, and on the far side of the room several pairs of French windows stood open, giving access to a lantern-lit terrace and garden.

On a raised dais, an orchestra was playing, and already several couples were dancing. Everyone appeared to be extremely well-dressed, the women wearing designer gowns and the men in immaculate evening clothes.

Joanne could only be pleased that at least she wouldn't look out of place.

They had just reached the archway and paused to survey the glittering scene, when a nice-looking man of medium height, with dark hair and a thin, intelligent face, made his way through the crowd to join them.

'Good to see you,' Brad greeted him.

The pair shook hands.

'Joanne, this is Paul Randall... Paul, my secretary, Joanne Winslow.'

Holding out her hand, she smiled. 'How do you do?'

For a moment he appeared nonplussed, then, his answering smile pleasant, he said, 'Nice to meet you, Miss Winslow... It *is* Miss Winslow?'

'Yes.'

As they shook hands he went on, 'Forgive me if I seem a bit confused. You see, I thought I knew Brad's secretary…small, ravishingly pretty, red-gold hair, bright blue eyes… I've even flirted with her…

'Now I find it's the same name, but a completely different girl…though equally beautiful,' he added gallantly.

When Brad stood, his face enigmatic, making no effort to explain, Joanne gathered herself and said steadily, 'Perhaps Mr Lancing should have introduced me as his *temporary* secretary. I'm just filling in for my sister.'

'Your sister? Oh, I see. You're not a bit alike…' Then with genuine concern, 'I do hope she isn't ill?'

'No, Milly's fine. It's just that she left, rather suddenly, to go to Scotland with her husband.'

'Her husband? When did she get married?'

'Last spring. Shortly after she started working for Lancing's.'

'Oh, I'm sorry.' He looked surprised. 'I didn't realise. She doesn't wear a wedding ring, and I've always known her as Miss Winslow.'

Frowning, Joanne was wondering why Milly hadn't worn her ring to work, when a tall, heavily built man with bushy eyebrows and a thatch of iron-grey hair appeared, and said, 'Glad you could come, Randall.'

'Thank you for inviting me,' Paul answered civilly as they exchanged handshakes.

Big and bluff and handsome, wearing impeccable evening dress, the newcomer looked to be in his late sixties or possibly early seventies.

'Brad, how are you?' He spoke excellent English, but with a slightly guttural accent.

'Very well… And you?'

'Starting to feel my age.'

The two men shook hands. Neither smiled.

There was a kind of careful cordiality there, Joanne realised, but no warmth.

An arm lightly encircling her waist, Brad drew her forward. 'Joanne, may I introduce Mr Reiersen... Harald, this is my secretary, Miss Winslow.'

'How do you do, Miss Winslow?'

Taking her hand, he smiled at her and, though the smile didn't reach his pale blue eyes, she recognised instantly that here was a man well-used to charming the ladies.

'How do you do?' she murmured, returning his smile.

Lifting the half-empty champagne glass he held, he toasted her. 'You look absolutely beautiful.'

More than a little uncomfortable under his admiring gaze, she said, 'Thank you.'

A waiter came hurrying up with a tray and, swapping his now empty glass for a full one, Reiersen turned again to Joanne and asked, 'How long are you intending to stay in Bergen?'

'I'm not really certain,' she answered carefully. 'It all depends on what Mr Lancing's plans are.'

His tone jocular, Reiersen admonished, 'Now, don't try to tell me that, as Brad's confidential secretary, you don't *know* what his plans are.'

Unsure what to say, she was relieved when Erika, dazzling in an aquamarine gown that shimmered when she moved, bore down on them.

'Brad, darling! So here you are at last. I've been watching out for you.' Then chidingly, 'You're so late I was starting to think you weren't going to come after all...'

She gave Joanne a cursory glance, before putting a possessive hand on Brad's arm and adding, 'Do come and dance with me.'

He hadn't moved when, doing a double take, Erika's ice-blue eyes swung back to Joanne.

Staring rudely, she said in a sharp voice, 'What an expensive-looking dress. Do tell me how you came by it. I'm sure you didn't buy *that* on the kind of wages a secretary earns.'

Feeling the hot colour rise in her cheeks, Joanne cursed

herself. Knowing the score, she should have been prepared for just that kind of remark.

Before she could find her voice, Brad cut in smoothly, 'As you've asked so nicely, my dear Erika, I'm quite sure Miss Winslow won't mind telling you where she got the dress.'

Joanne bit her lip. She certainly *did* mind. In fact she hadn't the slightest intention of admitting that she was wearing clothes Brad had paid for. Nor did she propose to lie.

Stepping into the breach, Paul said blandly, 'Perhaps you two girls can chat about clothes later? The orchestra has just started to play my favourite tune, and I was about to ask Miss Winslow to dance with me.'

Relieving Joanne of her glass, he set that and his own down on a side-table, and held out his hand to her. She took it gratefully and followed him onto the dance floor.

'It's an awful long time since I last danced,' she warned him as, clutching the evening purse in her left hand, she went into his arms.

'Dancing is like riding a bike, it's something you never forget how to do. And if you should happen to make a mistake it won't matter. I can assure you that while you're wearing that dress no one will be looking at your feet.'

Then quizzically, 'Does that make you feel better or worse?'

Smiling, she said, 'I'm not quite sure. But thank you for rescuing me.'

'Always at your service.' Then he added seriously, 'I presume you would have politely told that spoilt brat to mind her own business?'

'I'm just glad I didn't have to. It would have made it difficult for…everyone.'

'Brad in particular?'

'Well, yes.'

'There are times it would give me the greatest satisfaction to take that girl over my knee...

'Though I don't suppose I ever will,' he said regretfully. Adding with a grin, 'For one thing, she's bigger than me.'

Joanne gave a little choke of laughter.

'Seriously though, I often wonder how Brad puts up with her.'

'I don't suppose he comes to Norway very often.'

'Not all that often, but Erika stays in London a fair bit. Reiersen has a house near Hyde Park. He lived there for a number of years while his wife was ailing and needed specialised treatment.

'When they moved back to Bergen he kept the house, and shortly after Erika's marriage broke up he gave it to her...

'As you'll no doubt discover when you get to know them better, he absolutely dotes on her.'

'I take it she's an only child?'

'Can't you tell? And a late one, to boot. Apparently Reiersen waited years for a son and heir, and had given up hope of having any children.

'He was in his late forties by the time Erika was born, and after waiting so long for a child he was over the moon. Unfortunately his wife died while his daughter was still quite young, so she was all he had left.'

'That's sad,' Joanne said, feeling a quick sympathy for them both.

'I agree. She could well have turned out to be a much nicer person if it hadn't been for her father's influence...'

That was pretty much what Brad had said.

'In my opinion he's been the ruin of her. If he hadn't allowed her to marry that cousin of hers...'

'Perhaps he wasn't able to stop her.'

Paul shook his head. 'When she fell in lust with Lars he was about to marry someone else. Erika has always had everything she's ever wanted, so she appealed to her father...'

'But surely even he couldn't manipulate *people*—'

'That's just where you're wrong. Because that branch of the family have always been the poor relations, Daddy was able to buy his daughter the man of her choice by putting a vast amount of money into the company Lars was struggling to keep afloat.

'Of course, it suited him. Reiersen was hoping to groom his son-in-law to follow in his footsteps and be the son he never had.

'But I gather Lars soon got tired of playing the dutiful husband and, realising he'd sold his soul, opted out...'

As casually as possible Joanne asked, 'So what do you think she'll do now?'

'Erika's a very beautiful woman, and there's fire under that ice... If it wasn't for her father there would be plenty of men only too willing to chance getting burnt.'

There was something about the way he spoke that made her hazard, 'You amongst them?' Then quickly, 'I'm sorry, I shouldn't have said that.'

'Why not? We're having a very frank conversation. And yes, you're right, myself amongst them...'

The tune they were dancing to came to an end, and with scarcely a pause the band slipped into an old classic.

Paul's arm tightened around her, and as they moved off once more he continued, 'Believe me, I've no delusions about what kind of woman she is, and I wouldn't expect to change her overnight. But I do believe that with the right man...' He let the sentence tail off.

Curiously Joanne asked, 'How would you describe the right man?'

'In my opinion the right man would be someone strong, who genuinely loves her but isn't willing to spoil her rotten.

'The trouble is, she always seems to choose the wrong man.'

'You sound as if you think she's already chosen?'

'I'm fairly sure she has. But this time, if I'm any judge of character, she'll be on her own.'

'You're saying…?'

'I'm saying that on this occasion she may have set her sights on one of the few men Daddy won't be able to influence.'

CHAPTER EIGHT

'You mean Brad,' Joanne said flatly.

'Yes. As you may have noticed, she's crazy about him.'

Knowing she shouldn't, but doing it all the same, she asked, 'How do you think he feels about her?'

'Hard to say. Up till now, Brad has played it cool. He's not a man to wear his heart on his sleeve, so it's difficult to know which way he'll jump.

'He's always seemed fairly tolerant of her faults and failings...'

Remembering lunch time, and how he'd defended the blonde's rudeness, Joanne couldn't argue with that.

'If he *did* decide to take her on he's certainly strong enough, and I don't think he'd spoil her. But whether or not...'

As he was speaking she caught a glimpse of Erika and Brad on the far side of the dance floor. The blonde and he were closely entwined, her arms around his neck, her cheek resting against his.

Joanne felt such a stab of pain that she missed a step and stood on Paul's toe.

'Sorry,' she mumbled.

'That's all right,' he said, his eyes following hers before returning to her face.

Then thoughtfully, 'I guess we're both suffering from the same malady. But let's put our lacerated feelings aside and try to enjoy the rest of the evening... Oh, hell!'

'What's wrong?' she asked in alarm.

'Reiersen's heading this way, and I've noticed that he's been knocking it back a bit. I'm afraid he's always liked a spot too much of the bubbly...

132

'He may be going to ask you to dance, so if you don't want to take the risk, say so quickly, and I'll try to head him off while you run and hide in the loo.'

Suddenly liking this man enormously, she laughed and said, 'Thanks, but I think I'll take my chances on the dance floor. As I've already practically crippled you, I think Mr Reiersen is the one most at risk.'

'Nonsense,' Paul disagreed stoutly, 'when not distracted, you dance better than Erika.'

'I should hope so,' Reiersen remarked, appearing at their side. 'That daughter of mine has two left feet. That's why I take care not to dance with her.'

'I don't believe a word of it,' Joanne said lightly as they watched Brad and the blonde glide past.

'Elegance itself,' Paul commented.

Reiersen offered Joanne his hand. 'Shall we show them what we can do? You don't mind, Randall?'

'Not at all,' Paul said accommodatingly. 'I may try my luck with Erika.'

'I doubt if you'll get anywhere. She seems to prefer the partner she already has. Young Knut tried to cut in, and she soon sent him packing.'

'Oh, well, "Faint heart never won fair lady,"' Paul quoted cheerfully, and took himself off.

As though to confirm that Paul had been right in his assumption that Reiersen had been drinking, he moved clumsily and, catching Joanne's arm, knocked her purse from her hand.

'I'm so sorry,' he apologised, and stooped to pick it up.

'It's a bit of a nuisance,' she admitted. 'I should have left it somewhere.'

'Allow me.' He reached to put the small purse on a side-table.

'Thank you.'

Rather to Joanne's surprise, he proved to be a good

dancer, easy to follow, and light on his feet for so big a man.

As they moved round the floor, smiling and genial, he set himself out to charm her. 'Erika tells me you were lunching up Floyen. What did you think of the view from there?'

'I thought it was glorious,' she said sincerely.

'Then you like Bergen?'

'Oh, yes.'

'It was once Norway's largest city, and the undisputed capital of trade and shipping...'

Genuinely interested, she listened while he talked about Bergen's past. After a little while he paused to ask, 'Where are you staying?'

Startled by the abrupt change of subject, she answered, 'At Lofoten.'

'I understand Brad has a suite there?'

She said nothing, and after a moment Reiersen went on, 'Erika's fairly broad-minded about Brad paying for a little fun on the side, but she's keen that he should stay with her, as he has done in the past...'

The words coiled like a cold tentacle around Joanne's heart and squeezed, so that a sudden pain blotted out the rest of the sentence.

After a moment she recovered enough to hear Reiersen continuing, 'So you won't mind if he doesn't go back with you tonight?'

Realising he'd only asked her to dance in order to put this rather heavy-handed message across, she said, 'Not at all; I can always get a taxi,' and was pleased that her voice was steady.

'It may not be too easy to find a taxi. I happen to know there are several functions going on tonight, which means most taxi firms will already be fully booked.

'However, Randall is renting a house not far from

Lofoten, so I've no doubt he will be happy to take you back.'

'If Mr Randall can get a taxi, and he'll allow me, I'll be pleased to share it.'

'He came in his own car.'

Without thinking, she said, 'Oh, but I thought his car was off the road.'

'There was a spot of trouble with his brakes, I gather, but he's obviously had them fixed.

'Randall isn't the kind of young man to let grass grow under his feet. If he wasn't working for Brad *I* wouldn't mind employing him.' Almost to himself, he added, 'It didn't take him long to get on to Mussen…'

The name rang a distant bell, but before she could think why Reiersen was going on, 'But I'm talking too much, which is probably due to the fact that you're a very good listener…'

It was more probably due to the champagne, Joanne thought wryly.

After a moment or two of silence, his manner conspiratorial, he went on, 'I've heard a whisper that the DSL is having more trouble, including a fire in one of their hotels. Any idea what Brad's going to do about it? Is he considering calling in the police?'

'I'm afraid I don't know,' she said coolly.

'Suppose you have time to think about it? After all, there's such a thing as misplaced loyalty, and once Brad's had his fun…'

He left the sentence hanging in the air, but there was no mistaking his meaning.

There was a short pause, then he went on, 'I'm sure you're sensible enough to keep this conversation to yourself, and make any useful information pay big dividends.

'Perhaps you'll give an old man the pleasure of taking you out to lunch? Say tomorrow, or maybe the day after?'

Shaking her head, she said jerkily, 'I really don't think I'll be free...'

'That's a pity. I'd like to show you around the new leisure complex I've just had built. There are some wonderful shops in the arcade selling jewellery and clothes—'

'May I have my partner back?' Suddenly, like a knight in shining armour, Paul was there.

Just for an instant Reiersen looked ugly, then the geniality back, he said, 'Though I find it hard to part with her, how can I refuse?'

Releasing Joanne's hand, he added, 'If you should find you're free for lunch after all, just let me know.'

'Thank you, but I'm sure I won't be.'

Paul took her in his arms, and as they moved away she found her legs were distinctly wobbly.

When they were out of earshot he murmured, 'You were starting to look desperate, so I thought I'd better rescue you.'

'I can't tell you how grateful I am,' she said shakily.

'What did the old devil do? Make a pass?' As she shook her head he added, 'I thought he might have done when lunch was mentioned.'

'No. He'd heard a whisper that the DSL was having more trouble—'

'Now, where on earth did he hear that?' Paul sounded startled.

'He didn't say, but he did ask what Brad was doing about it. I told him I didn't know. Obviously believing I'm the kind of woman who can be bought, he hinted that if I gave him the information he wanted he'd make it worth my while...

'I don't understand why he approached me in this way, why he didn't just ask Brad,' she added helplessly.

'Perhaps he knows Brad wouldn't tell him.' Then thoughtfully, 'I presume he asked you to keep quiet?'

'His exact words were, ''I'm sure you're sensible enough

to keep this conversation to yourself, and make any useful information pay big dividends.'''

Paul nodded. 'I'm starting to realise that's the way Reiersen works. Though I imagine he's usually a lot more careful, and a better judge of character. It must be the drink that made him believe you could be bought.'

'I think it's more likely to be the dress,' she said evenly.

Diplomatically, Paul made no comment, and for a while they danced in silence, moving mechanically, each busy with their thoughts.

When the music came to an end and the doors into the adjoining room were opened Paul suggested, 'Shall we go and get some supper?'

Still feeling rattled, and with so much on her mind, Joanne wasn't very hungry, but she followed him through to where a long buffet table had been set up.

When they had helped themselves to a selection of delicious-looking food and a glass of wine they sat down at one of the small round tables that dotted the room.

There was no sign of either Erika or Brad, and to Joanne's great relief Reiersen too had vanished. Suddenly weary, she wished the evening were over.

But when it was she would be returning to Lofoten alone. She wondered bleakly why Brad had pressured her into coming in the first place if he was going to spend the *whole* evening with Erika. It made no sense...

'At least Reiersen puts on a good spread,' Paul remarked, breaking into her thoughts. 'That caviare is first class, some of the best I've ever tasted. Care to try some?'

She shook her head. 'I don't think so, thank you.'

'You don't seem to be eating much. Sure you're feeling all right?'

'Quite sure, thank you.'

Smothering a sigh, she picked up her fork and began to eat, tasting little, the expensive delicacies wasted on her as her whole mind focused on Brad.

In some ways he was a complete enigma. If Erika was already in Bergen, why had he needed a mistress as well as a secretary?

But maybe he hadn't...

What if, because of his reputation, she had made a mistake? Jumped to the wrong conclusions? Perhaps he had never *intended* her to sleep with him?

But in that case, why had he let...no, *encouraged* her to believe he did?

All at once it was painfully obvious.

Thinking about her behaviour, the names she had called him, the way she had smacked his face, she realised that forcing her to come with him, *making her think the worst,* had simply been his way of getting even.

Now she was looking at it from a slightly different perspective, she could see clearly that he had never *meant* to sleep with her. If he had he would have come through to the bedroom rather than making up the couch.

He hadn't needed her. *She* had needed him.

She recalled all too clearly how she had gone looking for him, how he'd said, 'As you've come to me, I guess we can do something about it...'

Then later, when he'd taken her back to bed, he hadn't slept beside her. He'd gone back to his solitary couch.

Which said everything.

Feeling a burning sense of shame, she realised that she had made a complete fool of herself. He had probably felt sorry for her, been amused by her lack of experience, laughed at her gullibility...

Don't get mad, get even.

Well, he had made her pay for her stupidity. Got even. That being the case, she could no longer believe he would carry out his threat to ruin Steve, so tomorrow she would get the first flight possible back to London...

'Do you want anything else?' Paul asked. 'A sweet, or some coffee?'

Feeling slightly sick, she shook her head. 'No, thanks.'

'Then shall we return to the fray?'

As she rose he urged, 'Cheer up; you look as if you're about to climb the steps to the guillotine.'

Though she couldn't admit it, she was experiencing something of the same despair.

'Paul,' she asked impulsively, 'how long were you planning to stay tonight?'

'Not too long. Why? Oh, don't worry, if Brad hasn't put in an appearance I'll stay as long as you need me.'

'Thank you, you're an angel…but I was going to ask, when you *do* go, could I beg a lift with you?'

'Of course. Though surely Brad will—'

'Mr Reiersen told me Brad will be going home with…' She broke off suddenly, realizing she might be about to hurt him.

'With Erika?' Paul hazarded. 'Well, if you take my advice, you won't believe all Reiersen tells you. I've discovered that he's adept at manipulating people.'

When they returned to the glittering ballroom the band leader was just making an announcement in Norwegian.

'This is a traditional lovers' waltz,' Paul translated as couples began to crowd onto the floor.

A lovers' waltz… In her mind's eye, she could see Erika and Brad dancing together, closely entwined…

It shouldn't matter, she thought fiercely.

But it did.

Seeing her face, Paul urged, 'Come on, don't look so tense. It's nowhere near as complicated as it may first appear, and you can keep the same partner.'

Her stomach tied in knots, she had started to shake her head, when Brad appeared from nowhere and said firmly, 'Our dance, I think.'

He had just taken her hand, when Erika came storming up and spoke to him in Norwegian.

He replied evenly, in English, 'The last time I saw you you were dancing with Knut.'

'I don't want to dance this one with Knut,' she said urgently. 'I was saving it specially for you.'

'Sorry, but I've just asked Miss Winslow to be my partner.'

'If you *must* dance with her, surely you can leave it until later?'

'I'm afraid not.'

'Please, Brad...' Seeing her appeal was having no effect, she said furiously, 'How could you? You know perfectly well that this is a lovers' waltz.'

She had raised her voice, and heads were starting to turn.

'Then we mustn't waste it.' An arm around her waist, Paul swept Erika onto the floor.

When she began to protest he stopped in his tracks, turned her towards him and, holding her upper arms, said something quietly.

After a moment he released her and, stepping back, held out his hand, unsmiling.

Looking shaken, and oddly vulnerable, she took it, and together they joined the throng of dancers.

'She may well have met her match there,' Brad remarked. Then, putting an arm around Joanne's waist, 'Let's dance.'

Why had he insisted on dancing with *her* rather than his girlfriend? Joanne wondered as he led her onto the floor. Perhaps he was using these tactics to bring the blonde to heel? Emphasising who was master?

If he was she shouldn't be allowing him to use her, shouldn't be playing his rotten game. But she loved him so much that she had been unable to forgo this last chance of being held in his arms...

She loved him so much...

Deciding that what she felt for Brad was a purely physical thing, she had called it lust rather than love. But all the time her subconscious had known the truth. It was love.

And love brought such pain. If Erika truly loved him she could find it in her heart to be sorry for the girl...

The orchestra started to play and, smiling down at her, Brad took her in his arms, making her whole body come alive with longing.

Suddenly terrified that he would realise how she was feeling, she looked anywhere but at him as they began to waltz.

'Relax,' he said in her ear. 'You were moving much more easily when you were dancing with Paul.'

Dancing with Paul hadn't affected her, so she had been *able* to relax.

Brad's arm tightened a little, drawing her closer, and he bent his dark head to put his cheek against hers. He moved with a lithe masculine grace that made him easy to follow and a pleasure to dance with.

She reminded herself that this would be the only time she would ever get to dance with him. If she wasted this chance she would regret it forever.

Giving herself up to the sheer pleasure of being in his arms, feeling the slight roughness of his cheek against hers, she let the tenseness drain out of her and her body melt against his.

They had circled the dance floor a couple of times, when he said in her ear, 'Unless you want to change partners, which is allowed at this point, keep hold of my hand.'

With an awful feeling that Erika might still claim him, she held tightly to his hand as the dancers parted to form parallel lines.

Amid much laughter and good-natured banter, some partner-swapping took place, but Joanne was reassured by a glimpse of Erika and Paul further down the line, and still hand in hand.

The lines of dancers, still holding hands and moving in unison, circled the ballroom before forming into sets.

At the end of each figure, the couples raised linked right hands above their heads and, smiling, faced each other through the arch.

When the last movement was completed Brad's left arm drew her closer and, smiling into her eyes, he bent to kiss her.

She should have been prepared, but she wasn't. The flood of feeling that swept over her left her clinging to him as a drowning person might cling to a rock.

His lips still lingered when most of the other couples were drawing apart, and when he finally lifted his head she was dazed and confused.

Out of the sea of faces, she became aware that Erika's burning gaze was fixed on them, and her father was standing close by, apparently waiting to talk to Brad.

Pulling herself free, she fled.

There was no sign of Paul and, feeling an urgent need to escape, she made her way through the nearest French windows and onto the terrace, which seemed to be deserted.

The air, though appreciably cooler than it had been, was still far from cold. Finding a corner furthest away from the lights, she sank down on a wrought-iron bench and looked blindly out over the moonlit garden.

So much had happened over the past three days, making her feel so many things she had never imagined herself feeling. Turning her world upside-down. Altering her life.

Tomorrow she would go back to her everyday existence and do her best to pick up the threads. But she already knew that nothing would ever be the same again.

Still, at least she had *lived*. She knew what it was like to love a man, to feel passion and rapture and jealousy— oh, yes, she was as bitterly jealous of Erika as the blonde was of her—to be truly *alive*.

No one could ever take that away from her. And though

her love was misplaced and foolish, and had brought almost as much pain as pleasure, it was still the most wonderful thing that had ever happened to her. A gift to be cherished.

If she sometimes found herself longing for what might have been, she wouldn't harbour regrets. She was one of the lucky ones. Some people grew old without ever knowing real love. As she would have done if she hadn't met Brad...

A movement caught her eye, and she turned her head to see the tall figure of a man strolling across the terrace towards her.

Though his back was to the light, his face in shadow, she would have known him from a million other men. Known that easy carriage and the tilt of his dark head...

'So this is where you're hiding,' Brad said.

Somehow she found her voice, and denied, 'I'm not hiding. I just needed a breath of fresh air.'

'Would you like to dance any more?'

'No... No, thank you.' Then hopefully, 'Is Paul ready to leave?'

'What has Paul got to do with it?'

'Well, I...I asked him if he'd give me a lift back.'

'I thought you two were getting on well,' Brad remarked coldly. 'But when I take a woman out I make a point of seeing her home.'

'Oh, but I—'

'I'm afraid you've missed your chance to change partners, which means you're stuck with me. So if you're ready to go?'

As she rose to her feet he added, 'We have a very early start tomorrow.'

She took a deep breath, and blurted out, 'I intend to go home tomorrow.'

'Do you, now?' he said grimly. 'What about your brother? Or have you decided you don't care what happens to his company?'

'Of course I care what happens to it.'

'Then I shall expect you to stick to our bargain.'

'If your intention is just to use me to bring your girlfriend to heel—'

'What makes you think that?' he broke in.

'Well, isn't that why you insisted on dancing with me? Why you kissed me the way you did? Because Erika was watching?'

'Is Erika watching now?'

'No...'

Pulling her into his arms, he kissed her with a punitive thoroughness that left her breathless.

Then, letting her go so suddenly that she staggered, he informed her curtly, 'That's just to prove I find you quite kissable enough not to need the kind of underhand motive you've credited me with...

'Now, if you're quite ready? Our taxi should be here. I've already thanked our host and hostess, and said our goodnights to them and to Paul...'

Joanne could only be thankful for that.

His hand beneath her elbow, he escorted her back through the press of people in the ballroom, and across the hall.

A word to a hovering attendant produced her wrap, and a moment later Brad was helping her into the waiting taxi.

The journey back to Lofoten was a silent one. Brad, his face set, stared straight ahead, while Joanne struggled to get her chaotic thoughts into some kind of order.

Without success.

The only thing that seemed to matter was that she wasn't going home tomorrow after all. The only thing she could feel was joy. She would see him, hear his voice, be with him for a little longer.

But on what terms?

He had insisted, 'I shall expect you to stick to our bargain...'

That *bargain* was still fresh in her mind.

When she had said, 'I won't be your mistress,' he had answered, 'If you really want to save your brother, you'll be anything I want you to be.'

So where did that leave her?

She hadn't the faintest idea.

But one thing she was certain about, knowing he hadn't *intended* to make her his mistress, she wouldn't go to him...

Her thoughts were interrupted by the taxi drawing up outside Lofoten. When Brad had helped her out and paid the driver, without touching her he escorted her across the smoothly pebbled frontage.

She could sense his pent-up anger simmering just beneath the surface, and this time she went in without a glance at the dragons.

As they crossed the lobby he paused to ask a young, fresh-faced man at the night-desk to have a pot of coffee and a plate of sandwiches sent up to their suite.

'Straight away, Mr Lancing,' the youth answered smartly.

He was as good as his word.

By the time Brad had taken Joanne's wrap, removed his own jacket and tie, and rolled up his sleeves to riddle the stove and pile on more logs, a knock announced the arrival of their supper.

Brad took the tray with a word of thanks, and set it down on the long table. Then, indicating the couch, he asked ironically, 'Won't you join me?'

Joanne, who had been hovering uncertainly, went to sit down, taking care to keep her distance. The skirt of her dress parted, exposing a silk-clad knee and shapely thigh.

She hastily rearranged it.

Smiling wolfishly, he queried, 'Coffee?'

'Please.'

He poured two cups, and put one in front of her before offering her a sandwich.

'No, thank you,' she refused politely.

'Have you had anything to eat tonight?'

'Yes. Paul and I went through to the buffet.' Hoping to get back on an amicable footing, she went on, 'He remarked that the caviare was some of the best he'd ever tasted. What did you think?'

'I didn't get to eat,' Brad replied brusquely. 'And before you jump to conclusions, I wasn't with Erika all the time. I was talking to Reiersen.'

It had been an emotionally fraught evening; upset by his coldness, and feeling the sudden prick of tears behind her eyes, she said huskily, 'Brad...I'm sorry if you're angry with me...'

He sighed. 'Forgive me if I've seemed short with you, but I don't take kindly to being brushed aside for another man, not even Paul.'

'B-but I thought you were going home with Erika,' she stammered.

'What on earth gave you that idea?'

'Mr Reiersen told me she wanted you to.'

Frowning a little, he suggested, 'Perhaps you'd better tell me exactly what Reiersen said to you.'

'He said, "Erika's fairly broad-minded about Brad paying for a little fun on the side."'

As she paused to try and steady her voice Brad said, 'Presumably the "paying for a little fun on the side" is a reference to the dress. But do go on.'

Her voice under control once more, she continued, 'Then he added, "But she's keen that he should stay with her, as he has done in the past. So you won't mind if he doesn't go back with you tonight?"'

'I see,' Brad said slowly. 'Of course, I've always known that Reiersen's not above lying and trying to manipulate people, to achieve his own ends...'

Paul had said much the same.

'Or Erika's, for that matter. He'd do anything to get his daughter what she wants.'

'And she wants you,' Joanne said flatly.

'I won't deny that she gave me a very pressing invitation to go home with her and stay. An invitation I declined. Which didn't please her.

'That's probably why Reiersen found it necessary to try and make trouble.'

When Joanne just looked at him he assured her. 'I have *never* stayed with Erika. The only time we've ever slept under the same roof was at Reiersen's house one night last winter.

'She was living at home after the break-up of her marriage, and I'd been invited to talk business over dinner. A blizzard blew up, and Reiersen offered me a bed for the night. So I slept there. Alone.'

Joanne felt such a rush of gladness and gratitude that, afraid he'd see, she looked away.

'I presume you think I'm lying?'

Turning to face him, she said, 'No. I don't think you're lying. Though there's no need to explain yourself to me.'

'Does that mean you don't care whether I've slept with Erika or not?'

'It means I don't consider it's any of my business.'

'In the normal state of things, what happened before I met you wouldn't be. But this is a little different, so I prefer to set matters straight.'

Sardonically, he added, 'I'm getting more than a little tired of being misjudged.'

'I'm sorry, truly I am, but with your…' Too late she stopped herself.

'*Reputation?*' he suggested.

Flushing, she said, 'Well, you have to admit it isn't a good one.'

Looking quietly furious, he said, 'I don't have to admit

anything of the kind. The only people who think badly of me in that respect seem to be you and your brother. Though I haven't lived like a monk, I'm certainly no Casanova.'

Angry in her turn, she demanded, 'Then how do you explain trying to seduce an eighteen-year-old married woman?'

A white line appearing round his mouth, he said, 'No matter what lies your sister may have told you, in the past I've always left married women and other men's fiancées strictly alone. And I can honestly say that, so far as I know, no woman has been worse off for knowing me.'

'I suppose you mean *financially*?' Looking down at the dress, she said caustically, 'I certainly can't deny you're generous.'

He made a sudden movement, and, realising she'd gone too far, she flinched away.

'You're quite safe,' he informed her icily. 'It isn't my style to strike a woman. All the same, it might be as well if you went to bed.'

Wanting to weep, because she hadn't meant it to be like this, she got to her feet and went blindly out of the room.

Closing the bedroom door behind her, she hovered helplessly, feeling sick and shaken. When her intention had simply been to apologise, how could such an ugly quarrel have flared?

But somehow it had. And it was very largely her fault. She hadn't meant to bring up his reputation, nor taunt him with the dress.

If only she had been more careful, guarded her tongue instead of saying the things she had, it could have been so different.

After all, he had chosen to come back to Lofoten with her, rather than go with Erika, and he had taken the trouble to deny the lie Reiersen had told her.

Would he listen if she went back and told him she was sorry?

No, after last night she couldn't bring herself to go back in there. He was bound to think the worst. In any case, it was too late. Too much damage had been done.

A cold space around her heart, she knew she had spoilt whatever chance there might have been of putting things right between them.

And no matter what he was, what kind of reputation he had, she loved him. Completely. Hopelessly.

In the past she had sometimes wondered how sensible women could choose to love, and keep on loving, totally unsuitable men.

Now she knew. It wasn't something one *chose* to do, it just happened, and there was no help for it.

All the unaccustomed emotion, the passion, the jealousy, the despair that she had been feeling suddenly became too much. Overwrought, she sank down on the bed and, burying her face in the pillow, began to sob uncontrollably.

CHAPTER NINE

HER misery was so great that she failed to hear either the tap, or the door being opened, just Brad's voice saying gently, 'Come on, now, there's no need to cry like that.'

Gulping, she sat up and, tears running down her face in tracks of shiny wetness, mumbled, 'I'm not crying.'

'As that statement is patently a lie, I shall ignore it.' He was wearing a short, dark silk robe and his hair was still a little damp from the shower.

'But why weep all over the pillow when I've got a perfectly good shoulder?'

He held out his arms, and like someone going home she went into them.

Now, rather than despair, she shed tears of relief, while his hand moved up and down her spine in a soothing gesture almost as old as time.

After a while, when her sobs had lessened, he queried, 'About done?'

Sniffing, she lifted her head and reluctantly moved out of his arms. He produced a folded handkerchief and handed it to her.

'Thank you.' She sat on the nearest chair and, scrubbing at her face, went on unsteadily, 'I'm sorry... I didn't mean to quarrel with you. I shouldn't have said what I did. I would have come back and told you so, but I thought you might think...'

A gleam of amusement in his eyes, he queried, 'And if I had thought what you imagined I might think, what would you have done?'

'Felt ashamed...after last night,' she added awkwardly.

'It's perfectly natural to want a man...'

150

She didn't just *want* him, she *needed* him, as she needed air to breathe.

'So why feel ashamed?'

'I thought you might not have wanted me.'

'How can you doubt it?'

'You didn't *plan* to make love to me.'

When he made no effort to deny it, she sighed. 'You didn't need to, when Erika was already here and more than willing.'

'It had nothing to do with Erika.'

'But you didn't want to make love to me. If you had, you wouldn't have made up the couch.'

'You're wrong about my not wanting to make love to you. I wanted to very much. But no matter what you may believe about me, I've never taken a woman who was remotely unwilling...'

'I thought you *might* want me, but I couldn't be sure. So I decided to let you make the first move.'

'And if I hadn't?'

'You would still be a virgin.'

Feeling the hot colour rise in her cheeks, she bit her lip. Since meeting Brad her usual cool control had totally deserted her.

Instead of behaving like the modern woman she was, she had acted as though she were in some Victorian melodrama, she thought crossly. She had fluttered and palpitated, blushed and cried. The only thing left to do was to swoon or get the vapours.

And she had no intention of doing either.

'Well, I can't say I'm sorry not to be a twenty-five-year-old virgin,' she said crisply. 'There's something almost laughable about the idea.'

'I don't think so,' he disagreed soberly. 'Even in today's world, virginity is a precious gift, often parted with much too lightly. Or simply thrown away...'

'And you're not twenty-five until tomorrow.'

'How do you know it's tomorrow?'

'I heard your birthday mentioned, and I asked your brother when it was. He told me with the greatest reluctance. He seemed to think I would use the occasion to ply you with diamonds and have my wicked way with you...'

While he was speaking the clock in the living-room chimed twelve.

Greatly daring, she asked, 'And are you going to?'

He shook his head regretfully. 'I'm afraid I forgot to buy any diamonds, and I've already had my wicked way with you.

'However, once I've unfastened your dress, which is what I came in to do, I might want to have it all over again.'

'Only *might*?'

'Intend?'

'That's better.' Then, catching sight of her ravaged face in the mirror, 'Or perhaps you don't want me all swollen-eyed and blotchy?'

He stooped to kiss her pink and puffy eyelids. 'I want you any way I can get you.'

Suddenly needing to know, she asked, 'Brad...last night...why did you go back to sleep on the couch?'

Standing looking down at her, he answered, 'It occurred to me that in the cold light of day you might change your mind and wish the whole thing had never happened.

'If that had been the case it could have come as a nasty shock waking up to find a man you regard as a lecher lying beside you.'

She winced. But then, she had asked for it. Taking a deep breath, she pleaded, 'You will stay with me tonight?'

'If you want me to. But if you think you might have regrets in the morning, you'd better tell me now.'

She could feel her pulse beating in her throat and wrists as she answered, 'I won't have any regrets.'

*   *   *

When they were both naked in bed he rolled over and held himself above her, looking down into her face. 'You're sure about this?' he asked.

'Quite sure,' she assured him huskily. And, on fire for him, begged, 'Please don't make me wait.'

He didn't. His lovemaking intense, focused, direct, he carried her to the heights until, like a sky-rocket, the spiralling ecstasy he was engendering exploded in a shower of golden stars.

Lying beneath him, she enjoyed the weight of his dark head on her breast, the feel of his body against hers, until their heart-rate and breathing had returned to something approaching normal.

She was waiting for him to lift himself away and draw her close, when, raising his head, he said, 'That was specially to please you.'

'It did.'

'Well, now I'm going to please you a whole lot more.'

Completely sated, she said contentedly, 'That's not possible. At least at the moment.'

'We'll see, shall we?' Rolling over and taking her with him, so that his body was supporting hers, he put his hands either side of her ribcage and, his arms propped on his elbows, lifted her.

She gasped as his tongue laved a nipple before he drew it into his mouth and, tugging a little, began to suck, sending the most exquisite sensations darting through her.

Immediately, the hunger she had thought was more than satisfied sprang to life, demanding to be appeased.

Lowering her, he turned again, so that she was lying on her back and he was stretched out beside her. Then, nuzzling his face against her breasts, he slid his hand between the warm, velvet skin of her inner thighs.

Her breath was coming in shallow gasps when he paused in his administrations to ask, 'Still think it's not possible?'

'No.'

His voice full of satisfaction, he queried, 'Then I take it you'd like me to go on?'

He was so sure of himself, so *complacent* that she wanted to shake him by saying no, but somehow she found herself saying weakly, 'Yes, please.'

This time his lovemaking was lazily assured, wonderfully inventive, and teasing to the point of near-madness. He knew exactly where to touch to drive her wild, to have her shuddering and begging...

When at length she could stand no more he sent her tumbling and spinning into the abyss, before settling her head on his shoulder, and saying, 'Sleep now. We need to set off quite early in the morning.'

Joanne awoke to find they had been sleeping on their sides, knees bent and lying spoon-fashion. Her back was against Brad's chest, her buttocks resting on his thighs. The weight of his arm lay across her ribs, and his chin pressed lightly on the top of her head.

She could feel the strong beat of his heart, and the rise and fall of his chest as he breathed. Filled with an utter and complete contentment, she gave silent thanks to whatever gods look after the happiness of mere mortals.

'Good morning,' he said.

'How did you know I was awake?'

'Your breathing altered.'

Daylight was just starting to filter through the greeny-blue curtains, and the room had the dimly lit quiet of an underwater cave. 'What time is it?' she asked idly.

'Time I was making a move. The car I hired will be arriving soon, and we still have to eat breakfast.'

Watching him climb out of bed, and admiring the lean elegance of his body as he pulled on his robe, she stirred herself. 'Then I'd better—'

Drawing back the curtains, he said, 'Stay where you are. It's breakfast in bed for the birthday girl.'

'It sounds very decadent. I don't ever recall having breakfast in bed before.'

'Well, you know what they say about trying everything once?'

Settling back against the pillows, she asked curiously, 'Why do we need to get off so early?'

'As a special present I'm taking you to see the Briksdal, and it's a fair distance away.'

'The Briksdal? What's that?'

'If you don't know then we'll keep it as a surprise.'

'What sort of clothes should I wear?'

'Something casual. A shirt and jeans would do fine. Oh, and sensible shoes… We'll be staying overnight, so you'll need to pack a bag… Ah, this sounds like breakfast.'

When he returned wheeling a trolley covered with a white cloth, she was sitting, black hair tumbling around her shoulders, the duvet pulled up high enough to hide her breasts and tucked modestly beneath her arms.

Having brought the trolley to the bedside, Brad spread his palms for her inspection, and intoned, 'Nothing in my hands, nothing up my sleeves…' Then, with a grin, he whipped off the cloth and, like a magician producing a rabbit from a hat, produced a posy of fresh flowers and handed them to her.

'Happy birthday.'

Flushing with pleasure, she buried her nose in their scented freshness. 'Thank you, they're lovely.' Impulsively, she added, 'Much better than diamonds.'

'A lot of women would find that debatable,' he countered drily.

Sitting on the edge of the bed, he handed her what was clearly a birthday card, though in Norwegian.

He had written a few words on it, but, as they too were in Norwegian, the only thing she could decipher was his name.

The picture was of a male elk with a soppy grin on its

face, handing a bunch of flowers to a female elk with inch-long eyelashes.

It was so ridiculous that she started to laugh. When she stopped laughing she asked, 'What does it say?'

'I'm not sure if the wording's appropriate. Perhaps I'll tell you when I've known you longer.'

His words reminded her that, though she was closer to him than she had ever been to any man, it was only four days since they'd met.

It was a strange and sobering thought.

'Now last, but not least...' He handed her a package no bigger than her thumb.

She tore off the paper and once more began to laugh helplessly.

The small wooden figure, which was dressed in a jerkin and boots, was grotesquely ugly, with long wisps of griz-zled hair, a wart, and a huge hooked nose and pointed chin which almost met.

'What on earth is it?' she managed.

Straight-faced, he told her, 'A lucky troll. His name's Olaf. As you're a woman of discerning taste, I'm sure you'll get to love him.'

'I do already. I'll take him with me everywhere.' Then impulsively, 'Thank you; I don't know when I've had so much fun on a birthday.'

'The day's hardly started, so hopefully there's lots more to come.

'Now for some breakfast...'

He helped her to a bowl of something resembling muesli mixed with delicious wild berries, then a kind of toasted croissant filled with a mixture of smoked ham and creamy cheese.

Wiping her buttery fingers on a napkin, she murmured, 'Mmm...delicious,' and reached to replace the empty plate.

The movement exposed one shapely pink-tipped breast.

Feeling ridiculously shy, she used her left hand to re-anchor the duvet.

He sighed and, cocking an eyebrow at her, asked hopefully, 'You don't think you're in any danger of putting on weight?'

Remembering their conversation over brunch at the airport, she said, 'No. As I told you, I have the kind of metabolism that burns off fat... In any case,' she added firmly, 'I'm getting plenty of...exercise.'

'You can never have too much of a good thing.'

'I could...after a meal like that.'

Leaning forward, he whispered a suggestion in her ear that made her blush rosily.

'I thought you said we needed to be off early.'

He dropped a light kiss on her lips and remarked mockingly, 'You're starting to sound just like a wife.'

Though she knew perfectly well that this was a brief affair, nothing more, nothing less, she felt such a tug at her heartstrings that her eyes filled with tears.

Luckily he had turned away without noticing.

Less than an hour later, casually dressed in well-cut trousers, a fine polo-necked sweater and a light jacket, Brad helped a similarly-dressed Joanne into the four-wheel-drive he had hired.

As soon as he had stowed their overnight bags, he tossed a picnic hamper in beside them and slid behind the wheel. Within minutes they were heading north-east out of Bergen and into central fjord country.

The day was golden and glorious. Fluffy cotton-wool clouds hung motionless in a sky of cornflower-blue, while early-morning sunshine warmed the grey rocks and brought the reds and golds of autumn to glowing life.

'Isn't it gorgeous weather?' she remarked.

He gave her a smiling sideways glance, and, his green eyes dancing, told her, 'I ordered it specially for you.'

They were soon travelling through scenery that was truly magnificent, with towering snow-capped mountains, deep-blue fjords, picturesque woodland and waterfalls that ranged from delicate plumes, fine as spun silk, to raging cataracts.

Joanne sat silent and awestruck, poignantly aware that she had never been so happy in her life.

Though in places the road surface was dusty and full of potholes, the sturdy jeep made light work of the rough and mountainous terrain, and they were approaching their destination by lunch time.

'Won't be long now,' Brad told her as, leaving the road, they began to follow a narrow track through wooded country.

When they reached a wide clearing he stopped the car and said, 'This is where we use other means of transport.'

The 'other means of transport' was a string of ponies and traps drawn up beneath the shade of the overhanging trees. All the traps were black and Victorian-looking, their green hoods folded neatly back. The ponies were light tan-coloured, with creamy tails and manes.

He lifted a hand, and the driver at the head of the queue detached his vehicle from the rest and came ambling over.

Brad helped Joanne into the high, open carriage, and, having tossed up the picnic basket, joined her on the wooden seat.

The driver mounted with the agility of a monkey, and turned to give them a gap-toothed grin. A wizened-walnut of a man, with wispy grey hair and a big, hooked nose, he was so like Olaf that, catching Brad's eye and seeing the unholy gleam there, Joanne was hard put to it not to laugh.

Her bottom lip caught in her teeth, she looked resolutely away as the driver chirruped to the pony, and they started at a leisurely trot up a fairly steep path.

They had gone about a mile when they came to a tremendous gorge, where a spectacular waterfall plunged down the rocks and disappeared into the depths.

Spanning the chasm was a frail wooden bridge which seemed to shake beneath the thunderous onslaught of the water. Spray was flung high into the air, drenching everything in a rainbow cloud.

Turning, the driver pulled the hood over their heads, before urging the pony into a gallop.

They were shaken and thrown about as the trap bumped and rattled over the uneven planking, and when Brad put his arms around her Joanne clung to him tightly, half laughing, half afraid of the abyss beneath their feet.

As though reaching for the sky, the road climbed even higher, and after a word with the driver they left the trap and, with Brad carrying the picnic basket, began to walk.

When they reached the edge of the trees he put the basket down, and, with one hand over Joanne's eyes and the other cupping her elbow, urged her a few steps.

'Now look.'

She gasped in wonder.

An awe-inspiring glacier filled the end of the narrow valley like a massive pile of sparkling candy sugar. Pale blue fissures scarred its rough surface, and as she watched an enormous piece broke away with an ear-splitting crack.

'So this is Briksdal?' she breathed.

'Yes. It's the most accessible arm of the Jostedal glacier.'

'I've never seen a real glacier before.'

'Well, if you want a closer look, there are guides who take tours over the safe parts, but we'll have to leave that until we come again.'

Until we come again... The words wrapped themselves warmly around her heart.

Below the giant ice fall, water flowed from a tunnel it had cut for itself through the slow-moving mass. Despite the heat of the day, large chunks of ice floated in the clear aquamarine water of the lake like miniature bergs.

Completely entranced by the spectacle, Joanne stood motionless until Brad picked up the basket and led the way along the side of the lake.

He chose a grassy bank in the sun, and, having discarded his jacket, opened the basket, put a blanket down to sit on, and spread out the picnic.

Enjoying the pine-scented air, the sunshine and the lovely view, they sipped a glass of white wine and began to eat in companionable silence.

Then, opening a small container of gleaming black caviare, Brad spread some onto a tiny biscuit and popped it into her mouth, enquiring, 'Is this as good as the one Paul praised?'

Wondering why he'd brought that up, she ate the morsel before answering, 'I'm afraid I don't know. I didn't try it.'

His voice even, he went on, 'You saw quite a lot of my right-hand man. What did you think of him?'

Recalling how he had said, 'I don't take kindly to being brushed aside for another man, not even Paul,' she hesitated, before admitting, 'I liked him very much.'

If it hadn't been so ridiculous, she might have suspected Brad was jealous as, his jaw tightening, he said a shade curtly, 'That was the impression I got.'

'I was grateful he took pity on me, otherwise I would have been alone.'

With a sigh, Brad reached for her hand and lifted it to his lips. 'I'm sorry I neglected you. But Reiersen wanted to talk business, and I felt it was important to hear what he had to say.'

To her great relief he let the matter drop, and after a moment became his old relaxed self again.

When they had finished tucking into the food they shared a flask of coffee before repacking the basket. Then, Brad's arm around her shoulders, and their backs against an outcrop of smooth grey rock, they lifted their faces to the warmth of the sun.

Contented and at ease, totally relaxed once more, Joanne closed her eyes, and in a moment or two she slept, a deep, quiet sleep that, after so much emotional turmoil, was curiously healing.

After a while she dreamt Brad was kissing her, softly, sweetly… When he began to draw away, afraid that he was going to leave her, she clutched at his sweater, muttering, 'No, no…'

'Wake up, Sleeping Beauty.'

The teasing words wrenched her back to consciousness and the realisation that she had been sound asleep, cradled in the crook of his arm.

Sitting up straight, she said, 'I'm sorry.'

'There's no need to be sorry.' He was looking at her, an expression on his face that could have been mistaken for tenderness. 'It seemed a shame to disturb you, but the sun's going down and we ought to be getting back.'

'How long have I…?'

'Almost two hours.'

'Two hours!' she exclaimed.

'You must have needed it, so regard it as therapy.'

The air was appreciably cooler now, and she reached for her jacket.

As Brad helped her into it she noticed he moved his right arm awkwardly, and wondered how long he had been enduring the pain of cramp, rather than disturb her.

As soon as he had replaced the blanket and fastened the lid of the wicker basket, they set off back to where the pony and trap were waiting.

'Thank you,' she said simply when he'd helped her into the trap and jumped in beside her. 'It's been a perfect day.'

Slanting her a glance, he reminded her, 'And the night is still to come.'

'Where are we spending the night?'

'At a little town called Lanadal. It's about an hour's drive away. Rather than one of the larger, newer hotels, I thought it would be fun to stay at Trollfoss, a small place that used to be a private house.

'It was built in the Victorian era, and what it lacks in modern amenities it makes up for in character. The beds are large and comfortable, with brass bedsteads and feather mattresses. I think you'll like it.'

'I'm sure I will,' she said contentedly.

The small, picturesque town of Lanadal lay at the foot of a hill and straddled a shallow, fast-flowing river that tumbled over a rocky bed.

By the time they drove through its narrow cobbled streets lined with colourful timber houses, it was dusk and the old-fashioned streetlights were adding an almost Dickensian atmosphere.

Trollfoss stood alone on the outskirts of town and partway up the hill. Built of clapboard and painted green, it was topped with gables and turrets, spires and curlicues.

When they drew up on the lantern-lit forecourt, and Brad helped her out, Joanne laughed with delight. Peering down from a niche above the door was a large child-sized replica of a troll.

'I thought you could introduce Olaf to his namesake,' Brad told her with a grin.

'I did wonder about the name Trollfoss,' she said.

Lifting out their overnight bags, he explained, 'You can't see them from this side of the house, but if you listen the muted roar in the background is the Troll Falls.'

Once inside, she saw that the hotel, as Brad had said, was very Victorian, with rich red carpets, heavily framed pictures, velvet, gold-tassled curtains and a riot of filigree carving.

At the polished desk was an elderly man with a cheerful, ruddy face who, at first, seemed a little confused about their booking.

When Brad had confirmed that they only needed one

room he led them up a curved staircase to one of the surprisingly large turret rooms.

Loving it on sight, Joanne exclaimed, 'I've never stayed in a round room before!' Then curiously, 'Why did he think you'd asked for two rooms?'

'Because I had, originally. You see, I booked it on Saturday, shortly after we arrived at Lofoten. At that point I presumed we would need two.'

Trying not to blush, she said, 'Oh, I see...'

'Would you prefer a separate room?'

Going pink all the same, she shook her head.

'The good news is we have the only guest room in the house that has its own bathroom.'

Seeing he was waiting expectantly, she asked, 'What's the bad news?'

'That it's down a flight of stairs, and it has no shower.'

'I don't see either of those as being too much of a problem. Does it have a bath?'

'Oh, there's certainly a bath. Come and look.'

She following him through a small door, down a wooden staircase and into a bathroom the size of the bedroom.

As she stood admiring the huge bathtub that stood on gilded feet in the centre of the room, he gave her a glinting look from beneath thick, dark lashes. 'I don't know what you think, but in my opinion a bath might prove to be even more fun than a shower.'

'I'm sure you're right,' she agreed demurely.

He threw back his head and laughed joyously. 'A woman after my own heart! I'm convinced that if you've never made love in a Victorian bathtub, you haven't lived.

'Now, let's see, champagne hardly seems in keeping. What about a glass of mulled wine? Then later we'll go into town and I'll take you to a rather special restaurant for a birthday dinner.'

'It all sounds marvellous!'

'I hope it will be.'

* * *

Given the option of walking the half-mile or so down to town or being driven, the night being fine and clear, Joanne chose to walk.

'Don't forget it will be uphill on the way back,' Brad teased.

'Well, if I find I can't manage it, I'm sure you'll carry me,' she said insouciantly.

'Won't you be sorry if I use up all my strength?'

'I'm rather surprised you haven't already.'

He raised an eyebrow at her, leaving her covered in a glow of confusion.

The restaurant he had chosen was in the centre of the town, but on the far side of the river. Moonlight glinted on the fast-flowing water as it tumbled over smooth grey boulders, and the lamps on the embankment cast golden pools of light.

As they crossed the old cobbled bridge Brad pointed, and said, 'There it is, To Kokker. The name simply means two cooks. It's owned by twin brothers.'

To Joanne's surprise, the restaurant appeared to be nothing more than a large hut.

The inside did little to dispel that impression. Heated by an old black stove at either end, and lit by brass-bound oil lamps, it couldn't have been less pretentious.

Its dozen or so tables, most of which were full, were of scrubbed wood, the floor was sanded, and the crockery was thick and plain. But the welcome they received was a warm one, and the food, when it came, was out of this world.

They had pickled artichoke hearts followed by lobster in *beurre blanc* sauce, then *krumkake*, a wafer-thin shell of pastry filled with delicious blackberry cream.

Along with the excellent coffee, they were given a bottle of home-made dessert wine, which they shared with the brothers and the one remaining couple in the restaurant.

It developed into something of a party, and it was quite

late before they finally said their goodnights and left.

As hand in hand, like young lovers, they strolled across the bridge and headed out of town, he asked, 'Are you OK to walk? Or would you like me to carry you?'

'While it's a tempting offer, I think if you have any strength left I'd prefer you to keep it.'

'Practical as well as beautiful,' he said appreciatively.

At this time of night, apart from the odd car, there was very little traffic about, and even fewer pedestrians.

They had gone only fifty yards or so when the engine of a parked car roared into life. Dazzling headlights blinded them as the vehicle swerved onto the pavement and headed straight for them.

As Joanne stood momentarily paralysed Brad swept her off her feet, his impetus sending the pair of them sprawling into the safety of a narrow alleyway between two buildings. A split-second later the car careered harmlessly past, and went racing up the street.

Scrambling to his feet, Brad helped her up, asking urgently, 'Are you hurt in any way?'

'No, not a bit.' His arms had been around her, her body protected by his.

'Sure?'

'Quite sure. Are *you* all right?'

'Fine.'

'My lucky troll must be doing his stuff.'

She saw the glint of his smile in the gloom, before, setting her back against the wall, he said, 'Stay just where you are for a minute.'

'Why? Where are you going?'

'I just want to make sure they've gone.'

So he thought it had been deliberate. He thought who-ever was responsible might possibly be back for a second try.

'I'm coming with you.'

'It might be safer if you waited here.'

She shook her head.

'Please, Joanne.'

'I've no intention of skulking in an alley while you go alone,' she said firmly.

'You're one stubborn woman,' he said. But he squeezed her hand.

As they emerged from the alleyway a car drew up with a rush and stopped by the kerb. Her heart in her mouth, Joanne recognised the people inside as the couple who had shared the wine in the restaurant.

The man jumped out and spoke to them in Norwegian. He seemed to be advocating a course of action Brad was reluctant to agree to.

After some further conversation, when Brad mentioned Trollfoss the man nodded and, apparently glad to be of help, opened the car's rear passenger door and ushered them inside.

When they were seated the woman turned her head and seemed to be asking anxiously if they were all right. By the time Brad had reassured her, they were drawing up outside the hotel.

He said, *'Tusen takk,'* while Joanne added her thanks in English. They clambered out and, repeating their thanks, stood for a moment to wave the pair off, before going inside.

Apart from a quick word with the desk clerk in the dimly lit lobby, Brad was silent until they reached their room.

It wasn't until he'd helped her off with her jacket and turned to hang it up that she got a proper look at him.

In the light from the red-shaded wall-lamps she saw his own jacket was torn and dirty, his left cheek was badly bruised and scraped, and trickles of blood had oozed down his face.

If he hadn't had his wits about him they might have both been killed or badly injured.

Reaction suddenly setting in, she turned icy cold, and, sinking down on one of the over-stuffed chairs, began to shake like a leaf.

Seeing her tremble, and taking in her pallor, he asked quickly, 'Are you certain you're all right?'

'Quite certain.' Through chattering teeth she added, 'But you've hurt your face.'

'It's just a graze,' he said dismissively.

'All the same it ought to be cleaned up. Do you think the hotel will have a first-aid box?'

'I'm sure they will. But I always carry an emergency kit.'

Having taken off his jacket and tossed it aside, he reached into his overnight bag and produced a small box. 'There should be everything necessary in there.'

Glad to have something positive to do, she got to her feet and, opening the lid, looked through the contents. 'These are just what we need.' Tearing open a pack of antiseptic wet-wipes, she instructed, 'Sit down there.'

He sat down like a lamb, his face the picture of innocence.

When she got near enough he threw his right arm around her waist and pulled her onto his knee. Then kissing the side of her neck, he remarked, 'I've always thought a nurse should get close to her patient.'

'Not that close,' she said severely.

But when she tried to wriggle free he merely held her tighter. 'Oh, very well,' she gave in, 'but turn your head that way…' A hand on his jaw, she pushed his face away.

When she had finished cleaning the wound she reached for a tube of ointment and put a thin smear over the raw area. 'There, that should do.'

'Thank you, Nurse. But you've forgotten something.'

'What have I forgotten?'

'When I was a very small boy and I hurt myself the nurse always used to kiss me better.'

'You're not a small boy any longer....'

'For which I'm truly thankful. My nurse had a moustache that prickled.'

Joanne was trying not to laugh, when he wheedled, 'Now I've told you my childhood secrets, what about that kiss?'

'All right. But just one.' She leaned forward to touch her lips to his good cheek.

'Call that a kiss?' he said contemptuously. '*This* is a kiss.' Growling and making horrendous slurping noises, he proceeded to demonstrate.

By the time he released her she was laughing helplessly, and the colour was back in her face.

'Feeling better?' he asked gently.

'Much better.'

And it was true. His fooling had lightened the atmosphere and allowed her to get her grip back.

Which was, she realised, why he'd done it.

CHAPTER TEN

'BRAD, I—'

A soft tap sounded through her words.

'This should be the coffee and brandy I ordered,' he said, and, pushing her gently into the chair he'd just vacated, headed for the door.

She heard the quiet murmur of voices, and a moment later he came back carrying a tray, which he set down on the bedside table.

Picking up the squat bottle, he poured a measure of the amber liquid into both glasses and handed her one. 'That should complete the cure.'

She took a cautious sip, coughed, and took another, feeling the brandy's fiery warmth dispel any lingering coldness.

When their glasses were empty he filled two coffee-cups and, sitting down on the edge of the bed, admitted soberly, 'I'm only sorry I ever involved you in all this.'

She shook her head. 'I'm not. Up till now my life has been sadly lacking in adventure.'

He saluted her spirit, before saying, 'Our friends, who left the restaurant shortly after we did and saw the whole thing, wanted to call the police.'

'Why didn't you let them?'

'It would have been a complete waste of time. With things happening so fast they didn't get the number of the car, and weren't sure of the colour, except that it was dark.

'In any case, the police would no doubt have regarded the incident simply as a drunken driver who had momentarily lost control.'

'And you're sure it wasn't?'

'Quite sure.'

'So this is part of the same trouble that brought you to Norway?'

'Very much a part. As I said, it's easier to deal with the opposition on home ground. Though not *too* close to home. It's my guess that it was planned to stage "the accident" well away from Bergen.

'I believe whoever was driving the car got to Lanadal ahead of us, and simply waited for the right opportunity. If we hadn't played into his hands by walking tonight I think he would have found some other way.'

'But who knew we were coming up to Lanadal?'

'Any number of people. You're probably the only one who didn't. I mentioned it to Erika when she asked me to go home with her. Helga, who packed our picnic basket, knew. So did the garage I hired the car from... Paul certainly did, and I've no doubt there were others.'

'I suppose you've still no idea who might be behind it all?'

'Having thought long and hard, I'm fairly sure I know. It's the only option that makes any real sense.'

'In that case, couldn't you go to the police?'

'It wouldn't do any good at this stage. I haven't any evidence as such, and this person is no common criminal. He's a rich and powerful man who most people would regard as being above suspicion.'

Puzzled, she asked, 'Have you any idea *why* he's doing it?'

'I believe there may be two connected reasons... The first is that his fleet of cargo vessels and the Dragon Shipping Line are in direct competition.

'The second, which sounds like the storyline to a soap opera, goes back over fifty years to when he and my grandfather were childhood friends.

'Both their families owned a shipping business, but as well as a lot of mountains Norway has a long coastline and a great deal of sea, so with more than enough space for them both to operate the two families never had a problem.

'Everything was fine until both young men happened to fall in love with, and want to marry, the same girl. They each proposed, and Grandfather won.

'Though later the other man married someone else, he and Grandfather ended up as lifelong rivals, not to say enemies, and he promised that one day, no matter how long it took, he'd find a way to even the score.

'When Grandfather died and I inherited the DSL he made me an offer for it, a very generous one, I might add, but it had been my grandfather's wish to keep the business in the family, so I refused to sell...

'He's made me two further offers since, both of which I've turned down.'

Frowning, Joanne asked, 'If, as you say, there's plenty of space for both shipping lines to operate, why does he want your company so badly?'

'He might well consider that a good way to even the score would be to take over and close down a business that Grandfather had spent a lifetime building up.'

Watching her expressive face, Brad added, 'While they're convincing-enough reasons for suspecting him, they're nowhere near good enough to enable me to make any firm accusations.'

'Yes, I see what you mean,' she said slowly. 'But if you can't find some way to stop him, presumably he'll go on with his campaign?'

'I think the answer to that is yes. Though it'll never get him what he wants.'

'Surely if he knows you he'll realise you won't bow to pressure?'

'Perhaps he doesn't know me that well. In any case I don't think he'll give up too easily. Beneath his outward respectability, he's a ruthless man. I believe he'll just try harder.'

She shivered. 'You don't mean to *kill* you?' Despite his grazed cheek, the whole thing seemed strangely unreal.

'I think he'd prefer *not* to have to go to those lengths. Tonight might just have been meant as a warning. A show of strength.

'On the other hand, if I didn't stand in his way and he only had Blake to deal with, he'd find the going a lot easier.

'As things stand at the moment, my cousin is next in line to inherit the Lancing empire.'

Sounding wearily cynical, he continued, 'Unfortunately, despite having a wife and two children, Blake makes a better playboy than a businessman. Which means he's always in need of money, and I couldn't trust him not to sell the DSL.

'Our competitor has probably checked him out and discovered as much.'

Horrified, she cried, 'But if that's the case, and he's as ruthless as you say…'

'It could well bump up the risk factor,' Brad admitted quietly.

'Even so, you've no intention of letting him have DSL?'

'Not the slightest! Would you?'

'No, I wouldn't.' Her answer was unequivocal. 'But there must be *something* you can do to stop him.'

'My best, maybe my only chance is to get some evidence that points directly to him. Faced with that, I hope and believe he'll back off. As a pillar of the church, and someone looked up to by the local community, he can't afford to lose his good reputation…

'Tomorrow when we get back to Bergen I'll talk to Paul and see if between us we can work out some sort of strategy.'

'Does Paul know his identity?'

Brad shook his head. 'Not yet. I was waiting to see if, off his own bat, he came up with anything that might corroborate my suspicions…

'But it's getting late and we've had more than enough of worries for one night... Would you like to use the bathroom first?'

When Joanne had washed her face and hands and cleaned her teeth she climbed the stairs back to the bedroom, and sank into the luxurious warmth and comfort of an old-fashioned goose-feather bed, while Brad took his turn in the bathroom.

Despite the upset the night had brought, and her anxiety over his safety, she was half-asleep by the time he returned.

As she lay watching him strip off his robe she noticed one arm seemed stiff, and when he turned she caught her breath. His left shoulder and arm, and his hip, were badly bruised.

'You told me you weren't hurt,' she said accusingly.

'I'm not.'

'What about all the bruising?'

Green eyes gleaming, he suggested, 'You could always try my favourite healing method.'

'I doubt if kissing will do much good.'

'Well, at the very least it'll take my mind off it.'

Next morning they woke to another fine, sunny day, and after a late-ish breakfast made a visit to the Troll Falls, which were spectacular, before starting back to Bergen.

Though Brad appeared to be relaxed and carefree, she knew by his frequent glances in the rear-view mirror and the caution with which he drove that he was on his guard.

Early afternoon they stopped for a meal at a roadside restaurant that smelt of sun-warmed wood and pine-resin.

'Would you like to eat indoors or out?' Brad asked.

'Oh, alfresco, I think.'

Out front was a wooden deck with tubs of bright flowers, and small tables covered with red-checked cloths. From it, there was a good view of the dusty road winding down the mountainside in a spectacular series of horseshoe bends.

While they sat enjoying the sunshine and waiting for their food he said, 'If you'll excuse me, I must phone Paul.'

'Of course.'

When Paul answered Brad told him crisply, 'We'll be back in Bergen by late afternoon, and I'd like to talk to you... Yes, that might be best... You have...?' Then sharply, 'You're not hurt...? Well, take care. See you then.'

As he dropped the phone back into his pocket she asked anxiously, 'Is Paul all right?'

'Yes, thank God. He was on one of our wharfs last night, checking out a report of an intruder, when a piece of heavy lifting equipment came adrift and missed him by inches.'

This latest news made the threat to Brad's life seem all the more urgent, more *real*, and she shivered. If anything happened to him...

Watching all the colour drain from her face, he said, 'There's really no need to worry. Paul assured me he'd escaped without a scratch.' Then sardonically, 'I hope this extreme reaction doesn't mean you've fallen for him?'

'Of course I haven't fallen for him.'

'That's just as well. He's carrying a torch for Erika.'

'Yes, I know. He told me.'

Brad raised a dark brow. 'Paul's not usually given to personal confidences.' An edge to his voice, he added, 'You two must have found an instant rapport?'

Steadily, she agreed, 'I suppose we did.'

'Is that why, thinking I was going off with Erika, you immediately decided to ask him to take you home?'

'I didn't *immediately decide* anything of the kind,' Joanne told him. 'My first thought was to get a taxi, but Mr Reiersen said, owing to the amount of functions taking place, most taxi firms would be fully booked.

'He suggested that, as Paul had come in his own car, and

was living quite close to Lofoten, *he* would no doubt be pleased to take me.

'I thought Paul's car was off the road, but—'

'Did you mention that to Reiersen?'

'I'm afraid so. Though I didn't tell him *why*.'

'What did he say?'

Joanne's recollection was good, and she was able to answer, 'He said, "There was a spot of trouble with his brakes, I gather, but obviously he's had them fixed."'

'Did he say anything else?'

'Yes, he added, "Randall isn't the kind of young man to let grass grow under his feet. If he wasn't working for Brad *I* wouldn't mind employing him. It didn't take him long to get on to Mussen…"'

She stopped speaking as a waiter brought a colourful dish of meatballs in tomato sauce, on a bed of green fettucini.

When they had been served, his face oddly tense, Brad asked, 'You're sure he said Mussen?'

'Quite sure. The name seemed to ring a bell, but I couldn't think why…'

'I presume Reiersen was not altogether sober?'

'No. Before he asked me to dance, Paul warned me that he'd been drinking.'

Brad frowned. 'I hope it wasn't too much of an ordeal?'

Remembering how shaken she'd felt, she said, 'No, of course not.'

'The lies fairly hop out of you.'

'All right, it wasn't very pleasant. But there's no harm done.'

His face relaxing, Brad squeezed her hand. 'I think you'll find an awful lot of good will come out of it.'

By the time they reached Lofoten it was early evening and dusk was starting to cover the bright day with cobwebby veils of lilac and blue.

Brad stopped the car by the main entrance and, carrying their bags and the picnic basket, ushered Joanne inside.

Paul was sitting in front of the stove in the deserted foyer, waiting for them. Watching them cross to the desk, he raised a hand in salute.

When Brad had returned the picnic basket with a word of thanks Helga said, 'I hope all went well?'

'Very well.'

'I will get Edvard to take up your bags.'

'And perhaps you can manage a pot of tea?'

'Of course.'

'Enjoy your birthday trip?' Paul asked cheerfully as they joined him.

'Very much,' Joanne answered.

'Though we did have a spot of bother in Lanadal,' Brad said, and proceeded to explain briefly what had happened.

Paul whistled through his teeth. 'Could have been nasty... And it ties in with the report I had back from the garage. There's no doubt that the car's braking system had been deliberately tampered with... Which seems to suggest that we're all targets.'

'It also suggests that it's high time we did something about it.'

'What *can* we do?' Paul asked gloomily.

'Now, I might just be able to answer that...' Brad broke off as their tray of tea arrived.

'Shall I pour?' Joanne offered.

Paul grinned. 'Thanks, Joanne.'

She had just started to pour, when a voice said sarcastically, 'My, but isn't this cosy?'

Beautifully made-up and dressed in a glacier-blue costume that matched her eyes, Erika was watching them in a derisory fashion.

Her gleaming silvery-blonde hair falling straight to her shoulders, her flawless skin pale, she looked like some exquisite ice maiden, totally out of place in the golden warmth of the foyer.

The two men rose to their feet.

'Won't you join us?' Brad asked politely.

'I wanted a word in private.'

'Tell you what,' Paul suggested to Joanne, 'shall we take a walk and—?'

'There's really no need,' Brad said firmly. 'I'm sure that whatever Erika has to say can be said in front of you both.'

Looking furious, Erika said, 'Very well. If that's how you want it.'

Then, addressing Joanne, 'I have something of yours. You left it at the party.' From her own handbag she produced the small silver evening purse.

'Thank you.' Joanne held out her hand.

Making no attempt to hand the purse over, the blonde went on, 'I must say, I'm surprised you went without it. But I suppose when you realised you'd left it you dared not kick up a fuss in case Brad found out what you'd been up to.'

'I'm afraid I don't know what you're talking about,' Joanne said flatly.

'I might have expected you to act the innocent.'

'Perhaps you could come to the point?' Brad suggested.

'The point is, your *secretary* has been selling information. When, having heard some odd rumours, Daddy casually asked her how things were with the DSL, she hinted that her answer should be worth money...'

'He was shocked, but clearly *someone* took her up on the offer.'

'What utter rubbish,' Joanne exclaimed.

'Then how do you account for the money?'

'What money?'

'Would you mind telling me what's going on?' Brad demanded.

'If you want to know what's going on, I suggest you look inside this bag.' Erika thrust the purse into his hand.

His voice icy, Brad informed her, 'I've no intention of looking in Miss Winslow's purse.'

'Don't be a fool!' Erika snatched back the purse, and, opening it, turned it upside-down. Onto the table fell a comb, a small compact, a tube of lipstick, a couple of tissues, and a thick wad of kroner.

As Joanne stared blankly at the money Erika said with unconcealed triumph, 'There! What did I tell you? While she was dancing the common little tart was obviously selling—'

'That's quite enough!' Though quiet, Brad's voice cracked like a whip. 'I'm sure Miss Winslow was doing nothing of the kind.'

'Instead of trying to defend her, why don't you ask her how the money got there?'

Her temper rising, Joanne said, 'I haven't the faintest idea. Unless you or your father put it there.'

'How dare you suggest such a thing?'

Catching Erika's eye, Paul asked mildly, 'May I say something?'

Darting an angry look at Brad, Erika said, 'It would be nice to hear from someone who isn't biased.'

'I'm glad you agree I'm not biased, because I'm in a good position to give you the facts.

'You see, I was with Miss Winslow for most of the evening, and when I wasn't actually *with* her I was keeping an eye on her, as Brad had asked me to—'

'There you are—' Erika began.

'I don't mean for any reason other than she knew no one there, and Brad wasn't expecting her to be made particularly welcome.

'Now, I can tell you categorically that, apart from myself, the only people Miss Winslow danced with were Brad and your father. I certainly didn't give her the money, and I really can't imagine Brad did…'

'I hope you're not accusing—'

'I'm not *accusing* your father of anything.'

'That's just as well. You can take it from me, Daddy never *touched* her purse.'

Paul shook his head. 'I happened to see him put it on a side-table.'

'When was that?' Brad asked sharply.

Her face paper-white, Joanne explained, 'It was when Mr Reiersen asked me to dance. I dropped the purse and he picked it up. When I remarked that it was a bit of a nuisance, he disposed of it for me. I'm afraid I'd forgotten all about it…'

Gathering up the purse and the items that went with it, Brad turned to Paul and said abruptly, 'Perhaps you'll be good enough to see Erika to her car?'

'Of course. How long before you want me back?'

'Fifteen minutes.'

'Fifteen minutes it is.'

Without another word, Brad took Joanne's arm and hurried her upstairs.

When they reached their suite he tossed the purse and the rest of the things onto the table, and pushed her gently into a chair. 'Do you feel up to telling me exactly what Reiersen said about the DSL?'

'He said he'd heard a whisper that there'd been more trouble, including a fire in one of the hotels. He wanted to know what you were doing about it, if you were considering calling in the police.

'When I told him I didn't know he said perhaps I needed time to think about it, and that useful information could pay big dividends…I told Paul all about it.'

'Take your time, and if you can remember I'd like the whole conversation verbatim.' Brad's voice held suppressed excitement.

As closely as she could, Joanne repeated what had been said word for word, stumbling a little over the more personal parts like, 'There's such a thing as misplaced loyalty, and once Brad's had his fun...' but leaving nothing out.

'He'd just offered to show me round the new leisure complex he'd built, and mentioned some wonderful shops in the arcade when Paul rescued me.'

Looking furious, Brad muttered, 'I'd like to break his damn neck.'

'It's all right—' she began awkwardly.

'But it *isn't* all right.' He took her cold hand. 'I'm sorry. The whole thing is my fault. I should never have put you in a position where you could be insulted like that.

'If he hadn't had too much to drink he would no doubt have been a great deal more cautious about what he said...

'When he sobered up he must have realised he'd made a mistake approaching you in that way.

'Presumably, afraid you'd tell me, he thought up this scheme to turn the tables and try to discredit you—'

A knock at the door made him release her hand and call, 'Come in.'

'All sorted out?' Paul asked. At Brad's nod, he went on, 'I've been wondering about Reiersen for some time now. When Joanne told me he'd tried to bribe her I made up my mind to talk to you about it. Now this money seems to clinch things.'

'You don't think it might have been Erika's doing?'

'I did wonder about that. I must admit that I wouldn't put it past her.

'But when I asked her how she came by the purse she said one of the servants had brought it to her, and she thought she recognised it as Joanne's.

'She swears that when she looked inside the money was already there. I think I believe her.'

'And I'm inclined to think you're right.'

'So *you* believe Reiersen's behind everything?'

'I've thought so for a little while. The problem was getting some evidence. Now, thanks to Joanne's memory for conversations, we may be able to find something that leads directly back to him.'

Picking up the wad of money, Brad thrust it into his pocket.

'You're going to tackle Reiersen now?'

'Yes, but first I want to call on Mussen.'

'You want me with you?'

'No. I'd like you to keep Joanne company.'

Everything falling into place to make a far from pleasant picture, she said quickly, 'I don't need anyone to keep me company. It would make more sense to take Paul with you.'

'I think Joanne's right,' Paul urged.

Seeing by the look on Brad's face that they were both wasting their breath, she promised, 'If it makes you feel any happier, I'll bolt the door and I won't set foot out of the suite.'

'You may need a witness to what's said,' Paul pointed out practically.

Apparently seeing the sense of that, Brad agreed, 'Very well.'

As Joanne breathed a sigh of relief he reminded her, 'Don't forget to bolt the door as soon as we've gone.'

'I won't.'

He clapped Paul on the shoulder. 'Come along, then. While we go I'll fill in the gaps.'

Despite the music-centre and the well-stocked bookcases, Joanne found herself unable to settle to anything.

For a while she pottered about, changing the water in the flowers Brad had given her, washing out her stockings and hanging them over the towel-rail, taking a shower...

And all the time *waiting*.

It seemed an age before she heard a rap at the door and

Brad's voice calling her name. A glance at the clock showed it was under two hours since he had left.

Hurrying to let him in, she asked eagerly, 'Is everything all right?'

'Thanks to you, everything is fine.'

Relief turning her knees to water, she sank down on the couch. 'I'm so *glad*, though I'm sure it isn't thanks to me.'

Taking a seat beside her, Brad disagreed, 'That's just where you're wrong. If you hadn't remembered Reiersen mentioning Mussen…'

'Though the name rang a bell, I'm still not sure…'

'As we were walking back from Bryggen, if you recall, I told you how Paul set a trap and caught a cargo-handler named Mussen… The man admitted bearing a grudge because his brother had been sacked for stealing…'

'Of course… I'm afraid at the time I was only half listening…'

'Perhaps your mind was on other things,' Brad suggested smoothly.

Remembering just what *had* been occupying her mind, she felt the colour rise in her cheeks. 'So what happened when you went to see him?' she asked hurriedly.

'We had a talk, and he admitted that a man named Andersen had suggested the way to work off his grudge, and had actually paid him.'

Seeing Joanne was looking a little blank, he explained, *'Andersen is one of Reiersen's top men.'*

'I see!' she breathed.

'After Mussen was caught, knowing he'd been a fool, and grateful that both he and his brother had been allowed to keep their jobs, he told Andersen to get someone else to do his dirty work.

'When I laid my cards on the table, and Mussen realised how serious things were getting, he gave me the names of a couple of men he felt sure were now working for Andersen.

'Armed with that information, and having decided to try a little bluff, Paul and I went to see Reiersen. First I gave him back his money, then, without involving Mussen, named a few names and told him that if the attacks didn't stop immediately and for good we had a complete dossier ready to put before the police. Faced with the threat of being exposed, he backed off, as I'd guessed he would.'

'You mean he *admitted* he was behind it?'

'No, he's too clever for that. He simply said he was sure we'd have no further trouble.

'Then he asked me if I wouldn't reconsider the offer he'd made the night of the party... Remember I told you we were talking business...?'

Joanne nodded.

'Well, in a nutshell, his offer was this, that our two business empires should merge, and that I should marry Erika and stay in Norway to run both of them.

'He said, "It's time there was a younger man at the helm. If I'd had a son I would have handed over the reins sooner. I'm nearly seventy-four now. When I'm gone you can have complete control."'

Her throat dry, Joanne managed, 'He said *reconsider*, so presumably you turned him down the first time?'

'Yes. I think the car incident in Lanadal was his response to that refusal.

'Tonight, in Paul's presence, he offered me complete control as soon as Erika and I had our first child. He said, "If you agree, one day your son, and my grandson, will take over a vast empire...

'"This time I hope you'll say yes. It's what Erika wants you to do."'

Feeling as though she was bleeding to death, Joanne asked though dry lips, 'So you agreed?'

He raised a dark brow. 'Have you ever noticed me doing what Erika wants me to do?'

'No… But it's obvious that she's in love with you, and—'

'Erika is a spoilt child who *thinks* she's in love with me. And before you ask, I've given her no encouragement to think that.'

'Oh… So what did you say?'

'I refused, of course. I told him politely that, having lodged the "dossier" with my bank, I intended to leave Paul in Norway to run DSL for me.'

'Paul won't mind?'

'No, he loves Norway, and he's still prepared to take his chance with Erika. Once I'm out of the picture, he may well succeed.

'For both their sakes I hope so… Though I would certainly class that marriage as a "noble daring".'

Filled with joy, she asked, 'So what will you do? Stay on for the holiday you were talking about?'

'I'm not sure,' he said abruptly. 'I may take a day or two to think about it. In the meantime I'll book you on the first plane back to London…'

Shock drained the joy away.

So it was over.

'I should never have forced you to come to Norway in the first place. Never made you wear that dress.'

'It's a lovely dress. And at least some good came out of it.'

But as though she hadn't spoken he went on, 'I've made so many mistakes, and all because I was furious at being misjudged… If you'd checked your "facts" you would have found that it was Blake who has the bad reputation. I don't know why his wife stays with him.'

'Perhaps she loves him.'

'If she does, he doesn't deserve it.'

'Brad…I-I'm sorry I misjudged you… If it hadn't been for what happened while we were having dinner that night, and then later on in the taxi…' Her words tailed off.

He sighed. 'When it became obvious what you were up to I decided to play along. I wanted to frighten you, to teach you a lesson.

'I've never had any designs on your sister. To be brutally honest, she's not my type. When I told you I'd never treated her as anything other than a good secretary, it was perfectly true.

'It's also true that I didn't know she was married. She started work as Miss Winslow and she never reported any change of status. If you don't believe me you can check with Personnel.'

'I do believe you,' Joanne said. 'Though with so much going on at the time it scarcely registered that Paul wasn't aware that she was married. He remarked that he'd always known her as Miss Winslow.'

'Well, I'm glad you have some kind of proof.'

'I don't need any proof. While I've been trying to tell myself you were the womaniser I first thought you, I knew in my heart you were nothing of the kind.

'Every single thing you've done or said has gone to prove the opposite.'

'Apart from the fact that you were a virgin when you came, and now you're not.'

'That was my choice,' she said firmly, 'and, as I told you, I don't regret it. Though I do regret listening to Milly. I'm sure that, fancying herself in love with you, she saw things as she *wanted* them to be...

'When you said Milly was merely your secretary I should have believed you. The mistakes that have been made are all mine.'

He shook his head. 'I've made my share, that's why I don't intend to make any more.'

Desperately wanting just a few more weeks of happiness, she pleaded, 'You don't think sending me back to London might be a mistake? You said you wanted companionship, someone to share things with... If you don't love Erika...couldn't I...?'

'You're not the kind to have affairs.'

'Oh, I don't know... I'm enjoying my first.'

'I don't happen to want to carry on having an affair with you,' he said flatly.

Ashamed that she'd thrown herself at him, she flushed scarlet.

Taking her hot face between his palms, he said, 'If you intend to stay, it'll have to be on my terms.'

'What are your terms?' she asked unsteadily.

'I want you to marry me.'

Unable to believe it, she shook her head. 'You can't want to marry me.'

'This isn't some sudden decision,' he told her. 'I've been waiting all my life for a wife who looks like you, and enjoys life the way you do, and laughs at the same things that make me laugh, and eats like a navvy, and kisses me back as though she loves me, even if she doesn't—'

'Oh, but I do.'

'I'm glad about that. If you'd simply gone back to London I don't know what I would have done. But I had to give you the chance.

'Do you want to be married in Norway? Or would you like to wait until we return to England?'

'I'd love to be married in Norway.'

'In Norway women tend to wear their wedding rings on the right hand, but if that bothers you I'll buy you one for each.

'And, speaking of rings, first thing tomorrow I'd like you to send Trevor's ring back and break the news to your family.'

A faint cloud appearing on the horizon, Joanne said worriedly, 'It's OK. I've already broken things off with Trevor; I rang him at the airport, when I realised I wanted to be with you. I don't know what Milly will think...'

'As you've told me repeatedly, your sister is a married woman. She's made her choice, and you are entitled to make yours. So does it really matter what Milly thinks?'

The cloud lifted. 'No, I suppose it doesn't.'

'There, now, everything's settled, so before I take you out to dinner, come and shower with me...'

Mischievously she said, 'I had a shower while I was waiting for you to come back.'

'I thought you agreed with the sentiment "Gather ye rosebuds while ye may".'

'Do you know, you're the only man I've ever known who can quote Herrick?'

He leered at her. 'I have other, more exciting talents that are best put to use in the shower.'

She pretended to consider. 'Well, I suppose I could always enjoy another.'

'I'll make sure you do.'

He took her hand and led her into the bedroom.

Propped on the bedside table, alongside the flowers he'd given her, was her birthday card.

'Now I'm going to marry you, you could at least tell me what my card says.'

He grinned at her, his green eyes gleaming through thick, sooty lashes.

'Well, I suppose it's appropriate now. It says, "A happy birthday to my very own deer." And my personal message reads, "PS I love you."'

THE MILLIONAIRE'S VIRGIN MISTRESS

by

Robyn Donald

Robyn Donald has always lived in Northland in New Zealand, initially on her father's stud dairy farm at Warkworth, then in the Bay of Islands, an area of great natural beauty, where she lives today with her husband and an ebullient and mostly Labrador dog. She resigned her teaching position when she found she enjoyed writing romances more, and now spends any time not writing in reading, gardening, travelling and writing letters to keep up with her two adult children and her friends.

CHAPTER ONE

'MARK, do you think she's one of the strippers? Or...' a significant pause followed by a little laugh '...do they parade her now and then as a horrible example of what can happen if you aren't careful?'

Heat stung Paige Howard's skin, although she acquitted the speaker of deliberate rudeness; the woman couldn't know that a trick of acoustics carried every cut-glass syllable from the foyer of the old hotel to the top of the staircase.

And the posters for the club on the upper floor, offering lap dancing and massage, were too blatant to miss. It was an understandable mistake to assume that Paige was one of the women who offered their services to any man with the money to pay for them.

However, she wasn't going to tell them that she'd never seen the inside of the strip bar! She had more important things to worry about than a momentary humiliation. Frowning, she glanced at the baby in her arms, worried by his increasingly flushed little face.

The woman and her Mark would be tourists on one of the routes that showed off Napier's stunning collection of Art Deco buildings, built after a devastating earthquake seventy years previously. The small city on the sweep of New Zealand's Hawke Bay was now a destination for pilgrims who enjoyed both the architecture and the superb wines of the region.

Paige knew she'd never see this couple again, and she didn't care a five-dollar note what they thought of her.

Although five dollars, she thought grimly, would come in handy right now. She had been made redundant a few weeks previously, and her meagre savings had almost disappeared.

When baby Brodie's temperature had got to the worrying stage she'd had to break the strip club's rules and contact his mother, who worked there. Sherry had thrust money for the doctor into her hands, and gone back to dancing with tears in her eyes.

Brows pinching together, Paige smoothed the shawl back from Brodie's crumpled little face, checking it with real fear building beneath her ribs. Dusky patches darkened the skin around his eyes and he was panting between pale, dry lips.

How could a baby—perfectly normal an hour ago—deteriorate so quickly?

At that moment he jerked in her arms, his face screwing up in pain although he made no noise. Increasing her speed as fast as she dared down the stairs, she pitched her voice to a low soothing murmur.

'Hush, darling. Shh, little man, we're on our way to the doctor and you'll soon feel much, much better...'

She'd almost reached the bottom of the staircase when the couple turned from their admiration of the panelled reception area. Unwillingly she glanced up. Her astounded gaze clashed with brilliant blue eyes in a dark, arrogantly aristocratic face—eyes that blazed with incredulous disbelief across the distance between them.

Not Mark, she thought sickly. *Marc.*

Marc Corbett.

'Paige!'

Irrational panic kicking her in the stomach, she missed the last step and pitched forwards. Hampered by the child in her arms, she instinctively twisted to protect him from the marble floor.

Cruelly strong hands bit into her waist, hauling her up against a lean, hard body, supporting her until she could gasp, 'I'm all right!'

Brodie's high-pitched wail cut through Marc Corbett's reply, but she could hear his deep voice reverberate through his chest, and for a moment—a brief, shocked second—she remembered what it had been like to be held in those arms as music swirled around them on the dance floor...

He let her go and demanded harshly, 'What the hell are you doing here?'

Brodie stiffened and shrieked again, the sound abruptly cutting off as though someone had clamped a hand across his mouth. His little body jerked, arms and legs thrashing wildly.

'What's the matter with that child?' Marc's voice cracked liked a whip.

Terror squeezing her heart, Paige scanned Brodie's unconscious face; his eyes were closed and his lips had turned an ominous purple.

'Oh, God, he's so sick,' she whispered, touching his forehead. The fine, soft skin burned the back of her hand. Terrified, she tightened her arms around him and swivelled, heading as fast as she could for the doors.

The woman with Marc said on a concerned note, 'I think it's having a convulsion.'

'Where's the nearest doctor?' Marc gripped Paige by the elbow, ignoring her mute resistance as he steered her up the street. 'Get into the car.'

He indicated a large BMW a few metres along the pavement, as timelessly elegant as the surrounding buildings. Paige bolted into the front passenger seat and gabbled directions at Marc, barely registering the woman who climbed into the back.

Marc glanced once over his shoulder before forcing his way into the stream of traffic, judging the narrow gap to a nicety. Heart hammering, Paige felt Brodie's small body relax. Oh, God, she thought feverishly, please, no. *Please*, no!

Almost sagging with relief, she saw his eyelids twitch; seconds later his lips gained a little healthy colour. He blinked a couple of times before giving a pathetic little wail.

In a voice she didn't recognise, she said, 'He looks better,' and tucked the shawl carefully around the little body.

Marc Corbett didn't take his eyes from the road. 'How's his breathing?'

Unevenly she said, 'Regular.' And, indeed, Brodie seemed to have slipped into a deep, natural sleep that was immensely reassuring.

'His colour?'

'Normal.'

She sneaked a rapid sideways glance. Bad move.

An ache rasped her throat and she turned her face resolutely to the front. Not fair, she thought fiercely. It simply wasn't fair that Marc Corbett should turn up when her life seemed to have crumbled into dust around her. It was a wonder he hadn't arrived in a clap of thunder, with lighting effects and a sinister laugh.

She knew that handsome face—the strong jaw and high cheekbones—as well as her own. Six years hadn't dimmed the brilliance of his eyes—a blue so intense they blazed with the colour and fire of sapphires. Looking into Marc Corbett's eyes was like being spun into the heart of an electrical storm.

How many times had she caught a glimpse of a tall dark

man and suffered this passionate, shameful excitement? Too many to count…

But until now it had never been the man she'd unconsciously been looking for; just as well, because six years previously he had married her childhood friend Juliette.

And two years ago Juliette had died in a tragic, senseless road accident. Paige's throat closed as she remembered the girl who'd been a charming substitute older sister to her.

The woman in the back seat leaned forward to say, 'Poor little boy! What is the matter with him? Do you know?'

She sounded so genuinely worried that Paige almost forgave her the sly comment about her being a horrible example.

Unevenly she answered, 'He's feverish and he has a rash; I think he might have chickenpox.'

But she couldn't banish the terrifying word *meningitis* from her mind.

She'd expected to have to repeat the directions to the surgery, but Marc Corbett didn't need his mind refreshed. As the building came into view, she said woodenly, 'You can stop here—pull left.'

'I know I am in New Zealand.' A faint, alien inflection to his intonation betrayed the influence of his French mother.

Without thinking, Paige turned her head. A royal blue gaze seared across her face before returning to the road.

Very appropriate! Royal blue eyes for a man who owned and ruled a commercial empire. Nerves wound tight in unbearable tension, Paige swallowed. Meeting Marc again had been a hideous, meaningless coincidence. He'd drop her off here and disappear from her life.

Which was exactly what she wanted.

The luxurious car drew into a miraculously empty length of kerbside. Anxiously searching Brodie's face, Paige wondered if Marc had ever had to search for a parking space like ordinary people. Probably not; his combination of ruthless determination and compelling charisma seemed to magic obstacles away.

'Thanks very much,' she said awkwardly, releasing herself from the seatbelt to scrabble for the door handle.

'Wait there.'

But as he strode around the front of the car she fumbled the door open. From the back came the woman's voice, amused yet chiding.

'It's best to do what he says. He's a very—dominant— man.'

She invested that word *dominant* with a lingering amusement that made Paige feel sick. If this was Lauren Porter, she was obviously still very much in Marc's life.

Why not? A man who'd maintained a mistress during the four short years of his marriage wasn't likely to let his wife's death break up the relationship.

When he opened the door Paige attempted to scramble out, but worry and shock made her awkward, and after a moment Marc plucked her and Brodie from the car with a leashed violence that destroyed the last pathetic shreds of her composure.

Once he was sure she was steady on her feet, he dropped his hands as though she'd contaminated them. 'Are you all right?'

His voice was cold and hard as iron, and as smoothly disciplined. Sensation flayed her with a diabolical combination of stimulation and fear—and, stronger than both, a weird, unnerving sensation of relief, as though she'd been lost and was now found again.

Clutching the baby, Paige stepped back and said tonelessly, 'Fine, thank you,' before racing into the sanctuary of the surgery.

While the woman at the counter pulled Brodie's records from the computer she turned her head and watched Marc's companion—slender, dressed in the signature good taste of a fashionable designer—ease gracefully into the front seat of the car with a flirtatious hint of long, superb legs. As soon as the door closed the vehicle pulled smoothly from the kerb and merged into the flow of traffic, disappearing almost immediately.

No doubt he was as glad to get rid of her as she was to see him go. A sour jab of disillusionment, goaded by that acute, painfully physical awareness, propelled Paige across to the waiting area.

She sat down in a chair apparently chosen for its lack of comfort and rocked a now wakeful—and very fretful—Brodie. Marc's companion fitted the description Juliette had given of a height to match Marc's six foot three or so. Even their colouring matched. Her black hair was cut into a style that suited her fine features. And Juliette had admired her eyes—'Grey as an English dawn,' she'd said.

The accent fitted too.

'She is English and clever—an executive in Marc's organisation. Marc says she is brilliant,' Juliette had told her, modern technology delivering the catch in her voice perfectly across the twelve thousand miles that had separated her from Paige. 'At least he doesn't shame me with his choice of a mistress; she is lovely and wears clothes like a Frenchwoman.'

Paige's knuckles gleamed white on the receiver. 'You might be getting it all wrong, you know. Unless—has he admitted it?'

'Oh, no.' Juliette sounded shocked. 'I am not going to ask him—I don't need to. I have seen them together, and that is enough. They are very discreet, but there is a connection between them that is impossible to miss.'

'What do you mean? Surely they don't—?'

'Flirt?' Juliette had sighed. 'Marc would never humiliate me like that. I can't describe the link between them except to say that it is there, like an invisible chain binding them together.'

And let's not go there now, Paige thought wearily, rocking the whimpering baby. Just concentrate on getting Brodie to the doctor, and working out how you can make your pathetic savings last until you get another job.

Half an hour later, when she walked out into the bright winter sunshine and heard a deep voice say her name, she wasn't surprised, although her heart contracted into a tight, hard lump in her chest. She'd known he'd be waiting for her.

'Did the doctor agree with your diagnosis of chickenpox?' he asked in a hard voice with a disturbingly abrasive undernote.

Warily she thrust the prescription into her jeans pocket as Brodie snuffled beneath the shawl. Although bright sunlight gilded the city, a sharp wind blustering in from the sea promised a cold night.

Marc was alone, she realised with humiliating relief. Not breaking stride, she returned in a tone as chilly as the air, 'Yes, she did. I'm sorry, I haven't time to talk. I need to fill a prescription and then take Brodie home.'

Marc fell in beside her, saying inflexibly, 'I'll drive you there.'

To a grotty little flat down an alleyway behind a hamburger joint? *Never.* She said quickly, 'It's all right; it's not far.'

'It's not all right. The child is ill.'

'The doctor was certain that it's the first stage of chickenpox, which is not a serious illness.' She paused, then

said with a touch of malice, 'I hope you've had it.
Chickenpox is very infectious.'

'I believe I had all the childhood diseases.' His hard,
handsome face revealed nothing. 'Have you had it?'

'Juliette and I had it together,' she said stonily. 'I gave
it to her, I believe.'

A rapid glance took in the symmetry of angles and
planes in the outrageously good-looking face that radiated
formidable, uncompromising power. His dead wife's name
brought no flicker of remorse or sorrow.

She dragged her eyes away, but it was too late; he'd
seen her survey him and something kindled in the depths
of his striking eyes. His voice, however, was all controlled
assurance. 'Nevertheless, I'll take you home. Give me the
prescription form and you can wait in the car with the
child.'

No doubt his formidable brain was slotting her involuntary response into a mental file. Marc Corbett hadn't
turned a large family fortune into a stupendous one by the
age of thirty-two without an incisive, analytical intelligence backed by relentless determination. He'd used his
father's legacy to become a player on the world stage.

And he knew women.

Masking her jumping nerves with a frozen façade, she
said crisply, 'Thank you, but you don't need to go to the
trouble.'

The door to the pharmacy beckoned; she turned
abruptly, feeling him follow her, noiseless and purposeful
as a predator.

Which, she reminded herself, was exactly what he was.
His father had been called the Robber Baron in the business press; no one dared whisper that about Marc, but
she'd read enough to know that his name inspired respect
mingled with fear.

Brodie began to cry again, his head turning restlessly inside the shawl. 'Hush, darling.' Paige juggled him as she fumbled in her jeans pocket. Her voice softened into a murmur. 'It's all right, sweetheart, you'll feel better once we get some of this stuff inside you.'

'Give him to me,' Marc commanded.

Shock whipped her head up; she looked directly into his autocratic face, its bold, chiselled features set in a mask of impatience.

'He doesn't like strangers,' she said raggedly.

One black, ironic brow shot up, and memories squeezed her heart painfully.

Marc said crisply, 'Then give me the prescription form.'

'I can manage.' But Brodie chose that moment to stiffen alarmingly.

Fortunately it didn't turn into another convulsion—it was only the prelude to a shriek. While she was hushing the baby, Marc gave her a glittering glance in which irritation and concern were blended, and before she had time to object his fingers had invaded her pocket and hauled out the piece of paper.

'Wait here,' he commanded, and strode up to the pharmacy counter.

Where, of course, he got instant service. Body throbbing at his unexpected touch, Paige's gaze followed him as she rocked the baby, trying to soothe him with softly spoken nonsense. Marc's overwhelming physical presence owed something to wide shoulders and lean hips and long athlete's legs, but more to an intangible aura of power and effortless authority that had cut a path through the other customers. Sensation twisted inside her, paradoxically sharp and smouldering.

And forbidden.

She noted with a pang of fear that inexplicable feeling

of rightness, as though the past six years had been a nightmare and she'd just woken to a new dawn. Don't be so ridiculous, she told herself staunchly. He's just like Dad. Marriage vows mean nothing.

Subsiding into whimpers, the baby stuffed a tiny fist into his mouth and sucked noisily until he realised he wasn't going to get nourishment from there. His desperate roars once more filled the pharmacy when Marc arrived back with the medication in one lean hand.

'Let's go before he eats that hand,' he said, turning with his other hand on her elbow, steering her out onto the footpath.

Paige didn't fool herself that she had any choices; for some reason Marc Corbett had decided he was going to take her home, and those fingers resting so casually on her arm would clamp if she tried to run. Although she hated to surrender, it meant nothing against the need to get the medicine and some liquid into Brodie immediately—and to ring Sherry, his mother, as soon as she could to reassure her that Brodie only had chickenpox.

Back in the car, with the lingering perfume of his previous passenger floating around her, Paige gave directions in a flat, remote voice. Sexy and modern, the scent breathed money and leisure and privilege, taunting her with its lazy exclusiveness.

She stiffened her shoulders and stared through the windscreen. It was difficult to find a dreary part of Napier, but today she saw her street with fresh eyes—the eyes of a man accustomed to the best. Subdued, out at the elbows, the collection of small shops and houses was only redeemed by bright flowers and shrubs.

'Number twenty-three,' she told Marc, the taste of defeat bitter on her tongue.

He turned down the drive between the fast food bar and an electrical goods shop that had seen better days.

'It's the second unit,' Paige said reluctantly.

The car drove down the row of cheaply built units; an elderly, failed motel had been turned into cramped apartments. Parking in the space allotted to her unit, Marc killed the engine.

Without taking his hands from the wheel, he surveyed the red-brick building with its aluminium ranch-slider windows and small concrete terraces separated by flower boxes. Most were desolate except for a few rugged weeds scraping an existence in dusty earth. Only the one outside Paige's unit radiated colour—brazen marigolds, their gold and lemon and rich mahogany defying the general hopelessness.

'Thank you,' she said levelly as Brodie, soothed into sleep by the motion of the car, woke with another weary little whimper. She wanted Marc out of there, safely banished to his world of luxury where the last thing *he'd* have to worry about was the state of his bank balance.

'Give the baby to me,' he ordered.

Startled, she said, 'I can manage.'

His beautiful mouth compressed into a thin line. 'It will be easier for you to get out if I have him.'

She hesitated.

'What are you afraid of?' he asked softly, blue eyes sardonic. 'That I'll kidnap him?'

'Of course not.'

'I won't drop him either.' His tone mocked her.

Flushing, she handed over the baby and leapt out of the car, only to see Marc emerge too, Brodie held with firm confidence in his arms. No stumbling or hesitation either, she noted; his distinctive ease and power made every movement graceful in a very masculine way.

'I'll bring him in,' he said, when she came towards him. 'You'll manage your keys more quickly if you aren't carrying him.'

Thus neatly forestalling her plans of taking the child and walking away, leaving him with no option but to drive off.

Not that he would have. Seething at her helplessness, Paige swung on her heel and walked across the bare concrete to insert the key with a vicious twist.

When she turned Marc was just behind her, and as she pushed the door back he walked in, dark head a few centimetres below the lintel, with Brodie traitorously silent in his arms.

Marc stopped in the middle of the threadbare carpet in all shades of mud, dwarfing the shabby, nondescript room. Paige burned with futile resentment as his narrowed, bright gaze checked out the elderly sofa, the table with two chairs—its scratched top covered by a sewing machine draped in a swathe of gleaming fabric—and the tiny kitchen overlooking a wall and a clothesline.

In spite of her efforts to cheer it up, she knew the room reeked with defeat. Not even the pots on the sill, fragrant with growing herbs, made any difference.

So what? she thought, stiffening her spine. She wasn't ashamed of living here.

He looked down at the baby in his arms, just as Brodie turned his head and sputtered a small amount of liquid over his shirt.

'Oh, I'm sorry,' Paige said, hoping her tone drowned out any defensive note as she came over and held out her arms for the baby. 'I'll take him now.'

'It's nothing.' Marc's voice was hard and autocratic, but when Brodie forced a small fist into his mouth and began to suck noisily his expression changed, some fugitive emotion softening the dominant features. 'I don't know much about children this small, but surely that indicates that he needs food?'

'He needs changing and medicine first. I'll heat a bottle,' she muttered unhappily, racing into the kitchen to grab a cloth and run it under the tap. She held it out to Marc, but he ignored it.

'I'll hold him until you've prepared it,' he stated, his pleasant inflection not hiding the steel in the words.

She did *not* care what he thought of her or the flat—not a bit. In fact, she was probably doing the world a service, showing him how the other half lived!

But the bitterness of rejection scraped across her skin. Stubbornly silent, she yanked open the refrigerator door and took out a sterilised bottle filled with formula. The electric kettle with its frayed cord spat sparks when she plugged it in.

'Be careful!' Marc snapped.

A knot somewhere inside her loosened a fraction, only to tighten again when he glanced at her. Above Brodie's wails, she said, 'It's all right; I'm used to it. All it does is spit.'

'It's dangerous.'

But not as dangerous as you, she thought angrily. And she couldn't afford a new one anyway.

A frown knotting his dark brows, Marc looked at the sewing machine on the table, and the swirl of bright fabric beside it. 'What the hell happened? When last I heard you and your mother were living with a cousin near a village called Bellhaven. You were working for him in his farm office.'

Juliette must have told him, and he'd remembered.

Then he killed the tiny flicker of warmth this had engendered by finishing abrasively, 'How did you get from there to a slum in Napier?'

Paige's chin jerked up. She stared at the kettle. 'This might be a slum to you, but most of the world would consider it basic but perfectly adequate,' she said politely. 'As for how I got here, that's simple. Lloyd, my mother's cousin, died and his farm was sold.'

He watched her with hooded eyes. 'When was this?'

'About a year ago. We moved to Napier because my mother thought it would be a good place to live.' She swallowed and finished in a flat voice, 'Unfortunately, for her it was a good place to die.'

'What happened?' he asked in an oddly gentle voice.

'She went for a walk along the beach and got caught by a rogue wave.'

'I'm very sorry,' he said. 'I know how close you were. When was this?'

Something in his tone—a touch of rare gentleness— made her blink ferociously. 'Five months ago.'

The silence was broken by the sound of the kettle boiling. Paige switched it off and poured the water into a jug.

Marc looked from her to the child in his arms. 'Where is the child's father?'

Until then it hadn't occurred to her that he'd think Brodie was *her* child. Which just shows what an idiot you are, she told herself wearily. One look at Marc and your mind turns into candyfloss!

Before she could tell him about Sherry and Brodie the baby broke the silence with a wail, and she said swiftly, 'He isn't here. I'll take Brodie now; he needs changing and some lotion on his rash to stop the itching.'

She bore him off through a door without a backward glance. Marc's mouth curved in a sardonic smile as she closed that door firmly behind her.

Clearly she wanted him in her home as little as he wanted to be there. At any other time he'd be ironically amused at how much she resented the outrageous coincidence of their meeting, and the fact that the baby's illness meant she'd had to rely on a man she viewed with wary distaste.

But one thought burned holes in his self-control: she didn't want him there, but every time he came near her she reacted like a cat faced with an unknown threat, spitting defiance and acute awareness.

CHAPTER TWO

A FIERCE, very male smile curling his mouth, Marc looked around the room. It must have been dingy indeed when Paige moved in, yet without spending much she'd made it as welcoming as it could be, given its depressing furnishings. He'd be prepared to bet that she had painted the walls the soft, buttery gold that both warmed and lightened the small room, and the touches of colour were hers too.

The pool of vivid material on the table caught his eye; he walked across to examine it.

It looked like a fancy dress costume, brief and shrieking with colour, but he recognised it for what it was—a costume intended to tease and titillate, designed to reveal its wearer's breasts and waist and legs.

So, Lauren had been right; as well as being a single mother and a woman down on her luck, Paige was a stripper or a lap dancer—or some such thing. Life hadn't been easy for her since her mother died; she had already developed the bright, hard shell of a woman who'd been rejected too often to trust any man.

Who the hell was her lover? Marc totted up months and realised that it had to be someone from Bellhaven. Why wasn't he here for Paige and his son?

Marc's lip curled with contempt as he thrust hands that bunched into fists in his pockets. He'd like to have the father of her child to himself for a few minutes, he thought with cold, aggressive anger; he'd show him exactly what he thought of a man who got a woman pregnant and then abandoned her.

But beneath the contempt was another, more primitive emotion—anger that some other man had taken the woman he wanted. Facing the admission with a slow burn of fury, he tried to rationalise this degrading infatuation.

It was nothing more than simple, basic lust, and if he gave it free rein it would reduce him to the same level as the men who paid to see her remove the cheap satin bra and scanty, high-cut briefs.

And although he mightn't be able to evict the mindless hunger from the weak part of him that bred it, he could certainly control it.

A memory leapt into his mind, shiny and precise as though it had been continually polished. They had danced at his wedding, the conventional dance of bridegroom and bridesmaid. He remembered the fresh, faint scent that had been hers alone, the way her slim body had moved against his with natural grace and an innocent seductiveness. She'd been seventeen, overwhelmed and excited, yet she'd glanced up through her lashes with a purely female need.

Desire gripped him, powerful, laden with temptation— and completely despicable.

She'd be a good stripper, he decided cynically. Not only did she move like a houri, but she looked like one—a walking, breathing challenge even now, when grief and pregnancy and sleepless nights with a sick child had leached much of the radiance from her fine, soft skin and ground away her vitality.

Nothing had been able to dim the rich honey glaze of her hair, or the gold lights in her great green eyes, or the full, sensuous contours of her mouth.

And she faced the world with a dogged independence that jutted her jaw and kept her shoulders squared.

In Sherry's bedroom, Paige fastened a clean napkin and manoeuvred Brodie into new leggings. The lotion she'd smoothed on seemed to have eased the itchy rash; he still wriggled, but without the frantic restlessness of a few minutes ago.

'Those red cheeks haven't gone away yet, though,' she murmured, kissing him as she picked him up. 'Better get some of that medicine inside you right now.'

But she had to force herself to take the first step towards the living room. No other man sent subtle electrical shocks through her with the accidental, meaningless brush of his skin against hers. Even in the dark she'd know Marc by his touch, she thought dazedly.

And he felt it too. Her spine had tingled when she'd seen the ruthless, swiftly concealed awareness in his eyes.

She wanted him and he wanted her.

Which was why she'd let him go on believing that Brodie was her child. Marc was no lover for a virgin to cut her teeth on.

What was he doing in Napier?

Not, she thought with bitter pragmatism, looking for her—when their eyes had duelled across the hotel foyer he'd been as astonished as she had.

And because that thought hurt much more than was safe, she went through the door and out into the cramped living room.

'I measured out the dose of medication,' Marc said, his voice cool and detached.

'Thank you.'

Brodie hated it; he spluttered and choked, thrusting out his tongue in disgust, but eventually she managed to get the drops into him.

Marc asked curtly, 'Why doesn't the baby's father live here?'

'He's in Australia.' She tested the temperature of the milk on her wrist. Exactly blood heat, so she carried both baby and bottle over to the shabby sofa. Deliberately she shook a swathe of hair across her face to serve as a fragile barrier against Marc's penetrating eyes.

'Are you joining him?' Marc asked, as though he had the right.

'No.' Keeping her eyes on the baby's face, she said neutrally, 'The rash looks much more like chickenpox now.'

Brodie began to suck with enthusiasm, but the milk didn't bring its usual satisfaction. After a few seconds he turned his head away and whimpered.

'Come on, sweetheart,' she encouraged him. 'You've got to get some liquid into you; you don't want to dehydrate.'

Achingly, violently aware of the man who watched her with a shuttered sapphire gaze, she risked a swift glance from beneath the curtain of her hair.

Apart from the hardening of his wide, sculpted mouth, no emotion showed in Marc's expression. Yet beneath the charismatic combination of tanned skin and brilliant eyes set off by hair as dark as sin she sensed cool speculation. Skin tightening, she shook her hair back and met his eyes.

With a brisk, no-nonsense emphasis, she said, 'Thank you. You've been very kind. Would you mind closing the door when you leave?'

The long, powerful muscles in his thighs flexed as he lowered himself onto the other end of the sofa.

'Tell me why you're living like this,' he said, a purposeful note in his voice making it more than clear that he had no intention of going until he'd got what he wanted.

Fighting back a rapid flare of resentment at his probing, she parried, 'Compared to the way some people live, this isn't bad.'

One black brow lifted in cool disbelief, but his voice

was perfectly courteous. 'You're being evasive. I presume your mother's death left you badly off financially?'

Her composure began to unravel. 'Funerals cost money.'

He was silent for a heartbeat. Quietly he said, 'Why didn't your cousin provide for you and your mother in his will?'

'Why should he? He had a son.' Paige knew her voice sounded flat, but she couldn't change it. She added, 'Lloyd was very good to us; he gave us a home for years.'

He didn't look convinced. 'Juliette said your mother kept house for him and you organised his books.'

Keeping her eyes on Brodie's face, Paige said quietly, 'He paid us.' Not a living wage, but they'd managed.

'Keeping you home was selfish of him and your mother,' Marc observed austerely. 'They should have sent you to university.'

Paige bit her lip. It seemed like a betrayal to be discussing her mother's tragic affliction with this man, intimidating in his strength and confidence. 'Mum needed me. After my father left us she suffered from bouts of depression.' Sometimes she had lain in bed for weeks at a time, staring into the grey world she'd inhabited.

Marc frowned. 'There are drugs available.'

'None of them worked.' Brodie snuffled a little and jerked his head around. As she coaxed him to drink some more Paige said, 'Anyway, we were happy here; it mightn't look much to you, but Mum settled in well. I got a job in an office and everything—everything seemed to be humming along. Then I was made redundant, and Mum died.'

She'd been so thrilled to get that job; her only employable skills were farm bookkeeping, and her previous experience didn't cut much ice. But she'd been given a chance and she'd been determined to make the most of it.

Then she'd discovered that her boss had a roving eye and hands that followed suit. An even greater blow to her pride followed: when she'd threatened him with a sexual harassment charge he'd let slip that he'd hired her because he'd seen her as an easy mark, a victim.

Well, she'd soon disabused him of that idea; startled by her angry response, he'd left her alone, but a month later she'd been made redundant. Yet another rejection, she thought cynically.

She hadn't been able to get another position. In summer there'd be plenty of casual work, but summer was several months off. No one wanted a woman with practically no employment history and a reference so subtly non-committal the only thing a prospective employer could take from it was that she'd been hopeless in the one job she'd had.

Marc looked at the pale, proud profile and swore silently in rapid French, deciding not to push further, although the green glitter in her eyes told him there was more to the story than that.

Had she been raped? The thought made him feel both sick and coldly, furiously angry. He didn't want to force her confidence; besides, there were other ways of finding out what he wanted to know.

'How long had your mother suffered from depression?' he asked casually.

'Since just after Juliette and her family went back to France.'

When that ironic brow shot up again she elaborated in an offhand voice, 'My father left us for his secretary. It shattered my mother.'

He frowned, eyes hard and blue as diamond shards. 'Are you in touch with your father still?'

She said briefly, 'He's dead too.'

'How long did you live next door to Juliette?' Marc asked with what sounded like idle interest.

Her expression softened. 'About eight years.' Juliette's father had been a diplomat, and in spite of the difference in their ages Juliette had been incredibly kind to her.

Marc leaned onto the painfully uncomfortable back of the sofa. It smelt clean, as did the unit, although a faint lingering taint in the air hinted at too many cigarettes smoked years ago, too much beer spilt on the thin carpet. He hated to see her in such surroundings.

Resisting any impulse to ask himself why, he said, 'What are your plans now?'

She skewered him with sword-points of green-gold fire. 'At the moment I have none beyond getting another job,' she said politely, setting the bottle down on the plywood table beside a small blue vase that held a single marigold, bright and flamboyant as the sun. She lifted Brodie and held him to her shoulder, patting his back until he brought up the last of his wind.

'Doing what?' When she didn't immediately answer he indicated a book on the floor by the sofa, a large tome she'd borrowed from the library written by a famous plantsman about his travels in search of new varieties. She'd been thoroughly enjoying it. 'I see you're interested in plants.'

'I like flowers. I find the whole business of breeding plants fascinating,' she said in a cool voice, silently mourning a lost dream. At school she'd planned to study botany and biology, and then work in a nursery. That had gone by the board when she'd realised that her mother couldn't cope without her.

Marc said calmly, 'Juliette would be upset to see you in such a situation.'

Didn't he realise that his unfaithfulness had distressed

Juliette infinitely more than anything else ever could? Outrage made Paige's reply brutal. 'I can manage. And Juliette has been dead for almost two years.'

'It was such a complete waste.' His voice was sombre, and when she looked up she saw his eyes close briefly.

But when he opened them again they were cold and clear and unreadable.

'Utterly,' Paige agreed unsteadily, deciding that he was an unfeeling, insensitive clod.

He'd rung her to tell her of Juliette's death; when she'd wept he'd been kind but icily remote.

She'd read more in the newspapers. Her friend had been in the back seat of a limousine inching up a steep mountain road in Italy. A truck with failed brakes had hurtled around a corner and pushed them off the cliff. Juliette, the chauffeur and the truck driver had died.

At least it had been immediate. Beyond one horrified second she'd probably not even known what had happened.

Blinking back tears, Paige coaxed a reluctant Brodie to accept more milk. He wriggled and turned his face sideways, before relenting and sucking again.

'I'm sorry. You must miss her too,' Marc said, his deep voice with its fascinating hint of an accent almost gentle. He touched her hand.

Paige's gaze flew to his face as that secret, blinding charge of electricity jolted her into a fiery oblivion where nothing else mattered but this man.

Before she could do anything stupid—like sighing or leaning towards Marc—Brodie gave a little choking splutter followed by an indignant wail.

Shaken, and intensely grateful to be saved from setting herself up for a rebuff, Paige lifted the baby and patted his back until he settled down. Marc Corbett belonged to a world as distant from hers as it was possible to be—a world of untold wealth, of power and privilege and social position.

He might want her, but the gap between them was impassable. Don't ever forget that, she told herself silently, tucking the bottle back into Brodie's mouth. He whimpered, spitting the milk out with disgust, and began to cry softly.

Accepting defeat, Paige got to her feet. 'He's ready for bed.' She looked directly at Marc, and her heart contracted in useless pain. 'Thank you for bringing us home,' she said formally.

He had risen when she did; she was tall enough, for a woman, but he towered over her, battering her with the power of his presence and his forceful personality.

'Can you get a babysitter for him?' he asked, long thick lashes narrowing his gaze.

She swallowed and banished a craven impulse to lick her lips. 'Why?'

'Answer me, Paige.'

She lifted defiant eyes. 'I don't have to answer you,' she said in a low, intense voice. 'I'm not your employee or someone who wants to curry favour with you. The question of a babysitter doesn't arise because I won't leave Brodie.'

Another evasion, but with any luck she'd made him angry enough not to notice. She turned away with the almost sleeping child in her arms and headed for the door that led to two small bedrooms and a minuscule bathroom.

Marc's voice came from behind, cool and deliberate. 'In that case, I'll come along tomorrow morning and bring breakfast for us both.'

Paige froze. 'No,' she said tautly.

'Why not?'

She was shaking her head, knowing only that she didn't dare see anything more of him. The only way she could think of to counter that inflexible will involved threatening him with harassment, and she couldn't trust herself to berate him without waking Brodie.

Fuming, she opened the door into the tiny hall. 'Because I don't want you here,' she said between her teeth.

'Tough,' he said, just as bluntly. 'We have things to talk about.'

She swivelled around. 'What on earth do *we* have to talk about? Juliette is dead, and she was the only thing we had in common.'

A sardonic brow lifted as he surveyed her with infuriating confidence. 'Unfortunately, that's not true. At the moment you're too concerned about Brodie to concentrate. He'll almost certainly be feeling much better in the morning and we can discuss things then.'

Paige pressed her lips together as he walked out into the sunshine and closed the door behind him.

Cradling the baby, she watched the sun strike fire from Marc's head. He seemed a creature from another planet—virile, radiating a potent energy that transformed the tired, drab surroundings and set her thrumming with deep, hidden desires.

Dangerous, frightening desires, doomed to be frustrated. She turned away, sickened by her body's treachery.

As she tucked the baby into his crib and stood patting his back, she thought of Juliette. It had been only a couple of years after her marriage that she'd rung Paige from New York and recounted her suspicions about Marc and Lauren, her lightly accented voice wry and steady.

Paige, her own life smashed to splinters after her father had walked out on her and her mother, had said immediately, 'Dump him.' And wondered why she'd felt so desolate.

But Juliette replied, 'That would be stupid. This is only a fling.'

Astounded, Paige said, 'But you'll never be able to trust him!'

'I trust him not to abandon me, as your father did your mother,' Juliette said with complete conviction. 'Marc won't betray me like that.'

And when Paige spluttered into silence her friend continued, 'He and I understand each other. He is not like your father and I am not like your mother, eating out my heart for something I can't have. We have a very good marriage, and if common sense and practicality sound a little boring, they are not such bad foundations for a union that will last a lifetime.'

'If that's the case, why are you upset about this affair?' Paige asked, honestly bewildered.

'Oh, it hurts a little.' Her friend gave a soft sigh. 'But I'm not all fire and passion, like you, and Marc and I came to an understanding of the sort of marriage we would have before we married. He was very honest.'

'He told you he'd have affairs?' Paige asked in shocked astonishment.

Where had Marc acquired such an arrogantly medieval attitude towards loyalty and honour in marriage? Surely Juliette didn't believe that it was merely a practical arrangement for the propagation of children and advancement of family fortunes?

Juliette laughed with real amusement. 'Of course not! He said he didn't seem able to feel the sort of love that poets write about, but that he liked me very much and wished for me to be the mother of his children. And I was glad, because between you and me, Paige, I'm not roman-

tic either. I don't think I could cope with a *grande passion*;
I've seen how they can tear people to bits, and they don't
last. My children won't worry about their parents divorcing
because one or the other falls in love with someone else.
Marc and I will always be together, and there for them.'

Even now Paige could remember the shiver down her
spine. Such a bloodless union might have suited Juliette,
but she'd never accept so little from a man.

Actually, she had no intention of accepting anything
from a man. Life without men was much more peaceful.
She shuddered, recalling her mother's years of anguished
despair after the break-up of her marriage. Laying yourself
open to pain was foolhardy.

Voices from outside jerked her from her memories. With
a final pat on Brodie's back, she hurried across to the window and peered through the curtains to see Sherry hurtle
across the concrete, groping for her key as a taxi drew
away.

By the time Paige got to the living room Brodie's
mother had managed to unlock the door and was pushing
it open, her small, voluptuous body quivering with frantic
impatience.

'How is he?' she demanded.

Soothingly Paige told her, 'The doctor's sure it's chickenpox. I've put the prescription lotion on his rash and it
doesn't seem to be worrying him nearly as much.'

'His temperature?' Sherry asked, rushing across to the
door into the tiny hall.

'He's still flushed, but it hasn't been long since he took
the medication.'

Sherry nodded and disappeared, leaving Paige listening
to the low hum of a perfectly tuned engine. Her breath
catching in her throat, she glanced through the window
and saw the BMW turn back into the car park.

Incredulously she watched Marc get out, lift a parcel from the passenger's seat and walk purposefully towards the flat.

Mindful of Brodie, he knocked quietly. And it was only because she didn't want the baby to wake that she flew across to open the door. 'What do you want? I told you—'

He held out the parcel. 'Here.'

Paige stared at it with wary suspicion. 'What's that?'

'An electric kettle,' he told her, and strode past her and into the kitchen, where he dumped the parcel on to the counter.

White with temper, she gritted, 'I don't want it. Please go.'

'Not until I've collected this.' He picked up the old electric jug and its dangerously frayed cord. With a hard-edged smile he carried it across to the door.

Keeping her voice low, Paige said vehemently, 'I don't want anything from you.'

'Is it just me?' His eyes narrowed into steel-blue slivers. Into the heated silence he finished, 'That's the second thing you've refused to take from me.'

Paige's lashes flickered down over her eyes. 'I don't know what you mean,' she said in a wooden voice.

'You didn't want to accept the locket,' he said evenly.

She froze, and he smiled and touched her mouth with a long forefinger. Heat sizzled through her, and she clenched her eyes shut.

'That's not going to help,' he said with contempt. 'It's lust, Paige. ''The expense of spirit in a waste of shame,'' as Shakespeare said. We saw each other and we wanted each other, and neither of us can forget it.' He paused. 'Because it's still there.'

Her eyes flew open as the colour drained from her skin, leaving her cold and shivering. The anger and bitterness openly displayed in his face dried the words on her tongue.

His smile was savage. 'In spite of everything.'

And he kissed her, punishing her—and punishing himself too, she dimly realised as passion roared like a holocaust through her.

It only lasted a moment. He swore against her mouth, chilling words in a language she only dimly recognised to be French, and then let her go as though she disgusted him.

Swaying, Paige clutched the chair and watched him stride noiselessly out of the door.

Almost gibbering with a mindless mixture of rage and cold terror, she dammed the reckless words that threatened to tumble out and watched the car drive away, taking him out of her life.

'Wow!' Sherry breathed, easing herself around the door. 'And double wow. If any guy could make my little heart go pitter-patter again, it would be that one.'

'Don't even think about it,' Paige said furiously. 'There's a woman already in residence. She's tall and dark and super-elegant, and she suits him perfectly.' She dragged in a painful breath. 'Satisfied that Brodie's getting better?'

Sherry nodded. 'He's sound asleep.' She came across and looked at the parcel. 'What's this?'

'An electric kettle. Your triple wow of a man doesn't like ours.' Paige tried to smile.

'I don't blame him. Talk about living dangerously! What are you going to do with it?'

'Well, the original kettle belonged to you, so you choose.'

'Then I choose to keep it.'

Paige turned away, listening as Sherry unpacked the box. She felt as though her emotions had been flung into the heart of a cyclone and were whirling around in uncontrollable violence, destroying everything in their path.

'It's a good one. I'll christen it with a cup of coffee for us both,' Sherry said on a sigh. 'It's been a bastard of a day and I could do with something to give me some zip.'

Collapsing onto the sofa, Paige decided she could do with some extra zip too. Her mouth stung from Marc's kiss and she felt like a stalk of overcooked asparagus. This, she decided, must be an adrenaline crash.

CHAPTER THREE

SHERRY looked across the counter. In an elaborately casual voice she asked, 'Who was the guy?'

'My best friend's husband.'

'The friend who was killed in a car accident?' At Paige's nod her eyes widened. 'The French guy?'

'His mother is French,' Paige said scrupulously. 'His father was a New Zealander; they used to call him the Robber Baron.'

'This one looks pretty French to me.' Sherry filled the new kettle. 'Mediterranean macho to the nth degree. What do they call *him*? Lord of all he surveys?'

'It fits,' Paige told her with an acid smile, 'but I think they take him too seriously to call him anything but sir.'

'So what's he doing here? Did he come looking for you?'

Paige snorted. 'Why would he do that? It was sheer coincidence that we met in the foyer of the hotel. Don't worry; we won't be seeing him again.'

'You met him coming down from the club?' Sherry looked unhappily at her. 'I hope you told him you aren't a stripper—that you're just looking after Brodie for me until you get another job?'

'I didn't tell him anything because it's none of his business,' Paige said firmly. 'And I'm really sorry I had to visit you at work. I hope your boss wasn't too angry, but Brodie got sick so quickly. He was fine when I went down to pay the rent, but we were only halfway home when I

36

could see he had a temperature, and I didn't have enough money to take him to the doctor.'

'Oh, the boss was a bit snippy, but she's got kids of her own so she understood. She let me off early without squealing.' Yawning, Sherry poured water into two mismatched mugs and brought one across to Paige.

Who sighed and asked, 'Why don't you give up stripping? You hate it and—'

'I'll give it up when I've paid off the debts my rat of a husband ran up in my name and when I've saved enough money to make a future for Brodie,' Sherry said firmly. 'I'm not brainy, like you. All I've got to offer is a good body and a sense of rhythm. Where else would I get decent money unless I worked the streets? And I'm not going to do that.'

Paige grimaced. 'Of course you won't.'

'Bloody men,' Sherry said, lowering herself onto the sofa. 'I'll bring Brodie up to think a lot more highly of women than his conman of a father ever did, I can tell you.' She glanced down at her finger, as though remembering the wedding ring that had once been there. 'He's going to be educated. He won't mortgage the house and gamble it away, then skip to Australia when he's found out.'

Paige raised her coffee mug. 'Here's to responsible men,' she said mockingly.

'I'll drink to that.'

But both women laughed.

Much later, as the sleepless night stretched before her, Paige lay in bed and deliberately let herself recall the first time she'd met Marc Corbett.

Only seventeen, she'd been so giddy with excitement she'd hardly been able to put two coherent thoughts to-

gether. With Juliette's bombshell request to be her bridesmaid had come an invitation to her mother and first-class
tickets to Paris. Although her mother had refused to travel,
Lloyd had insisted that Paige go, offering to pay her expenses.

She thought now that she'd have been safer staying in
her pleasant pastoral sanctuary at Bellhaven.

Yet it had all started so well. After the reunion with
Juliette she'd discovered that their friendship still held.
And then—oh, Paris! She'd loved the fittings for her gor-
geous dress, the art galleries, the museums, the wonderful
gardens—especially the gardens! Thoughtful as ever,
Juliette had organised visits to several.

Marc had been on a business trip in Asia, not returning
until two days before the wedding. They had met at a chic
private dinner put on by his even more chic mother in her
splendidly opulent apartment.

Introduced by a proud Juliette, Paige had looked into
his remote, handsome face with sharp awareness and a
terrifying, heated interest. Bewildered by the intensity of
her response, she'd been formal and quiet, hoping that no
one had noticed.

Restlessly Paige turned over in the bed and opened her
eyes. Lights flashed across the window as a car rumbled
into the forecourt, its engine kicking oddly before it died.
Its door thudded shut, followed by the front door of a unit.
Somewhere towards the port a siren sounded, eerily dis-
cordant.

In Paris the bridal party had stayed in a hotel, and after
Marc had brought them back from his mother's dinner
party Paige had gone to her room, tactfully leaving him
with his fiancée.

But about half an hour later he'd knocked on the door.

When she'd opened it her silly heart had looped a wild circle in her chest.

'I think you should have this tonight,' he said, holding out a small, exquisitely wrapped parcel. 'As you are to wear it tomorrow.'

Eyeing it, she said wonderingly, 'What is it?'

His smile melted her spine. 'It's traditional for the bridegroom to give the bridesmaid a gift,' he told her. And when she didn't reach for it he said a little impatiently, 'This is it.'

Almost reluctantly she took the small parcel, flushing because her hand shook when his fingers touched hers. 'Thank you,' she half-whispered, mortified by the small betrayal.

She should have closed the door then, and opened the gift in her room, but by then she'd already started fumbling with the bow and the ribbon, so acutely conscious of him watching her that she felt he could see her forbidden excitement.

It was a jeweller's box. Paige's breath stopped in her throat. All she could hear was the feverish tattoo of her heart as she flicked it open.

It dazzled her with its beauty—a round gold pendant on a heavy gold chain, the link set with a diamond that flashed and gleamed as blue as his eyes.

'It's perfect,' she said huskily, keeping her head down. 'Thank you so much.'

'It's a locket,' he told her. 'For keeping pictures of one's lovers.' His voice deepened. 'Or one particular lover.'

Heat flamed through her. 'Thank you,' she said again, because she couldn't find any other words.

Silence, thick and pulsing with hidden intensity, linked them in a frightening cell of intimacy.

Marc broke it with a quick, harsh question. 'Are you going to put it on?'

She hesitated, then took the lovely thing from the velvet box and looped it around her neck. Every tiny hair on her body stood upright; her skin, oddly too tight, prickled with sensation as she fumbled the catch.

'Turn around,' Marc told her, that note of impatience roughening his voice again.

Mouth dry, she obeyed, and he did it up, his fingers cool on the nape of her neck. Excitement rode her hard with a jolt of pure fusion—fire and ice and a rushing thrill that almost overwhelmed her.

'There,' he said, his voice oddly clipped, and stepped back.

Slowly, afraid of what she might see in his face, she turned towards him. He looked at the locket against her skin.

'Very pretty,' he said distantly, his voice as steady as his eyes. But in his jaw a muscle flicked once, twice, three times.

'Thank you,' she said, a cold unease spreading beneath her ribs. She didn't know how to close this, so she gave a brief, meaningless smile and stepped back, shutting the door against him and leaning back on it with her stomach lurching.

He had looked at her as she had seen her father look at the woman he'd left her mother for. And, although Paige was a virgin, she'd seen enough of illicit desire to recognise its heavy, ominous throb.

Snatching off the locket, Paige dropped it into the box and snapped it shut, horrified by the sensations rioting through her—an aching sweetness and a reckless urgency that made her breasts tingle and her body throb.

Sick at heart, she despised herself. Tomorrow Marc was

going to marry her best friend, but for a moment she'd wanted him with a desire that scared her witless. A few words, a touch, an exchange of glances had been all it took to transmute her innocent awareness into a heated, urgent need.

For the whole of the next day, the locket that Juliette insisted she wear burned like fire against her skin.

A month later, Paige staggered out of bed and struggled into her clothes before tiptoeing past Sherry's firmly closed door. Brodie's chickenpox was now a dim memory, and although he'd graduated to sleeping right through the night, she didn't want to disturb either him or his mother.

Paige glanced at her watch. He usually didn't stir until the shift worker next door slammed his car door and revved out of the car park. She had a bit more than an hour to do her part-time job and pick up the newspaper so she could scan the situations vacant.

She fought back a clutch of panic; although she wasn't any closer to finding a job, she could now claim the dole. However, that wouldn't be enough to pay Sherry back for the last three weeks' rent, so Paige was now walking two dogs every morning from Monday to Friday.

It helped, but not enough. If she couldn't get a job, she'd have to leave; Sherry couldn't afford to keep supporting her, even if she did look after Brodie in return. Her own dreams had been put on hold; she wasn't going to shatter Sherry's.

Her charges, a large German Shepherd and a vigorous Jack Russell, welcomed her with their usual seething energy; once in the park she threw a ball for them to scrap over.

When they'd worked off most of their high spirits they set off along the riverbank, the Jack Russell making eager forays into the scrub after rabbits, the gentler German Shepherd bitch at Paige's heel, except for occasional side trips when a particularly exciting smell seduced her.

Fortunately they kept her busy enough supervising so that her brain couldn't wander in forbidden directions. As swiftly as he'd appeared Marc had dropped out of her life. A note the day after they'd met had explained that he'd been called overseas on business and he was hers, Marc.

Not that she'd expected to see him again, but she'd been furious with herself for the terrible desolation that had swept over her. He meant nothing to her, and he couldn't have made it more obvious that she meant nothing to him.

Which was just the way she'd expected things to be.

The wind, cooled by thousands of miles of southern ocean, pounced onto her, flattening the thin material of her jersey against her skin. She firmed her mouth against a shiver. Unfortunately, her recovery from the shock of his arrival wasn't helped by his appearance every night in her dreams.

The sudden alertness of the bigger dog, followed almost immediately by an aggressive fusillade of barking from the smaller, swivelled her head around. A man was striding towards her from the direction of the road, his long legs covering the ground with rapid efficiency.

Pulses leaping, she faltered, then stopped. Tall, dark and dominant, it could only be Marc. Talk about the devil...!

For one horribly embarrassing moment she found herself wishing she'd worn something better than threadbare jeans and an elderly jersey that matched the colour of her eyes but had long since seen off its better days.

Then embarrassment was banished by a disturbing jolt of energy that jump-started both her heart and her breathing.

So much for getting over it, a small inner voice jeered silently.

'Sit,' she said sharply as the dogs danced protectively around her. When they'd obeyed she turned to face the man striding towards her, shoulders squared, jaw jutting at a deliberate angle.

Her stomach contracted as though expecting a blow. He wasn't smiling, but she sensed a leashed satisfaction behind the impassive mask of his face. It was unfair that the sun should bronze his aquiline features with such besotted accuracy. Goaded, she lifted her head so high her neck muscles began to protest, and directed a carefully cool gaze at him.

He said, 'Are you all right?' When she stared blankly at him, he said, 'Sherry said you'd had the flu. What the hell are you doing walking dogs on these cold mornings?'

Rallying her defences, Paige returned, 'I'm better now.'

'You don't look it,' he said bluntly, surveying her with a hard blue gaze. 'You're pale and you've got great dark circles under your eyes.'

When he'd first met her she'd been a glowing, sensuously vibrant girl, her warmth reflected in her skin and dark honey hair, in the green-gold depths of her large, black-lashed eyes. A month ago she'd been tired, but now—now, he thought forcefully, she looked like a woman whose reserves had been plundered too often— fragile, strained and exhausted. An inconvenient protectiveness stirred to life in him, followed by a deep, uncompromising anger.

'It was a nasty virus, but I'm feeling a hundred per cent better than I did this time last week,' she said stiffly, and clenched her teeth on another shiver.

'You shouldn't be out in this cold wind.'

He stripped off his jacket and, before she realised what

he was doing, slung it around her shoulders, turning her to wrap it around her. The body heat still clinging to the leather enveloped her, bringing a rapid lick of fire scorching up through her skin.

'I don't—' she muttered, trying to shrug the jacket from her shoulders.

Hard hands clamped it on. He said in a voice that sent shocks charging through her veins, 'If you don't keep it on, I'll pick you up and carry you back to the car.'

Even if she hadn't glanced into his unyielding face, she'd have known by the tone of his voice that he meant it. And the jacket was wonderfully warm, faintly scented with a fragrance that was as natural as his warmth.

Awkwardly, she muttered, 'Thanks. What are you doing here?' She stopped, the colour fading as she met eyes as cold and blue as polar ice.

He'd met Sherry.

Her gaze slid sideways. Then she rallied. 'I hope you didn't wake Sherry and Brodie.'

'They were already awake,' he said indifferently. 'I'm glad to see Brodie is over his chickenpox.'

Baffled, she said, 'He's fine. Why did you come back?'

'I told you last time. We have things to discuss.' The silky note in his voice tightened her skin.

'And I told you we have nothing to discuss,' she returned, her voice cold and remote, her eyes hard. 'We belong to different worlds.'

'If you believe that you're deliberately deluding yourself. But you don't believe that.' His words were cool and deliberate, at odds with the formidable aura he projected.

The Jack Russell growled.

Paige said sweetly, 'Tiger is an attack dog.'

Correctly judging the smaller dog to be the natural pack

leader, Marc held out an authoritative hand, letting it and then the German Shepherd sniff his fingers.

To Paige's irritation it was obvious that they accepted him as an Alpha male. After polite nasal inspections of the hems of his trouser legs, both sat down and panted cheerfully at him, tongues lolling.

He read Paige's expression correctly. Still in that smooth tone, he said, 'I like dogs; I have one of my own. Why did you deliberately let me think Brodie was yours?'

Paige shook her head. 'You didn't ask,' she pointed out, hoping her low voice hid the clammy pool of dismay beneath her ribs.

She didn't want him here, especially not in Napier, but even somewhere in the same country was too close. Why didn't he go back to the château in France, or the huge New York apartment, or the gracious Georgian house in London—anywhere but New Zealand?

He was too much, and the reactions she'd managed to ignore during the past month had exploded into life again.

'Why do he and his mother live with you?' For a moment she considered telling him to mind his own business, but he said satirically, 'I'm sure that if I offered Sherry a big enough sum of money she'd tell me.'

'How lucky you are to be overbearingly rich and famous,' she purred, her wits revitalised by another swift surge of adrenaline.

At this rate she'd overdose on it, but she'd shaken off the lethargy and depression that had followed her bout with the flu. Why had it taken this man, one she despised, to make her feel alive again?

'It's one of the perks,' he agreed without shame. 'Well?'

Marc decided that the insolent composure with which she met his lifted brows was a challenge in itself—one he was finding it more and more hard to resist.

She said with delicate scorn, 'Offer Sherry money to tell you, then. She needs it.'

Marc almost smiled. He never knew what she was going to say; the unexpectedness of her reactions was refreshing and intriguing. 'Why did you let me think that you were a stripper?'

'Because it was none of your business whether I was a stripper—or even a horrible example,' she returned crisply.

He frowned, recalling Lauren's teasing question in the foyer of the hotel. 'She didn't know you could hear.'

'I know. It's a quirk of acoustics.' Paige shrugged and called the restless dogs to heel. 'It doesn't matter—she's entitled to her opinion, even though she's pretty quick to judge.'

True, but he hadn't come to talk about Lauren. 'Last time I was here something blew up and I had to leave before I'd planned to. It took longer than I expected, but I always intended to come back. We do need to talk, Paige.'

'No.'

Marc noted absolute determination in her slender spine, straight and strong as steel reinforcing. This, he thought, with the relish he usually brought to boardroom battles, was going to be a fight—one he'd enjoy winning.

Which meant taking her by surprise. She was braced for battle, so he said, 'I'm calling this off. You're not making much of a fist of hiding those shivers.'

He whistled at the dogs. Maddeningly, both frisked towards him as if pulled by invisible strings. Made temporarily witless by such highhanded tactics, Paige even passed over the leashes when he held out a peremptory hand for them, watching with increasing resentment as he hooked on each dog with efficiency and speed.

Determined not to give in so easily, Paige glanced at

her watch. 'It's time we turned back, anyway,' she said, knowing it was surrender. Whether she wanted to go back or not, Marc was the one in control here.

White teeth flashed in an ironic smile. 'I'll go with you.'

'The dogs are my responsibility.' She held out her hand for the leashes.

Nodding, he gave them to her, then set off beside her, his tall, lean, graceful body shielding her from the sharp nip of the wind. Not that much got through his jacket, but his consideration made her melt inside.

It wasn't personal, she told herself scornfully. He'd do it for any woman.

Her senses seemed to have sharpened; the sun beat more warmly on her skin and the grass glowed iridescently green, while she was sure she hadn't ever noticed the faint, evocative perfume of some flowering plant before. Even the birds called with a more seductive sweetness.

Stop it! she commanded her traitorous body. Last week had been the second anniversary of Juliette's death; if he'd thought about her at all he could have found her any time in those two years. He'd have only needed to tell someone, Find this woman, and it would have been done.

But he hadn't done it. Keep that in mind, she told herself grimly.

After a few steps she asked, 'Where's your car?'

Walking beside him was boosting this terrifying, tantalising tension. She needed to stride out briskly and clear her mind of the fumes of desire summoned by the heady chemistry of his smile.

'Over by the road.' He nodded at a shape in the distance.

Baffled, she tamped down her anger and decided to make the best of the situation. 'All right, tell me whatever it is you want to—now.'

'Very well.' He sounded amused, but the humour left his voice with his next words. 'Juliette left you a legacy.'

She stopped abruptly. 'What?'

Long fingers around her elbow urged her on. 'In her will she left you a box. I don't know what it is. She also left you a sum of money.'

'I see,' she said colourlessly.

She pulled free of his grip, but she thought she could still feel the imprint of his fingers traced in molten outline on her skin. Oh, yes, right through your jersey and shirt, she scoffed, struggling to keep her equilibrium in a world suddenly tumbled off its axis.

'It's very kind of you, but you didn't have to come all the way here to tell me about Juliette's legacy,' she returned with crisp brevity. 'You can post the box to me. And I don't want any money. Give it to charity.'

'Ungracious as well as stubborn,' he observed in a pleasant tone that barely hid his contempt.

She stiffened. 'I'm not—I didn't mean to sound like that.' He waited in aloof silence until she finished lamely, 'I assume the box is a memento. I'd like that very much. But not money.'

'One comes with the other, I'm afraid,' he said flatly. 'And there are conditions.'

One simmering glance at his unyielding face told her he wasn't going to move on this. And that she wasn't going to like the conditions. 'What are they?' she asked, forcing the words out between her gritted teeth.

'Come to breakfast with me and I'll tell you.'

'Why can't you tell me here?'

He lifted his brows. 'Because you're already cold,' he pointed out. 'You're shivering, and your lips are starting to turn blue. And because Juliette's bequest deserves more than a few words exchanged in a park. I'd have thought you felt the same. Although you didn't see anything of each other in the last few years of her life, I know she kept in touch; I think in many ways you were her best friend. Is it too much to ask that you give me time to tell you about this?'

She went white. 'That's unfair and manipulative,' she flung back at him.

His broad shoulders lifted. 'The truth can't be manipulation,' he said, without giving an inch.

After a short hesitation she muttered, 'Oh, all right. I have to drop the dogs off, but I'll be at the flat in twenty minutes.'

'I'll take you and the dogs back,' he said implacably.

And, in spite of everything she could say, ten minutes saw both dogs transported to their home and Paige back at the flat.

When she emerged from the quickest shower she'd ever had, she could hear conversation in the living room—or rather she heard Sherry laughing over Marc's deep tones. Biting her lip, she took down a pair of chocolate-brown trousers and topped them with a corduroy shirt in a shade of spicy red that flattered her hair and her skin. Because the shower hadn't been able to warm her completely, she wore a creamy-white turtleneck beneath the shirt.

Lipstick gave her pale face a bit of warmth, but she still felt like something discovered under a stone—no fit state to have breakfast with Marc Corbett.

And, she thought masochistically, about as far removed from his original companion as anyone could be. In fact, the woman's scarf had probably cost more than her entire wardrobe was worth.

Not that Paige cared.

Yet she went out with a cake-mixer churning in her

stomach and had to force her face into an expression of cool disinterest as she came through the door.

Marc's vitality hit her like a blow to the solar plexus.

His uncomfortably perceptive eyes blazed and his mouth relaxed into a smile that held more than a hint of mockery. Casual though his clothes were, Paige recognised the superb tailoring that covered broad shoulders and long legs with loving fidelity.

He was—overpowering. The first time she'd met him she'd sensed the heat that smouldered behind the cool restraints of his will power—sensed it and been scared by it.

It was still there, and she was still afraid.

But she was more afraid of the excitement infiltrating her body, heating into a subtle arousal, as they said their goodbyes to Sherry and went out to the car.

CHAPTER FOUR

ONCE in the passenger's seat, Paige pasted a brittle skin over her turbulent emotions. 'It's going to be a glorious day when this wind dies down.'

'How long is it since you've had the flu?'

So much for the cheering effect of a bright shirt and some lipstick. 'Surely I don't look that bad?' she retorted.

And immediately clamped her lips in disbelief. Oh, what an opening! Marc took it, too, examining her from the top of her head to the hands that linked so tensely in her lap.

'You look as though you haven't fully recovered,' he said calmly, twisting the key. The engine purred into life, soft as the sound of luxury—yet, like its driver, it reeked of dangerous, barely curbed power. 'Sherry told me that you wouldn't let her call the doctor.'

'Doctors can't do anything for viruses,' she returned, wishing her flatmate had kept her mouth shut.

Efficiently backing the car out, Marc said with a touch of irritation, 'They can prescribe medication for any complications.'

'I didn't have any. It was just plain old ordinary flu—nasty, like flu always is, but I've recovered.'

After a stiletto-sharp, disbelieving glance, he commented, 'It's good to see little Brodie looking so much better.'

Welcoming a neutral subject, Paige said, 'The medication worked fast; he didn't have another convulsion and you guessed right—he was much better the next day.'

The big car moved smoothly out onto the street. A few

hundred metres later, Marc said coolly, 'I gather you've been looking after him while Sherry works?'

'Yes.'

'What hours?'

'From the middle of the afternoon to whenever she comes home.' Her voice was stiff and prickly.

'Every day?'

She shook her head. 'She has two days off each week.'

To her relief he didn't speak again until he'd parked the car outside a house up on the Port Hill.

'I thought we were going to a restaurant,' she objected, looking around with suspicion she didn't try to hide.

'I'm staying here,' he said laconically.

With his girlfriend? 'In a *house*?'

'Hotels bore me. I prefer being with friends.'

A cold emptiness expanded under her ribs.

His glance sliced through her. 'Paige, I'm not planning to murder you and tip you over the cliff,' he said, each word an exercise in icy precision. 'If you don't want to eat here I'll take you to the nearest restaurant and we can talk about Juliette's legacy in front of anyone who's interested.'

Murder had been the last thing on her mind, but she was being stupid; Marc was too worldly—and had far too much self-control—to give in to any wild clamour of the senses.

It was her own responses she was afraid of. However, as she certainly wasn't going to fling herself into his arms and pant, Take me! she'd be safe enough.

But she continued, 'What about your friend—the person who owns the house? I haven't been invited.'

'They're not here at the moment.' His hooded blue glance skimmed her face. 'They work. They know that you're coming to breakfast, and if it makes you feel better

I'll take you to meet them on the way home and introduce you.'

He sounded thoroughly fed up. 'That won't be necessary,' Paige said uncomfortably, and at last got out.

She could just imagine what his friends would be like—Hawke Bay aristocracy, with children who went to exclusive and expensive boarding schools and a circle of friends as sophisticated as Marc.

Sure enough, the house was luxurious—and superbly decorated. A crawling tension knotted her stomach as he escorted her into a dining room filled with sun and reflected light from the sea below.

'Sit down,' he said, indicating a table set with cheerful napkins and china. 'You look as though you could do with a jolt of caffeine.'

Once she was seated he brought in toast, fruit, porridge and coffee and juice, moving with the confidence of someone who had done this frequently.

Surprised, because she'd understood from Juliette that they had lived in some state—even his New Zealand home in the Bay of Islands had a resident housekeeper—Paige managed to eat a piece of toast and sip orange juice while he demolished a plate of porridge.

With a swift quirk of his lips he said, 'My father was one of the old school—he firmly believed that a man couldn't work on anything other than a plate of porridge.'

She smiled. Clearly robber barons had traditional tastes. 'Mine loved sausages and bacon.' Her mother had tried to convince him that he'd die of a heart attack. And he had.

But not until he'd been long gone from their lives.

Marc's sharp scrutiny sent a swift jab of sensation up her spine, but he began to discuss the upcoming election and she relaxed—as much as it was possible when she felt as nervous as though she was perched on the lip of an active volcano.

Eventually he said without preamble, 'The box Juliette left you is at Arohanui, my home in Northland. In her will she asked that you come to the island and collect it. She wanted you to stay a week there.'

Paige was already shaking her head. 'No,' she said huskily. 'It's impossible.'

'Why?'

Impatiently she retorted, 'I have to look after Brodie.'

He drank from his cup of coffee then set it down. 'Is that the only reason? Do you have someone who'd object? If so, bring him.'

Paige flushed. 'There's no one,' she said shortly, secretly resenting his indifference at the idea of her with another man. 'Brodie's the main reason I can't come, but I also walk the dogs every morning. You'll have to post it to me.'

'It's not that easy.'

Her voice settled into syrupy sweetness. 'It's not too hard to post a parcel, you know. You just wrap it up—possibly the housekeeper could do that for you—and take it to a post office. They'll do the rest.'

'Provocation isn't going to get you anywhere,' he drawled. 'The dogs and Brodie can be taken care of.'

Paige looked at him with simmering dislike. 'I've no doubt you can do that, but I need to earn some money until I get a job.'

'Do you have any interviews scheduled?'

'No,' she admitted reluctantly. 'Still, I'm not going to find jobs in Napier advertised in the local newspaper in the Bay of Islands!'

'I can organise that too,' he said casually. 'Most of the local papers will be on the Internet; if they're not, I'll get someone down here to look at the Sits Vac while you're away. Juliette wanted you to come up to Arohanui, and I think it's the least you can do for her.'

Paige bit back caustic words. *And your mistress? Will she be there too?*

Instead she spread her hands in bewilderment. 'What made her think of leaving me something? She couldn't have had any idea that…that she was going to die so tragically.'

'I insisted she made a will after we were married,' Marc said evenly. 'As for leaving you a memento—why not, for a friend she loved dearly? It's often done.'

She peered up through her lashes, saw his tanned skin tighten over the thrusting bone structure beneath. He looked completely self-assured, but his eyes were sombre beneath their heavy lids.

Reluctantly she accepted that although he might have hurt Juliette, he could miss her and grieve for a life cut so unfairly short.

The taste of coffee bitter in her mouth, Paige said, 'I didn't expect anything from her.'

'I know. And if you're wondering why you weren't told of this sooner, she specifically stated that her bequest not be given to you until two years after her death.'

Startled, she glanced at his face, met eyes as coldly crystalline as the blue depths of a glacier.

'Why?' she asked blankly. 'It seems odd to wait for two years, then ask me to go to Arohanui. She wasn't a person to indulge in whims, and she didn't even like—'

'The island? I know.' He lifted his shoulders in an eloquent shrug. 'She would have had a reason. Unfortunately, I have no idea what it was. But I intend to see that her wishes are met.'

Paige stared at the lazily swirling surface of her coffee.

Some part of her wished violently that Juliette hadn't remembered her like this. 'Do you know what it is, whatever she left me?'

One black brow shot up. 'No. It's small, so I suspect it's a piece of jewellery or some keepsake.'

'I can't afford to go,' she said baldly. 'I mean it; I haven't got the money to get there or home again.'

'That isn't relevant.'

She bristled. 'I don't want charity.'

Marc fixed her with another frigid shaft of ice-blue. 'She wanted to give you this,' he said, crushing and blunt. 'Is it too much of a sacrifice? A week of your time to fulfil the last thing she will ever ask of you?'

Paige scrambled to her feet and faced him across the table. 'You're a devious, manipulative swine,' she whispered.

He rose also. 'But you already knew that,' he said, his courteous tone a more pointed sword than any insult.

'I know exactly what you are,' Paige said between her teeth.

With a contemptuous smile Marc returned, 'Whatever you think of me, be assured that I have enough self-control not to force myself on women who don't want me.'

'I—I don't think…I mean, I wasn't thinking of that,' she said huskily.

But she had been, and he knew it. Humiliation ate into her composure; she was being ridiculous, because although he might find her attractive his self-control was legendary. She was making too much of this fierce awareness; what did she know about sex? Or the relations between the sexes, come to that? Her last boyfriend had been at high school, and she was that rare and exotic creature, a twenty-three-year-old virgin whose experience was confined to a little mild groping and a few enthusiastic but innocent kisses.

Marc was probably laughing at her.

He said calmly, 'If it makes you feel more confident, I plan to fly to Australia the day after I drop you off at the island.' He watched her with narrowed, piercing eyes, yet his voice warmed into a reassurance that sapped her will. 'Paige, please come up to Arohanui. I'll fly you up, and you can come back any way you choose to travel.'

Marc examined her pale, set face, despising himself because a ruthless need burned beneath the honest desire to do this last thing for Juliette.

A sardonic twist to his lips matched his emotions. He could do this; he could master his hunger.

Even as he monitored Paige's face for clues to her decision he was wondering what made him want her. Something subtler, more enigmatic than beauty, although his eyes appreciated skin like satin and the fine regular features that weren't particularly memorable—if you excluded green-gold eyes on a tantalising tilt, and a very determined chin.

Not to mention a lush mouth that beckoned with sultry promise in spite of its tight discipline, and a body that hinted of sensuous delights—slender and lithe and rounded. He tried to ignore the inconvenient stirring in his loins.

She was no push-over, but at the moment her defences were almost breached; she looked exhausted, and he resented the protective feeling that gripped him again.

'Don't make a big deal out of it,' he said, and took her cold hands in his, producing his trump card. 'I don't know why Juliette made it a condition that you come up to Arohanui, but as she did I'd like to see that her wishes are carried out.'

She shivered, shadows darkening her eyes to a defeated green as she lowered her lashes and looked away, and he knew he had her.

Pulling her hands free, she walked across to the window, her jerky movements revealing her agitation. When she turned back to face him he couldn't see her expression against the brilliance of sky and sea outside, but the tension in her shoulders told him she'd made a decision.

'All right,' she said, reluctance flattening her voice, 'but I'll have to organise things. I'm not going if Sherry can't get the time off to look after Brodie.'

Marc reined in a surge of satisfaction that eroded his control. 'I can help there.'

She gave him a slanting, rebellious look, but said with polite dismissal, 'Thank you, but that won't be necessary.'

A realist, and more than a little cynical, Marc knew that even without his wealth he'd be attractive to the opposite sex, so he was accustomed to women who looked at him and saw the promise of security. Or, at the very least, relished the prospect of fattening their bank balance while enjoying sex with him.

It was, he admitted wryly, unusual to have a woman treat him with barely concealed distrust. Was that why she was such a challenge?

No, he wasn't that cynical—or that shallow. For some reason she intrigued him at a primal, gut level that had the power to overthrow the checks and restraints he'd imposed on his passions.

'We'll see,' he said levelly. 'Now, I'm going to have bacon and eggs. Would you like to join me?'

Paige was astonished to feel her stomach growl softly in response. 'I—thank you.'

'Sit down and I'll bring some through—or you can come and watch me cook, if you like.'

'You can cook?' She didn't try to hide her astonishment.

When he smiled her body's demands changed to hunger of a different sort. 'Of course I can cook,' he said calmly, opening the door into a room that turned out to be a kitchen.

Not just any old kitchen, either; this one was a chef's dream. He stood back to let her through, the courtesy so automatic it meant nothing.

'And I suppose you can climb mountains without oxygen and fight grizzly bears with your bare hands?' she scoffed, but she went ahead of him.

'No, I only tackle lions bare-handed. For grizzly bears I carry a knife between my teeth,' he said cheerfully.

Paige laughed spontaneously. After a swift, heart-shivering smile, he set about grilling bacon. Paige watched his efficient handling of kitchen tools with something like wonder.

She'd become accustomed to thinking of him as the man who sparked her hormones into a sexual frenzy—and as Juliette's husband. Forbidden fruit, in other words. His relationship with Lauren Porter had reinforced her view of him as a predator whose only interest outside business was sexual intrigue.

The man deftly cooking her breakfast bore no resemblance to the bogeyman she'd manufactured. And that made him more risky, because she could despise a sexual predator.

An hour later Paige got out of the car and said pleasantly, 'Thank you for breakfast. It was delicious.'

He glanced at the thin gold watch on his tanned wrist. 'I'll see you at nine.'

With a scintillating, seething glance she spluttered, 'That's ridiculous. I can't organise everything in such a short time.'

'In two hours, then,' he said inexorably, concealing his keen scrutiny with a veil of long lashes.

Used like that, they were weapons. Fighting their effect, she said stiffly, 'I can't promise anything.'

He smiled and said, 'At ten o'clock, Paige. Don't worry, I'll take care of everything.'

Watching Marc taking care of everything was an education in raw power.

Standing at the window, Sherry watched his car leave the car park and said in a stunned voice, 'Whew! Talk about dynamite. I can see how he got to be a zillionaire!' She looked self-consciously at Paige. 'I'm sorry you disapprove of him paying for me to stay home with Brodie.'

Paige continued firing clothes into the only case she possessed—a pack Lloyd had given her one Christmas. 'I don't disapprove,' she said lightly. 'It's got nothing to do with me. But won't your boss object?'

Looking slightly smug, and rather too self-conscious, Sherry shook her head. 'No. I know I shouldn't have taken Marc's money, but he's not going to miss it.'

It wasn't a question, but Paige answered it. 'No, of course not.' She added more clothes and her sponge bag, wishing with futile foolishness that she had some outfit that didn't proclaim its provenance—a mail-order catalogue. 'I hate surprises! I wish you hadn't told him where I was this morning.'

Sherry flushed and patted Brodie's back. 'He's not the sort of man you refuse,' she said a little guiltily.

'I know. Don't take any notice of me—I'm just angry at being more or less railroaded into this.'

'Are you sure it's a good idea?'

'No,' Paige said on a sigh. 'But—well, if Juliette wanted me to go to Arohanui to pick up her bequest, I feel I'd be letting her down if I didn't.' She tucked a pair of socks into her sandshoes and zipped up the pack. 'That will have to do.'

In the sitting room, Sherry sat down on the sofa and smiled at her son. He lifted a small arm and waved it around, cooing as his mother kissed his face.

'How come you were such great friends with his wife?' she asked. 'This dude of yours is seriously loaded; that sort marry their own kind. And usually they make friends with their own kind.'

'He's not my dude!' Paige filled the new kettle. Above the sound of running water, she said, 'Juliette and I lived next door to each other in Wellington. She was five years older, but she adored kids—she used to call me her pretty little sister, although she was the pretty one. When they moved I cried so much that she promised me I could be her bridesmaid. At eleven that's a big deal.'

Sherry looked intrigued. 'You're right. And she followed through?'

'Yes, with a week in Paris and the most gorgeous dress.' And Marc's locket.

Sherry said drily, 'So Juliette was loaded too?'

'I never thought of it, but her family must have been. Her father was in the diplomatic service.'

'She sounds nice.'

'She was great—kind and fun. She kept in touch even after she was married.' Heat stung Paige's cheeks as she poured boiling water into the mugs.

'And then she got killed,' Sherry said sympathetically. 'That's tough.'

What was tougher was that for Marc the marriage had been a sham, a marriage of convenience entered into because he'd needed a suitable wife.

'Yes.' Frowning, Paige looked around. 'Now, are you sure you'll be OK?'

'We'll be fine,' Sherry repeated patiently. 'How did you get on with the dogs?'

'Mrs Greig grumbled, but the high school boy next door will do them until I come back.' She carried the two mugs of coffee across and sat down on a chair.

Sherry put Brodie down on the sofa to kick. 'You can't get out of this, so you might as well treat it like a mini-holiday,' she said, looking up from rapt admiration of his chubby legs. 'Heaven knows, you could do with it. You've had a rotten spin in the last year. It'll be warmer up in the Bay of Islands—see if you can get a little bit of tan.'

Paige looked up as a car drew up outside and Marc got out. 'Time to go,' she muttered, her heart jumping.

Sherry picked Brodie up and turned to scrutinise Marc. 'Oh, boy, he really is something,' she said softly. 'You be careful, Paige.'

Skin tightening, Paige went across and opened the door. 'Ready?' Marc asked.

'Yes.'

She stood back to let him in, and Paige wasn't surprised when Sherry, dazzled out of her usual cynicism where men were concerned, proudly handed the baby over to him.

Marc cradled him with confidence, smiling into the little face. For once the baby didn't deliver the usual roar he kept for strangers. Solemn-faced, he stared up at Marc, before producing a one-sided smile and clenching his fists in an energetic fashion.

'I think he knows me,' Marc said, smiling with immense charm.

Clearly dazzled, Brodie lifted an arm and waved it vaguely above his head while he produced soft gurgles.

Sherry nodded briskly and took the baby back. 'Looks

like it. Before you go, I'd better have an address and a phone number—just in case I need to contact you, Paige.'

'I'll give you my card.' Marc pulled a sleek wallet from his pocket and took out a card, scribbled on the back and handed it to Sherry.

She made no bones about reading it. 'Arohanui Island. Where's that?'

While Marc told her, Paige watched the corners of his mouth tuck in as he fought a smile. Of course he knew what Sherry was doing—her implied warning wasn't very subtle.

Sherry nodded, and, being a loyal daughter of the dry province of Hawke Bay, said, 'It rains a lot up there, I hear.'

'Not all the time,' Marc said with another dizzying smile. He stowed his wallet back in his pocket and looked across at Paige, a silent spectator. 'We should be going. The plane's waiting.'

He meant that quite literally. Half an hour later they were heading north in a chartered plane big enough to take ten or so people. Normally Paige would have enjoyed admiring New Zealand's wild central plateau, with its three snow-covered volcanoes marching southwards from Lake Taupo—its serene blue-grey waters the biggest crater of all—but there was nothing normal about the luxurious little plane or the trip.

She picked up a fashion magazine from the several the steward had presented to her after she'd refused his offer of champagne. The cover featured in loving and explicit detail a stunning red-headed woman clad in a swathe of silk and ostrich feathers; she appeared to be making love to a classical pillar.

Paige put the magazine down.

From the corner of her eye she could see Marc's hands

across the aisle as he sorted papers. They were beautiful—
long-fingered and strong, competently shuffling the documents. What would they feel like—?

Don't go there! Now that she was actually on her way
to his island she wondered how on earth she'd made such
a decision. He must have bewitched her.

No, she'd let herself be overborne by his stronger will,
and by a need to give Juliette whatever she had wanted
with this odd request.

Why had she made it? And why ask that Marc wait so
long after her death before contacting Paige? It didn't
make sense.

She glanced sideways again, this time lifting her eyes
to his face. He was now absorbed in reading one of the
documents, his profile an autocratic harmony of lines and
angles, but beneath the veneer of smoothly civilised power
pulsed a dark arrogance, an uncompromising force of will
that made her shiver inside.

He'd be a formidable enemy.

Dragging her eyes free, Paige leaned back and watched
cloud shadows chase themselves over the green, green
countryside beneath, Sherry's last words echoing in her
mind.

As Marc had carried Paige's bag out to his car, her
flatmate had muttered, 'Standing directly between you is
like walking into a furnace.' She watched Marc close the
boot of the car. 'I bet he's good,' she said, and smiled
reminiscently. 'Be careful, Paige. But why don't you have
some fun for once?'

Fun?

Paige stole another glance at the man reading papers
with efficient speed. Her stomach clamped on a spasm of
roiling sensation, sweet and strong and potent.

It wouldn't be fun. He might make love like a dark angel, but she stood to lose her heart if she—

Her mind closed down. She was *not* falling in love with him. Glaring at the hands in her lap, she forcibly reminded herself that he'd married Juliette for convenience, and the equally convenient Lauren Porter was still in the picture.

OK, so she felt something for him, but it certainly wasn't love. Lust, Marc had called it, and quoted Shakespeare with such contempt that she still felt cold when she thought of his voice, detached and brutally uncompromising, as he'd let her know exactly what he thought of this disruptive chemistry between them.

CHAPTER FIVE

SHE woke to hands at her waist and a darkly masculine voice forcing its way through compelling, X-rated dreams.

When she forced her lashes up Marc's tanned face swam into vision—too close, the hard features intent and purposeful. Her heart slammed into her throat as her dazed eyes met the burning blue of his. He was crouched in front of her, broad shoulders blocking out the aircraft cabin.

'What—?' she stammered, still fighting sleep and the corroding pleasure of his nearness. 'What is it? Are we there?'

'Not quite.'

His voice sounded guttural even to his own ears, and he took in a deep breath, watching her pupils dilate and darkness swamp the green-gold fire in an involuntary signal—one his body recognised and responded to with helpless, instant hunger that consigned caution to the rubbish bin. Every cell reacted with violent appreciation to her provocative, heavy-lidded gaze and the soft lips slightly parted in unconscious seduction.

'What are you doing?' Although the words emerged with a crisp bite he noted their husky, sensuous undertone.

'We'll be landing soon,' he said roughly. 'The seatbelt warning is on. I tried to fasten yours without waking you.'

Yet his hands refused to move, curving almost possessively against her midriff, just below her soft breasts. A feral, sensual heat set fire to his will power.

He knew love was a heartless cardsharp of an emotion, something he neither offered nor promised. Nevertheless he'd always made sure that his lovers—and his wife—understood that he liked and respected them.

And then the night before his wedding he'd looked into Paige's gold-green eyes and wanted her with a merciless craving. He despised men who used women; it had struck at some hidden vulnerability when he'd discovered that one glance from a girl he'd just met—a girl still at high school!—stripped back his controlled assurance to expose raw arousal.

It was like being taken over by an alien. Resentment couldn't kill it—didn't even dampen it. And neither had long years of denial.

When she moved her hands to cover his, and said in a lazy, throaty voice, 'I'll do it,' an odd sideways sensation, as though the world had shifted beneath his feet, catapulted him into unknown territory.

Her eyes trapped him in a smouldering snare and the touch of her hands sent forbidden messages straight to his brain and his loins. He'd never experienced hunger like this before, so intense it rolled over him like lava—dangerous, beautiful, lethally destructive.

In one lethal movement he snapped the ends of her seatbelt together and stood up, towering over her in deliberate intimidation.

'All right?' he asked, unable to drag his unwilling gaze from the pulse that jumped in her slender throat.

'Yes.' She flushed and looked away, straightening her shoulders with obvious effort. 'Sorry, it always takes me a while to wake up.'

Disgusted by his lack of control, Marc sat down quickly, before his body could betray him further. Fiercely disciplining his hands, he latched his own seatbelt across his flat stomach and fixed his eyes on the scene through the window, watching the panorama of sea and sky tilt below them.

It was no use; the loveliness outside faded as his mind supplied images of how Paige would look in his bed after a night spent making love, and how sensually, exquisitely magical it would be to wake her slowly...

God! If merely touching her could summon erotic fantasies, he should have stayed overseas and let his office organise this trip to Arohanui.

So why hadn't he?

The embarrassing answer sat beside him, her head turned away so that a dark honey-coloured swathe of hair hid her face. Although they weren't touching he could feel her closeness, smell the faint natural perfume of her skin, and see her hands from the corner of his eye. They lay loosely clasped in her lap, yet he sensed a tension to match his own.

She had long, competent fingers, and his treacherous mind supplied another sizzling picture of those hands on his skin, pale gold against bronze...

Perhaps, he thought coldly, he should follow this through and see where it took them both. It was nothing more than sexual chemistry, but when he was with her he felt—he felt like a lesser man, he warned himself with merciless honesty. Paige had power over him, power he refused to yield to her, because once she knew she possessed it she might be able to possess him.

In spite of that he wanted her, and he was experienced enough to read desire in a woman. So, why not accept what she unconsciously offered?

Because it *was* unconscious, and he didn't take advantage of innocents.

Yet how many women of her age were as inexperienced as she seemed to be? Perhaps it was a ruse...

Dressed properly, pampered and groomed, she'd make a stunning mistress. It would be a partnership of equals— she'd see the world, have some fun, learn a lot, and when he'd got her out of his system he'd make sure she never had to work again if she didn't want to.

Surely that would be better than the life she was leading now?

'Where do we land?' she asked, her voice tight and remote, as composed as the face she turned towards him.

He raked her with a hard gaze, noted the colour rising through her silky golden skin. She swallowed and her tongue stole out to moisten her parted lips. Yes, she wanted him.

Temptation riding him hard, he said, 'Kerikeri. It's the nearest commercial airport to the Bay.'

Paige turned back to watching the sea spin beneath the plane, and dragged a juddering breath into painful lungs. Every instinct shrieked a warning—too late. Because in the mindless, temporary no-man's land between sleep and awakening she'd betrayed herself.

Marc had recognised her response as sexual excitement. She'd seen disgust ice his eyes and freeze his face.

Juliette had told her about the women who chased him, the open lures they'd tossed in his way, the subterfuges they'd used to try and coax him into their beds. And she'd told her about his contempt for them.

Pride stiffened Paige's shoulders, clenched her jaw. So he assumed she was just like them—sexually available, light-heartedly promiscuous. Her soft lips tightened. He'd probably laugh if he knew she had never made love. Not that he'd ever find out.

From now on she'd be as aloof as he was.

Jaw jutting, she stared blindly through the window, her

self-possession evaporating when his voice—too close—sounded above the roar of the engines.

A subtly abrasive note threading each word, he said, 'We're turning over the Bay of Islands. You should be able to see Arohanui Island.' He leaned forward and pointed across her. 'There.'

Tensely aware that he took great care not to touch her, Paige followed his finger.

Heart-shaped, mysterious, his island lay in a glinting, swirling sea the colour of a blue-green opal. Around it more scraps of land dotted a huge bay, some sombre with native bush, others a bright, sharp green. She blinked at beaches so bright they made her think of diamond dust, and others an elusive shade that reminded her of the champagne she'd drunk at his wedding—pale and soft with a tawny glow.

'Is it called Arohanui because of its shape? The name means great love, doesn't it?' she asked.

Shocked by the sultry, too intimate tone of her voice, she discreetly cleared her throat and kept her eyes fixed on the island.

'Yes. But its name refers to an old Maori legend about doomed lovers, not its shape,' he said drily. 'It was called that long before the first Corbett settled here.'

'It's very beautiful.' She cast around for something else to say, falling back on a banal comment. 'I've seen photographs, of course, but I didn't realise how many islands there are in the Bay.'

'Over a hundred and fifty, I'm told. It depends on exactly what you call an island. Haven't you been here before?'

'Not that I know of. When I was a kid we used to go to Fiji and the Gold Coast in Australia.' Her reminiscent smile faded. 'And when I was eleven my mother took me to Disneyland in California.'

It had been an almost perfect holiday, spoiled only because her father hadn't gone with them. He hadn't been at home when they'd arrived back, either; while they'd been away he'd moved in with his secretary, taking holidays and colour and laughter with him.

'My father was born on the island,' Marc told her. 'He loved it. My mother thinks it a little unsophisticated. She prefers her scenic beauty well tamed and controlled.'

Paige remembered his mother well—a worldly woman with the effortless, casual elegance of a daughter of France. She and Juliette had got on well.

His face hardened into cold, bleak bronze. 'She says she always knew that the island would claim him. He went out to see if he could rescue a boatload of idiots who took off for a day's fishing without checking the forecast or bothering about life-jackets, radio or flares. They all died.'

Paige made a shocked noise. 'I'm so sorry.'

He shrugged. 'He enjoyed risky enterprises. He'd rather have gone down like that than dwindle into old age.'

Chilled, Paige looked into cold, crystalline eyes. Marc, she realised, didn't think like that; he was too responsible to indulge in grand gestures for the adrenaline rush.

For some obscure reason this insight comforted her. She turned back and stared resolutely down. Trees crowned the intricate tucks and folds of Arohanui, but from the air she could see the red-brown shape of a roof surrounded by large gardens. It must have rained recently, because the island gleamed like polished greenstone.

'It looks mysterious, enchanted,' she said softly. 'A place removed from time and space where everyday rules might be suspended.'

'That's the lure of islands. They offer a hint of the forbidden, the exotic, a dangerous beauty.'

His almost indifferent words echoed in her mind like a challenge.

Don't even consider it! Paige commanded, quashing a piercing excitement to fix her attention solely on the island that slipped away beneath the aircraft wing, swift and inevitable as the remnants of a lovely dream.

'I thought you preferred Paris,' she said.

'I love Paris. I like London and New York too. But Arohanui has always been my home.'

She had to stop herself from turning to look at him. Juliette had complained of boredom and the lack of sophisticated entertainment on Arohanui, and after the first year of their marriage Marc had visited it alone.

Paige fixed her eyes on the view and concentrated on reminding herself that, like her father, Marc had been unfaithful to his wife.

It didn't work. She couldn't think of anything else but the man beside her. Barely discernible, how did his natural scent make such an impact, kicking her heart into a gallop and drying her mouth?

Sex, she told herself robustly. Think pheromones and moths dying dramatically in candle flames. If you give in to it, you'll be betraying your friendship with Juliette.

And you might fall in love with him…

Not likely, she scoffed. Oh, there must be some men who could love selflessly, but she'd seen precious few of them. Betrayed love had driven her mother into the acute depression that had ruined her life; Sherry's husband had promised her a love for all eternity, then robbed her and abandoned her when she'd told him of her pregnancy. Even Marc's mother had been left alone and forlorn after her husband's gallant, foolhardy death.

Paige jutted her jaw and watched a couple of small seaside towns race beneath the wings; as long as she stayed independent, no one could hurt her.

'The villages are Paihia and Russell,' Marc said in a manner that hinted at mockery—and not the pleasantly teasing kind, either. 'Holiday towns, both of them, although Russell has some interesting old buildings. We'll be coming in over Kerikeri any minute—you'll see orchards and vineyards.'

Almost immediately a formal chequerboard landscape divided by hedges began to slip by; kicked by swift panic, Paige closed her eyes and gulped, wondering what the hell she was doing here.

Warmth enclosed her hand as Marc took it. 'It's all right,' he said, his voice deep and calm. 'Relax, we're just coming in to land.'

Feeling unutterably stupid, she let her hand lie in the warmth of his, wondering how so comforting a grip could also send charges of excitement up her arm to shut down her brain. She forced her eyes open as the plane levelled off over farmlands.

'Kerikeri Airport,' Marc said calmly, nodding towards a small cluster of buildings. 'We transfer to the helicopter here.' He dropped her hand to indicate a machine parked off the runway.

Paige swallowed. Marc was rich; she'd always known that. The locket he'd given her had been valued at an extraordinary price because of its workmanship and the quality of the diamond. He had houses scattered over the globe and, because he liked his privacy, he'd bought several islands.

Even his clothes, casual though they were, breathed an aura of wealth.

But this offhand use of chartered planes brought home to her just how much money—and power—he had.

Her mind raced, chanting, *You shouldn't have come, you shouldn't have come.*

She looked down at her faded jeans. He was a different species, she told herself with a hard practicality that somehow didn't ring true. You're only here to pick up Juliette's legacy. Tomorrow he's going back to his world and after a pleasant, uneventful week in beautiful surroundings you'll go back to yours, back to real life.

And you'll never see him again.

The sombre words emptied out her heart and rang through the furthest reach of her brain.

As the engines changed in pitch and the plane slowed she asked something that had been niggling in the back of her mind since she'd looked up to see him come towards her and the dogs. 'How did you know where I was this morning? Sherry said she could only give you general directions; I don't always go to the same place with the dogs.'

He paused, before telling her calmly, 'I had you checked out. My private detective told me you walked the dogs every week day and that you kept to a regular routine between parks and the beach.'

Her temper flashed. Staring straight ahead, she said rigidly, 'That is completely outrageous.'

'Just another perk of being obscenely rich,' he said blandly. 'It wouldn't have been necessary if you'd been a bit more forthcoming instead of clamming up and hissing every time I tried to find out anything.' He sounded cool, even mildly amused.

The plane touched down with a slight bump and taxied towards the buildings. As Paige sat fuming he ended with a caustic note, 'And I'm sure nothing would have persuaded you to tell me that you'd been sacked because you wouldn't sleep with your boss.'

'How did you find—?' Bright coins of colour standing out on her cheeks, she grated, 'Don't you dare say I've just told you.'

'All right, then, I won't,' he said obligingly. 'It wouldn't be true. I'll bet he wondered what the hell had bitten him when he tried to force you into bed.'

'He didn't get the chance,' she said with cutting disdain. 'The first time he groped me I told him I'd complain of harassment if he ever tried it again.' Colour touched her skin. For weeks she'd felt dirty, as though the man's touch had contaminated her.

'So he sacked you?'

A swift glance revealed a dangerous razor-edge of light in the depths of his eyes. Shaken, Paige looked away to marshal her thoughts. 'I was made redundant. Last hired, first off. And it was a bad year for farmers so the firm didn't have enough work for me... Actually, I was glad to go.'

Although if she'd known how difficult it was going to be to get another job she might have fought to stay, in spite of the creep.

Marc said in a voice that contradicted his searching gaze, 'He's spread it around the city that you're a predatory female who backs demands for an increase in wages with threats.'

Angry and bewildered, she stared at him. 'Threats? Threats of *what*?'

'According to him, you said that if you didn't get a rise you'd accuse him of sexual harassment.' He spoke in a detached, judicial tone that lifted the hairs on the back of her neck.

The plane slowed, easing to a stop. Her voice molten,

Paige said, 'So *that's* why I've had no luck finding a new job. I should have put his pot on.'

'Why didn't you? You weren't the first woman he'd tried it on with, and you must have known he'd do it again. Sleazes like him always do.'

Trust him to unerringly pinpoint the one thing that still worried her. She said defensively, 'It was my word against his. He's a well-known personality in Napier; why would anyone believe me? How did your private detective find out?'

'By asking questions of a couple of women who'd left that office suddenly. One of them was your predecessor.' The plane rolled smoothly to a stop. Marc got to his feet and said, 'It doesn't matter, anyway.'

And when she looked up in disgust he gave her a cold, merciless smile that jetted an icy touch the length of her spine. 'His firm now knows exactly what's been happening. He's got one chance to keep his job, and that's to keep his hands, his innuendoes and everything else to himself. He's also been—persuaded—to stop spreading slander about you. I don't think you'll have any trouble getting a similar position when you go back.'

Paige's jaw dropped, but the pilot's voice over the intercom stopped the hot words tumbling from her lips.

'Here we are in lovely sub-tropical Kerikeri,' he announced, 'gateway to the Bay of Islands. Hope you had a good flight.'

Pasting a jaunty smile on her lips, Paige said, 'Coincidence is a funny thing. Just think, if I hadn't come down the stairs of the hotel at the exact moment you turned around, you'd never have known that I lived in Napier.'

Marc's eyes were cool and opaque, as unreadable as the expression on his gorgeous face. 'New Zealand's not that big—I'd have found you.' He stood back to let her out into the aisle.

Something about his tone made her deeply uneasy. Trying to ignore the crawling tension between her shoulderblades, she got up.

The steward emerged to open the door, nodding respectfully as they stepped out into sultry sunlight and air that even the taint of aviation fuel couldn't sully.

Refusing to look at Marc, Paige decided there was a difference about the atmosphere up here—somehow the countryside glowed, softer yet more vivid than the crisp clarity she was used to. The grass radiated green light around them as they walked across to the helicopter where another pilot waited.

Not that he was needed. The helicopter belonged to Marc, and it was he who flew them to the island, landing the chopper precisely on a hard pad several hundred metres from the homestead.

The big house sprawled in magnificent gardens beside a half-moon of beach; as they'd flown down Paige had noted a grass tennis court and a swimming pool, and what appeared to be a large two-masted yacht in the bay, anchored beside a motor cruiser.

Rich man's paradise, she thought, struggling for balance and common sense, trying not to be overwhelmed. She knew Marc worked hard; Juliette had told her about his frequent absences and the long hours spent at his desk. But it didn't seem fair that Sherry had to display her body to earn enough for a place of her own when Marc had all this—and it was just one of his residences!

The rotors died, and she realised Marc was turning around. Into the sudden silence he said formally, 'Welcome to my home.'

'Thank you,' Paige said, enmeshed in an odd, swift shyness, because it seemed as though he was making some sort of statement.

Which was ridiculous. No doubt the formal welcome had been just a bit of old-world courtesy.

Marc was disloyal, a breaker of vows. Quite possibly the executive-cum-mistress whose existence had shattered Juliette's life was already in residence, honing her cutting English accents for more put-downs.

The house seemed to grow in size as they walked through the garden towards it. Clinging desperately to her composure, Paige refused to gawk like a sightseer—although that was difficult once they were inside.

Not that the house was decorated in incongruous splendour. For all its size it breathed a warm, casual sophistication that made her feel instantly at home. After being introduced to the housekeeper, a middle-aged woman called Rose Oliver, Paige was ushered by her to a bedroom overlooking the bay.

Paige eyed the vast bed, its white calico spread tucked into a box frame of dark, warmly coloured wood. White walls breathed understated elegance; one displayed a magnificent kimono in black and cinnamon and a blue almost the same intense hue as Marc's eyes, and on the wall behind the bedhead a triptych glowed like a jewel in the cool, beautiful room—a spare, exquisitely painted Japanese scene of mountains and river.

Apart from a terracotta pot holding a flourishing banana tree there were no other decorations, although the wall of stained wood shutters onto a terrace gave the room texture and pattern.

'The wardrobes are in here,' the housekeeper said, gesturing towards a door in the wall. 'Would you like me to unpack for you?'

'No, thank you.' Paige tried to sound at ease. The last

thing she wanted was to let someone who probably regularly ministered to heiresses see her clothes.

After showing her the bathroom, Mrs Oliver said, 'I'm sure you'd like a shower. I'll call for you in about an hour, shall I? If there's anything you need, don't hesitate to ring.' She pointed to a telephone tucked into a shelf below the headboard. 'The numbers are on the set.'

She smiled and left the room.

All very polite and friendly, Paige thought as she headed into the large tiled bathroom. A huge shower covered an indecent amount of the floor, and an even larger spa bath took up another corner. Sunlight shimmered through palm fronds and dark shutters onto creamy marble and gleaming glass.

A delicious perfume led her to the soap; she lifted the cake and smelt it, then set it down again with a firm, set smile. Her own brand was fine. It was stupid, but if she used the soap that Marc's money had provided she'd feel she'd been bought.

As she wallowed in hot water from four directions, she wondered if anyone quite so poverty stricken had ever been a guest in Marc's house before.

Who cared? 'Enjoy it while you can,' she told her reflection defiantly.

Her scruples, if scruples were what they were, didn't extend to not using the hairdryer, also bought with his money!

She got into a pair of olive-green trousers before tucking in her bittersweet red shirt. A final glance in the mirror revealed that the trousers hung a little loosely on her hips. Frowning, she pulled out the shirt to cover them.

Only just ready when someone knocked on the door—according to her watch, twenty minutes early—she opened it. Her smile set when she saw who waited outside.

CHAPTER SIX

LIKE her, Marc had changed. In trousers that skimmed his strongly muscled thighs and a sports shirt one shade paler than his eyes he looked big and unyielding—and forbiddingly attractive.

Paige's heart kicked into a gallop, and she had to swallow hard to dislodge her breath from its sticking place in her throat.

'Oh—I thought you were Mrs Oliver—the housekeeper,' she blurted, only just saving herself from stammering.

Narrowed, steely eyes examined her face. 'Would you like a look around before lunch?'

'Thank you.' She wanted to ask him about Juliette's legacy, but it seemed crass and greedy. Instead she walked sedately beside him down the wide hall and out onto a terrace running along the front of the house.

She had to admit that Marc was an excellent host. With impeccable courtesy he showed her the garden between the house and the beach, a sub-tropical fantasy that fascinated her with its skilful mingling of colour and form and scent.

On the way back towards the house they passed the tennis court, and he asked if she played.

'I used to,' she said. 'But not for a while.'

'Perhaps we could have a game some time.'

Which meant never, of course. 'Perhaps,' she said noncommittally. She turned away and looked out over the bay. 'Are those boats—the yacht and the cruiser—yours?'

80

'Yes. Do you like sailing?'

'I loved it when I was a kid,' she told him, adding, 'My father had a yacht.'

He frowned. 'I'll take you out one day.'

Like the suggestion of tennis, she knew he didn't mean it. What was the sense of all this? Tomorrow he'd be gone.

He was just being polite, as though she was a real guest here, not someone he'd been obliged to host by his dead wife's will—the wife he'd betrayed.

Abruptly she asked, 'Where is Juliette's box?'

Thick black lashes concealed his eyes for a second, then lifted to reveal intensely blue depths, unreadable and enigmatic. 'I'll have it sent to your room.'

In crackling silence, they walked up the steps to the wide terrace.

'It's a wonderful house,' Paige said woodenly. 'So warm and sunny, yet the eaves must keep out the summer sun. And the garden is magical!'

Marc watched her face, saw something like wistfulness there, and silently summoned a raw French oath at the wave of protectiveness he felt. It had to be because she was Juliette's friend. And because she'd had a rotten time with that bastard she'd worked for. As well, she hadn't entirely recovered from the flu.

A man who prided himself on facing the truth without flinching, he let the comforting lies lodge in his brain for a betraying moment, until cold anger banished them.

Yes, he felt some responsibility for Juliette's friend, because she was in trouble. But this strange need to care for her was something he'd never experienced before.

He was gentle with women because they were smaller and more fragile, although he respected their different kind of strength and their endurance when many men gave up.

And he didn't prey on the weak; he chose only those so-phisticated enough to look after themselves.

Even Juliette, he thought with a brief, hard smile, young as she'd been, had known exactly what she wanted.

But Paige got to him; he resented the fact that any offer of help would be flung back in his teeth. Determination shone from her face, from the set of her shoulders and the resolute line of her soft, tantalising mouth.

Although he admired her for it, he wanted to smash that challenging pride into shards and make her totally, completely dependent on him.

He'd never felt like that before.

Brusquely he said, 'Lunch must be ready.'

It was served at a table on the terrace, under the benign and hopeful gaze of a golden retriever called Fancy, each mouthful of delicious food accompanied by enthusiastic, fearless chattering from a pair of fantails, tiny birds that swooped through the warm air as they sought unseen insects.

Desperate to subdue the rising tension, Paige said brightly, 'They're such friendly little birds, aren't they? It's difficult to think of them as mighty hunters.'

Marc's smile hardened. 'Like them, we're all hunters,' he said, 'and we're all prey.'

Shocked, she lifted her lashes. He was watching her with half-closed eyes, and as little rills of flame ran wild through her body he lowered his gaze to her mouth.

Deliberately intimate, blatant as a kiss, the brief glance burned through her defences. Colour flamed into her skin and she couldn't think of anything to say—she who had been extremely vocal when her sleazy employer had tried to hit on her!

Finally she managed, 'That's an interesting perspective on personal relationships.'

With a slight Gallic shrug he stated inflexibly, 'It's the truth. Look at your flatmate.'

'Sherry?' She bristled. 'She's not a victim and she's certainly not—'

'She wants money from the men who watch her strip.' His coolly dispassionate voice doused her spurt of temper. 'The more provocative her routine—the more she promises with each gesture and movement—the more money she makes. But I doubt if she follows through on it.'

'She doesn't,' Paige snapped. 'She's a dancer.'

'So it's a coldly commercial transaction—she encourages her customers to fantasise about her without giving them any warmth or tenderness or respect.'

Paige blinked and cast a swift glance at his angular features. It seemed an odd thing for a man who kept a mistress to say. How much warmth or tenderness or respect had he given Juliette? She could glean nothing from his face beyond a quizzical gleam in the blue eyes.

She said stiffly, 'She's doing it for Brodie's sake. As for warmth and tenderness and so on, I don't imagine many of the men who watch her dance go to the club for that.'

'Your loyalty is praiseworthy,' he drawled, not hiding the mockery in his tone. 'So why aren't *you* stripping for a living? She's earning more than you are.'

Her appetite vanishing, Paige put down her fork and looked him straight in the eye. 'Because I can do other things, and I don't have a child to plan for,' she stated coldly. 'Sherry grew up in a horrifying family situation and ended up on the streets when she was only fourteen. She got herself off them by sheer guts, then she married, sure it was going to last for ever. When she told her husband she was pregnant with Brodie he scarpered off to Australia, leaving a pile of debts he'd run up in her name. She doesn't enjoy working as a stripper, but her long-term plan is to make enough money to get out and give Brodie a decent life.'

'That makes her prey,' he said calmly, and changed the subject with an insulting blandness. 'Eat up—it's a long time since breakfast, and you didn't have anything on the flight, so you must be hungry.'

He was right. Although Paige's mouth set mutinously, she was hungry, and while she cleared her plate of a delicious salad that combined beans and strawberries Marc told her Arohanui's ancient legend of two Maori lovers who laid down their lives for each other.

Lulled by sunshine and a deep, highly suspect pleasure, Paige clung to her common sense by sheer exercise of will. When he'd finished she said lightly, 'How very romantic and tragic—*Romeo and Juliet*, South Pacific-style.'

His answering smile was smoothly mocking. 'And you don't believe a word of it.'

'If it happened, I'll bet they were very young.'

'Meaning that only the young and naïve consider love worth dying for?' He leaned back in his chair, long fingers curved around the stem of his wine glass, those thick lashes hiding his thoughts. 'You could be right.'

Uneasily aware that for all his relaxed grace he was focused intently on her, she opened her mouth to answer, but was forestalled when his brilliant gaze took her prisoner.

'How old are you? Twenty-three? From my perspective that's pretty young,' he finished on a note of amusement.

Heat washed through her in a smooth, feral response, shutting down her mind until the dog sat up to snap at a fly and the familiar, tiny sound dragged her back to reality.

Paige looked away and said stiffly, 'If it's cynical to believe that love is a much overrated emotion, then I suppose I must be cynical.'

His brows rose above glinting, metallic eyes, but he said mildly, 'I agree entirely with you that love is a much over-rated emotion.'

Well, she'd known that—so why did her heart contract painfully? 'How astonishing! We have something in common,' she flashed, then bit her lip.

He nodded. 'My parents supposedly loved each other, but all I remember of them was the sound of their quarrels. And their silences.'

Paige looked down. A gleam of sunlight probed a knife-blade with metallic glitter. 'My parents didn't quarrel. My mother told me that she'd had no idea—she thought they had a wonderful marriage until we arrived back from Disneyland to find my father living with his secretary. I think that was why she never got over it.'

The moment the words were said she wished them back; wincing internally, she braced herself for his response.

Sunlight collected in mahogany pools in his hair as he looked down at her. 'That must have been a difficult time.'

'As I suppose you know, there's no easy way to deal with marriage disasters. I managed,' she said curtly, accepting a cup of coffee from him.

'But your mother didn't.'

Shocked, she looked up into eyes that were steady and sympathetic. 'Your private detective has been busy.'

'Drink up,' he said, not disturbed by her bitterness. 'After you've finished your coffee, why don't you rest for an hour or so?'

In her bedroom, Paige decided ironically that he was good; he'd managed to cloak a desire to get rid of her with common courtesy. She'd even believed him—until she was free of his overpowering magnetism.

Stretching out on the daybed, she tried emptying her mind, but it kept replaying that enigmatic conversation over the table. She'd said too much, revealed more of herself than was wise. It gave Marc an advantage, because all she knew of him was that he had a particularly continental way of running his sex-life.

Well, no, now she knew that his parents' marriage had been unhappy. Had he intended to tell her? He was so controlled a man that his oddly intimate disclosure had to be deliberate.

When she found herself daydreaming of other intimate disclosures—sexy, basic, urgent fantasies that smoked through her brain in a drugging miasma—she leapt to her feet and paced across the room to peer through the shutters into the sunlight, frowning ferociously as she reined in her vivid imagination.

Trying to be dispassionate and worldly, she decided that it was a pity she was still a virgin, at the mercy of her imagination when it came to men and sex! With even one lover tucked in her background she'd be more rational about Marc's elemental effect on her.

Feverish shivers chased each other down her spine. Looking like a lover from an erotic fantasy didn't make him some super-stud who'd automatically whisk her to the stars if he ever took her to bed.

First experience, she'd read, usually failed dismally to live up to expectations. Marc was dangerously attractive—and powerful and arrogantly confident—but he was only a man. He couldn't work miracles, and if she'd made love previously she'd have outgrown these romantic, overblown illusions of the perfect lover.

'Anyway, it's not going to happen,' she muttered, turning back to the daybed. An experienced man, Marc probably demanded all sorts of sexual expertise and techniques from his lovers.

She willed herself to think of more sober things, like

the fact that when she went back to Napier she might find
herself a job...

Thanks to Marc.

Slowly, inevitably, as the island drowsed under the afternoon sun, sleep took over and her secret desires wound
through her dreams.

She was smiling when a sharp noise forced her from
Marc's arms, hurling her into the cold water splash of reality.

Dazed and disorientated, she tried to hide a yawn as she
stumbled off the daybed and across the room, conscious
only of the imperative knock as she opened the door.

Marc looked down into her bemused face, black brows
drawn together, his beautiful mouth hardening.

'Are you all right?' he asked abruptly.

Colour swarmed up through her skin, heating it into
acute sensitivity. Not only was her body aching with a hot,
forbidden hunger, but her clothes were crumpled, her hair
tangled around her face—and it seemed utterly elderly to
sleep in the afternoon.

'I'm fine,' she croaked, adding with a brave attempt at
poise, 'for someone who a moment ago was being chased
by pirates.'

One pirate, actually.

And why had she said that? Marc's raised brow made
her feel insignificant and stupid, yet she couldn't drag her
eyes away from his face. Deep inside her something shattered into shards so fine she knew she'd never be able to
put them together again. She suspected it was her precious
independence. Every instinct shrilling an alarm, she took
a step back from the door.

'Then it's just as well I woke you up,' he said promptly,
but something had changed. A raw undertone deepened his

voice and darkness swallowed some of the brilliance of his eyes.

'I—yes.' Her lips were dry, but she didn't dare lick them. 'I'll just wash my face.'

The words fell into a charged silence, one made even more significant by Marc's slight shrug. 'Of course,' he said non-committally. 'I'll be out on the terrace. I thought you might like to walk up the hill behind the house.'

Desperate to shatter the disturbing intimacy, Paige nodded. She needed violent activity to burn off the adrenaline that alerted every cell in her body; climbing a mountain would be ideal, but a walk should help.

'I won't be a moment,' she said, and stepped back, closing the door behind her.

When he turned that lethal male charm onto her she had to guard every response in case she fell into the oldest trap in the world—the sex trap. Paige washed her face and took a couple of deep, grounding breaths before going out to join him.

She stopped in the wide doorway onto the terrace, her heart picking up speed. Tall, darkly dominant against the light, he stood with his hands in his pockets and a broad shoulder leaning against one of the columns that held up the pergola. The dog Fancy sat beside him, following his gaze out to the gleaming sorcery of the ocean and the islands.

Because he had his back to her Paige could allow her eyes to appreciate the way the superbly tailored fabric strained over his lean hips and moulded the strong muscles in his thighs.

An odd, twisting sensation caught her by surprise, as did a swift pulse of heat in the pit of her stomach.

Paige set her teeth and moved out to join him, pointing

to a line of cloud bulging ominously over distant hills on the mainland. 'Is that rain on the way?'

His hands emerged from his pockets as he straightened up to cast a knowledgeable eye at the dark bar along the horizon. 'The wind's gone round to the south-west, so it's more than likely.' Frowning, he examined her with a swift, perceptive survey, then returned his attention to the distant hills. 'It's not travelling fast enough to worry us, and often clouds like that don't make it this far out in the Bay. Will you be warm enough?'

Too warm. In fact, she was heatedly, uncomfortably, *unbearably* aware of him.

And also aware that probably no other guest in his house had worn clothes as undistinguished as hers. Not that Marc gave any indication he'd noticed, but he'd have to be obtuse not to realise that her T-shirt and cotton trousers couldn't compare with the exquisite outfit of the woman who'd been with him that first day in Napier.

And he was far from obtuse.

'It's not cold,' she said, a shiver of alienation driving her to the edge of the terrace, where she pretended to scan the flamboyant combination of tropical and traditional garden forms.

After he'd left the island she'd spend some days storing this place in her memories. The plantswoman she longed to be relished the way fan palms set off native New Zealand shrubs and trees, and was excited by the exotic touch of upright cannas and bird of paradise flowers in electric blue and orange against the sprawling, extravagantly sombre splendour of two ancient pohutukawa trees.

She observed, 'I suppose if you live on an island you need to understand the weather.' And then flushed, remembering too late the circumstances of his father's tragic death.

'It's not so vital as it used to be; we have the latest gadgets for forecasting, and the locals are pretty good at reading the signs.' He gestured towards a path across the lawn. 'This way.'

As they set off, with the dog racing ahead, he added with an inflection that came too close to mockery, 'It's steep, so we should work off some of the tension of being inactive all day.'

The tension twisting along her nerves, Paige thought grimly, didn't come from inactivity.

The path led through a gate into a stand of huge, gnarled old pohutukawa trees, then struck off up a bush-clad hill. Paige liked the fact that apart from rock steps in the steepest pinches the track hadn't been formed, winding its way up beside a little stream that chattered musically over rocks. Nikau palms and the softer, feathery fronds of tree ferns crowded close in stately, graceful profusion, blending into the dark mass of bush.

'It smells deliciously fresh,' Paige said. Oh, wonderful—just be as banal as you can! Other women—the woman with him in Napier, for one—would have been able to entertain him with lively, witty conversation. 'And green, and somehow ancient,' she added defiantly, stepping from one rock to another across the creek as Fancy splashed gloriously through the water.

'It's never been cut over, so some of these trees are centuries old.' Marc was right behind her.

She concentrated fiercely on setting a cracking pace. Of course he kept up with her—and *he* wasn't breathless with exertion within ten minutes! Paige was grateful that he didn't try to speak, seemingly content to climb the slope in silence apart from an occasional command to the dog.

Sunlight stabbed golden shafts through the thick, scented canopy. 'Oh—look!' Paige breathed, slowing her pace and pointing, entranced by an arrow of light glowing like a halo around a small violet toadstool.

But the light vanished as though someone had yanked a shutter across, turning the green solitude into a murky gloom, still and threatening.

She said, 'Has that cloud—?'

'Quiet!'

Like him, she stopped, following his frowning gaze up into the sky, suddenly dark through the tangle of leaves. Above the short, soft sounds of her breathing she heard a bird cry out with shocking clarity in the tense silence. Fancy whined and pressed herself against Marc's legs.

'Thunder,' Marc said tersely, clearly angry with himself. 'I should have seen it coming.'

The distant mutter startled Paige, but not as much as the hand on her shoulder.

Exerting considerable pressure, he turned her and propelled her down the track. 'That squall is blowing in fast. We're almost at the top of the highest hill around, and under trees—perfect targets for lightning. Fancy, *come*!'

Another clap of thunder, nearer now, reinforced his warning. Fingers tightening on her shoulder, he gave her a little push, ordering curtly, 'Faster!'

Paige began to run, picking her way down the path as the thunder rumbled closer and closer and the light faded into a waiting, taut dimness. She could feel the turbulent, dangerous energy building within the clouds.

Although she skidded a couple of times she kept her balance. Marc could have easily outrun her, but he stayed a step ahead, positioning himself so that if she fell she'd land on him.

Always the protective male, she thought, trying to quench a warm glow in the most secret region of her heart. It meant nothing—a male hangover from prehistoric times when a man had to be ready to defend his woman against predators both animal and human.

He had no need to worry about wild animals in New Zealand, and she wasn't his woman, but she began to understand the seductive lure of masculine strength and power.

A strange exhilaration blossomed beneath her heart, expanding to fill her with bubbles of delight. Instinct warned her she'd always remember this mad dash down the hill through the moist gloom; time wouldn't overcome the steamy rich aroma of leaf-mould, or the sight of Fancy tearing down ahead, gold hair flying, ears lifting and falling.

And Marc, moving silently and powerfully, all controlled, huntsman's grace.

He glanced over his shoulder. 'OK?'

Oh, more than OK—foolishly, crazily exultant! 'Fine!'

Trying to curb this wild intoxication of the spirit, she began to count the intervals between the lightning that pulsed in staccato flashes through the trees and its accompanying thunder.

'We're lucky—the full force of the squall is going to miss the island,' Marc said into the waiting silence. 'Keep going—we're nearly there.'

But a few hundred metres from the garden he grabbed her hand and hauled her ruthlessly into a stand of graceful small trees, their sinuous branches holding up huge leaves that formed an umbrella.

'These will keep us reasonably dry,' he said.

She protested, 'We could make the house—'

'Not without soaking you—and this rain will be cold. It feels like hail.'

Sure enough, the temperature had dropped noticeably.

'I'm not made of sugar,' Paige said, but her heart wasn't in it.

Eyes glinting in the premature dusk, he surveyed her upturned face. 'Far from sugary,' he said in a detached, impersonal tone. 'Rain is one thing, but hail can kill.'

Although they couldn't see the rapidly approaching storm through the tree canopy, its presence was all around—borne on the wind that propelled its hissing advance towards them.

That cold breath flowed over Paige, rapidly banishing the heat from her headlong race down the hill. She clenched her teeth together, but couldn't stop a shiver. Marc pushed her behind him, sheltering her from the full onrush of the squall.

He said, 'Here it comes.'

Rain pounced, spattering noisily on the huge, glossy leaves before settling into a solid, heavy drumming that blocked out any thunder and turned twilight into darkness. A sudden gust lashed the trees, spattering huge drops over them. Marc stood foursquare onto the thrust of the storm, Fancy pressed against his legs.

Although cold, and a little damp around the edges, that suspicious euphoria still bubbled through Paige like the very best champagne. Groping for a steady place to anchor her emotions, she reminded herself of all the reasons she had to distrust this man.

Yet he'd put himself between her and the full force of the storm, and because of him her blood sang a primitive, taboo song while her body seethed with eager life.

She thought wildly that she'd remember this moment on her deathbed.

And, because that terrified her, she tried to push past him, saying hoarsely, 'I'm already wet—I might as well go on.'

He turned and grabbed her wrist, giving it a swift shake as he yanked her back. Harshly he snapped, 'Don't be an idiot. It could still hail. It will be over in a few minutes, so—'

The words fell into a silence that wasn't real, a silence conjured by pitiless awareness. I won't look up, she thought defiantly. I will not look up...

But she did, straight into the blue heart of fire, into eyes both penetrating and molten at the same time.

He said something she'd never learned in high school French and let her wrist go. Some unregenerate part of her realised that it took him a huge effort to release her, and gloated.

She didn't step back; she couldn't. As the thunder muttered and grumbled above them she said one word.

'That's the first time you've ever said my name.' His voice was harsh and deep and textured with hunger. 'Paige.'

Only one syllable, yet it was a caress, a note of raw need, a sensual promise.

But he waited, his eyes keen and measuring as they raked her face.

What was he doing? Demanding that she take the first step to surrender?

A stray raindrop plopped onto her lips, startling her into licking it off. He made a soft, feral sound that sent chills scudding the length of her spine, and the next moment she was being strained against his big, aroused body and he was kissing her, his mouth cool and controlled against hers—for a mini-second.

Until his steely discipline shattered into splinters and they kissed like long-separated lovers, as though they had kissed a thousand times before—as though after this there would be no other kiss, no other touch.

CHAPTER SEVEN

THE day her boss had tried to force her mouth open beneath his, Paige had efficiently backed away before scorching his ears with a contemptuous verbal assault.

Yet now, when Marc did the same thing, she opened to him gladly, linking her hands behind his back and dizzily surrendering to the desperate urgency that surged through her like fire in dry fern. More thunder hammered in her ears, her heart's insistent counterpoint to the tumult around them.

This, she realised as his mouth took hers again in fierce possession, was what she'd recognised in herself the first time she'd seen Marc—a wild hunger that knew no boundaries and suffered no restraints.

His arms tightened, bringing her against his hardening body. Every instinct of self-preservation shrieked at her to wrench free and race through the dying storm to the safety of the house.

But older, more basic instincts challenged her to stay, to find out what made Marc Corbett the only man with the power to smash down the conditioning of a lifetime.

And while she hovered between the promise of safety and the dazzling, embargoed beauty of danger, he kissed her just under the line of her jawbone, and one long-fingered hand traced the soft curves of her breast. Shockwaves of sensation exploded through her.

Trembling, she whispered his name again.

Marc ran his thumb over the demanding centre of her breast. Her breath lodged in her throat as fire scorched along secret pathways from his touch. Although lightning flashed against her closed eyelids and thunder roared around them, nature couldn't produce as powerful a storm as the one that conquered her.

And then Marc lifted his head and with narrowed, blazing eyes watched her realise what she was doing.

Surrendering.

The heat in his gaze changed to coldly crystalline brilliance when shocked horror robbed her face of colour and twisted her mouth into a grimace of self-contempt. Marc had expected his wife to accept the presence of his mistress in their lives. And Paige had kissed him as though he was her one true lover, a man to die for.

'Let me go,' she croaked through numb lips.

Immediately he stepped back and gave her room. 'What do we do about this?' he asked uncompromisingly.

Shame flooded her face in a wash of colour that drained away to leave her skin painfully stretched. Cold and alone and empty, her glittering anticipation crumbling into ashes, she shook her head and said, 'Nothing.' But no sound came out.

However, he understood. She'd expected some protest—something!—*anything* but the hard, humourless smile that curled the corners of his mouth.

'Then we'd better go into the house and forget that it ever happened,' he said courteously. 'The rain's stopped and the storm is over.'

As Paige stepped out of the shelter of the trees the sun burst out in radiance.

From behind her came Marc's voice, sardonic and infuriatingly self-assured. 'But there will be other squalls, and I doubt if either of us will forget.'

'There won't be,' Paige told him stiffly, adding with a swift resentment she instantly regretted, 'As for forget-

ting—you'll do that easily. Women are expendable, after all.'

A heartbeat of silence pulsed around them before he
drawled, 'What exactly do you mean by that?'

'I'm sure you know.'

'And I'm sure I don't.' Iron ran like a threat through
his tone. 'Explain it.'

She bit her lip. Her damnable temper had to erupt at the
very worst time, summoned by the intense frustration that
tore her composure to tatters. If he hadn't lifted his head
and looked into her face she'd have willingly co-operated
in her own seduction.

This humiliating knowledge spurred her on. 'Simply that
whatever you want from women is easily found. It means
nothing more than momentary pleasure.'

His smile was cynical, almost cruel. 'Indeed?' he said
with cool indifference, and stooped and crushed her startled mouth beneath his.

The kiss was over in a heartbeat, but while it lasted her
lips had shaped to his.

'Momentary?' he murmured, his tone insultingly relaxed.

Shame burned like acid, concealing a pain she refused
to face. She was too unsophisticated to play teasing, sexual
games. Keeping her face averted, she walked beneath the
bold heat of the sun and tried to ignore the man beside
her.

He said, 'And what makes you think I see sex as a game
between men and women? Did Juliette tell you that?'

The ice in his words scraped along her nerves. 'I'd have
to be stupid not to know that women are, always obtain-
able—' her voice invested the word with scorching disdain
'—when you're rich.'

'A certain sort of woman,' he agreed silkily. 'But greed

is not exclusive to the female sex—a certain type of man is always on the lookout for rich women. And you're evading my question.'

They had reached the limits of the garden; automatically courteous, he reached to unlatch the gate and stood back to let her go through it first. Moving as carefully as though he were a tiger in ambush, she walked past him.

'You have no right to ask that question,' she said with steady composure. 'My conversations with Juliette were private.'

He said with clinical assurance, 'So she did.'

Paige waited tensely for him to reject the accusation, but he remained silent while they walked through the splendid gardens, past the tennis court and between two large citrus trees, glowing with burnished fruit like a treasure beyond price.

He startled her by observing with a judicial lack of emotion, 'Your father's defection presumably hit you hard, and making friends with Sherry would reinforce your belief that people exploit each other.'

Anger lit her eyes and tightened her lips—lips that still stung from his kisses. 'We've had this conversation before.'

'I'm just surprised that you accept her solution.' He held back a wet branch so that she didn't get drenched. Great drops fell like tears at his touch.

Paige cast him a glinting, dangerous glance. 'She does what she has to,' she said steadily. 'Women do, you know—we survive, and for some of us it's not easy or particularly pleasant.'

'Then why aren't you stripping with your friend on the stage?' He slashed her with a survey as blue and hard as the gleam in a diamond.

Paige stiffened as his gaze travelled from the vulnerable

length of her throat to her breasts, and then on to the apex of her body, assessing the contours of her legs beneath her trousers, and back up to her face, by then pale and set.

He said with brutal frankness, 'You've a good body, and you dance like a dream. You could probably earn as much as she does.'

Paige's teeth ravaged her bottom lip. 'It's not my scene,' she said finally.

'Then how about this—I will pay you to stay with me for—oh, shall we say a year? At the end of the year you'll be free to go.'

Paige gasped, her breath almost strangling her. He couldn't mean it—no, of course he didn't mean it. 'Don't be ridiculous.'

Smoothly, with enough cruel irony in his tone to set her skin crawling, he finished, 'Those kisses made it more than clear that there is nothing ridiculous about the proposition. I'd guess it would take us a year at least to tire of each other.'

Pain blocked her throat. She could only walk beside him and listen to his silkily dispassionate voice tear down dreams she hadn't known she'd been harbouring.

'Of course when it was over I'd make sure you had enough money to set you up in whatever business you desire, and keep you for a couple of years while it was getting onto its feet.' He paused, but when she said nothing he went on, still in that coldly amused tone, 'All you have to do is satisfy me. I can certainly promise to satisfy you.'

'I am not a prostitute,' Paige ground out, staring wretchedly at a hibiscus flower, brazenly scarlet with its silken petals gleaming. She didn't dare look at Marc, because he might guess that just for an instant—for a shameless fraction of a second—she'd been tempted.

'I rest my case.'

She stopped and jerked around to face him, eyes glittering in her stormy face. 'But I don't know what I'd do if I had a baby to look after! Sherry believes that all she's got to offer is her body. She wants to make sure Brodie never has to endure the sort of childhood she had, and to do that she's got to have a financial stake. She's getting it the fastest way she can.'

She stopped, infuriated by the inflexible expression on his boldly marked features. 'And you—' she finished with loathing '—you're a narrow-minded snob.'

His expression didn't change. 'Whereas your loyalty seems to be exceeded only by your gullibility. Women like Sherry move through any level of society. The ones I meet are more sophisticated, but essentially they have the same practical attitude.'

Something in the deep voice caught her attention, yet she couldn't decide what it was. Was he thinking of his mistress?

She began to walk towards the house, saying unsteadily, 'It would probably do you good to be in her shoes for a year. Then you might learn not to judge people.'

Marc watched her march away, shoulders erect, her stiff-legged fury unable to overcome the seductive, entirely unconscious sway of her hips. Fickle sunlight poured over her hair, turning it into a fall of dark honey-amber, still tousled by the rake of his fingers when he'd kissed her. Her skin echoed the colour, softened it and turned it into a pale, delicate glow so that she shimmered like a figurine, rare and precious and too delicate.

Heat slammed through him—heat that resisted the icy chill of logic and common sense. He bit back searing words and followed her, catching her up in two smooth, powerful strides.

At the intersection of two paths presided over by a superb marble Pan, she hesitated, not sure which way to go.

'To the left,' Marc directed abruptly, looking past her down that path. The cold control that had locked his features into stillness altered as he said smoothly, 'Ah, Lauren's arrived. She's an executive in Corbett's. In fact, although you haven't been formally introduced, you've met her—she was with me in Napier. She has a special interest in New Zealand.'

Paige swung around and watched with an oddly kicking heart as the tall woman came towards them. So this *was* the woman who had darkened Juliette's life. She suspected that she knew exactly what that special interest was—the man beside her.

Pain raked her with unsheathed claws; she took in a long, silent breath, stiffened her spine and angled her chin, wounded pride providing the courage to smile as she was introduced to the woman whose mocking voice she'd never forgotten.

Sleekly elegant, Lauren Porter possessed something a lot more special than conventional beauty—intelligence, and a knowledgeable sophistication that irradiated her fine features. And she had the same aura of confidence as Marc, an inbuilt assurance that set Paige's defences slamming up. She looked younger than Marc, but probably only by a couple of years.

Juliette would have had no defences against a woman like this.

After that initial softening Marc's unbreakable control masked his emotions, but his executive gave Paige a warm smile.

'So we meet again. Are you enjoying your visit to the island?' Lauren Porter asked.

'Very much, thank you.' Paige's voice sounded stiff but pleasant.

Before the other woman could answer Marc interpolated smoothly, 'And we're both a little damp, thanks to that last shower. Let's go inside.'

Back in her bedroom, Paige changed and showered and wondered at the smiling regard Marc's mistress had turned on her. She seemed very—well, pleasant. But *pleasant* was a nothing word, emotionless and without juice. And beneath that charming exterior there had to be much more than mere pleasantness.

Raging sexual desire, perhaps.

Paige's hand stole up to touch her lips. She clamped them tight to stop them trembling, feeling as though she'd walked through a barred gate onto a pathway leading down to destruction.

Which was ridiculous; she'd been kissed before.

Not often, she admitted reluctantly. As her mother had sunk into illness her friends had fallen away, so there had been no kisses after the unpractised ones stolen by the occasional boy at high school.

Perhaps her response to Marc was an indication of how utterly green and inexperienced she was; his lovemaking might not be anything special at all.

Perhaps any man might have that effect on her.

She shuddered with disgust, remembering her boss. Well, not *any* man…but any man she wanted. As for Marc; next time—if there was a next time!—his touch set off erotic explosions all through her, she had to remember why she disliked and distrusted him.

If she weakened at all towards him she could expect eventual rejection and bitter desolation.

Changing into jeans and a white shirt, she wondered miserably where Lauren Porter had bought her sleek black trousers and the pure red top made from merino wool as fine as silk. The black jacket over it was certainly leather, and so were the red gloves tucked dashingly into the pocket.

A very classy lady, Paige thought wearily. She examined herself in the mirror, then shrugged. She was no competition.

So why had Marc kissed her senseless? What would Lauren think if she knew? Perhaps a worldly woman wouldn't care how many other lovers he had.

Whereas if he was hers she'd scratch the eyes out of—

'No!' she said as her appalled gaze flew to the hands curling into claws at her sides.

Oh, no. Apart from being the most appalling disloyalty to Juliette, she was so far out of her league she might as well be a sparrow hunted by an eagle.

Not that she liked that idea, either. A nice domestic tabby, she decided with a mocking smile at her idiocy, in the den of a blue-eyed tiger.

Paige swallowed an uncomfortable obstruction in her throat and fastened an interested, alert, uninvolved look to her face before sallying out to confront Marc.

But when she steeled herself to walk casually into the room Marc had told her they'd meet in she found it empty. Not for long, however; the housekeeper arrived hot on her heels.

'I'm sorry,' Mrs Oliver said without preamble, 'but Marc asked me to tell you that there's an emergency— business, not personal—so he won't be able to dine with you tonight.'

Paige fought down the infuriating spasm of disappointment underlying her quick relief. 'I hope it's nothing too bad?'

Mrs Oliver said with complete confidence, 'Marc will

deal with it, whatever it is. He thrives on challenges. Shall I bring dinner here?' She indicated a table at one end of the informal room that shared the same warm, appealing elegance as the rest of the house.

'Thank you. Can I help with anything?'

The older woman smiled at her. 'That's very thoughtful of you, but I'm too set in my ways to work comfortably with anyone else in the kitchen. Dinner will be in half an hour or so. Afterwards, would you like to watch television? Or a film? Marc gets them flown in.'

'That sounds great.'

But later, after she'd made herself eat a delicious meal, sat in a fabulous home theatre and watched a taut, well-acted drama that hadn't yet reached New Zealand, she refused coffee or tea in favour of an early night and walked back to her room feeling stupidly abandoned.

'Ridiculous!' she said sternly, closing the door behind her too vigorously. So Marc admitted to wanting her—that didn't give her licence to develop a humiliating fixation.

His kisses had been dynamite. And her response had been scary. Somehow he'd smashed down all her barriers to reach some hidden, subversive part of her that gloried in the wildness and the heat and the urgent need his touch summoned.

However, although she'd wanted Marc with a desperation that scared the hell out of her, lust wasn't love, so she had no reason to feel this stupid, useless, embarrassing sense of betrayal. Love meant need and dependence and sacrifice—and eventual rejection—whereas lust, a simple physical itch, was much safer.

In fact, if she were an experienced woman she might even be tempted to have an affair with him.

Getting ready for bed, she toyed recklessly with the idea of yielding to the tormenting desperation that ran like hot honey through her body whenever she remembered those moments in his arms. Perhaps indulging in a wild conflagration of passion would eventually exorcise it, because nothing so intense could last—the human frame wasn't equipped to deal with prolonged exposure to such hunger.

'Don't be an idiot,' she scoffed, stamping out of the bathroom. 'Starting your sex life with an arrogant, autocratic, *cheating* magnate would be a very bad move.' Yet an unknown emotion tightened painfully around her heart.

Some time during the evening the housekeeper had removed the white bedspread and replaced the bolster with large, continental pillows. Beside the jug of water on a chest were a bowl of fruit and some crackers.

Clearly Marc gave great thought to his guests' comfort.

Not likely, she thought with an ironic smile. Apart from making sure he employed well-trained staff, he probably took it all completely for granted.

Why had he been so determined to fulfil the conditions of Juliette's will?

Her lip curled as she marched across the room. The most cynical answer was the right one; he knew he'd hurt Juliette with his unfaithfulness, so this was a sop to a guilty conscience.

And it wasn't costing him anything—not even time, because he was leaving tomorrow.

Aching with a desolate tiredness, she crawled into bed and switched off the light, waiting impatiently for sleep to shut down the chaos in her mind.

Only to have it play and replay with loving fidelity each delicious, forbidden kiss, every erotic stimulus, from the subtle friction of his shaven jaw to the vivid impact of flame-blue eyes, the experienced, knowledgeable touch of his hand on her breast, the blatant hunger of his hardening body...

Her own body sprang into eager life. Groaning, Paige turned her head into the pillow.

The telephone beside the bed shocked her with a soft, insistent warble. Heart jolting, she bolted upright, groping for the receiver. 'Hello?' she muttered.

Marc said, 'I thought you might like to ring Sherry and reassure her that you got here safely.'

Adrenaline sizzled through Paige like a charge of lightning. 'I—now?' But guilt bit deep; she'd meant to ask if she could contact her flatmate, and she'd been so caught up in her own concerns she'd forgotten.

'It's not late,' he said smoothly. 'I'll put you through.'

Paige opened her mouth to say something—she never knew what—but the number clicked up automatically and within a couple of seconds Sherry said, 'Hello?' into the receiver.

'It's Paige here. How's everything going?'

She relaxed at Sherry's soft, unforced laugh.

'Everything's fine. How are you? What's your guy's place like?'

'He's not my guy,' Paige said automatically.

'He wants to be,' Sherry teased. 'Talk about vibes!'

Paige said curtly, 'We have nothing in common.'

'You mean he's rich and you're not?'

Amongst other things. They also had completely different standards and values. Paige said lightly, 'Yep. Now I know how a fish out of water feels!'

'Rubbish,' her friend said indignantly. 'You'd fit in anywhere—you're pretty and nice and you're clever. What more could anyone want?'

Paige laughed, but Sherry's quick support warmed her. 'Thanks.'

'Still, be careful, all right?' Sherry's voice changed into

an almost maternal warning. 'Men like him aren't used to having women say no to them.'

Paige stated with such utter conviction she startled herself, 'You don't need to worry; he's not the sort to turn ugly. Besides, the long-term girlfriend is here, and they're taking off for parts unknown tomorrow.'

'Oh. Pity,' Sherry said, clearly not convinced.

'The house is lovely—old, but beautifully restored and added to, and only a few steps from a fabulous beach with huge old pohutukawa trees along the beachfront. It will be breathtaking in summer—great crimson domes against the sea. And not another house in sight, although there must be a place for the housekeeper.'

'A housekeeper?' Now Shelley was impressed.

'Yes. And the island is covered in native bush, so from the air it looks like a greenstone heart—fairytale stuff! Marc's helicopter met us at the airport and flew us over.'

'Cool!' Sherry didn't have an envious bone in her body. 'You enjoy it—every minute of it. Don't worry about me and Brodie, we're fine and enjoying our holiday together, so don't think of coming back until you're ready. You might as well make the most of whatever good fortune comes your way.' She paused, then said, 'And, Paige, I've been thinking. If you want to stay—'

'I don't. I'll be back home in a week's time.'

'Oh.' Sherry sounded startled, but she went on swiftly, 'Well, you might see a chance of a job or something there. You haven't had much luck in Napier, so if one comes up, take it. Don't worry about us. As a matter of fact, I think I might be getting a job myself—a *proper* job. I interviewed for it this afternoon—nice people.'

She sounded so elaborately offhand that Paige realised it was a job she wanted very much. 'Where?' she asked. 'Doing what?'

'In the country—well, about twenty kilometres out of Napier. I saw it in the paper after you left, and when I rang they were quite keen.' She gave a little laugh. 'It's light housework and taking care of a couple of kids after school. There's a free flat for me and Brodie.'

'It sounds perfect.' If Sherry got that job, Paige wouldn't be able to afford the unit. She pushed the thought to the furthest reaches of her mind and said heartily, 'I'll keep my fingers crossed for you.'

'Yeah, well, the money's not as good, of course, but I'll be able to save most of it. And it's more wholesome for Brodie to grow up there. Oh-oh, he's stirring. I'd better hang up.' Dropping her voice, Sherry said, 'Have a great time, and for once start looking out for yourself, OK?'

Paige's smile faded as she hung up. She switched off the light again and lay down, blessing the employer who was prepared to look past the stripper to the warm, responsible woman that Sherry was.

The telephone rang again. Lifting herself onto her elbow, Paige stared at it, then slowly reached for the receiver.

Marc asked, 'Is everything all right?'

'Fine, thank you.' She heard Lauren Porter's voice, sharply urgent.

Marc said, 'I'm sorry, I have to go. Goodnight, Paige.'

'Goodnight.'

But it seemed hours that she lay listening to heavy showers hiss across the sea and pounce onto the house. Was the emergency an all-night affair? Or was Marc with Lauren, making love on a bed even bigger than this one?

She turned over onto her stomach, thrusting her face into the pillow, and tried to block out the images that flashed through her brain. Eventually she drifted off to sleep, but she spent the rest of the night tormented by dark, agitated dreams, and woke with a jolt, aching all over, to the sound of the helicopter taking off.

Marc was leaving. Without conscious thought, she bolted out of bed.

CHAPTER EIGHT

BY THE time Paige had pushed the curtains back, and wrestled open the shutters onto the terrace, the sound of the chopper's engines had faded across the sea. The sudden hollowness beneath her ribs was invaded by a pain so acute she had to lean against the wall; narrowing her eyes, she frantically searched for the helicopter.

And when at last she caught the tiny silver glint buzzing across a cloudless sky, she whispered, 'Goodbye,' on a silent sob.

'Good morning,' Marc said from far too close.

Stiff with shock, she whirled around. Clad in well-cut trousers and nothing else, he'd walked out through another set of doors only a few feet from hers. The sun gilded his broad shoulders and magnificent torso and revealed the shadow clinging to his unshaven jaw. He looked like a buccaneer, sexy and sinful and formidably dangerous in every meaning of the word.

Heat exploded deep in the pit of her stomach. Squelching her first impulse to flee back into her bedroom, drag the curtains across and hole up there until the helicopter arrived back to rescue her from such reckless temptation, Paige stood firm and took a deep breath. If only she'd combed her hair before she came out! She could feel it rioting around her head like spun toffee.

Refusing to glance down at the shabby T-shirt she slept in, she said, 'Good morning.' And, while the smile curling his sculpted mouth wreaked untold damage on her nervous system, she blurted, 'Where's the helicopter going?'

110

'It's taking Lauren to Kerikeri. She has to catch the eight o'clock plane to Auckland.'

Dry-mouthed, she said, 'I thought you were leaving with her?'

'I'm not going until after lunch,' he said, almost as though she had the right to ask.

She met his eyes steadily, but couldn't read anything in his enamelled blue eyes and calm, outrageously handsome face.

The smile returned, high voltage this time. 'Did you sleep well?'

Tamping down a wild response, she told him shortly, 'Very well, thank you.' No lie, either. Once she'd chiselled those images from her brain she'd gone under like a drowning victim! But some masochistic urge persuaded her to ask, 'How about you?'

'When I finally got to sleep.' And before she had time to torture herself further with pictures of him in bed with Lauren he said, 'I'm sorry about last night. I had to deal with something that wouldn't wait.'

'It doesn't matter.' A cool breeze from the sea breathed on her, puckering her skin. 'It was a pleasant evening, and I enjoyed the film.'

He frowned. 'You'd better get into some warmer clothes.'

Did he ever miss anything?

He finished, 'I'll see you at breakfast in half an hour.'

'Certainly,' she said crisply, and walked inside, closing the shutters behind her.

Half an hour later he was coming along the passage when she emerged from her bedroom.

'A punctual woman,' he said. He regarded her with sardonic amusement. 'Hungry?'

She had been, but the sight of him, shaven and with his

splendid torso concealed by a shirt that darkened his eyes to smoky sapphires, stole her appetite.

Trying to marshal her tumbling emotions into some sort of order, she went with him to the room where she'd eaten her solitary dinner the night before. The dog Fancy ambled in through the open doors of the terrace to gaze adoringly at Marc, her tail wagging with expectation until he greeted her. Then, politely, she came across and let Paige stroke her head.

'She must miss you when you're away,' Paige observed, approaching the chair Marc held for her.

'I don't think so.' He looked down at the dog with a half-smile. 'I probably miss her more. According to Rose Oliver she sleeps a lot.'

It felt as though a century had gone by since this time yesterday, when she'd been walking the dogs in Napier, Paige thought despairingly as he slid the chair in beneath her.

Well, things *had* happened—she'd flown up here, and she'd kissed Marc Corbett. A truly life-changing event, she mocked.

She surveyed her empty plate with absorbed interest while the scents of breakfast teased her nostrils—toast and bacon, the sweet tang of orange juice straight from the tree, the delicious promise of coffee.

Kisses didn't have to mean anything, common sense assured her bracingly.

But Marc's kisses had spun her world off its axis. When she'd caught fire her surrender had shattered her life's safe, prosaic foundations into splinters.

'Something wrong?' Marc enquired. 'No, I remember— it normally takes you a while to wake up in the morning. Do you need a kick-start—coffee, perhaps?'

Sitting mute as a fish was hardly cool. She said evenly, 'Coffee helps.'

'Pour yourself a cup, then. And one for me, if you don't mind—black.'

It figured. Glad to have something to do, she lifted the pot and, while he made a sortie to the sideboard, carefully poured two large cups of coffee.

When he sat down she glanced at his plate, and in a voice she hoped sounded amused and light, asked, 'Do you eat porridge every morning?'

'At home I do.'

'Like father, like son.' The moment she said the words she'd have given anything to call them back. His father's nickname of the Robber Baron hadn't been affectionately given.

Marc shrugged. 'In matters of breakfast,' he confirmed blandly. 'What would you like?'

'Fruit, thank you, and toast.'

She got up and helped herself. Spooning yoghurt over tamarillos, she wondered angrily how just being in the same room as him made her respond so much more vividly; the yoghurt blazed like white fire against the ruby-coloured fruit, and the air stroking her skin was potent with fragrance.

While she ate Marc made polite conversation, his ease chipping away at her self-confidence. If those searing kisses had meant anything to him he'd be like her, almost raw with awareness, instead of giving off an aura of self-possession that meant he was fully in control.

'As the weather has settled we'll go around the island this morning,' he said urbanely. 'It will give you some idea of what the place looks like from the sea.'

It took all her will power to answer sedately, 'That's very kind, but you don't have to entertain me.'

His brows rose. 'It would be a pity if you don't see some of the Bay while you're up here.'

'You don't have to feel obliged—'

'Paige,' he said, his pleasant tone failing to hide a steely note, 'I won't kiss you again.'

A tumult of colour scorched her skin. Outside a dove cooed seductively, the soft sounds floating across the terrace and in through the wide doors.

'You won't get the chance,' she said, hurrying the words out so fast they arrived joined together. She breathed in deeply, and asked with stilted steadiness, 'Is there any chance of me seeing Juliette's legacy this morning?'

She felt greedy, and somehow sordid, but she wasn't going to pretend that this was a simple, carefree holiday, with yesterday's exchange of kisses a diversion to be easily ignored.

'Certainly,' he said with a hint of frost in his tone. It had disappeared when he said, 'I'll make a bargain with you.'

Startled, she looked up into eyes as cool and crystalline as the heart of a sapphire. 'What?' she asked, oddly breathless.

'I'll get Rose to bring the box along to your room after we come back. In return, promise to stop looking at me as though I'm going to leap on you. I'm sorry for kissing you yesterday.' His eyes were opaque blue gems against the tanned skin of his angular face as he scanned her face. When she moved uncomfortably in her seat, he said calmly, 'I won't make any excuses—you are deliciously desirable, and I temporarily lost my head—but it won't happen again.'

Because he'd spent last night in Lauren Porter's arms? Perhaps he did feel some loyalty towards his long-term mistress after all.

And she was very happy about his promise, Paige told herself, lying like an expert. 'All right,' she said gruffly.

'Now, do you think you'll be able to eat your breakfast instead of pushing it around the plate?'

Well, of course he was amused. He probably thought she was gauche and green and still wet behind the ears. No doubt he was kicking himself for losing his head temporarily yesterday, and this hideously embarrassing and painful conversation was his attempt at damage limitation.

'Yes,' she said stiffly, and began to force the food past the obstruction in her throat.

Marc's motor cruiser was smaller than the big yacht; nevertheless, Paige decided, eyeing the galley and comfortable cabin, it was nothing like the family boats owned by so many New Zealanders. As well as looking like a rich man's toy it exuded modern technology and luxury.

An uncharacteristic melancholy stole some of the warmth and colour from the day.

'Do you know anything about boats?' Marc asked, standing back to let her climb a set of steps from the deck to a high cabin above the main one.

'I can row,' she told him, going up nimbly. 'That's about it.'

At the top of the stairs he said, 'This is the flybridge.' He indicated an impressive bank of dials and screens in front of a leather chair fixed to the deck. 'Sit down and we'll get moving.'

Leather sofas stretched around the sides beneath windows that provided a panoramic view on three sides. The fourth opened towards the rear of the boat. Gingerly Paige sat down and watched Marc, big and dark and competent, take the wheel and deal with the array of dials.

Once they were out of the Bay and moving slowly down

the coast he said, above the noise of the engine, 'Glad I made you put on a jacket?'

She smiled and bent to stroke Fancy's gleaming head. 'Yes.'

'It's always colder on the sea. Would you like to try a stint behind the wheel?'

She hesitated, met a gleaming challenge in his eyes, and shrugged. 'Provided you don't abandon me there,' she said carefully.

'Trust me.'

Into a silence heavy with unspoken thoughts, she said, 'I hope you know the way.'

'I know the Bay like the back of my hand.'

He stepped aside and showed her how to hold the wheel. Trying not to notice that he avoided touching her, for a glorious half-hour she steered the boat with Marc beside her as he showed her his island.

Finally he took over again and brought them into a small cove where white sand gleamed against a thick forest of cabbage trees. Behind their spiky, surreal tufts of leaves reared forest giants, tall and dark and sombre as they climbed the hills backing the beach. Massive, sprawling pohutukawas clung to the cliffs of both headlands, their reddish aerial roots dangling in the spray.

The sound of the engine muted into a low throb, barely noticeable. 'Cabbage Tree Bay,' Marc told her.

'I can see why.' She admired the clumps of tall-stemmed plants, each slender trunk finished by a tuft of long, strap-like leaves. 'It's a lily—did you know? The biggest lily in the world.'

When he smiled her heart performed an aerial ballet in her chest.

'I didn't know. My father told me that the Maori and

the early settlers used to eat the tender end of the inner leaves, which is why it's called a cabbage tree.'

'They were a prosaic lot, our forebears,' she agreed, ruthlessly ignoring the expanding bubble of excitement in her breast.

'Have you always been interested in plants?'

Paige fiddled with a button on the jacket she'd discarded. 'Always. I used to drive my mother crazy long before I went to school. I'd haul up her seeds and seedlings to see what was happening under the ground. When I got older I was fascinated by the whole miracle of it—how you could plant a tiny seed and this glorious plant would grow from it.'

'So you're more interested in plants than in landscaping?' Marc asked with a lift of his brows.

She concealed her self-consciousness with a half-smile. 'There are two sorts of gardeners: artists who paint pictures with plants, and jewellers who treat each plant like a precious gem and try to find the perfect setting for it. I'm the second sort.'

When the silence stretched too long she risked a glance upwards. He was looking above her head towards the shore, his expression hard and ruthlessly aggressive.

Chilled, Paige felt Fancy push her head into the palm of her hand. Without looking down, she stroked the dog's head.

Marc said, 'Would you go to university if you could afford it?'

She shrugged. 'Of course. But it's not going to happen in the near future.'

He leaned forward and pressed a button. Startled, she heard a chain rattle.

'It's the anchor going down,' he told her. 'What sort of career do you have in mind?'

Career? She was silent, realising that her fight to survive had banished every dream she'd once had into a grey limbo.

Eventually she said slowly, 'I'd like to hybridise plants. New Zealand does so well in that field because we can grow such a wide variety. There's nothing I'd get more pleasure from than seeing a plant of my breeding flower for the first time.'

The silence that followed her words assumed overtones she couldn't decipher.

With a narrow smile Marc nodded at the dinghy on the stern. 'I'll put the dinghy out and you can show me how well you row.'

'Why?' Paige knew she sounded bewildered.

Blue eyes gleaming, he said smoothly, 'Because you might feel like puddling around in it. The homestead is just over the hill there; it's an easy row from there to here. Satisfy me that you know what you're doing and you can take the dinghy out whenever you want to, provided you wear a life jacket.'

Paige picked up the life jacket he'd given her and put it on, then ran lightly down the steps from the flybridge. After Marc had showed her how to heave the rubber dinghy over the stern he ignored Fancy's excited barks and stood watching as with calm competence Paige worked the oars to move the little craft away from the cruiser.

It had been over a year since she'd rowed anywhere, but it was like riding a bike; you didn't forget. This dinghy was wider and more clumsy than Lloyd's old plyboard one, but it slipped through the water far more easily.

Under Marc's assessing gaze she rowed around the cruiser and then out into the centre of the Bay, returning when the palms of her hands indicated that this was as much work as they were prepared to deal with that day.

'You can row,' he said as she shipped the oars and brought the dinghy against the stern of the boat. 'Stop whining, Fancy—see, she's back.'

Paige took his outstretched hand and was hauled up, up, up—almost into his arms. He let her go just before she got there and smiled down at her, his eyes narrowed into gleaming sapphire slivers.

'Fancy loves going out in boats,' he said, a note of mockery threading through his tone, as though he could read the mute, dark frustration that weighted Paige's limbs. He glanced at his watch. 'We'd better get back.'

Neither spoke in the few minutes it took the cruiser to reach Home Bay. Marc was withdrawing, his expression stern, as though the world beyond this idyllic island was already taking him over with its demands and pressures.

But as they walked up to the house he said, 'Promise me you'll ask Rose Oliver whenever you want to take the dinghy out. She was born on the island and she knows it well. She's also pretty good on the weather.'

'I'll tell her where I'm going and listen to her if she says it's not safe,' Paige said evenly. 'I'm not stupid.'

He gave her a glinting look, hard mouth curling into a smile that sent a million tiny darts of pleasurable excitement through her. 'Far from it.' And as they reached the door he said, 'I'll send Rose along to your room with Juliette's parcel.'

In her bedroom, Paige sat down on the chair, struggling against a stupid urge to cry. She stared tensely across the subtle, sophisticated room; through the dark wooden slats of the shutters the sea danced and glittered in shards of pure, brilliant colour.

Someone knocked on the door.

Mrs Oliver carried a small box—one Paige thought she

recognised. Why, she thought in bewilderment, would Juliette leave me her mother's bracelet?

'Mr Corbett asked me to bring you this,' the older woman said. 'And there's this too.' She looked down at an envelope.

'Thank you,' Paige said thinly. She held out her hand, and after a moment's hesitation the housekeeper gave both the box and the envelope to her.

Clutching them, Paige backed into the room and closed the door, waiting long, hushed seconds before putting the box down on the white cover of the huge bed. A dark fingertip of premonition touched her soul.

'Open it!' she told herself, but it took her several more minutes before she overcame the sick panic clogging her chest and unsealed the lid.

She blinked back tears. A gold chain-link bracelet met her eyes, its heart-shaped lock set in small diamonds.

As a child she'd admired the little bracelet extravagantly, convinced it was the most beautiful thing she'd ever seen. Juliette had occasionally let her wear it, and she'd strutted around feeling like a princess.

And now Juliette was dead, and this was all she had of her—the bracelet, and the letter that had come with it. With tear-blurred eyes she picked up the envelope and read her name, written in Juliette's distinctive handwriting. Paige tore it open and took out the note inside. Slowly, carefully, she unfolded the paper.

Dearest P, if you ever read this it will mean that Marc was right to persuade me to make a will! Sorry it has taken a couple of years to get this to you—there is a reason for it, but it is not important. If it ever does become important, you'll find out why.

I know Marc will make it possible for you to stay here

*at Arohanui, no matter what your circumstances are
now. Have fun—and that is an order. I want you to stay
for a week because you work far too hard, and I know
that you will not have had a proper holiday since your
father left.*

*Are you wondering if I have any words of wisdom for
you? Sorry, I have not. Just that you should grab life
and enjoy it—especially the time you're spending here.
Lots of love, J.*

She'd added a PS.

*You were always my best friend, as well as the little
sister I never had.*

Clutching the letter, Paige got to her feet and walked
across to the window. She stared out with unseeing eyes
until another knock at the door broke into the shell of
silence.

Silently she dashed across the room and stuffed the letter
beneath the coverlet.

Sure enough, Marc stood outside the door. 'You've been
crying,' he accused, his voice clipped and hard.

'No. Just—remembering.' Before she could stop herself,
she asked, 'Was Juliette happy?'

He looked at her with an enigmatic hooded gaze. 'She
was always bright and serene, and she seemed perfectly
happy.'

In spite of Lauren's presence in his life? Not likely.

Paige said 'Why did she insist I come up here to collect
the bracelet?'

'I have no idea.' He paused, then added, 'You didn't
see much of her after she went away to boarding school,
did you?'

'No,' Paige said distantly.

'Nevertheless, you must have had a strong friendship, to last so long and bridge distance and the years so successfully. Juliette always knew what she wanted, and she wanted you here.' Marc glanced at his watch. 'Lunch is ready—come and have it with me.'

He didn't ask her what had been in the letter—not then, and not before he left. Paige sat on her bed listening to the helicopter engines fade into the distance, bitter tears aching at the back of her eyes and clogging her throat.

That night Marc rang from Australia, and the next night from Singapore, and the evening after that from Tokyo in Japan. The calls continued, and Paige found herself waiting expectantly through each lovely, lonely day for his ring.

He didn't spend much time talking, but with the brutal intensity of physical awareness muted by distance she discovered a new Marc; he told her a little of his day, described each city with economy and a flair for bringing it to life. He joked with her, teased her a little, and asked her what she'd done.

She stored small discoveries to tell him—that the fruit on the loquat tree was being eaten by a pair of large, beautiful native pigeons who sat on the branches and peered interestedly down at her with heads tipped to one side. She told him she'd been rowing around Home Bay with Fancy for a figurehead, that Mrs Oliver was making guava jelly and had shown her how bake the perfect pavlova.

Later she'd realise that she fell in love with him during those telephone calls, but for now she just knew that they satisfied something deep inside her.

On her second to last night at Arohanui he didn't ring. Painfully disappointed, she resisted the stupid feeling that because she couldn't talk it over with Marc her day had been wasted and barren.

The next morning she came in from the terrace after breakfast and said to the housekeeper, 'Summer's come early this year.'

'It's certainly a glorious day.' Mrs Oliver smiled, efficiently continuing her dusting.

'I thought I might row around to Cabbage Tree Bay,' Paige said, tracing the outline of a flower on a blue Japanese bowl.

Her sleep had been punctuated by long periods of wakefulness when her brain had twisted and turned in futile, anguished resentment. In the end she'd had to accept that she'd allowed herself to become subtly dependent on Marc for—oh, not her happiness, but for an intangible support.

She needed exercise, something physically draining, to stop her remembering that after she left Arohanui she'd never see him again.

Mrs Oliver nodded. 'The forecast is excellent. I'll pack you a lunch.'

'Thanks, but you've got your own work to do. I'll make it.'

'It's no problem,' the housekeeper said, casting a knowledgeable eye across the sky. 'Start back about two o'clock; at half-tide a current sets in around the headlands on that side of the island, and you won't want to be caught in it. Once you get out to sea there's nothing between here and South America.'

Half an hour later Paige stacked a change of clothes, sunscreen, her hat and enough food and drink for a regimental exercise into the dinghy. Fancy got in, taking up her usual position in the bow.

'Here's her leash,' the housekeeper said, handing it over. She smiled at Paige's surprise. 'There are kiwis on the island, and they're fatally attractive to dogs. Last summer Marc had a run-in with some yachties who brought their Jack Russells ashore in Cabbage Tree Bay; he sent them packing in no time. Fancy's obedient, but even she finds it hard to resist kiwis, and you might want to take her for a walk.'

'OK.' Paige put it in with the pile. 'I look as though I'm doing a Robinson Crusoe,' she observed, smiling. 'I hope you don't expect me to eat all that?'

'You'll be surprised. Sea air makes you hungry.' As Paige got into the dinghy Mrs Oliver said, 'You're not going to swim by yourself?'

'No, I haven't got my togs with me.' She organised Fancy and the oars. 'Don't worry, I know how to deal with the water. I lived beside a river for years.'

Mrs Oliver nodded. 'If anything goes wrong, just stay at Cabbage Tree and I'll send my husband for you.'

'OK.' Paige waved and set off.

CHAPTER NINE

AT THE Bay Paige and a leashed Fancy explored the grove of cabbage trees, and when the sun reached its full height Paige sat down on a rug beneath a sprawling pohutukawa and confronted lunch.

It looked and smelt delicious; Rose Oliver was a superb cook. Yet Paige's appetite refused to be aroused. In the end she ate a slice of perfect bacon and egg pie, followed it with the scented, custardy white flesh of a small cherimoya fruit, drank lime juice and water, and looked helplessly at the rest of the food.

Fancy lay a few feet away, eyes fixed on the hamper. She'd already drunk her fill from the small stream that trickled into the sea between the cabbage trees.

'We'd better not waste it all, I suppose. And you've done a lot of dashing about and swimming,' Paige said, and fed her a sandwich.

Tomorrow she was leaving this beautiful place, this dog she'd come to love, and the man who owned both island and dog. She wouldn't come back, and he wouldn't seek her out.

Even if he did, she'd refuse him. With Lauren Porter still in his life, Paige knew that the most he could offer her was less than she wanted.

After a glance at her watch she lay down on the rug and watched the sun dazzle across the sea. She had time to rest before she needed to set off again for Home Bay. Firmly, she closed her eyes.

Not a good idea. Helplessly, without mercy, her mind

replayed everything Marc had ever said to her, every touch, each eloquent lift of his brow, the stunning brilliance of his eyes, his heart-shaking smile, the angular, powerful symmetry of his face...

And the way she'd gone up in flames when they'd kissed. The violent, incandescent heat of sensation he'd summoned so effortlessly.

She startled Fancy by getting abruptly to her feet. 'Come on, let's go,' she said raggedly.

The dog snatched up a stick from the sand and dropped it at Paige's feet. Paige sighed, but said, 'Well, why not? I suppose you're missing Marc too.'

Ears pricked, Fancy looked around, as though expecting him.

'He won't come back until I've gone,' Paige told her drearily, and picked up the stick.

Although the very simple game involved only hurling the stick into the waves and watching Fancy retrieve it, kill it on the sand and then bring it back to her, it should burn off some of the reckless energy that pulsed through her.

And perhaps it might keep at bay for a few minutes the secret unhappiness that had stolen like a thief into her heart.

She strode along the beach towards the rocky headland that separated this beach from Home Bay, trying to smile as Fancy pounced on the stick before dancing it back through the tiny waves, golden hair flying, sheer joy in every movement.

Pain gripped her. After tomorrow she'd never see the dog again. She'd never see Mrs Oliver, or her silent, shy husband, never see the vivid garden and the lovely, gracious house at its heart.

Never see Marc, her heart whispered.

Once more Paige threw the stick, then set off towards the dinghy, trying to banish the bitter taste of loss.

She stopped, shading her eyes to watch the dog. Sunlight sultry with the promise of summer beat down on her head and shoulders. The hollow emptiness eating into her self-sufficiency terrified her.

She had no idea when she'd made the decision never to rely on another person for her happiness; it hadn't been a conscious one. Living with a mother whose sense of self-hood had depended completely on the man she'd married had produced that unspoken determination to keep her own identity intact.

And now it was under threat. Marc's potent masculinity had bulldozed through her defences, but that was only part of the problem; she wanted much more from him than the promise of magnificent sex. She wanted the companion-ship he'd given her in those telephone calls—she wanted a future with him.

A shiver tightened her skin, chilled her heart. She crossed her arms and rubbed from her wrists to her elbows, staring blindly out to sea.

'I'm not in love with Marc Corbett,' she said aloud, despising the sound of her thin, unsure voice.

This acute physical awareness wasn't love, and neither was her fascination with him. Naturally she found him interesting to talk to—intelligence always intrigued her. So did competence. And Marc was nothing if not competent.

If he'd been born without that solid wealth behind him he'd have made it for himself. Articles in the financial pages praised his raw ability and dynamic initiative, tem-pered by a disciplined, incisive brain and will; they were his defining qualities, not the results of his privileged back-ground.

'And don't forget the fact that he looks like some romantic dream,' she said on a whiplash of self-contempt.

Shaking her head, she narrowed her eyes against the brilliant light. The more she let Marc invade her mind, the greater power she yielded to him.

Frowning, she focused on the water, trying to pick out the stick in the shimmering, deceptive webs of gold the sun spun on the surface of the sea. Fancy was swimming steadily on.

'Ah, there it is,' Paige muttered, then drew in a quick breath.

The stick had acquired momentum, and was moving slowly, purposefully away from the beach. Squinting against the sun, Paige realised that it had been caught in a current.

She cupped her mouth and shouted, 'Fancy, come back! Get back here!'

But Fancy ignored her. And she too was being dragged inexorably towards the rocky end of the far headland.

Fear coagulated in an icy pool beneath Paige's ribs. Once past the cliffs there was nothing between Fancy and the open sea.

Marc loved this dog; if she'd thrown sticks along the beach, instead of into the water, Fancy would be safely on firm ground.

Paige raced over the hot sand to the dinghy. It took her precious moments to pull on and secure the life jacket, but she didn't dare go out without it. And it seemed to take an age to drag the dinghy to the water's edge.

Once it was floating she heaved it seawards with all her strength and flung herself in, snatching up the oars to row as hard and as steadily as she could. Within a couple of minutes she heard the current chuckle under the boat, and felt its inexorable grip carry her towards the dog. A brisk wind whipped her hair into her eyes; she shook it free and concentrated on getting to Fancy.

From what she remembered of the tour Marc had given her, the headland straightened out into a long line of cliffs facing the open sea, rock stacks cluttering their base. Although the sea couldn't be more calm, there'd be no safe harbour there, so she'd have to make it back to Cabbage Tree Bay. And with wind and tide against her that could take some effort.

Fortunately that combination of wind and current meant she got to Fancy before the dog exhausted herself.

'All right, girl,' she said, steadying the little craft against the current; she shipped the oars and leaned over to grab Fancy's collar.

'Up, girl,' she coaxed, and hauled.

It took a couple of heaves, but Fancy's scrabbling co-operation and the dinghy's inherent stability finally brought the dog safely in—where, of course, she promptly shook herself, drenching the only other inhabitant.

'Sit *down*, you daft dog! We have to get back.' Paige risked a glance at the headland, now ominously close, and wished fervently that the dinghy had come equipped with an anchor.

'Well, it hasn't,' she said, beginning the row back to Cabbage Tree Bay. To hearten herself she told Fancy, now in her usual place as figurehead, 'It's do-able. We'll just take it steadily.'

But the current showed its teeth. And the dinghy, so stable and safe, caught enough wind to make progress slow and difficult. After ten minutes Paige glanced up and real-ised with an abrupt arrow of foreboding just how far she still had to go.

She was only just making headway against that lethal

combination of tide and wind; if either increased in strength she'd be swept out to sea.

Setting her jaw, she concentrated on rowing evenly, letting her mind concentrate on getting the dinghy a little closer to land with each stroke.

Where the hell were the boats that usually dotted the Bay? She could see sails, and some motor cruisers, but they were all too far away to be hailed and none came closer.

'It's a conspiracy,' she muttered, trying to smile at the absurd idea.

The muscles in her shoulders were beginning to burn resentfully when Fancy barked. Paige cast a glance over her shoulder, and if she'd had any energy to spare might have cheered at the sight of the motor cruiser purling around the headland that separated Cabbage Tree Bay from Home Bay.

Waving frantically, she croaked above the growing roar of its engine, 'There, old girl, everything's fine now! We're safe!'

An alteration in the pitch of the engines confirmed that the driver had seen her and answered her call for help. But, just in case, she kept rowing. The big cruiser idled closer; frowning, she scanned its lines, then looked up into the flybridge. Her pulses raced when she recognised Marc behind the wheel.

Such potent, overwhelming delight blazed through her that she realised just how much she'd been fooling herself.

'Oh, God,' she whispered, face white beneath her hat. 'What have you *done*?'

Limp with reaction, she shipped the oars and waited until the cruiser eased to a halt between them and the flow of the current. At the helm, Marc cut the engines to a mere throb in the water.

Paige waited tensely as he manoeuvred the big craft with skilful, delicate precision; a couple of times she had to use the oars, until eventually the dinghy was swept gently against the diving platform at the stern. He left the engines idling and came rapidly down from the flybridge, hauling the dinghy onto its platform with raw energy that spoke of strong emotion.

'Are you all right?' he demanded, his voice abrasive with anger.

Paige looked up into his blazing eyes. 'Fine,' she said tonelessly.

'Get out and I'll deal with Fancy.'

He made it sound easy, but when she tried to stand up her legs buckled like straws. Strong hands grabbed her and hauled her up into the cockpit. Violently tempted to collapse against him, she forced herself upright.

'I'm all right,' she muttered. 'Why have my legs given way? It's my arms and shoulders that have done all the work.'

'Shock.' He plonked her down onto a padded bench and turned to fasten the dinghy after ordering, 'Don't move.'

By now Fancy was aboard, frisking around Marc until he spoke with crisp authority to her. When he bent to deal with a rope Paige watched the muscles in his shoulders bunch and flex, appalled at the power of the sexual instinct in humans. Although waves of tiredness were draining the energy from her, something feral and uncontrolled stirred in the depths of her body. She'd have to be dead, she thought, her palms clammy with fear, not to respond to him.

Marc straightened and gave her a very level, very blue glare. 'Why didn't you anchor and wait for someone to come looking for you?'

'There's no anchor in the dinghy.'

His jaw hardened and he swore beneath his breath. 'I'm sorry. From now on there will be,' he said grimly.

Fancy chose that moment to shake herself again, sending drops of water flying around her like silver bullets.

Paige watched spots darken Marc's fine cotton shirt and the tailored trousers that clung to his lean hips and long legs, and started to laugh helplessly. For that moment the world shone with the promise of delight, because Marc had come home.

His hard face relaxed into a grin, and her laughter faded as she realised with a spasm of sheer, mindless panic that she'd fallen in love with him.

Common sense warned her that she didn't know him well enough. A deeper, more primitive instinct told her she'd loved him—painfully, hopelessly, fiercely—since the moment she'd first seen him.

Some hidden part had recognised him as the man she could give her heart to. And she had; in spite of trying so hard to convince herself that it was nothing more than a crude sexual urge, she'd always known that she loved Marc.

She turned her head sideways to hide the tears that stung her eyes.

But he'd seen. 'You're exhausted,' he said, his amusement obliterated. 'Come into the cabin—I'll make you a drink.'

'I'm wet,' she blurted.

'So am I.' When she still didn't move he picked her up, ignoring her squeak of astonishment to shoulder his way into the main cabin.

Paige blinked desperately, fighting the lure of that strong shoulder. 'It was my fault,' she muttered. 'I was throwing a stick for Fancy and it got caught in the current off Cabbage Tree Bay and she took off.'

'So you rescued her. It's all right.' He sat her down on one of the seats and stood back, his eyes searching her face. 'Do you want a shower?'

Paige could have killed for a shower, but she had no other clothes to get into, and the thought of climbing back into salty wet clothes was distasteful. 'I'll wait until we get back ho—to the house.'

Scarlet with humiliation, she closed her eyes. She had almost called the homestead home—as though she had some claim to the place!

She felt him look at her, but kept her eyes obstinately closed. However, when she heard soft sounds from the galley she forced herself onto her feet, wondering why her body felt like lead.

'Sit down,' he said, arriving with a glass of very pale orange juice.

She looked at him with a spark of defiance. 'If I stay there I might never get up again.'

'You will,' he said coolly. 'You don't give up.'

She accepted the glass. 'I try not to.'

'We have that in common,' he said, and put a hand on her shoulder, urging her back onto the banquette. 'Stay there until you've got some liquid into you. It's water with a splash of orange juice to flavour it. Straight juice isn't good for anyone who's dehydrated.'

'It looks wonderful,' she said, abruptly dry-mouthed and incredibly thirsty. 'But I don't need flavouring for water; I like the taste.' She sipped slowly.

His gaze burned like a blue flame. 'Honest and straight-forward,' he said curtly. 'Yet you're complex too, layer after layer after layer, and you resist every attempt to peel you back.'

Deluged by a slow, simmering tide of honeyed sensation, she veiled her eyes with her lashes. 'You make me sound like an onion. Peeling them makes people cry.'

'Some men might take that as a challenge.' His mouth curved in a smile that had mockery and speculation blended in equal parts.

'I'm not up to challenges at the moment,' she returned promptly.

'How do you feel? How stiff are your arms and shoulders?'

She wriggled experimentally. 'Not too bad,' she said, surprised.

'You're probably fitter than you think. Show me your hands.'

Blinking, she held them out. He startled her by taking them in his and turning them over so that he could inspect the palms. A sharp sizzle of electricity banished exhaustion; she drew in a sharp breath and had only just enough will power to force them to lie limply in his.

He felt it too, that hidden, dangerous warmth. Sparks glinted in his eyes and he let her go, saying harshly, 'Another five minutes or so and you'd have had raw patches. When we get home I'll get you some cream for those blisters. Stay there and drink your water slowly while I get us back.'

Silently she watched him go out and up the set of stairs that led to the flybridge. Her breath eased out between her lips and her heart-rate steadied, although it still raced. And, because it was inexpressibly pleasant to be looked after by Marc, she did as she was told, sipping slowly in bemused compliance.

Too soon, however, she began to swelter. She got up and stripped off the life jacket, then went out into the breeze. Fancy was snoozing in the cockpit; she opened one eye as Paige went up the steps to the flybridge.

'Oh,' she said, startled because they were in Cabbage Tree Bay. 'I thought we were going back to the homestead.'

The anchor went into the water with another swift outcry of chain. Marc gave her a keen glance that settled into a scrutiny. 'It won't take us a moment to pick up your gear. I'll do it; you and Fancy can stay on board. You look feverish.'

She raised a self-conscious hand to her flushed face. 'Just a bit hot; I was stewing in the life jacket.' She cleared her throat and found an innocuous subject. 'Fancy looks very relaxed. I hope she's all right—she was in the water for quite a long time.'

'She spends summers mostly in the water. She'll be fine. You'll be the one who'll be stiff tomorrow morning,' Marc said, a definite note of reserve in the words.

'I don't think so. One thing taking care of a baby does is strengthen your arms and shoulders.'

She squinted into the sun and he said, 'Go down and get into the cabin. You're turning slightly pink, and the reflection from the water will make it worse.'

He watched her walk to the top of the companionway and disappear, using her hands carefully. No sign of stiffness yet; she moved freely, with the swaying natural grace he'd noticed the first time he'd seen her—an unconscious, elemental invitation to every male in sight. His groin stirred and he turned back to the wheel with a silent, impatient oath.

This, he thought with biting irritation, was getting to be inconvenient.

It had been a bitch of a trip. He'd been presented with a clear case of corruption by one of his senior executives, and apart from his cold fury at the deception tidying it up was going to cost; keeping it quiet was going to be damned near impossible. As well, a subsidiary in Asia had managed to offend someone very important in the government, which had meant a side trip to smooth things over there.

Yet for the first time he'd had to fight to keep his mind on the issues. It had exasperated him; he'd resented this woman's ability to infiltrate an area of his life that had always been inviolate.

So he'd come back early, and realised just how much Paige had subverted his mind when Rose Oliver told him she wasn't there. He'd taken the launch out because it was the quickest way to get to her.

And his blood had run like ice in his veins when he'd rounded the point and seen her rowing valiantly across the current.

The sooner they went to bed the better, he decided bleakly. Then he'd be able to get her out of his system.

He set off down the companionway, but Paige met him at the door of the cabin.

'You took a bottle of beer out of the fridge,' she said. 'Do you want it?'

He'd intended to drink it, until touching her hands had driven the idea completely from his mind. 'Thanks.' He lifted the small cold bottle to his mouth to take a good gulp, relishing the honest taste and the refreshing chill of the liquid.

'I didn't know you were coming home today,' she said out of the blue. She was keeping her head turned away on the pretext of looking at her juice, but her knuckles were white against the frosted glass.

'Just as well I did,' he said curtly. 'I won't tell you what I felt when I saw you being carried out to sea by the current.'

Her full mouth quivered, then tightened. 'I was making

headway,' she objected. 'I'd have got there. But I was very glad to see the boat come around the point.'

'The most sensible thing would have been to let Fancy go. A dog's life is not as valuable as a human's.'

Paige's head shot up. 'Intellectually I know that, but I couldn't just let her drown.'

'You're too soft for your own good,' he said drily, eyes very blue as he surveyed her.

'Ha!' The word and the smile that accompanied it were pure challenge.

'A woman who gave up her chance of a career to stay at home and care for her mother, then asked a pregnant down-on-her-luck stripper to move in has to be soft-hearted,' he pointed out ironically.

'How did you know that?'

'Sherry told me you rescued her from almost certain destitution.'

'Rubbish!' she interposed robustly.

'When her husband left her. You offered her a bed, helped her get benefit from the government, and you sat with her during her labour and the birth with all the devotion of a sister.'

'Who wouldn't?' she asked matter-of-factly.

'Not everyone would have taken in a stripper,' he said drily.

Made uncomfortable by his keen scrutiny, Paige shrugged. 'She stopped stripping as soon as she got pregnant. And all she needed was support.'

His brow lifted. 'For which she's eternally grateful, as she should be. She also made sure I knew that while you were soft she was not, and more or less warned me to watch myself.'

Paige's jaws met with an audible click, damming the hot words that threatened to spill out.

'Your eyes turn pure green when you're angry,' he said conversationally. 'And they gleam gold when you're aroused. It's like being drowned in fire. I'll see you in ten minutes or so.'

Stunned, she watched him free the dinghy and push it into the water, tell Fancy severely that she wasn't going with him, and row for the shore.

He was back in the ten minutes he'd promised, and unloaded her gear onto the cruiser with another stern word to Fancy, who showed signs of wanting to leap into the water again. He looked up as Paige came out of the cabin to help.

'Stay out of the sun until we get back to Home Bay,' he said austerely.

'Yes, sir.'

One dark brow lifted. 'You're not up to it,' he said softly, and went up to the flybridge.

Once the wooden planks of the Home Bay jetty were safely under feet, Paige smiled in Marc's general direction and said, 'I'll have that shower now.'

'I'll see you later.'

Which sounded ominous. Keeping her face and eyes averted, she picked up the rug and her bag and walked steadfastly away from him.

CHAPTER TEN

MARC caught her up as she reached the door of the house. 'Get under the shower and let the water play on your shoulders and back. You know how to alter the head setting?' At her nod he said, 'Stay under it for as long as you can. I'll send Rose along with that cream for your hands.'

Safe at last in her bathroom, Paige leant into the heavy pulse of the spray, trying to relax as the jets massaged away the ache in her upper arms and shoulders. Although the pummelling hot water brought her superficial ease, a deep inner tension still knotted her nerves.

What a naïve, weak-willed idiot she was! Somehow, in spite of everything she'd done to prevent it, she'd allowed herself to fall in love with Marc Corbett, world-famous tycoon and heartbreaker. Helpless against her hidden desires, she'd let herself be carried along by a force of nature, and inevitably she'd succumbed.

'Like so many other women,' she muttered, pushing her wet hair back from her face. 'Like Lauren.'

A profound grief shadowed her soul. She couldn't give way to it because she still had the rest of the evening and the night to get through, not to mention tomorrow morning before she left for Napier. Marc had organised it all; at nine the helicopter would take her across to Kerikeri, and the same executive jet that had brought her to Arohanui would take her away.

Only this time he wasn't coming with her.

Choking back a sob, she grimly washed the sweat and the salt from her hair. 'I can cope,' she said beneath her breath. But the words echoed with bitterness, and she added silently, *Because I have to. I'm not going to let myself end up like my mother, so fixated on one man that life without him was a dead end.*

Eventually, when her hands started to wrinkle, she got out and wrapped herself in a large white bath towel before picking up the hairdryer. The play of warm air on her head normally soothed her, but not now. Raw grief waited like a predator, ready to catch her the moment she let her guard down.

She'd just finished when she heard the knock on the door. Tightening the knot that kept the towel safe, she shook her hair back and hurried across the bedroom.

Only it wasn't the housekeeper with cream for her hands. Marc stood outside. He too had showered and changed, and he was utterly overwhelming—a proud prince of darkness—with the leaping blue lights in those astonishing eyes the only sign of emotion in his handsome, ruthless face.

Heart jumping in her chest, Paige opened her mouth to say something—anything!—and seized gratefully on the arrival of Fancy, who demanded a pat.

Stooping, one hand on the knot between her breasts, Paige stroked the dog's head and tried to think of something sensible to say. 'Oh,' she murmured vaguely, 'she's still damp.'

'I've just washed the salt water out of her coat. Here's the cream I promised you for your hands.'

His voice was steady, almost deliberate, but the rasping note beneath the banal words tightened her every muscle, set every cell humming.

She straightened and without meeting his eyes said brightly, 'Thank you. My palms are starting to regret the last ten minutes in the dinghy.'

Marc held out the tube. With a foolish nod she took it, careful not to touch him. Tiny drums beat in her ears, and she resisted a strong urge to say his name and look at him.

Clumsily she stepped back, and tripped over Fancy, who'd sidled behind her to check out the bedroom. Paige cried out and time slid backwards, replaying itself in slow motion. Again she jerked sideways, this time trying to avoid falling on the dog.

Once again strong arms caught her. Once again she was turned into Marc's arms and looked up into eyes whose brilliant colour was being overwhelmed by darkness.

Paige's breath came fast and soft through her lips. Mutely she stared at him.

'This is getting to be a habit,' Marc said in a silky voice that sent the blood beating through her veins in a merciless tide.

'No,' she whispered, but whether it was an answer or a weak plea for him to let her go she didn't know, because her brain had turned to marshmallow the moment he touched her.

When his lips met hers it was like diving into the heart of the sun. Yet she tried to resist until her newborn love, reinforced by the bleak knowledge that after tomorrow she'd never see him again, flamed into a need so potent, so urgent, she surrendered to its insistent demand.

They kissed with a starving desperation that consumed her in a storm of sensation. Her hands stole up to clasp his neck and she opened her mouth and lost the last bit of herself in the taste, the scent of him, the heat from his body and his unleashed male power. Helplessly she responded to the rhythm of those kisses, falling further and further under the dark enchantment he wrought with his mouth and his touch.

She shuddered when he cupped her breast, shuddered

again when his thumb moved across the urgent nipple. Sensations so exquisitely fresh they were almost anguish sliced through her in sweet ferocity. At last she was going to find out what real desire was like—and she was fiercely glad that she had waited until she loved him before yielding.

She had no sexual tricks, no sophisticated techniques to offer him, and he didn't want her love, but this she could give—the untrained, honest responses of her body and her heart.

Yet he didn't know she was a virgin, and he might not value her gift. For a moment she froze, assailed by a chill of shyness.

'Paige. Look at me.'

The way he said her name and the kiss that accompanied it mixed desire and tenderness, as though he understood her fear.

She looked up, and he smiled and kissed her again, little kisses along her throat and across her shoulder, his mouth warm and seeking.

Her knees gave way; with a low, triumphant laugh he picked her up and lifted her high. Marvelling at the easy flexion of his body against hers, she looked up into his face. Passion emphasised the hawkish angles, gleamed darkly in his eyes, heated the skin across his sweeping cheekbones.

And then she remembered Juliette, and Lauren Porter. If she surrendered she'd be joining all those other women who'd loved Marc, only to discover that their love hadn't been enough for him.

He saw it happen. His expression hardened into distaste, the blue eyes glittering like frozen fire. 'You little tease,' he said, in a voice that blended savage anger and contempt, and set her down on her feet.

Humiliated, because her damned knees still wouldn't hold her upright, she had to grab his arm for support. But she found the strength to let him go and step back, although each movement weighed her down as though she was walking through quicksand.

'I take it that's a refusal,' he said with a slow, dangerously threatening smile.

She shook her head, feeling the heavy weight of her hair hot and tumbled on her neck. 'I'm not into fulfilling temporary needs,' she said huskily, despising herself for the bitter ache of grief.

His brow shot up, devastatingly ironic, but his voice was straight disdain. 'What do you want? A promise of permanence?'

'What would you know about permanence?' she asked in a low, scornful tone. 'Juliette wasn't enough for you, and even with Lauren Porter to cater to your every whim you're unable to keep faithful to her.'

White around the mouth, he surveyed her with hooded, molten eyes. 'Did Juliette tell you that?'

'Who else would?'

'She was wrong.' When she lifted her brows in disbelief he said with freezing distaste, 'Lauren and I are good and close friends, but there is nothing romantic or sexual between us.'

A wild tumult of emotions rocketed through her—a reckless desire to believe him, mixed with disgust and angry resentment. 'So why did Juliette think there was?'

'Like me, she grew up in a household where the husband couldn't keep his hands off other women.' He watched her with an unyielding expression. 'Unlike my mother, hers accepted her father's mistresses as a fact of life. Juliette grew up with a pragmatic outlook; she didn't believe in friendship between men and women. For her, there had to be a sexual component to any relationship.'

Horrified by the strength of her need to believe him, Paige remained obstinately silent.

He said harshly, 'I had no idea she saw Lauren as a threat until just before she was killed. I told her what I'm telling you—when I make vows I keep them. I was faithful to her.'

Paige couldn't formulate any answer. The hunger to believe him ate into her will power, but she didn't dare give in to it. Appalled, she realised that she was wringing her hands, and with an effort forced them apart to hang limply by her sides.

'Look at me,' he commanded.

Her hair swirled round her face as she shook her head.

'Paige, I don't believe this. You're such a valiant fighter I'd never have taken you for a coward.'

The note of amused gentleness in his voice shredded her determination. She glanced up and was lost, her gaze ensnared by the piercing brilliance of his.

He said roughly, 'I want you so much—so much—but not if you don't believe me. If there is nothing else between lovers, there must be truth.'

No man could speak with such blazing honesty and lie.

A shudder of need tightened her skin; she felt the small hard points of her breasts peak beneath the soft material of the bath sheet.

'Paige,' he said between his teeth, his voice so guttural she had difficulty discerning the words, 'turn around while I leave this room. Then lock your door after me.'

She'd intended to ask him whether Juliette had married him for practical reasons; she'd wanted to watch his face when he answered. But the idea fled as she met his eyes, points of sapphire flame in the golden skin of his sculpted face.

Longing and frustration combined like fire and petrol, urged on by an intensity of relief that Juliette had known the truth before she'd been so tragically taken; she said unevenly, 'Thank you for—I needed to know that. And I'm so glad Juliette didn't die believing that you had—that you were—'

He reached out to catch a tear slipping from the corner of her eye. In a hard voice he said, 'So am I. I don't deserve your tears, Paige, and she wouldn't have wanted you to cry for her.'

And as if he couldn't help it he lifted his hand and licked the tear from his finger. 'I have to go,' he said harshly. When she shook her head, he waited for a heart-stopping moment, then asked on a rough note, 'Are you certain, *mon coeur*?'

My heart—probably an everyday endearment in France, but she'd cherish the way he'd said it for the rest of her life.

'Yes.' She had never been more sure of anything in her life.

Her clamouring senses demanded satisfaction, but it was an upwelling of love that drove her to hold his hand against her cheek. Nothing, she realised with a swift, intense relief, had ever been more right than this. The last virginal tremors dissipated like dew under a benign sun as passion rioted through her, dazzling her with its stupendous intensity.

He turned and closed the door on Fancy. Then he pulled Paige gently against him and his mouth came down on her forehead.

'Are your arms and shoulders very painful?' he murmured.

Dimly she understood that he was giving her another chance to pull back. In some distant recess of her brain common sense drummed out warning and instructions, but she couldn't concentrate on anything but the clean, salty scent that was his alone. Essence of Marc, she thought desperately, fighting off the impulse to push her nose into his chest and inhale.

And his heat, curling around her like smoke, driving away the warnings until they turned into vapour and disappeared. Slowly, captured by the dilating intensity of his eyes, she slid her hand up to rest on his chest and luxuriated in his closeness.

Huskily, her mind finally surrendering to the barrage of sensory input, she said, 'My shoulders and arms are fine, but I think I can feel a chill coming on.'

His heart kicked against her palm. The heavy catch in its steady rhythm filled her with astonished triumph.

'We can't have that,' he said thickly, picking her up again and walking across the room.

Beside the bed she expected him to put her down, but instead he stopped and looked down into her face, his eyes almost black. Very quietly he asked, 'Are you sure you know what you're doing?'

Did he guess that this was the first time for her? She didn't care.

'Oh, yes,' she said huskily. And because she suspected that he was going to spell out that making love to her meant nothing beyond a momentary pleasure—a statement she wouldn't be able to bear—she lifted her head and kissed the words from his mouth.

When his arms tightened around her, and his demanding mouth turned that tentative kiss into an avowal of naked hunger, she accepted that she'd regret this surrender. Yet she knew she'd regret much more not making love with Marc.

And then she could no longer think. Banishing the last remnants of fear, she slipped the leash on her senses and allowed them to run riot.

Some time—a long time—later, her feet touched the floor. She swayed on boneless legs, dragging air into her famished lungs when he slid his hands beneath the towel and opened it. The damp bath sheet fell to the ground and she was exposed to him.

Swift colour stained her skin, turning it rose-gold. He was probably accustomed to women in silk and satin, she thought wildly, and wished she had some sexy, sensuous garment to wear.

He cupped a breast in his lean, strong hand. 'Look,' he said, his voice a deep rumble that reverberated through her.

She obeyed, sensation knotting in the pit of her stomach at the contrast of his long, tanned fingers against her gleaming skin.

'You're the colour of a peach,' he said quietly, and met her eyes with a stark urgency that splintered the last of her resistance.

All that mattered now was Marc, and her need to give him everything she could.

'Don't be shy,' he said, the slight French intonation in his voice strengthening. 'You are so beautiful, and I want you so much that I'm scared.'

'You?' she croaked as his thumb stroked the pleading nub of her breast with a skill that indicated his experience.

Sheer, astonishing pleasure shot from there to the rest of her body, scintillated across her nerves, lit up every cell in a parade of sensuous fireworks. Her breath choked in her lungs, then came and went swiftly through her part-ed lips.

He gave a soft, ironic laugh. 'Is that so surprising? Any man would be terrified by such beauty.' Before she could answer he buried his mouth in the hollow of her throat.

The touch of his lips fuelled her runaway anticipation, and when he nipped the spot where her neck joined her shoulder the sharp edges of his teeth produced an almost painful excitement.

She clung to him, gasping as he moved his hand upwards. For a moment she hung on the cusp between fear and violent anticipation, until he kissed her throat again and claimed her other breast with one teasing stroke of his fingers.

And then he said quietly, 'Take off my shirt.'

Her hands were shaking so much that she could barely push the buttons through their holes. When Marc shrugged free of the shirt she sighed, devouring him with shadowed eyes.

'You're so—so broad,' she breathed. Her fingertips lingered on smooth, hot, supple skin, sleekly taut over the hard swell of a muscle.

'I won't hurt you,' he said harshly.

She gave him a swift glance and looked away, her hand falling to her side. 'I know.'

And clearly he knew that she wasn't experienced. Was she being awkward and gauche? Should she explain that this was the first time for her—and run the risk of having him pull back?

No.

'How do you know that?' He caught her hand and rested it lightly against his chest, the soft abrasion of the pattern of hair a stimulus in itself.

She bit her lip. 'Pain is barbaric,' she murmured, 'and you're very civilised.'

He gave a bark of sardonic laughter. Paige looked up in surprise.

'At the moment,' he said, curving his hand around her breast, 'I'm very *un*civilised—almost purely primitive, in fact. But I won't hurt you.'

And he bent his black head and drew the tight, expectant nub of her breast into his mouth.

Paige froze, captured by impossible pleasure, by intolerable excitement. When he lifted his head she could have cried out in protest.

In a voice made deep and slow by carnal hunger, Marc said, 'Yes, you are beautiful, delicate and fragile as a flower, yet like a flower there's strength and determination in you.'

He picked her up and lowered her onto the bed. Still flushing, she watched with dilating eyes as he stripped. She was under no illusions; although she'd loved him for ever, and he wanted her now, his desire was deceptive and illusory as moonshine, a fleeting, beautiful thing. She would make love with him, and when it was time she'd leave with her pride intact and without a backward glance.

With slow, drugging expertise Marc kissed every thought from her head, and when he lifted his mouth he was beside her on the bed, an arm around her shoulders holding her against his lean, eager body.

A primal thrill scorched through Paige. Somewhere outside a gull screeched, its angry, spiteful call jaggedly reminding her that there was a reality outside the room and this man.

She didn't care.

Turning her head, she kissed his shoulder, then licked where she'd kissed; the faint salty taste of his skin was fiercely erotic to her, as was the tight sound from his throat and the dark flames in his eyes.

He ran a hand down her body, beginning at her throat and finishing at the place where her thighs met, and while her lashes slowly fluttered down he gave a crooked smile and began to show her exactly what magic a man and a woman could make together.

The instinct that had warned her he'd be a consummate lover had been dead on target. Marc seemed to understand more about her body than she did. He knew that his mouth on her breast twisted sensation inside her, tightening it until she sobbed on a shivering wave of heated rapture.

He explored her with his mouth, unlocking a reckless response that built and built and built until she was sobbing with a delicious frustration, her hands clenched by her sides and her body a taut, pleading bow under his ministrations.

Eventually she whispered in a hoarse, desperate little voice, 'Please. Marc, I can't—I want—'

His kiss pressed her head back into the pillow with its depth and demand, and while she was lost in that sorcery he moved over her, prolonging the kiss as he eased into her.

A sharp jab brought Paige's eyelashes bolting up. Dazedly she stared into Marc's eyes and read astonishment there, and then—amazingly—a white-hot satisfaction.

Harshly he said, 'I'm sorry—I didn't know.'

'It's all right,' she said, desperation cutting across the words as the ardent delight receded a little.

He kissed her again, and against her lips he murmured, 'Try to relax.'

'I can't,' she said, starkly honest, her hands gripping his shoulders. 'I want you too much.'

'So?' The muscles beneath her hands bunched and he pushed, slowly widening that path until the fragile barrier ripped.

Urgently she said, 'It's not—it's fine.'

'Good.' And he drove home.

What followed was pure drama. Never losing control, he wooed her with his body and his voice, driving her further and further up the sides of some insurmountable cliff, a long, pleasure-drenched journey where he was guide and mentor. At last, poised on the brink of rapturous knowledge, she reached the top and spun off into delight, ecstatic waves breaking through her body until she could bear it no longer.

Almost immediately he followed her, big body taut as a bow, and without realising it made her his for all time.

Her last thought, barely coherent before she slipped into sleep, was that whatever happened to her in the future she had this memory of delight to treasure.

It was dusk when she woke, with the distant noise of a helicopter buzzing in her ears. She turned towards the empty side of the bed, unconsciously questing, then re-membered, and blushed, and lay for several moments while the memories flooded through her.

Stretching luxuriously, she thought that no other woman in the world could have had such a long, idyllically sensual introduction to making love. Marc had been gentle and skilful, until gentleness and skill had been abandoned in raw male fire as desire overtook him.

It had been perfect. Marc had been perfect. She thought idly that she was no longer a virgin, and smiled, enjoying the tiny signals of his possession—her tender lips, a small ache between her legs, the deep, lingering sensuality.

Loving Marc had opened her to change, shown her that if this once was all she'd ever have of him—well, it would be enough for a lifetime. Because after this there would be no other man for her.

But she knew now that she wouldn't retreat from life as

her mother had; instead, she'd live it richly and fully, because love meant much more than a cowardly dependence.

She moved restlessly on the bed, turning to look at the indentation on the pillow beside her where Marc's head had rested. Satiety bred appetite; instead of being satisfied with the miracle he'd made for her she wanted to loosen the bars on the wild need that sang in forbidden cadences through her body, demanding a like response from him too.

She wanted him to lose control as she had lost it; she wanted him to know the almost aggressive craving that felt as though it might tear her apart—to feel it and to be forced to surrender to it.

'It isn't going to happen,' she said aloud. 'So take what you got and be contented.'

If she made love with him again it would shatter her self-esteem and break her heart. Marc might have ravished her soul from her body, but neither that afternoon or now had he said anything about a future.

So she'd have to resist this intense love that undermined every warning, every sensible thought and decision.

'Why?' she asked suddenly. After all, she'd made love to him knowing that he wasn't going to offer her permanence—he'd made sure of that with brutal frankness.

Resisting him would be cutting off her nose to spite her face.

She had tonight—their last night together. And, because she wasn't wasting a moment of it, she sprang out of bed and into the shower, then dressed swiftly before going out to see where he was.

Marc looked up from his desk. His eyes narrowed when he saw Paige wander across the lawn towards the beach.

She looked forlorn, he thought, and found himself on his feet, setting off to make everything better for her.

Fortunately logic kicked in before he'd taken more than a couple of steps. His mouth compressed into a straight line and he strode back to his desk, stepping over a comatose Fancy.

This desire to smooth the way for her was suspicious. He swore beneath his breath; he'd assumed that at her age she'd have had some experience. Her virginity had surprised the hell out of him.

And pleased him far too much, he thought with a twist of self-derision. He hadn't ever made love to a virgin before and, damn it, it changed things.

So what to do now?

The telephone rang. Impatiently he picked it up and barked, 'Yes?'

'Darling, I'll be with you in an hour,' Lauren said, not at all discomposed. 'I've got everything ready; there's just a couple of things to finalise, papers for you to sign off, and then it will be done. See you soon.'

Marc put the telephone down and frowned, his eyes on the solitary figure walking along the beach. Fancy had gone out to join her and they made a pretty picture in the dying glow of the sun, outlined in a crimson glow against the shimmer of the sea.

Closing down the computer took a couple of seconds while he sorted the papers he'd need later that night, when he spoke to his office in London.

Then he went out into the soft spring dusk, scented with the sea and the perfume of the season, a sensuous breath of growth and fertility. His mouth quirked cynically when he noted a glow behind the hill that promised a full moon. A cliché if ever there was one!

Yet clichés had power, and in spite of himself his instincts woke, strong and powerfully primal within him. But not tonight, he thought. For too many reasons; Lauren would be here, and Paige would…

She'd gone down to the edge of the water and was standing very still as she stared out to sea, her slender body held upright by that steel spine.

As he watched she straightened already straight shoulders and stooped to pick up a stone, hurling it across the water.

It skipped five times before sinking.

'You've practised that,' Marc said drily, walking down to join her.

Paige's heart jumped. Sheer force of will stopped her from whirling around, but her voice sounded breathy and startled when she said, 'For about three months when I was ten.'

'It must be a ten-year-old's rite of passage.' He strolled down onto the sand, Fancy a silent shadow at his heels. 'My father taught me how to do it here.'

He stooped, picked up a flat, round pebble and sent it out with a deft twist of his wrist. Both watched it skip six times before falling into the water.

'Do you take everything so competitively?' Paige asked wryly.

He shrugged. 'I wasn't trying to beat your score, but competition was bred into me.'

He kept so much of himself hidden that Paige held her breath, wondering if she dared follow up this tiny hint. What had his father been like? Had he shown his son a softer side?

'No quarter given?' she asked.

'He played to win, even when I was four and he was teaching me chess.'

Her heart twisted at the thought of a small boy faced

with his father's determination to beat him. 'I'll bet he was a bad loser.'

He laughed. 'The first time I got him he admitted defeat with gritted teeth, but I heard him bragging about it to a friend. He was proud of me.'

'Ah,' she said softly, 'one of those supreme moments, like the instant you realise that it's you, not the bike, in control.'

There was amusement in his voice when he agreed, yet through the comfortable silence that followed a familiar wild hunger simmered through her veins.

She gestured at the crimson afterglow of the sunset over the mainland and said, 'I can see why you call this place home. It's completely, ravishingly beautiful.'

And she'd eat her heart out for it—and its owner—after she left.

'Beauty beyond compare,' he agreed, turning his head so that for a moment the crimson light from the sea was reflected onto his profile. His beautiful mouth sketched an ironic smile. 'But if we don't want to see a very stern Rose Oliver we'd better get inside and think about a drink before dinner.'

It was a definite closing of the door that had so temporarily opened. Paige flinched internally, but turned with him and went across the lawn and into the house.

'I'll change,' she said quietly.

As she got into a simple straight skirt and a sleeveless scoop-necked top in a soft bronze that gave a deeper glow to her hair, she heard a helicopter fly in, fast and low, its rotors thumping as it landed on the pad.

Bringing someone? She stopped combing her hair and bit her lip, but she had no right to complain.

Yet outside the door to the morning room she stopped and gathered her courage in both her hands. Through it she could hear voices, so, yes, someone had arrived. And she was almost sure she knew who it was.

Her skin chilled, and she opened the door.

Marc and Lauren were looking out of the window at the sunset. Although they weren't touching, something about the silence that encompassed them clamped every muscle in Paige's body into punishing rigidity.

Anguish stabbed her in a region of her heart she hadn't known existed. He had lied, she thought painfully; *this* was how Juliette had known they were lovers. Their intimacy was so obvious it blazed as brightly as Marc's eyes.

She hadn't expected commitment, but she had believed him when he'd said he and Lauren weren't lovers—only to be betrayed. And he'd betrayed Lauren too.

Did any man keep his promises?

Forced to watch as Lauren looked into Marc's face and laughed, she recognised love in that soft sound—and a teasing inflection that hurt even more because it spoke of knowledge and equality.

'Oh, Marc,' his lover said, 'you darling idiot!'

CHAPTER ELEVEN

BEYOND thought, acting on a desperate instinct to protect herself from utter humiliation, Paige made a production of closing the door behind her. When she turned back to the room both Marc and Lauren had swung around.

Side by side, the link between them blazed as obvious as the posters at the strip club. A slow anger began to boil inside her as she saw them focus their attention onto her, deliberately concealing that silent, intangible connection.

Whipping up the remnants of shattered pride to stiffen her spine, Paige went towards them, her head held high enough to strain her shoulders and neck.

His handsome face impassive, Marc said, 'What would you like to drink before dinner, Paige? There's wine and sherry, or orange juice if you'd rather.'

Paige would much rather. Anything alcoholic might loosen the fierce leash she'd clamped on her emotions. Forcing herself to overcome an anguish so strong she could barely breathe, she said, 'I'd love orange juice, thank you,' wondering if she sounded as stilted to them as she did in her own ears.

Marc glanced at the woman beside him. 'Lauren? The usual?'

'Thank you.' She smiled at Paige—a warm smile that hurt its recipient more than anything else since she'd come into the room.

She could see why, in spite of everything, Juliette had liked this woman.

Who said now, 'How lucky you are to live in Hawke

Bay. When I'm in New Zealand I always like to try your superb wines, especially the *sauvignon blanc* and *pinot gris*. And your winemakers are producing some excellent reds.'

She had what sounded like an impeccable French accent. As well as wine, she'd probably be able to eloquently discuss food and the latest books and shows.

If Paige's smile was as ragged as it felt on her lips, neither seemed to notice. 'Living in a wine-growing district means that I've absorbed information by osmosis, but I have to admit I don't know much about it.' Grateful for the steadiness of her voice, she added, 'When it comes to discussing the finer points of New Zealand styles and vintages I'm lost.'

But after Marc had given them their respective drinks he began to talk of Northland's new boutique wineries. Paige didn't have to feign attention; he had the rare ability of being able to invest any subject with interest.

And even knowing that he's lied to you and betrayed you you'd listen to him for the pleasure of hearing his voice, an inner demon jeered.

Cynicism was good; it stopped her from remembering how it had felt to be in his arms, to—

Ruthlessly she dragged her mind back to the conversation, which had moved onto new industries in New Zealand's northernmost province. Northland's long, slender peninsula, pointing to the tropics, had traditionally been an agricultural and holiday area, but this was changing, and from what he and Lauren said Marc was a major player in that change.

Paige found that she could cope if she pretended she was acting in a play—as the foil for the main characters, she thought bitterly. Every second since she'd walked in had reinforced the bond between them; they knew each other very, very well.

By the time the housekeeper called them for dinner her throat had tightened, and after a couple of surreptitious swallows she knew she wasn't going to be able to eat.

Yet to save face she'd have to force food past the hard, heavy lump in her chest. A judicious lubrication of wine might help; she nodded when Marc offered a glass of red, and when it was poured took a slow, cautious sip.

'Do you like that?' he asked, startling her.

She looked no further than his chin. 'It's delicious,' she said politely.

'Tell me what you taste when you drink it.'

'Is this some kind of test?' she asked, her tone a little too sweet.

Lauren made a soft noise that could have been a stifled laugh.

Long fingers relaxed around the base of his glass, Marc leaned back and looked across the table. Candlelight flickered sensuously across his dark face, accenting the hawk-like features. Paige's stomach clenched into a knot and her spine went into instant meltdown.

I have to get away before I make a total fool of myself, she thought feverishly.

'I'm interested in your opinion,' he said mildly, yet a steely note ran through the words and his hard, blue gaze didn't leave her face.

She shrugged. 'It's—well, the word that comes to mind is earthy—yet I think I can taste plums. And a hint of liquorice.' She hesitated before adding with a touch of defiance that hid, she hoped, her wounded outrage, 'All in all, an arrogant vintage with hidden depths.'

Lauren's laughter broke the silence. 'She got you there, Marc. As clever a piece of subtext as I've come across in a while.'

One raised black brow indicated Marc's mocking amusement. 'You have a palate.'

Shamefully flattered, Paige said stiffly, 'Doesn't every-one?'

'Not as naturally sensitive as yours.'

When he smiled at her it was hard to remember that this was the man who'd lied to her, then seduced her, even though he must have known his mistress was arriving later that day.

She glanced at Lauren, caught an odd little smile curling her perfect mouth, and decided she was either depraved or she didn't know what sort of man she loved.

Paige called on every ounce of composure she possessed to say, 'How gratifying.'

'Another accomplishment to add to your list,' he said urbanely.

The note of irony in his words told her he'd recognised her withdrawal. Heat stung her skin. What did he mean by that?

Staring at the food on her plate with dogged determi-nation, Paige responded, 'A good sense of taste is hardly an accomplishment.'

'And that's a reply that shows a charming humility.' Marc's dry voice altered, becoming infused with a coolly goading irony that stopped Paige's heart. 'You should be proud of your many and varied talents.'

Surely he wouldn't mention those frenzied hours in his arms—not in front of the woman who was listening with every appearance of composure—even, she thought on a spark of anger, *amusement*—to this conversation.

There was a deadly little silence before he finished, 'Lauren has been remarking on your sense of style, and Sherry told me you have green fingers.'

The glimmer of the candlelight hid any expression in

his eyes. And was that a sleekly patronising smile from the high-powered executive beside him?

Paige refused to respond with anything other than a wooden, 'Thank you,' and when Lauren stepped in with an innocuous comment about gardening she could only summon a resentful gratitude.

She chewed grimly and made herself swallow even when her stomach showed signs of rebelling. And she made stilted conversation about her interest in plants.

'A friend of mine breeds roses,' Marc said deliberately. 'You might have heard of him—Adam Curwen.'

Her gaze, pure green in the subdued light, crossed swords with his. 'He's brilliant,' she said thinly. 'A trend-setter, yet his roses are tough and healthy and their scent is glorious.'

'I'll introduce him to you one day. He'd be—'

Rain drowned his voice—sudden, tempestuous pellets slashing onto the roof and across the windows. Paige noted the way one of Lauren's brows shot up as she sent a swift glance at Marc.

In spite of everything she could do to quench it a tiny fugitive flame of hope flickered into life in the cold region of her heart. He'd spoken as though there was some sort of future for them...

No, she thought fiercely. She wasn't like Juliette or Lauren—she wouldn't share him. It was demeaning and humiliating; it would be a slow death of the things that mattered most—her integrity, her self-respect.

If she couldn't be the only woman in his life she'd rather not have him in hers. Sometimes the price of love came too high.

When the fusillade of rain had passed, Lauren said sym-pathetically, 'It's a pity it's been so wet while you're here.'

Carefully avoiding Marc's eyes, Paige smiled. 'Actually,

it's been lovely in between the showers, and I expected the rain—Northland is notorious for its humidity.'

'Spoken like a loyal daughter of Hawke Bay's drier, more Mediterranean climate,' Marc said. He paused for a second, then added in an aloof tone underlined with a subtle taunt, 'Rain has its benefits—lush fertility, and an abundance of natural beauty.'

Light collected in his wine as he raised the glass to his mouth, then flashed crimson when he drank. Paige felt her colour deepen, and because her hand quivered she set her fork down with a sharp little crash that seemed to reverberate around the room.

She wondered if she was being absurdly sensitive. It was ridiculous to suspect an underlying meaning in everything he said!

Lauren murmured, 'But all of New Zealand—all that I've seen, anyway—is beautiful. Even your cities are set in glorious surroundings.'

'We're very lucky,' Paige agreed, welcoming the change of subject with galling relief. 'Of the cities you've visited, which one did you enjoy the most?'

'Paris,' Lauren said promptly, with a wistful smile that made her seem more vulnerable. She was silent a moment. 'But there are so many wonderful places in the world— and I hate to think that in one lifetime I'm never going to get around them all!'

And she talked charmingly of some of her favourites.

Later, as Paige prepared for bed, she prayed she'd been able to hide her turbulent emotions. She thought she'd managed to behave like an adult—one who'd never touched Marc, never kissed him, never lain with him in this bed and given him everything she had.

After dinner he'd asked courteously if she wanted to

watch a film. Equally courteous, she'd told him that she was a little tired so she'd go to bed.

He had got to his feet. 'How are your shoulders?'

'Just a bit stiff.'

'Shower before you go to bed and let the water play on your back again,' he'd advised.

'I'll do that,' she'd told him colourlessly.

Only twelve hours of this farce to go, she had reminded herself as she'd smiled meaninglessly in their general direction and turned towards the door.

Now, sitting on her bed, she wondered how on earth she was going to get through the night.

A bitter, aching sense of loss submerged her. And that was stupid, because how could she lose what she'd never had? Her involuntary, electric awareness of him—even her reluctant love—seemed indecent now she'd seen that invisible, undeniable bond between Marc and Lauren. But worse was the corroding jealousy that came dangerously near resentment.

'Brooding isn't going to help.' She climbed to her feet with the effort of someone determined not to give in to pain, and went into the opulent, scented bathroom.

And she was not going to surrender to self-pity. She'd find the guts and determination to make something of her life. Marc's sexual initiation of her might have been without the emotion she craved from him, but he'd given her a rare and precious gift—knowledge of her own sensuality and complete satisfaction.

Gripping the counter, she stared at herself in the mirror, meeting eyes tormented by secrets above a mouth with fuller, more ardent contours than she'd seen before.

In Marc's arms she'd crossed the perilous border from inexperience to knowledge.

'You already know that life can be tough—learn to deal with it,' she advised tautly.

She had to, because after the next day she was never going to see him again.

Grimacing, she fought back another wave of pain. She'd been such an idiot—so eager to co-operate in her own undoing, willingly tricking herself into believing that making love to Marc would mean something to him, even when he'd told her it wouldn't.

At least he'd made sure that there would be no unwanted results from their loving. She blinked hard, because now she knew why Sherry was so determined to do the best for Brodie; she too would have protected Marc's child, no matter what she had to do.

She tried hard to feel thankful that it wasn't going to happen.

Unbidden, a thought clawed its way through the tumult in her brain. Perhaps the closeness between Lauren and him was the rapport of ex-lovers who were now friends?

Her heart leapt, but Paige had done enough wishful thinking that day to learn her lesson. 'No,' she said with scornful contempt.

There had been real affection in their attitude to each other, a kind of unspoken empathy they didn't notice because it was so familiar.

Was Lauren like Juliette, sweetly complaisant and docile, content with the sort of relationship that gave Marc freedom to do what he wanted when he wanted with any other woman he wanted?

'She might be, but I'm not,' Paige said grimly. In the mirror she saw anger contort her face, and thought painfully, I can't bear this. I'm turning into a different person and I hate it. It's better to find out now that I'll never be able to trust him.

But oh, it *hurt*.

Back in Napier, away from his disturbing effect on her, she'd pick up the shards of her life and cement them back together; she'd find a job that had something to do with her interests. Certainly she'd opt out of the battle between the sexes. Love was a war zone, with far more losers than winners.

Until tomorrow she had to grit her teeth, keep reminding herself of the sort of man Marc was, and endure.

Although the prospect of life without him crumbled something strong and vital in her, she'd cope. Time was on her side, because she was stronger than her mother— she wasn't going to waste her life yearning for a man she couldn't trust.

Yet as she got into the shower she knew that some part of her would never recover; oh, she'd manage, but for her there would be no other man—she'd go to her grave wanting Marc.

'Don't be so melodramatic,' she scoffed.

Safely camouflaged by the rush of water, she let the tears fall, giving in—just this once—to the grief sifting through her soul like a grey mist.

Once in bed she kept her restless mind busy by working out vicious ways of paying Marc back. For what? she mocked. Making her want him? Making her lose her head? He hadn't even tried; she'd fallen headlong and with insulting ease.

But anger gave her strength, whereas desolation leached it away. And right now she needed strength.

And she was not in love with him! If you loved someone you were supposed to want their happiness above all else.

What she wanted above all else was to get away from Marc and lick her wounds and remake her life...

After what seemed hours of tossing in the bed she

opened her eyes, blinking at the hard, white slabs of moonlight that fell through the shutters and tiger-striped the floor.

She switched on her light and peered at the bedside clock.

She'd been in bed under thirty minutes. It was, she thought, her bravado fading under a wave of weary misery, going to be a long night.

'Yeah, that's good. You're getting the hang of it. That graft'll take.'

Paige flushed. The elderly nurseryman was sparing with his praise so this was a rare moment.

They stood for a couple of moments evaluating the rose bush before he remarked, 'I don't know why you're so set on going to university—it's a waste of time. Breeding new plants is mostly knowing what they want, and you get that by growing them. After that it's gut feelings and persistence and a good eye. I reckon you've got those already.'

Paige too had been wondering whether the money Juliette had left her would be wasted on university fees. 'I don't have to make a decision for a couple of months.'

'Well, you're doing pretty good. Don't forget to clean that grafting knife.'

'I won't.'

He strode off, then turned. 'Knew I came out here for something. There's a joker out front wants to talk to you.'

During the past three months Paige had thought she'd blocked out the fantasy that Marc might walk back into her life, but there it was again, painfully sharp and instant. Stop it now, she thought, putting the grafting knife down. It's not going to happen.

She was knitting her life together with dreams and will power, and she wasn't going to let a stupid obsession ruin her progress.

'Who is it?' she asked casually.

'Never seen him before.'

She glanced at her watch. 'I'm not expecting anyone. He can wait until finishing time.'

'Ten minutes won't do him any harm,' her boss agreed. 'But you worked all through lunchtime so you might as well go now.'

It took her ten minutes to wash her hands and take off her overalls, then run a comb through her hair without scanning her face. She knew what she'd see there—opaque eyes, a mouth that had somehow tightened over the past three months, a general air of tense control.

It was hot in the cloakroom; she pulled her T-shirt away from her body and puffed out her cheeks. She had a long ride home.

Small pack on her back, she wheeled her bicycle around the shabby building, part office, part greenhouse, then stopped in the shade of a huge silk tree. Dismay hammered at her—dismay and a wild exhilaration that broke through the crust of ice she'd moulded around her emotions. Only one man in her acquaintance would be driving a car like this expensive European saloon.

Marc had seen her coming. The car door opened and he got out, wearing strength and power with a formidable authority that reinforced his height and the spread of his shoulders.

'Paige,' he said with uncompromising self-possession, scrutinising her. 'How are you?'

Dry-mouthed, she returned, 'Stunned.' And grubby and angry, she told herself fiercely. It had to be anger that drove the colour into her skin and stirred up her energy levels, sending blood racing through her body.

That satirical eyebrow shot up and he smiled narrowly. 'Stunned? I'm surprised—surely you didn't expect your coldly formal farewell at Kerikeri airport to be the final words between us?'

She was staring at him as though he'd walked out of a spaceship and demanded to be taken to her leader. It was, Marc thought with cold self-derision, patently obvious she hadn't been expecting him. He knew why, too; all the men in her life had abandoned her in their various ways.

As he had.

Damn, she'd lost weight since he'd put her on the plane. Her face was more finely drawn; perhaps the heat and working two jobs were grinding her down. But her mouth still beckoned with lushly sensuous impact, and he still wanted her as much as he had before.

More.

'I think we've said everything there is to say to each other,' she retorted, not giving an inch, her square jaw lifting a fraction and her eyes gleaming green.

'Do you?' He held her gaze until the thick black lashes swept down and her colour faded.

'Yes,' she said coldly, hating him for doing this to her. 'And I'm afraid I'm running late, so I have to go.'

'I'll give you a ride home.'

'No, thank you.' She sent a savage, meaningless smile in his direction. 'I need my bike to get me here tomorrow morning.'

'You work on Sundays?'

Feeling like a total idiot for forgetting that today was Saturday, she held his eyes steadily. 'On Monday, then.'

'Your bike will go in the boot.'

Her laughter lacked humour. 'It will also scratch the paint.'

She stiffened at his negligent shrug, and the anger that was holding her upright intensified into cold rage when he said indifferently, 'So?'

'So I don't want a lift home.'

'I need to talk to you—'

'What about what *I* need?' she demanded.

Coolly arrogant, he returned, 'You need it too.'

'Like a hole in the head,' she said inelegantly, adding with rigid disdain, 'If it's my welfare you're interested in, as you can see I'm fine. I'm thoroughly enjoying working here, and learning a lot.' She dragged in a swift, shallow breath and hurtled on, 'Sherry and Brodie are settled and well. She loves her employers; they love her. She adores living in the country and she's switched from saving every cent she can for the deposit on a house to investing in stocks and shares.'

'The share market had better watch out,' he said with a lazy smile that scorched the length of her spine. 'Are you pregnant?'

Her fingers clenched on the handlebars. Well, of course! She should have thought of that. In spite of the precautions he'd taken, Marc Corbett covered all bases; he wouldn't want an inconvenient child on the periphery of his life!

Fighting back a buzzing in her head, she said baldly, 'No.'

'You're sure of that?'

She met his assessing eyes with a fiercely independent glare. 'Absolutely one hundred per cent sure. But even if I were, what would you do about it?'

'Marry you,' he said grimly.

Astonishment widened her eyes, but she made a swift recovery. 'Not even you,' she said, the metal in her words as cutting as steel, 'can do the impossible. I wouldn't marry you if I were pregnant, but it isn't relevant because I'm not. Now, go back to your world and leave me in mine.'

He reached her before she had time to swing her leg

over the bicycle. Strong hands closed over the handlebars and stopped the machine from moving.

'Once you asked me if Juliette had been happy. Now I'm asking you—are you happy?' he asked, his voice aloof.

But when she looked up she read an iron, uncompromising will in the hard angles and planes of his face.

She folded her lips together firmly and met his scrutiny with defiance that covered, she prayed, the pain beneath. 'Let my bike go, please,' she said between her teeth.

'I'd like to explain some things to you.'

'I can't talk to you. I have to get home because I go to another job, and I'm due there in an hour.' She hated lying to him, but she had to get out of here—his closeness was melting her resolve like a blowtorch on ice.

Her father's rejection had scarred her life and coloured her attitudes. Without realising it, she'd organised her life so that no man could get close enough to her to spurn her love. Somehow she'd twisted her feelings so much she'd even welcomed Marc's statement that he wasn't offering anything but sex because it freed her from her fear of rejection.

But she could no longer lie to herself. In spite of everything, she loved him, and every moment she spent with him brought her closer to admitting it.

'Coming home with me will make up time,' he said crisply. 'Get in—I'll put this in the boot.'

Mind racing, she hesitated; a seething glance told her he wasn't going to move, and short of yelling for help she had no chance of getting away. And perhaps this talk he wanted would give her an ending, a way to finally cut him out of her heart.

'Is this how you got to be a tycoon?' she asked scornfully. 'By nagging and harassment?'

He lifted the bike and dumped it in the car's big boot, lowering the top carefully to avoid scratching the gleaming paint. 'I prefer to call it bloody-minded perseverance,' he told her gravely.

Once they were purring down the road she asked, 'What is so important that it brings you here again?'

'I'll wait until we get home,' he said with infuriating self-possession. 'Tell me what you've been doing.'

Almost she snarled, but it wouldn't do any good, so she unclenched her jaw and kept her eyes on the road ahead. 'Working,' she returned steadily. 'And playing with Brodie when Sherry comes into town. He's grown such a lot—he can sit up and make noises, and laugh.' With the slightest of snaps she said, 'How's Lauren?'

'She's fine, and sends her regards.'

'Oh.' Disconcerted, Paige sent a sideways glance at him, and met eyes the polished blue of a gun barrel.

Her stomach jolting into free-fall, she turned her gaze ahead again.

Marc asked, 'Why are you working two jobs?'

Shrugging, she said, 'I need to earn as much as I can before the start of the next academic year.'

'So what sort of job takes up your Saturday night?'

'Oh, of course. Today's Saturday,' she said lamely. 'Ah, during the week I clean offices.' Ashamed, she stared out of the side window.

He didn't say anything, for which she was grateful. She should have known better than to lie; her mother had used to tell her she was the world's worst fibber.

CHAPTER TWELVE

BACK at the unit, Paige turned and fixed her gaze just past Marc's ear. 'I'm grubby. I need to shower and change.'

'I'll make you coffee.' Marc looked across at the kitchen and observed with irritating blandness, 'I'm glad to see you're using the electric jug I bought.'

'I don't cut off my nose to spite my face,' she said shortly, and disappeared.

After showering in record time, she changed into clean jeans and a dark green T-shirt. For the first time since she'd left Arohanui, she realised with a sinking feeling in her stomach, she looked human again. Sparks of gold glittered in her green eyes, her cheeks were pink, and her heart pumped blood so vigorously through her system that she felt alert and vital and ready for anything.

But when Marc left she'd be right back where she started—desolated and wretched.

So? She could cope, even if it took every ounce of will power she possessed.

She set her chin at a jaunty angle and walked into her tiny living room.

Marc's glance registered nothing more dangerous than cool assessment. Handing her a mug of coffee, he said abruptly, 'When I told you I was faithful to Juliette, I was lying.'

'I know.' She tried to hide her raw, exposed emotions with an expressionless voice.

A muscle flicked in his arrogant jaw. 'You don't know why.'

Paige bit back the scornful words that threatened to spill out and waited in an agony of apprehension for him to tell her that he loved Lauren.

He said levelly, 'When I met you, I looked at you and I wanted you—the classic *coup de foudre*.'

Bewildered, she stared at his harshly angular face. 'I don't—'

'Thunderbolt,' he translated with bleak brevity. 'And, like a thunderbolt, it scared the hell out of me. And it wasn't one-sided. Don't shake your head—do you think I don't recognise when a woman wants me, even a seventeen-year-old virgin who doesn't know what the hell has happened to her? You did your best to resist it, and you succeeded in hiding it from anyone else, but I knew—and was infuriated and humiliated, because there was nothing more to it than mindless, elemental hunger.'

'I—yes, I know,' she said inaudibly, bracing herself.

Whatever she'd expected, it wasn't this. He was going to tell her that he'd been exorcising an old obsession when they'd made love.

The thought made her sick. Get on with it, she told him silently. Just do what it is you need to do and then go! Clenching her teeth together, she stared into the depths of her coffee and watched the liquid swirl lazily around.

Tonelessly he said, 'So I ignored it. I had made a promise to Juliette and I kept it.' He paused, before continuing in a tone laced with self-disgust, 'But I couldn't forget you. I carried you like a shining talisman, a memento of something precious that never happened, in my head and in my heart. I don't know whether Juliette sensed that, but I suspect it was what convinced her that Lauren was my mistress.'

Coffee slopped over the side of her mug. Ignoring it, Paige whispered, 'Oh, *no*!'

'She never knew,' he said swiftly, taking the mug from her and setting it down on the table. 'She valued your friendship highly. From the start we both understood that ours was a practical marriage. She wasn't in love with me and she knew I wasn't in love with her. I liked her very much, and I was sure I could make her happy. It never occurred to me she'd decide that Lauren and I were having an affair.'

'How could she not?' Paige still didn't believe him, although something niggled at the back of her mind. She added trenchantly, 'When I saw you and Lauren together there was such a sense of—of love and trust—and a deep, deep connection that can't be mistaken. If she's not your lover, what *is* she?'

He didn't answer straight away. Paige couldn't look at him; in an agony of suspense she waited, listening to her heart thud noisily in her throat.

Without inflection he said, 'I must ask you to keep this confidential, although I have her permission to tell you. She's my half-sister.'

Paige's jaw dropped. Incredulously, she repeated, 'Your *half-sister*!'

That small muscle flicked again in his jaw. 'Her mother and my father had an affair—one of his many affairs—and Lauren was the result.' He spoke austerely, his body language indicating his contempt. 'She doesn't want anyone to know because her parents are still alive and her father believes she is his child—as she is in everything but genetic heritage. She loves him, and he has a weak heart. She's worried that if he ever found out not only would it wreck her parents' marriage but it could kill her father.'

Stunned, Paige picked up her coffee mug and took a fortifying sip. All she could think of to say was a feeble, 'How did she learn about it?'

'A medical emergency when she was twenty-two—I donated bone marrow.'

'But surely her father realised then—?'

His mouth twisted. 'Her mother was desperate and contacted me, hoping I might be a compatible donor. Fortunately I was; apparently she told her husband that I was on the worldwide register. She asked me not to tell anyone. So I didn't—not even Juliette. But I was determined to keep in touch with Lauren; when she asked if she could join the firm I agreed. She is extremely good at her work, and utterly loyal.'

'I'm not surprised; you saved her life. I don't know how I missed it, but you have the same bone structure,' Paige said quietly, wondering now at her own blindness. It was too early, and too presumptuous, to be relieved. 'And you both lift your left eyebrow; I noticed that, but not anything else except that special rapport between you.'

'Juliette never saw the physical resemblance,' Marc said remotely, his lashes hiding all but narrow slivers of blue.

Paige's fingers twisted together. 'But she knew that there was something not right about your marriage. I feel that I betrayed her.'

He stared at her as though she was crazy. She expected an explosion, and for a moment she thought she was going to get one, but eventually he closed his eyes and dragged in a breath. When he opened his eyes and expelled the air from his lungs he'd re-established control.

'How?' he asked, almost temperately.

'If you kept on wanting me, even when you were married to her—' She stopped, because so much had been unsaid.

His brows drew together. 'Go on.'

The words tied themselves in knots on her tongue, but

she had to keep going. 'I can't bear to think I made her unhappy.'

He exhaled again, and ran a hand through his black hair. 'If anyone made her unhappy,' he pointed out in a tone that strove for reason, 'I did. You were totally innocent.'

She bit her lip. 'I wanted you.'

'Paige, stop staring at me as though I'm the enemy.' He strode across to the door and stared for a moment outside, as though working out what to say next. After a charged moment he swung around. 'Sit down. You look as though you've been run over by a Jumbo Jet.'

Reluctantly she obeyed, crossing her legs at the ankle, setting the mug on the table and then locking her nervous fingers together in her lap.

'I need to tell you about my marriage, and to do that I have to tell you about my family,' he said in a crisp, un-emotional voice. 'To begin with, my father was notorious for his affairs.'

Paige realised he was hating this. She asked soberly, 'Is that why they called him the Robber Baron?'

He paused. 'Only partly. He conducted business like one of the old robber barons of industry. He always vowed he loved my mother—and I think in a strange sort of way he did.'

Paige snorted, and he smiled without humour. 'I couldn't agree more. My mother loved him desperately. She couldn't cope with his amours, and he didn't seem to be able to stop himself. Not that he was a rake; he chose sophisticated women, not innocents. I think I told you once that my childhood was punctuated by hideous rows and even more hideous silences; what I didn't tell you was that there were at least three suicide attempts by my mother. There may have been more.'

Paige made a shocked, sympathetic noise. Outside, the sun blazed down, silhouetting him against its brazen light.

Still in that toneless voice he said, 'I decided that I wouldn't ever put a woman through that; I wanted no part of love. I wanted a sensible marriage, where both of us knew exactly where we stood.'

'I can see why,' she admitted, horrified. Her own father's behaviour was nothing compared to this—at least he'd stayed with his second wife until he died.

'I chose Juliette because she loved children, she knew her way around the world I live in, and she was intelligent and kind. And she was beautiful—going to bed with her would be a pleasure.'

Outraged, Paige snapped, 'It sounds as though you made a list!'

His mouth tightened. 'And because although she liked me, and found me sexy and interesting, she wasn't in love with me. You noticed that Lauren and I share a family resemblance—Juliette never did. Doesn't that give you some indication of our marriage?'

She bit her lip. 'I'm good with faces.'

'Is that the real reason?' She flushed, and he went on quietly, 'With Juliette I knew there would be no loss of control, no passionate craving, no handing my heart over to someone who might treat it as carelessly as my father had treated my mother's. I chose the easy, safe, coward's path.'

Silence drummed between them until he said harshly, 'So it serves me right that when I saw you—a child of seventeen—two days before our wedding, I fell so hard and so fast I went into shock.'

Unable to speak, Paige sat stiffly, her eyes fixed on his hard face.

He finished, 'I don't believe in love at first sight, not

even now, but that's what happened to me. I married Juliette because I had made a vow to her and because I knew I would be safe with her. And if she hadn't died I would still be married to her.'

That flat, emphatic statement lifted Paige's heart, allowing her to hope. This man would keep a promise, no matter how much it cost him.

'I regret bitterly that she thought I was unfaithful,' he said bluntly. 'But, although she was pleased when I convinced her that it was untrue, she wouldn't have left me if it had been, Paige. She was content with what she had of me.' He paused. 'Just as I tried to convince myself that I was content with the path I'd chosen.'

She looked mutely at him, blinking at the blazing heat of his eyes. 'Then I saw you walk down the staircase from the strip club, and I knew that for six years I'd been lying to myself. The unruly passion I thought I'd killed had been hiding, and the moment I saw you with the child in your arms it burst out again—stronger for its repression, more violent than ever. And you felt it too—I saw it when you looked at me.'

'That's not love,' she said unsteadily.

'Perhaps not. But then I found that as well as being unbearably desirable you're compassionate, strong-willed, spirited and intelligent,' he said, his voice strained. 'And I want you in my life until I die. Is that love, Paige? Because if it is, I'm in love with you.'

Unable to believe what she'd heard, she stared at his dark, angular face in shock. 'In love?' she whispered.

'I don't know what else it can be.' He made an explicit Gallic gesture, his decisive hand slashing downwards. 'Passion is wonderful, and when we made love it was like nothing else I've ever experienced, but it is only part of what I feel for you.'

She jumped to her feet and advanced towards him, eyes glittering with tears. 'If you love me,' she demanded, 'why did you let me leave Arohanui? Why did you stay away for these past three dreadful months? You must have known how I felt about you, yet you, you—'

She grabbed his upper arms and shook him. It was like trying to move the Rock of Gibraltar. He didn't try to stop her, and when she made an exclamation of disgust at her own weakness he locked his fingers around her wrists, preventing her retreat.

In a low, caustic voice he said, 'I didn't want to feel this need. I dreaded being like my mother, weak-willed and dependent, enacting jealous rages, an abject slave to love. That's why I let you go, only to realise that without you there is nothing.'

He paused, a lethal gaze fixed intently on her face. 'And I hope you love me too. You were a virgin, yet you gave yourself to me—was that easy, ordinary lust?'

Colour flooded her skin, and just as rapidly faded. 'No,' she admitted on a long sigh. 'But, Marc—I'm not—I won't be a suitable wife for you.'

'I know,' he said, solemn-faced. 'In fact, you're outrageously unsuitable. I'll probably lose every cent of this money you find such a burden because I can't think of anything but you.'

She smiled, as he had meant her to, but it left her with twisted lips and she said uneasily, 'Your mother won't—'

'My mother wants me to be happy, and when she sees us together she'll know that I am.'

Paige stared up, read the complete conviction in his expression, and let herself hope. But before surrendering completely she said quietly, 'It's not that simple, Marc. You know that.'

'I know that together we can do anything we want to.'

His voice deepened. 'I know that my life is a desert without you. If you can't live in my world then I'll leave it and live with you, anywhere you want.'

Swift, hot tears ached behind her eyes. 'You'd get bored in a few months, and I wouldn't—I won't be happy unless you are.' She took a deep, ragged breath and fixed her eyes on his face. 'So if that means I have to learn how to behave in your world, I'll do it. I'm a quick learner, and if your mother will help—'

'She will,' he said, but he made no attempt to pull her where she longed to be, into his arms, against his heart.

He waited until she let down every barrier and took that first, terrifying step into the unknown.

'I do love you.' Her voice quivered, but she managed a smile in spite of the shimmer of tears. 'I've always loved you. And I want to make you so happy you won't ever regret it. If that's enough—'

'I want more than that.' His voice was slow and sure, vibrant with determination. 'I want to take such care of you that you never get ill again, or are unhappy again, or want—'

'Oh, Marc,' she whispered. 'You can't promise that.'

'I know.' He laughed softly and, finally yielding to his emotions, pulled her against him. 'But I'm going to try, my heart.'

At last convinced that this man would never use her or betray her, that she could trust him with her life and her love, she smiled crookedly at him. 'I will too,' she vowed. 'And I can see that we'll both be so over-protective we'll drive each other crazy.'

His arms closed around her as though she was something rare and preciously fragile. 'I can't wait. And I *can* promise that if you marry me we will always be together, that I'll always be there to support you, and that when you hybridise plants and call them after me and our children I'll be the proudest man in the world.'

She lifted a glowing face and kissed him, and after that there was no more talking, except in the deep, exquisite tenderness of love.

Later, lying in his arms on her bed, she traced a path through the pattern of fine hair across his chest and said sleepily, 'Now you can confess that you got Sherry her job.'

The wall of his chest lifted sharply beneath her finger. 'How did you know? She doesn't.'

'I guessed. It came very conveniently, and when I thought about it I couldn't really believe in people who'd overlook her past to hire her to look after their children— unless they knew more about her than that she was a stripper. Or unless they owed someone a favour.'

His eyes gleaming with lazy satisfaction, he pulled her exploring hand up to kiss the palm and then her wrist. Against the tumultuous pulse he admitted, 'They're friends. And they're delighted with her—so much so that now they owe me another favour for finding her for them.'

Paige looked at him with adoring delight. 'What made you do it for her?'

He paused, then shrugged, his skin sliding silkily, sensuously against hers. 'I liked her, and thought she deserved a better chance, but the main reason was that you were worried about her.'

'What about Juliette's legacy—the money?' When his mouth settled into a firm, inflexible line she leaned over and bit his earlobe. Into his ear she breathed, 'That came from you too, didn't it?'

'I can see I'm not going to have any secrets,' he complained wryly, easing her over onto her back. 'When did you work that out?'

'When you said you'd helped Sherry.' She lifted a hand and stroked his cheek, fingers tingling at the soft roughness of his beard beneath the sensitive tips.

He turned his head into her palm and said in a muffled voice, 'I couldn't bear the thought of you struggling on with no financial base to keep you safe. I had to make sure you were protected, that you had choices and options.'

Ten minutes before—only five minutes before!—Paige had believed that making love to Marc had more than sated her every desire. So she was surprised when that subtle heat began to smoulder again, this time reinforced by a deep, abiding gratitude to whatever fortunate fate had brought them together.

'I do love you,' she said, turning the simple words into a vow. 'I wish I hadn't thought you were such a horrible man.'

'You can make amends.' He slid his hand up to enclose one soft breast.

She laughed softly and kissed his shoulder. 'So I can,' she said wonderingly. 'I'm so happy! Everything seems newborn, as though loving you, knowing that you love me, has remade the world.'

'Good.' He traced the full contours of her mouth, his own softening into tenderness. 'I wondered if you could trust any man enough to love one. Your father left you, your boss harassed you, and your cousin died without making sure you and your mother had some sort of security. And I coldly and deliberately turned my back on a temptation I found unbearably enticing and married Juliette.'

'I fell in love with you on the telephone,' she confessed, 'at Arohanui when you rang every night. So I loved you before I knew you'd kept Lauren's secret, and that you were loyal to Juliette. I couldn't stop myself. It just happened.'

'I don't believe in fate. But then I didn't believe in love at first sight either! Perhaps we were meant to find each other, meant to love, meant to live a long and happy life together,' he said, and kissed her.

They were married on the island, a quiet simple ceremony with his mother and Lauren and Sherry and several of Marc's close friends. Afterwards, in the room she'd first slept in, Paige changed her ankle-length oyster-coloured silk gown for travelling clothes. They were spending their honeymoon on an island Marc owned in Tahiti, a small one in an isolated lagoon. Later they would fly to Paris, and then on to Venice.

Anticipation mingled in her with a tiny stab of foreboding. She looked down at her cream linen shirt and matching trousers and hoped she'd pass muster.

A brilliant blue flare from the ring Marc had given her comforted her. She turned it a little, admiring the colour. He'd suggested an emerald, but she'd decided on a Burmese sapphire the colour of his eyes. Glittering against the band of her wedding ring, it was a symbol of his commitment.

Not only was she utterly confident in Marc's love, confident enough to take on the world, but she had his mother's backing. At their first meeting Mrs Corbett had hugged her, and the last week had made it more than clear that Marc had been right—his mother only wanted his happiness, and was prepared to do whatever she could to forward it.

And she and Lauren were well on the way to becoming friends too. Marrying Marc had given her a family once

more. And there would be others—children, with his habit
of raising an ironic brow…

Smiling, she picked up her bag, and was making sure
she had everything she might need when a knock on the
door lifted her head. 'Come in,' she called.

But it was the housekeeper who came in, not Marc. She
looked a little worried, but she said, 'Mrs Corbett, I promised the—' she looked flustered, then recovered herself
'—the previous Mrs Corbett that I'd give you this if you
ever married Marc—Mr Corbett.'

'This' was an envelope with *Paige* written on it in
Juliette's elegant handwriting. A little chill ran down
Paige's spine.

'I hope it's all right,' the housekeeper said worriedly.
'She left me the two letters, you see—laughing a bit, because of course she didn't expect to die. One was to be
delivered when you came up to collect the bracelet, and
the other was if you married Marc.'

'Of course it's all right,' Paige said, hiding her momentary unease with a smile. 'Juliette was my friend.'

But the cold foreboding wormed its way into her as she
waited for the housekeeper to leave. Once the door had
closed behind Mrs Oliver, Paige slowly opened the envelope, sitting on the edge of the bed to read the note inside.

Dearest Paige,
If you're reading this then I'll have been dead for at
least two years and you'll have married Marc. I want
you to know that you have my blessing.
   I feel silly writing this, but I need to. Not long ago I
had a dream. I was lying in a swan boat with flowers
all around me, lovely carnations and roses and long
branches of mock orange in full white flower. Although

*it was strange, I was happy and excited, because I knew
I was going somewhere wonderful, and that once I got
there I'd meet someone wonderful. Then you and Marc
walked out of the mist and stood looking down at me.
You were crying, and Marc's face was all stony, the
way it goes when he doesn't want anyone to know what
he's thinking, yet you were linked in a shining glow, a
kind of radiance. I tried to tell you both that I was
happy, not to worry about me, not to grieve, but I
couldn't talk or move.*

Paige's heart clenched in her breast. She put the sheets
of paper down on the bed, but picked them up almost
immediately with trembling hands and read the rest.

*I knew that this was the way things were meant to be.
It was a lovely sureness, a certainty, and it stayed with
me when I woke up. Of course it was just a dream, but
in case it wasn't, dearest Paige, sister of my heart, then
I know that one day you'll be reading this and that you
and Marc will make each other very happy.*

*It's why I left you my bracelet on such strange con-
ditions. I wanted you to stay on the island so that you
and Marc would get to know each other, but it had to
be long enough after my death for neither of you to be
constrained by sorrow. Two years, I decided, was a
good period.*

She'd signed it *My love to you both*, and under the signature she'd added:

*By the way, Marc told me he has never had an affair
with his English executive, and I believe him. There is*

a connection there, but it is not sexual or romantic.
Dearest Paige, be very happy.

Paige was still sitting on the bed, her eyes drowned in
tears, when Marc came in.

'What is it?' he demanded, quick anger abrading his
voice.

Wordlessly she held the letter out to him.

He frowned, but took it and read it. Then he pulled her
up into his arms and said into her hair, 'I didn't know—
she never told me.'

Shivering, Paige leaned gratefully against him, absorbing his warm strength, the unfailing support she knew
would be hers always. 'It's—uncanny. And not like
Juliette—she was so pragmatic.' She drew in a shaking
breath. 'I hope—I hope that after the accident she woke
up in her golden swan boat, surrounded with her favourite
flowers and drenched in their perfume.'

He said soberly, 'The accident investigators told me
she'd have had one moment of fear, perhaps, and then
oblivion. She didn't suffer, my dearest heart. And if this
dream gave her some sort of comfort, I'm glad. As glad
as I am that she tried to set us up together. Some unconscious part of her must have recognised the—the affinity
between us.'

Paige nodded into his shoulder.

He went on, 'After she died I told myself I'd wait the
two years she'd stipulated and then hand her keepsake over
to you and that would be an end to this inconvenient obsession. But the moment I saw you again I knew I'd lied.
It was never going to end, and it wasn't obsession. It was
love. Not that I was ready to admit that to myself—I was
too afraid.'

Startled, Paige looked up. 'Afraid? You?'

'You still don't know how much you mean to me,' he told her, smoothing a strand of bright hair back from her temple. He held her away from him and looked into her face, his own at last naked and open to her, not trying to hide the deep, powerful emotions she saw there.

Blue fire leaping in his eyes, he said thickly, 'If I were a poet I could find new ways to tell you what I feel. But I can only say what so many men have said before, that I love you. I'll spend the rest of my life trying to convince you that those three words contain everything important to me.'

Paige met his brilliant gaze with courage and a happiness that turned her eyes to pure shimmering gold. 'And I love you,' she said very softly. 'With all my heart, all that I am. I always will.'

He laughed, the deep, triumphant laugh of a lover, and dropped a swift kiss on her nose. 'Then let's go. We've got a whole, glorious, magnificent lifetime together to discover all the facets of our love. I can't wait to start.'

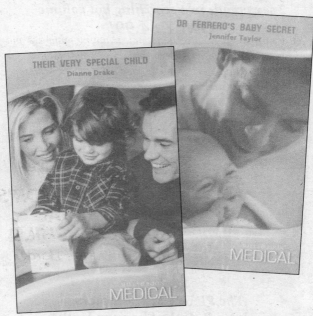

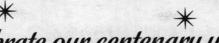

Celebrate 100 years of pure reading pleasure with Mills & Boon®

To mark our centenary, each month we're publishing a special 100th Birthday Edition. These celebratory editions are packed with extra features and include a FREE bonus story.

Plus, starting in February you'll have the chance to enter a fabulous monthly prize draw. See 100th Birthday Edition books for details.

Now that's worth celebrating!

15th February 2008

Raintree: Inferno by Linda Howard
Includes FREE bonus story Loving Evangeline
A double dose of Linda Howard's heady mix of passion and adventure

4th April 2008

The Guardian's Forbidden Mistress by Miranda Lee
Includes FREE bonus story The Magnate's Mistress
Two glamorous and sensual reads from favourite author Miranda Lee!

2nd May 2008

The Last Rake in London by Nicola Cornick
Includes FREE bonus story The Notorious Lord
Lose yourself in two tales of high society and rakish seduction!

Look for Mills & Boon 100th Birthday Editions at your favourite bookseller or visit
www.millsandboon.co.uk